Lecture Notes in Computer Sci

Commenced Publication in 1973
Founding and Former Series Editors:
Gerhard Goos, Juris Hartmanis, and Jan van Leeuwen

Roberto Moreno-Díaz   Franz Pichler
Alexis Quesada-Arencibia (Eds.)

Computer Aided Systems Theory – EUROCAST 2011

13th International Conference
Las Palmas de Gran Canaria, Spain
February 6-11, 2011
Revised Selected Papers, Part II

 Springer

Volume Editors

Roberto Moreno-Díaz
Alexis Quesada-Arencibia
Universidad de Las Palmas de Gran Canaria
Instituto Universitario de Ciencias y Tecnologías Cibernéticas
Campus de Tafira, 35017 Las Palmas de Gran Canaria, Spain
E-mail: rmoreno@ciber.ulpgc.es, aquesada@dis.ulpgc.es

Franz Pichler
Johannes Kepler University Linz
Institute of Systems Science
Altenbergerstrasse 69, 4040 Linz, Austria
E-mail: pichler@cast.uni-linz.ac.at

ISSN 0302-9743   e-ISSN 1611-3349
ISBN 978-3-642-27578-4   e-ISBN 978-3-642-27579-1
DOI 10.1007/978-3-642-27579-1
Springer Heidelberg Dordrecht London New York

Library of Congress Control Number: 2011945104

CR Subject Classification (1998): H.1.1, J.1, I.4, I.5.4, I.5, J.2, C.2.1, J.6

LNCS Sublibrary: SL 1 – Theoretical Computer Science and General Issues

Typesetting: Camera-ready by author, data conversion by Scientific Publishing Services, Chennai, India

Printed on acid-free paper

Springer is part of Springer Science+Business Media (www.springer.com)

Preface

Franz Pichler organized at the University of Linz the first CAST (Computer-Aided Systems Theory) Workshop in April 1988, which had the acceptance of prominent systems scientists. Next, the University of Las Palmas de Gran Canaria joined the University of Linz to organize the first international meeting on CAST (Las Palmas February 1989), under the name EUROCAST 1989. This first EUROCAST was a successful gathering of systems theorists, computer scientists and engineers from most European countries, North America and Japan.

It was agreed that EUROCAST international conferences would be organized every two years, alternating between Las Palmas de Gran Canaria and a continental European location, later being decided to celebrate them in Las Palmas. Thus, successive EUROCAST meetings took place in Krems (1991), Las Palmas (1993), Innsbruck (1995), Las Palmas (1997), Vienna (1999), Las Palmas (2001), Las Palmas (2003), Las Palmas (2005), Las Palmas (2007), and Las Palmas (2009), in addition to an extra-European CAST conference in Ottawa in 1994. Selected papers from those meetings were published by Springer as *Lecture Notes in Computer Science* nos. 410, 585, 763, 1030, 1333, 1798, 2178, 2809, 3643, 4739, and 5717, and in several special issues of *Cybernetics and Systems: An International Journal*. EUROCAST and CAST meetings are definitely consolidated, as has been shown by the number and quality of the contributions over the years.

EUROCAST 2011 took place in the Elder Museum of Science and Technology of Las Palmas, Canary Islands, during February 6-11, following the approach tested at previous conferences. It was an international computer-related conference with a true interdisciplinary character. There were different specialized workshops which, on this occasion, were devoted to the following topics: Systems Theory and Applications, chaired by Pichler (Linz) and Moreno Díaz (Las Palmas); Computation and Simulation in Modelling Biological Systems, chaired by Ricciardi (Napoli); Intelligent Information Processing, chaired by Freire (A Coruña); Traffic Behavior, Modelling and Optimization, chaired by Galán-Moreno, Rubio-Royo and Sánchez-Medina (Las Palmas); Computer Vision and Image Processing, chaired by Sotelo (Madrid); Mobile and Autonomous Transportation Systems, chaired by García-Rosa and De Pedro (Madrid); Computer-Aided System Optimization, chaired by Huemer and Lunglmayr (Klagenfurt); Modelling and Control of Mechatronics Systems, chaired by Schlacher and Scheidl (Linz); Heurist Problem Solving, chaired by Affenzeller and Jacak (Hagenberg) and Raidl (Vienna); Model-Based Systems Design, Simulation and Veriffication, chaired by Ceska (Brno); Biomimetic Software Systems, chaired by Braun (Sydney) and Klempous (Wroclaw) and Chaczko (Sydney); Computer-Based Methods for Clinical and Academic Medicine, chaired by Klempous (Wroclaw) and Rozenblit (Tucson); Mobile Computing Platforms and Technologies, chaired by Mayrhofer and Holzmann (Linz); and Modelling and Design of Complex Digital Systems by Signal Processing Methods, chaired by Astola (Tampere), Stankovic (Nis) and Moraga (Asturias, Dortmund). The Chairs of the workshops, with the advice of the International Advisory Committee, selected near 200 extended abstracts for oral presentation at the meeting.

There were three plenary invited speakers: Markus Schwaninger from St. Gallen (Modeling the Economic Crisis: System-Dynamics-Based Approach to Prevention), Jerzy Rozenblit from Tucson (Models and Techniques for Computer-Aided Surgical Training) and Luigi Ricciardi from Napoli (Uncertainty, Probability, Functionality).

With the additional help of the Session Chairs, a final selection was made of papers personally presented at the conference, final full versions of which are included in these volumes.

The conference was possible thanks to the efforts of the Chairs of the workshops in the selection and organization of all the material. The organizers must express their acknowledgement to the Director of the Elder Museum of Science and Technology, D. Fernando Pérez, and to the members of the museum. Special thanks are due to the staff of Springer in Heidelberg for their valuable support.

A group of Eurocast 2011 participants, on the Friday, 11 February afternoon post-conference excursion to the north of Gran Canaria.

June 2011   Roberto Moreno-Díaz
                                                          Franz Pichler
                                              Alexis Quesada-Arencibia

Organization

Organized by

Instituto Universitario de Ciencias y Tecnologías Cibernéticas
Universidad de Las Palmas de Gran Canaria, Spain

Österreichische Gesellschaft für Technologie-Politik
Wien, Austria

Centro de Automática y Robótica
Consejo Superior de Investigaciones Científicas y Universidad Politécnica de
Madrid

Museo Elder de la Ciencia y la Tecnología
Las Palmas de Gran Canaria, Spain

In cooperation with
International Federation for Automatic Control (IFAC)
(co-sponsorship applied)

Conference Chair

Roberto Moreno-Díaz (Las Palmas)

Program Chairman

Franz Pichler (Linz)

Organizing Committee Chairs

Alexis Quesada-Arencibia (Las Palmas)
Ricardo García-Rosa (Madrid)

Local Organizing Committee Chair

Alexis Quesada-Arencibia
Instituto Universitario de Ciencias y Tecnologías Cibernéticas
Universidad de Las Palmas de Gran Canaria
Campus de Tafira 35017 Las Palmas de Gran Canaria, Spain
Phone: +34-928-457108
Fax: +34-928-457099
e-mail: aquesada@dis.ulpgc.es

IN MEMORIAM

PROF. LUIGI M. RICCIARDI

Professor Luigi M. Ricciardi passed away last May 7 in Naples. He was a proud student of Eduardo Caianiello among other historical personalities in cybernetics. His own contributions to cybernetics and complex systems opened new frontiers that were to result in the fruitful works of many other researchers.

Luigi graduated in Physics in 1964 ("Laurea in Fisica"), in 1967 he obtained his Degree of "Perfezionamento in Fisica Teorica e Nucleare", and in 1971 his "Libera Docenza" in Cybernetics and Information Theory. From 1976 to 1981 he was full professor of Cybernetics and Information Theory at the Universities of Turin and of Salerno, and from 1981 he was full professor of Probability at the Department of Mathematics and Applications of Federico II Naples University. From 1983 he was Chairman of the Graduate Program for Research Doctor in Computational and Information Sciences and Director of the Graduate School in Mathematical and Informatics Sciences. Before being awarded his full professorship in Italy, he was a Research Staff Member with the Institute of Cybernetics of the Italian National Research Council and a faculty member with the Department of Theoretical Biology of the University of Chicago. His research activities, centered on applications of the theory of stochastic processes to biomathematics and on biomathematical and computational modeling, were carried out in collaboration with scientists from different countries, particularly from Japan, mainly within the framework of international bilateral research contracts sponsored by CNR and by the Ministry of Education and-Research. He therefore spent frequent periods in foreign universities and research centers as visiting professor and lecturer, in particular at the universities of Osaka and

Kyoto where he taught courses in the local graduate schools and supervised research activities of doctorate students and post-doctoral students. He authored, or co-authored, over 200 publications, mainly appearing in international journals and various books. He was an Associate Editor of *Scientiae Mathematicae Japonicae*, of the *International Journal of Cybernetics and Systems*, a member of the International Advisory Board of *Mathematica Japonica* and of *Ricerche di Matematica*, and the President of the Scientific Council of the International Institute for High Scientific Studies "Eduardo Caianiello" (IIASS). He organized and chaired numerous international workshops and was a member of the editorial board of several international journals. He was also a member of the Osterreichische Studiengesellschaft für Kybernetik (honorary member), the New York Academy of Sciences (life member), and the Naples Accademia di Scienze Fisiche e Matematiche (life member).

Besides his many scientific and professional values, Luigi Ricciardi was very much esteemed for his friendly personality, good and optimistic character to the very last moment, his teaching abilities and his special capacity to attract disciples, friends and colleagues everywhere. Some of us had the good luck of enjoying his magnificent hospitality in Naples. We have all lost a great scientist, a friend and a valuable and constant collaborator with EUROCAST. EUROCAST 2011, where he brilliantly delivered his last great plenary lecture, besides chairing his usual Workshop on Biocomputing, presents this modest tribute to his memory.

June 2011   Roberto Moreno-Díaz
                                                        Franz Pichler
                                               Alexis Quesada-Arencibia

Table of Contents – Part II

Modeling and Control of Mechatronic Systems

Biomimetic Software Systems

Computer-Based Methods for Clinical and Academic Medicine

Modeling and Design of Complex Digital Systems

Mobile and Autonomous Transportation Systems

Traffic Behavior, Modeling and Optimization

Mobile Computing Platforms and Technologies

Engineering Systems Applications

Table of Contents – Part I

Computation and Simulation in Modelling Biological Systems

Intelligent Information Processing

Heuristic Problem Solving

Computer Aided Systems Optimization

Model-Based System Design, Simulation, and Verification

Computer Vision and Image Processing

Optimization of a Magnetic Flux Leakage Measurement Set–Up Using FEM–Simulations

Johannes Atzlesberger* and Bernhard G. Zagar

Johannes Kepler University, Institute for Measurement Technology,
Altenbergerstr. 69, 4040 Linz, Austria
{johannes.atzlesberger,bernhard.zagar}@jku.at
http://www.emt.jku.at/

Abstract. This paper describes simulations of magnetic field strength distributions for magneto–conductive material in order to be able to optimize a measurement set–up that should be capable to detect minute changes of the magnetic field strength at the surface of a specimen containing some kind of material inhomogeneities or anisotropies of magnetic properties. The sensitivity which ultimately is limited by the noise figure of the sensing effect (GMR = giant magneto resistive effect) can be evaluated with respect to the detection of deviations in eddy current patterns caused by inhomogeneities of the material's conductivity or the anisotropy of magnetic properties of the specimen's material.

Keywords: Finite Elements Method (FEM), Magnetic Flux Leakage (MFL), Non–Destructive Testing (NDT), Giant Magneto Resistor (GMR).

1 Introduction

Tomographic methods applied to the analysis of inhomogeneous anisotropic properties of metals demand for the measurement some easily sensed parameters at some distance from the specimen's surface and the solution of a typically ill–posed mathematical problem. The measurement of magnetic properties is simplified by the advent of readily available highly sensitive GMR [1] sensors. In Fig. 1 a schematic set–up of the MFL–method [2] is shown. An electro magnet induces a magnetic flux which mainly flushes through the ferromagnetic specimen. Due to inhomogeneities inside the specimen[1] the magnetic flux leakage changes close to the positions of these inhomogeneities and can be detected by sensors which are positioned near the specimen's surface. Only for very uncomplicated geometries, the distribution of the magnetic field strength can be calculated or approximated by analytical methods [8]. But for more complex

---

* The authors gratefully acknowledge the partial financial support for the work presented in this paper by the Austrian Center of Competence in Mechatronics (ACCM).

[1] This inhomogeneities can be caused by corrosion [3], by surface–defects [4], through specimen thickness variations [5], or non–metallic inclusions, flaws, cracks [6], material blemishes and/or even residual stresses [7].

R. Moreno-Díaz et al. (Eds.): EUROCAST 2011, Part II, LNCS 6928, pp. 1–8, 2012.
© Springer-Verlag Berlin Heidelberg 2012

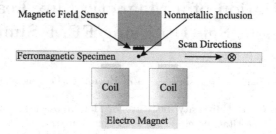

Fig. 1. Schematic test set–up of the magnetic flux leakage method (aka magnetic anomaly detection)

geometries and inhomogeneous, anisotropic, nonlinear material properties the application of numerical methods are essential.

2   FEM Simulation Model

If there exists no relative velocity between the electro magnet[2] and the specimen, no eddy–currents are driven and the magnetic field strength depends only on the distribution of the material's inhomogeneities. For this case the Maxwell's equations are [9]

$$\mathrm{curl}\boldsymbol{H} = \boldsymbol{J} \tag{1}$$

$$\mathrm{curl}\boldsymbol{E} = 0 \tag{2}$$

$$\mathrm{div}\boldsymbol{B} = 0 \tag{3}$$

$$\mathrm{div}\boldsymbol{D} = 0 \tag{4}$$

and the material equation is

$$\boldsymbol{B} = \mu\boldsymbol{H} \tag{5}$$

with μ, permeability[3], $\boldsymbol{H}$, magnetic field strength, $\boldsymbol{B}$, magnetic flux density, $\boldsymbol{J}$, current density and $\boldsymbol{E}$, electric field strength. Using the relation

$$\boldsymbol{B} = \mathrm{curl}\boldsymbol{A} \tag{6}$$

with $\boldsymbol{A}$, the scalar potential, the problem can be resided as a differential equation (Poisson's equation)

$$\Delta\boldsymbol{A} = -\mu\boldsymbol{J} \tag{7}$$

with Δ as the laplace operator and can subsequently be approximately solved by FEM–programs that are readily available.

---

[2] Direct–Current (DC) flows through the coils of the electro magnet, thus the magnetic flux density time–invariant: $\frac{\partial \boldsymbol{B}}{\partial t} = 0$.

[3] Only for homogeneous isotropic materials $\mu = \mu_0\mu_r$ is a scalar with μ_0, permeability of free space and μ_r, relative permeability. In general μ is a tensor which means not only the magnitude but also the direction of $\boldsymbol{H}$ and $\boldsymbol{B}$ are different.

3 Simulation Results

The result of a two–dimensional FEM–simulation[4] for an MFL set–up (excitation current $I = 4$ A, number of coil windings $N = 2 \times 110$, single air gap width $a = 1$ mm) and the zoomed area of the ferromagnetic specimen containing a defect can be seen in Fig. 2. The color represents the magnetic flux density and the dashed line indicates the measurement plane of the magnetic leakage field characteristic for comparing the simulation results of a defective and a non–defective specimen as shown in Fig. 3(a). The difference of this two curves can be measured experimentally. (An exemplary measurement result of a steel plate containing real holes and a magnetizable spiral drill is presented in Sec. 4 in Fig. 8.) The magnetic flux density inside the specimen in the center between the two pole shoes in Fig. 2 is nearly homogeneous and approximately constant along a short distance for a homogeneous, isotropic material. Thus the axis of symmetry is the optimal measurement position for a sensor that detects the variation of the magnetic leakage field in the horizontal direction.

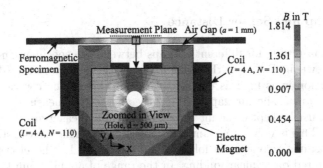

Fig. 2. Two–dimensional FEM–simulation of the magnetic circuit (excitation current $I = 4$ A, number of coil windings $N = 2 \times 110$, air gap $a = 1$ mm). The zoomed in view containing a defect, which causes a field displacement the location of the sensor. The material next to the hole (red area) is driven into magnetic saturation. Please note that the coordinate system's origin is positioned at the left hand side pole shoe inner surface.

3.1 Magnetic Excitation

The magnetic field distribution for the same model as in Fig. 2 but using an excitation current of only 1 A is shown in Fig. 3(b). For this case the material is not driven anywhere into magnetic saturation therefore the field variation at the sensor position due to the hole is much smaller than in Fig. 3(a). In order to get a magnetic leakage field variation as large as possible, the magnetic circuit has to be driven into magnetic saturation due to inhomogeneities[5].

---

[4] All FEM–simulations in this paper were made with *ELEFANT2D* (=ELEctromagnetic Field ANalysis Tools 2D, www.igte.tugraz.at).

[5] To be precise only the hole's adjacent material should be driven into magnetic saturation.

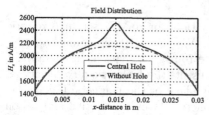
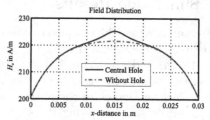

(a) Simulated magnetic leakage field along the measurement plane of Fig. 2 at an excitation current of $I = 4$ A.

(b) Simulation result for the same specimen as in (a) at an excitation current of only $I = 1$ A. The material is not driven anywhere into magnetic saturation.

Fig. 3. Simulation results for the model in Fig. 2 for different excitation currents. The largest magnetic leakage field variation is obtained for driving the hole's adjacent material into magnetic saturation thus displacing field lines out of the specimen.

3.2 Air Gap and Sensor Distance

The simulation results for different air gaps between the specimen and the pole shoes are shown in Fig. 4(a). For this example the field variation due to the air gap variation is as high as the field variation due to the centric hole (diameter = 500 μm). The air gap significantly affects the measurement results, therefore it must be kept constant through the whole measurement cycle in the experiments. This is very important especially for observing curved steel sheets, thus the specimen's contour is followed automatically by the electro magnet which is mounted on a linear guiding. In the range of about 1 mm the sensor's y–distance)to the specimen's surface[6]) affects the results only marginal. For smaller distances the results would be influenced more, but due to the housing of the sensor it cannot be positioned closer to the specimen than 1 mm. Anyway in the test set–up presented in Sec. 4 the sensor is mounted on an adjustable linear guiding in order to have a constant sensor distance.

3.3 Lateral Sensitivity

In Fig. 5(a) the effect of asymmetrically positioned inhomogeneities is shown. The excentric hole can be detected by an excentric sensor ($H_2 = 334$ A/m) but also by a sensor positioned in the center between the pole shoes ($H_1 = 63$ A/m). A centric hole (Fig. 5(b)) can be detected by a centric ($H_3 = 363$ A/m) but also by an excentric sensor ($H_4 = 82$ A/m). Therefore a total surface scan is possible by using a rather coarse sensor array or coarse scanning grid. The largest sensitivity, however, is obtained for positioning both the hole and the sensor at the center.

---

[6] Depending on the vertical position of the measurement plane (dashed line) in Fig. 2.

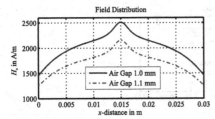

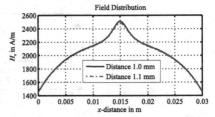

(a) Simulated magnetic leakage field for different air gaps.

(b) Simulated magnetic leakage field for different y–distances between the sensor and the specimen's surface.

Fig. 4. Simulation results for different air gaps and sensor distances from the specimen's surface

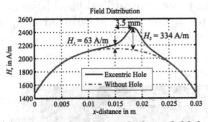

(a) Simulated magnetic leakage field for a hole positioned 3.5 mm lateral to the center.

(b) Simulated magnetic leakage field for a centric hole.

Fig. 5. Simulation results for an excentric and a centric hole and the obtained signal amplitude of centric and excentric positioned sensors

3.4   Vertical Position of the Inhomogeneity

An important point is the distinction of the inhomogeneity's vertical position. In Fig. 6 the results for specimen containing no deficiency, a central inclusion and an inclusion with a diameter of 500 μm located 650 μm underneath the surface are shown. The altitude–to–width ratio of the subsurface inclusion is about twice as large as the ratio of the central inclusion. For a known inclusion size its vertical position can be estimated and vice versa for a known vertical inclusion position its size can be estimated. In general inhomogeneities on or near the surface produce a large signal with a small spatial dilatation compared to the signal amplitude and inhomogeneities deep inside the specimen produce a small signal with a widely spread dilatation compared to the signal amplitude. From this size/depth dependency can be calculated that both parameters are measurable with a top and bottom scan or a single sided scan with two distinct distances y.

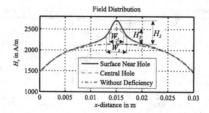

Fig. 6. Simulated magnetic leakage field along the measurement plane of a specimen containing no deficiency, a central and a surface near inclusion. Altitude–to–width ratios: $H_1/W_1 = 182$ A/(m·mm), $H_2/W_2 = 95.5$ A/(m·mm)

4   Experimental Arrangement

A hot rolled steel sheet (thickness = 3.3 mm) containing drilled blind holes and a broken magnetizable spiral drill (diameter = 500 μm) was scanned using a GMR magnetometer and a GMR gradiometer type system[7].

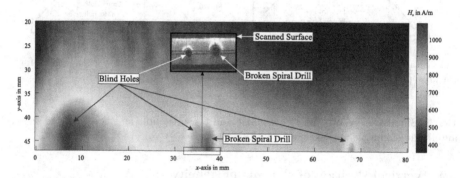

Fig. 7. Two–dimensional magnetometer scan of a ferromagnetic specimen (thickness = 3.3 mm) and a microscopic image of the specimen's front side containing a blind hole and a broken magnetizable spiral drill with diameter of 500 μm.

The holes and the air gap between the specimen and the broken spiral drill (which is partly filled with magnetizable swarf and therefore the effective air gap is even smaller) simulate elongated, nonmagnetic, subsurface inclusions. In Fig. 8 a two–dimensional magnetometer scan and two line scans (obtained by a magnetometer and a gradiometer) are shown. The peaks in the magnetometer signal and the steep flanks in the gradiometer signal indicate the hole's and the spiral drill's position. The signal peak (Fig. 8(a)) produced by the spiral drill is higher than the peak produced by the blind hole next to it, because the spiral drill is

---

[7] The magnetometer measures the magnetic field strength and the gradiometer measures the gradient of the magnetic field strength along their sensitive axes.

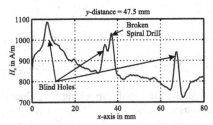

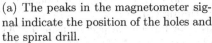

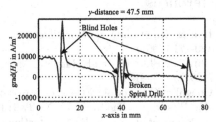

(a) The peaks in the magnetometer signal indicate the position of the holes and the spiral drill.

(b) The steep flanks in the gradiometer signal indicate the position of the holes and the spiral drill.

Fig. 8. A magnetometer and a gradiometer line scan of a ferromagnetic specimen (thickness = 3.3 mm) containing blind holes and a broken magnetizable spiral drill with a diameter of 500 μm

closer to the specimen's surface than the blind hole as it is shown in the microscopic image in Fig. 7.

5   Conclusion

A measurement set–up applying the magnetic flux leakage (MFL) method was analyzed using FEM–simulations. The results allow an optimization of the arrangement in order to get a highly sensitive measurement system which is able to detect magnetic anomalies in ferromagnetic material. The simulation results were verified by observing a ferromagnetic specimen with a real life measurement set–up. The following items summing up the most important findings obtained by the simulations:

- Inhomogeneities can be detected easier by observing the surface parallel magnetic field strength component (H_x) than the surface normal component (H_y).
- The largest sensitivity is obtained, if the magnetic circuit is driven into magnetic saturation locally due to inhomogeneities.
- A variation of the air gap between the specimen and the pole shoes significantly affects the measurement results.
- The largest sensitivity is obtained for positioning the sensor and the hole (inhomogeneity) in the center between the pole shoes.
- Also an asymmetrically placed inhomogeneity affects the central magnetic leakage between the pole shoes therefore a total surface scan is possible by scanning the specimen's surface using a coarse sensor array or scanning grid.
- Inhomogeneities on or near the surface produce a large signal with a small spatial dilatation compared to the signal amplitude.
- Inhomogeneities deep inside the specimen produce a small signal with a widely spread dilatation compared to the signal amplitude.

References

1. Hauser, H., et al.: Magnetoresistors. In: Magnetic Sensors and Magnetometers, pp. 129-171 (2001)
2. Blitz, J.: Electrical and Magnetic Methods of Non–destructive Testing, 2nd edn. (1997)
3. Coughlin, C.R., et al.: Effects of Stress on MFL Responses From Elongated Corrosion Pits in Pipeline Steel. In: NDT&E International, vol. 33, pp. 118–188 (2000)
4. Atzlesberger, J., Zagar, B.G.: Detection of Inhomogeneities in Magneto–Conductive Objects. In: Proc. of the SSD 2011, Sousse, Tunisia (2011)
5. Niese, F.: Wall Thickness Measurement Sensor for Pipeline Inspection using EMAT Technology in Combination with Pulsed Eddy Current and MFL. In: ECNDT (2006)
6. Göktepe, M.: Non–destructive Crack Detection by Capturing Local Flux Leakage Field. In: Sensors and Actuators, 70–72 (2001)
7. Ricken, W.: GMR and Eddy Current Sensor in Use of Stress Measurement. Sensor and Actuators A91, 42–45 (2001)
8. Foerster, F.: On the Way from the Know–How to Know–Why in the Magnetic Leakage Field Method of Nondestructive Testing, pp. 1154–1398 (1985)
9. Strassacker, G., Strassacker, P.: Analytische und numerische Methoden der Feldberechnung, Teubner, Germany (1993)

Comparison of RF Power Amplifier Behavioral Models with Respect to Their Modeling Capabilities in Adjacent and Alternate Bands

Markus Hoflehner and Andreas Springer

Johannes Kepler University, Altenberger Str. 69, 4040 Linz, Austria
m.hoflehner@nthfs.jku.at

Abstract. In this work a comparison of three different behavioral models for radio frequency (RF) power amplifier (PA) is done. The used models were a Volterra series model, the memory polynomial model (MPM) and the generalized memory polynomial model (GMPM). A special focus is put on their modeling capabilities in the adjacent and alternate band. It was found that the Volterra model gives the best modeling performance but also has a high amount of parameter. The GMPM has a significantly lower amount of parameter yet a comparable modeling performance. The MPM uses only very few parameter but still achieves a good modeling performance. The modeling performance for each model was highest in the inband, is less in the adjacent band and decrease further in the alternate band. It also is highly dependent on the used order of nonlinearity.

Keywords: Power Amplifier (PA), behavioral modeling, nonlinear filters, normalized mean square error (NMSE), adjacent channel error power ratio (ACEPR).

1 Introduction

In mobile communication terminals the constraints for power amplifier (PA) constantly get tighter with respect to power consumption and spectral efficiency. The tradeoff in PA design is always between efficiency and linearity. As modern wireless communication standards demand the use of higher-order QAM modulation formats, linearity of the PA, is a must. To ensure this linearity, digital predistortion (DPD) [1], known from applications in base stations, is increasingly considered in mobile stations. A necessary perquisite for DPD is an accurate model of the PA which accounts for inband but also for adjacent and alternate band distortion.

In this paper we compare the modeling abilities of different Volterra-based models [2] regarding their adjacent and alternate band behavior. For evaluation we use the normalized mean square error (NMSE) and the adjacent channel error power ratio (ACEPR). The NMSE is calculated for the whole spectrum and separately in the inband, the adjacent band and the alternate band.

R. Moreno-Díaz et al. (Eds.): EUROCAST 2011, Part II, LNCS 6928, pp. 9–16, 2012.

2 Behavioral Models

Our comparison is limited to the following behavioral models: Memory Polynomial Model (MPM) [3], Generalized Memory Polynomial Model (GMPM)[4] and Volterra Model. These models seem to be the most promising candidates for an implementation of a DPD for a mobile terminal. This is because the model parameter estimation is a linear process and can be done in one step. A major selection criterion was the complexity/accuracy tradeoff [5] as in a terminal resources are limited.

One of the simplest models is the Memory Polynomial Model (MPM), also known as parallel Hammerstein Model. It consists of a nonlinear function for each memory tap, alternatively it can be seen that the contributions for each polynomial order are filtered by a dedicated filter. Because of the possibility to estimate the parameters by linear least squares, the estimation procedure is fairly simple.

$$y\,[n] = \sum_{\substack{p=1 \\ p\in\mathbb{O}}}^{P} \sum_{q=0}^{Q-1} h_{pq} x\,[n-q]\,|x\,[n-q]|^{p-1}. \tag{1}$$

Here $\mathbb{O}$ denotes the set of natural odd numbers, P is the maximum order of the nonlinearity and Q is the memory length. $x\,[n]$ and $y\,[n]$ are the input and output sequence of the PA, respectively. Finally h_{pq} are the model coefficients.

Morgan et. al. propsed the Generalized Memory Polynomial Model (GMPM) in [4]. The difference to the MPM is the generalization term G which increases the modeling capabilities, but also the number of coefficients.

$$y\,[n] = \sum_{\substack{p=1 \\ p\in\mathbb{O}}}^{P_h} \sum_{q=0}^{Q_h-1} h_{pq} x\,[n-q]\,|x\,[n-q]|^{p-1}$$

$$+ \sum_{\substack{p=1 \\ p\in\mathbb{O}}}^{P_a} \sum_{q=0}^{Q_a-1} \sum_{g=1}^{G_a} a_{pqg} x\,[n-q]\,|x\,[n-q+g]|^{p-1}$$

$$+ \sum_{\substack{p=1 \\ p\in\mathbb{O}}}^{P_b} \sum_{q=0}^{Q_b-1} \sum_{g=1}^{G_b} b_{pqg} x\,[n-q]\,|x\,[n-q-g]|^{p-1}. \tag{2}$$

In this comparison the Volterra model is assumed to be the most general polynomial model. The above introduced models are in principle simplifications of the Volterra model. Due to this the best modeling performance is expected for the Volterra model. However this comes at the price of a high number of model coefficients to be identified.

$$y[n] = \mathbb{H}(x[n]) = \sum_{\substack{p=1 \\ p \in \mathbb{O}}}^{P} \left(\sum_{q_1=0}^{Q-1} \sum_{q_2=0}^{Q-1} \cdots \sum_{q_p=0}^{Q-1} h_p(q_1, q_2, \ldots, q_p) \right.$$

$$\left. \prod_{i=1}^{\frac{p+1}{2}} x[n-q_i] \prod_{j=\frac{p+3}{2}}^{p} x[n-q_j] \right). \tag{3}$$

3   Error Criteria

For the evaluation of model performance two different measures were used. The normalized mean square error (NMSE) and the adjacent channel error power ratio (ACEPR). The NMSE is a commonly used figure of merit in behavioral modeling. It is defined as

$$NMSE_{(dB)} = 10 \log_{10} \frac{\sum_n |y_{\text{meas}}[n] - y_{\text{model}}[n]|^2}{\sum_n |y_{\text{meas}}[n]|^2}, \tag{4}$$

were $y_{\text{meas}}[n]$ is the measured amplifier output and $y_{\text{model}}[n]$ is the output of the estimated model. Due to signal characteristics it mainly compares the in-band performance of the model. We circumvented this by brickwall filtering the signal for each band (in-band, adjacent- and alternate-band) and separately calculating the NMSE.

The ACEPR is a measure for the out of band performance. Because the modeling capability for the upper and lower bands can vary they have to be calculated separately. For the performance evaluation only the inferior value was used. It is defined as

$$ACEPR_{(dB)} = 10 \log_{10} \frac{\sum_{\text{adj. Band}} |Y_{\text{meas}}(f) - Y_{\text{model}}(f)|^2}{\sum_{\text{channel}} |Y_{\text{meas}}(f)|^2}, \tag{5}$$

where $Y_{\text{meas}}(f)$ is the discrete Fourier transform (DFT) of the measured output signal and $Y_{\text{model}}(f)$ is the DFT of the model output. The summation in the numerator is performed over the upper or lower adjacent band while the denominator is always summarized over the channel.

4   Measurement Setup

For the measurements a system, as described in [6] and [7], was used. A vector signal generator (R&S SMJ 100A) and a vector signal analyzer (R&S FSQ40) were used to generate the PA input signal and analyze the PA output signal, respectively.

4.1 PA and Signal

As a reference PA a solid state power amplifier was used and driven close to saturation. At 2 GHz the 1-dB compression point is 23 dBm with a small signal gain of 23 dB.

As test signal different realizations of an QAM16 signal with 2 GHz center frequency and 2.4 MHz bandwidth were used. The peak-to-average ratio (PAR) of the used signals were around 7.8 dB. These signals were generated in the vector signal generator (VSG) and the output of the PA was fed to the vector signal analyzer (VSA) which sampled the baseband signal with 20 MHz.

4.2 Signal Processing

The signal generation, model estimation, synchronization, and error calculation was done in Matlab. Over 150 different measurements were made and the measured data streams were split into identification data and validation data. The signal synchronization was done in two steps. First a crosscorrelation was used to find the integer sample delay between the input and output signal. For the subsample synchronization a three point interpolation method as described in [8] was used.

Calculation of the NMSE was done for the measurements and estimated models as well as for their in-band, alternate band and also adjacent band components separately. To have a better understanding of the NMSE in the different bands the corresponding ACEPR was calculated.

5 Results

Results show that the in-band modeling capabilities for all models are generally very good. As expected, the Volterra model almost always gives the best results for the overall NMSE but also has the biggest amount of parameter and thus needs much more resources (time and/or power). The memory polynomial model has a significantly lower number of parameters but also shows a good modeling ability (see Fig. 1). A direct comparison with the generalized memory polynomial model is difficult. This is due to the generalization factor that increases the memory length for some input terms (see Fig. 2). This leads to the expected result that for a low amount of memory taps the Volterra model is inferior to a GMPM with an, relative to the amount of memory taps, high generalization factor.

As can be seen in table 1, the modeling accuracy for all three models is best in the inband, less in the adjacent band and decreases significantly in the alternate band. The modeling capabilities in the adjacent and alternate band mainly depend on the order of the model and significantly less on the amount of memory used. This can be seen for the ACEPR but also for the NMSE in the corresponding band. Higher order models show better capabilities for modeling in the adjacent band due to the wider bandwidth their mixing products cover.

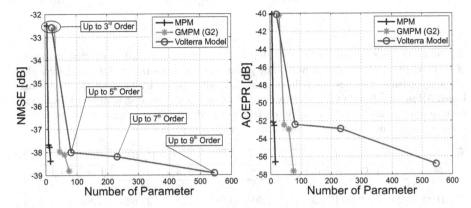

Fig. 1. Modeling performance of all models with respect to the amount of model parameter is shown here. The order of nonlinearity is varied from 3rd to 9th whereas the memory length is alway three. For the NMSE the Volterra model has the best result however also the highest amount of parameters. When regarding the ACEPR the GMPM leads to the best result. This can be seen in table 2.

Simulations were done from 3rd up to 9th order, however, the performance in the alternate channel, despite it was increasing, was always poor.

All models showed an improvement of modeling accuracy with an increasing amount of memory. This is also true for the modeling in the out of band regions. As stated earlier the improvement in the adjacent and alternate band depends on the used order of nonlinearity, i.e. good improvements are only possible in regions covered by a sufficiently high order. This increase in modeling performance is dependent on the used model. Here the Volterra Model showed the best performance increase, followed by the GMPM, while the MPM showed the least increase. This is attributed to the amount of additional available parameters with each increase of the memory length.

When comparing the NMSE values of the three different models in the adjacent and alternate band the results are comparable to the behavior of the NMSE over the whole spectrum. The MPM also shows good modeling performance, however is outperformed by the Volterra model and GMPM. For a generalization factor of one the Volterra model clearly outperforms the GMPM. With a generalization factor of two or higher the GMPM shows a lower NMSE than the Volterra model for short memory length (see Fig. 2).

Also it was found that more coefficients not always lead to a better NMSE if different models are considered. This is also the case if the NMSE is considered only for inband, alternate band or adjacent band. Despite its relative small number of model coefficients the MPM has shown very good results with respect to its modeling capabilities for adjacent and alternate band.

When comparing the ACEPR and the NMSE in the adjacent channel (see Fig. 1) one can notice that the overall behavior is similar (see table 2).

Table 1. The performance of the three models in terms of NMSE for different orders of nonlinearity (NL) is shown here. The global NMSE gives the performance over the whole spectrum, whereas the following NMSE values are calculated for the according band. All models in this table have a memory length of 3. The degradation of modeling performance outside the inband is clearly noticeable, also the increase of modeling accuracy with the order of the used nonlinearity is apparent.

Model	NL Order	# param	NMSE/dB					
			Global	low alt.	low adj.	inband	high adj.	high alt.
MPM	3	6	-32,50	-0,62	-17,69	-34,61	-17,76	-0,71
GMPM (G2)	3	30	-32,60	-0,68	-17,81	-34,68	-17,87	-0,75
Volterra	3	21	-32,58	-0,67	-17,72	-34,70	-17,77	-0,75
MPM	7	12	-37,78	-4,60	-29,98	-38,64	-30,49	-4,72
GMPM (G2)	7	60	-38,10	-4,90	-30,41	-38,93	-30,64	-4,96
Volterra	7	231	-38,20	-4,86	-30,36	-39,03	-30,57	-4,88
MPM	9	15	-38,38	-7,23	-34,06	-39,00	-34,94	-7,24
GMPM (G2)	9	75	-38,80	-7,64	-35,18	-39,36	-35,24	-7,62
Volterra	9	546	-38,92	-7,55	-34,39	-39,49	-34,49	-7,42

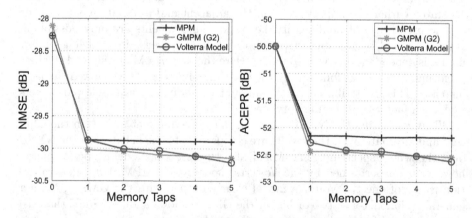

Fig. 2. This shows NMSE and ACEPR values in the adjacent band for a variable memory length. The used order of nonlinearity was five. It can be found that for a lower amount of memory (here < 4) and a generalization factor of > 2 the GMPM gives better results. This is attributed to the fact that for these cases the GMPM already has high number of parameter relative to the Volterra model. Also due to its structure it has a larger memory length than the compared Volterra model.

Table 2. A comparison of the behavior of the NMSE and the ACEPR in the adjacent band for all models is given here. One can see that the GMPM while usually having a lower overall modeling performance as the Volterra model gives better results in the adjacent channel. This is especially true for 9th order.

Model	NL Order	# param	Global	NMSE/dB low adj.	NMSE/dB high adj.	ACEPR/dB low adj.	ACEPR/dB high adj.
MPM	3	6	-32,50	-17,69	-17,76	-40,22	-40,11
GMPM (G2)	3	30	-32,60	-17,81	-17,87	-40,35	-40,22
Volterra	3	21	-32,58	-17,72	-17,77	-40,26	-40,12
MPM	7	12	-37,78	-29,98	-30,49	-52,51	-52,84
GMPM (G2)	7	60	-38,10	-30,41	-30,64	-52,95	-52,99
Volterra	7	231	-38,20	-30,36	-30,57	-52,90	-52,92
MPM	9	15	-38,38	-34,06	-34,94	-56,59	-57,29
GMPM (G2)	9	75	-38,80	-35,18	-35,24	-57,72	-57,59
Volterra	9	546	-38,92	-34,39	-34,49	-56,92	-56,84

6 Conclusion

In this work three different behavioral models for power amplifier were compared for their overall modeling capability and their modeling capability in the adjacent and alternate band. Also the number of parameters of each model was an additional evaluation criterion. The compared models were the Volterra series model, the memory polynomial model (MPM) and the generalized memory polynomial model (GMPM).

It was found that the Volterra series model has the best modeling performance when comparing models with equal order of nonlinearity and memory depth. When the amount of model parameters is included in the comparison the MPM is due to its low amount of model parameter clearly advantageous despite its slightly poorer NMSE/ACEPR values. Due to the generalization factor the amount of parameter for the GMPM reaches comparable modeling performance as the Volterra model with a lower number of parameters.

It was found that for all models the modeling performance is highest in the inband, less in the adjacent band and decrease further in the alternate band. Also the absolute modeling performance largely depends on the order of the model. The modeling performance of the different models in the adjacent and alternate band is analog to their overall performance, thus the MPM has the worst NMSE but also the lowest amount of parameter. Whereas the Volterra Model and the GMPM have a much higher amount of parameter but also better modeling performance.

Acknowledgments. The research leading to these results was conducted partly in the frame of the European ENIAC project, MIRANDELA, and received funding from the ENIAC Joint Undertaking under grant agreement number

120221 together with funding from the COMET K2 Center "Austrian Center of Competence in Mechatronics (ACCM)". The COMET Program is funded by the Austrian Federal government, the Federal State of Upper Austria and the Scientific Partners of ACCM.

References

1. Ding, L., Zhou, G.T., Morgan, D.R., Ma, Z., Kenney, J.S., Kim, J., Giardina, C.R.: A robust digital baseband predistorter constructed using memory polynomials. IEEE Transactions on Communications 52, 159–165 (2004)
2. Schetzen, M.: The Volterra and Wiener Theories of Nonlinear Systems, Revised edn. Krieger (2006)
3. Kim, J., Konstantinou, K.: Digital predistortion of wideband signals based on power amplifier model with memory. Electronics Letters 37, 1417–1418 (2001)
4. Morgan, D.R., Ma, Z., Kim, J., Zierdt, M.G., Pastalan, J.: A generalized memory polynomial model for digital predistortion of RF power amplifiers. Electronics Letters 54, 3852–3860 (2006)
5. Tehrani, A.S., Cao, H., Afsardoost, S., Eriksson, T., Isaksson, M., Fager, C.: A Comparative Analysis of the Complexity/Accuracy Tradeoff in Power Amplifier Behavioral Models. IEEE Trans. on Microw. Theory and Techn. 58, 1510–1520 (2010)
6. Isaksson, M., Wisell, D., Ronnow, D.: A comparative analysis of behavioral models for RF power amplifiers. IEEE Trans. on Microw. Theory and Techn. 54, 348–359 (2006)
7. Landin, P.N., Fager, C., Isaksson, M., Andersson, K.: Power Amplifier Behavioral Modeling Performance Comparison of the LSNA and the Modulation-Domain System. In: 72nd ARFTG Microw. Meas. Conf., Portland, pp. 73–78 (December 2008)
8. Wiens, T., Bradley, S.: A Comparison of Time Delay Estimation Methods for Periodic Signals, Technical report, University of Auckland, Auckland, New Zealand (2009)

A Network and System Level Approach towards an Accurate Simulation of WSNs

Georg Möstl[1], Richard Hagelauer[1], Gerhard Müller[2], and Andreas Springer[2]

[1] Research Institute for Integrated Circuits
{moestl,hagel}@riic.at
[2] Institute for Communications Engineering and
RF-Systems Johannes Kepler University, Austria
{g.mueller,a.springer}@nthfs.jku.at

Abstract. Since wireless sensor networks (WSNs) are used increasingly in industrial applications, new tight constraints on the timing and power consumption behaviour arise. These constraints cannot be investigated properly by using state-of-the-art simulation tools. In our work we consider and model the WSN at different levels of abstraction in the domains hardware, software, and network. Additionally, the behaviour of the software component executed on a node, which has a major impact on its timing and power consumption, is included in the simulation while maintaining acceptable performance. We show the usefulness and accuracy of our developed methodology using a simple but expressive TDMA-based networking scenario.

Keywords: Hardware/software/network co-simulation, wireless sensor networks, source level simulation, real-life code.

1   Introduction

A network consisting of several resource-constrained sensing devices, i.e. sensor nodes, that monitor a variety of environmental conditions (temperature, sound, acceleration, etc.) and communicate by means of wireless transmission is called a wireless sensor network (WSN). In the past few years, the relevance of WSNs has increased, since they have been employed in a growing range of application domains, such as building automation, car-interior devices, car-to-car communication, container monitoring and tracking, health care and environmental monitoring.

Nowadays, WSNs in control and feedback control systems deployed in industrial environments are becoming increasingly interesting to developers. This recent application area imposes new tight constraints on the network. In addition to reliability and low power consumption, the ability to operate in real-time – and therefore the timing behaviour of the nodes – is of primary interest.

Since development and evaluation of WSNs are complex tasks (due to their distributed nature, diversity of operational scenarios, repeatability, number of nodes, etc.), the only feasible approach is simulation. Simulation always goes

R. Moreno-Díaz et al. (Eds.): EUROCAST 2011, Part II, LNCS 6928, pp. 17–24, 2012.

hand in hand with abstraction, which can lead to a loss in accuracy. Existing simulators can be divided into three broad categories. The first category of simulators (e.g. Castalia [1]) support efficient development of algorithms in an early protocol design phase, using abstract and highly tuneable modules (e.g. MAC) but with the drawback of neglecting timing effects of the hardware components and the software running on a node. Simulators in the second category (e.g. TOSSIM [7]) include the application code in the simulation and are based on an operating system. The drawbacks of this category are (i) the component view of the hardware peripherals and (ii) limited support for interrupt processing in the execution model, which leads to inaccurate timing behaviour. The third category of simulators (e.g. AEON [6]) uses a cycle-accurate instruction-level emulator, which reflects the timing aspect of the software component but is bound to a specific platform and is unfeasible for simulating dozens of nodes.

From our point of view, meeting the needs of WSN development for control and feedback control systems requires introducing a new category of WSN simulation located between categories two and three. The key task is to establish a methodology which allows accurate simulation of (i) the energy consumption and (ii) timing behaviour of all essential network components while maintaining acceptable simulation performance. We achieve this by combining established concepts, namely *system level modelling*, *source level simulation (SLS)* and *network simulation*. Nodes in the network are modelled at the system level using different abstraction levels corresponding to the impact of the hardware components. To include real-life applications, i.e. the software component, in the simulation, we use natively executed and time-annotated code. Since the source code is used as the functional representation and for annotation, this approach is called source level simulation. To investigate phenomena related to the radio frequency channel (throughput, reliability, etc.), we use network simulation.

The contribution of this paper is twofold. First, we combine several established concepts into a new general methodology for WSN simulation with acceptable simulation performance and increased accuracy concerning timing and power consumption behaviour. Second, we show the practical feasibility and usefulness of our methodology based on the implementation of a typical networking scenario. We implemented our system using the PAWiS [18] framework, which builds upon the discrete event network simulator OMNeT++ [17].

The remainder of this paper is organised as follows: Section 2 gives an overview of related work done so far. We introduce our concept in section 3. Application of the concept and example simulation results are presented in section 4, and section 5 comprises the conclusion of this paper and future work.

2   Related Work

Since determining the energy consumption of nodes and including real-life application code are crucial tasks when simulating and developing WSNs, only those existing simulation environments are considered which offer these aspects.

Landsiedel et al. developed AEON [6], which builds upon Avrora [16]. While Avrora offers cycle-accurate instruction-level simulation of wireless sensor networks consisting of AVR-based nodes, it does not have any power-profiling mechanism. AEON integrates an energy model (i.e. pre-measured current draws of each state of sensor node components) into Avrora and extends the implementation of each emulated hardware component by monitoring its power usage.

PowerTOSSIM [15] is an extension of the TOSSIM [7] simulator and enables estimation of the energy consumption of Mica2 network sensor nodes. TOSSIM is located at the operating system abstraction level using TinyOS [8] and is therefore highly scalable. An energy model (i.e. pre-measured current draws) in combination with *Power State Transition Messages* is used to determine the energy consumption of a node.

In [4], Eriksson et al. presented a simulation environment consisting of the COOJA [13] sensor network simulator, the MSPSim [3] instruction level emulator of MSP430-based nodes, and a power profiler integrated into the Contiki [2] operating system. The Contiki power profiler is based on a linear energy model which uses pre-measured current draws and the on/off times of the node components to estimate the energy consumption.

Nguyen et al. [12] presented a SystemC-based cycle-accurate simulator for wireless body area networks (BSN). The simulator contains a model of the MSP430 microcontroller architecture and executes application code written in NesC and compiled with TinyOS. A power monitor module is added to monitor and accumulate the energy consumed by each component in the BSN node.

SensorSim [14] is a simulator for sensor networks and builds upon an NS-2 [9] 802.11 network model. Although the authors added power, battery and CPU models, the high level of abstraction results in inaccurate and coarse-grained approximations. Another drawback is that the developers have withdrawn the public release of the SensorSim suite of tools.

In [5], Fummi et al. presented an energy-aware simulation setup targeting the AquisGrain-2 node. TinyOS-based application code is executed on an instruction set simulator (μCSim), while hardware and network components are modelled in SystemC and executed by the SystemC simulation kernel. The transceiver is abstracted to a finite state machine model of the IEEE 802.15.4 MAC protocol with associated power consumption values for each state.

Our approach differs from the aforementioned simulation environments in several ways. First, we use native execution of real-life application code in the simulation. This approach, in combination with a homogeneous simulator, provides the fastest possible simulation principle. Second, arbitrary application code can be simulated, i.e. there is no need for using an underlying operating system on the target platform. Third, building upon the sophisticated energy model of PAWiS [18], it is possible to establish a simple electrical network of power consumers and suppliers which influence each other. Finally, the presented methodology allows modelling the network at different abstraction levels and running cross-level models of the nodes in one simulation.

3   Methodology

Our methodology comprises three concepts to model the software, hardware and network components of the WSN.

Software. Applications targeting embedded systems are typically written in the C programming language and must somehow be linked into the simulation. Because an interpretive approach using an instruction-level emulator decreases simulation performance dramatically, a different approach is used, namely native execution. The application is compiled for and run on the host processor and linked into the simulation using a glue logic. A special software architecture is needed to separate code related to microcontroller peripherals, i.e. low-level drivers, from other parts of the application. This enables portability between (i) different hardware platforms and (ii) between simulation and hardware.

Since the application is executed on the host processor, the correct timing behaviour of the application on the target architecture is lost. To establish a time-accurate simulation, the code used for simulation is annotated at the source level. Annotation uses estimated time values related to the execution of the code on the microcontroller. A more detailed description of the software component was published in [10].

Hardware. Modularity, a notion of time, concurrency, and specification of wait conditions (event/time) are the fundamental concepts of hardware modelling and are provided by PAWiS [18]. Using PAWiS, the nodes of the network are broken down and modelled at the system level (CPU, digital I/O, timer, etc.). As each of these components has a different impact on the power consumption and timing behaviour of the node, they are modelled at different abstraction levels. For example, the transceiver module, a major power consumer, is modelled in more detail, reflecting the state machine, fifos, registers, etc. This leads, on the one hand, to a more accurate simulation but, on the other hand, results in decreased simulation performance. To compensate for this, other modules such as the serial peripheral interface (SPI) are modelled at a higher abstraction level, and in fact, model only a time delay for data transmission.

A special module is the CPU, which corresponds to the targeted microcontroller. This module is a somewhat abstract model responsible for correct interrupt processing and for correctly delaying the application task (using the annotated time values). Furthermore, the CPU logs the different operating modes with the corresponding current and voltage values, i.e. the power consumption.

Network. Network simulation is handled by the PAWiS framework with underlying OMNeT++ [17] message handling. PAWiS uses a propagation model that considers only attenuation effects and is based on the signal to noise ratio (SNR). The SNR can further be used to derive the bit error rate (BER). Since other nodes can disturb an ongoing transmission, the SNR, and therefore also the BER, changes during a transmission. PAWiS provides the ability to specify the granularity of transmission from the bit-level up to the packet-level.

4 Experiments and Results

To demonstrate the functionality, practical feasibility and usefulness of the presented methodology, we modelled a networking scenario that is typical of industrial applications targeting feedback control systems. The simulation setup consisted of PAWiS v2.0, OMNeT++ v3.3, GCC v4.2 and GNU make v3.81.

Our application is visualised in Figure 1. There are two types of nodes: one *base node* (BAN), which corresponds to the data sink, and several *action nodes* (ACN), which represent the sensing devices. Every node in the network is statically assigned a unique identifier and a time slot in which it is allowed to send a packet. Since the nodes are separated in time, this is a classical time division multiple access (TDMA) scheme. The BAN regularly sends a synchronisation frame, which marks the start of a new round. Subsequently, the ACNs respond to this beacon frame with a packet containing the sensed data.

The action nodes are distributed uniformly in a 100x100 m^2 area with the BAN positioned in the center. Each of the eight ACNs is equipped with a MSP430F2274 microcontroller, while the BAN uses a MSP430FG4618 microcontroller. All nodes use a CC2500 transceiver to transmit a packet consisting of 4 bytes of preamble, a 4-byte synchronisation word, 3 bytes of header (length, address, packet type), 2 bytes payload and 2 bytes CRC using 2-FSK modulation at a datarate of 2.4 kBaud. The chosen slot time is 100 ms, which yields a round time of one second.

A parameter of major interest when developing a WSN is the energy consumption of individual network components, which depends on the currently active state, given by voltage and current values, and the duration of that state. The accuracy of our system level models was investigated in [11]. In an embedded system, the hardware is largely controlled by software. Therefore, the modelling of the timing behaviour of the software directly influences the accuracy of the energy consumption of the nodes. From the software engineer's point of view, it is crucial to obtain a quick overview of the principal energy consumers and to subsequently identify potential software optimisations.

We studied three different implementations of the aforementioned TDMA scheme at the ACN, focusing on the two greatest energy consumers – the CPU and the transceiver. The different approaches are visualised in Figure 1, and the simulated results for the energy consumption of several hardware components are summarized in Table 1. A simulation duration of 10 s was chosen.

Case 1: This case reflects the most energy consumptive but direct approach, in which the CPU is always keept in active mode (AM). First, the transceiver is in the receiving state (RX) to receive the beacon, then it sends its packet within the assigned time slot, and subsequently stays active until the next beacon is received. Address filtering is used to dismiss erroneously received packets. As shown in Table 1, the primary energy consumer is the transceiver (rfmod). A light emitting diode (LED) is used to visualise the sending of a packet.

Case 2: In this case, as a first optimisation strategy, the transceiver is set to idle state (ID) when neither a packet must be transmitted nor the beacon is expected. A timer wakes up the transceiver before the next beacon is sent. Simulation results reveal that the CPU is now the primary energy consumer, and – compared to the first case – the total energy consumption is reduced.

Case 3: The final investigated case is the most energy-saving approach, in which the transceiver and the CPU are set to idle and low power modes respectively. As the low power mode zero (LPM0) of the MSP430 architecture is utilised for the CPU, it only has to be active during beacon processing and sending of the sensed data. The total amount of energy consumed decreases further.

Conclusion. In addition to the obvious finding, that the utilisation of idle and low power modes for the primary energy consumers decreases the total energy consumption dramatically, more subtle insights are revealed by the data in Table 1 which verify the timing accuracy of the simulation. In the first case, the timer module is used only to pause until the assigned time slot is reached and is then deactivated. In contrast, cases 2 and 3 make heavy use of the timer to awaken components from their idle or low power modes. Consequently the absolute energy consumption of the timer is lower in case 1 compared to cases 2 and 3. However, the energy consumption of the SPI in case 1 is higher than in cases 2 and 3 because the transceiver always receives packets (waiting for the next beacon), which leads to higher SPI utilisation because of the need for RX strobes (ID → RX).

Table 1. Simulated energy consumption of sensor nodes

case	rfmod [%]	spi [%]	cpu [%]	timer [%]	led [%]	$\sum$ [mJ]
1	68.27	0.26	30.05	$0.23*10^{-3}$	1.43	289.35
2	42.47	0.10	54.82	$7.22*10^{-3}$	2.60	158.62
3	71.32	0.16	24.13	0.012	4.37	94.45

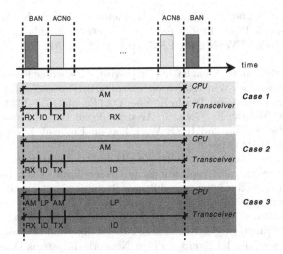

Fig. 1. Simulated TDMA schemes utilising different power modes

5 Summary and Future Work

In this paper, we have presented a general methodology to establish an accurate simulation of WSNs. The methodology is based on and combines well-established concepts – system level modelling, source level simulation and network simulation. Although the goal is accuracy, the need to maintain simulation performance is addressed by natively executing application code. We have shown the practical feasibility, usefulness and accuracy by means of a TDMA-based networking scenario typical of industrial applications. Future work will include improvements to the timing annotation process, first to automate it and second to increase the accuracy of the timing values used for annotation.

Acknowledgments. This work was funded by the COMET K2 Center "Austrian Center of Competence in Mechatronics (ACCM)". The COMET Program is funded by the Austrian Federal government, the Federal State of Upper Austria and the Scientific Partners of ACCM.

References

1. Castalia - A Simulator for WSN (April 2010),
   http://castalia.npc.nicta.com.au
2. Dunkels, A., Gronvall, B., Voigt, T.: Contiki - a Lightweight and Flexible Operating System for Tiny Networked Sensors. In: 29th Annual IEEE International Conference on Local Computer Networks, pp. 455–462 (November 2004)
3. Eriksson, J., Dunkels, A., Finne, N., Österlind, F., Voigt, T.: MSPSim - an Extensible Simulator for MSP430-equipped Sensor Boards. In: Proceedings of the European Conference on Wireless Sensor Networks (EWSN), Poster/Demo session (January 2007)

4. Eriksson, J., Österlind, F., Finne, N., Dunkels, A., Tsiftes, N., Voigt, T.: Accurate Network-Scale Power Profiling for Sensor Network Simulators. In: Roedig, U., Sreenan, C.J. (eds.) EWSN 2009. LNCS, vol. 5432, pp. 312–326. Springer, Heidelberg (2009)

5. Fummi, F., Perbellini, G., Quaglia, D., Acquaviva, A.: Flexible Energy-Aware Simulation of Heterogeneous Wireless Sensor Networks. In: Proceedings of the Conference on Design, Automation and Test in Europe (DATE), pp. 1638–1643 (April 2009)

6. Landsiedel, O., Wehrle, K., Gotz, S.: Accurate Prediction of Power Consumption in Sensor Networks. In: 2nd IEEE Workshop on Embedded Networked Sensors (EmNetS), pp. 37–44 (May 2005)

7. Levis, P., Lee, N., Welsh, M., Culler, D.: TOSSIM: Accurate and Scalable Simulation of Entire TinyOS Applications. In: Proceedings of the 1st International Conference on Embedded Networked Sensor Systems (SenSys), Los Angeles, California, USA, pp. 126–137 (2003)

8. Levis, P., Madden, S., Gay, D., Polastre, J., Szewczyk, R., Woo, A., Brewer, E., Culler, D.: The Emergence of Networking Abstractions and Techniques in TinyOS. In: Proceedings of the 1st Symposium on Networked Systems Design and Implementation (NSDI), San Francisco, California (2004)

9. McCanne, S., Floyd, S.: The Network Simulator - NS-2 (April 2010), http://www.isi.edu/nsnam/ns/

10. Möstl, G., Hagelauer, R., Springer, A., Müller, G.: Accurate Power-Aware Simulation of Wireless Sensor Networks Considering Real-Life Application Code. In: Proceedings of the 13th ACM International Conference on Modeling, Analysis, and Simulation of Wireless and Mobile Systems (MSWiM), Bodrum, Turkey, pp. 31–38 (2010)

11. Möstl, G., Hagelauer, R., Springer, A., Müller, G.: Including Real-Life Application Code into Power Aware Network Simulation. In: Proceedings of the 3rd International ICST Conference on Simulation Tools and Techniques (SIMUTools), Torremolinos, Spain (2010)

12. Nguyen, K., Cutcutache, I., Sinnadurai, S., Liu, S., et al.: Fast and Accurate Simulation of Biomonitoring Applications on a Wireless Body Area Network. In: 5th International Summer School and Symposium on Medical Devices and Biosensors (ISSS-MDBS), pp. 145–148 (June 2008)

13. Österlind, F., Dunkels, A., Eriksson, J., Finne, N., Voigt, T.: Cross-Level Sensor Network Simulation with COOJA. In: Proceedings of the 31st IEEE Conference on Local Computer Networks, pp. 641–648 (November 2006)

14. Park, S., Savvides, A., Srivastava, M.B.: SensorSim: A Simulation Framework for Sensor Networks. In: Proceedings of the 3rd ACM International Workshop on Modeling, Analysis, and Simulation of Wireless and Mobile Systems (MSWiM), Boston, Massachusetts, United States, pp. 104–111 (2000)

15. Shnayder, V., Hempstead, M., Chen, B.-r., Allen, G.W., Welsh, M.: Simulating the Power Consumption of Large-Scale Sensor Network Applications. In: Proceedings of the 2nd International Conference on Embedded Networked Sensor Systems (SenSys), Baltimore, MD, USA, pp. 188–200 (2004)

16. Titzer, B., Lee, D., Palsberg, J.: Avrora: Scalable Sensor Network Simulation With Precise Timing. In: 4th International Symposium on Information Processing in Sensor Networks (IPSN), pp. 477–482 (April 2005)

17. Varga, A.: The OMNeT++ Discrete Event Simulation System. In: Proceedings of the European Simulation Multiconference (ESM) (June 2001)

18. Weber, D., Glaser, J., Mahlknecht, S.: Discrete Event Simulation Framework for Power Aware Wireless Sensor Networks. In: 5th IEEE International Conference on Industrial Informatics, vol. 1, pp. 335–340 (June 2007)

On the Modelling of Resonating Fluid Sensors

Martin Heinisch, Erwin K. Reichel, and Bernhard Jakoby

Institute for Microelectronics and Microsensors,
Johannes Kepler University Linz,
Altenbergerstraße 69, 4040 Linz, Austria
martin.heinisch@jku.at, erwin.reichel@biw.kuleuven.be,
bernhard.jakoby@jku.at
http://www.ime.jku.at/

Abstract. The modeling of three different types of resonating viscosity sensors is presented. The results from these analytical, closed-form models relating measurement data to the viscosity are compared to measurement results from sample liquids.

Keywords: modelling, fluid sensors, resonators, rheometers, Lorentz force excitation.

1 Introduction

Resonating fluid sensors aim at measuring liquid's properties such as mass density and viscosity in a certain frequency range. The three sensors presented here were primarily designed for measuring viscosity with the focus on facilitating large penetration depths (of shear waves which are excited in the examined liquid by the resonating device). Large penetration depths become important when examining complex liquids such as multi-phase fluids such as, e.g., emulsions. To allow for large penetration depths (several micrometers in case of aqueous liquids), the oscillator's resonance frequencies should be in the low kilohertz range. The principle of the presented sensors is based on the analysis of the resonant response (including the fundamental harmonic) of an oscillating mechanism interacting with a sample liquid. The oscillations are excited by means of Lorentz forces

$$F_{\mathrm{L}} = I_{\mathrm{in}}\, B\, l^* \tag{1}$$

(I_{in}: sinusoidal input current driving the oscillator with angular frequency ω; B: magnetic flux density of an external magnetic field, provided by a NdFeB permanent magnet; l^*: effective length of an electrical conductor used for excitation)

The oscillations are read out with a lock-in amplifier via the motion-induced voltage in an electrical conductor following the movement of the resonating device. In case of the wire viscometer [1], [2], see section 2, only one wire is used for both, excitation and readout. The sensors discussed in the following two sections (suspended plate rheometer, [1] - [3] and double membrane rheometer, [4] - [6]) use two galvanically isolated conductors, see section 3 and 4. In general, a model of a resonating sensor can be formally split into three building blocks: First,

R. Moreno-Díaz et al. (Eds.): EUROCAST 2011, Part II, LNCS 6928, pp. 25–32, 2012.

the input, relating the input signal to the forces driving the sensor. Second, the interacting model relating the fluid-structure interaction to the motion-induced voltage, containing the information for the quantity of interest. And third, the output, incorporating the motion-induced voltage as well as side-effects such as e.g., electrical cross talk and offset.

2 Wire Viscometer

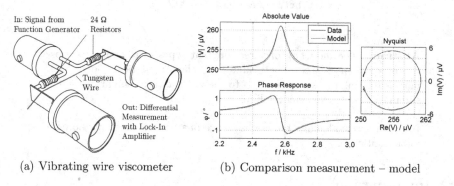

(a) Vibrating wire viscometer   (b) Comparison measurement – model

Fig. 1. In (a) the schematic drawing of the wire viscometer is depicted. A 100 μm thick tungsten wire carrying sinusoidal currents is placed in an external magnetic field (not depicted) and thus oscillating due to Lorentz forces. For excitation, a function generator is connected to two 24 Ω resistors being connected in series with the tungsten wire. These resistors are used to limit the excitation current. In (b) a comparison between measured data in Isopropanol and the fitted closed-form model is illustrated (Isopropanol: mass density $\rho = 0.78\text{g/cm}^3$, dynamic viscoisty $\mu = 2.05\text{mPa\,s}$, values measured with an Anton Paar viscometer SVM 3000 @ 25 °C.)

For the modeling of the wire viscometer [1], [2], see Fig 1(a) the transversal movements $u_x(z,t)$ of the wire subjected to an axial force N, driving Lorentz forces F_L and the loading of the fluid forces F_F can be described by the following linear, inhomogenous, partial differential equation [7]:

$$E\,I\frac{\partial^4 u_x(z,t)}{\partial x^4} - N\frac{\partial^2 u_x(z,t)}{\partial x^2} + m'\frac{\partial^2 u_x(z,t)}{\partial t^2} = F_L'(x,t) + F_F'(x,t) \quad (2)$$

(E: Young's modulus, I: second moment of inertia, m: wire's mass, $'$: quantity in respect of unit length) Eq. 2 is transformed to the frequency domain and the forces per unit length on the right hand side of Eq. 2 acting on the wire are substituted by

$$\underline{F}_L' = \underline{I}_{\text{in}}(\omega)\,B \quad (3)$$

and [8]:

$$\underline{F}_F'(z,\omega) = -j\,\omega\,\underline{g}_1(z,\omega)\,\underline{u}_x(z,\omega) + \omega^2\,\underline{g}_2(z,\omega)\,\underline{u}_x(z,\omega) \quad (4)$$

(Quantities in the frequency domain are underlined.) $\underline{g}_1$ and $\underline{g}_2$ can be calculated by using the analytical relation of the fluid forces acting on a prism with cylindrical cross-section [9], [10]:

$$\underline{F}'_F(z, \omega) = \pi \rho_f \omega^2 R^2 \left(1 - \frac{4j K_1 \left(j \sqrt{-j\,Re} \right)}{\sqrt{-j\,Re}\, K_0 \left(j \sqrt{-j\,Re} \right)} \right) \underline{u}_x(z, \omega) \qquad (5)$$

where $Re = \frac{\rho_f \omega R^2}{\mu}$ is the Reynolds number.

(ρ_f: mass density of the liquid, R: wire's radius, $j^2 = -1$, K_0, K_1: modified Bessel functions, μ: dynamic viscosity) After the calculation of the deflection of the wire $\underline{w}(x, \omega)$, the measured voltage is calculated as follows:

$$\underline{V}_{out} = j\omega B \int_0^L \underline{u}_x(z, \omega)\, dx + R_w \underline{I}_{in}(\omega) \qquad (6)$$

(L: wires lenght, R_w: wire ohmic resistance) Fig. 1(b) shows a comparison between this model and measured data for Isopropanol as sample liquid.

3   Suspended Plate Rheometer

For the suspended plate rheometer, [4] - [6], see Fig 2(a), the platelet is the main interacting part with the sample liquid. The influence of the wire and the platelet's height are neglected in this modeling approach. Thus, one-dimensional

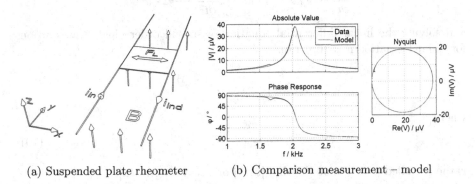

(a) Suspended plate rheometer   (b) Comparison measurement – model

Fig. 2. In (a) the schematic drawing of the suspended plate rheometer is illustrated. The sensor consists of two parallel wires placed in an external magnetic field **B**. In this figure, the left wire is used for exciting lateral vibrations by means of Lorentz forces. The second wire on the right, used for pick-up, is coupled to the excitation wire with a rigid plate, thus following the movement of the left wire. The induced voltage in the second wire is used as read-out. The platelet, inducing (one-dimensional) shear waves into the liquid, is the main part interacting with the sample liquid. In (b) a comparison between measured data and the model relating input and output signals for Isopropanol is depicted.

shear wave propagation can be assumed to calculate the influence of the fluid forces acting on the resonator. The intrinsic parameters (mass, damping and stiffness) of the Lorentz forces-driven oscillator are take into account by considering a mechanical spring-dashpot oscillator. This semi-lumped element modeling yields the relation of the platelet's lateral deflection to Lorentz forces, which in turn can be used to calculate the induced voltage in the pick-up wire, thus finally relating the input to the output voltage.

3.1   One-Dimensional Shear Waves in Viscous Liquids

To analytically describe the propagation of shear waves in a viscous liquid induced by a plate resonating at an angular frequency ω and amplitude $\hat{x}$ and considering a no-slip boundary condition at the solid-liquid interface and under the assumptions first, that the infinitely extended plate is oscillating in x-direction (thus imposing only shear stress in x-direction), second that gravitational forces are negligible, and third that the convective term in the Navier-Stokes equations can be neglected, the equation of motion and relation for the stress tensor can be drastically simplified to the one dimensional problem [5]

$$\rho \frac{\partial^2 u_x}{\partial t^2} = \frac{\partial T}{\partial z} \quad \text{with} \quad T = \mu \frac{\partial^2 u_x}{\partial z \, \partial t}. \tag{7}$$

Substituting T in the equation of motion, transforming the problem to the frequency domain assuming a time dependence $e^{j\omega t}$, with $j = \sqrt{-1}$

$$\frac{\partial}{\partial t} \circ\!\!-\!\!\bullet j\omega \quad \text{and} \quad \frac{\partial^2}{\partial t^2} \circ\!\!-\!\!\bullet -\omega^2 \tag{8}$$

and solving the linear differential equation of second order yields the solution for the deformation in x-direction

$$u_x(z, \omega) = \hat{x}\, e^{-\frac{z}{\delta}(1+j)} \tag{9}$$

where

$$\delta = \sqrt{\frac{2\mu}{\rho\omega}} \tag{10}$$

is the so-called penetration depth [5], [11] or decay length [12].

3.2   Lumped Element Model

For modeling the damped in-plane oscillation, a linear spring-mass-damper oscillator, is used to describe the oscillator's intrinsic resonant behavior (in air) for the fundamental harmonic i.e., lateral oscillations in x-direction. The influence of the fluid on the oscillation is taken into account by considering a no-slip boundary condition at the platelet-liquid interface and assuming a one-dimensional shear wave propagation on both sides of the platelet. As the platelet's lateral dimensions are much larger than its thickness and as its surface A is much larger than the wires surfaces, side effects emerging from displacement of the liquid at the platelets front sides as well as the flow around the wires are not taken into account. Thus, the fluid forces on the platelet are

$$F_F = -2\,T(z=0)\,A \qquad (11)$$

where the shear stress

$$T(z=0) = \hat{x}\,(1-j)\sqrt{\frac{\mu\,\rho\,\omega^3}{2}} \qquad (12)$$

is calculated by substituting Eqs. 9 and 10 into the the shear stress T in Eq. 7 and evaluating for $z=0$.

With this, the transfer function of the mechanical oscillator, which in this case, is the quotient of displacement in x-direction and Lorentz forces can be written as

$$G_m = \frac{u_x}{F_L} = \frac{1}{-\omega^2\left(m + A\sqrt{\dfrac{\mu\,\rho}{2\,\omega}}\right) + j\,\omega\left(r_0 + A\sqrt{\dfrac{\mu\,\rho\,\omega}{2}}\right) + k_0} \qquad (13)$$

Finally the motion-induced voltage in the pickup wire (coupled to the movement of the excitation wire) can be written as

$$V_M = j\,\omega\,G_m B^2\,l^{*\,2}\,I_{in} \qquad (14)$$

Depending on the wiring of the sesnsor it may be necessary to consider the effect of electrical cross-talk in the measured voltage as well, which can be easily taken into account with

$$V_{ct} = j\,\omega\,M\,I_{in} \qquad (15)$$

where M is the mutual inductance describing the inductive coupling between excitation and read-out circuit. As the the input resistance of the lock-in amplifier is 10 MΩ it is assumed that $I_{out} \approx 0$ and thus

$$V_{out} = V_M + V_{ct} \qquad (16)$$

4 Double Membrane Rheometer

Here, for modeling the double membrane rheometer, see Fig. 3, a lumped element model is presented which decomposes the measured voltage into two parts: A motion induced voltage and another induced voltage due to electrical cross talk from the excitation to the readout path.

The motion-induced voltage in the readout path (beeing placed in an external magnetic field and following the movement of the membrane and assuming that the occurring terms are in perpendicular) can be written as:

$$V_M = N\,v_z\,B\,l^* \qquad \text{where} \qquad v_z = j\,\omega\,u_z = j\,\omega\,G_m\,F_L \qquad (17)$$

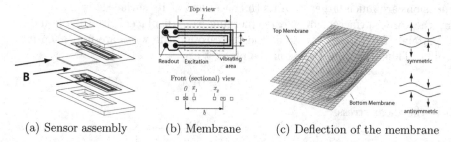

(a) Sensor assembly   (b) Membrane   (c) Deflection of the membrane

Fig. 3. In (a) the exploded view of the double membrane rheometer is illustrated. Two polymer membranes carrying conductive paths for excitation and readout are bonded to rigid platelets. The bonding, also acting as sealing, ensures that the membranes' sides carrying the conductive paths do not get wetted with the liquid. I.e., the liquid is only in the space between both membranes. The arrows on the left side indicate the direction of the external magnetic field provided by two NdFeB magnets on each side of the sensor. In (b) one of both membranes is depicted in detail. In (c) the deflection of the membranes in the (2,1)-eigenmode is depicted. Depending on the direction of the electric current in the particular excitation path, the deflection can either be symmetric (opposite direction) or antisymmetric (same direction).

(N: number of turns of the readout path (coil); v_z: mean velocity of the vibrating readout paths; In the following it is assumed that $l^* \approx l_{\text{in}}^* \approx l_{\text{out}}^*$, where the latter are the effective lengths of the excitation and readout path respectively.) G_m is the quotient of deflection in z-direction and Lorentz forces:

$$G_m(s) = \frac{u_z(s)}{F_L(s)} = \frac{G_0}{-\dfrac{\omega^2}{\omega_0^2} + 2j\,d\,\dfrac{\omega}{\omega_0} + 1}, \qquad (18)$$

(G_0: mechanical amplification; $d = d_M + d_L$: total damping accounting for intrinsic damping of the membrane, d_M, and damping due to the liquid loading, d_L; $\omega_0 = \sqrt{\frac{k}{m}}$: mechanical (undamped) eigenfrequency; k: spring constant of the oscillator (represents the stiffness of the membrane); $m = m_M + m_L$: total effective mass considering the intrinsic effective mass of the membrane, m_M and the inertial component of the liquid loading, m_L)

To account for the induced voltage due to electrical cross talk the mutual inductance M describing the inductive coupling between excitation and readout path can be estimated from (see Fig. 3(b))

$$M \approx 2\,M_s \qquad \text{where} \qquad M_s = \frac{\Psi_{21}}{I_{\text{in}}} = \frac{l\,\mu_0}{\pi} \int_{x_1}^{x_2} \left(\frac{1}{x} + \frac{1}{b-x} \right) dx \qquad (19)$$

(M_s: mutual inductance for one membrane; Ψ_{21}: flux linkage of output and input circuit; μ_0: permeability in air)

Assuming that the output current in the readout path is negligible the induced voltage due to cross talking in the readout path is calculated as

$$V_{\text{ct}} = s\,M\,I_{\text{in}} \qquad (20)$$

and thus,

$$V_{\text{out}} \approx V_{\text{M}} + V_{\text{ct}} \tag{21}$$

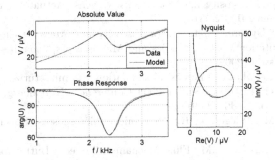

Fig. 4. Comparison between the model and measured data for the viscosity standard S3 (Cannon Instrument Company ®): $\rho = 0.864\text{g/cm}^3$, dynamic viscoisty $\mu = 3.3\text{mPa s}$. Here, the sensor was operated in the symmetric mode.

5 Conclusion and Outlook

Three different approaches for modeling Lorentz force-driven, resonating viscosity sensors were reviewed. The wire viscometer, section 2, is modeled by a closed form model. A semi-lumped element approach is used to model the suspended plate rheometer, section 3, where the influence of the sample liquid on the oscillation is analytically incorporated. For the double membrane rheometer, section 4, a purely lumped element model was used. From Figs. 1(b), 2(b) and 4 it can clearly be seen that the presented models can be fitted into a measured frequency response with high accuracy. However, at this point it is clearly pointed out, that for measuring and sensing, lumped elements are hardly suited for reliably gleaning the quantities to be measured from the readout signal.

Acknowledgements. We are indebted to the Austrian Centre of Competence in Mechatronics (ACCM) for the financial support. We also want to thank Prof. Isabelle Dufour from Université de Bordeaux, Laboratoire de l'Intégration du Matériau au Système, France, for the enriching discussions.

References

1. Heinisch, M., Reichel, E.K., Jakoby, B.: A Study on Tunable Resonators for Rheological Measurements. In: Proc. SPIE, vol. 8066, p. 806629 (2011), doi:10.1117/12.887103
2. Heinisch, M., Reichel, E.K., Jakoby, B.: Miniaturized Resonating Viscometers Facilitating Measurements at Tunable Frequencies in the Low kHz-Range. In: Proc. Eurosensors (in print, 2011)

3. Heinisch, M., Reichel, E.K., Jakoby, B.: A Suspended Plate In-Plane Resonator for Rheological Measurements at Tunable Frequencies. In: Proc. Sensor+Test, pp. 61–66 (2011)

4. Heinisch, M., et al.: A resonating rheometer using two polymer membranes for measuring liquid viscosity and mass density. Sens. Actuators A: Phys. (2011), doi:10.1016/j.sna.2011.02.031

5. Reichel, E.K.: Dynamic Methods for Viscosity and Mass Density Sensing, PhD Thesis, Institute for Microelectronics and Microsensors, Johannes Kepler University, Linz, Austria (2009)

6. Voglhuber, T., et al.: Semi numerical simulation o fa miniaturized vibrating membranerheometer. In: Proc. Sensor 2009 Conference, Nuremberg, Germany, May 26-28, vol. 1, pp. 41–46 (2009)

7. Elwenspoek, M., Wiegerink, R.: Mechanical microsensors. Springer, Heidelberg (2001)

8. Landau, L.D., Lifshitz, E.M.: Fluid Mechanics, 2nd edn. Butterworth-Heinemann, Butterworths (1987)

9. Rosenhead, L.: Laminar Boundary Layers. Clarendon, Oxford (1963)

10. Sader, J.E.: Frequency response of cantilever beams immersed in viscous fluids with applications to the atomic force microscope. Journal of Applied Physics 84, 64–76 (1998)

11. Riesch, C.: Micromachined Viscosity Sensors, PhD Thesis, Technical University Vienna, Austria (2009)

12. Martin, S.J., Granstaff, V.E., Frye, G.C.: Characterization of a Quartz Crystal Microbalance with Simultaneous Mass and Liquid Loading. Anal. Chem. 63, 2272–2281 (1991)

Extension of Static Non-linear DoE Identification Algorithms to Dynamic Systems

Markus Hirsch and Thomas E. Passenbrunner

Institute for Design and Control of Mechatronical Systems,
Johannes Kepler University, 4040 Linz, Austria
{markus.hirsch,thomas.passenbrunner}@jku.at

Abstract. The excitation of a system is a crucial task in system identification. If the data was not captured with persistent excitation, the parameter estimation degrades and the parameter variance increases. Application of Design of Experiment (DoE) algorithms helps to overcome these problems. This work presents the extension of the well known Wynn-Algorithm for non-linear but static systems to non-linear dynamic systems. Instead of optimizing the input only for the next sampling instant, an input sequence is optimized over a receding horizon.

The developed algorithm is used to identify the model of a hydrodynamic brake used on a combustion engine test bench as load machine.

Keywords: System identification, Optimal input design, Polynomial NARX models, Non-linear dynamic systems, Hydrodynamic dynamometer, Water brake.

1 Introduction

Identification of non-linear multi-input systems is a challenging task often addressed using approximators like artifical neural networks or fuzzy models [9,14]. "Practical approximators" like hybrid models, local linear models [5] or polynominal models [10] are also utilized.

A persistent excitation is important in parameter estimation. White noise is the classic choice. However, the non-linear behaviour affects the convergence properties of the estimation and thus its variance (see e. g. [2]), if the measurement length is short, a very common situation. In this case the model describes more the data then the real system (see [9]). Different experiments tend to significantly different models.

The choice of the input sequence used for system excitation during data acquisition is a crucial task. Optimal Design of Experiments (DoE) can improve the convergence rate of the parameter estimation and contribute to identify unique parameter.

Research on optimal input design algorithms for non-linear dynamic systems is a discussed topic [2,6,8,11]. However, most approaches are based on algorithms for linear dynamic systems or include some extensions for specific non-linear properties.

R. Moreno-Díaz et al. (Eds.): EUROCAST 2011, Part II, LNCS 6928, pp. 33–40, 2012.

The Wynn-Algorithm (see [16]) used for the iterative generation of D-optimal experimental designs provides an opportunity in case of non-linear but static systems. It is able to cope with general constraints on the input range. Iteratively that point is added to the experiment where the prediction of the model would be worst.

This paper presents a modified approach: The iterative procedure is extended to deal with dynamic systems. The state vector of the next sampling instant is taken into account instead of the input, the definition of the normalized prediction variance is the same as for static models. However, the state also depends on the past input values, so the online optimization has to be done over a receding horizon instead of the next sampling instant. This approach offers the opportunity to approximate D-optimal designs for non-linear dynamic systems.

The paper is organized as follows: Section 2 and 3 deal with the identification of NARX models and the optimal input design for these models. In Sect. 4 the method is used to identify a model of a real plant namely a hydrodynamic dynamometer for a combustion engine test bench. The paper is concluded with comments on the proposed methodology and a future outlook in Sect. 5.

2 NARX Model Identification

The general form of a multi-input polynomial NARX model is given by the recursive equation

$$y(k) = f^l(x(k), \theta) + \varepsilon(k).$$ (1)

The actual system output $y(k)$ is defined by $f^l(.)$, an l-th degree polynomial function of its arguments given by the vector $x(k)$ and θ defining the parameters of the polynomial which are estimated during the model identification. The error term $\varepsilon(k)$ is assumed to be white noise. $x(k)$ is composed of delayed outputs (up to maximal lag of n_y) and the r inputs (up to maximal lag of n_{ui}, $i = 1...r$):

$$x(k) = [y(k-1) \ldots y(k-n_y) \quad u_1(k-1) \ldots u_1(k-n_{u,1}) \\ u_2(k-1) \ldots u_2(k-n_{u,2}) \, u_r(k-1) \ldots u_r(k-n_{u,r})]^T.$$ (2)

A polynomial NARX model of full factorial l-th degree can be defined as follows:

$$y(k) = \theta_0 + \sum_{m=1}^{l} \sum_{\substack{i_1 \ldots i_m=1 \\ i_1 \leq i_2 \leq \ldots \leq i_m}}^{n} \theta_{i_1 \ldots i_m} \cdot \prod_{p=1}^{m} x_{i_p}(k) + \varepsilon(k).$$ (3)

Once a model structure has been defined by specifying the maximum polynomial degree l, the values of the parameters can be estimated by optimization. Since the model is linear in the parameters, these estimates $\hat{\theta}$ can be computed using standard least squares algorithms minimizing the sum of the squared prediction error over N measured samples (see e. g. [7]):

$$\hat{\theta} = \arg\min_{\theta} \sum_{k=1}^{N} \left(y(k) - f^l(x(k), \theta)\right)^2.$$ (4)

In general, a model assumption for a polynomial system as in (3) will contain some regressors with little relevance. Hence, some kind of regressor selection seems useful. Several possibilities for selecting the proper regressor set can be found in the literature. [1] presents algorithms especially for the NARX structure.

3   Optimal Input Design for NARX Models

The main purpose of input design is to increase the information content of data utilized for identification. The information content can be evaluated by the size of the information matrix $M(u, \sigma(u))$ which contains the correlations of the polynomial regressors defined by the inputs u and the system outputs $\sigma(u)$ (see [7]). For the polynomial NARX model class it is defined by

$$M = \mathrm{E}\left\{\frac{1}{\sigma^2}\sum_{k=1}^{N}\frac{\partial f^l(x(k),\theta)}{\partial\theta}\frac{\partial f^l(x(k),\theta)}{\partial\theta^T}\right\}, \tag{5}$$

where $\mathrm{E}\{\cdot\}$ indicates the expected value. As the covariance matrix of the parameters which defines the uncertainty of the estimated parameters is proportional to the inverse of M, the input $u(k)$ should be defined to maximize the size of M. Several criteria exist to evaluate the size of a matrix by a scalar criterion (see e. g. [12]). In this work we use the D-optimal criterion which defines optimal inputs

$$u^*(k) = \arg\max_{u(k)\in\Omega}\det(M), \quad k = 1\ \ldots\ N, \tag{6}$$

where $\Omega \subset \mathbb{R}^R$ defines the closed input set that is allowed for input design, by maximizing the determinant of M.

3.1   Wynn-Algorithm

Solving (6) is difficult as the complete input sequence of length N has to be optimized. Since such an optimization would overstrain most optimization algorithms (especially as the problem is non-convex), we want to define the optimal input $u^*(k)$ iteratively. For static systems approximated by a static model

$$\hat{y}(k) = f(u(k),\theta), \tag{7}$$

where the system output $\hat{y}(k)$ at sampling instant k just depends on the input $u(k)$, the Wynn-Algorithm [16] presents a possibility to iteratively generate optimal designs. This algorithm can cope with general constraints on the input range Ω and iteratively adds that point to the experiment where the prediction of the model would be worst. The prediction quality of the model can be evaluated by means of the normalized prediction variance

$$d(\xi(k), u(k+1)) = u^T(k+1)\ \bar{M}(\xi(k))^{-1}\ u(k+1), \tag{8}$$

a function depending on the observed normalized information matrix

$$\bar{M}\left(\xi\left(k\right)\right) = \frac{1}{N}\sum_{k=1}^{N}\frac{\partial f\left(u\left(k\right),\theta\right)}{\partial\theta}\frac{\partial f\left(u\left(k\right),\theta\right)}{\partial\theta^{T}}. \tag{9}$$

The Wynn-algorithm defines the next optimal input $u^{*}\left(k+1\right)$ by

$$u^{*}\left(k+1\right) = \arg\max_{u(k+1)\in\Omega}d\left(\xi\left(k\right),u\left(k+1\right)\right). \tag{10}$$

3.2   Extension to Dynamic Systems

The idea of the advanced algorithm is to adapt this iterative procedure so that it can be used for dynamic systems too: Assuming that the system is stable and taking the state vector of the next sampling instant $x\left(k+1\right)$ instead of the next input $u\left(k+1\right)$ into account, the definition of the normalized prediction variance is the same as for static models. As the states also depend on the past input values, the whole state vector cannot be optimized by only adapting the next input $u\left(k+1\right)$. Nevertheless, adaptation of the states is possible if online optimization is done not only for the next sampling instant $k+1$, but for a sequence over a receding horizon. Hence, assuming that n_h, the length of the receding horizon, is sufficiently large to affect all regressors, that the stochastic components in the state vector are small such that they can be neglected and that a model $\hat{f}\left(\cdot\right)$ for the the prediction of the future outputs is available, a D-optimal design for NARX models is iteratively obtained by the first component $u^{*}\left(k+1\right)$ of

$$u^{*}\left(k+1\ \ldots\ k+n_{h}\right) = \arg\max_{u(k+1\ \ldots\ k+n_{h})\in U}\sum_{i=k+1}^{k+n_{h}}d\left(\xi\left(k\right),x\left(i\right)\right) \tag{11}$$

with

$$x\left(k\right) = [y\left(k-1\right)\ \ldots\ y\left(k-n_{y}\right)\quad u_{1}\left(k-1\right)\ \ldots\ u_{1}\left(k-n_{u,1}\right)$$
$$u_{2}\left(k-1\right)\ \ldots\ u_{2}\left(k-n_{u,2}\right)\ u_{r}\left(k-1\right)\ \ldots\ u_{r}\left(k-n_{u,r}\right)]^{T}$$

and

$$y\left(i\right) = \hat{f}\left(y\left(0\ \ldots\ i-1\right),u\left(0\ \ldots\ i\right)\right),\qquad i > k.$$

Following it is shown that (11) generates a D-optimal design. D-optimal designs maximize the determinant of the information matrix. Dividing the observed normalized information matrix into two terms, a sum of already done measurements and a sum containing the future inputs for optimization yields to

$$\bar{M}\left(k+n_{h}\right) =$$
$$= \frac{1}{k+n_{h}}\sum_{i=1}^{k}\left[\varphi\left(x\left(i\right)\right)\varphi^{T}\left(x\left(i\right)\right)\right] + \frac{1}{k+n_{h}}\sum_{i=k+1}^{k+n_{h}}\left[\varphi\left(x\left(i\right)\right)\varphi^{T}\left(x\left(i\right)\right)\right]$$

$$\tag{12}$$

with

$$\varphi\left(x\left(i\right)\right) = \frac{\partial f^l\left(x\left(i\right),\theta\right)}{\partial \theta} \tag{13}$$

the regressors of the polynomial NARX model. In (12), the future terms can be replaced by a matrix multiplication

$$\bar{M}\left(k+n_h\right) = \frac{k}{k+n_h}\bar{M}\left(k\right) + \frac{n_h}{k+n_h}W\left(k+1\right)W\left(k+1\right)^T, \tag{14}$$

where the matrix $W\left(k+1\right)$ contains the future states and therefore the future inputs for optimization.

For D-optimality, the determinant of the matrix $\bar{M}\left(k+n_h\right)$ should become maximal. Hence, next optimal inputs $u^*\left(k+1 \ \ldots \ k+n_h\right)$ are defined by

$$u^*\left(k+1 \ \ldots \ k+n_h\right) =$$
$$= \arg \max_{u(k+1 \ \ldots \ k+n_h)\in U} \det\left(k\,\bar{M}\left(k\right) + n_h\,W\left(k+1\right)W\left(k+1\right)^T\right). \tag{15}$$

By means of the Matrix-Determinant Lemma, the sum within the determinant can be resolved and as only $W\left(k+1\right)$ can be adjusted, we obtain:

$$u^*\left(k+1 \ \ldots \ k+n_h\right) =$$
$$= \arg \max_{u(k+1 \ \ldots \ k+n_h)\in U} \det\left(I + \frac{n_h}{k}W\left(k+1\right)^T \bar{M}\left(k\right)^{-1} W\left(k+1\right)\right). \tag{16}$$

Since the second term in (16) will become small for large k, an approximation by a first order Taylor series can be set up:

$$\det\left(I + \frac{n_h}{k}W\left(k+1\right)^T \bar{M}\left(k\right)^{-1} W\left(k+1\right)\right) =$$
$$= \det\left(I + \varepsilon X\right)$$
$$= \det\left(I\right) + \frac{\partial \det\left(I + \varepsilon X\right)}{\partial \varepsilon}\varepsilon + O\left(\varepsilon^2\right)$$
$$= 1 + \text{trace}\left(X\right)\varepsilon + O\left(\varepsilon^2\right). \tag{17}$$

Here, $X = W\left(k+1\right)^T \bar{M}\left(k\right)^{-1} W\left(k+1\right)$ and $\varepsilon = \frac{n_h}{k}$. For $k \to \infty$ the approximation error term $O\left(\varepsilon^2\right)$ can be negelected and (16) is equivalent to

$$u^*\left(k+1 \ \ldots \ k+n_h\right) =$$
$$= \arg \max_{u(k+1 \ \ldots \ k+n_h)\in U} \text{trace}\left(W(k+1)^T\bar{M}\left(k\right)^{-1} W\left(k+1\right)\right)$$
$$= \arg \max_{u(k+1 \ \ldots \ k+n_h)\in U} \sum_{i=k+1}^{k+n_h} d\left(\xi\left(k\right),x\left(i\right)\right). \tag{18}$$

4   Application to a Hydrodynamic Dynamometer

Dynamic engine test benches are used to reproduce load conditions a combustion engine would undergo in a passenger car, truck or other vehicle without the vehicle. A test bench reduces the costs and time required for developement and configuration and guarantees reproducible conditions in terms of temperature, pressure, etc. Typically the engine under test is connected to an electric machine via a flexilbe shaft.

Hydrodynamic dynamometers provide especially in case of high power ratings a cost-efficient alternative to these type of brakes. Moreover, they combine high power ratings with a low moment of inertia and cover the entire range of combustion engines. Despite these advantages water brakes are not widely used in dynamic testing as their nonlinearities make them hard to control.

A model-based control for the water brake itself and an optimal control for the entire engine test bench should be developed on the basis of a mathematical model. However, models for systems with varialbe fill level are rare. In a series of papers [13,3,4] the authors developed a stationary model for a variable fill hydrodynamic dynamometer, extended this model to transients and finally designed a closed loop control. [15] compares a first principles approach with a black box model and a gray box model. Best results were achieved by using the gray box model which combines the simple structure of a first principles model with a data-based part.

The inlet and the outlet valve position are the two inputs of the water brake. The flow to and from the brake and as consequence the fill level and the torque are changed using these valves. However, a higher flow through the brake results in a less increased water temperature at the outlet. Running a test cycle the rotational speed is a measured input disturbance resulting from the engine torque and the load torque.

Fig. 1 shows the stationary torque of the brake for a fixed speed as non-linear function of the inlet and the outlet valve position as well as the optimized combination of valve positions for measurement. Similar maps can also be recorded for different speeds, only the maximum torque increases with increased speed and the steep increase shifts to higher values of the valve positions.

The dynamics of the plant results from the dynamics of the actuators and mainly from filling and emptying the brake. The behaviour of the brake is described by

$$
\begin{aligned}
y\left(k\right) = {}& \theta_0 + \theta_1 y\left(k-1\right) + \theta_2 u_1\left(k-1\right) + \theta_3 u_2\left(k-1\right) + \\
& \theta_4 u_1{}^2\left(k-1\right) + \theta_5 u_1\left(k-1\right) u_2\left(k-1\right) + \theta_6 u_2{}^2\left(k-1\right) + \\
& \theta_7 u_1{}^3\left(k-1\right) + \theta_8 u_1{}^2\left(k-1\right) u_2\left(k-1\right) + \\
& \theta_9 u_1\left(k-1\right) u_2{}^2\left(k-1\right) + \theta_{10} u_2{}^3\left(k-1\right)
\end{aligned}
\tag{19}
$$

the parameters are determined using the proposed approach. The model has successfully been used to develop a model-based torque controller for this type of load machines.

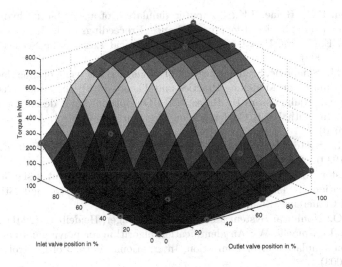

Fig. 1. Stationary torque of the hydrodynamic dynamometer for a fixed speed of $n_D = 1000$ rpm and optimized combinations of valve positions for measurement

5   Conclusions and Outlook

The paper proposes the extension of the Wynn-Algorithm to dynamic systems. The depency of the state on current inputs as well as previous states is considered by optimizing over a receding horizon. Hence, D-optimal designs are iteratively obtained also taking general non-uniform input sets into account.

The paper summarizes the steps of the design procedure and shows the application to a specific non-linear real life plant, namely a hydrodynamic brake for combustion engine test benches.

Acknowledgments. The authors gratefully acknowledge the sponsoring of this work by the COMET K2 Center "Austrian Center of Competence in Mechatronics (ACCM)".

References

1. Billings, S.A., Chen, S., Korenber, M.J.: Identification of mimo non-linear systems using a forward-regression orthogonal estimator. International Journal of Control 49, 2157–2189 (1989)
2. Hjalmarsson, H., Martensson, J.: Optimal input design for identification of nonlinear systems: Learning from the linear case. In: 2007 American Control Conference, New York, US (2007)
3. Hodgson, P.G., Raine, J.K.: Computer simulation of a variable fill hydraulic dynamometer. Part 2: steady state and dynamic open-loop performance. Proceedings of the Institution of Mechanical Engineers, Part C: Journal of Mechanical Engineering Science 206(13), 49–56 (1992)

4. Hodgson, P.G., Raine, J.K.: Computer simulation of a variable fill hydraulic dynamometer. Part 3: closed-loop performance. Proceedings of the Institution of Mechanical Engineers, Part C: Journal of Mechanical Engineering Science 206(53), 327–336 (1992)
5. Kozek, M., Sinanovic, S.: Identification of wiener models using optimal local linear models. Simulation Modelling Practice and Theory 16(8), 1055–1066 (2008)
6. Larsson, C., Hjalmarsson, H., Rojas, C.R.: On optimal input design for nonlinear systems. In: 49th IEEE Conference on Decision and Control, Atlanta, Georgia, USA (2010)
7. Ljung, L.: System Identification: Theory for the User. Prentice-Hall, Englewood Cliffs (1999)
8. Manchester, I.R.: An algorithm for amplitude-constrained input design for system identification. In: 48th IEEE Conference on Decision and Control and 28th Chinese Control Conference, Shanghai, P. R. China (2010)
9. Nelles, O.: Nonlinear System Identification. Springer, Heidelberg (2001)
10. Piroddi, L., Spinelli, W.: An identification algorithm for polynomial narx models based on simulation error minization. International Journal of Control 76, 1767–1781 (2003)
11. Pronzato, L.: Optimal experimental design and some related control problems. Automatica 44, 303–325 (2008)
12. Pukelsheim, F.: Optimal Design of Experiment, 2nd edn. John Wiley & Sons, Chichester (2006)
13. Raine, J.K., Hodgson, P.G.: Computer simulation of a variable fill hydraulic dynamometer. Part 1: torque absorption theory and the influence of working compartment geometry on performance. Proceedings of the Institution of Mechanical Engineers, Part C: Journal of Mechanical Engineering Science 205(33), 155–163 (1991)
14. Sjöberg, J., Zhang, Q., Ljung, L., Benveniste, A., Delyon, B., Glorennec, P.-Y., Hjalmarsson, H., Juditsky, A.: Nonlinear black-box modeling in system idenfication: a unified overview. Automatica 31, 1691–1724 (1995)
15. Vetr, M., Passenbrunner, T.E., Trogmann, H., Ortner, P., Kokal, H., Schmidt, M., Paulweber, M.: Control oriented modeling of a water brake dynamometer. In: 2010 IEEE Multi-Conference on Systems and Control, Yokohama, Japan, September 8-10 (2010)
16. Wynn, H.P.: The sequential generation of d-optimum experimental designs. The Annals of Mathematical Statistics 41, 1655–1664 (1970)

Automatic Tuning Methods for MPC Environments

Harald Waschl[1], Daniel Alberer[2], and Luigi del Re[2]

[1] JKU Hoerbiger Research Institute for Smart Actuators
[2] Institute for Design and Control of Mechatronical Systems
at the Johannes Kepler University of Linz, Austria
{harald.waschl,daniel.alberer,luigi.delre}@jku.at

Abstract. Model predictive control is a powerful method for controlling multivariable systems, in particular when constraints have to be taken into account. However, MPC also has negative attributes, like a high computational effort but also a non intuitive tuning. While the first issue can be addressed by use of numerically efficient optimizers, the non intuitive tuning still remains. To this end, an approach for efficient tuning of a MPC environment consisting of controller and state observer is proposed. The idea is to provide an automatic tuning strategy, such that even an unexperienced user can design a satisfactory controller within reasonable time. The proposed tuning of the state observer is done by a combination of multi model and adaptive estimation methods and for the weight tuning of the MPC objective function an additional optimization loop is applied which also accounts for the numerical condition. Finally an example is presented, where the proposed strategies were used to tune the MPC for controlling a pipeline compressor natural gas engine in a nonlinear simulation environment, yielding promising results.

Keywords: Model predictive control, self tuning, MPC tuning, Kalman filter tuning.

1 Introduction

Especially at multivariable control problems in the chemical and process industry model predictive control (MPC) has turned out to be a suitable choice [9]. Due to recent developments in available computational power and efficient online optimization algorithms, this control strategy prompts an upcoming interest also for fast and complex applications. MPC provides several positive attributes, like explicit use of a plant model to predict the future outputs, the possibility to consider disturbances and constraints and of course the optimal control action depending on the minimization of a user defined objective function.

Unfortunately MPC has two major negative attributes, firstly the high computational effort and secondly a demanding and non intuitive tuning. Furthermore, in many applications the MPC control formulation and the state observers are combined to a control structure, hence the tuning task has to be carried out for

R. Moreno-Díaz et al. (Eds.): EUROCAST 2011, Part II, LNCS 6928, pp. 41–48, 2012.
© Springer-Verlag Berlin Heidelberg 2012

both elements. The first negative attribute can be overcome by the use of formulation and fast efficient realtime capable QP solvers, like [7]. An alternative is to transfer the computational burden to an offline calculation and to implement an explicit MPC [3], which, however, leads to a high memory requirement. In this work we will focus on the second issue and present an automatic tuning method for a structure for an online MPC in combination with a Kalman filter.

Considering the Kalman filter, different adaptive tuning approaches for the weighting matrices can be found in the literature. For example in [4] a multiple model structure is presented where multiple filters run parallel and the state is estimated by a hypothesis test. Another common approach is the innovation based adaptive estimation like analyzed in [10] and [8].

Several tuning guidelines for MPC can be found in the literature (e.g. in [11]). A strategy for automatic tuning of MPC for large scale two dimensional actuator systems, is presented in [6]. In [12] norm based approaches for automatic MPC tuning are used in combination with a multi objective optimization. Another automatic tuning strategy is presented in [1] which is based on a linear approximation of the closed loop system and with a priori defined time domain performance specifications. In [5] a different method is suggested, where the unconstrained closed loop behavior of the MPC was matched to a given desired controller. However, none of these strategies take the numerical condition and the limitations of a realtime application into account.

The application example for the proposed approach is the control of a natural gas engine used in compressor stations in the US pipeline network, like described in [2]. In this work it could be shown that by application of an MPC environment it was possible to reduce emission levels of such legacy engines especially during load changes. The intended implementation of MPC on many different types of engines would lead to a high effort, if the tuning was done manually. To this end, the proposed approach should allow a "non-expert in control" to setup a satisfactory MPC within a reasonable time.

Finally it should be noted that in the presented work the term automatic tuning is understood in a non conventional way. In the particular case the systems is already identified and assumed to be not time varying. Furthermore the strategy is essentially based on offline analyses due to limitations on the target system and in view of reduced complexity for the setup engineer.

2   System Description and Requirements

The considered integral gas engine consists of a two stroke turbocharged reciprocating gas engine and a reciprocating compressor acting on the same crankshaft. The main control objective is to regulate the engine to a constant value of the relative fuel to air ratio ϕ – which corresponds to constant NO_x emissions – and the secondary objective is to keep the engine speed n at the desired value. The two main control inputs are the injected fuel amount, with the according control signal GFC (governor fuel command) and the wastegate position of the turbocharger WG, which determines the boost pressure and thus the air supply to the combustion chambers. An additional input is the desired load which is changed by the clearance volume of the compressor, which can be varied in a discrete way by enabling pockets. This input can be seen as a measured disturbance, since it cannot be used actively and is predetermined by the pipeline conditions. However, an upcoming load change is already known in advance, which is a valuable information for control. The used control scheme can be separated into four parts, the integral engine with the inputs GFC, WG (normalized between $0 - 100\%$) and the compressor load torque T_c, an MPC to control n and ϕ based on load information, system states and given setpoints, a state observer and a load handler as depicted in Fig. 1.

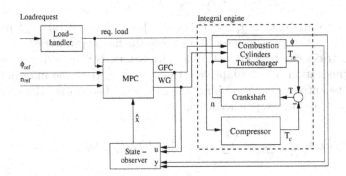

Fig. 1. System structure

A more elaborate description can be found in [2]. The engine model is defined in a linear discrete state space formulation

$$x_{k+1} = A_p x_k + B_p u_k \quad y_k = C_p x_k \tag{1}$$

with the input $u_k = [GFC, T_c, WG]^T$, the output $y_k = [n, \phi]^T$ and the according system matrices A_p, B_p and C_p.

3   State Observer

For the proposed MPC control structure a state observer is necessary. In a previous work [2] a linear Kalman filter in discrete state space formulation was used which was tuned at the station. To ensure a steady state offset free tracking the system was extended with an output error model.

3.1   Kalman Filter and Adaptive Strategies

The Kalman filter has become a widely used and valuable tool for state estimation. In the following the main principle and adaptive strategies will be reviewed shortly. For the Kalman filter the system model is extended with two additional white noise inputs w_k and v_k

$$x_{k+1} = A_p x_k + B_p u_k + w_k \quad y_k = C_p x_k + v_k \tag{2}$$

to account for measurement and process noise. In the case of a linear plant the algorithm can be separated into two steps, first a prediction of the estimation

$$\hat{x}_k^- = A_p \cdot \hat{x}_{k-1} + B_p \cdot u_{k-1} \tag{3}$$

$$P_k^- = A_p \cdot P_{k-1} \cdot A_p^T + Q_k \tag{4}$$

and afterwards an update with

$$K_k = P_k^- \cdot C_p^T \left(C_p \cdot P_k^- \cdot C_p^T + R_k \right)^{-1} \tag{5}$$

$$P_k = (I - K_k \cdot C) P_k^- \tag{6}$$

$$\hat{x}_k = \hat{x}_k^- + K_k \left(y_k - C_p \cdot \hat{x}_k^- \right). \tag{7}$$

The covariance matrices of $Q_k = E\{w_k \cdot w_k\}$ and $R_k = E\{v_k \cdot v_k\}$ have to be known a priori. However, in most cases these stochastic properties are unknown and the matrices can be seen as tuning parameters. For more details see [4].

In the innovation based adaptive estimation (e.g. [10]) the information contained in the output estimation innovation ν_j is used to update the error covariance matrices at each step k according to

$$R_k = \frac{1}{N_{IAE}} \sum_{j=k-N_{IAE}+1}^{k} \nu_j \nu_j^T - C_k \cdot P_k^- \cdot C_k^T \tag{8}$$

$$Q_k = \frac{1}{N_{IAE}} \sum_{j=k-N_{IAE}+1}^{k} \Delta x_j \Delta x_j^T + P_k^+ - A \cdot P_{k-1}^+ \cdot A^T \tag{9}$$

$$\nu_j = y_j - \hat{y}_j, \quad \Delta x_j = \hat{x}_k^+ - \hat{x}_k^-. \tag{10}$$

This strategy requires initial matrices for R_0 and Q_0 and additionally the definition of a window length N_{IAE}. In the evaluation the choice of these parameters showed an impact on the quality of the state estimation.

The multiple model filter approach (e.g. [4]) uses a group of n_μ different Kalman filters that run parallel and with the output estimate $\hat{y}_{\mu,k}$ of each filter a hypothesis test is performed to determine the probability of each estimation with respect to the measurements. The likelihood of one estimate is given by the probability density function

$$f(y_k|\mu) = \frac{1}{\sqrt{2\pi^{n_\mu} C_\mu}} e^{-\frac{1}{2}(y_k - \hat{y}_{\mu,k})^T C_\mu^{-1}(y_k - \hat{y}_{\mu,k})} \tag{11}$$

$$C_\mu = C \cdot P_{k,\mu} \cdot C^T + R_\mu, \tag{12}$$

the probability is calculated with

$$p_j(k) = \frac{f(y_k|\mu_j) p_j(k-1)}{\sum_{h=1}^{n_\mu} f(y_k|\mu_h) p_h(k-1)}, \quad p_j(0) = \frac{1}{n_\mu} \tag{13}$$

and the estimated state is defined by $\hat{x}_k = \sum_{j=1}^{n_\mu} p_j(k) \hat{x}_{k,\mu}$.

3.2 Offline Automatic Tuning Approach

In view of the later application an offline strategy was designed which is based on an iterative multi-shooting algorithm which combines innovation based adaptive estimation and multi model filters to provide optimal weightings. By the combination of both methods the choice of window lengths and initial matrices becomes less important. For the training of the algorithm only measurement data, e.g. obtained during the identification process, and an identified model are necessary. The steps of the automatic tuning are summarized as follows:

Initialization. Load measurement data and set of initial covariance matrices and window lengths for the adaptive filter.

Adaptive Kalman Filter. Run the adaptive filter with the set of initial matrices and the first window length; repeat until all sets are adapted.

Multiple Model Filter. Select the most appropriate filter for this window length with a multi model filter and store the covariance matrices.

Repeat. these two stages for the other window lengths with the initial matrices

Final Multiple Model Filter. A final multi model filter run is used to select the best filter out of the collection of stored matrices.

4 Model Predictive Control Setup

In this work a multivariable MPC in QP formulation, based on linear state space models, is used and as objective the weighted sum of the output tracking error and the control effort is applied. The determination of the control signal can be formulated as optimization problem, where the values of u_k are optimized for the control horizon n_{CH} according to the evaluation of the objective function over the prediction horizon n_{PH}. Due to the multivariable structure the setpoints are defined as $y_{ref} = \begin{bmatrix} y_n \\ y_\phi \end{bmatrix}$ and the control action is given by $u_k = \begin{bmatrix} u_{k,GFC} \\ u_{k,WG} \end{bmatrix}$ which both are constrained. The objective function is defined by

$$\min_u \frac{1}{2} \sum_{k=0}^{n_{PH}} (y_k - y_{ref,k})^T S (y_k - y_{ref,k}) + \Delta u_k^T T \Delta u_k \tag{14}$$

$$\begin{aligned}
s.t. \ & u_k = u_{k-1} + \Delta u_k \\
& x_{k+1} = A_p x_k + B_p u_k, \ y_k = C_p x_k \\
& \underline{u} \leq u_k \leq \overline{u} & k = 0 \dots n_{CH} - 1 \\
& \underline{\Delta u} \leq \Delta u_k \leq \overline{\Delta u} & k = 0 \dots n_{CH} - 1 \\
& \Delta u_k = 0 & k = n_{CH} \dots n_{PH}
\end{aligned}$$

where the tracking error is weighted by $S = \begin{bmatrix} S_1 & 0 \\ 0 & S_2 \end{bmatrix}$ and the actuator movement is penalized by $T = \begin{bmatrix} T_1 & 0 \\ 0 & T_2 \end{bmatrix}$ with weighting factors $\{S_1, S_2, T_1, T_2\} > 0$.

In the actual case of a linear state space representation, the MPC optimization problem (14) can be stated in the form of a standard QP which can also be used directly for the online solver on the hardware

$$\min_u \frac{1}{2} u^T H u + u^T f \tag{15}$$

$$s.t. \ lb_G \leq Gu \leq ub_G, \quad lb \leq u \leq ub,$$

where the Hessian H remains constant and the gradient f and the constraint vector have to be updated at every time instant. Further the gradient can be split up into two parts $f = f^* \cdot \Theta$, a fixed one f^* and the feedback vector $\Theta = [x_k, u_{k-1}, y_{ref}]^T$ with the current state and reference information.

4.1   Automatic Tuning

The automatic tuning of the MPC in our case focuses only on the weights S_1, S_2, T_1 and T_2 of the objective function, while the horizons are predetermined by the application and the hardware. The idea is to use the optimal unconstrained solution of the QP formulation $\left(U_{opt} = -H^{-1} \cdot f^* \Theta = K_{MPC} \cdot \Theta\right)$ to determine a closed loop representation of the system, which depends only on the four tuning parameters and contains the MPC, the plant and the state observer. Moreover, the MPC is approximated by the linear state dependent formulation K_{MPC}. The inputs of the closed loop plant are the setpoints for y_{ref} as well as the torque T_c and the outputs are the according values y_k and u_k.

The idea is to apply an overlying optimization loop to determine the parameters corresponding to a tuning scenario defined in the time domain. This scenario should lie within the representative operating range and contain different reference and load changes. Another aspect is to incorporate the numerical condition of the QP in the parameter optimization. This is motivated by the fact that on the hardware only single precision hardware is available and thus the iterative solution of the QP strongly depends on its conditioning. In particular the connection between both numerical condition and computational effort is that the online QP solution is essentially done iteratively, whereas a better condition can reduce the number of necessary iterations and hence the needed runtime.

To determine the parameters an optimization problem is defined, where the tracking error and the applied actuator energy are used as objectives. In this case the numerical condition of the Hessian $\kappa(H)$ is implemented as a nonlinear constraint for the optimization problem

$$\min_{S_1, S_2, T_1, T_2} \left(J_{e,n} + sc_1 J_{e,\phi} + sc_2 J_{u,GFC} + sc_3 J_{u,WG}\right) \tag{16a}$$

$$\text{s.t.} \quad \{S_1, S_2, T_1, T_2\} > 0, \quad \kappa(H) \le \kappa_{ub} \tag{16b}$$

$$\text{with:} \quad J_{e,n} = \sum_{k=0}^{N} \left(y_{k,n} - y_{k,n_{ref}}\right)^2 \quad J_{e,\phi} = \sum_{k=0}^{N} \left(y_{k,\phi} - y_{k,\phi_{ref}}\right)^2$$

$$J_{u,GFC} = \sum_{k=0}^{N} \left(u_{k,GFC}\right)^2 \quad J_{u,WG} = \sum_{k=0}^{N} \left(u_{k,WG}\right)^2 \quad N = \frac{t_{ref}}{T_s},$$

the sampling time T_s and the time length of the reference trajectory t_{ref}. Notice that this optimization task is different to the MPC formulation to determine optimal parameters for the MPC in dependency of the given input profile and objective function. The scaling factors (sc_x) in (16a) are used to provide appropriate weightings for all criteria and κ_{ub} was set to 100.

5   Results

Both automatic tuning strategies were applied to a nonlinear simulation model of the compressor station which was matched to the real system [2]. The automatic tuning is compared against a controller and observer setup which was done by an experienced control engineer directly at the station. As evaluation scenario a load change after 20 s and a reference step change on ϕ at 110 s was used. In Table 1 the results of the nonlinear simulation are summarized and additionally also the number of maximum and average necessary iterations is listed. The resulting in- and output trajectories for both cases are depicted in Fig. 2.   The overall

Table 1. Comparison of automatic to on-site tuning

Tuning	$J_{e,n}$	$J_{e,\phi}$	$J_{u,GFC}$	$J_{u,WG}$	$\kappa(H)$	max. iterat.	avg. iterat.
On-site	100 %	100 %	100 %	100 %	7.4 10^5	10	4.69
Self tuning	59.9 %	87.72 %	99.5 %	99.3 %	100	6	0.01

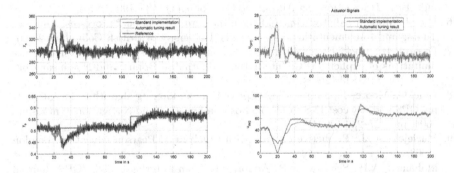

Fig. 2. Comparison of output tracking and control action with on-site and automatic runing result

tracking performance with the automatic tuning could be increased while the applied actuation energy remained almost identical. A significant improvement of the numerical condition was achieved and also the immediate consequence, namely the number of necessary QP iterations, was reduced significantly.

6   Conclusions and Outlook

In this work an automatic tuning strategy for a MPC environment was presented, addressing both the control formulation of the MPC and the state observer. On a simulation model it was possible to achieve a similar performance as with control setup tuned on-site by an experienced engineer. Furthermore the numerical condition of the problem was significantly improved. The future work will focus on an implementation on a real engine to further evaluate the self tuning methods.

Acknowledgments. The authors gratefully acknowledge the sponsoring of this work by the COMET K2 Center "Austrian Center of Competence in Mechatronics (ACCM)". The COMET Program is funded by the Austrian federal government, the Federal State Upper Austria and the Scientific Partners of ACCM.

References

1. Al-Ghazzawi, A., Ali, E., Nouh, A., Zafiriou, E.: On-line tuning strategy for model predictive controllers. Journal of Process Control 11(3), 265–284 (2001)
2. Alberer, D., Ranzmaier, M., del Re, L., Huschenbett, M.: MIMO model predictive control for integral gas engines under switching disturbances. In: IEEE CCA 2008, pp. 317–322 (2008)
3. Bemporad, A., Morari, M., Dua, V., Pistikopoulos, E.N.: The Explicit Solution of Model Predictive Control via Multiparametric Quadratic Programming. In: Proceedings of the American Control Conference, Chicago, pp. 872–876 (2000)
4. Brown, R., Hwang, P.: Introduction to random signals and applied Kalman filtering. Wiley, New York (1997)
5. Di Cairano, S., Bemporad, A.: Model predictive control tuning by controller matching. IEEE Transactions on Automatic Control 55(1), 185–190 (2010)
6. Fan, J.: Model predictive control for multiple cross-directional processes: Analysis, Tuning and Implementation. Ph.D. thesis, University of British Columbia (2003)
7. Ferreau, H., Bock, H., Diehl, M.: An online active set strategy to overcome the limitations of explicit MPC. International Journal of Robust and Nonlinear Control 18(8), 816–830 (2008)
8. Hide, C., Moore, T., Smith, M.: Adaptive Kalman filtering algorithms for integrating GPS and low cost INS. In: Proc. Position Location and Navigation Symposium 2004, pp. 227–233 (2004)
9. Maciejowski, J.: Predictive control: with constraints. Pearson education, London (2002)
10. Mohamed, A.H., Schwarz, K.P.: Adaptive Kalman Filtering for INS/GPS. Journal of Geodesy 73(4), 193–203 (1999)
11. Soeterboek, R., Toumodge, S.: Predictive control: A unified approach. Prentice Hall, Englewood Cliffs (1992)
12. Vega, P., Francisco, M.: Norm based approaches for automatic tuning of Model Based Predictive Control. In: Proceedings of ECCE-6, Copenhague (2007)

On-board Implementation of a Decentralized Algorithm for Deployment of a Swarm

Thomas E. Passenbrunner and Luigi del Re

Institute for Design and Control of Mechatronical Systems,
Johannes Kepler University, 4040 Linz, Austria
{thomas.passenbrunner,luigi.delre}@jku.at
http://desreg.jku.at

Abstract. The area of operation of UAS (Unmanned Aircraft Systems) has increased substantially due to falling prizes and increased on-board computational power. Many of these applications are intended to increase the safety of the civil population or to support disaster operations. One of these applications is the measurement of the concentation of toxic gases after an incident in a chemical plant to estimate the release rate.

The optimal distribution of the agents of the swarm equipped with pollution sensors in the area to be scanned is an important challenge. The communication between the individual agents as well as with the ground station is limited. Furthermore, a simple function allows a weighting of a distinguished part of the area to be scanned. This paper presents technical basics and a simple, decentralized but yet effective on-board implementation as well as results in simulation.

Keywords: UAS (Unmanned Aircraft Systems), Swarm, Decentralized algorithm, Deployment, Geometric optimization, Partitioning, Geometric center, Center of gravity.

1 Motivation and Introduction

The desire for security has increased significantly in recent years in Austria as well as in other western countries. In Austria the greatest fears seem to be caused by natural disasters like avalanches, mudslides or floodwaters and hazardous events like an incident in a chemical plant.

Successful applications of UAS in military but also civil operations (see e. g. [4], [6] and [7]) combined with reduced costs, increased availability on the market and increased on-board computation power motivate the usage of a swarm of low-cost UAS with limited pay-load for information collection. In the project SkyObserver such a swarm is amongst others applied to provide measurements to estimate the release rate of toxic gases after an incident.

Therefore, each agent is equipped with an autopilot system including a GPS sensor and an altimeter to determine its own position, a transmitter respectivelly a receiver and a pollution sensor. All agents are equipped equally. The airfield is considered free of stationary obstacles and therefore no additional sensors are used. (More details on the project can be found in [5].)

R. Moreno-Díaz et al. (Eds.): EUROCAST 2011, Part II, LNCS 6928, pp. 49–56, 2012.

Robustness and scalability are key requirements for the entire system. It must be possible to add agents at any time and the loss of individual agents may not jeopardize the whole mission. An update of the area to be scanned caused by additional knowledge or the transport of the toxic gas by wind must also be feasible during the operation. These requirements suggest a decentralized implementation of all algorithms. So the computation is not centralized e. g. at a ground station or a leader, instead it is done by each agent itself.

According to [2] and [3] an optimal distribution of the agents is achieved using the following procedure: *Each agent transmits its own position and receives its neighbors positions, then it computes the geometric center of its own cell. This is done in each communication round between the communication rounds each robot moves towards the center of its own cell.*

On the one hand each agent has to calculate its trajectory and implement it by an autopilot, on the other hand rules for communication between agents and between an agent and the ground station are necessary. To determine its trajectory each agent has to calculate its own cell, its geometric center and the next way point.

This paper is organized as follows: The partitioning of a given set and the calculation of the geometric center of a cell are treated in Section 2 and Section 3 respectivelly. Section 4 presents results in simulation. Conclusions and Outlook complete the paper.

2   Partitioning

The computation of cells – a partitioning – is equal to the subdivision of a set S into connected subsets. For a given set $S \subset \mathbb{R}^d$ in the Euclidean space $\mathbb{R}^d$ and n distinct points $\mathcal{P} = \{p_1, \ldots, p_n\}$ in S the Voronoi partitioning can be calculated by

$$V_i(\mathcal{P}) = \{q \in S \mid \|q - p_i\| \leq \|q - p_j\| \text{ for all } p_j \in \mathcal{P} \setminus \{p_i\}\}. \tag{1}$$

$V_i(\mathcal{P})$ denotes the set of all points in S closer to p_i than to any other point in $\mathcal{P}$.

The maximum flight altitude of the used agents is limited in Austria by law to 150 m over ground, the minimum one was set to 50 m to avoid collisions with statinary obstacles. By introducing fixed altitudes at 50 m, 100 m and 150 m over ground, the challenge is reduced to a 2D-problem for each of these altitudes.

Subsequent the calculation of the own cell $V_i(\mathcal{P})$ of an agent $i \in \{1, \ldots, n\}$ located at p_i only based on vector analysis and geometry for a given set $S \subset \mathbb{R}^2$ bounded by the edges of a convex polygon $\mathcal{B}_0 = \{b_1, \ldots, b_m\}$ with $m \in \mathbb{N}$ and $b_k \in \mathbb{R}^2$, $1 \leq k \leq m$ is described in detail:

0. Fig. 1 shows the initial configuration with three agents. The supposed exit site of the toxic gas is located at (0 m, 0 m), the area to be scanned results from the direction and the strength of the wind and the elapsed time respectively. Every vertex of the boundary polytope $\mathcal{B}_0$ is marked by a circle.

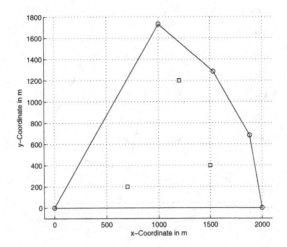

Fig. 1. Initial configuration with three agents (squares) located at $\mathcal{P}$ = $\{(700\text{m}, 200\text{m}), (1500\text{m}, 400\text{m}), (1200\text{m}, 1200\text{m})\}$. The area to be scanned is defined by the sector of a circle with a radius of 2000m and a center point angle of $60°$, this area is approximately bounded by the polytope $\mathcal{B}_0$ = $\{(0\text{m}, 0\text{m}), (2000\text{m}, 0\text{m}), (1879\text{m}, 684\text{m}), (1532\text{m}, 1285\text{m}), (1000\text{m}, 1732\text{m})\}$.

1. In a first step agent i performs the following calculations with respect to agent $j \in \{1, \ldots, n\} \setminus i$:
   - Compute the vector $v_{i, j}$ connecting agent i with agent j and the corresponding normal vector $n_{i, j}$.
   - Determine the parameters $(k_{i, j}, d_{i, j})$ of a straight line such that this line runs in the direction of $n_{i, j}$ through the midpoint between agent i and agent j.
2. For an edge of the actual polygon $\mathcal{B}_q$, $q \in \{0, \ldots, n - 2\}$ bounding the area to be scanned the following calculations are done:
   - The parameters $(\bar{k}_{k, l}, \bar{d}_{k, l})$ of the edge connecting two points b_k and b_l of the boundary $\mathcal{B}_q$ are determined with

$$l = \begin{cases} k + 1 & k < m \\ 1 & k = m \end{cases}.$$

   - The intersection point P of these two straight lines is calculated treating special cases like horizontal or vertical lines separately.
   - If the projection of the intersection point P on the vector $v_{i, j}$ is between agent i and agent j as well as the distance of the projection to agent i is smaller than the one to agent j, the intersection point P is added to the new boundary polytope $\mathcal{B}_{q+1}$.
     b_k has to be added to the new boundary polytope $\mathcal{B}_{q+1}$, if $\frac{v_{i, j} \, \bar{v}_{i, k}}{\|v_{i, j}\| \, \|\bar{v}_{i, k}\|}$ $<= 0$ with $\bar{v}_{i, k}$ being the connection vector between agent i and the point b_k of the boundary. This guarantees for example that the point $(0\text{ m}, 0\text{ m})$ is added to the boundary polytope of the own cell of agent $i = 1$.

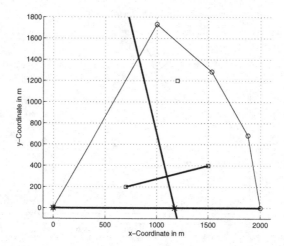

Fig. 2. Calculation of intersection point P for agent $i = 1$ with respect to agent $j = 2$ and the first edge ($k = 1$, $l = 2$) of the boundary polytope $\mathcal{B}_0$.

Fig. 2 shows the results of these calculations for $i = 1$, $j = 2$, $k = 1$ and $l = 2$. An other intersection point for $k = 5$ and $l = 1$ can also be seen.

3. The calculations in 2 are repeated until all edges of the boundary polytope $\mathcal{B}_q$ have been considered. The restricted area to be scanned by agent $i = 1$ taking agent $j = 2$ into account is depicted in Fig. 3 and marked by black lines and stars.

4. Agent i has to take all other agents j into account. Fig. 4 shows the Voronoi cell $V_i(\mathcal{P})$ of agent i (see (1)) bounded by $\mathcal{B}_{q+1}$.

3   Geometric Center of a Cell

The procedure to achieve an optimal distribution does not imply the usage of a specific geometric center. For example, the circumcenter $CC(S)$ of a bounded set $S \subset \mathbb{R}^d$ is the center of the closed ball of minimum radius that contains S. The set of centers of all closed balls of maximum radius contained in this set is the incenter $IC(S)$ or Chebyshev center. However, both definitions lead to an optimization problem.

In contrast, the center of mass for a given set $S \subset \mathbb{R}^d$ in the Euclidean space $\mathbb{R}^d$ can be calculated using the equation

$$CM_\varphi(S) = \frac{1}{A_\varphi(S)} \int_S q \, \varphi(q) \, dq \tag{2}$$

with

$$A_\varphi(S) = \int_S \varphi(q) \, dq \tag{3}$$

for a given density function $\varphi : \quad \mathbb{R}^d \to \mathbb{R}_{\geq 0}$.

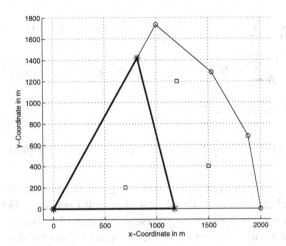

Fig. 3. Restriction of the area to be scanned by agent $i = 1$ taking agent $j = 2$ into account. The new boundary polytope is $\mathcal{B}_1 = \{(0m, 0m), (1175m, 0m), (820m, 1420m)\}$.

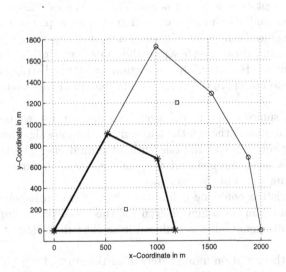

Fig. 4. The Voronoi cell $V_i(\mathcal{P})$ of agent $i = 1$ is bounded by the polytope $\mathcal{B}_2 = \{(0\text{ m}, 0\text{ m}), (1175\text{ m}, 0\text{ m}), (1007\text{ m}, 671\text{ m}), (526\text{ m}, 911\text{ m})\}$

For a given set $S \subset \mathbb{R}^2$, a cell $V_i\left(\mathcal{P}\right)$ bounded by a polygon $\mathcal{B} = \{b_1, \ldots, b_m\}$ with $m \in \mathbb{N}$ and $b_k \in \mathbb{R}^2$ the centroid of this cell (see [1]) is given by

$$x\left(CM\right) = \frac{1}{6\,A} \sum_{i=1}^{m} \left(x\left(b_i\right) + x\left(b_{i+1}\right)\right)\left(x\left(b_i\right)\,y\left(b_{i+1}\right) - x\left(b_{i+1}\right)\,y\left(b_i\right)\right) \qquad (4)$$

$$y\left(CM\right) = \frac{1}{6\,A} \sum_{i=1}^{m} \left(y\left(b_i\right) + y\left(b_{i+1}\right)\right)\left(x\left(b_i\right)\,y\left(b_{i+1}\right) - x\left(b_{i+1}\right)\,y\left(b_i\right)\right) \qquad (5)$$

with the area of the cell $V_i\left(\mathcal{P}\right)$

$$A\left(V_i\left(\mathcal{P}\right)\right) = \frac{1}{2} \sum_{i=1}^{m_i} \left(x\left(b_i\right)\,y\left(b_{i+1}\right) - x\left(b_{i+1}\right)\,y\left(b_i\right)\right), \qquad (6)$$

where $x\left(\cdot\right)$ and $y\left(\cdot\right)$ represent the x- and the y-coordinate respectivelly.

A simple weighting can be realized by a plane put over the area to be scanned. A higher weighting is expressed by a greater "distance" between the area to be scanned and this plane. The center of gravity can be calculated as mentioned in [8] for the now emerging set $\overline{S} \subset \mathbb{R}^3$. For example, the density of measurements in the area of release can be increased in this way.

4   Results

The usage of the procedure described in [2] and [3] applying the previously described implementation is shown below. The simulation shows the robustness of the algorithm and the implementation regarding a planned as well as an unplanned change in the number of used agents. Robustness against a change in the area to be scanned can be shown in the same way. Both events change the optimal distribution. However, after a certain time this distribution is reached again, the cells do not change and the agents remain in the geometric center of their own cell.

It is further assumed that only one agent can transmit its own position at each communication round. Although the transmitted data are significantly reduced, the partitioning converges to the one without limitations. The frequency with which data must be exchanged derives from the size of the area to be scanned and the maximum speed of the agents.

Another restriction could be a limited range of transmission. Nevertheless, convergence can again be achieved even for this case. In an improved implementation distant agents must be exluced from the calculation of the cell of an agent.

Fig. 5 shows the situation immediately after the start of the fourth agent. At this stage there are large distances between the actual position (squares) of some agents and the weighted center (triangles, up) of their own cell. The unweighted center of a cell is indicated by a triangle (down), the last position an agent has broadcasted information by a diamond. This leads to free spaces or overlaps of the individual cells.

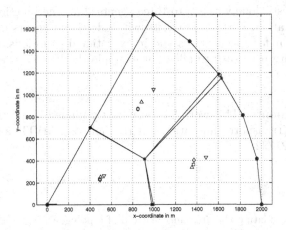

Fig. 5. Partitioning of a sector immediately after adding of the fourth agent at $t = 90$ s

The situation after about 300 s – 7 agents are available for coverage – is depicted in Fig. 6. All agents have reached the weighted center of their cell. Rotary wing aircraft can simply remain at that position, fixed wing aircraft should rotate around that position.

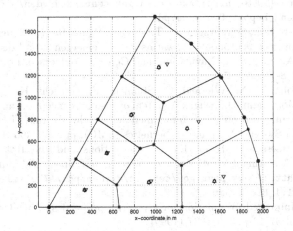

Fig. 6. Partitioning of a sector by 7 agents at $t = 300$ s

5   Conclusion and Outlook

This paper describes a simple, decentralized but yet efficient implementation for deployment of a swarm. Robustness against a varying number of agents, a varying size of the area to be scanned and a limitation of the communication has been shown in simulation.

First flight tests done with up to three agents show the function of the real-time implementation. Further tests also with additional agents must show the correct behaviour for special cases and in exceptional situations. Extensions of the algorithm are necessary to allow for example the launch of agents outside the area to be scanned.

Acknowledgements. This work has been partly funded by the Austrian Federal Ministry of Transport, Innovation and Technology (BMVIT) and FFG under grant FIT-IT-821732.

References

1. Bourke, P.: Calculating the area and centroid of a polygon (July 1988)
2. Bullo, F., Cortes, J., Martinez, S.: Distributed Control of Robotic Networks. Applied Mathematics Series. Princeton University Press, Princeton (2009), http://www.coordinationbook.info
3. Cortés, J., Martínez, S., Karatas, T., Bullo, F.: Coverage control for mobile sensing networks. In: IEEE Conference on Robotics and Automation, Arlington, Virginia, USA (May 2002)
4. Cox, T.H., Nagy, C.J., Skoog, M.A., Somers, I.A., Warner, R.: A Report Overview of the Civil UAV Capability Assessment. National Aeronautics and Space Administration (2005), http://www.nasa.gov/centers/dryden/pdf/111760main_UAV_Assessment_Report_Overview.pdf
5. Passenbrunner, T.E., Schwarzgruber, T., Ortner, P., del Re, L., Naderhirn, M.: The skyobserver project: Autonomous swarms in civil emergency and disaster management. In: AIAA Guidance, Navigation, and Control Conference, Portland, Oregon, USA, August 8-11 (2011)
6. Sebastion, Rohde, G.N., Wietfeld, C., Steinicke, F., Hinrichs, K., Ostermann, T., Holsten, J., Morrmann, D.: Avigle: A system of systems concept for an avionic digital service platform based on micro unmanned aerial vehicles. In: IEEE International Conference on Systems Man and Cybernetics (SMC), pp. 459–466 (October 2010)
7. Civil UAV Assessment Team. Earth Observations and the Role of UAVs: A Capabilities Assessment. National Aeronautics and Space Administration (August 2006), http://www.nasa.gov/centers/dryden/pdf/175939main_Earth_Obs_UAV_Vol_1_v1.1_Final.pdf
8. Wang, Z.J.: Improved formulation for geometric properties of arbitrary polyhedra. AIAA Journal 37(10), 1326–1327 (1999)

Modelling, Simulation and Control of a Heavy Chain System

P. Ludwig[1,*], K. Rieger[2], and K. Schlacher[1]

[1] Institute of Automatic Control and Control Systems Technology,
Johannes Kepler University Linz,
Altenberger Straße 69, 4040 Linz, Austria
{paul_felix.ludwig,kurt.schlacher}@jku.at

[2] Kappa Filter Systems GmbH, Im Stadtgut A1, 4407 Steyr-Gleink, Austria
k.rieger@kappa-fs.com

Abstract. This contribution deals with the modelling, simulation and control of a particular heavy chain laboratory system which consists of a pivoted disc connected to a chain. First, the Hamilton principle is applied to obtain the governing mathematical equations in form of (nonlinear) partial differential equations (with boundary conditions) and ordinary differential equations. The control law is derived by using the concept of passivity in combination with the backstepping method. Moreover, simulation and measurement results are provided.

Keywords: Heavy Chain System, Infinite-Dimensional Systems, Modelling, Passivity, Backstepping.

1 Introduction

This contribution is dedicated to the problem of stabilization of a heavy chain system. In the past years the passivity based control approach has been established for the control of distributed parameter systems, see [1,4,5]. Heavy chain systems can be found in several industrial areas, for instance, in form of a gantry crane [1,5], which is a linear guided heavy chain system. In this contribution we focus on a particular heavy chain system, see Fig. 1 for a picture of the corresponding laboratory model and a schematic diagram. It consists of a pivoted disc connected to the chain via a pivot bearing. The disc is directly driven by an electrical drive. The angle and the angular velocity of the disc as well as the angle and the angular velocity of the chain at the pivot bearing are available as measurements.

This contribution is organized as follows. In section 2 we deal with the modelling of the system in form of PDEs (partial differential equations) with boundary conditions and ODEs (ordinary differential equations). In section 3 we derive an energy based control law in combination with the backstepping method for the heavy chain system. Finally, in section 4 we show the performance of the proposed control approach in terms of a laboratory experiment.

---

* The authors gratefully acknowledge for the support of the Austrian Center of Competence in Mechatronics (ACCM).

R. Moreno-Díaz et al. (Eds.): EUROCAST 2011, Part II, LNCS 6928, pp. 57–64, 2012.

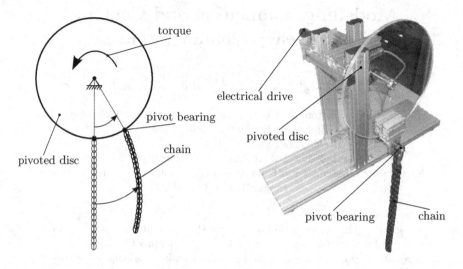

Fig. 1. This figure shows a schematic diagram of the laboratory model (*left*) and a picture of the laboratory model (*right*)

2   Modelling

This section mainly focuses on the derivation of a mathematical model for the heavy chain system. The chain is regarded to have an infinite number of elements and, therefore, can be modelled as a distributed parameter system described by PDEs. We suppose that the chain is only moving in the (x, z)-plane and, in addition, is inextensible as well as perfectly flexible, see, e.g. [1,3,5]. Furthermore, the assumption of a homogenous mass density of the chain is taken into account and we suppose that from bending and its total time derivative no friction torque arise. In contrast to the modelling task for control in this section the friction effects are not neglected for simulation purposes, see section 4. Hence, in contrast to, e.g., [1,3,5], the assumption of small chain displacements is dropped here for the reason that the chain is moved in vertical direction due to the disc rotation and, therefore, the effects of large chain movements have to be included to get a precise model. The mechanical degrees of freedom are the angle of the disc φ and the displacement of the chain u, w in the $x-$ and $z-$direction, see Fig. 2 for a schematic diagram of the system. The spatial coordinate is given by the arc length $s \in \mathcal{D}$ on the domain $\mathcal{D} = [0, l_c]$ and the boundary $\partial \mathcal{D} = \partial \mathcal{D}_0 \cup \partial \mathcal{D}_1 = \{0, l_c\}$ where l_c denotes the length of the chain. The equations of motion are derived by using the well known Hamilton principle and, accordingly, are given by PDEs (with boundary conditions) and ODEs. For this specific setup we introduce the mass moment of inertia Θ_d of the disc about the $y-$axis, the radius R and we suppose a homogenous mass density ρ for the chain. We further make use of the independent coordinates (t, s), the dependent coordinates (φ, u, w) and the derivative coordinates of the dependent coordinates with respect to the independent ones of first order $(\varphi_t, w_t, w_s, u_t, u_s)$

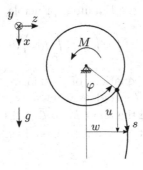

Fig. 2. This figure presents a schematic diagram for the modelling task

as well as the second order derivative coordinates $(\varphi_{tt}, w_{tt}, w_{st}, w_{ss}, u_{tt}, u_{st}, u_{ss})$. In addition we use the torque[1] M as the control input. For the purpose of deriving an adequate mathematical model we determine the position vector of a chain element which follows to $r^T = [R\cos(\varphi) + u, w]$. In order to eliminate the coordinate u from the equations we use the relation $u = \int_0^s u_s ds$ together with the constraint for the inextensibility of the chain $u_s^2 + w_s^2 = 1$. Therefore, the position and the velocity of a chain element in the (x, z)-plane only depends on the coordinates (φ, w) and their derivative coordinates with respect to the independent ones and, thus, it follows

$$r = \begin{bmatrix} R\cos(\varphi) + \int_0^s \sqrt{1 - w_s^2}ds \\ w \end{bmatrix}, \quad v = \frac{dr}{dt} = \begin{bmatrix} R\cos(\varphi)\varphi_t - \int_0^s \frac{w_s w_{st}}{\sqrt{1-w_s^2}}ds \\ w_t \end{bmatrix}.$$

The kinetic energy of the disc is given by $E_{kin}^d = \frac{1}{2}\Theta_d \varphi_t^2$ and the kinetic energy of the chain, defined by $E_{kin}^c = \int_D e_{kin}^c ds = \int_D \frac{1}{2}\rho v^T v ds$ with the kinetic energy density of the chain e_{kin}^c given by[2]

$$e_{kin}^c = \frac{\rho(l_c - s)w_s^2 w_{st}^2}{2(1 - w_s^2)} + \frac{\rho(l_c - s)w_s w_{st}R\sin(\varphi)\varphi_t}{\sqrt{1 - w_s^2}} + \frac{1}{2}\rho R^2 \sin(\varphi)^2 \varphi_t^2 + \frac{w_t^2 \rho}{2}$$

The potential energy of the chain, defined by $E_{pot}^c = \int_D e_{pot}^c ds = \int_D \frac{1}{2}\rho G^T r ds$ with the vector of gravity given by $G^T = [g, 0]$ and the potential energy density

$$e_{pot}^c = -Rg\cos(\varphi) - g(l_c - s)\sqrt{1 - w_s^2}.$$

Now we are able to determine the Lagrangian of the disc and the Lagrangian density of the chain

$$L = E_{kin}^d, \qquad l = e_{kin}^c - e_{pot}^c$$

---

[1] It is important to mention that the dynamics of the electrical drive can be neglected since an appropriate current controller realized by a power electronics, leads to a rising time of the current of about $t_{rise} \approx 90\mu s$. Therefore, the torque serves as the control input for the system.

[2] In order to simplify the energy densities we used Fubinis theorem for iterated integrals.

and define the functional for the Hamilton principle

$$\mathcal{L} = \int_{t_1}^{t_2} \left(L + \int_{\mathcal{D}} l \, ds \right) dt.$$

To determine the governing equations of motion we take the input M and the constraint[3] $\Theta^1 = w|_{s=0} - R \sin(\varphi) = 0$ into account. Hence, we extend the functional in consideration of the input M to $\bar{\mathcal{L}} = \mathcal{L} + \int_{t_1}^{t_2} M \varphi \, dt$. One possibility for considering the constraint $\Theta^1 = 0$ is to extend the functional $\bar{\mathcal{L}}$, by using the Lagrange multiplier λ, to

$$\bar{\bar{\mathcal{L}}} = \bar{\mathcal{L}} + \int_{t_1}^{t_2} \lambda \Theta^1 dt = \bar{\mathcal{L}} + \int_{t_1}^{t_2} \lambda \left(w|_{s=0} - R \sin(\varphi) \right) dt.$$

Now we are able to derive the equations of motion by the Hamilton principle which are given by a nonlinear PDE of second order with appropriate boundary conditions. Since the equations are too long to be presented here and due to the fact that for control purposes we are only interested in small motions around a predefined set point we linearize the geometry by means of small deflections w and small angles φ around the chosen set point. Therefore, we choose

$$\varphi = \tilde{\varphi} = 0, \; \varphi_t = \tilde{\varphi}_t = 0, \; w = \tilde{w} = 0, \; w = \tilde{w}_t = 0, \; M = \tilde{M} = 0$$

by means of the coordinate and input transformation

$$\varphi = \tilde{\varphi} + \Delta \varphi = \Delta \varphi, \; w = \tilde{w} + \Delta w = \Delta w, \; M = \tilde{M} + \Delta M = \Delta M.$$

The kinetic energy, respectively kinetic energy density of the linearized system[4] is derived by a Taylor series expansion up to second order terms leading to $E_{kin}^{d,lin} = \frac{1}{2} \varphi_t^2 \Theta_d$, $e_{kin}^{c,lin} = \frac{1}{2} \rho w_t^2$ and the potential energy density of the linearized system results in $e_{pot}^{c,lin} = \frac{\rho(l_c - s)g}{2} w_s^2$. Therefore, the functional for the Hamilton principle of the linearized system reads as

$$\bar{\bar{\mathcal{L}}}^{lin} = \int_{t_1}^{t_2} \left(E_{kin}^{d,lin} + \int_{\mathcal{D}} \left(e_{kin}^{c,lin} - e_{pot}^{c,lin} \right) ds + M\varphi + \lambda \left(w|_{s=0} - R\varphi \right) \right) dt.$$

Hence, by the Hamilton principle the equations of motion follow to the second order PDE on the domain $\mathcal{D}$

$$\mathcal{D} : \rho w_{tt} + \rho g w_s - \rho g \left(l_c - s \right) w_{ss} = 0$$

with the boundary conditions given by

$$\partial \mathcal{D}_0 : \varphi_{tt} = \frac{\rho R l_c g \, w_s|_{s=0} + M}{\Theta_d} \quad \text{and} \quad \partial \mathcal{D}_1 : \left[\rho g \left(l_c - s \right) w_s \right]_{s=l_c} = 0.$$

---

[3] By a slight abuse of notation we use the abbreviation $w|_{s \in \partial \mathcal{D}}$ for the restriction of the coordinate w to the boundary $\partial \mathcal{D}$.

[4] In order to increase the readability we omit the Δ in the coordinates whenever it is clear from the context.

3   Control

This section deals with the control design based directly on the distributed parameter system. The control aim is to stabilize a predefined set point. The main idea for deriving a suitable control law which meets the requirements is to focus at the chain subsystem and to induce damping into this subsystem by use of the passivity concept, see, e.g. [6]. To get a control law for the entire system this contol law is combined with the backstepping method, see, e.g. [2]. For this purpose the system is virtually split into subsystems, see Fig. 3, which depicts the domains of these subsystems as well as the energy ports connecting them. The source for deriving a suitable control law is the chain energy of the linearized system given by

$$H^{chain} = \int_{\mathcal{D}} \left(e_{kin}^{c,lin} + e_{pot}^{c,lin} \right) ds = \int_{\mathcal{D}} \left(\frac{w_t^2}{2} + \frac{\rho \left(l_c - s \right) g}{2} w_s^2 \right) ds.$$

We can see that if we take rigid body motions into account the energy function is not positive definite and, therefore, it cannot be used as a Lyapunov function candidate. To circumvent this problem we extend the energy function with a term that can be interpreted as the energy of a linear spring. Therefore, we use the extended Lyapunov function candidate

$$H_e^{chain} = \int_{\mathcal{D}} \left(\frac{\rho w_t^2}{2} + \frac{\rho \left(l_c - s \right) g}{2} w_s^2 \right) ds + \frac{1}{2} \alpha_1 \left(w|_{s=0} \right)^2 > 0, \quad \alpha_1 \in \mathbb{R}^+$$

and after some calculations it follows that the formal time derivative of the extended chain energy of the linearized system is given by

$$\frac{\mathrm{d}}{\mathrm{d}t} H_e^{chain} = \left(\underbrace{-\rho R l_c g \, w_s|_{s=0}}_{F} + \alpha_1 \, w|_{s=0} \right) w_t|_{s=0}$$

which immediately point out the energy port of the chain given by the collocated parameters $(F, w_t|_{s=0})$, see Fig. 3. Therefore, we conclude that a suitable control law $w_t^c|_{s=0}$ for the virtual input $w_t|_{s=0}$ will be

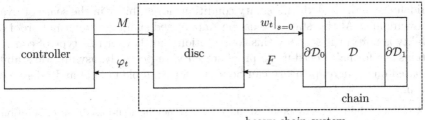

heavy chain system

Fig. 3. In this figure the seperation of the system into subsystems is pointed out

$$w_t^c\big|_{s=0} = w_t\big|_{s=0} = -\alpha_2 \left(F + \alpha_1 \, w\big|_{s=0}\right), \qquad \alpha_2 \in \mathbb{R}^+$$

Moreover, it can be seen that by regarding H_e^{chain} as a Lyapunov function candidate the necessary conditions for stability in the sense of Lyapunov are met[5]. Obviously, the velocity $w_t\big|_{s=0} = v\big|_{s=0}$ is not available as a control input and, thus, we use the backstepping approach. When we consider the boundary condition at the disc together with the coupling condition $\Theta^{1,lin} = w\big|_{s=0} - R\varphi = 0$ the disc system follows to the system of first order ODEs

$$\partial \mathcal{D}_0 : \begin{cases} w_t = v \\ v_t = \frac{\rho R l_c g \, w_s\big|_{s=0} + M}{R\Theta_d} \end{cases}.$$

To simplify the derivation of the control law we use the input transformation

$$u = \frac{\rho R l_c g \, w_s\big|_{s=0} + M}{R\Theta_d}.$$

Following the idea of the backstepping method the coordinate transformation

$$z = w_t\big|_{s=0} - w_t^c\big|_{s=0} = w_t\big|_{s=0} + \alpha_2 \left(F + \alpha_1 \, w\big|_{s=0}\right)$$

to the boundary system is performed and, thus, we use the Lyapunov function candidate $V = H_e^{chain} + \frac{1}{2}z^2$ for the closed-loop system whose formal time derivative results after some calculations in

$$\frac{\mathrm{d}}{\mathrm{d}t}V = \frac{\mathrm{d}}{\mathrm{d}t}H_e^{chain} + \frac{\mathrm{d}}{\mathrm{d}t}\left(\frac{1}{2}z^2\right) = -\alpha_2 \left(F + \alpha_1 \, w\big|_{s=0}\right)^2$$

$$+ \underbrace{\left(w_t + \alpha_2 \left(F + \alpha_1 \, w\big|_{s=0}\right)\right)\left(\frac{u}{R} - \alpha_2 \left(\rho g l_c \, w_{ts}\big|_0 - \alpha_1 \, w_t\big|_{s=0}\right)\right)}_{=-\alpha_3\left(w_t + \alpha_2\left(F + \alpha_1 \, w\big|_{s=0}\right)\right)}, \alpha_3 \in \mathbb{R}^+$$

Appointing the expression in brackets in this manner enables us to derive the control law for the transformed input

$$u = -\alpha_3 R \left(w_t + \alpha_2 \left(-\rho g l_c \, w_s\big|_{s=0} + \alpha_1 R\varphi\right)\right) - \alpha_2 R \left(-\rho g l_c \, w_{ts}\big|_0 + \alpha_1 R\varphi_t\right)$$

and for the sake of completeness we refer that the real control input M can be derived by inverting the input transformation. Applying this control law, it can be seen that the formal time derivative of the Lyapunov function is negative semidefinite and, thus, the necessary conditions for stability in the sense of Lyapunov are met. At this stage it must be emphasized again that a formal proof of stability is not in the scope of this contribution and that for this type of control systems the formal procedure to proof stability, respectively, asymptotic stability based on semigroup theory can be found for example in [4,5] and references therein.

---

[5] To claim stability at this point we have to assume the well-posedness of solutions in the sense of Hadamard which is indeed a strong restriction but a formal proof of stability is not in the scope of this paper. The formal procedure to proof stability for this type of control systems can be found in e.g. [4,5] and references therein.

4   Simulation and Measurement Results

This section is dedicated to the simulation of the heavy chain system as well as the comparison of simulation with measurement results in order to validate the mathematical model. Furthermore, the proposed control strategy will be demonstrated by measurement results, which arises from a laboratory experiment on the heavy chain laboratory model depicted in Fig. 1. For high-precision simulation purposes a large but finite number of chain elements is considered and, therefore, a simulation model consisting of a so called "n−Pendulum" connected to the model of the disc is developed. Friction is taken into account in form of a static friction model which means that we consider Coulomb and viscous friction in every bearing and between the chain elements as well as stick friction at the actuator. The parameters of the laboratory model are the mass moment of inertia $\Theta_d = 0.0144 \mathrm{kgm}^2$, the length of the chain $l_c = 0.675\mathrm{m}$, the line mass density $\rho = 2.77 \mathrm{kgm}^{-1}$ and the radius of the disc $R = 0.18\mathrm{m}$. The angle of the disc and the angle of the chain at $s = 0$ as well as the angular velocities are available as measurements. The controller parameters are chosen to $\alpha_1 = 5, \alpha_2 = 15$ and $\alpha_3 = 20$. In the first experiment we compare the controlled system with data from the laboratory model and the simulation model. Thus, Fig. 4 shows the simulation with the "n-Pendulum" compared to the measurement results from the laboratory model. As it can be seen, the simulation includes the main physical effects acting at the laboratory model and, therefore, fits well. To show

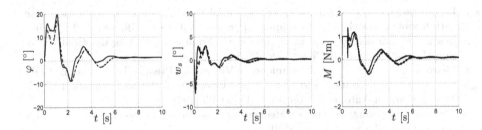

Fig. 4. The present figure demonstrates the comparison of simulation (*dashed line*) and measurement (*solid line*) results

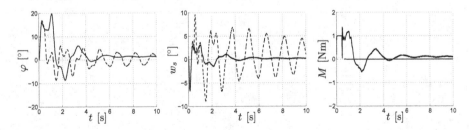

Fig. 5. This figure displays a comparison between measurement results of the controlled (*solid line*) and the uncontrolled (*dashed line*) laboratory model

the efficiency of the proposed control approach we finally compare the behaviour of the controlled system with the uncontrolled one, see Fig. 5. In this particular experiment we disturb the system with a filtered impulse generated by the input torque M and after this disturbance we activate the controller.

5 Conclusion

In conclusion it may be said that we have shown a model based control approach for disturbance rejection and stabilization of a set point directly based on the distributed parameter system by means of a passivity based control law combined with the backstepping approach. Laboratory model experiments pointed out the performance of the proposed approach. Some future works with focus to this configuration deals with the analysis of the full nonlinear distributed parameter system as well as the application of other control approaches.

Acknowledgements. The authors gratefully acknowledge for the support of the ACCM. This work was done in terms of a strategic research project of the ACCM Area 2 - Mechanics and Model Based Control with the title *Model based control for linear/nonlinear lumped/distributed parameter systems.*

References

1. D'Andrea-Novel, B., Coron, J.M.: Exponential stabilization of an overhead crane with flexible cable via a back-stepping approach. Automatica 36, 587–593 (2000)
2. Krstic, M., Kanellakopoulos, I., Kokotovic, P.: Nonlinear and Adaptive Control Design. John Wiley & Sons, New York (1995)
3. Meirovich, L.: Principles and Techniques in Vibrations. Prentice Hall, London (1997)
4. Morgül, Ö.: Stabilization and Disturbance Rejection of the wave equation. IEEE Transactions on Automatic Control 43(1), 89–95 (1998)
5. Thull, D.: Tracking Control of Mechanical Distributed Parameter Systems with Applications. Shaker, Aachen (2010)
6. Van der Schaft, A.J.: L2-Gain and Passivity Techniques in Nonlinear Control. Springer, London (2000)

On Modelling and Control of Compressible Non-Newtonian Injection Processes

H. Daxberger[1,*], K. Rieger[2], and K. Schlacher[1]

[1] Institute of Automatic Control and Control Systems Technology,
Johannes Kepler University Linz, Altenberger Straße 69, 4040 Linz, Austria
{harald.daxberger,kurt.schlacher}@jku.at
[2] Kappa Filter Systems GmbH, Im Stadtgut A1, 4407 Steyr-Gleink, Austria
k.rieger@kappa-fs.com

Abstract. This contribution is dedicated to the modelling and control of a particular injection process configuration with non-newtonian compressible fluids. First, the governing mathematical equations are derived in form of one-dimensional partial differential equations with (spatially moving) boundary conditions. Then, we propose control strategies for selected tracking problems. We follow the early lumping approach, where the controller design relies on an approximated model described by nonlinear ordinary differential equations. Simulation results highlight the tracking performance.

Keywords: Infinite-Dimensional Systems, Flow Control, Nonlinear Control, Tracking Control.

1 Introduction

Injection processes of compressible non-newtonian fluids are widely spread in industry, for example, in the domain of food processing and manufacturing industry. In this contribution we treat one possible configuration of a filling process, whose schematic diagram is shown in Fig. 1. A horizontally movable piston allows to transport fluid into the cavity. The piston itself is driven by an external force that serves as the control input. Moreover, the pressure and the volume flow at the piston are supposed to be available as measurements. Typically the operator wants the pressure or the volume flow at the piston to follow a desired trajectory during the filling process. For the controller design based on a mathematical model we propose control strategies for both tracking problems.

For similar problems model predictive control (see e.g. [1]) or iterative learning control (for instance [2]) have been proposed. We follow an adaptive approach, similar as presented in [3], but for a different application and in contrast to [4], where for the adaptive controller design a linear model is assumed, we use a nonlinear model derived from the governing equations.

---

* The authors gratefully acknowledge for the support of the Austrian Center of Competence in Mechatronics (ACCM).

R. Moreno-Díaz et al. (Eds.): EUROCAST 2011, Part II, LNCS 6928, pp. 65–72, 2012.
© Springer-Verlag Berlin Heidelberg 2012

This contribution is organized as follows. In section 2 the mathematical model is derived. Section 3 deals with the design of a volume flow controller as well as a pressure controller and the simulation results in section 4 demonstrate the performance of this approach. Finally, we conclude in section 5.

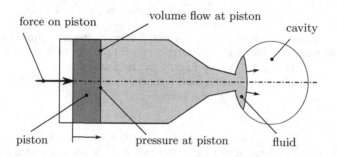

force on piston   volume flow at piston   cavity

piston   pressure at piston   fluid

Fig. 1. Example of a filling process

2 Mathematical Model

The governing equations for the fluid are obtained by applying the balance of mass, the balance of momentum and the constitutive equations. Since we consider a non-newtonian behaviour of the fluid, its viscosity depends on the shear rate. In particular, we confine here to the class of fluids, whose viscosity is described by the power law model [5]. In addition, we assume a rotationally symmetric geometry and a certain velocity distribution such that the governing equations simplify to one-dimensional partial differential equations. In the following arguments of functions are omitted, when the dependency is clear from the context.

2.1 Conservation Laws in Cylindrical Coordinates

Since we confine to a radially symmetric geometry of the cavity and the cylinder it is beneficial to formulate the governing equations in cylindrical coordinates (r, φ, z). Starting with the conservation law of mass in cylindrical coordinates [6] is given by

$$\partial_t \rho + \frac{1}{r}\partial_r \left(r\rho v_r\right) + \frac{1}{r}\partial_\varphi \left(\rho v_\varphi\right) + \partial_z \left(\rho v_z\right) = 0$$

with $\partial_r = \frac{\partial}{\partial r}$, $\partial_\varphi = \frac{\partial}{\partial \varphi}$, $\partial_z = \frac{\partial}{\partial z}$ and $\partial_t = \frac{\partial}{\partial t}$. The velocities v_r, v_φ and v_z in r-, φ- and z-direction and the mass density ρ are functions of the independent coordinates (r, φ, z, t). The differential momentum balance formulated in cylindrical coordinates (see [6]) reads as

$$\rho\left(\partial_t v_r + v_r \partial_r v_r + \frac{v_\varphi}{r}\partial_\varphi v_r - \frac{v_\varphi^2}{r} + v_z \partial_z v_r\right) = -\partial_r p + \frac{1}{r}\partial_r (\sigma_{rr} r) + \frac{1}{r}\partial_\varphi \sigma_{r\varphi} - \frac{\sigma_{\varphi\varphi}}{r} + \partial_z \sigma_{rz} + \rho b_r,$$

$$\rho\left(\partial_t v_\varphi + v_r \partial_r v_\varphi + \frac{v_\varphi}{r}\partial_\varphi v_\varphi + \frac{v_r v_\varphi}{r} + v_z \partial_z v_\varphi\right) = -\frac{1}{r}\partial_\varphi p + \frac{1}{r^2}\partial_r (\sigma_{r\varphi} r^2) + \frac{1}{r}\partial_\varphi \sigma_{\varphi\varphi} + \partial_z \sigma_{\varphi z} + \rho b_\varphi,$$

$$\rho\left(\partial_t v_z + v_r \partial_r v_z + \frac{v_\varphi}{r}\partial_\varphi v_z + v_z \partial_z v_z\right) = -\partial_z p + \frac{1}{r}\partial_r (\sigma_{rz} r) + \frac{1}{r}\partial_\varphi \sigma_{\varphi z} + \partial_z \sigma_{zz} + \rho b_z$$

with respect to the components of the viscous stress tensor $\mathbf{S}$ which is

$$
\mathbf{S} = \begin{bmatrix} \sigma_{rr} & \sigma_{r\varphi} & \sigma_{rz} \\ \sigma_{r\varphi} & \sigma_{\varphi\varphi} & \sigma_{\varphi z} \\ \sigma_{rz} & \sigma_{\varphi z} & \sigma_{zz} \end{bmatrix} = \mu(\dot\gamma) \begin{bmatrix} 0 & \left(r\partial_r\left(\frac{v_\varphi}{r}\right) + \frac{1}{r}\partial_\varphi v_r\right) & (\partial_r v_z + \partial_z v_r) \\ \left(r\partial_r\left(\frac{v_\varphi}{r}\right) + \frac{1}{r}\partial_\varphi v_r\right) & 0 & \left(\partial_z v_\varphi + \frac{1}{r}\partial_\varphi v_r\right) \\ (\partial_r v_z + \partial_z v_r) & \left(\partial_z v_\varphi + \frac{1}{r}\partial_\varphi v_r\right) & 0 \end{bmatrix} .
$$

The terms b_r, b_φ and b_z describe the body forces in in r-, φ- and z-direction. Since we deal with a non-newtonian fluid the viscosity μ depends on the shear rate $\dot\gamma$ (see [6]) which takes in cylindrical coordinates the form

$$
\dot\gamma = \Big(2(\partial_z v_z)^2 + (\partial_r v_z)^2 + 2(\partial_r v_z)(\partial_z v_r) + \tfrac{1}{r^2}(\partial_\varphi v_z)^2 + \tfrac{2}{r}(\partial_z v_\varphi)(\partial_\varphi v_z) + (\partial_z v_r)^2 +
$$

$$
+ 2(\partial_r v_r)^2 + (\partial_\varphi v_r)^2 + \tfrac{1}{r^2}(2r\partial_r v_\varphi - 2v_\varphi)\partial_\varphi v_z + 2\tfrac{v_r^2}{r^2} + \tfrac{4}{r^2}\partial_\varphi v_\varphi v_r + (\partial_z v_\varphi)^2
$$

$$
+ (\partial_r v_\varphi)^2 - \tfrac{2}{r^2}v_\varphi\partial_r v_\varphi + \tfrac{2}{r^2}(\partial_\varphi v_\varphi)^2 + \tfrac{1}{r^2}v_\varphi\Big)^{\frac{1}{2}} .
$$

The viscosity of the model is described by $\mu(\dot\gamma) = \mu_0 \dot\gamma^{n-1}$ with $n > 0$. The relation between pressure p and mass density ρ is given by the polytropic relation $p(\rho) = \left(b^{-1}\rho\right)^{\frac{1}{\beta}}$ for $\rho > 0$ with b, $\beta > 0$. The boundary condition (BC) at the piston follows from the velocity of the piston and since we assume that the fluid sticks to the walls of the cavity the velocity vanishes at the walls. At the flowfront ambient pressure is assumed such that the BC at the flow front is given by the corresponding mass density.

2.2   Reduction to a Spatially One-Dimensional System

We assume that the dynamical behaviour of the process is mainly influenced by the velocity and pressure distribution along the flow path whereas the pressure and the velocity distribution in radial direction is quasistatic, i.e, the system can be approximated by a 1-dimensional model.

First we assume that the BCs and initial conditions are rotationally symmetric, such that all derivatives with respect to the angle φ vanish and we assume that $v_\varphi = 0$. In addition the radial component of the velocity v_r is neglected and $(\partial_z v_z)^2 \ll (\partial_r v_z)^2$ is assumed. Under these assumptions the momentum balance equation in φ-direction vanishes and the equation in r-direction is neglected. One gets the simplified balance of momentum

$$
\rho\left(\partial_t v_z + v_z \partial_z v_z\right) = -\partial_z p + \frac{1}{r}\partial_r(\sigma_{rz} r) + \rho f_z \tag{1}
$$

with $\sigma_{rz} = \mu(\dot\gamma)\partial_r v_z$ and $\dot\gamma = |\partial_r v_z|$. For a convenient description we introduce the volume flow

$$
q = \int_0^R 2\pi r v_z \, dr . \tag{2}
$$

In order to derive a spatially 1-dimensional description we make use of the ansatz $v_z = f(q)\left(r^{\frac{n+1}{n}} - R^{\frac{n+1}{n}}\right)$ which is a solution of the incompressible, static case and describes the velocity distribution in a cross section with radius R. We determine $f(q)$ such that (2) is met and end up with the velocity distribution

$$v_z = q \frac{(3n+1)\left(1-\left(\frac{r}{R}\right)^{\frac{n+1}{n}}\right)}{\pi(n+1)R^2}.$$

If the change of the cross section area A in z-direction is neglected the one-dimensional mass balance reads as $0 = A\partial_t\rho + \partial_z(\rho q)$ and the integration of the conservation law of momentum over the cross section area A results in

$$0 = \rho\left(\partial_t q + \frac{3n+1}{(2n+1)\pi R^3}q(R\partial_z q - q\partial_z R)\right)$$

$$+A\partial_z p + \mu_0 g(n,R)|q|^{n-1}q \quad \text{with} \quad g(n,R) = \frac{2(3n+1)^n}{n^n \pi^{n-1}}R^{1-3n}.$$

Finally one ends up with the system

$$0 = \rho\left(\partial_t q + \frac{3n+1}{(2n+1)\pi R^3}q(R\partial_z q - q\partial_z R)\right)$$

$$+A(z)\partial_z p + \mu_0 g(n,R)|q|^{n-1}q$$

$$0 = A(z)\partial_t\rho + \partial_z(\rho q). \tag{3}$$

The BC at the piston $q(z_0,t) = A(z_0)v_0(t)$ results from the velocity v_0 of the piston at the position z_0. The velocity and the position are described by $\dot{z}_0 = v_0$ and $\dot{v}_0 = \frac{1}{m}(F - p(z_0)A(z_0))$ where m is the mass of the piston. The external force F that acts on the piston is the controller input. To describe the BC of the flow front one has to distinguish two cases. If the cavity is not totally filled, the flow front at position z_L moves with velocity $v(z_L) = \frac{q(z_L)}{A(z_L)}$ and the ambient pressure p_a is assumed to act on the flow front. Since the density depends on the pressure the BC reads as $\rho(p(z_L)) = \rho(p_a)$ with $\dot{z}_L = \frac{q(z_L)}{A(z_L)}$. If the cavity is filled the flow front has reached the end position z_E such that $z_L = z_E$ and the velocity at the flow front $v(z_L) = 0$ vanishes. In this case the BC at the flow front is given by $q(z_L,t) = 0$.

2.3   Model Reduction

The controller design for a system that is described by nonlinear partial differential equations is far from trivial. Moreover, in many cases the geometry of the cavity is not exactly known or too complex for this application such that it can't be considered for the controller design. In order to simplify the design of a controller we derive a simplified model.

Especially for fluids of rather high viscosity the acceleration in (3) can be neglected and one gets a simplified system

$$\partial_z p = c(z)q^{n-1}|q| \quad \text{with} \quad c(z) = \frac{\mu_0 g(n,R(z))}{A(z)}$$

$$A\partial_t\rho(p) = -\partial_z(\rho(p)q).$$

We take a look at the case $q > 0$ such that the absolute value can be omitted. Now the ansatz for the pressure distribution $p(z,t) = p_0(t) k(z, z_L)$ depending on the flow front position z_L is applied to the stationary conservation of momentum and for the volume flow we obtain

$$q = \bar{k}(z, z_L) p_0(t)^\alpha \qquad \bar{k}(z, z_L) = \left(\frac{\partial_z k(z, z_L)}{c(z)} \right)^{\frac{1}{n}} \qquad \alpha = \frac{1}{n}.$$

The integration of the law of mass conservation (3) with the additional condition $q(z_0) = q_0$ leads to

$$\int_{z_0}^{z} A(z) \partial_p \rho \partial_t p_0 k(\xi, z_L) \, d\xi = -\rho(p(z,t)) q + \rho(p(z_0,t)) q_0 .$$

If one plugs in the relation between the pressure and the mass density and uses the volume flow from above one gets

$$\underbrace{b p_0^{\beta-1} \beta \int_{z_0}^{z} A(\xi) k(\xi, z_L)^\beta \, d\xi}_{C(z_0, z, z_L)} \partial_t p_0 = -\left(b p_0^\beta k(z, z_L)^\beta \right) \bar{k}(z, z_L) p_0^\alpha + b p_0^\beta q_0$$

$$\partial_t p_0 = -\frac{\left(p_0 k(z, z_L)^\beta \right)}{C(z_0, z, z_L)} \bar{k}(z) p_0^\alpha + \frac{p_0}{C(z_0, z, z_L)} q_0$$

and for $z = z_L$ we end up with

$$\partial_t p_0 = \frac{p_0}{C(z_0, z_L, z_L)} (q_0 - \delta p_0^\alpha) \qquad \delta = k(z, z_L)^\beta \, \bar{k}(z, z_L) |_{z=z_L} .$$

Furthermore, the assumption $C(z_0, z_L, z_L) = \text{const.}$ is made. The conservation of momentum for the actuator with mass m and acting force F results in a differential equation

$$\dot{q}_0 = \frac{A}{m} (F - p_0 A)$$

for the simplified model. With the substitutions $p_0 = \bar{p}$ and $q_0 = \bar{q}$ ($\bar{p}$ and $\bar{q}$ are the states of the finitedimensional simplified model) the simplified process model reads as

$$\begin{bmatrix} \dot{\bar{q}} \\ \dot{\bar{p}} \end{bmatrix} = \begin{bmatrix} \frac{A}{m}(F - \bar{p}A) \\ \frac{\bar{p}}{\bar{C}}(\bar{q} - \delta \bar{p}^\alpha) \end{bmatrix} . \tag{4}$$

3   Control

The controller design relies on the approximated model of the process (4). For both the pressure and velocity tracking problem we propose a control strategy, involving a feedforward and a feedback part, and it is shown that the controller guarantees the stability of the tracking error system for the simplified model.

3.1 Velocity Control

For the controller design the simplified model (4) is used. To stabilise the tracking error the control law $F = F_{FF} + F_{FB}$ with the feedforward law $F_{FF} = \frac{m}{A}\dot{\bar{q}}_d$ and the feedback law $F_{FB} = \bar{p}A - \frac{\lambda_1 m}{A}(\bar{q} - \bar{q}_d)$ is suggested. With the tracking error $e_{\bar{q}} = \bar{q} - \bar{q}_d$ the controller leads to the closed loop system

$$\begin{bmatrix} \dot{e}_{\bar{q}} \\ \dot{\bar{p}} \end{bmatrix} = \begin{bmatrix} -\lambda_1 e_{\bar{q}} \\ \frac{\bar{p}}{C}(\bar{q}_d + e_{\bar{q}} - \delta\bar{p}^{\alpha}) \end{bmatrix} .$$

The tracking error $e_{\bar{q}}$ is obviously asymptotically stable if $\lambda_1 > 0$ is fulfilled.

3.2 Adaptive Pressure Control

The pressure controller design is also based on the simplified model (4). It is assumed that $\bar{p}$ and $\bar{q}$ can be measured and that the system parameters A, m, C and α are known. The parameter δ which is assumed to be constant but unknown describes the friction of the fluid. In a first step a feedforward controller is designed. Since δ appears in the feedforward law, an estimator that estimates the value of δ and a feedback law are proposed such that the closed loop system is locally uniformly stable. First, the model (4) is augmented by the state δ for the pressure controller design

$$\begin{bmatrix} \dot{\bar{q}} \\ \dot{\bar{p}} \\ \dot{\delta} \end{bmatrix} = \begin{bmatrix} \frac{A}{m}(F - \bar{p}A) \\ \frac{\bar{p}}{C}(\bar{q} - \delta\bar{p}^{\alpha}) \\ 0 \end{bmatrix} . \tag{5}$$

In order to design a feedforward law, we use the fact that any system variable (state, input, output) of a differentially flat system can be expressed as a function of the flat output and a finite number of its derivatives (see e.g. [8],[9] and references therein). For the system (5) the pressure $\bar{p}$ and the state δ are a flat output and one can obtain the feedforward law for the desired pressure $\bar{p}_d$

$$F_d = \frac{mC}{A}\frac{\ddot{\bar{p}}_d}{\bar{p}_d} - \frac{mC}{A}\frac{\dot{\bar{p}}_d^2}{\bar{p}_d^2} + \frac{\alpha\delta m}{A}\bar{p}_d^{\alpha-1}\dot{\bar{p}}_d + \bar{p}_d A$$

for which the nominal system exactly follows the nominal trajectory. Since δ is unknown, we use the estimated value $\hat{\delta}$ such that the feedforward law $\hat{F}_d$ and the desired volume flow $\hat{\bar{q}}_d$ read as

$$\hat{F}_d = \frac{mC}{A}\frac{\ddot{\bar{p}}_d}{\bar{p}_d} - \frac{mC}{A}\frac{\dot{\bar{p}}_d^2}{\bar{p}_d^2} + \frac{\alpha\hat{\delta}m}{A}\bar{p}_d^{\alpha-1}\dot{\bar{p}}_d + \hat{\delta}\bar{p}_d^{\alpha} + \bar{p}_d A \quad \text{and} \quad \hat{\bar{q}}_d = C\frac{\dot{\bar{p}}_d}{\bar{p}_d} + \hat{\delta}\bar{p}_d^{\alpha} .$$

Now we introduce error cordinates $e_{\bar{p}} = \bar{p} - \bar{p}_d$, $e_{\bar{q}} = \bar{q} - \hat{\bar{q}}_d = \bar{q} - \bar{q}_d + e_{\delta}\bar{p}_d^{\alpha}$ for trajectory the errors, $e_{\delta} = \delta - \hat{\delta}$ for the estimation error and $\dot{\hat{\delta}} = -f_{\delta}$. The feedforward law results in $\hat{F}_d = F_d - \frac{\alpha m}{A}\bar{p}_d^{\alpha-1}\dot{\bar{p}}_d e_\delta - \frac{m}{A} f_\delta \bar{p}_d^\alpha$. With the feedback law $F_c = -\lambda_2(\bar{p})\, e_{\bar{p}} - \lambda_1 e_{\bar{q}}$ we get the error system

$$
\begin{bmatrix} \dot{e}_{\bar{q}} \\ \dot{e}_{\bar{p}} \\ \dot{e}_\delta \end{bmatrix} = \begin{bmatrix} -\frac{A^2}{m}e_{\bar{p}} - \lambda_2(\bar{p})\frac{A}{m}e_{\bar{p}} - \lambda_1 \frac{A}{m}e_{\bar{q}} \\ \frac{\bar{p}}{C}e_{\bar{q}} - \frac{\bar{p}}{C}\delta\left((e_{\bar{p}}+\bar{p}_d)^\alpha - \bar{p}_d^\alpha\right) - \frac{\bar{p}}{C}e_\delta \bar{p}_d^\alpha + \frac{e_{\bar{p}}}{\bar{p}_d C}\dot{\bar{p}}_d \\ f_\delta \end{bmatrix}. \tag{6}
$$

We choose $\lambda_1 = \text{const.} > 0$, $\lambda_2(\bar{p}) = -A + \frac{\gamma_2}{\gamma_1}\frac{m\bar{p}}{AC}$ and $\dot{\hat{\delta}} = -f_\delta = \frac{1}{\gamma_3}\left(\gamma_2 \frac{\bar{p}}{C}\bar{p}_d^\alpha e_{\bar{p}}\right)$. Once the desired trajectory $\bar{p}_d$ is chosen, it is a function of time and therefore (6) is a nonautonomous system. To proof uniform stability we use Theorem 4.8 from [10]. If $\dot{\bar{p}}_d < \dot{\bar{p}}_{d,max}$, $\bar{p}_d > 0$, $\delta > 0$ with $\dot{\bar{p}}_{d,max} = \alpha\delta\bar{p}_d^{\alpha+1}$ is guaranteed and one chooses $V = \frac{1}{2}\gamma_1 e_{\bar{q}}^2 + \frac{1}{2}\gamma_2 e_{\bar{p}}^2 + \frac{1}{2}\gamma_3 e_\delta^2$ it follows that $\dot{V} \leq 0$ is locally fulfilled and therefore the uniform stability of the equilibrium point $[e_{\bar{q}}, e_{\bar{p}}, e_\delta]^T = 0$ follows.

4   Simulation Results

In order to simulate the filling process (3) is discretised by the method of finite differences which is suitably adapted to include the spatially moving BCs and one obtains a system of ordinary differential equations. The generation of this equation system is implemented in C++ and solved with the DASKR [7] solver. For the following simulations a geometry was chosen where the cross section area changes along the flow path. Figure 2 shows the tracking behaviour of the controlled system for velocity and pressure control. At the beginning both simulations show that the tracking errors decline and the proposed controllers are able to stabilise the tracking errors. Later on the volume flow and pressure of the controlled system follow the desired trajectories.

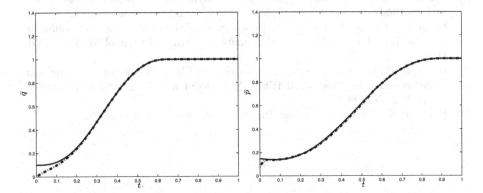

Fig. 2. The figure on the left shows the normalised desired volume flow $\bar{q}_d$ (*solid line*) and the normalised simulated volume flow $\bar{q}$ (*dot and dash line*) for the veloctiy controller, the figure on the right shows the normalised desired pressure $\bar{p}_d$ (*solid line*) and the normalised simulated pressure $\bar{p}$ (*dot and dash line*) for the adaptive pressure controller.

5 Conclusions

In this contribution we have dealt with a particular injection process configuration. We derived a distributed parameter model for simulation purposes and a lumped parameter model for controller design. Then we proposed a velocity controller as well as an adaptive pressure controller and provided simulation results that demonstrate the performance of this approach.

Acknowlegements. The authors gratefully acknowledge for the support of the Austrian Center of Competence in Mechatronics (ACCM).

References

[1] Dubay, R., Pamujati, B., Han, J., Strohmaier, F.: An investigation on the application of predictive control for controlling screw position and velocity on an injection molding machine. Polymer Engineering and Science Journal 47(4), 390–399 (2007)

[2] Havlicsek, H., Alleyne, A.: Nonlinear Control of an Electrohydraulic Injection Molding Machine via Iterative Adaptive Learning. IEEE/ASME Transactions on Mechatronics 4(3) (1999)

[3] Kemmetmüller, W., Fuchshumer, F., Kugi, A.: Nonlinear pressure control of self-supplied variable displacement axial piston pumps. Control Engineering Practice 18, 84–93 (2010)

[4] Yang, Y., Gao, F.: Adaptive control of the filling velocity of thermoplastics injection molding. Control Engineering Practice 8, 1285–1296 (2000)

[5] Chhabra, R.P., Richardson, J.F.: Non-newtonian Flow in the Process Industries. Butterworth-Heinemann, Butterworth (1999)

[6] Slattery, J.C.: Advanced Transport Phenomena. Camb. Univ. Press, Cambridge (1999)

[7] Brown, P.N., Hindmarsh, A.C., Petzold, L.R.: Differential-algebraic system solver with rootfinding (April 22, 2010), http://www.netlib.org/ode

[8] Fliess, M., Levine, J., Martin, P., Rouchon, P.: Flatness and defect of nonlinear systems: Introductory Theory and Examples. Journal of Control 61, 1327–1361 (1995)

[9] Rouchon, P., Fliess, M., Levine, J., Martin, P.: Flattness, motion planning and trailer systems. In: Proc. 32nd IEEE Conf. Decision and Control, San Antonio, pp. 2700–2705 (1993)

[10] Khalil, H.K.: Nonlinear Systems. Prentice-Hall, Englewood Cliffs (2002)

Model-Based Evaluation of a Linear Electro Hydraulic Direct Drive

Florian Poltschak[1,2], Peter Hehenberger[3], Babak Farrokhzad[4], Wolfgang Amrhein[1,2], and Klaus Zeman[3]

[1] Institute for Electrical Drives and Power Electronics, Johannes Kepler University Linz, Altenbergerstr. 69, 4040 Linz, Austria
{florian.poltschak,wolfgang.amrhein}@jku.at
[2] JKU HOERBIGER Research Institute for Smart Actuartors, Johannes Kepler University Linz, Altenbergerstr. 69, 4040 Linz, Austria
{florian.poltschak,wolfgang.amrhein}@jku.at
[3] Institute for Computer-Aided Methods in Mechanical Engineering, Johannes Kepler University Linz, Altenbergerstr. 69, 4040 Linz, Austria
{peter.hehenberger,klaus.zeman}@jku.at
[4] HOERBIGER Automation Technology
Südliche Römerstrasse 15, 86972 Altenstadt, Germany
babak.farrokhzad@hoerbiger.com

Abstract. The requirements of the desired applications can be evaluated at an early design stage based on mechatronic models that give an integrated description of the system. This is demonstrated for an electro-hydraulic linear motion actuator on a working machine that has the potential to replace standard hydraulic systems. The requirements differ for each use cases and unwanted side effects can deteriorate the key performance requirements. In this paper the advantage of a model-based evaluation is shown for the case of undesirable vibrations and possible concepts for their reduction. This method has the power to reduce the time to market significantly.

Keywords: model-based evaluation, mechatronic design, linear electro hydraulic drive.

1 Introduction

Mechatronics design is the competence integration of mechanics, electronics and information technologies. As mechatronic design processes have to handle a high degree of complexity and have to consider a wide variety of technologies, the question of optimum design becomes specifically challenging. Tackling this issue requires a novel, integrated approach to the design and engineering of products that capitalizes on the use of modern IT infrastructure and software throughout all design stages [1]. Based on models that give an integrated description of the electrical, mechanical and hydraulic components of the system the system performance can be evaluated in early design stages and compared to the requirements of the application. This enables the engineer to improve the design at an early stage, thus drastically reducing the time to market.

R. Moreno-Díaz et al. (Eds.): EUROCAST 2011, Part II, LNCS 6928, pp. 73–80, 2012.
© Springer-Verlag Berlin Heidelberg 2012

The advantages of such an approach can be well demonstrated for linear motion machines which perform working steps like punching, nibbling, marking, coining, calibration pressing, bending, etc. The key performance requirements of these machine tools concern motion: positioning and repeat accuracy, stroke rates, forces and noise generation. To meet these demands a linear drive combining the force density of a hydraulic system with the dynamics of an electric drive has been developed. The drive has the potential to replace the currently used purely hydraulic systems.

As the requirements of the machine tools are not identical for different applications (or use cases) the "optimal" actuator design differs for different machines. Thus, before applying the new system it has to be evaluated thoroughly. Here a model-base approach helps to identify the improvement potential of the design for the application in the early stages of the product development.

Especially interesting for a model-based evaluation are requirements and features that concern unwanted side effects such as vibrations that have to be reduced while increasing the key performance requirements (stroke rate).

This papers shows how a model-based evaluation is performed for an electro-hydraulic actuator and demonstrates the strengths of the approach compared to conventional approaches where the problems connected to vibrations are solved by introducing rest periods, although methods have been investigated to reduce them actively as the example of an active work piece holder in a column milling machine tool shows [2].

In addition to that the new possibilities of parameterization connected with the model-based evaluation allow boosting performance in a variety of ways.

2 Mechatronic Design Processes

As new functionality in products is realized to a large extent through integration of mechanics, electronics and software the need for knowledge integration between these disciplines becomes central. The interactions between product developers from the different disciplines are hindered by insufficient understanding between the disciplines and by missing common platforms for modeling of complex systems. As many sub-systems are delivered by suppliers, there is a need for both a horizontal integration within organizations and a need for a vertical integration between the sub-system suppliers and the suppliers of the full systems ([3-6]).

Specific design tools are required to support the engineer in solving mechatronic design tasks. The functional interaction between domain-specific (discipline-specific) components is the key of any mechatronic solution. Hence the selection or alteration of a solution in one domain may affect the solutions in other domains. The prediction and evaluation of the system performance of a particular solution implies the investigation of the system components from other domains (disciplines) as well as their interactions. This makes it difficult to guarantee the specific performance of a new mechatronic system in advance.

Therefore it is necessary to define and describe the system in a model that is consistent, manageable and suitable for serving a specific purpose. From all possible models the simplest model which will suffice should be preferred. For the building and usage of a simple, efficient and valid model, there are no formal rules, hence previous experience play a major role. A key guideline is that different design phases need a different level of detail. Moreover it is appropriate to modularize the system and portray the operational characteristics as interfaced sub-systems. Finally it has to be kept in mind that different domains require a different view of the system which arises from different domain specific needs.

Many researchers have carefully analyzed the different steps during the design process [7-10]. The development/design process is usually structured into four sub-processes [7], namely the phases of Problem Definition, Conceptual Design, Preliminary Design and Detailed Design.

For mechatronic projects, experience in the interdisciplinary nature of the design process plays an important role. Conceptual Design is one of the most important phases during product development, as the main parameters, properties and costs of the solution - and consequently also the main elements of success of the new product - are fixed here.

The determination of the product's overall function and of its most important sub-functions (main functions) and their interaction, lead to a functional structure. During this design phase, principal solutions with a structure of realizable modules should be established. In this stage the cooperation between the several design engineers is of vital importance for the success of the design process.

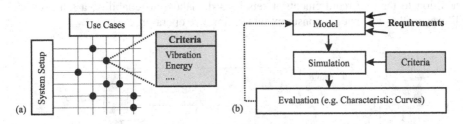

Fig. 1. Design process under the influence of different use cases

The creative and intuitive part is relatively high in the earliest design steps; the presented development method assists the design engineer during development of the models in a phase before the geometric design is carried out in detail. On the left side of Fig. 1 we can see the interaction between the defined use cases (e.g. punching, coinage) and the realized system setup. According to the list of requirements several criteria for evaluation are predicted (e.g. force, vibration, energy efficiency ...), which play an important role for the application. The right side of Fig. 1 presents a simple process model for simulation of the properties using different models.

The critical modules have to be specified and pre-designed preferably by the use of simulation tools. The influence of parameter changes in the sub-modules on other interacting modules and on the overall system have to be estimated and visualized.

It has to be kept in mind that the selected and used principal solution and its realization have the strongest impact on the product's success.

3 Application of Mechatronic System Design

3.1 A Hybrid Direct Drive for Linear Motion

A linear motion is common to many machine tools which perform working steps like punching, nibbling, marking, coining, calibration pressing, bending, etc. A single actuator that can be implemented in any of these machine tools is favorable, as it not only simplifies the setup but also boosts the development of multi-task machines. These multi-task machines reduce the overall needed machine space and handling costs significantly. Though the linear motion is a common feature of all mentioned tasks, the requirements of these machine tools are not identical. Therefore a single actuator for all applications is only reasonable if it combines the features and not the drawbacks.

The main requirements imposed on the given machine tools are connected with the motion: positioning and repeat accuracy, stroke rates, forces and noise generation. High stroke rates reduce the costs per unit and absolute web control allows the production of high-precision parts at low noise levels.

Fig. 2(a) shows the concept of mechatronic system design for this field of applications. It combines the advantages of servo-electric linear drive technology, such as dynamics and precision, with the power density and stability of hydraulics. The presented hybrid direct drive for linear motion (HDDL) has been developed by HOERBIGER [11] and is designed to set a new standard for punching drives. In addition to the key requirements it sets high demands on reliability, a long service life, as well as low energy consumption to minimize operating costs.

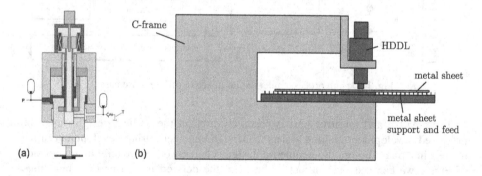

Fig. 2. (a) Hybrid direct drive for linear motion (HDDL) and (b) Punching machine with HDDL mounted to a C-shaped frame

Designed in the sense of mechatronic the high-performance linear drive, the power electronics unit, the hydraulic system and the control strategy show a high level of integration and interaction. Being directly coupled to the hydraulic amplifier the motor forms the basis for maximum dynamics and positioning accuracy. The internal mechanical feedback of the tappet position is carried out in directly linear fashion and is therefore absolutely without time-lag.

3.2 Requirements and the Interaction of Different Properties

Starting from the point that a solution for the required task already exists, new demands lead to a shift in the weighting of the values connected to the product. While most of the advanced requirements are defined to lead to faster, cheaper, smaller and more efficiency systems with a higher positioning accuracy and degree of reliability some requirements define a trade-off situation. Thus the use-case finally defines the weighting.

From the view point of Mechatronics the requirements to the actuator can be separated into two groups: one consisting of requirements that are directly connected with the linear motion and the second containing all not motion related requirements. These are requirements like a reduction of change over time, an increase in the durability of the tools, longer maintenance intervals or a tunable level of quality.

Moreover an existing solution that is implemented at the customers factory will only be changed to a new system if the new system outranges the existing significantly and is only connected with limited requirements to the customer, which are seen as costs. The level is here typically more demanding as in the case of a new acquisition. As main points the changeover time, the necessary training for the new control interface and the influence of the new actuator on other system components are seen.

Accordingly the requirements to the actuator as well as the costumer and the use case influence the requirements to the complete system, what often leads to trade-off situations. The requirements to the punching machine have the intention to provide for a proper punching result, namely the manufactured product. In this context not only the machine or its components, but also the processed material significantly affects the result. Thick and large sheet need high forces but limit the orthogonal feed and therefore the punching frequency. Welded frames, which are commonly used, bend up under the working load. Disadvantageous resonance frequencies can lead to deflections big enough to jeopardize absolute web control. Thus the actuator at the punching head as well as the working task and the material properties define the undesired effects of noise and vibrations that have to be considered additionally.

To achieve the desired properties of the punching machine and reduce the negative issues resulting from the process of machining several solutions are possible. However, their interaction has to be considered as well. This will be outlined in the next section for the example of unwanted vibrations.

3.3 Model-Based Simulation of Vibration Characteristics

3.3.1 Use Case (Application)

This paper refers to the HDDL mounted on a C-shaped frame for punching machines. Fig. 2(b) shows the principle setup of the system. This setup is used in a multi tool machine for punching, nibbling and marking of sheet metal. A combination with special tools allows tapping, laser cutting and bending, too. The punch cycle differs significantly between the tasks. Highest precision and frequency is needed in the case of marking. In this case strokes of about 1 mm with a frequency up to 3000 strokes/min are typical and precision is crucial as the marking tool only scratches the surface.

In the case of punching the focus is mainly on high punching forces. For a sheet of 1 mm thickness a frequency of up to 1300 strokes/min with a total stroke height of 3 mm is reached. The high stroke rates refer to the case of nibbling, which typically uses small tools and needs less punching force as larger punching tools.

3.3.2 Consideration of Vibrations

In our application the vibrations influence the main requirements significantly. To extinct the negative influences it would be best to solve the problem at its roots. However this is not possible in the case of punching. In this case the process forces will always be high enough to significantly bend the C-shaped frame open and leave it oscillate freely as soon as the sheet breaks through. However the first step will be to identify the eigenfrequencies and validate the results. This starts with the modeling on a CAD system and results in a model given in Fig. 3. Here the eigenmodes of the first two eigenfrequencies of the frame are shown.

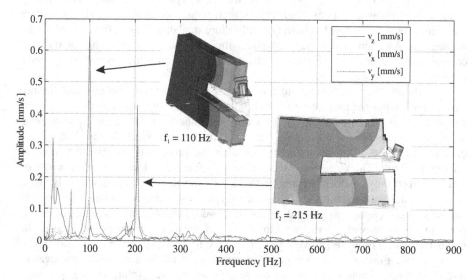

Fig. 3. Measurement of vibrations at the punching head

3.4 Validation of the Properties with Measurement Results

A validation is inevitable to verify the selected model. If not all quantities can be measured directly like it is here the case with the motor forces for example because of the integrated structure of the setup, a model consisting of measured and simulated data can be used. However care has to be taken that enough parameters are available in both measurement and simulation that can be used to validate the model.

The need for a validation lies in the fact that a model is always based on several assumptions. An example is in this case the mounting condition of the frame to the floor that directly affects the boundary condition of the model and has a strong influence on the resulting eigenvalues. Measurements have been taken with the punching head moving in air, so that the frame is not bending up due to process forces. The punching stroke is 1 mm and the measured results are given in Fig. 3.

Clearly visible are the peaks in the range of 110 Hz and 215 Hz that confirm the simulated results. The measured peaks in the range of 25-30 Hz under the lowest eigenfrequency cannot be found in the simulated analysis. Their origin is the rigid body movement of the whole frame which results from the excitation in combination with the elastic connection to the floor.

3.5 Concepts to Reduce Vibrations

The FE results show a high degree of deflection due to the way the HDDL is mounted on the frame using a relatively soft angle bracket. Thus the first measure taken is to remove the angle bracket and fix the actuator directly to the frame. However this does not eliminate but shift the eigenfrequencies further away from the desired region of operation. A further improvement will bring the use of an O-shaped frame in exchange to the currently used C-shaped frame. Returning the focus back to the C-shaped frame active and passive methods exist to damp the vibrations. The possibilities for passive damping are limited and mainly concern the connection of the frame to the floor.

Summing up the method of parameter variation and optimization is a sufficient tool to find an optimum solution for the concepts mentioned above. In these cases only mechanical models for FE-analyses or analytical calculations are necessary.

More interesting are concepts for active damping. The smartest concept is to directly use the HDDL actuator to suppress the vibrations. An estimation of the needed performance can easily be given looking at the measured data of the frame deflection evoked by a single punching stroke. The energy stored in the vibration can be estimated from measurements and model to 6.6 J. Though the energy of the vibrations is fairly small only the moving mass of the HDDL is available to damp the vibrations. Hence a single stroke of 1.5 mm at maximum speed inserted between the punching strokes can reduce the energy only by 0.9 J. Thus a completely integrated active damping is not feasible for the desired stroke rate with the current system. Either additional external damping devices or a redesign and multi-domain optimization of the system keeping the aspect of vibrations in mind is necessary. The latter would include a combined optimization in the mechanical, hydraulic and electro-magnetic domain.

4 Conclusion and Outlook

The system modeling process is well known for a single domain which represents the company's core competence. As the example of the vibrations of a punching machine shows a mechatronic and multi-domain approach is necessary to completely understand and optimize the system especially when different use cases have to be considered. Thus potential weaknesses of the system can be identified soon what allows to include these topics early in the product development cycle. This significantly reduces the time to market.

The key to success is the combination of a profound system model which is validated with a demonstrator before the actual prototype is built. Therefore the resulting model can consist of both: data from simulation and measurement ensuring enough overlap for a sound validation. In the case of suppliers when the developed system itself forms a sub-system the exchange between supplier and customer can lead to hints of how to optimize the complete machine.

Acknowledgments. Scientific advisory support was kindly given by the Austrian Center of Competence in Mechatronics (ACCM). This COMET/K2 program is aided by the funds of the state Austria and the provincial government of Upper Austria. The authors thank all involved partners for their support.

References

1. Hehenberger, P., Poltschak, F., Zeman, K., Amrhein, W.: Hierarchical design models in the mechatronic product development process of synchronous machines, Mechatronics (2010); ISSN 0957-4158
2. Brecher, C., Manoharan, D., Ladra, U., Köpken, H.G.: Chatter suppression with an active workpiece holder, Production Engineering. Springer, Heidelberg (2010)
3. Avgoustinov, N.: Modelling in Mechanical Engineering and Mechatronics. Springer Publishing Group, UK (2007)
4. Bishop, R.H.: Mechatronic Fundamentals and Modeling. The Mechatronics Handbook. CRC Press Inc., New York (2007)
5. De Silva, C.W.: Mechatronics – an integrated Approach. CRC Press Inc., Boca Raton (2005)
6. Eder, W.E., Hosnedl, S.: Transformation Systems – Revisited. In: Conference proceedings International Conference on Engineering Design, ICED 2007, Paris, France (2007)
7. Pahl, G., Beitz, W.: Engineering Design – A Systematic Approach. Springer Publishing Group, UK (1999)
8. Poelman, W.: Product Function Analysis for the Design of Goals. In: Conference Proceedings International Symposium Series on Tools and Methods of Competitive Engineering, TMCE 2008, Izmir (2008)
9. VDI 2206, Design Handbook 2206, Design Methodology for Mechatronic systems. VDI Publishing Group, Düsseldorf (2003)
10. VDI 2221, Design Handbook 2221, Systematic Approach to the Development and Design of technical Systems and Products. VDI Publishing Group, Germany (1993)
11. Ritzl, J., Kurz, M.: Hybridantrieb sorgt für Dynamik und Präzision bei Stanzmaschinen, MM Maschinenmarkt (2010)

Some Aspects of SysML Application in the Reverse Engineering of Mechatronic Systems

Martin Hochwallner[1], Matthias Hörl[1], Stefan Dierneder[1], and Rudolf Scheidl[2]

[1] Linz Center of Mechatronics GmbH, Altenbergerstrasse 69, 4040 Linz, Austria
`martin.hochwallner@lcm.at`
[2] J.K. University Linz, Institute of Machine Design and Hydraulic Drives,
Altenbergerstrasse 69, 4040 Linz, Austria

Abstract. The focus of this paper is the applicability of SysML [2] for modelling certain aspects of both, mechatronic systems and the corresponding engineering processes. SysML is derived from UML, which was developed for software engineering, with the intention to support the engineering of technical systems in general. Although the usefulness of UML is widely confirmed in the software context, the use of SysML in the more hardware oriented engineering domains and in Mechatronics is still an open issue.

Mechatronic relevant applications (like reported in [4]) have their focus on automation and software issues, mechanical and electrical hardware aspects, however, are rarely addressed. In an ongoing research project with industry the authors study the potentials of SysML to make the engineering of such systems more structured, better documented and, hence, more transparent.

In [6] SysML is nearly exclusively studied for the development of new systems. Its application for product improvement or design modification because of changing customer requirements is scarcely reported. In the following sections the authors will focus on these topics, first on mechanical sub-systems since this is seen most critical, and in future on overall mechatronic systems.

1 Introduction

In the authors' understanding, 'Reverse Engineering' describes the derivation of the underlying information structure and the design knowledge based on realised and existing systems. In other words, the recovery of information that already existed but has not been documented in a qualified way.

The examples, the authors focus on in this paper, are primarily dedicated to process oriented heavy machinery, especially systems from steel industry because of our industrial partner. A typical example shows Figure 1. The final realisations of this kind of mechatronic machinery are very customer specific. This applies also to other machinery, like paper industry or power plants, for which this work is applicable too.

R. Moreno-Díaz et al. (Eds.): EUROCAST 2011, Part II, LNCS 6928, pp. 81–88, 2012.

Fig. 1. L: Continuous Casting Machine, R: Steel Ladle (source: Siemens-VAI)

Characteristics of the studied systems:

- They are mechatronic systems with many technical disciplines involved in development and implementation.
- They have a high degree of automation.
- Design and realisation have a long lifespan – up to some decades.
- They are very customer specific. The design basis for all the customer-specific variants represents more or less a whole product family.
- The systems' aspect is crucial. The systems have a strong functional coupling between all the sub-systems. This also requires a strong coupling of the design and engineering processes.

Usefulness of SysML is seen most critical for mechanical sub-systems. The authors will discuss SysML application for a steel ladle (see Figure 1). A steel ladle is a pot used to transport liquid steel from steel production to the casting machine.

Future work is to apply SysML to overall mechatronic systems.

2   Reverse Engineering

For the kind of products and systems, mentioned in Section 1, order processing and ongoing product improvement are dominating. The development of new products is also important but happens less often and consumes only a smaller share of the overall work. For business success it is crucial that all the design tasks will be performed in an effective, efficient, and reliable way.

A significant improvement of this everyday product design work has been achieved by parametric CAD models, see [1], which enable a largely automatic design adaptation to specific customer's requirements. But such parametric models only reflect small part of all the knowledge about a product and its development. Certain structural information about the product should be given by SysML diagrams. This refers to models documenting the product, like CAD models, and models used for the design evaluation, like simulation models for dynamic performance or for strength analysis, ...). Existing information sources of the mechanical engineering domain are the main engineering documents like CAD drawings and CAD models. Information is lost, if it is not documented, hard to find or difficult to comprehend. Quite often, a lot of knowledge of a system or product is scattered over many minds. This knowledge cannot be accessed arbitrarily and gets largely lost over time. Typical examples of lost information are concepts, requirements, functional and logical structure and the systems' context.

Contrary to the technical drawings and other standardized or traditional documents the purpose of SysML diagrams and models has to be defined. In the focussed application area, namely process oriented heavy machinery, there are many engineering tasks where SysML model can be helpful.

The assessment of any product design leads to questions like "What is this good for?" or "Do we really need this?". Such questions are part of every product design process. As one can see in the Figures 2a and 3 a lot of global information can be made easier comprehensible by SysML diagrams than with text. This is not restricted to the systems environment and systems context. With SysML also the systems behaviour, the relations between the requirements on a product and the realizing components resp. their design parameters as well as the management of variants and configurations can be made visible. There are many more aspects of systems and system design which up to now are not documented properly, for which SysML models could be usefully applied.

3   SysML Models of the Physical Structure

3.1   Objective of Physical Structure Models

The physical structure of steel production systems, especially of its mechanical sub-systems is sufficiently documented. 3D CAD and PLM systems are routinely used. In addition to the geometric information, they also cover the organisation of components in assemblies and the geometric and some mechanical relations between components.

There are three main benefits from modelling certain aspects by SysML:

Traceability: One goal of SysML models is the modelling of relationships between various aspects; for example the relationship between physical components, requirements and stakeholders of these requirements. For that purpose, the model of physical structure is the SysML model's connection to the CAD model. For each component in the CAD model there is a corresponding block in the model of physical structure which can serve as entry point for tracing.

Interfaces: For the understanding of the system the system's interfaces (information, electrical, hydraulic, mechanical, . . .) are important and, thus, shall be modelled explicitly.

One way to model mechanical interaction points in SysML are so-called nonatomic flowPorts. They may have a regular or a conjugated form. This corresponds to usual mechanical interfaces which have a left and a right side. Of

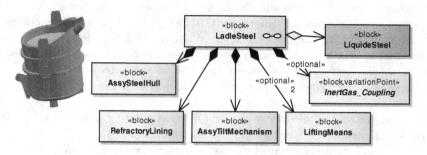

(a) Main Assembly – Optional Components

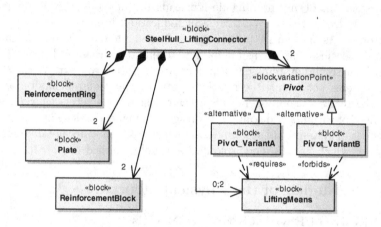

(b) Sub-Sub-Assembly – Alternatives

Fig. 2. Model of Physical Structure and Variants: Excerpt

course, for mechanical interfaces flowSpecification does not specify mass or energy flow but refers to geometric constraints.

Variant: In steel production systems several variants of a basic design are used. Variants, for example, can be additional components for optional functionality (see Figure 2a) or alternative designs (see Figure 2b). Some require certain other components to be altered, or there might exist incompatibility with certain components (forbids); see also [4]. These circumstances can be handled by SysML models as shown in Figure 2b. Additionally to structural variants (component / functionality is included or not) there are variants of design parameters. This type of design variation is best handled by parameterisation of CAD models. In the SysML tool used for this study (Enterprise Architect from SparxSystems), there is no obvious way to handle parameter variants directly. But add-ons to SysML tools are available which promise to handle parameter variants properly. Such tools have not been tested by the authors so far.

3.2   Reverse Engineering of the Physical Structure

To derive the SysML model of the existing physical structure the main engineering documents can be used as information source. The main sources in the mechanical domain are 3D CAD models, 2D drawings, parameter models (often in Excel), or PLM systems. In the example Ladle (see Figure 1) the 3D CAD model and its parameterisation did already exist and were available for the reverse engineering work.

The reverse engineering is partially a one-to-one transformation from the CAD model to the SysML model, but some information has to be processed, i.e. (analysed, organised, and simplified) manually. In future, tool support could automate the building of SysML models and could keep SysML and CAD models synchronised.

3.3   Results for the Ladle

For the example Ladle the reverse engineering of the model of the physical structure is straightforward. An excerpt of the derived diagrams is shown in Figure 2. This SysML model can handle design variants and can serve as interface between CAD models and other SysML models.

4   Modelling of the Context

The context definition based on [3,5] states:

> The context of the system is that part of the systems' environment that is relevant for understanding and defining the system.

In steel production machines the system of concern is usually a sub-system of a much bigger superior system; for example, the Ladle is part of the steel plant. The system of concern is not autonomous and depends strongly on its superior system.

4.1   Purposes of Context Modelling

System Partitioning: The superior system is partitioned into sub-systems. These are units with well defined functions, which are designed by own teams, and which are also sold as own units. The context of the system specifies what is part and what is definitely not part of the system.

Understanding: To understand what the system is doing and how it is working the superior system must be understood to some extent. The interfaces between the system of concern and its neighbour systems define their interaction.

System Integration: As stated before, adapting the design to the customer's needs and environment is one of the main parts of the ongoing product design work. Thus, a representation of the connections to other systems and their interfaces is an important knowledge. The interfaces have to be matched to those of the customer in the design process; see Figure 3.

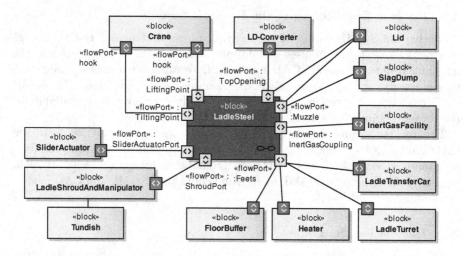

Fig. 3. Physical Context of the Ladle

4.2 Reverse Engineering of the Context

In contrast to the model of the physical structure usually less documentation is available on the system's context. In fact, no explicit documentation of the context of the Ladle was available. Some information was found in the documentation of the superior systems (LD converter, continuous casting machine), yet in a scattered way. The main knowledge sources were interviews and the extrapolations from the model of physical structure and from the CAD model, since interfaces in the physical structure model enforce at least one in the context model.

Actor or Block: In the SYSMOD approach [6] Actor blocks are used to represent systems in context diagrams. It the rental car unlock system example of SYSMOD, the context refers mainly to services and communication. The Ladle, however, is a system with a tight coupling to its superior systems. This requires understanding the superior system including its relevant behaviour. Therefore, a different approach was chosen.

The perspective is swapped by modelling the superior system. Abstraction, level of detail, and completeness are chosen according to the purpose of the context model. To clearly separate context and system, the context is placed in a separate package and colours are used to distinguish them in the diagrams; see Figure 3. Additionally, stereotypes can be applied. This approach now leads to an equal structure, as it has been set up by the original design in the past by the product designers on the superior system's level. With this 'swapped' view more than one sub-system's context can be represented in one diagram. Stereotypes with «context» would not work, but coloured diagrams and use of packages do.

The SysML models derived from a reverse engineering process should be the same as those constructed in a direct design process.

System Partitioning: For the Ladle the system's boundary is quite clear. For other, more complex systems, for instance a continuous casting machine as depicted in Figure 1, however, systems boundaries' definitions are nontrivial. In such cases the above approach - modelling the superior system - is advantageous, too. The superior system is modelled and then partitioned in sub-systems at all relevant aspects: physical, logical and behaviour.

Interfaces: Interfaces are the important elements of the context model. Figure 3 depicts how interfaces of the physical context can be modelled. A discussion about modelling of mechanical interfaces with FlowPorts is given in Section 3.1.

4.3   Results for the Ladle

Figure 3 depicts the model of the physical context of the Ladle. All physical interfaces of the Ladle and all systems which can be connected to them are shown. There are additional diagrams, not included in this paper, which depict the Ladle context in certain situations, like while casting, to supply more specialised views. These diagrams help in adapting the Ladle's design to a customer's environment by highlighting the interaction points.

5   Conclusion

SysML can be used to model several mechatronic system's aspects, also of mechanical sub-systems. Such models provide a substantial gain in documenting and communicating certain aspects. Since SysML models are stored electronically, if software tools are used, there is an option to automate some engineering work.

SysML can help in reverse engineering processes to effectively document the results. The SysML models derived form such processes can serve as templates for the reverse engineering of other similar systems, which would speed up such processes significantly.

The experience out of this study was that the lion share of reverse engineering work is to collect all required data and knowledge, which is to a great extent independent of the form of modelling or documenting. The mentally most challenging part was to find out which aspects should be modelled, how should these models be constructed, and which SysML elements are most appropriate for it, to get optimal benefit from the work and patterns which are best suited for a reverse engineering of other systems. This takes definitely more time than learning SysML language and the handling of software tools. A future reverse engineering of similar systems will tremendously benefit from such first work. Existing SysML models can serve as draft and reusing certain patterns will speed up the work significantly.

The usefulness of SysML models depends heavily on the used software tool. Usability, standard compliance, interfaces to other tools and functionality like tracing, searching and so on are important.

Catalogues with modelling patterns are necessary for an efficient work. SysML is so general that its application is nontrivial in a certain situation. Powerful patterns like shown in this work, for instance, how to model variants or mechanical interfaces, are required.

In this work modelling patterns have been developed for a quite simple mechanical system. It is still an open issue how the same could be done successfully for bigger systems and in a mechatronic context.

SysML is useful to represent the engineering process and the system's model itself. Especially if the model's model and the system's model are located in the same repository the model's model can help the system's model user to better navigate.

Acknowledgement. The authors gratefully acknowledge the sponsoring of this work by the 'Austrian Center of Competence in Mechatronics' in the framework of the COMET program of the Austrian government. This program is funded by the Austrian government, the province Upper Austria and the scientific partners of the Center in particular the Johannes Kepler University Linz.

References

1. Dierneder, S., Scheidl, R.: Parametric Design, criteria for its use, and the role of Complexity and Functional Decomposition for the optimal choice of the Design Parameters. In: Parkin, R.M., Al-Habaibeh, A., Jackson, M.R. (eds.) ICOM 2003 International Conference on Mechatronics. Professional Engineering Publishing, Loughborough (2003)
2. Friedenthal, S., Moore, A., Steiner, R.: A Practical Guide to SysML: The Systems Modeling Language. Morgan Kaufmann, OMG (2009)
3. International Requirements Engineering Board e.V.: Syllabus – CPRE Foundation Level (September 2010), http://www.certified-re.de/
4. Maga, C., Jazdi, N.: An approach for modeling variants of industrial automation systems. In: IEEE International Conference on Automation, Quality and Testing, Robotics, AQTR (2010)
5. Rupp, C., SOPHISTen: Requirements-Engineering und -Management, 5th edn. Hanser (2009)
6. Weilkiens, T.: Systems Engineering with SysML/UML: Modeling, Analysis, Design, p. 307. Morgan Kaufmann, OMG (2008), http://www.system-modeling.com/

Integration of SysML and Simulation Models for Mechatronic Systems

Matthias Hörl[1,2], Martin Hochwallner[2], Stefan Dierneder[2], and Rudolf Scheidl[3]

[1] TRUMPF Maschinen Austria GmbH & Co KG, Industriepark 24, A-4061 Pasching
[2] Linz Center of Mechatronics GmbH, Altenbergerstrasse 69, A-4040 Linz
[3] J.K. University Linz, Institute of Machine Design and Hydraulic Drives,
Altenbergerstrasse 69, A-4040 Linz
matthias.hoerl@at.trumpf.com

Abstract. Each engineering domain, such as mechanical, electrical, hydraulic and software engineering has developed specialized tools to support its engineering work. Also for the management of the design process a lot of customized tools are used. Most of them have independent programming interfaces making the coupling error prone and resource intensive. In order to better manage the overall system's aspects - what is essential for a well-founded mechatronic approach - appropriate models and corresponding tools for system description and simulation are necessary.

All systematic development processes, i.e. conceptual design, detail design and common product refinement process, have to focus on the functional requirements and constraints of the overall system under consideration. Describing and maintaining this structure and all the associated data and documenting its relations with the virtual or real experiments is very helpful for a systematic and reliable development process. This paper analyses the use of SysML as a system description language as well as a modeling and simulation language for the aspects of "System Requirements", "System Behavior", and "System Structure" and their interdependence.

1 Introduction

Mechatronic system development involves multiple disciplines and in most cases people from different departments of one or several companies. Cooperations between departments, vendors and sub-contractors require at least to share information and sometimes also development activities. Product development is never straightforward but requires multiple design cycles. The global approach in mechatronic system development according to the V-model – as sketched in Fig.1a – indicates an essential aspect of multi-disciplinary systems. The complete system view must be managed in at least two phases, the early conceptual design – it corresponds to the left part of the V-model – and in the integration phase. Of course, the V-model is just a rough picture of real design processes. System integration is done multiply and partly also in the domain specific design phases, since the specifications of the system design for the domain specific designs cannot always be met.

R. Moreno-Díaz et al. (Eds.): EUROCAST 2011, Part II, LNCS 6928, pp. 89–96, 2012.
© Springer-Verlag Berlin Heidelberg 2012

As indicated clearly in the V-model, assurance of properties is a central activity. Naturally, it happens not only in the system integration phase but also in domain specific design. Assurance of properties corresponds also to the analysis step in each design cycle according to Fig.1b. Assurance of properties can be done in various ways. Physical prototypes are the most direct and definitely most reliable, but in the majority of cases also the most expensive and most time consuming ones. In view of the iterative character of product design which starts from the specification of the requirements on the product and proceeds over to conceptual design to more and more detailing in many design cycles, adequate mathematical modeling and simulation in property assurance are extremely helpful. It goes without saying that computer assistance of these activities can often provide a real breakthrough in terms of model complexity, speed, labor cost, quality of results and their documentation.

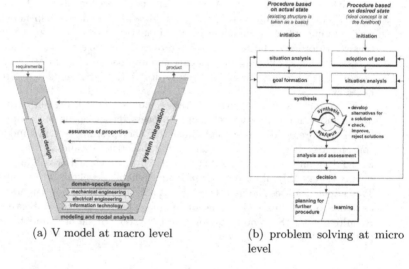

(a) V model at macro level   (b) problem solving at micro level

Fig. 1. Structure of mechatronic product development according to VDI2221 [10]

The V-model indicates a crucial aspect of mechatronic system design, which is the preservation of the holistic system view in all phases. The system aspects in product design not only comprise the chosen solution and its structure, but also the requirements on the system and the management of the design process. A different view but also emphasizing the unity of Requirements, Solution/Structure, and Management is also done by [5] by choosing the picture of three brains, created respectively filled by using the less restrictive agile methods.

Modern mechatronic product development uses computer based modeling and simulation tools quite frequently. This comprises models in the different engineering domains (e.g. Finite Element Methods for stress analysis, CFD tools for fluid flow, electric circuit analysis software) as well as multi-disciplinary system models (multi-disciplinary dynamic simulation methods, like Modelica) for assurance of properties and product definition by CAD, PLM, VHDL software, to name just a few. Although advanced tools for Requirements Engineering do exist, there is lack of standardized methods. This is mainly visible through the lack of adequate tools for representing and managing product structure, for design management, and for handling the interrelationship between requirements, product structure the models for assurance of properties. Furthermore, there is little awareness of the importance of documenting early phases of design, the models used there, and to establish relationships between these models and the models employed in later phases of design (see for instance [8]). The present paper addresses the use of SysML as a modeling method for the product structure/ requirements and for the requirements/ model relationships. SysML and the inner structure of these relationships will be briefly introduced in the next section. In Sect. 3 all this will be exemplified by a press-brake example.

2 Use of SysML in Mechatronic System Modeling

SysML is a system modeling language for systems engineering. It was derived from UML – which is a more software centered modeling language – to better handle general systems for modeling a wide range of systems engineering problems. SysML particularly addresses requirements, structure, behavior, allocations, and constraints on system properties [6]. SysML reuses a subset and extends the constructs of UML2 by adding new modeling elements and actually two new diagram types.

2.1 SysML and Mechatronic Design Methods

All the information is stored in a model repository, which is the data basis for all the diagrams. The structure view in SysML – called solution/structure in the previous Sect. – represents the global hierarchy of either the function- or of the building-structure, i.e. how the whole system is decomposed in sub-systems in various hierarchical levels, from application level down to the components level. Other diagrams define the context of the system, behavior diagrams describe the events and activities which the system has to execute. The requirements view represents the goals of and requirements on the system and their interconnections. The requirements can be linked to both, the structure and the other parts, to provide traceability between the requirements and the system design.

SysML allows structuring the components of the system model in a modularized and a hierarchical way (according to [11]). This allows the designer to represent structural aspects of the two main characteristics of mechatronic systems, namely functional interaction and spatial integration, on a systems level. Of course, only the topological aspects of spatial integration can be represented by SysML, not the real installation space issues. An important means to handle complexity of larger mechatronic systems is their decomposition into so called mechatronic modules [3] The most important aspect of modularization on a system level is their interrelations and their interfacing. These have to be clearly and unambiguously specified. SysML is able to represent these aspects within its structural diagrams. This is particularly helpful to reduce communication errors between all the different disciplines, departments, or even companies, which are involved in the development of a mechatronic system.

2.2 Describing Requirements/Models/Product Dependence in SysML

An exemplary dependence structure between requirements, models, and the product is shown in Fig. 3. As outlined in Sect. 1, quite different models are used at different design levels. Also the requirements structure develops with the design process. The overall system requirements are translated into sub-system or sub-function requirements (see e.g. [2]). For the analysis of a synthesized solution at a certain instance of the development process different methods - or test setups or prototypes - can be used. They all are denoted 'Models', further on. If several such models are available they form a library of models for a certain testcase. Between requirements and the evaluation of their fulfillment a test scenario must be defined. The definitive test of a product is its use by the customer. The specified requirements should map the criteria for customer satisfaction to the design process. The evaluation by models will only be useful if the underlying test scenario – called 'TestCase' in Fig. 2 – anticipate the later real use reasonably, which means with an acceptable effort and in a statistical sense, since the actual use of the product by a specific user can only be predicted with a certain probability. Of course, for many products standards concerning certain requirements and the respective testcases (e.g., fuel consumption of a passenger car) have been established or are regulated by contracts. A 'TestCase' consists of a certain 'TestSetUp' and a 'LoadCase' (see Fig. 2). In case of experimental tests the meaning of 'TestSetUp' is obvious. The term 'LoadCase' is lend from the mechanical domain and means one out of possibly several scenarios of running a test by a 'TestSetUp'. For instance, in a system with controlled mechanical motion a 'LoadCase' could be to a step response with definite step height and system parameters. One 'TestSetUp' could be a specific simulation model with the appropriate properties, like the right initial or boundary conditions in case of initial or boundary values problems.

The relation to 'SystemModel' is required to match the modeling parameters with the corresponding product parameters and its structure, respectively. This makes sure that the analysis step and the synthesis step according to Fig.1b are properly linked with respect to the system properties. SysML is a language that offers standardized diagrams as a graphical user interface and a standardized data structure for an electronic representation of the established models. Additional functionality is offered by several SysML software tools, but there is no standard for these additional functions, hence, they are very tool specific. SysML is not intended to set-up simulation models, although there is an initiative to develop such a tool with SysML4Modelica [7] . In view of the manifold of models and simulations required in mechatronic system design, a direct integration of the many modeling and simulation worlds in one software environment seems

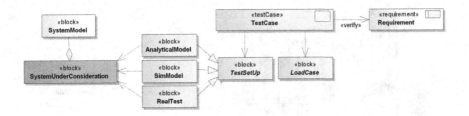

Fig. 2. Dependence between requirements and the system model described by a SysML diagram; this has natural links to system/structure models as well

much too complex. What, however, could be realized with a reasonable effort, is a tool to provide data exchange between various parts of a SysML model and some data linking and execution sequencing of external simulation models.

3   Case Study of a Press-Brake

3.1   System Model of a Press-Brake

As example the modeling of a press-brake (Fig. 3a) is studied. A simplified SysML model of its building structure is given by a block definition diagram shown in Fig. 3b, listing the main parts of a press-brake. This SysML model can be designed much freer than a CAD model of the press-brake, which also provides the building structure. The SysML model has less information than the CAD model and focuses on one aspect: which are the main parts of the press-brake. The basic SysML idea is to structure the view on a system into several diagrams. One SysML block may be refined by another elaborate diagram. SysML tools typically support this concept by representing different diagrams in different windows, which, for instance, pop-up on command.

3.2   Build and Document Testcases

For a press-brake design the precision of the bending angle at the workpiece is a crucial performance aspect. A typical quality level for the bending angle precision of modern machines is a deviation of 0.3°. In Fig.4 this requirement is given by the requirement block 'BendingAngleDeviation'. This block is linked to the corresponding testcase block. Two models of quite different complexity are used for analyzing this testcase: (i) an 'Analytical_Model' based on Castigliano's theory of elastic beam deformation [12] and (ii) a Finite Element model (denoted 'FEM_Model' in Fig. 4). Model (i) is more appropriate for earlier phases of design where rough estimates are appropriate, since very accurate models would miss information that is not available before detail design is accomplished. Such models often result in a compact formula which can be converted, to solve the

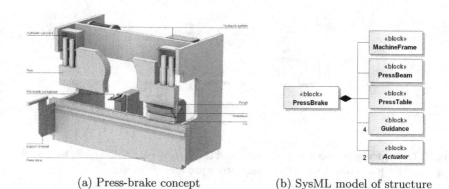

(a) Press-brake concept   (b) SysML model of structure

Fig. 3. Physical view at a Press-brake

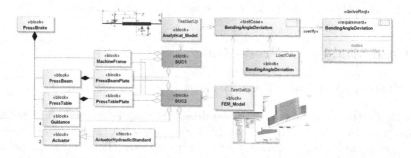

Fig. 4. Models for the analysis of the requirement 'BendingAngleDeviation'

so called inverse problem – that is the determination of the design parameters from the given requirements – immediately.

This SysML diagram also reflects clearly which product information is required for which model. The 'Analytical_Model' does not access the 'Guidance' and 'Actuator' blocks. Even this fact provides useful information, namely that these two parts of the press-bake will not have significant influence on the fulfillment of the bending angle requirement. Otherwise, the 'Analytical_Model' should consider their influence. Little coupling of the system parameters /requirements relation is essential to keep complexity low (see [9]). Thus, such SysML testcase models give a good impression of such complexity and allow also the automatic computation of complexity measures, as for instance proposed in [4].

Optimization and Automatic Processing

Another important aspect of advanced product design is the early recognition, documentation and visualization of possible optimization loops or design trade-offs. Such trade-offs are typical for any product development process and are the core aspect of Altshuller's TRIZ method [1]. This is strongly supported by a system modeling with SysML or comparable means. With the bending angle test-case model the relation between bending angle precision and cost requirements and the press-brake structure is revealed (see Fig. 5). Such simple diagrams can make such trade-offs structures evident to many people involved in the design and simulation of mechatronic systems. It is helpful to enhance this view on design modification impacts by modeling also the stakeholder of requirements and testcases. That may lead to standardize certain design cycles, which is an effective means to save cost and risk of design changes in the later phases of a product life cycle. Since in those phases the system architecture is not changed, the awareness of the design engineers of all possible implications of small changes is not much expressed.

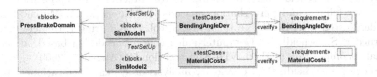

Fig. 5. Requirements coupling example of a press-brake

4   Conclusion

The system modeling language SysML is a means to model various aspects of mechatronic systems and their design. In this paper the aspect of assurance of properties is studied. To do this consistently the interrelations of requirements, simulation models, testcases, and product models needs to be modeled properly. SysML is an effective means for this. It has sufficient modeling capacity to repre-sent various testcases and various models and which information of the product is required in each case. Proper maintenance of testcases and the interrelations with the models is an important means for failure avoidance, since the testcases might change with time. Also the design trade-offs, which are so typical for any product development and are characteristic for a specific design solution, can be represented compactly. This is seen an excellent opportunity to better com-municate these essential properties to the many parties that are involved in the ongoing design changes in the later phases of design. That most likely would help to avoid failures which arise due to a misunderstanding of the possibly far reaching impacts of even small design modifications.

In the future work automated links between SysML models and the simulation models shall be established to create in this way a common SysML platform. It is also planned to use that platform to evaluate the traceability between require-ments and the product structure and to compute complexity measures of the requirements / system parameter relations.

Future research will also address the question in which way the various models and certain evaluations of them can be condensed to support a better decision finding in the development process by the main stakeholders.

Acknowledgment. The authors gratefully acknowledge the sponsoring of this work by 'TRUMPF Machines Austria GmbH' and the 'Austrian Center of Competence in Mechatronics' in the framework of the COMET program of the Austrian government. This program is funded by the Austrian government, the province Upper Austria and the scientific partners of the center in particular the Johannes Kepler University Linz.

References

1. Altshuller, G.S.: Creativity as an Exact Science. Gordon and Breach, New York (1984)
2. Dierneder, S., Scheidl, R.: Conceputal design, functional decomposition, mathematic modelling, and perturbation analysis. In: Kopacek, P., Moreno-Díaz, R., Pichler, F. (eds.) EUROCAST 1999. LNCS, vol. 1798, Springer, Heidelberg (2000)
3. Dierneder, S., Scheidl, R.: Computer-aided conceptual design based on the functional decomposition method. VDI-Konstruktion 52 (August 7, 2000)
4. Dierneder, S., Scheidl, R.: Complexity analysis of systems from a functional and technical viewpoint. In: Moreno-Díaz Jr., R., Buchberger, B., Freire, J.-L. (eds.) EUROCAST 2001. LNCS, vol. 2178, pp. 223–232. Springer, Heidelberg (2001)
5. Hruschka, P., Rupp, C.: Agile Softwareentwicklung für Embedded Real-Time Systems mit der UML. Hanser (2002), www.b-agile.de
6. OMG: Systems modeling language (omg sysml) ver. 1.2 (2010), http://www.omg.org/spec/SysML/1.2/
7. Paredis, C.J., Bernard, Y., Burkhart, R.M., de Koning, H.P., Friedenthal, S., Fritzson, P., Rouquette, N.F., Schamai, W.: An overview of the sysml modelica transformation specification. In: INCOSE (2010)
8. Scheidl, R., Winkler, B.: Model relations between conceptual and detail design. Mechatronics - Special Issue on Theories and Methodologies for Mechatronics Design 20 (2010)
9. Suh, N.P.: Axiomatic Design: Advances and Applications. The Oxford Series on Advanced Manufacturing. Oxford University Press, Oxford (1990)
10. VDI: Systematic approach to the development and design of technical systems and products. Tech. rep., VDI (1993)
11. VDI: Design methodology for mechatronic systems (VDI 2206). Tech. rep., VDI (2004)
12. Ziegler, F.: Mechanics of Solids and Fluids. Springer, Wien-New York (1995)

Modelling and Optimisation of Mechatronic Systems Using the Autogenetic Design Theory

Konstantin Kittel[1], Peter Hehenberger[2], Sándor Vajna[1], and Klaus Zeman[2]

[1] Otto-von-Guericke-University Magdeburg, 39106 Magdeburg, Germany
[2] Johannes Kepler University Linz, A-4040 Linz, Austria

Abstract. The interdisciplinary description and definition of product information from the various disciplines of mechatronics is a necessary requirement for mechatronic design models. Optimisation tools can use such design models in order to explore the potential of mechatronic systems. Such optimisations need to handle numerous parameters as well as goal criteria from different disciplines. This paper presents the first step in setting up such complex optimisation systems. The optimisation of infrared heating zones of industrial annealing simulators covers the most relevant physical aspects, e.g., geometry or heat radiation and allows to optimise the heating zone according to the main requirements such as maximum temperature or homogeneity of temperature.

Keywords: Mechatronics, Product Development, Autogenetic Design Theory, Multi Domain, Optimisation.

1 Introduction

Mechatronic design of machines, devices, and plants can help to create improved and enhanced products, processes, and systems. On the other hand, the complexity of these systems usually is increased due to the intended beneficial interaction between components and technologies from different mechatronic disciplines [1] [2]. Therefore new concepts are requested in order to assist mechatronic design engineers in handling the increased complexity of such systems and in reacting faster to market demands.

For the exploitation of the potentials of mechatronics, fully consistent design models for the product development process and for the description of complex systems are essential. The interdisciplinary description and definition of product information from the various disciplines of mechatronics is a necessary requirement for mechatronic design models. In view of product lifecycle management, it is necessary to consider all information relevant for the product from all phases of the product life cycle in a universal structure. With the ever-increasing need for integration and interaction of a growing variety of functions in modern mechatronics, the demand for a combined consideration of all product features arose. The individual product life phases and the involved mechatronic disciplines require investigations concerning different aspects of the product (object) under

R. Moreno-Díaz et al. (Eds.): EUROCAST 2011, Part II, LNCS 6928, pp. 97–104, 2012.

consideration. Hence, a general description of product properties and characteristics for different views, in different combinations and grades of detailing should be available. For example, this can be certain mechatronic characteristics (deflection, dynamics, transfer function, reference action of a control loop, etc.) during different development activities (design, modelling, analysis, testing, evaluation, etc.), the power demand, the complexity of manufacturing and assembling, or of operation and handling items. In addition, in view of product lifecycle management, it is necessary to consider product-relevant information from all phases of the product life cycle in a universal structure. In this context, different hierarchical models could be useful. On the one hand, these models can be elaborated in more detail during the product development process, which results in an improved significance. On the other hand, it is possible to define rough and simple dimensioning models for the concept phase by an appropriate reduction of more complex models [3] [4].

1.1 Autogenetic Design Theory (ADT)

The Autogenetic Design Theory (ADT) applies analogies between biological evolution and product development [5] by transferring the methods of biological evolution (and their advantageous characteristics) to the field of product development. Such characteristics are for example the ability to react appropriately to changing environments (requirements and boundary conditions), so that new individuals are in general better adapted to the actual environment as their ancestors. The ADT is not another variety of Bionics (where results of an evolution, e.g., the structure of trees, are transferred to technical artefacts). Rather, the ADT transfers procedures from biological evolution to accomplish both a description and broad support of product development with its processes, requirements, boundary conditions, and objects (including their properties).

The main thesis of the ADT is that procedures, methods, and processes of developing and adapting products can be described and designed as analogies to the procedures, methods, and processes of biological evolution to create or to adapt individuals. Main characteristics of biological evolution (with the underlying principle of trial and error) are continuous development and permanent adaptation of individuals to dynamically changing targets, which in general have to be accomplished in each case at the lowest level of energy content and with the minimal use of resources, i.e. the evolution process runs optimised in terms of energy consumption and resource employment. The targets can change over time because of (unpredictable) changing requirements, resources, conditions, boundaries, and constraints, and they can contradict each other at any time.

The result of a biological evolution is always a set of unique solutions having the same value but not being of similar type. Consequentially, the result of the ADT is for the very most part a set of equivalent, but not similar unique solutions that fulfil the actual state of requirements and conditions best.

At the present state, three major components of the ADT have been researched. First, a process model describing how the ADT works and what the steps are, which the product developer has to perform. Secondly, the solution space model, which shows how the space, in which product development takes place, is structured. The third component is the underlying product model, which holds the description of how product information is structured and used.

Although the research on the ADT is ongoing, a subset of its methods has been implemented in an optimisation tool called NOA (Natural Optimisation Algorithm). At present, basic procedures and first approaches can be applied already. With NOA, existing solutions can be improved by applying methods of natural evolution while considering certain boundary conditions. NOA applies a genetic algorithm with a universal design that makes it suitable to solve a huge range of optimisation problems on different kinds of computer hardware. The basic procedure of NOA can be seen in Figure 1.

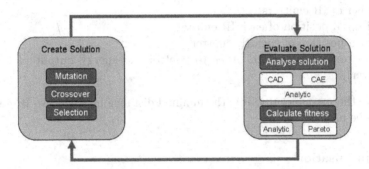

Fig. 1. General procedure of NOA

At the end of the optimisation, the designer has to interpret the results. NOA normally finds a set of equivalent solutions, from which the designer can choose his preferred solution.

2 Application

The main focus on using this approach is the optimisation of mechatronic systems (e.g. power train, heating zones of annealing simulators). In this contribution the optimisation of a heating zone will be shown.

The development of heating zones for industrial annealing simulators merges solutions from different engineering disciplines, like mechanical engineering, electrical engineering, control engineering as well as thermodynamics (see [6]). The goal of this work is to optimise the infrared heating zones (IR zone) of industrial annealing simulators with the help of computer-based models. These models cover the most relevant physical aspects, e.g., geometry or heat radiation, and enable engineers to customise the heating zone according to the main requirements such as maximum temperature or homogeneity of temperature.

In order to use the analytical model it is assumed that the resulting radiation distribution can be modelled as a superposition of the effects of all single IR emitters.

The Autogenetic Design Theory is applied to find the best design for the heating zone.

Problem Definition

The first step before the optimisation itself is to determine the key design parameters of the technical system. Therefore, an analysis on different already existing heating zones was performed, to figure out the differences and similarities of the different heating zones. The results of the analysis were also used, to define the solution space for the optimisation, which is defined by the following parameters:

- Number of IR emitters
- Horizontal position of each IR emitter
- Vertical position of each IR emitter
- Phase control factor (in order to control the energy output of each IR emitter)

To ensure the manufacturability, the minimal distance between two IR emitters needs to be at least 16mm.

2.1 Optimisation

One goal of the optimisation is to reach a high homogeneity of the heat distribution within the specimen to ensure the equal heating-up. This is achieved by minimising the deviation of the energy input along the specimen. The second optimisation goal is to reach a certain total energy input into the specimen. The reference value thereof is given by the heating zone of an existing annealing simulator.

Table 1. Weighting factors

	Energy Input Deviation	Deviation From Total Target Energy Input
Run 1	1	1
Run 2	2	1
Run 3	4	1
Run 4	1	2
Run 5	4	1

Within this project different optimisation runs with different set ups were tested. Five different combinations of weighting factors were used to analyse the behaviour of the system and to analyse the influence of the weighting factors (see table 1). The information gathered in this step is used to find the best combination of weighting factors for the actual problem.

2.2 Results

The results of the optimisation show that the distribution of the solutions within the solution space is highly dependent on the weighting factors for the optimisation goals. Depending on the weighting factors, the algorithm focused the search on different areas of the solution space. This results in different optimal solutions for each of the five runs.

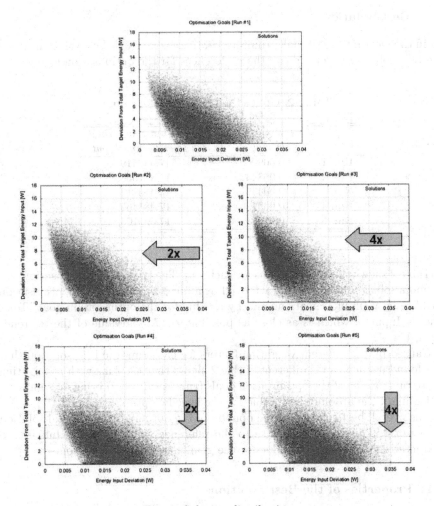

Fig. 2. Solution distribution

Figure 2 gives an impression on how the weighting factors influence the solution distribution (the weighting factor for each run is represented as green arrow).

The picture in the first row (see figure 2) shows the solution distribution when there is no weighting factor used. As expected, the genetic algorithm doesn't show a preference for one of the goals. Row two shows how increasing the weighting factor for the goal Energy Input Deviation leads to a concentration of solutions in the area of lower values for the goal Energy Input Deviation. Row three shows the same effect but for the goal Deviation Form Total Target Energy Input. The solutions concentrate in the area of lower values as soon as the weighting factor is increased.

2.3   Best Solutions

As in the most multi-criteria optimisations, there is no single best solution. What the best solution is depends on the preferences for the optimisation goals.

Table 2. Optimal solutions from each run

	Energy Input Deviation	Deviation From Total Target Energy Input
Run 1	0.009060	17.438419
Run 2	0.008437	17.437958
Run 3	0.004351	13.475713
Run 4	0.009423	17.484465
Run 5	0.010089	17.505103

Table 2 shows the best solutions for each run. The goal of the optimisation was to find a solution, which is characterised by a minimal value for the optimisation goal "Energy Input Deviation" and by a value for the optimisation goal "Total Energy Input" , which is as close as possible to 17.5W (value of the reference set up).

Caused by the different weighting factors for each run, the best solution that was found in each run is different. Table 2 shows that the runs with a weighting factor of 4 for one of the optimisation goals (run 1 and run 5) bring up solutions, which mark the absolute best value for the specific optimisation goal.

The overall best solution in the opinion of the authors is the optimal solution from run 4. This solution is close to the reference value of 17.5W, but is also characterised by a very low value for the goal energy input deviation.

2.4   Properties of the Best Solutions

The following section presents the key properties of the best solution in comparison with the reference set up.

Figure 3 shows the properties of the overall best solution and of the reference set up. The reference set up is characterised by 16 IR emitters, all on the same height of 90mm. The phase control factor has the same value (60%) for the IR emitters in the middle. The IR emitters closer to the boundary are characterised by higher phase control factors. The properties of the best solution from all five optimisation runs look less simple. The height of the IR emitters is also 90mm, except for eight IR emitters close to the middle. The phase control factor varies much more, compared to the reference set up. The highest values (100%) are found at the IR emitters closer to the boundary, whereas the IR emitters in the middle have a phase control factor of only 20%.

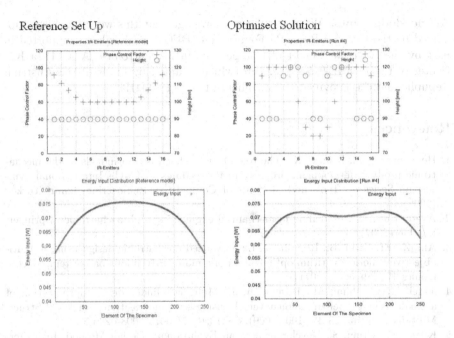

Fig. 3. Properties of the optimal solutions

The energy distribution along the specimen has a nearly parabolic distribution for the reference set-up (max. deviation 0,018750W), whereas the optimised solution has two smaller peaks with a maximal deviation of 0,09423W.

3   Conclusion and Outlook

The optimisation of the heating zone of the annealing simulator ends up with a set of equivalent solutions. Each of the best solutions of the different runs is an improvement compared to the original solution, which shows the potential of the algorithm. The results also show that the optimisation system reacts properly on changing weighting factors. NOA was able to find an overall best solution, which is close to the goal "Total Energy Input" and which has a maximal energy input deviation of only 0,09423W, which is half the deviation of the reference heating zone.

In the further work various modifications on the optimisation model are planned. These modifications shall enlarge the number of parameters and include changes on the geometry (e.g. more flexible IR emitter positions, mirrors to improve energy input into the specimen) and on the used components (type and shape of IR emitters and mirrors).

Another focus within the future work will be to transfer the actual model to more complex problems, which include more parameters and optimisation goals from different domains.

Acknowledgments. We gratefully acknowledge that this work has been supported by the German Research Foundation (DFG) and has been supported in part by the Austrian Center of Competence in Mechatronics (ACCM), a K2-Center of the COMET/K2 program (which is aided by funds of the Austrian Republic and the Provincial Government of Upper Austria).

References

1. Hehenberger, P., Zeman, K.: The role of hierarchical design models in the mechatronic product development process. In: Proceedings of TMCE International Symposium Series on Tools and Methods of Competitive Engineering, Izmir, Turkey (2008)
2. Avgoustinov, N.: Modelling in mechanical engineering and mechatronics. Springer, London (2007)
3. Affi, Z., EL-Kribi, B., Romdhane, L.: Advanced mechatronic design using a multiobjective genetic algorithm optimization of a motor-driven four-bar system. Mechatronics 17, 489–500 (2007)
4. Jodei, J., Ebrahimi, M., Roshanian, J.: Multidisciplinary design optimization of a small solid propellant launch vehicle using system sensitivity analysis. Struct. Multidisc. Optim. 38, 93–100 (2009), doi:10.1007/s00158-008-0260-5
5. Kittel, K., Vajna, S.: Development of an Evolutionary Design Method. In: Leifer, L., Skogstad, P. (eds.) Proceedings of ICED 2009, Design Methods and Tools, Part 2, vol. 6, pp. 147–156 (2009)
6. Follmer, M., Hehenberger, P., Geirhofer, R., Haslmayr, M., Zeman, K.: Conceptual design tool for the development of a heating zone of an industrial Annealing Simulator. In: Proceedings of Mechatronics 2010, Zurich, Switzerland (2010)

Model-Based Approach for the Reliability Prediction of Mechatronic Systems on the System-Level

Martin Follmer, Peter Hehenberger, and Klaus Zeman

Institute for Computer-Aided Methods in Mechanical Engineering,
Johannes Kepler University Linz,
Altenbergerstr. 69, A-4040 Linz, Austria
{Martin.Follmer,Peter.Hehenberger,Klaus.Zeman}@jku.at

Abstract. In general, mechatronic products merge solutions from different engineering disciplines and therefore a mechatronic design process must integrate multiple disciplines as well. There is a critical lack of tools supporting the inter-disciplinary aspects of the development process of mechatronic products, especially in the conceptual design phase. A general approach for the creation of mechatronic system models as well as a simulation-based design process based on system-level simulations was elaborated. Simulations on the system-level are different from those on the discipline-level. They should contribute to a better understanding of the overall system under consideration by the evaluation of system-specific (global) properties that cannot be evaluated on a discipline-specific level. In this paper a model-based approach for the reliability prediction of mechatronic systems on the system-level is presented.

Keywords: process model, product development process, system-level modelling, system-level models, system models, mechatronics, mechatronic systems, systems-of-systems, reliability prediction.

1 Introduction

The defining feature of mechatronic products, also known as systems-of-systems, integrated systems, or mixed systems (e.g., [1]), is that they merge solutions from different engineering disciplines. As a consequence, a mechatronic design process must integrate these multiple disciplines. In the individual engineering disciplines the conceptual design process is well understood, and some process models even provide valuable advice for the design of mechatronic systems (e.g., [2], [3]), however, well-established integrated approaches for mechatronic design processes are still missing in practice. The situation is similar for the various kinds of computer-aided systems (CAx-systems) used by highly skilled engineers of different disciplines [2]. There is a critical lack of tools supporting the inter-disciplinary aspects of the development process of mechatronic products, especially in the conceptual design phase [4], [5].

In the present paper, a general approach for a simulation-based design process of mechatronic systems, especially for the early phases of design, is elaborated. This approach consists of six phases based on the VDI Guideline 2221 [6] and aims at the continuous integration of simulation techniques from the very beginning of the design

R. Moreno-Díaz et al. (Eds.): EUROCAST 2011, Part II, LNCS 6928, pp. 105–112, 2012.

process in order to evaluate the properties of the actual system under design during each design stage. By this means, the match between actual and desired properties of the system under design should be facilitated, resulting in an improved design process itself.

Simulations on the discipline-level typically and traditionally are performed in later phases of the design process (e.g., during preliminary or detail design) when the granularity of information about the product is sufficiently fine, i.e., when information of the product is defined already in such detail, that well-established discipline-specific tools may be applied. Such simulations allow for the analysis of discipline-specific components as well as of entire systems that are composed of these components. Nevertheless, simulations in earlier phases of design (e.g., in conceptual design), when information about the product is still vague and incomplete, are an object of desire even on the discipline-level. A good deal more this is true for the design of multi-disciplinary products such as mechatronic systems. The reasons for this are twofold: The first reason originates from the fact that especially the early phases of design are even more challenging for multi-disciplinary products causing a higher demand for simulations there. The second reason results from the still existing general lack of multi-disciplinary modelling and simulation methods and tools, which affects all phases of the design of multi-disciplinary systems.

Simulations on the system-level (both for single- and multi-disciplinary products) are different from those on the discipline-level. They should contribute to a better understanding of the overall system under consideration by the evaluation of system-specific (global) properties that cannot be evaluated on a discipline-specific level, e.g. reliability prediction of the overall system. This should also prevent the design team from too many iterations during the design process. Typical questions ("load cases", "scenarios", evaluations) treated by these simulations are quite different from those addressed by discipline-specific simulations.

One of the major challenges in developing mechatronic products is the increasing complexity of the products themselves. This makes it difficult to overview the relationships of the involved engineering disciplines. Mechatronic System Models (MSM) can improve this unsatisfactory situation and allow a holistic view on complex mechatronic systems. Furthermore, a MSM offers the possibility to consider the required reliability of a multi-disciplinary system.

The presented approach for the reliability prediction on the system-level according to [8] is applicable during the early phases of the product development process (concept phase, preliminary design, ...), as well as for already existing products (optimization, update, ...). The aim of a reliability analysis during the early phases of the product development is benchmarking different design concepts of the system under design. The reliability prediction should also allow for optimizations and updates for already existing products. In that case, an exact analysis of the product's structure is feasible. For further information concerning mathematical models, methods, etc. for the prediction of the reliability of technical systems see [7], [8], [9] and [10].

2   Related Works

In [11] and [12] the authors presented an approach for the holistic description of a multi-disciplinary system with the consideration of the essential operating modes and the desired behaviour. According to this approach, aspects such as the environment, application scenarios, requirements, the system of objectives, functions, etc. should be considered in a certain specification technique. Furthermore, a procedure model for the conceptual design phase (which includes four sub-phases) was developed. The research group also developed the software tool "Mechatronic Modeller" that is based on the specification technique for modelling mechatronic systems.

A system-level (high-level) model of a multi-disciplinary system based on a functional description was introduced in [13]. The architecture of the system is primarily determined by the main functions which are already known in the conceptual phase of design. In later design phases, general functions can be decomposed into more concrete ones which lead to a more detailed functional structure of the system under design. The system-model should provide a better overview of the system and should also connect abstract models with more concrete ones. A verification of specific parameters against requirements can also be supported by the functional structure.

A concept for a software prototype supporting the development of mechatronic systems was presented in [14]. The software prototype called "Connection-Modeller" should allow various views on the system under design, e.g., requirements, functions, structure. These views are called partial models and can be developed using proprietary software-tools. The Connection-Modeller provides means to define cross-discipline connections between various partial models which can be used, e.g., for the propagation of design changes.

3   Mechatronic System Model (MSM)

In this section the basic principles of the Mechatronic System Model (MSM) are discussed in brief. For more information regarding the MSM see [4] and [15].

3.1   Process Model I: Creation of a MSM

The generic approach shown in Fig. 1 describes the necessary steps and their chronological order for the creation of a MSM both for top down as well as for bottom up modelling. In Fig. 1 the different levels of the MSM are depicted as rectangles representing sub-models of the MSM that can be used to structure the MSM with respect to various views. Different views allow for (i) the representation of different modelling aspects, (ii) a holistic depiction of the system under consideration, (iii) a multiple structured model by using different modelling aspects as well as (iv) the customization of the MSM. Views could be dedicated to, e.g., requirements, structure, behaviour, parametrics of the system. The white area of each sub-model of

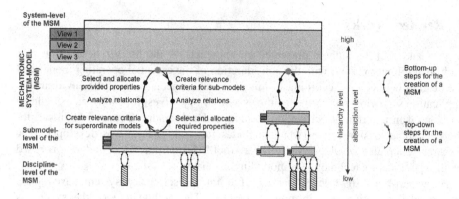

Fig. 1. Approach for the creation of a Mechatronic System Model (MSM) according to [15]

the MSM accounts for interfaces and communication between the connected sub- or discipline-specific models by transmitting input and output parameters (depicted as circles). The hatched rectangles represent discipline-specific models.

3.2 Process Model II: Simulation-Based Design Process

The approach shown in Fig. 2 consists of six phases based on VDI Guideline 2221 [6] and aims at integrating simulation techniques into the design process from its very beginning. As already mentioned, these simulations at the system-level allow for the evaluation of specific "global" system properties. The basis for simulations in the various phases of the product development process is a shared database. This database also provides interfaces to discipline-specific software tools and their related models, and has to ensure data consistency. Further investigations of the database are beyond the scope of this work.

The input to the process model is a specific "development task". The process model consists of six design phases, however, only the phases 1 to 5 are considered in more detail as they are most representative for the early phases of design. The design phases (depicted as large rhombuses) include specific working steps (depicted as rectangles) and corresponding working results (depicted as small rhombuses). Each design phase concludes with a query: Are the requirements reachable? If the requirements are attainable, the process is continued with the next design phase; otherwise, an "external" iteration is necessary, or the process must be terminated. The step "Validation/Evaluation" represents an "internal" iteration step (inside the actual design phase) at the end of each design phase. Phase 6 and the output ("further realization and documentation") are beyond the scope of this paper. For more information see [15].

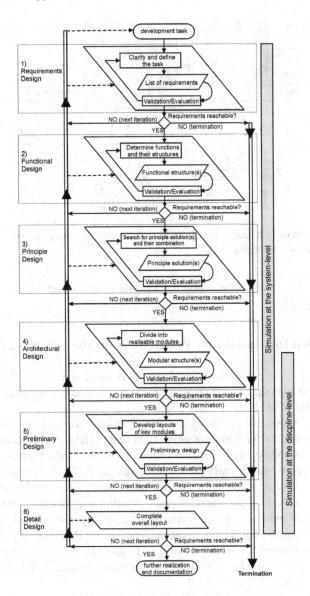

Fig. 2. Design process model

3.3 Process Model III: Model Based Mechatronic Design

Both process models presented here extend the common product development processes by additional investigations regarding simulation-based modelling on the system-level. Fig. 3 shows the integration of process model II into process model I as well as the specific working steps depicted as ellipses and "diamonds" leading to an integrated process model for model based mechatronic design. The relevance of the various design steps depends on both the phases of the product development process

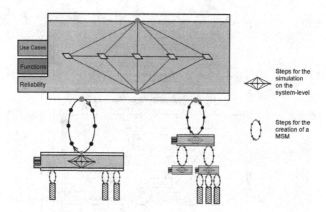

Fig. 3. Process model for model based mechatronic design with special views with respect to reliability prediction according to [15]

as well as on the specific abstraction level of the system under consideration and the corresponding MSM.

4 Approach for Reliability Predictions on the System-Level

According to [7], the reliability of a product is defined as follows: Reliability is the probability that a product performs its required function under stated conditions for a specified period of time.

Thus it is obvious that reliability is a very important aspect in product design and plays an essential role for costumer satisfaction (e.g., safety or availability aspects). In other words, reliability has significant influence on the product success. Integrating reliability analyses into the early phases of design should lead to designs which reach the defined reliability goals from the beginning and consequently helps to reduce iteration loops as well as development costs. A holistic approach for the prediction of the reliability of multi-disciplinary systems is currently not available and therefore each discipline involved has its own special analyses for the reliability prediction. For electronic components, for example, several handbooks containing the relevant data and models are available, however, for software, standardized approaches are currently not defined, [7], [8] and [9].

Fig. 4 shows an approach for the reliability prediction of a mechatronic system according to [8]. This approach consists of the following six steps: (i) identification of the main-functions of the system, (ii) creation of a detailed representation of the system, (iii) specification and classification of the critical components of the system, (iv) collection of the data necessary for the reliability prediction, (v) separation into qualitative respectively quantitative analysis and (vi) comparison of the evaluated reliability values with the defined reliability goals.

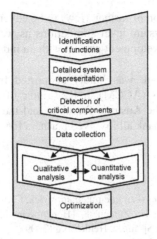

Fig. 4. Approach for the reliability prediction of mechatronic systems according to [8]

The first two steps of the above mentioned approach could be supported by a MSM. Step (i) could be supported by a view "functions" to identify the main-functions, main-malfunctions and sub-functions of the system. The second step could be supported by modelling the structure and specific use cases of the system under design (possible views: "Structure" and "Use Cases"). Both views could be based on standardized diagrams according to [16]. Fig. 3 schematically shows the required views ("Use Cases", "Functions" as well as "Reliability") of a MSM for supporting the reliability prediction on the system-level. In step (iii) the critical components of the system are specified and classified using an ABC-Analysis, for example. Some of the data which are necessary for the fourth step are listed in specific handbooks, others can be determined by tests or analyzing related systems or may be based on expert knowledge, for instance. Step (v) is dedicated to both qualitative as well as quantitative reliability analyses. Qualitative analyses contain, e.g., FMEA or FTA whereas quantitative analyses are based on statistics and probability calculations such as Reliability Block Diagrams and Markoff-Theory. In the last step, the reliability values identified by the analysis are compared to the defined reliability goals. If the goals cannot be reached, the critical components must be modified and another analysis has to be done, [8].

5 Conclusion and Further Activities

It is obvious that there still exists a substantial lack of methods as well as software tools that provide a holistic view of multi-disciplinary systems and support design engineers in executing simulations especially in the early phases of the product development process. In this article, the significance of system-level modelling and simulation especially in the design of multi-disciplinary systems is outlined. The potential of such an approach has been demonstrated schematically by the reliability prediction of mechatronic systems on its system-level. The next steps of the research work will focus on the creation of further views to be covered by the MSM in order to enable a broader range of system-level simulations as well as on the application of this approach to a product development project with an industrial background.

Acknowledgments. This work was kindly supported by the Austrian Center of Competence in Mechatronics (ACCM), a K2-Center of the COMET/K2 program, which is aided by funds of the Austrian Republic and the Provincial Government of Upper Austria. The authors thank all involved partners for their support.

References

1. De Silva, C.W.: Mechatronics – an integrated approach. CRC Press, Boca Raton (2005)
2. Vajna, S., Weber, C., Bley, H., Zeman, K., Hehenberger, P.: CAx für Ingenieure: Eine praxisbezogene Einführung. Springer, Heidelberg (2009)
3. VDI 2206: Design Handbook 2206, Design Methodology for Mechatronic systems. VDI Publishing Group, Düsseldorf (2003)
4. Follmer, M., Hehenberger, P., Punz, S., Zeman, K.: Using SysML in the product development process of mechatronic systems. In: 11th International Design Conference, Design 2010, pp. 1513–1522 (2010)
5. Aberdeen Group, System Design: New Product Development for Mechatronics (2008)
6. VDI 2221: Design Handbook 2221, Systematic Approach to the Development and Design of technical Systems and Products. VDI Publishing Group, Düsseldorf (1993)
7. Bertsche, B., Lechner, G.: Zuverlässigkeit im Maschinenbau. Springer, Heidelberg (1999)
8. Bertsche, B., Göhner, P., Jensen, U., Schinköthe, W., Wunderlich, H.-J.: Zuverlässigkeit mechatronischer Systeme Grundlagen und Bewertung in frühen Entwicklungsphasen. Springer, Heidelberg (2009)
9. Birolini, A.: Qualität und Zuverlässigkeit technischer Systeme. Springer, Heidelberg (1991)
10. Follmer, M.: Computer-aided reliability prediction of mechatronical systems. Diploma Thesis, Institute for Computer-Aided Methods in Mechanical Engineering. Johannes Kepler University, Linz, Austria (2007)
11. Gausemeier, J., Dorociak, R., Pook, S., Nyßen, A., Terfloth, A.: Computer-aided cross-domain modeling of mechatronic systems. In: 11th International Design Conference, Design 2010, pp. 723–732 (2010)
12. Gausemeier, J., Dorociak, R., Kaiser, L.: Computer-aided modeling of the principle solution of mechatronic systems: A domain-spanning methodology for the conceptual design of mechatronic systems. In: ASME 2010 International Design Engineering Technical Conferences & Computers and Information in Engineering Conference, IDETC/CIE (2010)
13. Alvarez Cabrera, A.A., Erden, M.S., Foeken, M.J., Tomiyama, T.: High Level Model Integration for Design of Mechatronic Systems. In: IEEE/ASME International Conference on Mechatronic and Embedded Systems and Applications, MESA 2008, pp. 387–392 (2008)
14. Stark, R., Beier, G., Wöhler, T., Figge, A.: Cross-Domain Dependency Modelling – How to achieve consistent System Models with Tool Support. In: 7th European Systems Engineering Conference, EuSEC (2010)
15. Follmer, M., Hehenberger, P., Punz, S., Rosen, R., Zeman, K.: Approach for the creation of mechatronic system models. In: 18th International Conference on Engineering Design, ICED 2011 (accepted for publication, 2011)
16. OMG, Systems Modeling Language SysML, Version 1.2. (2010)

Understanding the Relationship of Information in Mechatronic Design Modeling

Peter Hehenberger[1], Alexander Egyed[2], and Klaus Zeman[1]

[1] Institute for Computer-Aided Methods in Mechanical Engineering, Johannes Kepler University Linz, Altenbergerstr. 69, A-4040 Linz, Austria/Europe
{peter.hehenberger,klaus.zeman}@jku.at
[2] Institute for Systems Engineering and Automation, Johannes Kepler University Linz, Altenbergerstr. 69, A-4040 Linz, Austria/Europe
alexander.egyed@jku.at

Abstract. Understand the information flow during engineering processes of mechatronic systems is an important point for competitive mechatronic engineering. The paper gives an overview about product models used in mechatronic design and analyzes also the flow of information through tools. Furthermore, there is also the need for considering model consistency because if objects and models are independently created and maintained by the various disciplines then correctness is no longer guaranteed. The same is true for objects or models that are transferred from one discipline to another, from one abstraction level to another, or from one design phase to the next one – if such objects or models are subsequently modified on both ends just as proposed in simultaneous engineering.

Keywords: Mechatronic Design, Product Model, Change Propagation, Information Flow.

1 Introduction

Mechatronics can be considered to be an integrative methodology utilizing the technologies of mechanical engineering, electrical engineering/electronics and information technology in order to provide enhanced products, processes and systems [1, 2]. Mechatronic design of machines, devices and plants can help create improved and enhanced products, processes and systems. On the other hand, the complexity of these systems usually higher due to the intended beneficial interaction between components and technologies from different mechatronic disciplines. In all phases of the design process there is a need to build models which are simplified representations of corresponding originals, in many cases of the real world. In different phases, these design models have different aims. In the conceptual design phase, physical principles, functions, structures, etc have to be evaluated by building models. In most cases, analytical and virtual models are less expensive and less time-consuming than physical prototypes.

R. Moreno-Díaz et al. (Eds.): EUROCAST 2011, Part II, LNCS 6928, pp. 113–120, 2012.

Engineering processes and tools accentuate the capture of engineering solutions and possibly intermediate solutions generated along the way. What is typically not captured is the flow of information that led to these (intermediate) solutions. Indeed, the engineering process is based on a complex flow of information where results computed in one step (perhaps by one discipline) are consumed in other steps (perhaps by other disciplines). The aim of this work is in better understanding this flow of information.

Trivially, we can think of the flow of information as data exchanges and the computations as processing that produces this data and consumes it. The main goals of this consideration are:

- Understand the impact of changes during engineering processes (direct, indirect and transitive impact)
- Understand the flow of information through tools: For the most part, engineering tools are well established and internally reasonably well integrated. To understand the impact of changes, however, we require its knowledge together with external flow.
- Understand the direct and indirect flow across tools
- Understanding trade offs (completeness and correctness of flow vs. completeness and correctness of change impact)

2 Background

Models are very important for the design of complex engineering activities. For example, numerical modeling and simulation are fundamental to the engineering of high performance characteristics. Such modeling approaches require experimenting with computer-based models. From the viewpoint of engineering design, models are means of storing knowledge which is used by simulations for producing information that may improve product knowledge and potentially also the quality of many analyses and decisions made during the design process [3].

When designing a mechatronic system, it is possible to design the mechanical equipment, before any of the control system design has been initiated. An obvious drawback of this sequential approach is the (probable) lack of compatibility between the subsystems which results in additional efforts and costs to (optimally) meet the specifications of the total (integrated) system. Another drawback of this approach is that during the design process decisions have to be made about whether to use a mechatronical or just a mechanical solution. Design engineers have to balance mechanical, electr(on)ic and software solutions.

In general, a model is devoted to the task of mapping reality onto a significant representation of reality in order to make valid predictions and conclusions for reality. It should include the relevant phenomena/effects of interest ("views of the object", such as geometry, dynamics, stability, materials, electrodynamics, controllability, cycle time, maintenance, etc. During all phases of the design process there is a need to establish models. If these models are simplified representations of the product to be built then we speak of product models. The purpose of these models changes depending on the phases of the product development. During the conceptual design phase, physical principles, functions, structures, etc have to be modeled and evaluated. In most cases, analytical (mathematical) and virtual models are less expensive and less time-consuming than physical prototypes. Virtual models can be implemented and used to simulate and evaluate (significant representations of) reality with the help of computers.

Some aspects of change management in the design of mechatronical products are discussed in [4,5]. The parts of a product (e.g. engine, gearing, clutch) are classified as absorbers, carriers and multipliers depending on whether a change in the input parameters of a part causes less, equal or more changes than in the output parameters. Multipliers can cause avalanches of changes of the design of a product. As solution to avoid this, "safety" margins are proposed, so the change of one part does not necessarily affect the adjoining parts.

In [6], a change propagation index (CPI) is introduced based on studies of change propagation in the design of automotive platforms. With the CPI, the identification of parts or elements as absorbers, carriers or multipliers is done more easily. The largest set of change requests during the development of a sensor system was analyzed in [7] to get a better understanding of change and change development of large scale products. Based on the documentation of change requests, a design structure matrix (DSM) and a ΔDSM was developed representing the actual state of a change.

3   Information in Mechatronic Design Processes

3.1   Model Views

In the design process of mechatronic systems product models and data from different angles have to be analyzed – representing the different disciplines involved. This diverse viewpoint dimensions include the following aspects (Fig. 1):

- objects and models from different disciplines, which are involved in the development process of a mechatronical system
- model granularity (which differs across disciplines), denoting the extent to which an object or model is broken down into smaller parts (e.g., sub-models with a higher level of detail and a lower level of abstraction, respectively)
- design phases: The development/design process can be structured into four phases, namely problem definition, conceptual design, preliminary design and detailed design

Furthermore, there is also the need for consistency because if objects and models are independently created and maintained by the various disciplines then correctness is no longer guaranteed. The same is true for objects or models that are transferred from one discipline to another, from one abstraction level to another and from one design phase to the next one – if such objects or models are subsequently modified on both ends just as proposed in simultaneous engineering. This problem, of course, becomes increasingly pronounced with system size and complexity because likely more people and disciplines are involved. A proven strategy to handle this increasing complexity is to divide up the work as it is done in concurrent engineering. However, it is rarely possible to divide up a problem such that two people can work fully independently from one another and then, at the end, expect that the results of their work fit together without conflicts. Through good modularization, it is possible to achieve some degree of independence; however, it is never possible to avoid dependencies. The role of consistency is to characterize such dependencies – to identify the conditions that have to be met for objects and models to fit together.

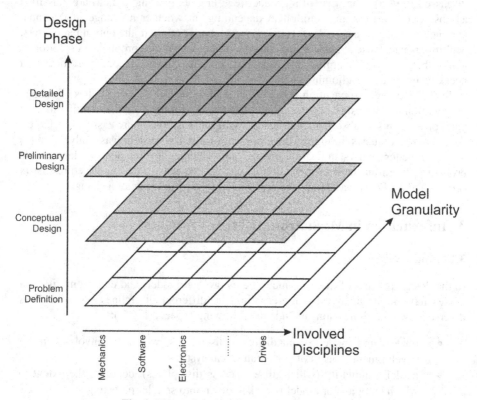

Fig. 1. Viewpoint of product models and data [8]

The aim of a behavioral model, i.e. a model of the (physical) system behavior, is to serve as a means of finding an answer to a design question. Each model is unique and it has a specific purpose. The preliminary design phase is often characterized by a cascading series of what-if questions. Many of these questions, which may be of divergent character, are related to the complex dependencies between geometry (shape), topological structure and (physical) behavior. The complex nature of engineering design, as well as the time and cost-constraints on this process, require highly efficient and flexible procedures to configure system models (overall models) for non-routine simulations. The modeling challenge may be addressed by a modular or an integrative model design. A modular sub-system has interfaces that are well defined and are shared with only a few other sub-systems. An integrative system has interfaces that may be more complex and shared across the whole system model. The physical behavior of a technical system depends on the properties of the sub-systems and their (internal and external) interactions [9]. An interface describes the relationship between a pair of mating features. Product models are important containers of significant product properties such as shape and material.

3.2 Consistency

Consistency rules are simply conditions on a model which evaluate to true or false – depending on whether the rule is satisfied by the model or not [8,10]. There are typically many such consistency rules and these rules need to be re-evaluated whenever the model changes. This re-evaluation is computationally expensive if done exhaustively with every model change. During a rule's evaluation, a consistency rule investigates typically a portion of the model only. We define the accessed portion of a model as the scope of a rule. For example, we want to analyze different design models during the development process of a gripper. Figure 2 shows different simplified models from different design stages.

The function structure is used to describe product functionality because in engineering design, the final goal is the creation of an artifact, product, system, or process that performs a function or functions under certain constraints to fulfill customer need(s). The conceptual design model is used to select, define and fix the main parameters of the gripper. In detailed design we have a CAD-model which describes the geometry (and other properties) of the gripper.

Consistency rules are written for a context element (a type of model element, e.g. a function) from where its evaluation starts. For consistency rule 1 (Fig. 2), the interaction between the function structure and the conceptual design model is described as "applies to <fix workpiece> requires(this).contains(<pneumatic cylinder>)". This means that for the function "fix workpiece" a drive like a "pneumatic cylinder" is required. In the second rule the interaction between the model parameter "distance piston" and the geometric representation in the CAD-model is defined as equal.

Large design models contain thousands of model elements. Designers easily get overwhelmed maintaining the correctness of such design models over time. Not only is it hard to detect new errors when the model changes but it is also hard to keep track of known errors. In the software engineering community, this problem is known as the consistency problem and errors in models are known as inconsistencies. Inconsistencies are detected through reasoning processes that require the existence of rules that describe correctness. Such consistency rules describe conditions that a model must satisfy to be considered a valid model (e.g., syntactic well-formedness and even coherence between different models). Such consistency rules obviously vary for different models. The validity (correctness) and invalidity depend on the modeling notation (language) and its semantics. However, for many mainstream modeling languages (e.g., SysML, UML) such semantics are well-defined and engineers have been able to identify consistency rules.

During the development stages of complex mechatronic systems many models are generated either manually or in an automatic manner. The nature of these models ranges from requirements expressed in text documents down to mathematical description of a physical effect.

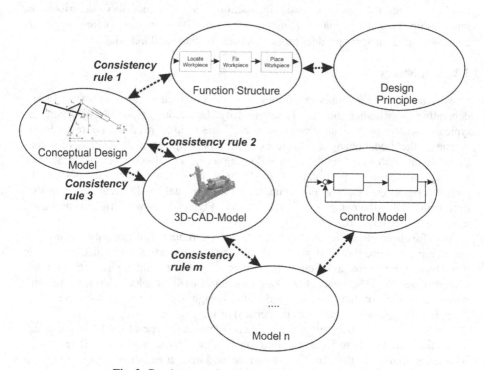

Fig. 2. Consistency rules between different models [8]

3.3   Information Flow

Understanding the relationships among different models is a nontrivial task and becomes harder the more complex a system is. Therefore one important topic is the analysis of these relationships. Traceability refers to the completeness of the information flow every step in a process chain.

The lack of information flow is most problematic in context of change management. If some (intermediate) solution changes - i.e., changed data - then engineers must be able to understand where this data was consumed because other solutions that were computed based in part on this changed data may change also. Fig. 3 illustrates this in a simple manner. We see that engineer 1 produces output $Data_B$ through some processing that requires $Data_A$ as input. $Data_B$ is then consumed by Engineer 2 who, through some other processing, produces $Data_C$. If $Data_A$ changes then $Data_B$ directly and $Data_C$ indirectly may be affected by this change where $Data_C$ should only be affected if $Data_B$ is affected. Change propagation thus requires knowledge about the flow of information where, in this particular case, $Data_B$ is a $Processing_{A-B}$ function of $Data_A$ ($Data_B = Processing_{A-B}(Data_A)$).

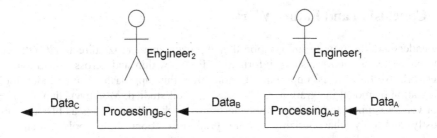

Fig. 3. The impact of successive processing onto the information flow

The data may also be abandoned if undesirable. The processing of data and hence the flow of information can be arbitrarily complex and also hierarchical. The flow of information in engineering processes is typically meant to accentuate information flow among tools and users (e.g., communication between two users, between two tools). We distinguishe the information flow between engineering tools (external flow) and information flow within engineering tools (internal flow). The main focus of this work is on external information flow. This focus is useful and necessary because engineering tools internally

1) may already have (limited) ability to track information flow and
2) even if they do not it is the tool builder's responsibility to providing this capability.

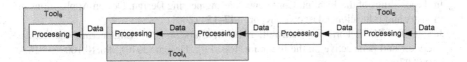

Fig. 4. Relationship between tools, processing, and data

Fig. 4 depicts the relationship between tools, processing, and data. Engineering tools mainly serve as means for processing data and internal data exchanges. Results produced by these tools are usually not forwarded to other engineering tools but rather stored persistently. Depending on the complexity of the tool, it may support a range of processing activities. In some cases, a tool may support multiple related processing activities where the flow of information among the activities is internal to the tool (as in $Tool_A$). In other cases, a tool may support one or more independent processing activities where the flow of information among these and other activities is external (outside the tool as in $Tool_B$). Not all processing may be tool supported and even for the ones that are, engineering tool support typically involve extensive manual activities. Individual tools may support multiple processing steps. These tools are typically well integrated and within a single tool there may even be support for the capture of the information flow.

4 Conclusion and Future Work

To understand the flow of information this approach characterize direct and indirect, internal, external, and transitive information flow - within and across user domains (network, verbal). It is important to note that this approach is not about tool integration or model integration. Both areas are well studied. Moreover, they require tool vendor support to be successful. The future work will treat tools as black boxes mostly and only characterizing certain properties about these tools which are important for understanding information flow and change propagation.

Acknowledgments. We gratefully acknowledge that this work was supported in part by the Austrian Center of Competence in Mechatronics (ACCM), a K2-Center of the COMET/K2 program, which is aided by funds of the Austrian Republic and the Provincial Government of Upper Austria and in part by the Austrian FWF grant P21321-N15.

References

1. De Silva, C.W.: Mechatronics – an integrated approach. CRC Press, Boca Raton (2005)
2. Isermann, R.: Mechatronic systems. Fundamentals. Springer, London (2005)
3. Hehenberger, P., Zeman, K.: The role of hierarchical design models in the mechatronic product development process. In: Proceedings of TMCE International Symposium Series on Tools and Methods of Competitive Engineering, Izmir, Turkey (2008)
4. Eckert, C.M., Zanker, W., Clarkson, P.J.: Aspects of a Better Understanding of Changes. In: Proceedings of the 13th Int. Conference on Engineering Design: Design Applications in Industry and Education, Glasgow, UK, pp. 147–154 (2001)
5. Jarratt, T.A.W., Eckert, C., Caldwell, N.H.M., Clarkson, P.J.: Engineering change: an overview and perspective on the literature. Res. Eng. Design (2010), doi:10.1007/s00163-010-0097-y
6. Suh, E.S.: Flexible Product Platforms. Doctoral Dissertation, Massachusetts Institute of Technology. Engineering Systems Division, Cambridge, MA, USA, (2005)
7. de Weck, O., Bounova, G., Keller, R., Eckert, C., Clarkson, P.J.: Change Propagation Analysis in Complex Technical Systems. ASME Journal of Mechanical Design 131 (August 2009)
8. Hehenberger, P., Egyed, A., Zeman, K.: Consistency checking of mechatronic design models. In: Proceedings of IDETC/CIE 2010, ASME 2010 International Design Engineering Technical Conferences & Computers and Information in Engineering Conference, Montreal, Quebec, Canada, Paper-Nr. DETC2010-28615 (2010)
9. Hehenberger, P., Poltschak, F., Zeman, K., Amrhein, W.: Hierarchical design models in the mechatronic product development process of synchronous machines. Mechatronics 20, 864–875 (2010); ISSN 0957-4158,
   http://dx.doi.org/10.1016/j.mechatronics.2010.04.00
10. Egyed, A.: Automatically Detecting and Tracking Inconsistencies in Software Design Models. IEEE Transactions on Software Engineering (TSE) 37(2), 188–204 (2010)

Modeling and Design of a Production Concept for Skinless Pretzel-Shaped Sausages

Stefan Punz, Peter Hehenberger, and Martin Follmer

Institute for Computer-Aided Methods in Mechanical Engineering, Johannes Kepler University
Linz, Altenbergerstr. 69, A-4040 Linz, Austria/Europe
{stefan.punz,peter.hehenberger,martin.follmer}@jku.at

Abstract. The development of a production concept for skinless pretzel-shaped sausages brings along several challenges, ranging from difficulties in automatically handling sausage meat to the compliance of applicable regulations for food production. In this design project, several companies with different tasks and experiences were involved, whereby the Johannes Kepler University Linz contributed systematic conceptual design knowledge. As a basis for the design cooperation, a systematic design approach was applied and supported by several methods when passing through different development stages in mechatronic product design. This paper gives a brief summary of the design activities in this project and summarizes the gained experience.

Keywords: Conceptual design, systematic product development, design methods, product development process, production concept.

1 Introduction

This paper is intended to give an overview of a project dealing with the development of a production concept for skinless pretzel-shaped sausages. This task brings along several challenges, ranging from difficulties in automatically handling sausage meat to the compliance of applicable regulations for food production. The project was realized with several small and medium-sized enterprises in Austria. It was tried to use various design approaches and methods when passing through different development stages in mechatronic product design, which will be focused on in the following.

One of the key elements in mechatronic design is the integration of the different disciplines involved. Several phases in the design process, ranging from the identification of the customer needs to the detail design of a mechatronic product, have to be mastered [1]. Therefore different systematic approaches and methods to support various tasks occurring in product design are known. In this project it was consciously tried to use common design guidelines and methods to gain experience in the application of systematic mechatronic product development and to demonstrate the usability of such advanced product development methods even for design projects in small and medium-sized enterprises.

R. Moreno-Díaz et al. (Eds.): EUROCAST 2011, Part II, LNCS 6928, pp. 121–128, 2012.

2 Problem Definition and Project Environment

An entrepreneur had the idea to produce and sell skinless pretzel shaped sausages and started a co-operation with a butcher who started with the manual production. In the manual production process, the raw sausage meat is filled manually into plastic molds (Fig. 1). Then the molds are put into the oven for a certain period of time and then the finished pretzels have to be knocked out of the molds that can be used again after cleaning. Thus, at least as much molds as pretzels per batch are needed.

Soon it was realized that an automatic production would be useful, because it would allow for a higher production output and it would be more cost-effective, primarily because of the reduction of personnel costs and due to the reduction of molds needed. The question was, how such a production system for pretzel shaped sausages could look like, and thus the project "Conceptual design of a production concept for pretzel shaped sausages" was initiated.

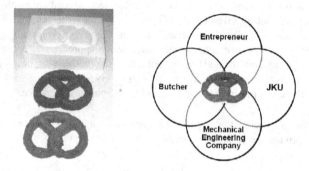

Fig. 1. Left: Manual production of pretzel shaped sausages using plastic molds. Right: The four companies involved in the development of the production concept.

In this project four companies, responsible for different tasks, were involved (Fig. 1):

- The Entrepreneur
  - o   Idea
  - o   Project leader
- A Butcher
  - o   Produces and processes sausage meat
  - o   Manual production using pretzel forms
- A Mechanical Engineering Company
  - o   Construct and build new production system
- JKU as a scientific partner
  - o   Support the design project through methodical know-how in systematic conceptual design
  - o   Adaption and application of several widespread methods supporting conceptual design
  - o   Bundling relevant knowledge of the several companies involved

3 Design Approaches and Methods Used

The VDI-guideline 2221 ([2], [3]) providing a "systematic approach to the development and design of technical systems and products" served as a basis both for the design cooperation and the several design steps. For the conceptual design of a product, steps one to four of this guideline are relevant. These steps comprise the activities "clarify and define the task", "determine functions and their structures", "search for solution principles and their combination" and "divide into realizable modules". To support the steps of conceptual design, several methods such as "Requirements list", "Quality Function Development (QFD)", "Creativity techniques" or "Axiomatic design" were applied (see Fig. 2). Some of these methods and their results will be explained briefly in the following.

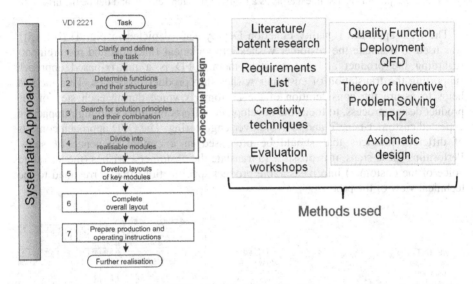

Fig. 2. The first 4 steps of the VDI-guideline 2221 ([2], [3]) were used as a basis for the conceptual design process, supported by several design methods, and served as a framework for cross-company cooperation

The first step in the project was to clarify and define the task. For this reason, the customer needs and boundary conditions were discussed in detail with the entrepreneur. The results were documented using a requirements list, shown in Fig. 3 in excerpts.

Soon it was realized that the task contained several tricky challenges such as difficulties in automatically handling raw sausage meat or in the compliance with applicable regulations for food production. Therefore, the knowledge of the cooperation partners was essential for the success of the project and especially for the evaluation of possible solutions.

Nr.	Question	Clarification, Requirement
1	Which product shall be designed?	A production system for the automatic production of pretzel shaped sausages
2	Where is the site of operation?	At the butcher's
3	Which unique features shall the sausage have?	- Pretzel shaped - Skinless - Organic meat
4	Which sorts of raw sausage meat have to be processed?	Just one sort at the beginning
5	Operating conditions of the production system?	Production rooms of the butcher's
6	Maximum cost of the production system	XY Euros
7	Maximum production cost per pretzel sausage	0,XY - 0,XZ Cent
8	Which supplies are available at the operating site?	Electric current. Compressed air, Water supply
9	Installation space available?	X x Y x Z m
10	Shall it be possible to produce other contours too?	No, just pretzel shape. Maybe change of size
11	...	...

Fig. 3. Requirements list in excerpts as a result of the step "clarify and define the task"

The QFD-approach (Quality Function Deployment, depicted in Fig. 4) ([4], [5]), was used to translate the customer wishes into technical functions and requirements regarding the product and to prioritize them. QFD is a matrix-based approach supporting the translation of customer wishes into product properties. This method helps to assure the consideration of the customer's voice during each step of the product design process, to focus the development efforts on areas with high impact on expected customer-benefit and to avoid over-engineering. The QFD approach consists of different matrices that should be processed in a certain sequence of steps. Performing these steps, it is possible to translate the customer's wishes (the so called voice of the customer) into measurable product specifications that correspond to the technical view of the product.

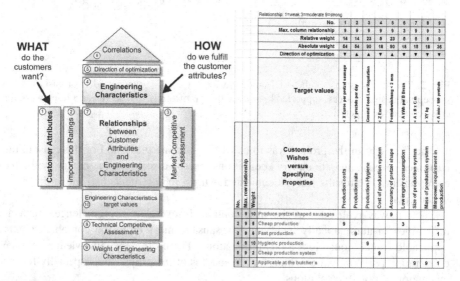

Fig. 4. The HoQ (House of Quality) ([4], [5]) was used to translate the customer's wishes into the specifications of the product

As to be seen in Fig. 5, the most important requirements for this task were "production hygiene", "accuracy of pretzel shape", "high production rate", "minimum staff requirements" and "minimum production costs". Functions, Specifying Properties and their weights are a good starting point for conceptual design and furthermore essential as assessment criteria for the evaluation of solutions [6].

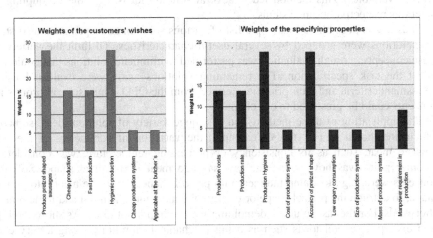

Fig. 5. The results of the HoQ (House of Quality) [4, 5] are the priorities of the Specifying Properties of the product on the basis of the customer's preferences

Following the phases of the VDI-guideline 2221 ([2], [3]), the next step was to determine the product's functions and their structures. The main functions of the production system are "transport the sausage meat to the production system", "bring the sausage meat into pretzel-shape" and "transport the shaped sausages to the cooking unit".

As a next step, suitable solution principles to realize these functions were searched for using several creativity techniques [7] such as (i) Individual Brainstorming, (ii) Group Brainstorming, (iii) Brainwriting, (iv) Progressive abstraction or (v) Search for analogies.

Another method used to support the search for solution concepts was the Theory of Inventive Problem Solving "TIPS" [8]. This problem solving method was developed by Genrich Altshuller and is based on the analysis of inventions documented in patent literature. The basic idea of this method is that inventive solutions often originate from the resolution of technical contradictions. Thus, general solution principles were gathered and arranged within a so called matrix of contradiction. The procedure of this approach is to formulate the contradiction, to have a look at this matrix of contractions and to find the appropriate inventive principles proposed. In our project, the task was to bring the raw sausage meat into pretzel shape and to ensure that it retains this shape. However, due to its smeary, slimy consistency it easily looses this shape. Generally speaking, the relevant contradiction is "shape of the object gets better, but the stability of the object decreases". The matrix of contradictions suggests several solution principles, such as (i) Principle 1: Segmentation, (ii) Principle 18:

Mechanical vibration or (iii) Principle 4: Asymmetry. These solution principles were included in the pool of solutions.

Another method used to support idea generation was "Axiomatic Design" ([9], [10]), a design methodology which is based on two design axioms, describing the connections between customer needs, functional requirements, design parameters and process variables. This method led to several solution ideas, e.g., the decoupling of functions respectively sub-systems.

Thus it was possible to make up a list of various solution concepts. As a next step, the solutions were grouped by several useful characteristics. To limit the variety of these concepts, a rough evaluation was performed to eliminate solutions that could not fulfill the task specification. The remaining solutions again were evaluated using assessment criteria and their priorities derived from the QFD. Thus, several promising concepts could be presented to our client.

The application of these methods led to a huge variety of solution ideas, some of which are shown in Fig. 6. For example, the variation of parameters of the raw sausage meat, such as its consistency or processing temperature, was considered. Another point was how to get the raw sausage meat into pretzel shape. Solution concepts were, e.g., to stamp the meat into pretzel shape, to roll the meat into pretzel shape, to extrude the pretzel shape or to press the meat into the mold and to demold it afterwards. For the last solution, demolding was an important topic. As shown in Fig. 6 in excerpts, several ideas such as using mechanical vibrations, using a very cool mold, a separating medium or an ejection mechanism could be found.

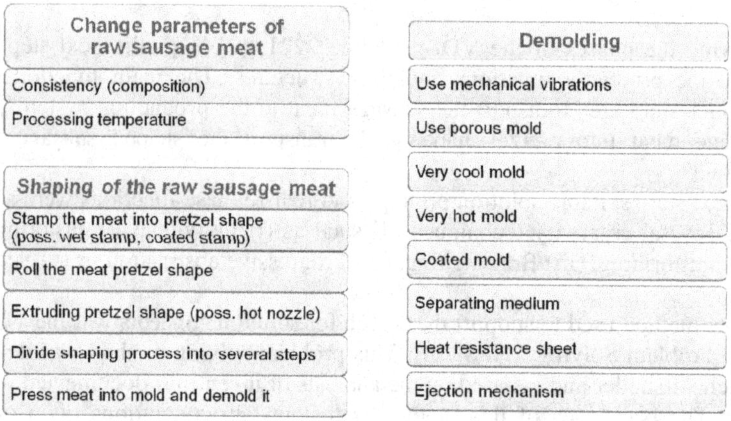

Change parameters of raw sausage meat	Demolding
Consistency (composition)	Use mechanical vibrations
Processing temperature	Use porous mold
	Very cool mold
Shaping of the raw sausage meat	Very hot mold
Stamp the meat into pretzel shape (poss. wet stamp, coated stamp)	Coated mold
Roll the meat pretzel shape	Separating medium
Extruding pretzel shape (poss. hot nozzle)	Heat resistance sheet
Divide shaping process into several steps	Ejection mechanism
Press meat into mold and demold it	

Fig. 6. Some of the solution ideas created by means of different creativity techniques

To prepare the decision for a basic technology concept, an evaluation workshop involving all cooperation partners was initiated. In a discussion know-how and evaluation criteria of all cooperation partners were considered. On this basis, a corporate decision for a basic solution concept was made.

The basic concept chosen can be seen in a schematic representation in Fig. 7. The raw sausage meat with a certain temperature is injected into the lower machine part, and pressed through a channel into the mold. Then the mold is shifted sideways, and

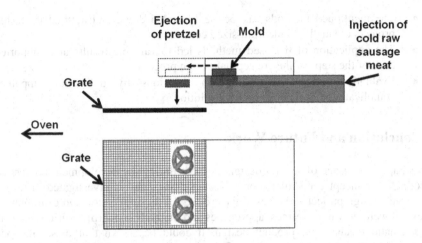

Fig. 7. Schematic representation of the basic solution concept

the pretzel shaped sausage meat is ejected and dropped onto a grate. This grate is transported into an oven, where the pretzels are cooked.

The basic concept leaves many questions concerning a technical realization unanswered. Therefore several solution variants were developed, for example, regarding the shape of the feed opening (it could be beveled, pretzel shaped, circle shaped etc.). The ejection mechanism for demolding could be, e.g., (i) two divisible parts, (ii) many divisible segments, (iii) a stamp or (iv) water or air pressed through tiny nozzles. Additionally, several possibilities concerning the arrangement of the grate were considered.

To decide for a final technology concept, a second evaluation workshop was initiated. Again, advantages and disadvantages for each solution were worked out. In this evaluation workshop, a problem occurred: Some of the evaluation criteria depended on decisions which were not yet taken.

For example, the shape of the feed opening depends on the kind of the feed of the raw meat or the quantities of pretzels produced. Or the ejection mechanism for demolding depends on the existing modular system of the mechanical engineering company or the infrastructure at the butcher's (clean water, filtered air supply). A final decision could not be taken within the period of this project, nevertheless, our documentation was handed over to the client for further activities. From this project many useful experiences could be gained that are summed up in the following chapter.

4   Experiences and Reflections

The project showed that systematic conceptual design provides a good basis for design cooperation of several companies, eases the alignment of design activities and facilitates the bundling of know-how. The methods applied had to be slightly adapted to be applicable to this project. Some experiences gained in the use of different methods are summarized in the following list:

- The mentioned methods can be easily scaled down and applied to design projects of small and medium-sized companies
- The application of the used methods led to valuable results and supported each of the steps of the conceptual design process
- Evaluation criteria depending on decisions by different companies complicate the decision for a final solution

5 Conclusion and Future Work

In this paper, the usage of several design methods during the development process of a production concept for skinless pretzel-shaped sausages is investigated. The use case of this design project served as a playground for the application and examination of several well known guidelines, approaches and methods supporting various aspects of systematic mechatronic product design. It could be shown that these methods - after slight adaptions - may be of significant benefit even for relatively small design projects. Moreover, systematic conceptual design provides a good basis for design cooperation between several companies, eases the alignment of design activities and facilitates the bundling of know-how. The experiences from the project may fertilize the further development of design process models.

Acknowledgments. This work was kindly supported by the Austrian Research Promotion Agency FFG. The authors thank Mr. Manfred Braun (Almbrezen OG, www.almbrezen.at) and all involved partners for their support.

References

1. De Silva, C.W.: Mechatronics – an integrated approach. CRC Press, Boca Raton (2005)
2. Pahl, G., Beitz, W.: Engineering Design – A Systematic Approach. Springer Publishing Group, UK (1999)
3. VDI 2221: Design Handbook 2221, Systematic Approach to the Development and Design of technical Systems and Products. VDI Publishing Group, Düsseldorf (1993)
4. DGQ, Deutsche Gesellschaft für Qualität e.V: QFD – Quality Function Deployment. DGQ Band, 13-21 (2001)
5. Shin, J.S., Kim, K.J.: Complexity reduction of a design problem in QFD using decomposition. Journal of Intelligent Manufacturing 11, 339–354 (2000)
6. Punz, S., Hehenberger, P., Follmer, M., Zeman, K.: Customer-Oriented Hierarchical Concept Development - Application of the HoC Approach in Mechatronic Design. In: Proceedings of the IEEE International Conference on Mechatronics, ICM 2011 (2011)
7. Winkelhofer, G.A.: Kreativ managen: ein Leitfaden für Unternehmer, Manager und Projektleiter. Springer, Berlin (2006)
8. Altshuller, G.S.: Creativity as an Exact Science: The Theory of the Solution of Inventive Problems. Gordon and Breach, New York (1984)
9. Suh, N.P.: The Principles of Design. Oxford Series on Advanced Manufacturing, New York (1990)
10. Suh, N.P.: Axiomatic Design, Advances and Applications. Oxford Series on Advanced Manufacturing, New York (2001)

Optimization of a Speedboat Simulator for Engine Calibration

Markus Hirsch[1], Thomas Schwarzgruber[1],
Michael Aschaber[2], and Herbert Pöllhuber[2]

[1] Institute for Design and Control of Mechatronical Systems,
Johannes Kepler University Linz,
Altenberger Straße 69, 4040 Linz, Austria
[2] Steyr Motors GmbH, Am Stadtgut B1, 4407 Steyr, Austria
{markus.hirsch,thomas.schwarzgruber}@jku.at,
{michael.aschaber,herbert.poellhuber}@steyr-motors.com

Abstract. This work covers the development of a virtual speed boat model for HIL (Hardware in the loop) simulations on engine testbenches. The virtual boat model is restricted to the longitudinal dynamics of the speed boat, as the purpose of the HIL setup is to calibrate the engine for optimal acceleration performance. Due to their high performance setup, speed boats are able to reach planing – a driving state where the boat planes over the water surface. The transition from displacement to planing and the different load characteristics in planing are crucial in the development of the virtual boat model for high speed boats. This work introduces a simplified model to take into account those transition effects.

Keywords: Simulation, HIL, Engine Calibration, Marine Application, Test bench.

1 Introduction

Fast acceleration and maximum velocity are a main focus for speedboats. Therefore engines are calibrated to optimize these demands. As the interaction of the engine and the boat is important for this aspect, final engine calibrations are done on the real boat or on an engine test bench using a virtual boat model and a HIL setup. A schematic of a HIL setup is shown in Fig. 1. Conducting the calibration on a test bench allows using more measurements and diagnoses tools and provides independence of environmental conditions. Nevertheless, test bench optimizations may be useless if the virtual boat given by the simulator does not represent the behavior of the speedboat well enough.

An important effect, that needs to be covered, occurs when the boat exceeds a certain speed (the hull or displacement speed), and changes from displacement to planing, where the boat is planing over the water surface, rather than displacing the water. This affects the resistance force acting on the boat enormously, as shown e.g. in [4], where the resistance force of a scaled model of a planing hull

R. Moreno-Díaz et al. (Eds.): EUROCAST 2011, Part II, LNCS 6928, pp. 129–136, 2012.

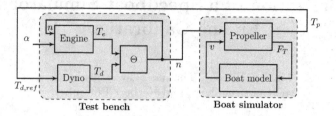

Fig. 1. Schematic of the virtual boat simulator for an engine test bench

is determined in laboratory conditions. Correct representation of this transfer from displacement to planing is crucial for satisfactory results on the test bench doing acceleration tests, especially as the operating point of the engine is the result of a closed-loop with the simulated boat.

2   Boat Model

A simulation model of a boat may be separated in two distinct parts: the propeller model, which represents both the load of the engine due to the propeller and the generated thrust accelerating the boat, and the longitudinal boat model, which represents the driving resistance acting on the boat hull and the resulting boat speed. The thrust F_T and the torque load produced by the propeller T_p may be modeled according to [1]

$$T_p = \rho_w n^2 d_P{}^5 \cdot k_Q\left(J\right) \tag{1}$$

$$F_T = \rho_w n^2 d_P{}^4 \cdot k_T\left(J\right) \tag{2}$$

with ρ_w being the density of the water, n being the rotational speed of the propeller, d_P being the diameter of the propeller and $k_Q\left(J\right), k_T\left(J\right)$ denoting nondimensional torque and thrust coefficients, respectively. Both of those characteristics depend on the *advance ratio* J which is defined as

$$J = \frac{v_a}{n \cdot d_P} \tag{3}$$

where v_a is the inflow velocity to the propeller. Assuming that the inflow to the propeller is not affected by the wake behind the boat, the boat velocity v may be used for this speed.

The longitudinal model of the boat (acceleration model) is described by

$$m\dot{v} = F_T - F_R \tag{4}$$

where m is the mass of the boat and F_R the resistance force acting on the boat. The resistance force is composed of various components, representing the viscous water resistance of the wetted surface of the hull, air resistance, spray and spray rail resistance and the wave resistance [2]. While one of the main components, the viscous water resistance, may be represented by (5) with S being the wetted surface area of the hull and C_F a frictional force coefficient depending on the Reynolds number, there is no simple formula expressing the wave resistance. The air resistance is defined by (6) where A is the projected surface of the boat and C_w is a resistance coefficient.

$$R_v = \rho_w \frac{v^2}{2} S \cdot C_F \tag{5}$$

$$R_a = \rho_a \frac{v^2}{2} A \cdot C_w \tag{6}$$

It is important to note that S and A are not constant and do depend on the driving state and the friction coefficient C_F depends on the Reynolds number and therefore on the water flow conditions. Additionally the values of the wetted surface and the projected surface are not known, as the pitch or trim angle of the boat during the test runs is unknown. Therfore a simplified model using a map $\tilde{F}_R(v)$ is used for modeling F_R:

$$F_R = v^2 \cdot \tilde{F}_R(v). \tag{7}$$

To account for an inertia effect in the change of the trim or pitch angle of the boat during the tranisition from displacement to planing, this formula is extended with a dynamic part, a low pass filter with a time constant k:

$$F_R = v^2 \tilde{F}_R(\tilde{v}) \tag{8}$$

$$\dot{\tilde{v}} = \frac{1}{k} \cdot v - \frac{1}{k} \cdot \tilde{v}. \tag{9}$$

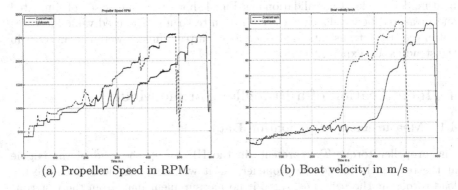

(a) Propeller Speed in RPM   (b) Boat velocity in m/s

Fig. 2. Upstream and downstream steady state measurments

3 Identification of the Resistance Force

The acting resistance force on the boat may be identified through a steady state boat measurement, setting constant engine rotational speeds and measuring the steady state velocity of the boat. With $v = $ const the longitudinal boat model yields $F_T = F_R$ and a way to determine the resistance force, if the thrust through the propeller is assumed to be known from (2). The map $k_T(J)$ for a given type of propeller is available in [1]. This is only an estimation as the according type of propeller is mainly used for large vessels and ships, and not speed boats. However it is the best available data, as usually no further data about the used propeller on the boat is available except for the diameter. Fig. 2 shows two time series data from an upstream and downstream test run with the speed boat, with the flow speed of the river compensated. From this data some steady state combinations of propeller speed and boat velocity are selected and with (2) and (9) the map $\tilde{F}_R(v)$ is calculated.

Additionally the data of acceleration test runs are available to validate the identified resistance model. Figure 3 shows the schematic of the longitudinal

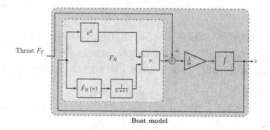

Fig. 3. Schematic of the longitudinal boat model

boat model, used in this validation and Fig. 4 shows the comparison of simulated and measured boat velocity for acceleration test runs. The used value for k was optimized using transients in the acceleration test runs as well as transients in the steady state experiments.

4 Identification of a Propeller Torque Model

4.1 Measurement of Validation Data

The propeller torque T_p represents in the HIL setup the load of the engine at the testbench due to the propeller. As it was not possible to measure the load torque at the test runs, there is no measurement data from the test runs available to identify $k_Q(J)$ in the propeller torque model of (1). Using the fact that throughout the acceleration test runs the engine was set to full throttle ($\alpha = 100\,\%$) and the rotational speed of the engine was recorded, it is possible

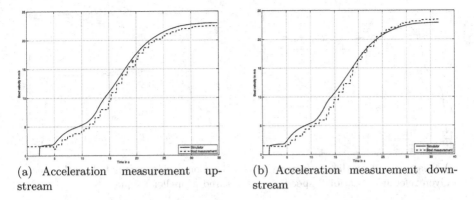

(a) Acceleration measurement upstream   (b) Acceleration measurement downstream

Fig. 4. Comparing the measured with simulated boat velocity – input: measured engine speed

to determine the propeller torque on the test bench. Using the identical engine and implementing an engine speed controller to follow the recorded engine speed at the acceleration test run on the boat, the resulting load approximates the propeller torque. The scheme of this setup is shown in Fig. 5, where n_{meas} is the reference value, and the necessary load T_d gives an approximation of the propeller torque.

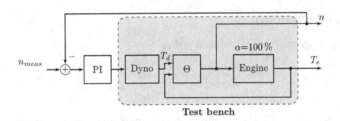

Fig. 5. Schematic of the test setup at the test bench to get an approximation of T_p

As the $k_Q(J)$ map shows typically similar characteristics as the $k_T(J)$ map [1], a first estimation of $k_Q(J)$ may be made based on the selected $k_T(J)$ map with some scaling applied [3]. With the torque measurement data available this model may now be validated with:

$$T_p = \rho_w n^2 d_P{}^5 \cdot k_Q(J) \tag{10}$$

$$J = \frac{v_a}{n \cdot d_P} \tag{11}$$

and using acceleration test run measurement data for n and v_a. With the engine speed being the same reference as in the test bench measurement, a valid model and especially a valid $k_Q(J)$ should result in a comparable propeller torque.

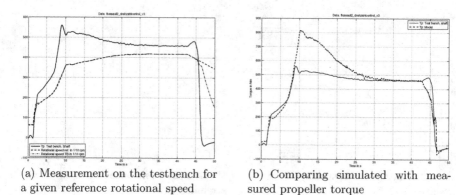

(a) Measurement on the testbench for a given reference rotational speed

(b) Comparing simulated with measured propeller torque

Fig. 6. Propeller torque

Fig. 6(a) shows the resulting propeller torque approximation created on the engine test bench, and a comparison of the measured engine rotational speed on the speed boat and at the test bench – the propeller torque approximation is reasonable, as it allows almost perfect tracking of the recorded engine speed. Fig. 6(b) shows on the other hand, that the propeller torque may not be reproduced by using this first approximation of the $k_Q(J)$ map and the measured $J(t)$.

4.2   Adaptation of k_Q

An exact k_Q map may be calculated using

$$k_Q(t) = \frac{T_p(t)}{\rho_w n(t)^2 d_P{}^5} \tag{12}$$

and the calculated $J(t)$. Fig. 7 shows $k_Q(t)$ over $J(t)$. Some ambiguity in the data becomes obvious in Fig. 7(b) showing that multiple values of k_Q belong to one value of J. Therefore there may not be a function $k_Q(J)$ that reproduces the propeller torque using the $J(t)$. A proper way to treat this situation is to exclude the ambiguous interval of the data, use the unambiguous intervals to calculate an approximated $\tilde{k}_Q$ map with a sensible choice in the missing interval (linear interpolation).This way there will be a discrepancy between the calculated T_p using this approximation of k_Q and the measured T_p in the excluded interval.

But the idea is that the data in this interval, more specific the J value, does not describe the state of the propeller correctly, and the real value of J is different to that one determined. A reason for the deviation in the J value may be the use of the measured boat velocity, which does not necessarily correspond to the inflow velocity of the propeller due to influences by the hull shape, the pitch angle of the boat due to hydrodynamic lift, the wake field behind the propeller and other hydrodynamic effects. Using the approximated map $\tilde{k}_Q\,(J)$ it is possible to calculate an ideal value $J^*\,(t)$, that reproduces the determined torque $T_p\,(t)$ with that map and define a ratio $\frac{J(t)}{J^*(t)}$. This ratio covers all effects causing a different inflow velocity (compared to boat velocity), and as boat pitch seems to be an important factor in this, we denote this as a (virtual) boat pitch correction factor γ:

$$\frac{J\,(t)}{J^*\,(t)} = \frac{\frac{v}{n\cdot d_P}}{\frac{v_i}{n\cdot d_P}} = \frac{v}{v_i} = \gamma \tag{13}$$

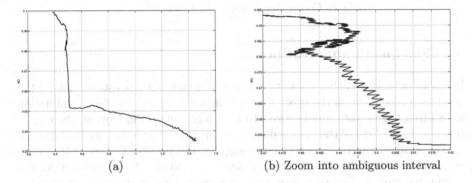

(a)   (b) Zoom into ambiguous interval

Fig. 7. Calculated k_Q over J with compensated time delay

4.3   Validation of Pitch

To validate the pitch correction factor and $\tilde{k}_Q$ map, a second test bench measurement with the same rotational reference speed (from an upstream acceleration test run) and a measurement with a different rotational reference speed (from downstream acceleration test run) are used.

   Figure 8(a) shows the result of the validation with the second data record of the same rotational reference speed, and Fig. 8(b) shows the results of using test bench measurement data from an experiment with different rotational reference speed (from downstream accleration test run). Keeping in mind that in a distinct boat acceleration test run the resulting wake field, the distribution and the exact velocity of the propeller inflow, the exact shape of bow and stern waves and other parameters will not be exactly the same, which all of it will influence the exact shape of the according (virtual) pitch correction, the results show a rather good match of the resulting propeller torque compared to the test bench measurement.

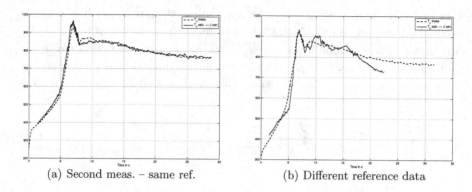

(a) Second meas. – same ref.   (b) Different reference data

Fig. 8. Comparing meas. T_p and validation T_p

5   Conclusion and Outlook

It has been shown in this work, that through a simplified resistance model the acceleration behavior of the speed boat is sufficiently reproduceable in simulation for a given engine rotational speed. To completely close the loop on the engine test bench, the load of the engine due to the propeller has to be modeled as well. As the available data showed some ambiguity, the necessary value $J(t)$ might not be calculated correctly in some ranges. Due to this fact a correction was introduced and applied to different measurement data, with promising results. In further work this correction factor may be improved and validated with additional data and by measurement of the speed boat pitch angle, possibly allowing to formulate the correction factor $\gamma(\alpha)$, in dependency of pitch angle α.

References

1. Carlton, J.: Marine Propellers and Propulsion, 2nd edn. Butterworth-Heinemann, Butterworth (2007)
2. Faltinsen, O.: Hydrodynamics of high-speed marine vehicles. Cambridge University Press, Cambridge (2005)
3. Pivano, L., Johansen, T., Smogeli, O.: A four-quadrant thrust estimation scheme for marine propellers: theory and experiments. IEEE Transactions on Control Systems Technology 17(1), 215–226 (2008)
4. Thornhill, E., Oldford, D., Bose, N., Veitch, B., Liu, P.: Planing hull model tests for cfd validation. In: 6th Canadian Marine Hydromechanics and Structures Conference, May 23-26 (2010)

WSN Clustering Using IC-SVD Algorithms

Zenon Chaczko

FEIT, University of Technology, Sydney, Australia
zenon.chaczko@uts.edu.au

Abstract. This paper presents a new biomimetic approach for sensor placement, clustering and data routing in Wireless Sensor Networks that can be deployed and managed in ubiquitous applications such as: security, business, automation, home and healthcare, precision agriculture, ecosystem monitoring and many more. Since hierarchical clustering can reduce the resource usage in sensor networks, we investigate Immuno-Computing and SVD-based algorithms for sensor clustering, routing and management of sensornet resources. The simulation results show that the proposed approach can improve robustness and extend the life-span of network infrastructures.

Keywords: WSNs, Resource Management, Immuno-Computing, SVD.

1 Introduction

Wireless Sensor Networks (WSNs) can be deployed in hostile environments such as: fires, space missions, oils spills or in situations where the recharging of sensor batteries is not possible. This is why resource management (i.e., energy, CPU, memory) is critical to the life-span of WSNs. In this research, a novel approach for sensor placement, their clustering and data routing that improves robustness and extends the WSN lifetime is being investigated. The method involves sensor clustering and routing that is adjusted according to multi-dimensional affinities (i.e., shape, size and minimal energy binding) among sensors, clusters of sensors and WSN routing paths to minimise use of resources, sustain communication and extend the system lifetime. This is achieved by generating a hierarchy of cluster-heads (CHs), according to their suitability to meet requirements of the sink with a minimal energy loss. The WSN lifetime can be defined as the time elapsed from the initialisation of the network infrastructure to the moment when critical functions can no longer be supported. For simplification, the WSN lifetime is determined by the time the first (last) node dies or when certain thresholds of the resource availability are reached. These thresholds, for example, can indicate that 50% of all active sensors are depleted of the basic resources. In the literature, there is a range of solutions for sensor clustering and routing to extend the WSN lifetime. Some of these approaches, consider heuristic methods of sensor organisation and data management[12]. Various issues related to WSN topology are increasingly receiving attention of the researach community[4],[5],[13].

R. Moreno-Díaz et al. (Eds.): EUROCAST 2011, Part II, LNCS 6928, pp. 137–145, 2012.
© Springer-Verlag Berlin Heidelberg 2012

2   Process of Sensor Clustering

A common sensor node clustering technique includes such procedural and decision making steps as:

1. *Presentation of the sensors.* The first stage involves assessment of sensor input vectors (i.e., data representation, quantities, categories and the scale of attributes) and a selection of the data transformation method(s).
2. *Selection of the basic method* involves cluster partitioning or agglomerative hierarchical approach.
3. *Selection of a specific clustering computation algorithm.*
4. *Selection of similarity (affinity) and dissimilarity (divergence) measures.* The selection of clustering algorithms involves the similarity/affinity metric and the criteria of clustering.
5. *Validity analysis of sensor clustering.* Validation includes making decisions on the number of clusters, their organisation, the assessment of validity of clusters and their stability.

For partitioning methods, an additional step of the initial grouping selection has to precede the assessment and validation tasks. Evaluation of sensor clustering can be intrinsic or extrinsic. For example, intrinsic evaluation [5] may involve measuring the cluster quality that tests the compactness of WSN clusters or checks if sensors in one cluster appear more alike when compared with sensors in other clusters.

2.1   Presentation of Sensors

When applying classification techniques in WSN it is necessary to transform the raw information about sensors into a more abstract, efficient and meaningful representation for further analysis and visualisation. A common approach is the space vector model where sensor parameters can be described by a numerical vector containing a list of the most important or relevant properties of the sensor (i.e. *3D* position, energy level, transmission range, precision, efficiency, error rates, cooperative capabilities, etc.). A sensor s_j can be represented as a vector:

$$s_j = (d_{1j}, d_{2j}, \ldots, d_{|n|j}) \qquad (1)$$

The d parameter is the set of descriptors defining the $|n|$ number of characteristic properties (columns) of a sensor and m is a number of sensors in the field (or a cluster), where p_{kj} represents a specific property of the sensor. In classification of sensors the weighting w_{jk} is introduced to address an importance of the property described by d_{jk}.

2.2   Selection of Basic Clustering Method

There are many methods of clustering that have been discussed by various authors [12],[13],[14]. Many clustering approches relate to applications in the WSN domain [8],[9],[11]. In general. these approaches can be divided into: agglomerative, partitioning, density, grid-based and dimensional reduction methods.

- **Agglomerative Methods.** In the agglomerative approach, initially all sensor nodes are separate and at the end of the process all nodes are somehow connected. These methods produce a tree-like class structures called dendrograms where the height of dendric branch gives an indication of similarity between sensor input vectors. There are two techniques of building the tree. One involves starting from a single sensor and the other starting from the entire set of sensors in the field. When starting with individual sensors, each sensor is initially inserted into a class of its own. Then, the two most similar sensors are put together into one class. The procedure is repeated until a predefined exit criteria is met.

- **Partitioning Methods.** In the partitioning method, at the start all sensor nodes are somehow interconnected, however at the end of the organisation process, nodes belong to separate clusters. Partitioning (Flat Clustering) methods are often used in the organisation of WSNs. Among these methods, commonly used are: the K-means (mobile centers), the K-medoids and the Dynamic Clouds methods. In the K-means method, the number of classes needed to be predefined. At first, the cluster centers need to be estimated and only then resolved. A sensor is put into a cluster if the distance between the sensor vector and the center of the cluster is the smallest when comparing the distances between the sensor vector and the centers of the other clusters.

- **Grid-Based Methods.** The Grid-based sensor grouping is based on the division of the sensor field space into multidimensional cells forming a grid, where sensors in the grid represent objects for grouping. Grouping of nearby cells occurs in terms of distance so that groups of sensors are built by aggregating the cells containing a sufficient number (density of) sensors. Multilayer grids can be used, each with an increased level of resolution.

- **Density-Based Methods.** A Density-based forming of sensor groups continues until the vicinity density exceeds a predefined threshold. The groups or sensor clusters are dense sensor zones separated by less dense zones. A sensor object is considered to be dense, if the number of its neighbours exceeds a given limit, and a sensor is close to another sensor while it is placed at a distance lower than a given (fixed) value. The discovery of a cluster is executed in two main steps: random finding of a sensor in a dense area of WSN and then forming a cluster by processing all attainable sensors starting from the first location, until the density limit is reached.

- **Dimension Reduction and Model Oriented Methods.** It is common for dimension reduction methods to follow a model of conceptual hierarchy where sensor classes relate to inherent sensor properties. The concept is based on a tuple (intention, extension) where the intention component expresses the maximum set of properties common to all sensor vectors and the extension component defines the maximum set of sensor vectors sharing the attributes. Self-Organising Maps (SOMs) method [11] is a prime example of dimension reduction and model-oriented approach. The SOM maps are made up of: (1) an input layer with classified sensors is represented by a multidimensional vector where for each individual sensor a neuron is assigned that represents the center of the cluster and (2) an output layer where various competing sensor nodes/neurons are activated according to a selected distance, where after an iterative process a single node is activated only.

2.3   Selection of Clustering Computation Algorithm

The choice and applicability of the computation algorithms used for sensor clustering remains an open problem. The difficulty mainly comes from the fact that an evaluation process is subjective by nature because there are often various possible relevant groupings for the same data set. However, the most common criteria used to select algorithms for clustering of sensors in the field are:

1. The ability to process large sets of unstructured data.
2. The sensor data must be as homogeneous as possible within each group, and the groups as distinct as possible. This aspect concerns the selection of a similarity measure.
3. A suitable representation that has a strong impact on sensor clustering.
4. Easy reading of results; the system needs to offer various modes of visualisation.

The model based clustering methods such as the SOM have been used in the domain of unsupervised learning for sometime[6]. There are a number of other competitive model driven techniques techniques that have been developed [10]. For example, the bi-clustering approach where both the sensor and the experiments are processed simultaneously to find appropriate context for clustering. In 2000, a graph-theoretic based method (CAST) that finds a minimum cut sets was proposed[2]; and relatively recently, the Bayesian Network model was introduced where observations are derived from modules (clusters) and processes [10]. Similarly to SOM, the proposed model based on SVD/IC clustering technique [5] orders the sensor groups into a topological map(s), that are inter-linked in the sensor field. The new technique considers that WSNs form an non-uniformed information space with a goal (sink) oriented set-up and minimum resource binding groupings.

2.4   Similarity (Affinity) and Dissimilarity Measures

The choice of similarity (distance), affinity (similarity in shape space) and dissimilarity/divergence measures (Table I) are an important area of research in bio-computing [1],[7]. The concept of shape-space was adopted from biology to help in quantifying the description of affinity between sensornets components. The shape-space is using a metric that is associated with distance affinity function. In the WSN domain, concerns with similarity/affinity measures are still not fully appreciated. One of the aims of this research is to demonstrate that both organisation and optimisation of sensornets can greatly benefit by departing from classical approaches to similarity measures for sensor classification and clustering to affinity measures seen as the problems representation space. It is well known that in biomimetic algorithms the measure of affinity can significantly affect the quality of the object selection and thus direct the computation to find

Table 1. Properties of Binary Vector Dissimilarity Measures

Measure	$S(X,Y)$	$D(X,Y)$
Correlation	$\frac{S_{11}S_{00}-S_{10}S_{01}}{\sigma}$	$\frac{1}{2} - \frac{S_{11}S_{00}-S_{10}S_{01}}{2\sigma}$
Dice	$\frac{S_{11}}{2S_{11}+S_{10}+S_{01}}$	$\frac{S_{10}+S_{01}}{2S_{11}+S_{10}+S_{01}}$
Jaccard-Needham	$\frac{S_{11}}{S_{11}+S_{10}+S_{01}}$	$\frac{S_{10}+S_{01}}{S_{11}+S_{10}+S_{01}}$
Kulzinski	$\frac{S_{11}}{S_{10}+S_{01}}$	$\frac{S_{10}+S_{01}-S_{11}+N}{S_{10}+S_{01}+N}$
Rogers-Tanmoto	$\frac{S_{11}+S_{00}}{S_{11}+S_{00}+2(S_{10}+2S)}$	$\frac{2(S_{10}+S_{01})}{S_{11}+S_{00}+2(S_{10}+2S)}$
Rogers-Tanmoto-a	$\frac{S_{11}+S_{00}}{S_{11}+S_{00}+2S_{10}+2S_{01}}$	$\frac{2(N-S_{11}-S_{00})}{2N-S_{11}-S_{00}}$
Russell-Rao	$\frac{S_{11}}{N}$	$\frac{n-S_{11}}{N}$
Sokal-Michener	$\frac{S_{11}+S_{00}}{N}$	$\frac{2(S_{10}+S_{01})}{S_{11}+S_{00}+2S_{10}+2S_{01}}$
Yule	$\frac{S_{11}S_{00}-S_{10}S_{01}}{S_{11}S_{00}+S_{10}S_{01}}$	$\frac{S_{10}S_{01}}{S_{11}S_{00}+S_{10}S_{01}}$

a better solution, if it actually exists (references). The affinity plays a crucial role in immuno-computing algorithms, as the majority of these algorithms use a one-shot technique when selecting candidates for further analysis. Using the one-shot approach for the selection of candidates in AIS/IC algorithms[7] can lead to more precise models. The methods does not eliminate a possible hybridisation with evolutionary approaches. Its true value lies in its simplicity, as the method allows implementation of a flexible learning process that still leaves a lot of space for extensions. However, an inappropriate choice of affinity measure in one-shot mechanism may limit, or even completely inhibit, chances for finding an optimal solution. Hence, departing from standard affinity measures, including Euclidean distance metric to more specialised metrics can offer a new class of interesting possibilities. The approach reflects specific aspects of the domain under investigation. The interaction between sensors can be evaluated via similarity measures between sensor attribute strings and there are many similarity measures methods available. The most common affinity measures for the generalised sensor or cluster shape can be described by a set of N parameters (size, type, resolution, charge, etc.) as: $S_k = <S_{k1}, S_{k2}, .., S_{kn}>$. Affinity for real-valued shape-spaces (distance measure) in $S^L \times S \to \mathcal{R}^+$ i.e. the Euclidean or the Manhattan metric while affinity for symbols shape-spaces in $S^L \times S \to \mathcal{R}^+$ can use the metrics such as Hamming distance, R-contiguous bits matching rule with transformation T-operator or R-contiguous bits matching rule without T-operator.

2.5   Validity Analysis of Sensor Clustering in WSN

Organisation of nodes in clusters needs to be interpretable for their internal homogeneity and external heterogeneity (i.e. internal validity indices). Considering large sensor populations, the number of clusters should be minimised. Clusters should be isolated from each other and their size should be selected carefully. The sensor classification should match sensor input vectors so that any variation in data should be self-evident. Nodes that belong to the same cluster should be

Algorithm 1. Pseudocode of MEBiC

1. *Initialization of clustering organisation selection*
2. *Obtain test set to determine goal of which to form cluster (X, Y, Z dims of the sink, 3D is the default)*
3. *Obtain training set to determine cluster formation. (X, Y, Z dimensions)*
4. *Execute SVD transformation on training set and return 3 largest singular values.*
5. *For each value 'v' in the right singular value matrix*
   (a) *Perform a dot vector operation on the inverted test set, right singular value of 'v' divided by the Eigenvalues in the matrix of dimension 'v,v' and return the result as binding energies vector.*
6. *Perform a Euclidean distance weight function of the inverted binding energies and the left singular value matrix and return as a single-dimension Euclidean distance weighting.*
7. *Sort the Euclidean distance weighting in ascending order, where the node ID with the lowest binding energy is ranked highest as it is closest bound to the test set.*
8. *Change new test set to coordinates of node ID with highest ranking (the most highly bound to input test set).*
9. *Divide sorted node ID list into number of nodes 'n' required for each cluster.*
   (a) *Randomly select the Cluster Head and bind each 'n' number of nodes to the cluster head into new cluster.*
10. *For each node in the sensor map*

Algorithm 2. SVD-Based Re-nomination of Cluster Heads

1. *Initialization of Re-nomination of Cluster Heads*
2. *Obtain test set to determine goal of which to form cluster (X, Y, Z dimensions of sink where 3D is a default)*
3. *For each cluster 'c' within the cluster formed sensor map*
   (a) *Obtain training set of all nodes belonging to cluster 'c' (X, Y, Z dimensions, 3D is a default)*
   (b) *Execute SVD transformation on training set and return 3 largest singular values.*
   (c) *For each value 'v' in the right singular value matrix*
      − *Perform a dot vector operation on the inverted test set, right singular value of 'v' divided by the Eigenvalues in the matrix of dimension 'v,v' and return the result as binding energies vector.*
   (d) *Perform a Euclidean distance weight function of the inverted binding energies and the left singular value matrix and return as a single-dimension Euclidean distance weighting.*
   (e) *Sort the Euclidean distance weighting in ascending order, where the node ID belonging in cluster 'c' with the lowest binding energy is ranked highest as closest bound to the test set.*
   (f) *Within the cluster "c", re-nominate the Cluster Head as the node ID with the highest ranking (the most highly bound to input test set).*
   (g) *For all other nodes "n" within the cluster set*
      − *Bind each node "n" to the newly re-nominated cluster head.*
4. *Exit on completion*

affine while nodes belonging to different clusters should somehow differ. Minor modifications in data or methods should not affect the results. Sensor clusters should correlate with external variable that are related to the given classification method but are not applied in clustering. A model driven biomimetic approach to sensor clustering and routing adapted for the realisation of WSN configuration and data delivery services was thoroughly examined. An integrated Cluster Validity Model (CVM) framework was developed to validate the quality of clustering in the simulated sensornet environment [5], [14]. The CVM integrates two separate sensor clustering validation tools: the Immuno-Computing Analysis (ICA) and the Cluster Validity Analysis Platform (CVAP) toolkits. The CVAP toolkit [14] can be used to validate the quality of sensor clustering (the unsupervised learning strategy) and the overall assessment of the WSN infrastructure. CVAP validation tests indicated that it is possible to significantly improve the WSN resource management using the IC-SVD-based renomination of CHs strategy and at the same time achieve levels of organisational quality comparable, and in many cases, superior to those achieved in systems based on the most popular unsupervised learning strategies. The aim of the approach is to quantify the organisational gain that translates to a better resource utilisation, increased robustness and improved cooperativeness in WSNs. This is achieved by supplementing the traditional and arbitrary clustering strategies by the IC-SVD-based techniques. The simulation results show that the IC-SVD-based CH renomination integrates well in WSNs. Addtionally, the IC-SVD-based CH renomination can improve the topology of WSN.

3 IC-SVD-Based Sensor Clustering

The experimental work in this section explores and verifies the suitability of IC-SVD based Minimum Energy Binding (MEB) algorithms for sensor clustering in WSN [5]. The MEB computations encapsulate a blend of autonomous behaviour in biological structures and aspects of non-uniform distribution of information in WSN infrastructures. The MEB algorithms address communication and energy constraints in networks made up of a large number of sensors that require effective mechanisms for the multi-hop data transmission. The most prominent feature of the MEB algorithms is their ability to allow individual sensors as well as and the entire WSN fields to monitor events by configuring nodes according to their affinity to events that occur in the environment and levels of resource availability. The configuration of the sensor field has an opportunistic character as the WSN resources that are organised according to the MEB model, reflect the needs and processing capability of the sink. The MEB class of algorithms can be applied to generate resource utilisation and quality of clustering/routing maps to support decision making in WSN. The MEB clustering and routing algorithms for WSN include: Minimum Energy Binding Clustering and Minimum Energy Binding Re-nomination of Cluster Heads algorithms (Algorithm 1 and 2). These algorithms use the SVD on a training set and then returns 3 largest singular values for each value $'v'$ in the right singular value matrix, then it performs a dot vector operation on the inverted test set, where the right singular value of $'v'$ is divided by the Eigen-values in the matrix of $'v,v'$ dimension and then the results are returned as the binding energy vector. In the following steps, the algorithms calculate the Euclidean distance weighting of the inverted binding energies and the left singular value matrix. Finally, the Euclidean distance weighting sorted in ascending order, such that the node ID with the lowest binding energy is ranked highest as it is the closest bound to the test set presented by the sink. The highlighted components in the listed algorithms indicate active SVD decomposition functions. The analysis of resource usage and areas for efficiency improvements can be aided by visual representations of resource distribution in the WSN (Fig. 1) that are generated by SVD-based MEB algorithms. The main application of the MEB clustering algorithm is to initiate and organise the process of IC-SVD reasoning in sensor clustering and routing.

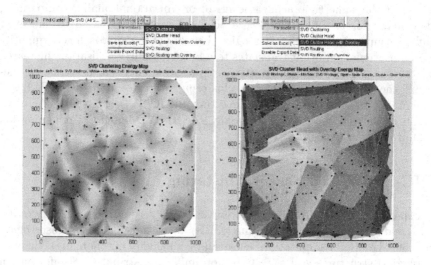

Fig. 1. Minimal energy binding maps for clustering in WSNs

4   Conclusion

The proposed biomimetic clustering and data routing approach performs better than many traditional cluster-based techniques. The simulation results indicate that using biology inspired sensor placement and IC-SVD algorithms for clustering and routing can increase the WSN lifetime. It is the author's s belief that the SVD-based CH renomination technique is a suitable strategy to be applied in many real-life WSN applications. When comparing the process cy'cles of IC-SVD with other approaches, it was found that SVD-based computation cycles run significantly longer.

References

[1]   Aickelin, U., Chen, Q.: On Affinity Measures for Artificial Immune System Movie Recommenders. In: Proceedings of the International Conference on Recent Advances in Soft Computing, RASC 2004, Nottingham, UK (2004)
[2]   Ben-Dor, A., Shamir, R., Yakhini, Z.: Clustering Gene Expression Patterns. Journal of Computational Biology 6(3/4), 281–297 (1999)

[3] Cao, Y., He, C., Wang, J.: A Backoff-Based Energy Efficient Clustering Algorithm for Wireless Sensor Networks. In: Jia, X., Wu, J., He, Y. (eds.) MSN 2005. LNCS, vol. 3794, pp. 907–916. Springer, Heidelberg (2005)

[4] Cerpa, A., Estrin, D.: ASCENT: Adaptive Self-configuring Sensor Networks Topologies. IEEE Trans. on Mobile Computing, Spec. Issue on Mission-Oriented Sensor Networks 3(3) (July-September 2004)

[5] Chaczko, Z.: Towards Epistemic Autonomy in Adaptive Biomimetic Middleware for Cooperative Sensornets. PhD thesis, UTS, Australia (July 2009)

[6] Chaczko, Z., Chiu, C.C., Moses, P.: Cooperative Extended Kohonen Mappings for WSN. In: Conference Proceedings of Computer Aided Systems Theory, Eurocast 2007, Las Palmas, Spain (2009)

[7] de Castro, L.N.: Fundamentals of Natural Computing: Basic Concepts, Algorithms, and Applications. Chapman and Hall/CRC, Taylor and Francis (2006)

[8] Dimokas, N., Katsaros, D., Manolopoulos, Y.: Node Clustering in Wireless Sensor Networks by Considering Structural Characteristics of the Network Graph. In: 4th International Conference on Information Technology, ITNG 2007, April 2-4, pp. 122–127 (2007)

[9] Fernandess, Y., Malkhi, D.: K-Clustering in Wireless Ad Hoc Networks. In: Proceedings of 2nd ACM Workshop on Principles of Mobile Computing, Toulouse, France, pp. 31–37 (2002)

[10] Friedman, N., Koller, D.: Probabilistic Graphical Models: Principles and Techniques. MIT Press, Cambridge (2009)

[11] Furuta, T., et al.: A New Cluster Formation Method for Sensor Networks Using Facility Location Theory, Nanzan University, Tech. Rep. 01 (2006), http://www.seto.nanzan-u.ac.jp/msie/nas/techreport/index.html

[12] Hussain, S., et al.: Genetic Algorithm for Energy Efficient Clusters in Wireless Sensor Networks. In: Proc. of the 4th International Conference on Information Technology: New Generations (ITNG 2007), Las Vegas, USA, April 2-4 (2007)

[13] Kang, T., et al.: A Clustering Method for Energy Efficient Routing in Wireless Sensor Networks. In: Proceedings of the 6th WSEAS Int. Conf. on Electronics, Hardware, Wireless and Optical Communications, Corfu Island, Greece, February 16-19 (2007)

[14] Wang, K.:Cluster Validity Analysis Platform, Version 3.5 (2007), http://www.mathworks.com/

Multi-dimensional Information Space View of Wireless Sensor Networks with Optimization Applications

Robin Braun and Zenon Chaczko

Centre for Real-time Information Networks, University of Technology, Sydney, Australia

Abstract. This paper presents an optimization example using a new paradigm for viewing the work of Wireless Sensor Networks. In our earlier paper [1] the Observed Field (OF) is described as a multi-dimensional "Information Space" (ISp). The Wireless Sensor Network is described as a "Transformation Space" (TS), while the information collector is a single point consumer of information, described as an "Information Sink" (ISi). Formal mathematical descriptions were suggested for the OF and the ISp. We showed how the TS can be formally thought of as a multi-dimensional transform function between ISp and ISi. It can be aggregated into a notional multi-dimensional value between $\{0, 1\}$. In this paper, this formal mathematical description is used to create a genetic algorithm based optimization strategy for creating routes through the TS, using a cost function based on mutual information. The example uses a connectivity array, a mutual information array and the PBIL algorithm.

1 Introduction

The optimization of Wireless Sensor Networks (WSNs) points to a need for a formal understanding of their underlying functions. Up to now, the emphasis has been on the functionality of the sensors, their interconnection and such things as power consumption. However, with the advent of so called ad-hoc networks, and the ability to deploy many hundreds of sensors in the field, there is a need to optimize this deployment for both energy consumption and efficacy in collecting the data. For example, the easiest way to collect information from a remotely located sensor may be a direct wireless link. However energy consumption for propagation is proportional to the square of the distance[2]. Therefore a multi hop solution may be more appropriate.

This paper expands [1] by extending the propositions to applications in the optimization of wireless sensor networks for energy efficiency.

The underlying assumption of this work is that the sensors, the information source, are attached to wireless devices that transfer the sensor information back to an information sink. The additional assumption is that these wireless devices are able to forward the information of other sensors until it ultimately reaches the information sink.

R. Moreno-Díaz et al. (Eds.): EUROCAST 2011, Part II, LNCS 6928, pp. 146–152, 2012.

This paper builds on the formal description of the Observed Field and its Information Space. It suggests ways to use these formal descriptions in the application of optimization methods such as Genetic Algorithms, or other biomimetic algorithms [3,4,5]

2   The Need for Optimization

There are a large number of areas in which WSNs need optimization. These mostly relate to the fundamental concept that the sensors are not wired, and hence cannot receive energy from a central source. The sensors are generally battery powered, which may be supplimented by harvesting energy from the environment. eg. Solar pannels or vibration generators.

This paucity of energy requires minimization of energy consumption. For example:

- There is no point in collecting information from one location that might be the same or very similar to the information from adjacent locations. Information collection and transmission all require energy
- If the communications link between any two locations is poor, this will result in corrupted packets and retransmissions, which all require energy
- If the information rate from a location is low, there would be no point in sampling it at the same rate as at another location with a high information rate
- The spatial sampling theorem also applies. No need to oversample a space
- etc.

Traditionaly our emphasis has been on functionality and robustness. This has mostly been to ensure connectivity, without a real understanding of the requirements of the underlying function of information collection. For example, if the temperature at a particular location on a bridge needs to be monitored over a few months, there is no problem if the temperature sample arrives a few days late - as long as it is date and time stamped.

The formulation described in this paper, and its predecessor, is designed to allow the creation of cost functions that can be used in the optimizations mentioned above. The next section describes an example.

3   An Example Using Population Based Incremental Learning (PBIL)

The PBIL algorithm was first described by Baluja [6,7] in 1994. It is a very simple but robust optimization algorithm. It relies on the problem space being describable by a binary string. A "population" of solutions is then created and tested against the cost function. The best of these solutions is then used to "steer" the generation of the next population. And so forth.

3.1 Connectivity

In our formulation, $\xi_{i,j}\,[nn, ne, ee, se, ss, sw, ww, nw] \in \{0,1\}$ we describe a factor that can be either 0 or 1, where $0 =$ no connection from i, j to its neighbour in that specific direction, and $1 =$ connected. We can view a small portion of the OF in tabular form.

$$
\begin{array}{|c|c|c|}
\hline
nw & nn & ne \\
\hline
ww & i,j & ee \\
\hline
sw & ss & se \\
\hline
\end{array}
=
\begin{array}{|c|c|c|}
\hline
i-1, j-1 & i, j-1 & i+1, j-1 \\
\hline
i-1, j & i, j & i+1, j \\
\hline
i-1, j+1 & i, j+1 & i+1, j+1 \\
\hline
\end{array}
$$

With an example

$$
=
\begin{array}{|c|c|c|}
\hline
0 & 1 & 1 \\
\hline
1 & i,j & 0 \\
\hline
0 & 0 & 1 \\
\hline
\end{array}
$$

In this case, $\xi_{i,j}\,[nn] = 1$, and $\xi_{i,j}\,[ww] = 1$, etc.

It can be seen that the connectivity from a particular node i, j to its neighbours, can be described by an 8 bit array of 0's and 1's. Remember that the origin of our OF is the top left hand corner of the array. Therefore, the fragment of the array at the origin would be;

$$
=
\begin{array}{|c|c|}
\hline
0,0 & 1 \\
\hline
1 & 0 \\
\hline
\end{array}
$$

We can see that an OF with N locations can be represented by an $8N$ array of values of either 1 or 0.

3.2 Mutual Information

We can use the same nomenclature as above to define the Mutual Information Im between a node and its neighbours.

$$Im_{i,j}\,[nn, ne, ee, se, ss, sw, ww, nw] = 0 \text{ for a perfect channel}$$

$$Im_{i,j}\,[nn, ne, ee, se, ss, sw, ww, nw] \neq 0 \text{ for a imperfect (noisy) channel}$$

If we sum up all the Mutual information for our TS, then we can use this as our Cost Factor.

We can see that $Im_{i,j}$ can be represented by an 8 element array of real values. Hence, an OF of N locations would be represented by an $8N$ length array of real values.

3.3 Formulation of the Problem for PBIL

PBIL requires an array of binary digits.

$\xi \rightarrow$	0	1	1	0	1	$\cdots$	0	0	1	1	0	0	1	1	Connectivity
$Im \rightarrow$	0.01	0.1	0.5	3	3	$\cdots$	0.001	2	4	1	1.5	1.3	2	2	Mutual Information
$\xi Im \rightarrow$	0	0.1	0.5	0	3	$\cdots$	0	0	4	1	0	0	2	2	Z = Sum this row

As a naive exemplar, let us assume that we have an OF of 16 locations (4 by 4). That implies a 128 bit array of connectivity bits C_k, and a 128 bit array of Mutual Information values.Im_k. Our cost factor is obtained by multiplying each connectivity bit by its Im and summing the products. The PBIL then works to minimise this to create a connectivity matrix that has the minimum added noise.

$$Z = \sum_{k=1}^{128} C_k Im_k$$

The PBIL algorithm starts with a 128 element Probability vector $Pv = 0.5$. It randomly generate C_k values based on Pv in epochs. It then analyses each epoch for lowest cost Z, using that one to modify the Pv. It iterates through this process until the Pv values are either 0 or 1. That is then the optimum solution.

There are obvious constraints that must be applied. For example, the result must include all actual paths that are required. Or, prevent circular paths.

4 Conclusions

In conclusion, we have shown how the Observed Field (OF) with its attendant Information Space (ISp) and the Information Theoretic Transform Space (TS) can be used to develop an optimization strategy for the path through a network. We have described the formulation based on a Genetic Algorithm, PBIL.

More work needs to be done so as to build a methodology for implementing this into a dynamically changing wireless sensor network.

Appensix A: The Information Space (ISp)

We include summaries of our the *Definitions, Propositions, Conditions* and *Assumptions* that we use here as originally described in our 2009 paper [1].

Definition 1. *We define the Observed Field (OF) as a three dimensional space, in which sensors with their wireless devices are located. We assume that the X and Y axis are equally divided to create an array of bins in which the sensors are located. These bins are defined by their i and j values. Sensors can be placed at any altitude Z in the bin, but the bin can contain only 1 or 0 sensors.*

Proposition 1. *We can define the Information Space for a particular information type (eg. temperature) by means of a two dimensional matrix.*

The central elements of the matrix are tupples that indicate the rate of flow of information for a particular location, the altitude of that location from the Base Plane, and the correlation between the information at that location and its nearest occupied neighbours, the connectivity between the nodes. The elements in matrix are "placeholders" for sensors that could be occupied or not. All of these elements are time variant. The elements are regularly located, with spacing such that the spacial sampling theorem is not abrogated.

No two sensors may be placed at the same location, even though their altitudes may be different. If this is neccesary, then the base plane needs to be rotated, or the granularity of the scale needs to be reduced.

Definition 2. *We make the following definitions*

- s_x and s_y are the grid spacings in the x and y dimension. Mostly $s_x = s_y$, and hence we define this as s_{xy}
- $0 \le i \le M$ is an integer indicating the index of the sensor location in the x direction, where the size of the field is $M + 1$
- $0 \le j \le N$ is an integer indicating the index of the sensor location in the y direction, where the size of the field is $N + 1$
- The physical location of the sensor is given by $xy_{i,j} = [s_x i, s_y j]$, or $xy_{i,j} = [s_{xy} i, s_{xy} j]$
- The rate of flow of information (the entropy $H(I)$) from a location is given by

$$H_{i,j} = \left\{ \begin{array}{ll} 0 & \text{no sensor at this location} \\ > 0 & \text{information rate in bits per second} \end{array} \right\}$$

- $a_{i,j} \ge 0$ is the altitude of the sensor at location i, j
- $\rho_{i,j}$ $[nn, ne, ee, se, ss, sw, ww, nw] \in \{-1, 1\}$ is an array of 8 valWe can now create the Global Mutual Information factor as follows:

Definition 3

$$I = \sum_{i=0}^{N} \sum_{j=0}^{M} \left(\frac{H(i,j) - \sum_{q=0}^{Q} x_{\left(P(I,J)_q\right),\left(P(I,J)_{q+1}\right)*}}{H\left(P(I,J)_q | P(I,J)_{q+1}\right)} \right)$$

- from $-1 \le \rho_{i,j}[n] \le 1$ which gives the correlation between the information coming from location i, j and its closest neighbouring location in the direction indicated. nn means North, ne means North East, etc.
- $\xi_{i,j}$ $[nn, ne, ee, se, ss, sw, ww, nw] \in \{0, 1\}$ is an array of 8 values from $0 \le \xi_{i,j}[n] \le 1$ which gives the connectivity between a node and its neighbour in that direction. nn means North, ne means North East, etc.
- Other parameters such as Trust, security and access rights could also be included.
- The Information Space can therefore be constructed as a multi-dimensional matrix

Appendix B: The Transformation Space (TS)

The TS is a multi-dimensional mathematical space that describes the transfer characteristics of information from any specific sensor to the IS.

Proposition 2. *The following is the summary of our conjectures.*

- We propose that for our firsts matrix, each of the sources has a direct single hop connection to each of the sinks
- We then propose that this can be expanded to describe a situation where the path from a particular information source to a particular information sink can be via other forwarders, that do not modifying the information in any way.
- We propose that the Connectivity can be described in terms of the Mutual Information between any two forwarders $Im_{i,j}$ or $Im_{j,i}$ and that these are additive along a path. (This is given effect by a cumulative subtraction as will be seen later.)
- In addition, we propose that the Cost of a connection $C(m)$ where m is the factor cost, can be described as $C(m)_{i,j}$ or $C(m)_{j,i}$. We further propose that this cost can be accumulated along the path.

Furthermore, we make the following definitions.

Definition 4. *First we need to define the Mutual Information along a path.*

- Assume we have a path A, B, C to D
- We define the Mutual Information between A and B as $I(A, B) = H(A) - H(A|B)$.
- We know that Mutual Information measures the information that A and B share[8]. Information is a measure of uncertainty. So, if A were perfectly known having observed B, there would be no uncertainty, and hence, no Mutual Information. Mutual Information increases as the artifacts of the channel add uncertainty about the source having observed the destination.
- We define the term, Path Mutual Information, as $I_p(A, D) = H(A) - H(A|B) - H(B|C) - H(C|D)$.
- Or more generally

$$I_p(1, N) = H(1) - \sum_{j=1}^{N-1} H(j|j+1)$$

References

1. Braun, R.C.: Towards a new Information-Centric view of wireless sensor networks. In: 4th International Conference on Broadband Communication, Information Technology & Biomedical Applications, Wroclaw, Poland, July 15-18 (2009)
2. Haykin, S.: Communication Systems, 4th edn. Wiley, Chichester (2000)

3. Chiang, F., Braun, R.: An event-based autonomic framework implementing bio-swarming intelligent mechanisms into ubiquitous service-oriented networks. International Journal of Pervasive Computing and Communications, JPCC 2006 (July 2006)
4. Chiang, F., Braun, R., Hughes, J.: A biologically inspired multi-agent architecture for autonomic service management. Journal of Pervasive Computing and Communications 2(3), 261–275 (2006)
5. Chiang, F., Braun, R.: Ant-based algorithms for resource management in vanets. LNCS (2007)
6. Baluja, S.: Population-based incremental learning. a method for integrating genetic search based function optimization and competitive learning. tech. rep., Carnegie-Mellon Univ. Pittsburgh PA Dept. of Computer Science (1994)
7. Baluja, S., Caruana, R.: Removing the genetics from the standard genetic algorithm. In: Machine Learning-International Workshop then Conference, pp. 38–46 (1995)
8. Golomb, S.W., Peile, R.E., Scholtz, R.A.: Basic Concepts in Information Theory and Coding: The Adventures of Secret Agent 00111, 1st edn. Springer, Heidelberg (1994)

Application of Morphotronic Theory to Parallel Robots

Zenon Chaczko[1] and Germano Resconi[2]

[1] Faculty of Engineering and Information Technology, University of Technology Sydney,
15 Broadway, Ultimo, NSW, Australia,2007
[2] Dept. of Mathematics and Physics,
Catholic University Brescia, I-25121, Italy
chaczko@uts.edu.au, resconi@numerica.it

Abstract. The main aim of this paper is to demonstrate the connection between parallel robotics and electronic circuits using the Morphotronic geometry. Parallel robotic system can be represented by a non Euclidean geometry which metric is the kinetic energy and the metric tensor is the mass metrics in the configuration space of the join angles. We can also remark that for electrical circuit we can have a similar non Euclidean geometry in the space of the currents or voltages. In this way we establish a morphological connection between the mechanical and electrical devises that we denote as Morphotronic. We present examples for the geometry in the kinetic space and example in the natural biological membrane represented by electrical circuits.

Keywords: Morphotronic geometry, parallel robotics, electronic circuits.

1 Introduction

The parallel robots have a number of advantages over the traditional serial robots due to their particular architecture. There are certain advantages of parallel robots, especially in the fields of assembly and medical applications. However, there are also some disadvantages associated with the parallel robots, which have impeded their wider use. The most notable drawback is that its particular architecture leads to smaller and irregular-shaped workspace and poorer dexterity. To achieve a parallel robot with acceptable workspace properties, the design parameters with regards to the geometric parameters must be optimized[1]. Based on the design goal, the optimal design of general parallel robots' kinematic parameters is classified into two categories. The first type of optimal design is where a set of parameters of a parallel robot [5, 6, 8] whose workspace is a maximized one, is found. The second type of optimal design is concerned with the dimensional synthesis of parallel robots and tries to fit a prescribed working region as closely as possible.

In this paper, we shall exploit the analogies between the electrical circuit and the mechanical system that would help us to apply concepts of the Morphotronic System theory [2, 12] in order to study the properties of the parallel robot system.

R. Moreno-Díaz et al. (Eds.): EUROCAST 2011, Part II, LNCS 6928, pp. 153–160, 2012.
© Springer-Verlag Berlin Heidelberg 2012

2 Kinetic Energy as a Metric

Under the geometry and geodesic model we can study physical and geometric properties. In fact, we know that in physics of the possible configuration we have free variables (independent) and conditioned variables (dependent). It is possible to identify these relations (constraints) between the free variables and conditioned variables. It is also known that the kinetic energy for all the variables, dependent or independent is the ordinary expression. For a spherical surface, we can define the constraints and we can show their geometric image.

$$T = \frac{1}{2} m \frac{dx^i}{dt} \frac{dx^j}{dt} \tag{1}$$

The relation between independent q variables with the dependent variables x can be expressed as

$$\begin{cases} x_1 = x_1(q_1, q_2, ..., q_n) \\ x_2 = x_2(q_1, q_2, ..., q_n) \\ ... \\ x_m = x_m(q_1, q_2, ..., q_n) \end{cases} \tag{2}$$

and

$$a_{i,j} = \sum_{h,k} \frac{\partial x_i}{\partial q_h} \frac{\partial x_j}{\partial q_k} \tag{3}$$

The kinetic energy can be denoted for independent variables q as a geodesic:

$$T = \frac{1}{2} m a_{i,j}(q) \frac{dq^i}{dt} \frac{dq^j}{dt} = \frac{1}{2} M_{i,j}(q) \frac{dq^i}{dt} \frac{dq^j}{dt} \tag{4}$$

where the tensor a is function of q:

$$a_{i,j}(q)$$

Include the action of field on the given n dimensional configuration space. The cost or geodesic function for the physical phenomena can be expressed as:

$$C = \int dt \sqrt{\frac{1}{2} M_{i,j}(q) \frac{dq^i}{dt} \frac{dq^j}{dt}} \tag{5}$$

The cost function can substitute in a geometric way the classical Hamiltonians and Lagrangians, as well as the Hamilton principle. It can be said that also in physics we have "Intentionality," but a physical system does not have the possibility to control its intentionality (geodesic). For example, in the brain, we have the intentionality that we can control.

2.1 Examples

For the spherical surface we have the constrains

$$y_1^2 + y_2^2 + y_3^2 = r^2 \tag{6}$$

The geometric image of the constraint is depicted in Fig 2.

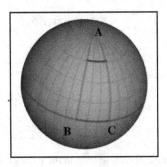

Fig. 2. Illustration of the geodesic principle. The geodesics shows lines (AB, AC) with a minimum cost.

The radium of the sphere is constant. The free (independent) variables are α and β and all the other variables are x_1, x_2, x_3. The relation between independent variables and the other variables is:

$$\begin{cases} x_1 = r\sin(\alpha)\cos(\beta) \\ x_2 = r\sin(\alpha)\sin(\beta) \\ x_3 = r\cos(\alpha) \end{cases} \tag{7}$$

This relation is a constraint that we can represent as the surface in figure 16. Now we compute the geodesic in the space (x_1, x_2, x_3) and the reduce space of the independent variables α and β. So we have:

$$\begin{aligned} T &= \frac{1}{2}m[(\frac{dx_1}{dt})^2 + (\frac{dx_2}{dt})^2 + (\frac{dx_3}{dt})^2] \\ &= \frac{1}{2}m[(\frac{dx_1}{d\alpha}\frac{d\alpha}{dt} + \frac{dx_1}{d\alpha}\frac{d\beta}{dt})^2 + (\frac{dx_2}{d\alpha}\frac{d\alpha}{dt} + \frac{dx_2}{d\alpha}\frac{d\beta}{dt})^2 + (\frac{dx_3}{d\alpha}\frac{d\alpha}{dt} + \frac{dx_3}{d\alpha}\frac{d\beta}{dt})^2] \\ &= \frac{1}{2}m[r^2(\frac{d\alpha}{dt})^2 + r^2\sin^2(\alpha)(\frac{d\beta}{dt})^2] \end{aligned} \tag{8}$$

And the function cost that must be at the minimum value is:

$$C = \int dt \sqrt{\frac{1}{2} m \left[\left(\frac{dx_1}{dt} \right)^2 + \left(\frac{dx_2}{dt} \right)^2 + \left(\frac{dx_3}{dt} \right)^2 \right]}$$

$$= \int dt \sqrt{\frac{1}{2} m \left[r^2 \left(\frac{d\alpha}{dt} \right)^2 + r^2 \sin^2 (\alpha) \left(\frac{d\beta}{dt} \right)^2 \right]} \qquad (9)$$

3 Parallel Robot System and Kinetic Energy as a Metric

Given the simple image of the parallel robot

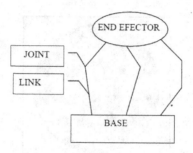

Fig. 1. Scheme of a close loop in the parallel robot system

We can define the two spaces, the space of the configuration given by the join angles and the end effector space [2, 6,]. Now the variables of the join space are not all independent so we have the systems of equations:

$$\begin{cases} \beta_1 = \beta_1 (\alpha_1, \alpha_2, \ldots, \alpha_n) \\ \beta_2 = \beta_2 (\alpha_1, \alpha_2, \ldots, \alpha_n) \\ \quad \ldots \\ \beta_m = \beta_m (\alpha_1, \alpha_2, \ldots, \alpha_n) \end{cases} \qquad (10)$$

Where the angles β are the independent joint angles and α are all the join angles. The positive definiteness of the inertial matrix follows directly from the fact that the kinetic energy of the manipulator is always positive and is zero only if the system is at rest. It actually defines a Riemannian metric in the joint space, so called the kinetic energy metric which in turn also defines a compatible kinetic energy connection, with respect to which the momentum and the velocity are covariant and controvariant tensors in the kinematic metric space.

$$P_j = M_{i,j}(q^i) \frac{dq^i}{dt} = M_{i,j}(q^i) v^i \qquad (11)$$

and

$$Force = \frac{dp_j}{dt} = M_{i,j} \frac{dv^i}{dt} + \frac{dM_{i,j}}{dt} v^i = M_{i,j} D_k v^k \qquad (12)$$

Fig. 3. An industrial parallel robotic system from Micos (USA) [9]

Where D_k is the covariant derivative in the kinematic metric space where the mass matrix is the metric tensor. The force is the general force (forces and torque) in the kinetic metric space. In we found that the previous Newton law in Kinematic metric space has these properties [1, 2]. The notation can be seen as compact and very useful for different formulations. However, the important point is the geometrical concept synthesizes all these various approaches and thus allows one to use a mix of different methods in dealing with the formulations of a complex system dynamics. The relationship between the different types of formulations can be viewed to be ultimately linked to the physical forces and Newton's Law for point masses. Hence, with this unifying concept it is possible to combine them together to form the dynamics equation for the entire system. In this sense, the presented approach is a mix of different dynamics formulations aiming at preserving merits of those other different approaches as they are applied to different areas of the problem. The discussed unifying concept also generalizes some of the principles used in the previous research work to remedy the drawbacks of different formulations for parallel manipulators, namely cutting of links and transformation of forces. An example of the industrial 6 axes parallel robot system is shown in Fig.3.

4   Geometry of Electrical Circuit in Morphotronics

Any electrical circuit defines the relation between voltages and currents in as follows:

$$v_j = f_j(i_1, i_2, \ldots, i_n)$$

(13)

Since the expression of the dissipate power W is

$$W = i^1 v_1 + i^2 v_2 + i^3 v_3 + \ldots + i^n v_n$$

(14)

hence

$$W = i^1 f_1 + i^2 f_2 + i^3 f_3 + \ldots + i^n f_n$$

(15)

When the edges are separate one from the others we have n free variables so the power can be write as follows:

$$W = R_1\,i_1^2 + R_2\,i_2^2 + R_3\,i_3^2 + \,.....\, + R_n\,i_n^2$$

$$for$$

$$v_j = R_j i_j^2$$

(16)

Here, when the edges in a circuit are connected, we can reduce the independent currents from n to $p < n$, we obtain:

$$i_j = \alpha_{1,j}\,i_1 + \alpha_{2,j}\,i_2 + \alpha_{3,j}\,i_3 + \,.....\, + \alpha_{p,j}\,i_p$$

(17)

We find that all the n currents are linear combination of the independent currents p. In this situation the power assume the following form:

$$W = R_1\,(\alpha_{1,1}i_1 + ... + \alpha_{p,1}i_p)^2 + R_2(\alpha_{1,1}i_1 + ... + \alpha_{p,1}i_p)^2 + R_3\,(\alpha_{1,2}i_1 + ... + \alpha_{p,2}i_p)^2 + ...$$

$$+ R_n\,(\alpha_{1,n}i_1 + ... + \alpha_{p,n}i_p)^2$$

(18)

Therefore, the power can be expressed in the following form

$$W = \sum_{h,k} g_{h,k}\,i^h\,i^k = g_{h,k}\,i^h\,i^k$$

(19)

the metric tensor g is given by:

$$g = \alpha^T R\,\alpha$$

(20)

where

$$\alpha = \begin{bmatrix} \alpha_{1,1} & \alpha_{1,2} & \cdots & \alpha_{1,p} \\ \alpha_{2,1} & \alpha_{2,2} & \cdots & \alpha_{2,p} \\ ... & ... & ... & ... \\ \alpha_{n,1} & \alpha_{n,2} & \cdots & \alpha_{n,p} \end{bmatrix}, \quad R = \begin{bmatrix} R_1 & 0 & ... & 0 \\ 0 & R_2 & ... & 0 \\ ... & ... & ... & ... \\ 0 & 0 & ... & R_n \end{bmatrix}$$

(21)

Since

$$i^j = \frac{dq^j}{dt} \quad j = 1,2,3,....., p \quad and \quad W = \frac{dE}{dt}$$

(22)

Where E is the energy and W the power an q the charge, the geodesic equation can write in this way

$$dE = \sum_{h,k} g_{h,k}\,dq^h\,dq^k = \sum_{h,k} \left(\sum_{j,i} \alpha_{k,j} R_{j,i} \alpha_{i,k} \right) dq^h\,dq^k$$

(23)

For Maxwell theorem in an electrical circuit, the dissipative power W assumes the minimum value. Thus, the power is comparable with the Lagrangian in mechanics (Hamilton'a principle) or the Fermat principle in optics (minimum time). Now, the geodesic in space of the charges can be expressed as:

$$\delta \int \sqrt{W}\, dt = \delta \int \sqrt{g_{h,k} i^h i^k}\, dt = \delta \int \sqrt{g_{h,k} \frac{dq^h}{dt}\frac{dq^k}{dt}}\, dt = 0 \tag{24}$$

Now for the Euler differential equations we have that the minimum condition can be found when

$$\frac{d}{dt}\frac{\partial \sqrt{g_{h,k} i^h i^k}}{\partial i^j} - \frac{\partial \sqrt{g_{h,k} i^h i^k}}{\partial q^j} = 0 \tag{25}$$

The geodesic as a power can be visualized as in Fig. 4.

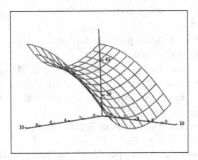

Fig. 4. Minimum electrical power in the geodesic trajectory

5 Conclusion

In conclusion, any electrical circuit generate a deformation of the currents space of the power and geodesic trajectories.

Between electrical circuit and the mechanics of the parallel robot system we have the similarity relations as follows:

Parallel robot	Electrical circuit
Position q	Charges q
Momentum p	Voltage E
velocity	Current I

This geometric similarity justifies the name "Morphotronic" that we use in our research work. Between velocity and momentum in parallel robot (mechanics) there is a well known relation:

$$p_j = a_{i,j} \frac{dq^i}{dt} = a_{i,j} v^i \quad (15)$$
(36)

That is the same relation between the voltages sources E and the current

$$E_j = Z_{i,j} \frac{dq^i}{dt} = Z_{i,j} I^i \quad (16)$$
(37)

References

1. Brockett, R., Stokets, A., Park, F.C.: A geometrical formulation of the dynamics equations describing kinematic chains. In: Proceedings of IEEE International Conference on Robotics and Automation (1996)
2. Chaczko, Z., Resconi, G.: Morphotronic system applications. In: Moreno-Díaz, R., Pichler, F., Quesada-Arencibia, A. (eds.) EUROCAST 2009. LNCS, vol. 5717, pp. 905–912. Springer, Heidelberg (2009)
3. Chaczko, Z.: Towards Epistemic Autonomy in Adaptive Biomimetic Middleware for Cooperative Sensornets, PhD thesis, University of Technology, Sydney, Australia (2009)
4. Chaczko, Z., Resconi, G.: Organising Software Infrastructures: EgoMorphic BIM Model. International Journal of Computing Anticipatory Systems 21, 372–385 (2008); ISSN 1373-5411 ISBN 2-930396-08-3
5. Clavel, R.: Conception d'un robot parallèle rapide à 4 degrés de liberté, Ph.D. Thesis, EPFL, Lausanne, Switzerland (1991)
6. Kuen, Y.Y.: Geometry, Dynamics and Control of Parallel Manipulators Thesis Submitted to the Hong Kong University of Science and Technology in Partial Fulfillment of the Requirements for the Degree of Doctor of Philosophy in Electrical and Electronic Engineering, Hong Kong (August 2002)
7. Tsai, L.-W.: Robot Analysis: Mechanics of Serial and Parallel Manipulators. John Wiley and Sons, Canada (1999)
8. Merlet, J.P.: Parallel Robots, 2nd edn., pp. 12–13. Springer, Netherlands (2006)
9. Micos   USA   (2011),   http://www.micosusa.com/old/_event/action/paros2.html (viewed on April 10, 2011)
10. Resconi, G.: Modelling Fuzzy Cognitive Map By Electrical and Chemical Equivalent Circuits. In: Joint Conference on Information Science, Salt Lake City, USA, July 8-24 (2007)
11. Resconi, G., Srini, V.P.: Electrical Circuit As A Morphogenetic System. GEST International Transactions on Computer Science and Engineering 53(1), 47–92 (2009)
12. Resconi, G., Chaczko, Z.: Morphotronic system (Theory). In: Moreno-Díaz, R., Pichler, F., Quesada-Arencibia, A. (eds.) EUROCAST 2009. LNCS, vol. 5717, pp. 9–16. Springer, Heidelberg (2009)
13. Resconi, G., Jain, L.: Intelligents Agents. Springer, Heidelberg (2004)
14. Resconi, G.: The Morphogenetic Systems in Risk Analysis. In: Proceeding of the International Conference on Risk Analysis and Crisis response, Shanghai, China, September 25-26, pp. 161–165 (2007)
15. Resconi, G., van der Wal, A.J.: Morphic Computing: Concepts and Foundation. In: Resconi, G., Nikravesh, M. (eds.) Morphogenetic Neural Network
16. Treyer, E. W.: Caltech laboratory, CNS 221 Spring 2006 Lecture 1, http://www.klab.caltech.edu/~cns221
17. Young E.: 5-3164 System Biology II Neural Network (580-422) Lecture 9 nonlinear cable theory, http://eyoung@jhu.edu

Mechatronics and the Bond Graph Theory Extended by the Morphotronic Systems

Germano Resconi[1] and Zenon Chaczko[2]

[1] Dept. of Mathematics and Physics,
Catholic University Brescia, I-25121, Italy
[2] Faculty of Engineering and Information Technology, University of Technology Sydney,
15 Broadway, Ultimo, NSW, Australia, 2007
resconi@numerica.it, chaczko@uts.edu.au

Abstract. Mechatronics plays an important role in surgical, automotive, food and industrial applications. To become smarter and more robust, mechatronic systems have to rely on numerous objects and controls that operate in a diverse range of conditions. These controls can exhibit undesirable and coupled behavior. Adjusting the controllers in hardware is difficult and time consuming, often resulting in de-tuning the system below acceptable performance levels. The Morphotronics theory aided by a new approach to the Bond Graph theory represents an improvement to traditional computation models used for the analysis of mechatronic systems. Morphotronics use non-Euclidean geometry for context shaping and defining the projection operators in an ideal network of mechatronic forms.

Keywords: Morphotronic theory, bond graph, mechatronics.

1 Introduction

In classical mechanics we can study the behaviour of the system by considering only two complementary variables, the velocity and the momentum. The bond between velocity and the momentum is the mass. With the bond we can move from the momentum to velocity and reverse. The mechanical energy is the scalar product of the velocity and the momentum. The energy structure offers the internal rules (differential equations) which can be used to compute the movement of the masses. Applying the Bond Graph theory we can compare mechanical and electronic systems[7] which are inherent parts of Mechatronics. It can be demonstrated that we can improve the bond graph characteristics and extend it to a more general mathematical model denoted as the Morphotronic system. When we substitute the velocity with the current and the momentum with the voltages, the bond is characterised by the impedances which we can then compute from the voltages, the current and reverse. The Morphotronics formal language is based on the *incidence matrix* that show the relationship (form) between the two classes of objects. In mechanical systems, the incidence matrix is the relationship between the velocity and the momentum, and in electrical circuits, the incidence matrix is the relationship between the currents and the voltage. In Morphotronics, the incidence matrix is the basic system where relation the flow and

R. Moreno-Díaz et al. (Eds.): EUROCAST 2011, Part II, LNCS 6928, pp. 161–169, 2012.

effort relation is set in as the two classes of variables. The bond is defined by the values of this relation and the power is the scalar value given by the scalar product in the general coordinates of the flow and effort. In our previous papers [3, 4, 10, 11] the flow is denoted as attributes and the effort is described by the objects. The electrical power is the scalar product of the voltages and currents that defines the internal structure of the electrical circuit. It is possible to reproduce the same structure for different domains and find analogies across different disciplines such as: mechanics, electronics, biology, thermodynamics, optimisation, fuzzy set , risk analysis, conceptual imaging, quantum computer and mechanics, constructal theory, heuristic algorithms, wireless sensor networks, cloud computing, system of systems, SVD decomposition and many other areas. Since, it is possible to build a prototype for the above listed cases of the system that resembles an electronic device, authors of this paper introduced the name of "Morphotronic System" [3, 10] for the purpose to describe a new general computation model and geometry (Morphotronic) that allows to study the elasticity of networks, the best trajectories or even the entire space of ideal kinematic chains (conformations) of the movements in the system at both macro and micro (nano) scale [1, 2]. Specifically, this work aims to show how the morphotronics can help in analysis and design of mechatronic systems

2 Morphotronic System and the Bond Graph in Mechatronics

Let us first introduce the Morphotronic system model that uses a novel mathematical representation of the bond theory that is extensively used when conceptualizing the mechatronic device that interconnects mechanical and electrical devices. We begin with a simple example of the electrical circuit (Fig. 1) to show the bond graph in a new form.

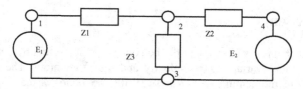

Fig. 1. Electrical Circuit with two generators and three impedances

In the electrical circuit we have two loops 123 , 243 that are associated with two currents (or flows) f_1 , f_2. There are also three voltages e_1, e_2, e_2 for the couple of points 12 , 23, 24. Hence, the incidence matrix between the currents and the voltages can be defined as:

$$
\begin{array}{c}
\begin{array}{cc} f_1 & f_2 \end{array} \\
\begin{array}{c} e_1 \\ e_2 \\ e_3 \end{array}
\begin{bmatrix}
1 & 0 \\
1 & 1 \\
0 & 1
\end{bmatrix}
\end{array}
\tag{1}
$$

Since the previous matrix assembles the individual loops 123, 243 in one network (Fig.1) , we denote the incident matrix as the assembling Boolean matrix. We remark that we take the direction of the currents all the same in the loops. Given the incidence matrix in (1) we can built the bond graph as depicted in Fig 2.

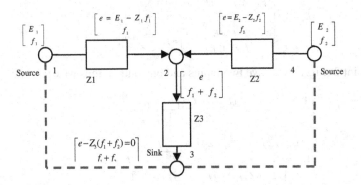

Fig. 2. Bond graph from incidence matrix (1)

Where

$$\begin{cases} e_1 = e - E_1 \\ e_2 = e \\ e_3 = e - E_2 \end{cases} \qquad (2)$$

The dashed lines (Fig 2) form the part of the circuit where the voltage generators are found that are input to the bond graph. In the below discussion, all the internal transformations given in the Fig.2 will be demonstrated. The first transformation is denoted as B_1 and can be expressed as:

$$\begin{bmatrix} E_1 - Z_1 f_1 \\ f_1 \end{bmatrix} = B_1 \begin{bmatrix} E_1 \\ f_1 \end{bmatrix}$$

That can write in this formal way

$A = B_1 C$

where

$$A = \begin{bmatrix} E_1 - Z_1 f_1 \\ f_1 \end{bmatrix}, C = \begin{bmatrix} E_1 \\ f_1 \end{bmatrix} \qquad (3)$$

Note that $A(C^T C)^{-1} C^T C = A$ thus $B_1 = A C^T (C^T C)^{-1}$, however $A(\Lambda^T C)^{-1} \Lambda^T C = A$ hence $B_1 = A(\Lambda^T C)^{-1} \Lambda^T$ The matrix Λ is a parametric matrix. So we have infinite number of solutions for B that in our case are given by the expression

$$B_1 = A(\Lambda^T C)^{-1} \Lambda^T = \begin{bmatrix} (E_1 - Z_1 f_1)\lambda_1 & (E_1 - Z_1 f_1)\lambda_2 \\ f_1 \lambda_1 & f_1 \lambda_2 \end{bmatrix} \frac{1}{\lambda_1 E_1 + \lambda_2 f_1} \qquad (4)$$

For example, with $\lambda_1 = 0.5$, $\lambda_2 = 0.5$ we obtain:

$$B_1 = \frac{1}{2}\left[\frac{(E_1 - Z_1 f_1)}{f_1} \quad \frac{(E_1 - Z_1 f_1)}{f_1}\right]\frac{1}{\frac{1}{2}(E_1 + f_1)} \tag{5}$$

$$B_1 C = \left[\frac{(E_1 - Z_1 f_1)}{f_1} \quad \frac{(E_1 - Z_1 f_1)}{f_1}\right]\frac{1}{E_1 + f_1}\left[\begin{matrix} E_1 \\ f_1 \end{matrix}\right]$$

$$= \frac{1}{(E_1 + f_1)}\left[\frac{(E_1 - Z_1 f_1)}{f_1} \quad \frac{(E_1 - Z_1 f_1)}{f_1}\right]\left[\begin{matrix} E_1 \\ f_1 \end{matrix}\right]$$

$$= \frac{1}{(E_1 + f_1)}\left[\frac{(E_1 - Z_1 f_1)(E_1 + f_1)}{f_1(E_1 + f_1)}\right] = \left[\frac{E_1 - Z_1 f_1}{f_1}\right]$$

At the cross point 2 (Fig.1) we have two inputs and one output, thus we can write

$$B_1 = \frac{1}{2}\left[\frac{(E_1 - Z_1 f_1)}{f_1} \quad \frac{(E_1 - Z_1 f_1)}{f_1}\right]\frac{1}{\frac{1}{2}(E_1 + f_1)} \tag{6}$$

$$B_1 C = \left[\frac{(E_1 - Z_1 f_1)}{f_1} \quad \frac{(E_1 - Z_1 f_1)}{f_1}\right]\frac{1}{E_1 + f_1}\left[\begin{matrix} E_1 \\ f_1 \end{matrix}\right]$$

$$= \frac{1}{(E_1 + f_1)}\left[\frac{(E_1 - Z_1 f_1)}{f_1} \quad \frac{(E_1 - Z_1 f_1)}{f_1}\right]\left[\begin{matrix} E_1 \\ f_1 \end{matrix}\right]$$

$$= \frac{1}{(E_1 + f_1)}\left[\frac{(E_1 - Z_1 f_1)(E_1 + f_1)}{f_1(E_1 + f_1)}\right] = \left[\frac{E_1 - Z_1 f_1}{f_1}\right]$$

At the cross point 2 we have two inputs and one output, so we have

$$\left[\begin{matrix} (E_1 - Z_1 f_1) = e & (E_2 - Z_2 f_2) = e \\ f_1 & f_2 \end{matrix}\right] \rightarrow \left[\begin{matrix} e \\ f_1 + f_2 \end{matrix}\right] \tag{7}$$

and

$$\left[e = E_1 - Z_1 f_1 = E_2 - Z_2 f_2 \quad f_1 \quad f_2\right] \rightarrow \left[e \quad f_1 + f_2\right] \tag{8}$$

the incidence matrix is

$$A = \left[\begin{matrix} e_1 & f_{1,1} & f_{1,2} \\ e_2 & f_{2,1} & f_{2,2} \\ \cdots & \cdots & \cdots \\ e_m & f_{m,1} & f_{m,2} \end{matrix}\right]$$

Now, the following equation needs to be solved

$$A w = B$$
$$where$$

$$A = \left[\begin{matrix} e_1 & f_{1,1} & f_{1,2} \\ e_2 & f_{2,1} & f_{2,2} \\ \cdots & \cdots & \cdots \\ e_m & f_{m,1} & f_{m,2} \end{matrix}\right], w = \left[\begin{matrix} w_1 \\ w_2 \\ w_3 \end{matrix}\right], B = \left[\begin{matrix} e_1 & f_{1,1} + f_{1,2} \\ e_2 & f_{2,1} + f_{2,2} \\ \cdots & \cdots \\ e_m & f_{m,1} + f_{m,2} \end{matrix}\right] \tag{9}$$

The equation $Aw=B$ can't be solved; hence the previous equation has to be modified:

$$A^T A w = A^T B$$
$$and$$

$$w = (A^T A)^{-1} A^T B = \begin{bmatrix} w_{1,1} & w_{1,2} \\ w_{2,1} & w_{2,2} \\ w_{3,1} & w_{3,2} \end{bmatrix}$$

$$= \left(\begin{bmatrix} e_1 & f_{1,1} & f_{1,2} \\ e_2 & f_{2,1} & f_{2,2} \\ \dots & \dots & \dots \\ e_m & f_{m,1} & f_{m,2} \end{bmatrix}^T \begin{bmatrix} e_1 & f_{1,1} & f_{1,2} \\ e_2 & f_{2,1} & f_{2,2} \\ \dots & \dots & \dots \\ e_m & f_{m,1} & f_{m,2} \end{bmatrix} \right)^{-1} \begin{bmatrix} e_1 & f_{1,1} & f_{1,2} \\ e_2 & f_{2,1} & f_{2,2} \\ \dots & \dots & \dots \\ e_m & f_{m,1} & f_{m,2} \end{bmatrix}^T \begin{bmatrix} e_1 & f_{1,1} + f_{1,2} \\ e_2 & f_{2,1} + f_{2,2} \\ \dots & \dots \\ e_m & f_{m,1} + f_{m,2} \end{bmatrix} \quad (10)$$

$$= \begin{bmatrix} 1 & 0 \\ 0 & 1 \\ 0 & 1 \end{bmatrix}$$

And the output in the node 2 is denoted as:

$$B = A w = \begin{bmatrix} e_1 & f_{1,1} & f_{1,2} \\ e_2 & f_{2,1} & f_{2,2} \\ \dots & \dots & \dots \\ e_m & f_{m,1} & f_{m,2} \end{bmatrix} \begin{bmatrix} 1 & 0 \\ 0 & 1 \\ 0 & 1 \end{bmatrix} = \begin{bmatrix} e_1 & f_{1,1} + f_{1,2} \\ e_2 & f_{2,1} + f_{2,2} \\ \dots & \dots \\ e_m & f_{m,1} + f_{m,2} \end{bmatrix} \quad (11)$$

Thus the description the Morphotronic network is obtained (Fig. 3)

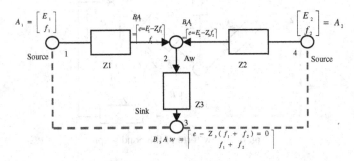

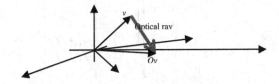

Fig. 3. Morphotronic Network

4 Extending the Bond Graph for Complex Mechatronics

An important optical geometric image can be obtained in 3D of the operator Q. Given v as a point in 3D, the Q is the ray that projects the point v into the point w perpendicular to the plane defined by the two vectors Z. Optical geometry representation [8, 9, 11] is shown in Fig. 4.

Fig. 4. Optical ray in 3D and the Projection Operator Q

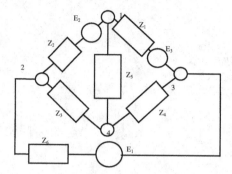

Fig. 5. Complex electrical circuit

For the given electrical circuit (Fig. 5) we have the tree or the bond graph

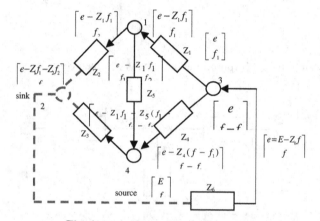

Fig. 6. A new form of the bond graph

In the circuit (Fig 6) the current and voltage (edge) incident matrix is defined as:

$$\begin{bmatrix} obj & edge & 124 = f_2 & 134 = f_3 & 243 = f_1 \\ Z_1 & 31 & 0 & 1 & 0 \\ Z_2 & 21 & 1 & 0 & 0 \\ Z_3 & 24 & 1 & 0 & 1 \\ Z_4 & 43 & 0 & 1 & 1 \\ Z_5 & 14 & 1 & 1 & 0 \\ Z_6 & 32 & 0 & 0 & 1 \end{bmatrix} \tag{12}$$

the currents are defined as:

$$f = \begin{bmatrix} 0 & 1 & 0 \\ 1 & 0 & 0 \\ 1 & 0 & 1 \\ 0 & 1 & 1 \\ 1 & 1 & 0 \\ 0 & 0 & 1 \end{bmatrix} \begin{bmatrix} f_2 \\ f_3 \\ f_1 \end{bmatrix} = \begin{bmatrix} f_3 \\ f_2 \\ f_2 + f_1 \\ f_1 + f_3 \\ f_3 + f_2 \\ f_1 \end{bmatrix} \tag{13}$$

and the power by generators are defined as:

$$P = \begin{bmatrix} f_1 \\ f_2 \\ f_3 \end{bmatrix}^T \begin{bmatrix} E_1 \\ E_2 \\ E_3 \end{bmatrix} = E_1 f_1 + E_2 f_2 + E_3 f_3 \tag{14}$$

and the power by the currents is:

$$f^T Z f = \begin{bmatrix} f_3 \\ f_2 \\ f_1 + f_2 \\ f_1 + f_3 \\ f_3 + f_2 \\ f_1 \end{bmatrix}^T \begin{bmatrix} Z_1 & 0 & 0 & 0 & 0 & 0 \\ 0 & Z_2 & 0 & 0 & 0 & 0 \\ 0 & 0 & Z_3 & 0 & 0 & 0 \\ 0 & 0 & 0 & Z_4 & 0 & 0 \\ 0 & 0 & 0 & 0 & Z_5 & 0 \\ 0 & 0 & 0 & 0 & 0 & Z_6 \end{bmatrix} \begin{bmatrix} f_3 \\ f_2 \\ f_1 + f_2 \\ f_1 + f_3 \\ f_3 + f_2 \\ f_1 \end{bmatrix}$$

$$= Z_1 f_3^2 + Z_2 f_2^2 + Z_3 (f_1 + f_2)^2 + Z_4 (f_1 + f_3)^2 + Z_5 (f_3 + f_2)^2 + Z_6 f_1^2 \tag{15}$$

The new bond graph can be defined as depicted in Fig. 7.

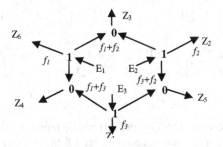

Fig. 7. Bond graph for complex mechatronic device

For example, an electrical (mechatronic) circuit with the current generator can be studied using a new type of bond graph (Fig.8).

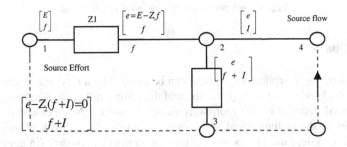

Fig. 8. A new type of bond graph

4.1 Morphotronic Model Equations

In Morphotronics, the basic system involves the relation between the flow and effort. This relation is set in as the two classes of variables.

$$
E - Z_1 f - Z_2 (f + I) = 0
$$
$$
E = (Z_1 + Z_2) f + Z_2 I \tag{16}
$$
and
$$
e - Z_2 (f + I) = 0
$$
$$
e = Z_2 (f + I)
$$

$$
\begin{bmatrix}
obj & effort \,/\, flow & f_1 & I \\
Z_1 & e_1 & 1 & 0 \\
Z_2 & e_2 & 1 & 1
\end{bmatrix} \tag{17}
$$

From currents to potential we have the system

$$
\begin{bmatrix} E \\ e \end{bmatrix} = \left(\begin{bmatrix} 1 & 0 \\ 1 & 1 \end{bmatrix}^T \begin{bmatrix} Z_1 & 0 \\ 0 & Z_2 \end{bmatrix} \begin{bmatrix} 1 & 0 \\ 1 & 1 \end{bmatrix}\right) \begin{bmatrix} 1 & 0 \\ 1 & 1 \end{bmatrix}^T \begin{bmatrix} f_1 \\ I \end{bmatrix} = \begin{bmatrix} (Z_1 + Z_2) f_1 + Z_2 I \\ Z_2 (f_1 + I) \end{bmatrix} \tag{18}
$$

$$
\begin{bmatrix} v_1 \\ v_2 \end{bmatrix} = \begin{bmatrix} E \\ e \end{bmatrix} = \left(\begin{bmatrix} 1 & 0 \\ 1 & 1 \end{bmatrix}^T \begin{bmatrix} Z_1 & 0 \\ 0 & Z_2 \end{bmatrix} \begin{bmatrix} 1 & 0 \\ 1 & 1 \end{bmatrix}\right) \begin{bmatrix} 1 & 0 \\ 1 & 1 \end{bmatrix}^T \begin{bmatrix} f_1 \\ I \end{bmatrix} \tag{19}
$$
$$
= \begin{bmatrix} Z_1 + Z_2 & Z_2 \\ Z_2 & Z_2 \end{bmatrix} \begin{bmatrix} f_1 \\ I \end{bmatrix} = \begin{bmatrix} g_{1.1} & g_{1.2} \\ g_{2.1} & g_{2.2} \end{bmatrix} \begin{bmatrix} i_1 \\ i_2 \end{bmatrix} = G \begin{bmatrix} i_1 \\ i_2 \end{bmatrix}
$$

The two port system described by (18 and 19) can be represented graphically (Fig. 10) with currents as the contravariant components of the voltages and with voltages sources as the covariant components where G is the metric tensor.

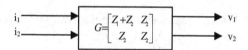

Fig. 9. Two port unity by new bond graph model

5 Conclusion

In conclusion, any morphotronic system can be defined by a rectangular metric where we locate the bond of the flow (currents) and the effort (voltages). The morpho-power is the internal distance of the morphotronic space and the N-dimensional geometric optics gives us the mathematical and geometric image of a network of morphotronic systems. The system morpho-power defines the system's geometry (in general, it is a non-Euclidean geometry). The "Morphotronic" approach can extend circuit analysis to include micro-machined devices. It is possible to use the Morphotronics to model mechatronic systems to comply with the executable specifications by uniquely describing the natural/controlled behaviour of objects in the mechatronic network.

References

1. Nils Becker, N.: Sequence Dependent Elasticity of DNA, Phd Dissertation Thesis, Technische Universität, Dresden, Germany
2. Brockett, R., Stokets, A., Park, F.C.: A geometrical formulation of the dynamics equations describing kinematic chains. In: Proceedings of IEEE International Conference on Robotics and Automation (1996)
3. Chaczko, Z., Resconi, G.: Morphotronic system applications. In: Moreno-Díaz, R., Pichler, F., Quesada-Arencibia, A. (eds.) EUROCAST 2009. LNCS, vol. 5717, pp. 905–912. Springer, Heidelberg (2009)
4. Chaczko, Z., Resconi, G.: Organising Software Infrastructures: EgoMorphic BIM Model. International Journal of Computing Anticipatory Systems 21, 372–385 (2008); ISSN 1373-5411 ISBN 2-930396-08-3
5. Chaczko, Z., Moses, P., Chiu, C.: Co-operative extended kohonen mapping (EKM) for wireless sensor networks. In: Moreno-Díaz, R., Pichler, F., Quesada-Arencibia, A. (eds.) EUROCAST 2009. LNCS, vol. 5717, pp. 897–904. Springer, Heidelberg (2009)
6. Chaczko, Z.: Towards Epistemic Autonomy in Adaptive Biomimetic Middleware for Cooperative Sensornets, PhD Dissertation thesis, UTS, Sydney, Australia (July 2009)
7. Jezierski, E.: On Electrical Analogues of Mechanical Systems and their Using in Analysis of Robot Dynamics. In: Kozlowski, K. (ed.) Robot Motion and Control - Recent Developments. LNCS, vol. 335, pp. 391–404. Springer, Heidelberg (2006)
8. Resconi, G.: Modelling Fuzzy Cognitive Map By Electrical and Chemical Equivalent Circuits. In: Joint Conference on Information Science, Salt Lake City, USA, July 8-24 (2007)
9. Resconi, G., Srini, V.P.: Electrical Circuit As A Morphogenetic System. GEST International Transactions on Computer Science and Engineering 53(1), 47–92 (2009)
10. Resconi, G., Chaczko, Z.: Morphotronic system Theory. In: Moreno-Díaz, R., Pichler, F., Quesada-Arencibia, A. (eds.) EUROCAST 2009. LNCS, vol. 5717, pp. 9–16. Springer, Heidelberg (2009)

Parallel Robot Vision Using Genetic Algorithm and Object Centroid

Anup Kale[1], Zenon Chaczko[2], and Imre Rudas[3]

[1,2] aculty of Engineering and Information Technology,
University of Technology Sydney, 15 Broadway, Ultimo, NSW, Australia, 2007
[3] Óbuda University, Bécsi út 96/B
H-1034 Budapest, Hungary
Anup.V.Kale@student.uts.edu.au, zenon@eng.ust.edu.au,
rudas@uni-obuda.hu

Abstract. Parallel Robots are playing a very important role in the medical, automotive, food and many manufacturing applications. Due to its high speed and efficient operation, it is gaining an increasing popularity in these application domains. For making the parallel robots more automated and an intelligent a machine vision system with robust performance is needed. Here, a Machine Vision Algorithm based on Genetic Evolutionary principles for object detection in the Delta Parallel Robot based systems is proposed. The solution applies a simple, robust and high speed algorithm to accurately detect objects for the application domain. The Image Acquisition of a robot's workspace is performed by using a camera mounted on the end-effector of the robot. The system is trained with the object database and with the most significant visual features of every class of objects. Images are assessed periodically for detecting the Region of Interest (ROI) within an image of the robot's workspace. The ROI is defined as an area in which a presence of object features is detected. The ROI detection is achieved by applying a random sampling of pixels and an assessment of color threshold of every pixel. The color intensity is assumed as one of the features for classification that is based on the training data. After classification process, the Genetic Algorithm is applied to locate the centroid of an object in every class. In a given application class, the Centroid is considered as the most important feature. Knowledge of an approximate location of the Centroid of objects helps to maintain a high speed and reliable pick and place operations of the Delta robot system. The proposed algorithm is tested by detecting presence of electronic components in the workspace. Experimental results show that the suggested approach offers a reliable solution for the Delta robot system.

1 Introduction

1.1 Parallel Robot

As per the definition by Merlet et al [8] a Parallel Robot is made of an end-effector with n degrees of freedom, and of a fixed base, linked together by at least two kinematic chains. In case of a parallel manipulator, number of chains is strictly equal

R. Moreno-Díaz et al. (Eds.): EUROCAST 2011, Part II, LNCS 6928, pp. 170–178, 2012.
© Springer-Verlag Berlin Heidelberg 2012

to number degree of freedom (d. o. f.). There are several advantages of these robots over the traditional serial robots. These include: high bandwidth motion capacity, load capacity and operational precision. Since kinematic chains work in parallel to each other, the friction produced is averaged while in serial robots the friction is accumulated. A mechanical structure of a parallel robot consists of a fixed base plate, a mobile plate, an end-effector and kinematic chains to join these two plates. In case of the three d. o. f. parallel robot, every kinematic chain has one universal joint [3]. The architecture of a parallel robot includes combined movement of kinematic chains which allows a three dimensional movement of the end-effector. Delta Robot is a best example of the three d. o. f. parallel robot and was originally developed by Clavel [4, 10]. In case of delta robot, three kinematic chains are placed at 120 degrees and driven by three different motors. The combined velocity produced by motors makes all three chains to move together and the position control is achieved by the vector addition of all velocities. Common applications of delta include surgical, industrial assembly, packaging, machine-tools, simulations and many others [1, 2, 5, 10, 12].

1.2 The Robotic Vision

The Robotic Vision [5] adds a great amount of flexibility and makes operation of a robot more efficient and intelligent. A robotic system without vision functions can operate correctly in fully known and constrained environments only. Another drawback relates to the fact the system requires a total knowledge of objects; and without this knowledge it is unable to work properly. In many industrial applications, the robot relies on a series of a pre-taught sequence of operations. In the cases of a pick-and-place or an assembly application the position sequence with respect to the geometry of an environment and an object location are necessary to operate the robot correctly. A variation in object location needs human intervention to a manually update of offset position values and failure to do so causes an operational malfunction. Thus porting machine vision to any type of robot, provides an additional value in terms of operational flexibility and an automated response to environmental and objects positional variations.

1.3 Robotic Vision from an Assembly and Pick-and-Place Point of View

Important issues to be addressed during pick and place and assembly applications from a robotic vision perspective include scale, orientation and position of an object. Depending on strategy selected for an application either scale is fixed in case of a fixed camera observing a workspace or it is variable in case eye in hand vision. Orientation is an important parameter from a pose estimation point of view. Position in 3 D Cartesian space as well is very important as Robot cannot simply reach to the desired position without its prior knowledge. In this work we propose an Object detection process for a Robotic Vision system to be ported in Parallel Robots of a type Delta (3 d. o. f.).Proposed approach uses eye in hand strategy to observe the workspace of Delta. Here we suggest scale, rotation and position invariant approach by detecting Regions of Interest containing classified objects and later applying a Genetic Algorithm to locate the centroid of every object.

In this section we have introduced topic and explored basics of problem space. Second section explores important issues to be addressed in Parallel Robot vision and previous attempts to solve these issues. Third section outlines the methodology of the proposed solution. This section provides a details of Algorithms and the System Architecture. Section four explains an experiment performed and result details. Section five discusses future directions of this work and conclusions.

2 Background and Previous Work

2.1 Robotic Vision Implementation Strategies

The Robotic Vision can be applied using various strategies. In case of serial Robots, 'Eye in Hand' and 'Eye at Hand' are very popular strategies. In case of 'Eye in Hand', vision camera is mounted at end effector and moves with it. This scheme is particularly useful for a precise localisation of objects. Whereas, "Eye at Hand" is effective to achieve a global picture of the scene as it has a camera mounted at fixed position to watch the end effector movements with respect to object. Both schemes are useful in different situations and can be even combined in certain cases. Both these schemes can provide position feedback to servo system or controller to achieve a goal of a visual servoing function. To this date, researchers have devoted plenty of effort researching the area of visual servoing techniques for Parallel Robots. In most of the cases, robotic vision strategies applied for the parallel robots are same as the one in case of serial robots.

2.2 Genetic Algorithms for Machine Vision

Genetic Algorithm is a class of algorithms which is inspired from a biological process of an evolution. Fundamental operations in a Genetic Algorithm include:

- *Initialization:* In this process random population of solution candidates
- *Selection:* During iteration of Genetic Algorithm chromosomes are selected for next sub-processes called fitness check, Crossover and Mutation. Chromosome selection can be performed by either by random selection, ranking or fitness.
- *Fitness Check:* Every chromosome is evaluated and rated with certain fitness.
- *Crossover:* Two random solutions or chromosomes from population are selected (called parents) and their certain bits out of their bit pattern are swapped with each other to create variations. Bit swapping is done by selecting crossover single point or multiple crossover points.
- *Termination:* Genetic Algorithm is terminated after solution is found or fixed numbers of iterations are executed or allocated time is over.

The algorithmic process starts with generation of random population of solutions, then every element of population is compared with fitness function which is a benchmark to evaluate population elements. If desired fitness level or optimization is not found than depending on strategy the population is selected for crossover and mutation operations. The application of GA in the Machine Vision has been studied by many researchers [3, 6]. In this case scale, rotation and translation variance is achieved by assuming these parameters as genes of every chromosome in the population.

2.3 Centroid in Object Detection

Centroid being a geometric center of an object can be very helpful to detect objects with orientation invariance. Wang et al [11] suggest the use of the centroid for detection of an irregular shaped object in the agricultural application. In this research images are sampled at a reduced frequency as it can limit the search space and time required. These parameters might have quite high values depending on the image size.

3 Methodology

3.1 Problem Formulation

In Delta parallel robots, the relationship between the robot's end-effector, camera and pixel co-ordinates can be expressed using a simple algebraic equation. Since end-effector and camera are placed on same moving plate of a robot, the relationship between can be expressed as:

$$\begin{bmatrix} X_c \\ Y_c \\ Z_c \end{bmatrix} = \begin{bmatrix} X_e \\ Y_e \\ Z_e \end{bmatrix} + \begin{bmatrix} a \\ b \\ c \end{bmatrix}$$

(1)

Where $[X_e \quad Y_e \quad Z_e]^T \in R^3$ are end-effector coordinates; $[X_c \quad Y_c \quad Z_c]^T \in R^3$ are camera coordinates and $[a \quad b \quad c]^T \in R^3$ is a translation matrix between end effector and camera coordinates. R is coordinate system of the Robot workspace. The relationship between image pixel co-ordinates and work space of robot can be expresses by translation matrix: $[X_p \quad Y_p]$ so that an image can be represented as a matrix I as follows:

$$I = \begin{bmatrix} f(x_1,y_1) & f(x_1,y_2) & f(x_1,y_3) & . & . & f(x_1,y_n) \\ f(x_2,y_1) & f(x_2,y_2) & f(x_2,y_3) & . & . & f(x_2,y_n) \\ f(x_3,y_1) & f(x_3,y_2) & f(x_3,y_3) & . & . & f(x_3,y_n) \\ . & . & . & . & . & . \\ f(x_{m-1},y_1) & f(x_{m-1},y_2) & f(x_{m-1},y_3) & . & . & f(x_{m-1},y_n) \\ f(x_m,y_1) & f(x_m,y_2) & f(x_m,y_3) & . & . & f(x_m,y_n) \end{bmatrix}$$

(2)

where $f(x_m,y_n)$ denotes the probability density function of image pixels and (m, n) are pixel co-ordinates.

3.2 Proposed Algorithm

Process starts with entering of object to be searched into the search area or an Image frame (Fig 1). The object and search areas are measured for its dimensions and color threshold band or range of an object. Then object is divided into 'n' equal sections, each section with dimensions proportional to size of an object. In the next step, the population of 'm' pixels is generated in every section (where population = m*n). For finding the elite set of pixels, the entire population is set at color threshold equal to an object. If elite count is bellow (m*n)*k then the population generation is performed again. Else, the parent chromosomes are created at every elite pixel. The fitness level is evaluated by passing the entire elite population through fitness function. After the fitness test, the process is stopped otherwise the process is continued by executing the crossover and mutation. After every crossover/mutation, the fitness is re-evaluated and if optimization level is achieved the process is stopped.

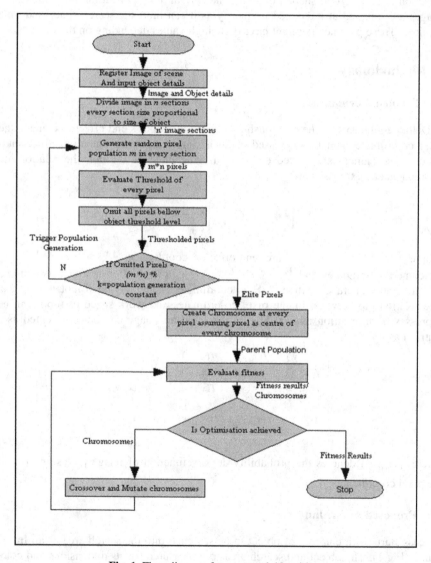

Fig. 1. Flow diagram for proposed Algorithm

Population Generation: Generating 'm' pixels in all 'n' sections of an image. Matrix representation on right side of equation (2) can be simply represented as:

$$I = \begin{bmatrix} l_{1,1} & l_{1,2} & l_{1,3} & l_{1,4} & \cdot & l_{1,y} \\ l_{2,1} & l_{2,2} & l_{2,3} & l_{2,4} & \cdot & l_{2,y} \\ l_{3,1} & l_{3,2} & l_{3,3} & l_{3,4} & \cdot & l_{3,y} \\ l_{4,1} & l_{4,2} & l_{4,3} & l_{4,4} & \cdot & l_{4,y} \\ \cdot & \cdot & \cdot & \cdot & \cdot & \cdot \\ l_{x,1} & l_{x,2} & l_{x,3} & l_{x,4} & \cdot & l_{x,y} \end{bmatrix} \qquad [3]$$

where every matrix l inside I is with size (i*j) and also $(i * j) \propto s$; where S is a scale of an object to be identified. The *Population* = (m*n) and Elite separation is defined using Filter Elites by thresholding the (m*n) population. In the chromosome creation process, the decimal value of pixels in elite population is converted into a binary string. In this case 10 bits each for x and y co-ordinate values are allocated. The Crossover/Mutation involves swapping bits in (x, y) co-ordinates to shift position of pixels. For the image frame, the bit swapping creates the pixel's positional deviation. The Region of Interest (ROI) Creation: Depending on how the z axis position co-ordinate value ROI of a particular size is created, we need to find presence of an object. The relation between size of ROI at the calibration time process and at the time object search is defined using the transformation [7]: Rm=Ra*(Za/Zm), where Ra= ROI size measured when calibration is performed and Rm= ROI size measured when object detection is performed, Za = Z position of camera at the time of calibration , Zm= Z position of camera when object detection is performed. In the case of Delta parallel robot, for the Fitness Check operation, the relationship between centroid measured in ROI is easily comparable with centroid measured during the calibration process. The *distance* and *scale* can be co-related here based on simple perspective projection rule. In case of delta robot distance of an object with respect to camera is Z axis co-ordinate value from current camera plane to object plane. Thus object scale and object-camera distance is defined as:

$$S_a = S_m * f / z \qquad (4)$$

where, Sa is the actual scale or scale when object dimensions were measured during calibration of object, Sm is an Object scale measured from any other distance than calibration position, f is focal distance of camera lens (in our experimental set up approximately = 3.2 mm) z is a distance between camera and an object at the time of recording frame to measure Sm. The centroid $\bar{I}_{x,y} = (\bar{x}, \bar{y})$ can be defined as:

$$\bar{x} = (\sum_{i=1}^{N} x_i) / A \qquad (5)$$
$$\bar{y} = (\sum_{i=1}^{N} y_i) / A$$

Now referring to equation (5) and (6) fitness function can be defined as:

$$f_f = ([\bar{x}_c / (f / z_c)] - [\bar{x}_a / (f / z_a)]) \qquad (6)$$

4   Experiment and Results

4.1   Machine Vision for Delta Parallel Robot

Experiments were carried out for checking versatility, accuracy and scalability of proposed system. For implementing proposed system the Delta model (Parallix) of the robot (Fig. 2) was used along with the camera and Matlab for implementing algorithms. During the experiments, results were obtained by assessing the capability of algorithms for sorting of electronic components. During experiment performed the following assumptions were made:

- There is only translation transformation between camera and the Robot's end-effector co-ordinates (no rotation transformation)
- End effector is placed at such position that it is able to scan the portion of work area where objects are placed.

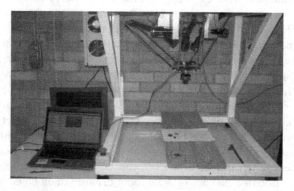

Fig. 2. Experiment Setup using the Delta robot model Parallix developed by the Instituto Politecnico Nacional, Mexico

- Since proposed solution can handle up to approximately 5% of occlusion in the image any of objects are not largely occluded.
- Object background is of fixed and contrast color with respect to objects.
- This solution can assess only broader category of object not specific ratings or in-prints on object. E.g. in our case, for resistor items checks for color, bands and ratings are not performed.

4.2   Experiment of Locating of Objects and Sorting

The experiment involved locating centroid location of object and sorting of objects from mixed group. In this experiment we used electronic components as target objects. During this experiment we assessed 40 different types of components for finding their centroid locations. During this experiment Parallix Robot was supposed to perform operations in following sequence: (1) move to detection position, (2) scan image of work area and run proposed algorithm, (3) once object centroid position is detected move end-effector to these co-ordinates, (4) pick-up the detected object and

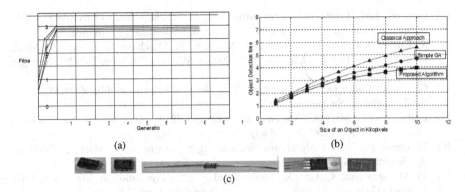

Fig. 3. Algorithm performance: optimization for different components (a), comparative analysis (b), detected objects (c)

place to its targeted bin or location. In the experiment for assessing performance at different positions of end-effector, it was moved to different Z axis positions and an object detection exercise was performed.

5 Future Directions

For making solution more versatile further work is needed to modify the Algorithm. This can be achieved by making Algorithm multi-objective. For improving accuracy and enhancing speed further work is needed to embed the solution into visual servoing process.

6 Conclusion

The proposed solution for the Parallel Robot Vision performs much faster if compared with conventional and other GA based solutions. An increased reliability of Algorithm is achieved due to the proposed approach that generate random population of pixels periodically in smaller sections or regions of image. An increased performance (processing speed) is achieved due to the population generation process in which initially a set of pixels is assessed for their color intensities before considering a particular region of interest. This approach avoids "wasteful" handling of large data size and enhances speed

References

[1] Brandt, G., Zimolong, A., Carrat, L., Merloz, P., Staudte, H.-W., Lavallee, S., Radermacher, K., Rau, G.: CRIGOS: a compact robot for image-guided orthopedic surgery. IEEE Transactions on Information Technology in Biomedicine 3(4), 252–260 (1999)
[2] Bruzzone, L.E., Molfino, R.M., Zoppi, M.: An impedance-controlled parallel robot for high-speed assembly of white goods. Industrial Robot: An Inter'l Journal 32(3), 226–233 (2005)

[3] Centeno, T.M., Lopes, H.S., Felisberto, M.K., de Arruda, L.V.R.: Object detection for computer vision using a robust genetic algorithm. In: Rothlauf, F., Branke, J., Cagnoni, S., Corne, D.W., Drechsler, R., Jin, Y., Machado, P., Marchiori, E., Romero, J., Smith, G.D., Squillero, G. (eds.) EvoWorkshops 2005. LNCS, vol. 3449, pp. 284–293. Springer, Heidelberg (2005)

[4] Clavel, R.: Conception d'un robot parallèle rapide à 4 degrés de liberté, Ph.D. Thesis, EPFL, Lausanne, Switzerland (1991)

[5] Corby, N.R.: Machine Vision for Robotics. IEEE Transactions on Industrial Electronics IE-30(3), 282–291 (1983)

[6] Cucchiara, R.: Genetic Algorithms for clustering in machine vision. Machine Vision and Applications 11, 1–6 (1998)

[7] Yi, M., Stephano, S., Jana, K., Sastry Shankar, S.: An invitation to 3-D Vision, From Images to Geometric Models, pp. 48–53. Springer, New York (2004)

[8] Merlet, J.P.: Parallel Robots, 2nd edn., pp. 12–13. Springer, Netherlands (2006)

[9] Nabat, V., de la O Rodriguez, M., Company, O., Krut, S., Pierrot, F.: Par4: very high speed parallel robot for pick-and-place. In: 2005 IEEE/RSJ International Conference on Intelligent Robots and Systems, IROS 2005, August 2-6, pp. 553–558 (2005)

[10] Pierrot, F., Reynaud, C., Fournier, A.: DELTA: a simple and efficient parallel robot. Robotica 8, 105–109 (1990)

[11] Wang, M., Wei, K., Yuan, J., Xu, K.: A research for intelligent cotton picking robot based on machine vision. In: International Conference on Information and Automation, ICIA 2008, June 20-23, pp. 800–803 (2008)

[12] Weck, M., Staimer, D.: Parallel kinematic machine tools: current states and future potentials. Ann. CIRP 51(2), 671–683 (2002)

Towards Sensomotory Coordination of Vision and Action in Humanoid Agents

Gerhard Hoefer and Manfred Mauerkirchner

Austrian Partner of International Universities (UDA), A-4060 Leonding, Austria
{g.hoefer,m.mauerkirchner}@htl-leonding.ac.at

Abstract. The classical approach corncerning the coordination of sensory and motor systems is characterized by purely reactive behaviour: all sensory input (tactile, accoustical, visual) is unidirectionally transformed into output signals that are sent to the motor system. Both involved cortical systems (parietal cortex and premotor cortex) act in a strictly unitary way. Recent progress in anatomical and neurophysiological research in primate brains has shown that both cortical systems are far from acting unitarily. They rather consist of several distinct coupled areas exhibiting specific functional properties called basic behaviours. These functional properties arise from the reciprocal coupling of one parietal area and its corresponding premotor area. This coupling is based on the bidirectional interaction of multimodal neurons located in both areas. Similar functional properties are arranged in streams: AIP-F5 enables grasping behaviour, LIP-F4 enables reaching behaviour, and LIP-FEF controls eye movement. These pragmatic streams together with semantic streams like PIP-IT may be regarded as the distinct building blocks of the associative cortex which is traditionally viewed as a monolithic computational unit. Basic behaviours act as active action detectors that are selected by overall controller systems like the ratiomorph apparatus.

1 Introduction of the Biomimetical Design Principles

The design of autonomously behaving agents is focused on the task-oriented coordination of their sensory and motor systems. This sensomotory coordination is based both on the structure of the sensomotory apparatus and on the sensomotory transformation processes carried out by the set of components comprising that apparatus. The structure of the apparatus is determined by the actual range of desired behaviours and the bodily structure of the agent as well as the structure of its ecological niche. Accordingly, the agents have to be realized as complete agents that are structurally coupled to their environment [1].

The sensomotory apparatus is made up by a set of parallel streams each performing one distinct task-oriented type of sensomotory transformation process. One individual stream biomimetically resembles one clearly segregated circuit of pariofrontal circuitry and should be regarded as the functional unit of distinct areas of the cortical system. Each of these functional units is able to carry out one distinct motor act like grasping, reaching, or searching. According to the traditional point of view, each stream transforms multimodal signal patterns from

R. Moreno-Díaz et al. (Eds.): EUROCAST 2011, Part II, LNCS 6928, pp. 179–186, 2012.
© Springer-Verlag Berlin Heidelberg 2012

one distinct associative area of the parietal cortex into a motor act controlled by an area of the premotor frontal cortex. These transformation process acts in an unidirectional way. As a prerequisite the parietal cortex integrates sensory input from various sensory cortices and generates multimodal sensory input patterns [2].

Based on the same traditional point of view, the premotor cortex has been considered to play essentially an executive role in motor control. Its role has been that of an passive executor of motor commands that originate from associative areas of the parietal and frontal cortices which may be responsible for higher-order cognitive functions. But quite contrarily the premotor cortex is now seen as the active controller of voluntary movements. It is formed by a mosaic of independent areas characterized by unique sets of connections with parietal, prefrontal, and cingulate cortices and involved in specific aspects of motor planning and execution. Therefore, sensomotory transformations are the result of a strict cooperation between certain parietal and premotor areas [3].

The parietal cortex is not acting in a purely associative way since its areas show characteristic motory properties that correspond with the properties of the reciprocal coupled areas of the premotor cortex. A stream should be regarded as a bidirectional transformational unit that fully integrates sensory and motor signals at both the parietal and premotor areas. The sensomotory transformation processes carried out by distinct streams depend crucially on reciprocal signal processing by multimodal neurons located in the parietal cortex as well as in the premotor cortex [2][4].

Generally, the coupled premotor and parietal areas are organized in an effector specific way (i.e. arm, hand, head, eyes) and are not modality specific (i.e. visual, acoustical, or tactile perception) . It appears that spatial positions and physical characteristics of objects as well as their semantics have multiple functional descriptions in the brain. Each has with different purposes according to the different effectors acting in a particular context [5].

The reciprocal coupling of one parietal area and one premotor area within a certain stream is based on the presence of multimodal neurons in both areas. Certain premotor areas all contain visuomotor neurons that in addition to their motor discharge respond also to the presentation of visual stimuli. Furthermore, areas of the parietal cortex targeting these premotor areas appear to be related to the effectors that are somatotopically represented in these areas [5].

Three distinct streams that coordinate vision and motion may be distinguished: The AIP-F5 stream enables grasping behaviour, the VIP-F4 stream enables reaching behaviour within the peripersonal space, and the LIP-FEF stream controls saccadic eye movement in order to focus single objects in the extrapersonal space [3][6].

These three streams may be regarded as acting in a pragmatic or action oriented way, but there also exist semantic streams that act in a content oriented way [7]. The pariotemporal PIP-IT stream is a semantic stream that enables a further classification of potentially useful affordances of objects that may be grasped by the agent.

2   Structure and Functions of the Pragmatic Streams in the Primate Cortex

Each stream is made up by a set of highly specialized basic behaviours or competences that are able to carry out a preconfigured spectrum of similar but slightly
different sensomotory transformations. Therefore, the AIP-F5 stream comprises
all basic competences for grasping acts, whereas the VIP-F4 stream contains the
complete set of all basic reaching competences. Therefore, streams are structured
as collections of certain characteristic competences and may be regarded as an
ensemble of hypotheses of acting. At a time one or more such hypotheses may
become applicable in certain environmental contexts. Consequently, these competences actively signal their potential applicability to the extended ratiomorph
apparatus which has to carry out the subsequent selection process [8].

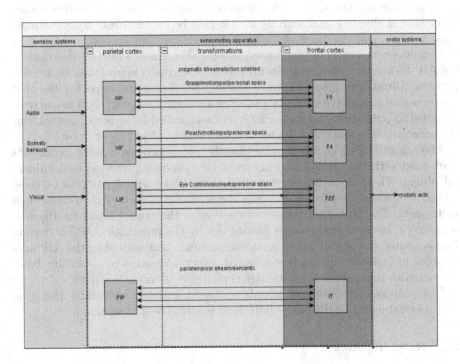

Fig. 1. Model of pragmatic and semantic streams

2.1   Grasping Acts

The pragmatic AIP-F5 stream and the semantic PIP-IT stream are both engaged
in basic grasping acts in a cooperative way.

Area F5 contains representations of hand and mouth movements that enable
goal-directed grasping acts. The representation of hand movements is made up

by a comprehensive set of goal-orientated motor acts or basic competences that are selective for the three particular types of grip: precision grip, finger prehension, and whole hand prehension. F5 is made up by motor neurons as well as visuomotor neurons in nearly the same amounts. Certain sets of motor neurons discharge during the actual grasping act while certain sets of visuomotor neurons become active when a particular type of graspable object is presented. Therefore, the three basic types of grip are coded selectively by the interaction of motor and visuomotor neurons [9].

Area AIP is made up by visual neurons, visuomotor neurons as well as motor neurons. Visuomotor neurons and motor neurons act in the same way as the corresponding types of neurons in area F5. Together with the visual neurons they code the shape, size, and orientation of tridimensional objects in an active way [10][11].

The pragmatic AIP-F5 stream may be regarded as a context-sensitive vocabulary of grasping acts. Each basic competence serves as an entry in this vocabulary that is able to signal actively that it may be executable in a contextually appropriate way.

Grasping acts mostly depend on exploitable affordances which are detected by the AIP-F5 stream in order to select the best contextually appropriate basic competence. Affordances may be regarded as embodied practical opportunities that are presented by an environmental object to a perceptive agent [12]. They may be regarded as parameters for motor interaction signalled by sensory cues without the necessary intervention of 'high-level processes' of object recognition [6].

The semantic PIP-IT stream classifies the potentially executable motor acts associated with the various affordances of the currently perceived environmental object. The PIP area provides the characteristic visual patterns of these affordances while the IT area provides the semantic content of their associated motor acts. The output of this stream serves as the crucial input for the sensomotory transformation process carried out by the pragmatic AIP-F5 stream. Consequently, the output of the semantic stream is transmitted to the AIP area in order to facilitate the context sensitive selection process of applicable basic competences that match the currently exploitable affordances [6][13].

Our proposed modelling of affordance based grasping acts differ from the already established FARS model [6][13]and is introduced in section 3.

2.2   Reaching Acts

Reaching acts are carried out within the peripersonal space of the agent and controlled by sensomotory transformation processes carried out by the basic competences of the VIP-F4 stream. This peripersonal space, although introspectively perceived as unitary, is not represented in a single cortical area as a multipurpose map. Quite contrarily, it is evident that there are at least as many spatial maps as there are motor effectors that act in the peripersonal environment. Therefore, the peripersonal space is dynamically constructed as the sum of all spatial locations that are reachable by all currently possible reaching acts [14].

The basic competences of the VIP-F4 stream integrate visual and somatosensory signals (VIP) and couple them reciprocally to the contextually most adequate motor act (F4). Therefore, a vocabulary of reaching acts is established in analogy to the vocabulary of grasping acts. A multimodal integration process anchors the visual receptive field of one movable body part in its associated somatosensory receptive field. All these body parts like the face, upper arm, or forearm act within their local system of coordinates made up by their individually associated somatosensory receptive field [14].

Such anchoring is based on motor neurons of area F4 that also respond to sensory stimulation. Based on these responses they are subdivided in two classes: Somatosensory neurons have superficial tactile receptive fields located on the body parts mentioned in the section above. Bimodal (somatosensory and visual) neurons respond in almost the same way as purely somatosensory ones but, in addition, these neurons discharge when a tridimensional visual stimulus is introduced inside the peripersonal space. Neuronal responses are enhanced if the stimulus is moved toward the receptive field of the bimodal neurons. The reaching process is facilitated by the congruence between the various visual receptive fields and the spatial position towards which the hand has to be moved [15].

The somatosensory and the visual receptive fields of one effector is determined by its current position and represented by distinct basic competences of the VIP-F4 stream. The activation of such a competence reflects a potential action directed towards a particular spatial location. The presentation of a visual stimulus evokes automatically one of these potential actions, which functionally represents the position in space in motor terms. This kind of representation within the peripersonal space renders the actual performance of reaching acts much more economical [5].

In summary, F4 contains a complete spectrum of action oriented basic competences that actively signal their individual potential applicability if they are able to carry out one contextually favourable reaching act.

2.3 Searching and Categorisation Acts

Sensomotory coordination carried out by the basic competences of the LIP-FEF stream structures the visual input in an action-oriented way. Especially, the agent is able to influence the structuring process via its motor system.

The FEF area controls the saccadic eye movement which directs the fovea towards objects located at the border of the field of vision. These objects are detected by the closely interacting LIP area. The LIP-FEF stream sensitively reacts on objects located within the extrapersonal space in a distance independent way. The system of coordinates used in this process is always centred along the focal axis and is exclusively employed in the motor control of the saccadic eye movements [16].

This kind of sensomotory coordination of object detection may be regarded as the basic process of the transformation of type2 in type1 categorisation problems [17].

2.4   Sensomotory Schemes

Sensomotory schemes are constructed by the task-oriented superposition of currently applicable basic competences of the pragmatic streams. The construction process of various task-oriented types of these sensomotory schemes must be conceived as a evolutionary and self-organizing adaptive process based on assimilation and accommodation. These mechanisms help the agents to react on environmental perturbations in order to create a broad range of behaviours that guarantee the viability of the agent. Viability states that there exists no isomorphic or iconographic relation between the structure of the agent and its environment [18]. Consequently, some acceptable degree of structural coupling must exist.

3   Proposed Modelling of Grasping Acts

Our proposed modelling of affordance based grasping acts may be regarded as a further development in the structure-function relation of the already established FARS model [6][13]. In our model all these acts are carried out by a set of grasp specific and independently acting basic competences. Each basic competence is comprised by a reciprocally and tightly coupled subarea of the AIP area and its corresponding subarea of the F5 area. These basic competences acting as autonomous affordance detectors make up a multi-agent based stream whereas the FARS model employs neural subpopulations of two distinct and comprehensively acting networks that represent the overall AIP area and the overall F5 area, respectively. Both areas are only lightly coupled in a reciprocal way but act clearly as distinct computational units. According to the FARS model the features of graspable objects are reflected in subpopulations of both relevant areas: The AIP area is modelled as a computational unit that extracts affordances from visual representations of attended objects. The F5 area is modelled as the controller of the phases of the execution of the chosen grasping act. The selection of the contextual most appropriate grasping acts is carried out by the AIP area by the means of the broadly tuned population code. This set of acts is passed to F5 which selects one of these acts. Now it is responsible for the unfolding of the phases of the grasping act in time. Each act is divided in five distinct phases (set, extension, flexion, hold, and release) that depend on the actual task like a pecision pinch or a power grip. This activity is broadcast back to the AIP, strengthening the affordance that corresponds to the selected grasp [6][13].

Our proposed model does not depend on the two quite separately acting computational units that make up the FARS model. Instead, all basic competences should be modelled as distinct attractor networks made up by various types of spiking neurons. These different types of neurons integrated in one such attractor network exhibit the important monomodal or bimodal features introduced in section 2. These networks actively signal their appliability in a certain contextual useful situations as an stable attractor state. This state is modelled as feedback activity of the tightly connected subareas of AIP and F5. If such a basic competence is chosen by the overall system (see section 4) the output activity of the F5 subarea is carried out in the clearly defined phases of subsequent feedback processes that control the complete grasping act. One completed phase specific process triggers the next one according to the close interaction of bimodal neurons integrated in coupled AIP and F5 subareas. These subsequent feedback processes make sure that the chosen grasping act is carried out correctly or may be abandoned if its complete execution is not feasible.

In conclusion, the main difference between both models is the recently discovered relation of structure and function in the parito-premotor cortex introduced in section 2.

4   Integration of the Sensomotory Schemes into the Overall System Architecture

The aim of the coupling process must be the viable establishment of both externally and internally grounded agents. Only such agents are able to exhibit a broad range of behaviours based on the interplay of internally and externally generated states. That broad range is necessary to cope with a more or less unpredictable environment. The grounding processes of the agent should be represented by an overall body scheme [19]. This body scheme is a body map that represents the actual states in a distributed and action oriented way. It is created by the content of the interoceptive, proprioceptive, and extereoceptive pathways in an emergent way.

Therefore, the body scheme integrates signals from the interoceptive and the proprioceptive pathway and represents them on a set of corresponding feature maps. This part of the body scheme is the base for basic drives and emotions [8].

Additionally, the activities of the sensomotory schemes of the exteroceptive pathway must also be represented in a second distinct part in the body scheme in order to establish the interplay of all three pathways. This part of the body scheme is the base for the intentional interaction with the environment of the agent. But it is not realized as a single multipurpose map but as the set of parieto-premotor circuits introduced in section 2 [19][20].

The interplay of these three pathways and the subsequent action generation is managed by the extended ratiomorph apparatus [8]. But its overall architecture has to be modified in an important way since the representational structures of the exteroceptive pathway have to be realized as part of the sensomotory streams introduced above. These structures are able to carry out all the tasks of the parietal associative cortex. The nature of the associative processes carried out by this cortex becomes much clearer when they are viewed as one part of the reciprocal and multimodal circuitry that make up the set of distinct pragmatic and semantic streams.

References

1. Pfeiffer, R., Scheier, C.: Understanding Intelligence. MIT Press, Cambridge (2000)
2. Gallese, V.: The inner sense of action: agency and motor representations. Journal of Consciousness Studies 7, 23–40 (2000)
3. Luppino, G., Rizzolati, G.: The organisation of the frontal motor cortex. News Physiological Science 15 (2000)
4. Gallese, V., Craighero, L., Fadiga, L., Fogassi, L.: Perception through action. Psyche 5 (1999)
5. Fadiga, L., Fogassi, L., Gallese, V., Rizzolati, G.: Visuomotor neurons: ambiguity of the discharge or 'motor' perception. International J. Psychophysiology 35 (2000)
6. Arbib, M.: From visual affordances in monkey parietal cortex to hippocampo-parietal interactions underlying rat navigation. Philosophical Transactions of the Royal Society 352 (1997)
7. Jacob, J., Jeannerod, M.: Ways of seeing. The scope and limits of visual cognition. Oxford University Press, New York (2003)
8. Hoefer, G., Mauerkirchner, M.: Biomimetic controller for situated robots based on state-driven behaviour. In: Moreno-Díaz, R., Pichler, F., Quesada-Arencibia, A. (eds.) EUROCAST 2009. LNCS, vol. 5717, pp. 398–405. Springer, Heidelberg (2009)
9. Murata, A., Fadiga, L., Gallese, V., Raos, V., Rizzolati, G.: Object representation in the ventral premotor cortex (area f5). Journal of Neurophysiology 78 (1997)
10. Sakata, H., Taira, M., Murata, A., Mime, S.: Neural mechanisms of visual guidance of hand action in parietal cortex of the monkey. Cerbal Cortex 5 (1995)
11. Murata, A., Gallese, V., Luppino, G., Kaseda, M., Sakata, H.: Selectivity for shape, size, and orientation of objects for grasping in neurons of monkey parietal area aip. Journal of Neurophysiology 79 (2000)
12. Gibson, J.: The ecological approach to visual perception. Houghton Mifflin, Boston (1979)
13. Fagg, A., Arbib, M.: Modelling parietal-premotor interaction in primate control of grasping. Neural Networks 11 (1998)
14. Rizzolati, G., Fadiga, L., Fogassi, L., Gallese, V.: The space around us. Science 277 (1997)
15. Fogassi, L., Gallese, V., Fadiga, L., Luppino, G., Matelli, M., Rizzolati, G.: Coding of peripersonal space in inferio premotor cortex (f4). Journal of Neurophysiology 76 (1996)
16. Colby, C., Goldberg, M.: Space and attention in parietal cortex. Annual Review in Neuroscience (1999)
17. Clark, A., Thornton, C.: Trading spaces. Behavorial and Brain Sciences 20 (1997)
18. Piaget, J.: The development of thought equilibration of cognitive structures. The Viking Press, New York (1977)
19. Gallese, V.: The "conscious" dorsal stream: Embodied simulation and its role in space and action conscious awareness. Psyche 13(1) (2007)
20. Gallese, V., Sinigaglia, C.: The bodily self as power for action. Neuropsychologia 48 (2009)

The Different Possibilities for Gait Identification Based on Motion Capture

Ryszard Klempous

The Institute of Computer Engineering, Control and Robotics
Wrocław University of Technology
11/17 Janiszewskiego Street, 50-372 Wrocław, Poland
ryszard.klempous@pwr.wroc.pl

Abstract. The domain of biometric motion identification undergoes an extensive research and development. An adaptation of one of the motion identification solutions can be the base for an implementation of a complex identification system. Such a system will always require well defined human skeleton, motion model, comparison algorithms as well as a properly constructed motion database. The results obtained while studying the system, greatly depend on the analysis methods. The main advantage of Motion Capture (MC) systems is the accuracy of recorded data. A Captured motion contains a lot of subtle details as their source is the life person (a human actor).

Keywords: motion capture, gait recognition.

> „I know her by her gait." The Tempest; 1611
> William Shakespeare

1 Introduction

Annual, global biometric industry revenues is growing rapidly from 3 billion US$ in the 2009, 5 billion US$ in this year and is expected to reach the 9 billion US$ in the 2014 according to the International Biometric Group [i,ii].

Biophysical features can be the source for recognition [i,ii], for example: face recognition, body (face) thermogram, fingerprints, eye-based features (e.g. iris), palm features, voice analysis, signature template, keyboard typing, motion analysis, vascular, hand geometry, DNA recognition, body scent, hand motion signatures, on-line handwriting analysis. And well known practical applications [i,ii] as for example: access control and privileges checking , suspect identification, security systems (also personal tracking), medical data analysis (diagnosis/treatment), patient identification, finding lost children in public venues, analysis of pedestrian patterns for space planning, analysis of where people go for marketing purposes. Human motion may also be an interesting source of information for biometric posture recognition [5, 10, 11, 24, ii, v, vi].

R. Moreno-Díaz et al. (Eds.): EUROCAST 2011, Part II, LNCS 6928, pp. 187–194, 2012.

2   The Process of Recording Human Movement

The main aim of this paper is to present various approaches and estimation methods for creating virtual human motion models; a special attention is given to an overview of methods that construct gait differentiating algorithms from data acquired by Motion Capture systems.

Motion Capture (MC) [7, 16, 19, 21] is an important data source for human recognition task. Actor's motion are captured using different kinds of sensors and recorded in 3D virtual space [8, 16, 17, 20, 23-27]. Data are saved using proper representation taking into consideration skeleton hierarchy [i].

2.1   The Main Ideas of MC Systems

The data motion registration process has several intrinsic requisites, as for example:

- The registration should be held in the studio equipped with an appropriate system of cameras (between eight and sixteen) as well as sufficiently powerful computer system.
- Special sensors (markers) should be attached to the characteristic points of the actor (or person identified.
- Actor's motion are captured using different kinds of sensors and recorded in 3D virtual space.

The level of the realism of the animation determines the quantity of attached sensors. It also depends on what we want to reach. In this technique many subtle details can be recorded, which are difficult to simulate using analytical motion model. Data are saved using proper representation, taking into consideration skeleton hierarchy. These data are sent to the computer which processes them then one receives the figure three-dimensional model in the result. There are several types of Motion Capture systems. Among the most popular are: *Optical Systems, Inertial Systems, Magnetic Systems and Electromagnetic Systems.*

Thanks to the application of various models of hierarchic skeletons together with their dimensionality, the development of the Motion Capture interception systems results in a more advanced generation of motion capture systems.

2.2   Skeleton Model

The skeleton model is organized in an invariable hierarchy and considerations usually consists of fixed number of bones (between15 and 23). Each bone can have at most one predecessor and one or more successors. The beginning of the whole hierarchy in the skeleton is a virtual root bone. Bones can move only by a rotation around given axes. The data related to the rotation of each bone is recorded. There are two most known types of data representations for rotations [3, 8, 10, 12, 14, 16, 17]: Euler's angles and rotational matrices and quaternions. Euler's angles are more more popular but quaternions determine representation that is invariant to coordinate system. Both systems are widely also used in animation systems, games and computer graphics software.

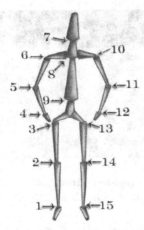

Fig. 1. Typical skeleton model [19]. Where the natural numbers denote skeleton parts as follows: 1 Left Ankle Joint ; 2 Knee Joint; 3 Hips Joint; 4 Wrist Joint; 5 Elbow Joint; 6 Shoulder Joint; 7 Neck-Head; 8 Torso-Neck; 9 Pelvis; 10 Shoulder Joint; 11 Elbow Joint; 12 Wrist Joint;; 13 Hips Joint; 14 Knee Joint ; 15 Right Ankle Joint.

2.3   Data Standards

Most popular data standards of motion captures [i] are listed below: BVA and BVH file formats; MNM file format; ASK/SDL file format; AOA file format ASF/AMC file formats; BRD file format; HTR and GTR file formats; TRC file format; CSM file format;V/VSK file format;1.11 C3D file format; GMS file format; HDF file format The three of them are of importance, namely: BVA and BVH file formats, ASF/AMC file formats, and C3D file format.

BVA and BVH File Format. The BVH (Biovision Hierarchical Data) replaced former BVA format. Both formats were introduced by a motion capture company called Biovision (vii). Company (vii) motion capture company. The standards are mostly used as a typical representation of human motion and provide skeleton hierarchy information as well as the motion data. There is a right handed coordinate system defined for the BVH hierarchy.

ASF/AMC File Formats. Acclaim Video Game Company(viii) introduced ASF/AMC formats. These formats are composed of one file for skeleton data and another one for motion data. The ASF file contains Acclaim Skeleton File, which can be used for different motions. The ACM file contains Acclaim Motion Capture data.

2.4   C3D File Format

The National Healt Institute in Mryland (ix) introduced very helpful the C3D binary (mostly ASCII files) format in the biomechanical applications. The system is mostly used for athletes or physically handicapped person needs. It carry

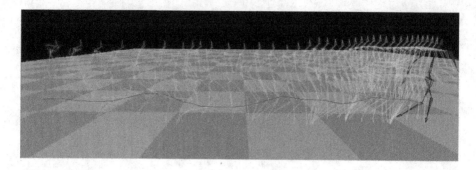

Fig. 2. Spring to walk motion registered from LifeForms(BHV format). Additionally, the motion of a point located at the knee is also shown.

the most complete amount of information useful for the biomechanics research, because of the following features:

- The storage of three-dimensional data are directly coming from the measure instrument.
- The storage of position marker, force captors, sampling rate, date, type of examination as well as name, age, physical parameter;
- The possibility of enlarging the data by adding new data to the ones already stored.

Main properties of the listed above Data Format: Acclaim ASF/ACM; Biovision BVH and C3D

Table 1. Main properties of the Data Format

Company	Acclaim	Biovision	C3D
Hierarchical Skeleton	Yes	Yes	No
No of registered person in one file	None	No limit (any)	No limit (any)
Data stored	text	text	binary)
Additional data stored	No	No	Yes, EMG,..

3 Methods of Motion Data Analysis

The following set of important observations can be made according to currently published research results:

- For the process of recognition, the analysis of motion of legs seems to be the most important. In many papers, for example [4- 7, 9], demonstrate that person can be identified using legs motion.

  Motion capture data can be obtained .both from the commercial system [iv] both free [v vii] to test proposed methods. In this paper we use LifeForms

3D database produced by Credo Interactive Inc. [iv]) motion library, which contains different action sequences played by real actors and processed using motion capture technique.

- The method of video analysis can be successful even when parts of the body are covered by clothes legs are easier to distinguish (for example by using Hough transform [8]).
- In the papers [10 - 12, 14] it is proposed to take into consideration rotation along one axis and only 3 coefficients of amplitude spectrum analysis (I, II amplitudes of X rotation of hip, I amplitude of X rotation of knee).
- Motion can be considered and analyzed as time-series [1].
- Many traditional time-series analysis methods have been successfully applied to human motion, including both deterministic and probabilistic approaches, stationary and time-varying statistical models, analysis in time and frequency domains.
- Among the more popular approaches of time-series modeling applied to human motion are Dynamic Time Warping (DTW), Hidden Markov Models (HMM), Markov Random Fields (MRF), algorithms directed towards time-series comparison such as Longest Common Subsequence (LCSS), spectral analysis methods including Fourier and wavelet transforms, dimensionality reduction methods including Principal Component Analysis (PCA), kernel based methods, and Latent Variable Model (LVM) [13, 19, 21].
- Variety of filtering techniques are used for filtering, estimation, prediction and tracking of motion data, including autoregressive models such as AR, ARMA or ARIMA, Kalman filter and Extended Kalman Filter (EKF), kernel based methods, and Monte Carlo based techniques such as a Particle Filter [20], [22] and MCMC.
- An emerging important and fruitful branch of human motion research is directed towards recovery of skeletal pose from video sequences without the use of special suits and markers, referred to as Markerless Motion Capture [23],[24],[25],[26].
- Monte Carlo filtering methods such as Particle Filter (Condensation method) are often used for markerless body tracking.
- Human body dynamics and inverse dynamics analysis can be used to provide informative constrains [2, 18] for filtering and tracking of pose from markerless video data.
- One of the most challenging problems in markerless motion capture, but offering a widespread application potential is that of estimation of body pose from single video sequence (monocular markerless tracking) [27].

The LifeForms 3D database is a very convenient tool to check the performance of the listed above methods. The 3D models are used in investigations in medicine (diagnosis of a variety of balance disorders as Parkinson, Multiple Sclerosis and other degenerative conditions), allow us to recognize easily pathological movements of a patient and would help to chose the way of a treatment, for analysis of athletic performance of sportsmen, ergonomic design, reconstruction of accidents involving humans. It is also possible analysis of crowd behavior or from detecting and recognizing people movements for security purposes. It can helpful to create and verify similar methods but using 2D database for gait recognition as well as for security goals.

Actually three methods can proposed to recognize gaits: using 2D data sources.

Dynamic Time Warping. The Dynamic TimeWarping (DTW) method[28 – 30] is considered to compare motion sequences. The method is based on dynamic programming and is widely used for different time-series [1] comparison applications (like voice recognition [12]). The application for motion processing and the data base structure proposal based on DTW was presented in different papers [11, 13, 14].

Spectrum Analysis. Some authors suggest that spectrum analysis of the motion signal can lead to interesting results concerning person identification [5 9]. I would like to to verify if the method is suitable also for motion capture data which are represented either by Eulers angles or by quaternions. The initial experiment consists of the comparison of the energy accumulated in the most important part of the spectrum of signals. We compared the first few spectrum amplitude coefficients in signals of rotations along 3 axes. The first 30 coefficients were taken into account, because one can notice it is the main band, where the majority of the energy is accumulated.

Worm-Like Chain. The worm-like chain (WLC) model in polymer physics is used to describe the behavior of semi-flexible polymers; it is sometimes referred to as the "Kratky-Porod" worm-like chain [15] model. The WLC model envisions an isotropic rod that is continuously flexible. In [15] it is proposed that adaptation WLC to the gait recognition will be very fruitful. The main problem solved is partition set of primitive motions according to similarity between motions. The motion models are constructed to easier extract features of given motions. Using these models the measure of discrepancy between motions is examined. Moreover, it normalizes length of motions and decreases high dimension of considered motion data, so clustering may take place in dimensionally reduced space. Human motion is a complex process and its various characteristics may be used in biometric analysis. Different motion representations is also considered.

4   Remarks

The goal of MC based modeling is to achieve a representation of the main human characteristics which allows to understand the essence of human gait phenomenon. A visually sensed human motion can be a very useful source of information for biometric posture recognition. This work summarizes methods and analysis that are applied at the consecutive stages of modeling as well as provides a comparison of various techniques and mathematical models that can be applied to a representation of human motion. This work shows different approaches to the problem of recognizing humans. It indicates directions of the future research into the design and implementation of biometric systems that use the human gait recognition for the identification purpose. The proposed solution uses data acquired by 3D Motion Capture systems and shows the methods and research directions that can also proof their usefulness in the process of identification of 2D data.

References

1. Batyrshin, I.Z., Sheremetov, L.: Perception Based Time Series Data Mining for Decision Making. In: IFSA (2), pp. 209–219 (2007)
2. Chaczko, Z., Klempous, R.: Anticipatory Biomimetic Middleware. In: 9th International Conference CASYS 2009 on Computing Anticipatory Systems, Lige, Belgium, August 3-8 (2009)
3. Kulbacki, M., Jablonski, B., Klempous, R., Segen, J.: Learning from Examples and Comparing Models of Human Motion. J. of Advanced Computational Intelligence and Intelligent Informatics 8(5), 477–481 (2004)
4. Murray, M.P.: Gait as a total pattern of movement. American Journal Phys. Med. 46(1) (1967)
5. Murray, M.P., Drought, A.B., Kory, R.C.: Walking patterns of normal men. Journal of Bone Joint Surg. 46A(2), 335–360 (1996)
6. Yam, C.Y., Nixon, M.S., Carter, J.N.: Extended Model-Based Automatic Gait Recognition of Walking and Running. In: Proc. of 3rd Int. Conf. on Audio-and Video- Based Biometric Person Authentication, pp. 278–283 (2001)
7. Yam, C.Y.: Automated person recognition by walking and running via model-based approaches. Pattern Recognition 37(5) (2003)
8. Cunado, D., Nixon, M.S., Carter, J.N.: Automatic extraction and description of human gait models for recognition purposes. Computer Vision and Image Understanding 90(1), 1–41 (2003)
9. Mowbray, S.D., Nixon, M.S.: Automatic Gait Recognition via Fourier Descriptors of Deformable Objects. In: Proc. of Audio Visual Biometric Person Authentication (2003)
10. Cunado, D., Nixon, M.S., Carter, J.N.: Using Gait as a Biometric, via Phase-Weighted Magnitude Spectra. In: Proc. of 1st Int. Conf. on Audio-and Video-Based Biometric Person Authentication, pp. 95–102 (2003)
11. Kuan, E.L.: Investigating gait as a biometric (Technical report, Department of Electronics and Computer Science. University of Southampton (1995)
12. Rabiner, L.R., Juang, B.: Fundamentals of speech recognition. Prentice-Hall, Englewood Cliffs (1993)
13. Itakura, F.: Minimum Prediction Residual Principle Applied to Speech Recognition. IEEE Trans. on Acoustics Speech and Signal Processing AS23(1), 67–72 (1975)
12. Bruderlin, A., Williams, L.: Motion Signal Processing. Computer Graphics 29, 97–104 (1995)
14. Kulbacki, M., Jablonski, B., Klempous, R., Segen, J.: Multimodel approach to human motion designing. In: Proc. IEEE International Conference on Computational Cybernetics, Siofok (2003)
15. Kratky, O., Porod, G.: Röntgenuntersuchung gelöster Fadenmoleküle. Rec. Trav. Chim. Pays-Bas. 68, 1106–1123 (1949)
16. Klempous, R.: Biometric motion identification based on motion capture. In: Rudas, I.J., Fodor, J., Kacprzyk, J. (eds.) Towards Intelligent Engineering and Information Technology. SCI, vol. 243, pp. 335–348. Springer, Heidelberg (2009)

194   R. Klempous

17. Klempous, R.: Movement identification analysis based on Motion Capture. In: Moreno Díaz, R., Pichler, F., Quesada Arencibia, A. (eds.) EUROCAST 2007. LNCS, vol. 4739, pp. 629–637. Springer, Heidelberg (2007)
18. Moulton, B., Pradhan, G., Chaczko, Z.: Voice operated guidance systems for vision impaired people: investigating a user-centered open source model. International Journal of Digital Content Technology and its Applications (September 12, 2009) (in press, accepted)
19. Kucharski, T.: Animated Human shape and movement modelling, Masters Thesis, Wroclaw University of Technology (2005) (in polish)
20. Cheng Changn, I., Lin, S.-Y.: 3D human motion tracking based on a progressive particle filter. Pattern Recognition 43, 3621–3635 (2010)
21. Lawrence, N.D.: Gaussian process latent variable models for visualisation of high dimensional data. In: Advances in Neural Information Processing Systems, vol. 16, pp. 329–336 (2003)
22. Saboune, J., Rose, C., Charpillet, F.: Factored interval particle filtering for gait analysis. In: International Conference of the IEEE Engineering in Medicine and Biology Society, pp. 3232–3235 (2007)
23. Corazza, S., Muendermann, L., Chaudhari, A., Demattio, T., Cobelli, C., Andriacchi, T.: A markerless motion capture system to study musculoskeletal biomechanics: visual hull and simulated annealing approach. Annals of Biomedical Engineering 34(6), 1019–1029 (2006)
24. Muendermann, L., Corazza, S., Andriacchi, T.: The Evolution of methods for the capture of human movement leading to markerless motion capture for biomechanical applications. Journal of NeuroEngineering and Rehabilitation 3(1) (2006)
25. Corazza, S., Mndermann, L., Andriacchi, T.: A Framework For The Functional Identification of Joint Centers Using Markerless Motion Capture, Validation For The Hip Joint. Journal of Biomechanics (2007)
26. Mndermann, L., Corazza, S., Andriacchi, T.: Accurately Measuring Human Movement using Articulated ICP with Soft-Joint Constraints and a Repository of Articulated Models. In: CVPR (2007)
27. Shahrokni, A., Lepetit, V., Fua, P.: Bundle Adjustment for Markerless Body Tracking in Monocular Video Sequences. In: ISPRS Workshop on Visualization and Animation of Reality-based 3D Models, Vulpera, Switzerland (2003)
28. Keogh, E.J., Pazzani, M.J.: Derivative Dynamic Time Warping. In: First SIAM International Conference on Data Mining, Chicago (2001)
29. Jablonski, B., Klempous, R., Majchrzak, D.: Feasibility analysis of human motion identification using motion capture. In: Proc. of the Int. Conference on Modelling, Identification and Control. Acta Press (2006)
30. Yers, C.S., Rabiner, L.R.: A comparative study of several dynamic time-warping algorithms for connected word recognition. The Bell System Technical Journal 60(7), 1389–1409 (1981)
i. www.ibgweb.com/products/reports/bmir-2009-2014
ii. www.btsbioengineering.com/
iii. http://en.wikipedia.org/wiki/List of motionandgesture file formats
iv. http://www.credo-interactive.com/
v. http://www.cs.wisc.edu/graphics/Courses/cs-838-1999/Jeff/BVH.html
vi. http://mocap.cs.cmu.edu/
vii. http://www.mpi-inf.mpg.de/resources/HDM05/
viii. http://www.biovision.com/
ix. http://www.computerhope.com/comp/acclaim.htm
x. http://www.nih.gov

Biomimetic Optimizers for Job Scheduling

Czesław Smutnicki

Institute of Computer Engineering, Control and Robotics
Wrocław University of Technology
Wybrzeże Wyspiańskiego 27, 50-372 Wrocław, Poland
czeslaw.smutnicki@pwr.wroc.pl

Abstract. In the paper, we proposed and tested a few biomimetic approaches for solving optimization problems derived from the practice of manufacturing. The main considered case is the cyclic flow shop scheduling problem with no-store constraints to minimize cycle time. Special problem properties are also shown. Quality of the proposed biomimetic optimization methods is evaluated in numerous computer tests.

Keywords: Nature, cyclic manufacturing, optimization.

1 Introduction

Combinatorial optimization problems, especially scheduling problems, create the real challenge for the efficient solution algorithms design. The strong NP-hardness of most of these problems disqualifies classical, exact approaches, as an example, branch-and-bound scheme (B&B) or integer linear programming (ILP), for instances coming from practice. On the other hand, the quality of solutions generated by approximate approaches influences immediately economic indexes (thus also profits). That's why many researchers continuously seek new, better fitted algorithms, which would be able to solve such problems with high accuracy in a short time. Optimizers, that mimics Nature, provide particularly efficient and promising optimization algorithms for the stated class of problems.

Manufacturing systems producing various products in large series with slow changeable assortment can fulfill market requirements either by (1) supplying series of uniform products with non-periodical change of product type, or by (2) cyclic supplying a mixture of various products. The quantitative and qualitative composition of the mixture depends on medium- and long-term orders of clients. Assuming that both solutions are achievable, the latter approach seems to be more attractive since eliminates or decreases the size of the output depot. Through the minimization of the cycle time (for the fixed set of products in the cycle) we can increase additionally the system efficiency as well the level of machine utilization. The further increase of efficiency one can obtain by elimination of storage between production stages. This leads to the specific constraints known as *no store* (no buffer) or *limited store* (buffer). Such type of restrictions appears also in the context of Just-in-Time (JIT) manufacturing systems.

R. Moreno-Díaz et al. (Eds.): EUROCAST 2011, Part II, LNCS 6928, pp. 195–202, 2012.

Models with regular job flows have been considered more frequently than others in the scheduling theory, because thanks to the simplicity of the problem formulation, algorithm designers can focus their attention chiefly on the efficiency of solution methods. The permutation flow shop problem with the makespan criterion is one of the most popular problems in this class. Until the eighties, two main approaches were applied to solve this class of problems: (1) B&B schemes and (2) constructive approximate algorithms. In the nineties, it became evident, that B&B reached the application limit despite the significant increase in computers power. Thus, heuristic methods and intelligent approximate approaches of iterative type became foreground tasks since the nineties, [1,3,7,8,9,11,12,15]. Several studies were carried out to improve efficacy of these algorithms, measured by the accuracy being opposed to the running time. Primal application of simulated annealing (SA), copying from physical processes of the Nature, [9], was only a small step toward the improvement of the quality. The newest history of methods began with the high quality approximate algorithm of Taillard, copying from the Nature an intelligent human solution method, [15], known as tabu search approach of Glover [2]. Next era came with tabu search algorithm TSAB, [7], based on the neighborhood with *blocks* and *accelerators*, which provided results of better quality in a considerably shorter time; the result was then strengthen in [7]. A few best features of TSAB, combined with the idea of path relinking, allow Reeves and Yamada [12] to improve their Genetic Algorithm, copying from Nature the evolution of organisms. Learning reinforcing has been observed by the use of space topology to control search processes, [17].

Systems without buffers or with limited buffer size have been already studied by many researchers because of the strong relevance for practitioners and troubles with designing of sufficiently efficient solution algorithms, [1,4,5,6,13]. Unfortunately, the majority of obtained so far results refer to noncyclic systems of such type. Deterministic *cyclic* problems with storage constraints are considered as the particularly hard combinatorial optimization case. Strong NP-hardness of even the simplest version of this problem, limits application of *exact optimization algorithms* to instances of a small size, leaving space for fast approximate methods with good quality. We refer next to the two-level decomposition of the problem: finding optimal sequence of jobs (upper level) and multiple finding of the minimal cycle time for the fixed sequence of jobs (lower level). Note, that the lower level in *classical scheduling problem with regular criteria* can be relatively simply solved using specific graph, whereas the lower level in the stated problem needs to solve certain Linear Programming (LP) problem. Therefore, any special properties of the problem are essential for the quality of the solution algorithm.

2   The Problem

The problem can be formulated as follows. Each of n jobs from the job set $J = \{1, 2, \ldots, n\}$, for $n > 1$, has to be processed in the cyclic way on m machines $1, 2, \ldots, m$ in the order given by the indexing of the machines. Thus job j, $j \in J$, consists of a sequence of m operations; each of them corresponding to the processing of job j on machine i during an uninterrupted processing time $p_{ij} \geq 0$. Machine i, $i = 1, 2, \ldots, m$, can execute at most one job at a time, and it is assumed that each machine processes the jobs in the same order. We represent the job processing order in the single cycle by the permutation $\pi = (\pi(1), \ldots, \pi(n))$ on the set J, and we let Π denote the set of all permutations on J. The overall job processing order, by repetition of the cycle, can be perceived as infinite concatenation $\pi \circ \pi \circ \pi \ldots$. Schedule of tasks from k-th cycle, $k = 1, 2, \ldots$, can be described by matrix $[S^k]_{m \times n}$ where $S^k_{i,j}$ is the time moment when processing of task j starts on machine i. Feasible schedule $[S^k]_{m \times n}$, for given π, must satisfy the following set of constraints

$$S^k_{i,\pi(j)} + p_{i,\pi(j)} \leq S^k_{i+1,\pi(j)}, \quad i = 1, \ldots, m, \quad j = 1, \ldots, n, \tag{1}$$

$$S^k_{i,\pi(j)} + p_{i,\pi(j)} \leq S^k_{i,\pi(j+1)}, \quad i = 1, \ldots, m, \quad j = 1, \ldots, n-1, \tag{2}$$

$$S^k_{i+1,\pi(j)} \leq S^k_{i,\pi(j+1)}, \quad i = 1, \ldots, m-1, \quad j = 1, \ldots, n-1, \tag{3}$$

$$S^k_{i,\pi(n)} + p_{i,\pi(n)} \leq S^{k+1}_{i,\pi(1)}, \quad i = 1, \ldots, m, \tag{4}$$

$$S^k_{i+1,\pi(n)} \leq S^{k+1}_{i,\pi(1)}, \quad i = 1, \ldots, m-1, \tag{5}$$

for $k = 1, 2, \ldots$. Inequalities (1) follow from technological order of operations inside each job. Inequalities (2) follow from the fixed processing order of jobs on machines. Inequalities (3) ensure the proper sequence of events in case of absence the buffer for job storing. Inequalities (4) – (5) express relations between events in k-th and $k + 1$-th cycles in case of job processing order (4) and buffering constraints (5). Such formulation of the problem allows one a freedom in schedule construction by preserving the rigid order of cycles, allowing simultaneously certain variation of start times in a small range. Nevertheless, we do not utilize this fact, tending toward formal deterministic periodic schedule. We assume next that not only the sequence π is repeated periodically but also the schedule $S_{m \times n}$ is periodical. It means that there exists constant T (period) such that

$$S^{k+1}_{i,\pi(j)} = S^k_{i,\pi(j)} + T, \quad i = 1, \ldots, m, \quad j = 1, \ldots, n, \quad k = 1, 2, \ldots \tag{6}$$

Value T depends on π and is called *cycle time*. Minimal value of T for fixed π will be called *minimal cycle time* and denoted by $T(\pi)$. Substituting (6) in (1) – (5) we obtain constraints referring to single cycle, and all cycles for $k = 1, 2, \ldots$ have the same form. This means that we can construct the schedule for single cycle and then translate it by kT, $k = 1, 2, \ldots$ on the time axis. Since obtained constraints are identical for any k, superscript k can be omitted in denotations. Value $T(\pi)$ and schedule S_{ij}, $i = 1, \ldots, m$, $j = 1, \ldots, n$ for fixed π can be found by solving the following optimization problem

$$T(\pi) = \min_{T, S} T \tag{7}$$

$$S_{i,\pi(j)} + p_{i,\pi(j)} \leq S_{i+1,\pi(j)}, \quad i = 1, \ldots, m, \quad j = 1, \ldots, n, \tag{8}$$

$$S_{i,\pi(j)} + p_{i,\pi(j)} \leq S_{i,\pi(j+1)}, \quad i = 1, \ldots, m, \quad j = 1, \ldots, n-1, \tag{9}$$

$$S_{i+1,\pi(j)} \leq S_{i,\pi(j+1)}, \quad i = 1, \ldots, m-1, \quad j = 1, \ldots, n-1, \tag{10}$$

$$S_{i,\pi(n)} + p_{i,\pi(n)} \leq S_{i,\pi(1)} + T, \quad i = 1, \ldots, m, \tag{11}$$

$$S_{i+1,\pi(n)} \leq S_{i,\pi(1)} + T, \quad i = 1, \ldots, m-1, \tag{12}$$

Without losing generality, we anchor the schedule at $S_{1,\pi(1)} = 0$.

The proposed mathematical model allow us to make quite natural two-level decomposition of the optimization problem. On the upper level we are looking for the best permutation $\pi^* \in \Pi$, where Π is the set of all permutations on the set N, so that

$$T(\pi^*) = \min_{\pi \in \Pi} T(\pi). \tag{13}$$

On the lower level we need to find $T(\pi)$, see (7) – (12). Searching π^* can be performed in any technology, as an example SA, TS, GA.

3   Lower Level Problem

Problem (7) – (12), for fixed π, is the linear programming (LP) task. However perceiving it in terms of LP seems to be computationally too time consuming. In the paper [4] there were proposed to find $T(\pi)$ and S_{ij}, $i = 1, \ldots, m$, $j = 1, \ldots, n$ by solving certain min flow problem in the specific network. Taking into account the size of the network $O(nm)$ and the computational complexity of the flow algorithm, we have obtained in the considered case algorithm of complexity $O(n^3 m^3)$. In the mentioned paper [4], there is also given the interpretation of T by using paths in a cylinder graph, however no algorithm was proposed there. Follow this idea, one can imagine quite sophisticated method with binary searching over T supported by modified Bellman-Ford algorithm, which implies certain approach with the complexity $O(n^2 m^2 \log_2 T^+)$, where T^+ is an upper bound on $T(\pi)$. In this section we propose two original methods with formal proofs of correctness (but not provided here). The former method finds lower bound T^* on $T(\pi)$ in the time $O(nm^2)$ on the base of typical grid graph for flow shop problem with buffering constraints. The latter method finds feasible schedule S for given T^* in the time $O(nm^2)$ on the base of the cylindric graph. Successive application of these methods allow us to find $T(\pi)$ and the proper schedule S in the time $O(nm^2)$ which is the best up to now result. Both methods analyze different graphs and are based on various following properties.

Property 1. *For each fixed π we have*

$$T \geq T(\pi) \geq T^* \stackrel{\text{def}}{=} \max_{1 \leq i \leq m} T_i \tag{14}$$

where

$$T_i \stackrel{\text{def}}{=} \begin{cases} \max\{S_{i,\pi(n)} + p_{i,\pi(n)}, S_{i+1,\pi(n)}\} - S_{i,\pi(1)} & \text{if } 1 \leq i < m \\ S_{i,\pi(n)} + p_{i,\pi(n)} - S_{i,\pi(1)} & \text{if } i = m \end{cases} \tag{15}$$

The value T_i evaluates minimal period of time for events linked through constraints (8) – (12). Notice, values $S_{i,\pi(n)}$ and $S_{i,\pi(1)}$ are generally correlated by the graph of precedence constraints of operations. Values T_i can be done with the graph and properties given below.

For the given processing order π we build the grid graph $G(\pi) = (V, R \cup E \cup F)$, having m rows and n columns, see interpretation in [7]. Nodes from $V = M \times N$ represents all operations of the job set J, whereas arc sets R, E, F correspond to performing operations and are defined accordingly to conditions (8) – (12) as follows

$$R = \bigcup_{i=1}^{m-1} \bigcup_{j=1}^{n} \{((i,j),(i+1,j))\}, \quad E = \bigcup_{i=1}^{m} \bigcup_{j=1}^{n-1} \{((i,j),(i,j+1))\}, \quad (16)$$

$$F = \bigcup_{i=1}^{m-1} \bigcup_{j=1}^{n-1} \{((i+1,j),(i,j+1))\} \quad (17)$$

Node $(i,j) \in V$ represents i-th operation of job $\pi(j)$ and its weight is $p_{i,\pi(j)}$. Arcs from sets R and E have weight zero. Each arc $((i+1,j),(i,j+1)) \in F$ has weight minus $p_{i+1,\pi(j)}$ and corresponds to constraint (10) converted to the form

$$(S_{i+1,\pi(j)} + p_{i+1,\pi(j)}) - p_{i+1,\pi(j)} \le S_{i,\pi(j+1)}, \quad (18)$$

where $i = 1, \ldots, m-1$, $j = 1, \ldots, n-1$. Graph $G(\pi)$ has regular structure not dependent on π, having weights on nodes and arcs from F dependent on π. Notice, that event $S_{i\pi(j)}$ associated with node $(i,1)$ influences on only certain subset of activities, which are successors in the graph.

Let d_{ij} denotes the length of the longest path in $G(\pi)$ going to node (l,j) (with this node weight) for i fixed in (15). Taking node $(i,1)$ as source we obtain from Bellman's algorithm the following recursive formula

$$d_{l,j}^{i} \stackrel{\text{def}}{=} \begin{cases} \max\{d_{l-1,j}^{i}, d_{l,j-1}^{i}, d_{l+1,j-1}^{i} - p_{l+1,\pi(j-1)}\} + p_{l,\pi(j)} & \text{if } 1 \le l < m \\ \max\{d_{l-1,j}^{i}, d_{l,j-1}^{i}\} + p_{l,\pi(j)} & \text{if } \quad l = m \end{cases} \quad (19)$$

where $p_{l,\pi(0} = 0$, $l = 1, \ldots, m$. In order to represent source properties we set $d_{l,0}^{i} = -L$, $l = 1, \ldots, i-1$, $d_{0j}^{i} = -L$, $j = 1, \ldots, i-1$, $d_{i,0}^{i} = 0$, $d_{0,i}^{i} = 0$, where L is a large number.

Property 2. *We have*

$$T_i = \begin{cases} \max\{d_{i,n}^{i}, d_{i+1,n}^{i} - p_{i+1,\pi(n)}\} & \text{if } 1 \le i < m \\ d_{i,n}^{i} & \text{if } \quad i = m \end{cases} \quad (20)$$

Property 3. T^* *can be found in the time* $O(nm^2)$.

Property 4. *There exists optimal solution of (7) – (12) such that* $T(\pi) = T^*$.

4 Schedule Construction

For the given π we built non-planar grid graph $H(\pi) = (V, R \cup E \cup E^* \cup F \cup F^*)$ having m rows and n columns (similarly as for $G(\pi)$) but wrapped around cylinder. Sets V, R, E, F are defined in (16) – (17); node and arc weights are defined in the same way. Sets E^* and F^* "closing" the cylinder are defined as

$$E^* = \bigcup_{i=1}^{m} \{((i,n),(i,1))\}, \quad F^* = \bigcup_{i=1}^{m-1} \{((i+1,n),(i,1))\} \tag{21}$$

Each arc $((i,n),(i,1)) \in E^*$ has negative weight $-T^*$ and represents constraint (12) converted to the form of

$$(S_{i,\pi(n)} + p_{i,\pi(n)}) - T^* \leq S_{i,\pi(1)}, \tag{22}$$

Each arc $((i+1,n),(i,1)) \in F^*$ has negative weight $(-p_{i+1,\pi(j)} - T^*)$ and represents constraint (11) converted to the form of

$$(S_{i+1,\pi(n)} + p_{i+1,\pi(n)}) - p_{i+1,\pi(n)} - T^* \leq S_{i,\pi(1)}, \tag{23}$$

We associate with the node (i,j) the event $S_{i,\pi(j)}$ having the sense of the longest path going to this node (without the node weight), $i = 1, \ldots, m$, $j = 1, \ldots, n$. Since graph $H(\pi)$ contains cycles (going around cylinder) and positive as well as negative weights on nodes and arcs, then in order to find path lengths we have to use the Bellman-Ford algorithm adopted to max path problem. Taking into account the size of $H(\pi)$ and complexity of Bellman-Ford method, we would obtain algorithm with the computational complexity $O(n^2 m^2)$. In the sequel we provide original more efficient algorithm with the complexity $O(nm^2)$.

At the begin we set $S_{1,\pi(1)} = 0$ and $S_{i,\pi(1)} = S_{i-1,\pi(1)} + p_{i-1,\pi(1)}$ for $i = 2, \ldots, m$. Next we repeat m-times the *iteration* consisting of calculation formula (24) for $j = 2, \ldots, n$ and then formula (25) for $j = 1$ (in the last iteration we do not perform (25))

$$S_{i,\pi(j)} = \begin{cases} \max\{C_{i,\pi(j-1)}, S_{i+1,\pi(j-1)}\} & \text{if} \quad i = 1, \\ \max\{C_{i,\pi(j-1)}, C_{i-1,\pi(j)}, S_{i+1,\pi(j-1)}\} & \text{if } 1 < i < m, \\ \max\{C_{i,\pi(j-1)}, C_{i-1,\pi(j)}\} & \text{if} \quad i = m \end{cases} \tag{24}$$

$$S_{i,\pi(1)} = \begin{cases} \max\{C_{i,\pi(n)} - T^*, S_{i+1,\pi(n)} - T^*\} & \text{if} \quad i = 1, \\ \max\{C_{i,\pi(n)} - T^*, C_{i-1,\pi(1)}, S_{i+1,\pi(n)} - T^*\} & \text{if } 1 < i < m, \\ \max\{C_{i,\pi(1)}, S_{i-1,\pi(n)} - T^*\} & \text{if} \quad i = m \end{cases} \tag{25}$$

where $S_{i,\pi(j)} + p_{i,\pi(j)} = C_{i,\pi(j)}$. Single iteration of (24) – (25) corresponds to single iteration of Bellman-Ford method with updating $S_{i,\pi(j)}$ along π. One can verify that in each iteration (8) – (10) are satisfied due to the form of (24). One need to check constraints (11) – (12). Since T^* s the lower bound of $T(\pi)$, there is enough to show that $H(\pi)$ does not contain cycle of positive length.

Let us assume, by contradiction, that $H(\pi)$ contains of positive length. The cycle must goes around cylinder since $G(\pi)$ was acyclic. Without losing generality we can assume that this cycle goes through the node $(i,1)$ for some i, $i \leq i \leq m$. Hence, from Property 20 (T_i as a path in the graph) we have $T_i - T^* > 0$, which yields $T_i > T^*$ and contradicts that T^* was maximal.

Table 1. Comparison of efficiency of solutions methods

Group	GA-E			SA			TS		
$n \times m$	MINB	AB	TIME	MINB	AB	TIME	MINB	ITER	TIME
20×5	0,75	1.92	3.5	0.5	2.43	0.5	0.68	40	3.8
20×10	0.43	1.73	13.2	0.41	1.84	2.3	0.53	300	14.8
20×20	0.30	1.31	48.6	0.22	1.57	9.1	0.54	250	51.7
50×5	2.94	4.21	13.7	0	2.16	4.4	3.50	50	18.8
50×10	2.58	3.93	30.9	0	1.52	14.4	3.07	50	50.1
50×20	2.02	2.94	115.2	0	1.32	61.1	2.61	50	171.2
100×5	5.86	6.94	29.1	0	1.93	20.6	18.53	10	48.5
100×10	4.88	5.88	61.0	0	1.62	58.4	12.10	10	97.8
100×20	3.01	3.77	228.8	0	1.10	223.9	7.09	10	288.7

5   Computer Experiments

The aim of the computer experiments was to evaluate quality of different bio-mimetic optimization technologies embedded on the upper level of the searching procedure. There have been considered: genetic algorithm from [10] with the new mechanism of gene expression (GA-E), simulated annealing method with auto-tuning and logarithmic cooling scheme (SA) [14], basic variant of tabu search approach TS (without using block properties and accelerator). Algorithms were programed in C++ and tested on first nine groups of Taillard's benchmarks [16]. Each group consists of 10 hard instances with the fixed number of machines m and number of jobs n. GA-E has been performed in the same way as in [10], in the version with full gene expression. Each algorithm dependent on random variables (e.g. GA or SA) has been run 10 times for each instance, excluding TS, which acts in deterministic way. For each instance, for each tested algorithm and for each of 10 runs, there have been calculated: minimal cycle time for running algorithm for this instance, relative error of i-th run of the algorithm A for this instance. Based on these values we found: AB mean relative error, $MINB$ minimal relative error, $TIME$ - mean running time per instance. Finally, for each algorithm and each group of instances, values of mentioned measures have been provided in Table 1.

6   Conclusions

Consequences of the introduced properties are manifold. Property 1 allow us to find minimal cycle time $T(\pi)$ without necessity of finding strict schedule S_{ij}, $i = 1, 2, \ldots, m$, $j = 1, 2, \ldots, n$, which can be very effectively used to good ac-count in SA, TS, GA technologies. Actually, detailed schedule is needed for the permutation generated on the output of optimization procedure. Property 3 states that $T(\pi)$ can be found more efficiently then the best known so far. Ad-ditionally, Property 2, through its relation to the path in the graph, allows one to introduce so called block properties, known for the problems with blocking, particularly useful for construction of promising neighborhood in the TS method and creation of accelerator. Property 4 allow us to find detailed schedule more efficiently than so far. Last but not least, approach allows us to attack more complex problems like job shop. We conclude from Table 1 that the best results, among those tested, provide SA. Algorithm TS does not reach the proper working conditions; because of the lack of accelerator it performs only 50 (or 10) iterations, but it should perform at least 1000...5000.

References

1. Grabowski, J., Pempera, J.: Sequencing of jobs in some production system. European Journal of Operational Research 125, 535–550 (2000)
2. Glover, F., Laguna, M.: Tabu search. Kluwer Academic Publishers, Massachusetts (1997)
3. Ishubuchi, M., Masaki, S., Tanaka, H.: Modified simulated annealing for the flow shop sequencing problems. European Journal of Operational Research 81, 388–398 (1995)
4. McCormick, M.L., Pinedo, M.L., Shenker, S., Wolf, B.: Sequencing in an assembly line with blocking to minimize cycle time. Operations Research 37, 925–935 (1989)
5. Leisten, R.: Flowshop sequencing with limited buffer storage. International Journal of Production Research 28, 2085–2100 (1990)
6. Nowicki, E.: The permutation flow shop with buffers: A tabu search approach. European Journal of Operational Research 116, 205–219 (1999)
7. Nowicki, E., Smutnicki, C.: A fast tabu search algorithm for the permutation flow-shop problem. European Journal of Operational Research 91, 160–175 (1996)
8. Ogbu, F.A., Smith, D.K.: The application of the simulated annealing algorithm to the solution $n/m/P/C_{max}$ flow-shop problem. Computers and Operations Research 17, 243–253 (1990)
9. Osman, I.H., Potts, C.N.: Simulated annealing for permutation flow shop scheduling. OMEGA 17, 551–557 (1989)
10. Pempera, J., Smutnicki, C.: Minimizing cycle time. The genetic approach with gene expression (Polish). Automatyka 9, 189–199 (2005)
11. Reeves, C.R.: A genetic algorithm for flow shop sequencing. Computers and Operations Research 22, 5–13 (1995)
12. Reeves, C.R., Yamada, T.: Genetic algorithms, path relinking and the flowshop sequencing problem. Evolutionary Computation 6, 45–60 (1998)
13. Smutnicki, C.: A two-machine flow shop scheduling problems with buffers. OR Spectrum 20, 229–235 (1999)
14. Smutnicki, C.: Scheduling algorithms (Polish). EXIT, Warszawa (2002)
15. Taillard, E.: Some efficient heuristic methods for flow-shop sequencing. European Journal of Operational Research 47, 65–74 (1990)
16. Taillard, E.: Home page. Internet, http://www.eivd.ch/ina/collaborateurs/etd/default.htm
17. Watson, J.P., Barbulescu, L., Whitley, L.D., Hove, A.E.: Contrasting structured and random permutation flow-shop scheduling problems: search-space topology and algorithm performance. INFORMS Journal of Computing 14, 98–123 (2002)

Task and Resources Assignment in Special Application Embedded Systems

Adam Handzlik[1], Andrzej Jablonski[2], Ryszard Klempous[2],
and Agnieszka Skotarczyk[1]

[1] Microtech International SA, Wołoska 20, 51-116 Wroclaw, Poland
{a.handzlik,a.skotarczyk}@microtech.com.pl
[2] The Institute of Computer Engineering, Control and Robotics
Wrocław University of Technology
11/17 Janiszewskiego Street, 50-372 Wrocław, Poland
{andrzej.jablonski,ryszard.klempous}@pwr.wroc.pl

Abstract. There are probably as many approaches to the design of the best embedded system as the number of design engineers. All they would review a set of given requirements and then take their favorite chips and tools to do the implementation. Although it seems that the approach to the design is typical, one thing is sure giving this task to ten different teams will result in ten different solutions. This situation takes place in spite of numerous methodologies and optimization schemes which should lead to the most optimized solution

Keywords: embedded systems, resources assignment, human-machine interfaces, electronic communication.

1 Task and Resources Assignment

Multiple mathematical tools, simulators, hardware and software codesign tools are employed to evaluate and predict all the functions, tasks, resources and interactions needed to fulfill requirements of the specific embedded system. However, even extremely well optimized solution will finally be confronted with seemingly unlimited choice of chips and platforms to be used as a final practical proof.

A real life example of an embedded system is presented in this paper to show how limited the choice of hardware and software becomes, if many physical, technical and human interaction aspects are to be taken on account.

At the same time the iterative nature of mastering of the human-machine interface may lead to even more critical hardware resource planning [2].

The practical example of an approach to the embedded system design conditions is based on an experience gained during realization of the research project entitled MoveON - Multi-modal and multi-sensor zero-distraction interaction interface for two wheel vehicles ON the move. The MoveON investigates the application of multi-modal and multi-sensor zero-distraction interfaces for enabling 2-wheel vehicle drivers to access online, in real-time and taking into account on the road safety issues, services and information resources.

Application description and resources are:

R. Moreno-Díaz et al. (Eds.): EUROCAST 2011, Part II, LNCS 6928, pp. 203–208, 2012.
© Springer-Verlag Berlin Heidelberg 2012

- Motorcycle control and communication system.
- Hands and eyes busy operation.
- Minimum distraction requirement.
- Multimode / Multilevel HMI.
- Harsh working environment.
- Extreme noise environment.
- Limited physical dimensions and weight helmet.
- Software architecture as simple as possible.
- Embedded system on chip vs PC architecture.
- Simplified interface solution.
- Standard component with Windows driver vs simple software procedures.

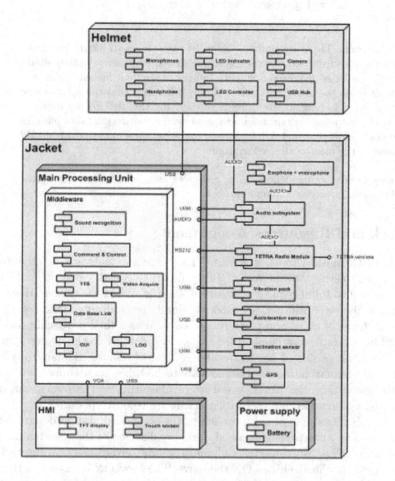

Fig. 1. Physical architecture of the MoveOn system

The main components are:

- The helmet.
- The motorcyclist jacket.
- The motor cycle

There is a wired connection between the jacket and the helmet and the sleeve display has a wired connection to the jacket. The rationale behind this system design is to have a fully wearable system, with everything in the jacket and in the helmet and nothing left on the motorcycle. However there is one exception to the system wearability, which deals with the scrolling device that is mounted on the mock-up handlebar. Indeed the user evaluation discarded the idea of using button-equipped gloves, for lack of ergonomics and usability, that is drivers remove their gloves when getting off the motorcycle. In the latter situation, the driver still has the possibility to use a gamut of interaction modalities to issue commands (e.g., speech recognition, touch screen).

The energy source is in the jacket (so the electronic devices in the helmet are powered by the wired connection between the jacket and the helmet). For the purpose of the evaluation and the demonstration, the user is static within an office environment or seated along a busy road. Instead of a motor cycle, a mock-up handlebar is used to run through the prototype functionalities in realistic conditions.

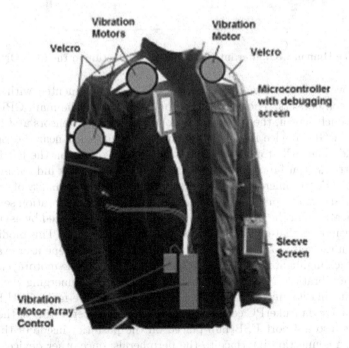

Fig. 2. MoveOn jacket with place holders affixed to the inner lining of the jacket to indicate the positions reserved for augmenting devices

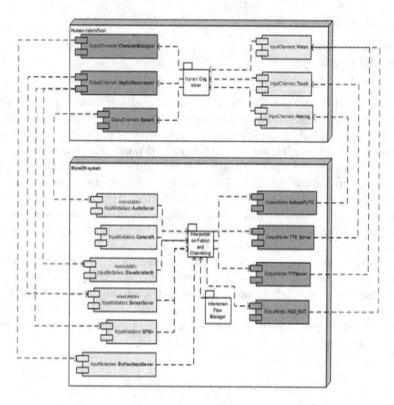

Fig. 3. The Human-Computer interaction loop architecture in the MoveON system

The MoveOn jacket is a classic motorcycle jacket augmented with assistive electronic components. These jacket components include the main CPU board, the LCD touch screen, the tilt/acceleration and vibration sensors and the USB hub. Also, a GPS device resides on the inside of the jacket near the right arm side-deltoid. The LCD touch screen acts as a sleeve screen on the left forearm. A dot-matrix screen functions purely as a debugging facility hidden inside the jacket, attached to a micro-controller that supports the functionality of the vibration motor array. The precision micro-drive 10mm shaftless vibration sensors, as had been featured in the design for prototype, have been replaced by asymmetric load rotary motors that give a more powerful vibration output. This modification was done in response to the results obtained from the prototype user evaluation process which highlighted the fact that the vibration from the motorcycle engine muffled the vibration output from shaftless sensors i.e. submerging their vibration and making it difficult to be sensed by the rider. The main CPU board is housed in a Travla AnkerPC casing affixed to the left posterior side of the jacket.

There is also a 4-port USB hub placed on the posterior inside of the jacket to provide a connection interface to the peripherals; once other devices e.g. accelerometers, helmet, etc., are integrated into the second jacket prototype, another USB hub will be installed to facilitate connectivity.

MoveON supports the complimentary use of speech, head nods and tactile modalities pushing beyond the state-of-the-art for motorcycle set-ups. The projects intended target users are the motorcycle drivers at large [3].

Apart from all other aspects of the project, from the electronic system point of view, it means a design of distributed embedded control and measurement system physically distributed around the driver and the motorcycle interacting with the driver and the surrounding environment.

The audio subsystem is responsible for real time operating with the following audio streams as following:

- Collecting synchronized voice data from all microphones and sending it using USB to the main computer for voice recognition.
- Routing PC outgoing audio channel from voice synthesis to helmet and ear set headphones.
- Routing microphone signal to Tetra audio output channel to provide outgoing voice communication.
- Routing Tetra audio input channel to helmet and ear set speakers to provide incoming voice communication.
- Mixing Tetra audio input channel together with PC audio channel.

Architecture of audio subsystem is presented in the figure below.

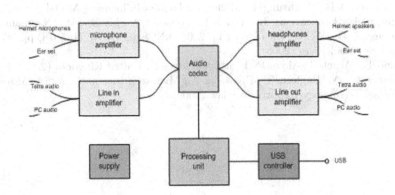

Fig. 4. Audio subsystem architecture

Problems of power consumption are:

- Battery operated system.
- Event driven activity.
- Switching off of unused hardware.
- Prioritizing of the software to be executed.
- Serialization of executed procedures.
- Low power silicon technology.

In this case an environment means not only communication between the driver and central information and command centers but a harsh and noisy field where speech recognition is to be used [4].

All those aspects created a set of different requirements which were driving substantially the way the electronic system was built.

2   Summary

In this document we have reviewed previous work about the physical architecture of the MoveOn System, that is now based on a wearable system, with all elements in the jacket and in the helmet. Problems for solving are:

- No tools for design of the complex embedded systems solutions.
- Variable requirements for parts of the system limit unification and resources optimization.
- Advanced power limiting techniques to be employed for battery operation.
- Custom hardware design as the only way of economical market approach.

References

1. Labrosse, J.: Embedded Software: Know It All. NEWNES, Weston (2007)
2. Naumann, A.B., Wechsung, I., Möller, S.: Factors Influencing Modality Choice in Multimodal Applications. In: André, E., Dybkjær, L., Minker, W., Neumann, H., Pieraccini, R., Weber, M. (eds.) PIT 2008. LNCS (LNAI), vol. 5078, pp. 37–43. Springer, Heidelberg (2008)
3. Handzlik, A., et al.: MoveON Prototype Series II, United Kingdom (2009)
4. Skotarczyk, A., Englert, T., Handzlik, A.: Microtech International SA. Move on. Internal Technology Report. Wroclaw (2009)

Diagnosis of Neurodegenerative Diseases Based on Multi-modal Hemodynamic Classification of the Brain

Gerald Zwettler[1], Robert Pichler[2], and Werner Backfrieder[1]

[1] Biomedical Informatics, School of Informatics, Communication and Media,
University of Applied Sciences Upper Austria,
Softwarepark 11, 4232 Hagenberg, Austria
{gerald.zwettler,werner.backfrieder}@fh-hagenberg.at
[2] Institute of Neuro-Nuclear Medicine at the State Mental Hospital Wagner-Jauregg,
Wagner-Jauregg-Weg 15, 4020 Linz, Austria
robert.pichler@gespag.at

Abstract. Accurate diagnostic assessment of metabolic processes in nuclear medicine diagnostic imaging, e.g. SPECT and PET, rely on specific localization of physiological activity. The major step in precise staging of neuro-degenerative diseases is robust, patient-specific classification of the brain. In this work a vascularization-based classification strategy for MRI datasets of the brain is introduced to handle variability of patient's anatomy. The vascularization-based classification utilizes skeletonization in combination with *m-adjacency* to construct a hierarchical vessel tree from binary pre-segmentations. Based on the vessel topology, the brain voxels are classified with respect to a minimal distance criterion from the vessel branches they are assigned to. This blood-supply oriented approach shows proper segmentation of respective anatomical regions of the human brain. Results are validated on T1-weighted brainweb database.

Keywords: vessel tree modeling, skeletonization, morphological classification.

1 Introduction

For diagnosis of neurodegenerative diseases like *Morbus Parkinson* or *Morbus Alzheimer* and other types of dementia, the combination of complementary information of high resolution morphological modalities, e.g. CT or MRI and functional modalities like SPECT and PET, provide a holistic view on the patient's anatomy and pathology. A vast majority of all clinical questions concerning neurodegenerative diseases necessitates accurate quantification of the metabolic activity for detection and assessment of the affected foci. For accurate assessment of the measured activity, patient-specific reference parameters concerning anatomy are needed as a base for comparison. Consequently, anatomical knowledge about volume and dimension of specific brain areas is required for relative analysis of the measured activity.

R. Moreno-Díaz et al. (Eds.): EUROCAST 2011, Part II, LNCS 6928, pp. 209–216, 2012.

Classification of the brain can be performed at different levels of granularity:

- according to *white matter, gray matter, cerebrospinal fluid, muscles,...*
- according to the main brain lobes, the *frontal, temporal, occipital lobe,...*
- according to the *Brodmann* areas [1][2] as detailed taxonomy of the brain windings.

In clinical practice, the ascertainment of the specific anatomical information is achieved based on MRI studies utilizing different imaging protocols. The segmentation procedure is a time-consuming semi-automatic process. More advanced applications utilize sophisticated and calculation-intensive deformable models [3], LevelSets [4] or statistical shape models [5] that automatically align an a-priori model to the patient data but do not account for the patient-specific variation of anatomy.

Analysis of image data shows that brain-vascularization is highly patient-specific and significantly differs from pre-defined anatomical models. Consequently, a strong need for individual classification of the brain according to the particular vascular system as prerequisite for accurate diagnostic evaluations arises.

2   Material

Image data from $n=20$ T1-weighted MRI datasets of *brainweb* database [6][7] and associated reference segmentations are used. Further test runs and validations are performed using $n=12$ anonymous multi-modal patient studies comprising morphologic image acquisitions (*T1, T2, PD,*) as well as functional images (*SPECT, PET*).

3   Methodology

A fully automated algorithm for vascular classification of the brain is presented, comprising several image-processing steps, see Fig. 1. Details of the particular processing steps are explained in the following sections.

3.1   Segmentation

An algorithm for vessel segmentation is used, based on characteristic vessel measures [8], extracted from volume image data by Eigenanalysis of the second derivatives, the Hessians, yielding the radius of curvature for tubular structures.

For segmentation of the gray and white matter, K-means clustering [9][10] is utilized to perform a preliminary segmentation of T1-weighted images. Based on this pre-classification, region growing is used to connect gray and white matter.

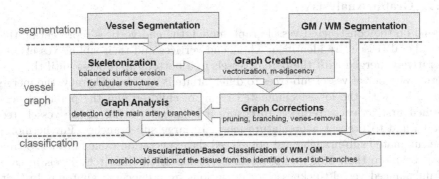

Fig. 1. Delineation of the image-processing pipeline for vascularization-based classification of the brain. After segmentation of vessels and the brain matter, the vessel graph is constructed and analyzed as required pre-processing for subsequent classification of the brain tissue.

3.2 Skeletonization

Skeletonization of the vascular structures is performed utilizing a morphologic operator for balanced surface erosion, an acceleration of Jonker's generic skeletonization approach [11] for the domain of tubular structures. Thereby elements on the surface of the object are eroded each iteration, until a thickness of one voxel for the remaining fully-connected medial axis is reached. Three constraints for N_{26} neighborhood prevent loss of connectivity, shrinking and skeleton artifacts due to grabbing into the surface during erosion process [12].

3.3 Graph Construction and Correction

The transformation of the binary medial axis representation into a graph model requires vectorization, i.e. transformation of a connected mask into a polyline. Bifurcation points of the resulting vessel tree's medial axis are identified by applying *m-adjacency* [13], defined for voxels p and q in N_{26} as:

> two voxels p and q are in mixed adjacency if
> I) $q \in N_6(p)$ or
> II) $q \in N_{12}(p) \ \wedge \ N_6(p) \cap N_6(q) = \emptyset$ or
> III) $q \in N_D(p) \ \wedge \ N_6(p) \cap N_6(q) = \emptyset \ \wedge \ N_{12}(p) \cap N_{12}(q) = \emptyset$.

The bifurcation points are then used for constructing a hierarchical and acyclic vessel tree. The root of the graph representing the vessel tree is identified with respect to a maximal vessel diameter and minimal distance from the *pons*, i.e. a structure located at the brain stem that connects cerebrum, cerebellum and medulla. In an iterative correction procedure the parent-to-child relations are analyzed with respect to hemodynamic properties. Furthermore, short child vessels are identified and merged with the parent segments until convergence is reached. This correction run removes artifacts and significantly reduces vessel graph complexity.

3.4   Graph Analysis

Based on the constructed vessel graph model, the end vertices representing the peripheral vessels are identified. These end vertices and their sibling vessels are iteratively merged with the parent vessels in a bottom-up process until the targeting number of vessel sub-trees to differentiate is reached. Thereby, the merge operation with the lowest cumulated result of children and the parent is performed first at each iteration to ensure a balanced tracing of the vessel tree model and to prevent a premature merge of large sub-branches. Furthermore, the cumulated sub-branch must not exceed the expectation value for the sub-tree sizes by more than *30%* to ensure conservation of the hierarchy levels in case of imbalanced vessel thicknesses or deviations from expected anatomy. In that case, the merge process finishes before the targeting number of vessel branches is reached. The described bottom-up merging for a targeting hierarchy of $N = 5$ is illustrated in Fig.2.

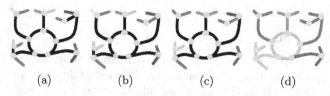

(a)   (b)   (c)   (d)

Fig. 2. Graph analysis for a targeting number of $N = 5$ vessel sub-trees. Child and parent vessels at the periphery are merged until the targeting number of remaining sub-trees is reached.

3.5   Vascularization-Based Classification

The voxels representing gray and white matter are classified with respect to minimal Euclidean distance to one of the pre-classified vessel sub-trees. In a pre-processing step, a distance map is calculated recursively, giving the minimal Euclidean distance of each brain matter voxel to the nearest vessel segment. For calculation of the distance map, the geodesic properties of the object to be classified are incorporated, i.e. possible inclusions necessitate detours from the direct path. Based on the pre-calculated distance map the vessel representations are iteratively eroded against the object to classify, starting at the surface of the vessel skeletons. For each iteration run, the distance of the voxels to consider for classification is increased by $\Delta = 0.5$ voxel width, see Fig.3.

To assure balanced morphological growth, collision-handling must be considered. If a particular voxel can be reached by multiple different vessel segments at a certain distance interval, a proper strategy for choosing the vessel segment to grab the voxel is required. In this work three different strategies were developed and evaluated for balanced collision-handling:

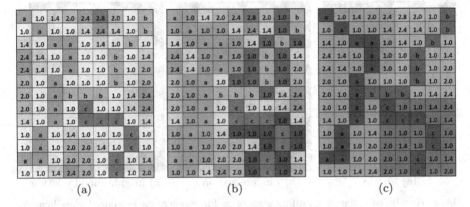

(a)   (b)   (c)

Fig. 3. Illustration of 2D vascularization-based classification for three segments *a*, *b* and *c*. The Euclidean distance map is calculated based on the pre-segmented vessel segments (a). The distance threshold is increased by *0.5* prior to each iteration. Every voxel within the distance threshold is classified according to the closest segment (b). Finally all voxels are assigned to one of the three segments (c).

4 Results

The presented vascularization-based classification is applied to brainweb T1-weighted MRI-data at $N=5$ target sub-branches. The vessel tree model is thereby derived from the arteries originating at the Circle of Willies [14] and utilized for classification the entire white and gray brain matter, see Fig.5. The primary artery branch is decomposed into *anterior*, *middle* and *posterior cerebral artery* for subsequently performing dilation-based assignation of the white and gray brain matter. The resulting cutting planes between adjacent vessel sub-branches are symmetric and well defined, see Fig.5(d).

- *first-in*: the first vessel segment to reach an unclassified voxel will assign the class value. Results highly depend on the vessel-segment processing order, see Fig. 4(a). Imbalances in the early iterations have an exponentially growing influence on the final results due to propagation of the volume deviations.
- *randomized order*: shuffling of the segments for randomized processing order can be applied to compensate this imbalance and guarantee equal growth of the segments at the cost of frayed border areas, see Fig. 4(b).
- *neighborhood relation*: incorporating the neighborhood count and distances of all segments adjacent to the particular voxel to classify. For each segment, distance weights of the neighboring voxels in N_{26} as $weight_i = 1.0 + 4 \cdot (\sqrt{3} - dist_i)$, with $dist_i$ as Euclidean distance between the adjacent neighbors in N_{26}, are cumulated, thus favoring proximity besides adjacent voxel count. The segment with the highest score, i.e. most and/or closest adjacent neighbors, is selected for classification of the particular voxel. For tie situations random selection is applied, see Fig. 4(c).

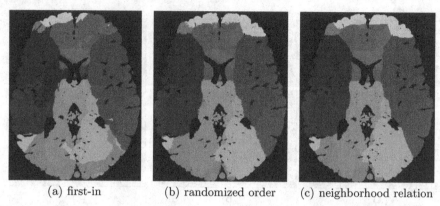

(a) first-in   (b) randomized order   (c) neighborhood relation

Fig. 4. Results of collision handling strategies for vascularization-based classification as axial views of T1-weighted brain MRI

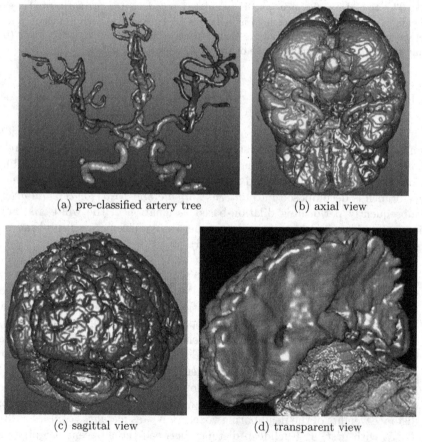

(a) pre-classified artery tree   (b) axial view

(c) sagittal view   (d) transparent view

Fig. 5. Results from processing patient dataset #4. Based on the pre-classified artery model (a) the vascularization-based classification of the gray and white brain matter is performed (b-c). The chosen collision handling strategy leads to well defined cutting planes, observable when transparently visualizing segments for inside (d).

Incorporating both, the neighborhood count and the Euclidean distances for collision handling leads to the best results as the volume assignment is balanced and the produced cutting areas are plane, see Fig.4.

5 Discussion

A vascularization-based classification concept, not limited to the neurological domain of brain datasets, has been presented in this work. In preliminary studies the applicability for Couinaud liver lobe classification based on *vena porta* model has been shown in the past [15][16]. The generic concept is applicable to all medical domains, where the vascularization system predetermines anatomical structures.

6 Conclusion

This classification strategy can be further refined according to the maximum segmented vessel tree hierarchy level that heavily depends on the specific image data quality and the imaging modality and protocol parameters. With the presented vascularization-based classification strategy, patient-specific variability of the vessel tree can be accounted for more precisely.

Future improvements will be aimed at incorporating additional a priori knowledge of hemodynamics for robustness of graph analysis and reliable modeling of the hierarchy levels besides analysis of mean parent-to-child vessel cross-sections.

Acknowledgements. The research work was accomplished in the context of project *INVERSIA*, part of the funding program *Regional Competitiveness Upper Austria 2007-2013* financed by *The European Regional Development Fund* (EFRE) and the government of Upper Austria.

References

1. Brodmann, K.: Vergleichende Lokalisationslehre der Grosshirnrinde - in ihren Principien dargestellt auf Grund des Zellenbaues. Johann Ambrosius Barth Verlag, Leipzig (1909)
2. Duus, P.: Neurologisch-topische Diagnostik, pp. 389–390. Georg Thieme Verlag, Stuttgart (1990)
3. McInerney, T., Terzopoulos, D.: Deformable models in medical image analysis - a survey. Medical Image Analysis 1(2), 91–108 (1996)
4. Sethian, J.A.: Level set methods and fast marching methods. Cambridge Monographs on Applied and Computational Mathematics (1999)
5. Lamecker, H., Lange, T., Seebass, M.: Segmentation of the liver using a 3d statistical shape model. ZIB-Report (2004)
6. Cocosco, C.A., Kollokian, V., Kwan, R.K.-S., Evans, A.C.: Brainweb - Online Interface to a 3D MRI Simulated Brain Database. NeuroImage 5(4), 425 (1997)
7. Kwan, R.K.-S., Evans, A.C., Pike, G.B.: MRI simulation-based evaluation of image-processing and classification methods. IEEE Trans. on Medical Imaging 18(11), 1085–1097 (1999)

8. Frangi, A.F., Niessen, W.J., Vincken, K.L., Viergever, M.A.: Multiscale vessel enhancement filtering. In: Wells, W.M., Colchester, A.C.F., Delp, S.L. (eds.) MICCAI 1998. LNCS, vol. 1496, pp. 130–137. Springer, Heidelberg (1998)
9. Kanungo, T., Mount, D.M., Netanyahu, N.S., Piatko, C.D., Silverman, R., Wu, A.Y.: An efficient k-means clustering algorithm: analysis and implementation. IEEE Trans. Pattern Analysis and Machine Intelligence 24, 881–892 (2002)
10. Ibanez, L., Schroeder, W., Ng, L., Cates, J.: The ITK Software Guide. Kitware Inc. Publisher (2005)
11. Jonker, P.P.: Skeletons in N dimensions using shape primitives. Pattern Recognition Letters 23, 677–686 (2002)
12. Zwettler, G., Swoboda, R., Pfeifer, F., Backfrieder, W.: Fast Medial Axis Extraction on Tubular Large 3D Data by Randomized Erosion. LNCIS, vol. 6(14), pp. 97–108. Springer, Germany (2010)
13. Pfeifer, F., Kastner, J., Freytag, R.: Method for three-dimensional evaluation and visualization of the distribution of fibres in glass-fibre reinforced injection molded party by μ-X-ray computed tomography. In: Proc. of the 17th World Conference on Nondestructive Testing, China (2008)
14. Hartkamp, M.J., van der Grond, J.: Investigation of the circle of Willies using MR angiography. Medica Mundi 44, 20–27 (2000)
15. Backfrieder, W., Zwettler, G., Swoboda, R., Pfeifer, F., Kratochwill, H., Fellner, F.: Automated segmentation of liver morphology for diagnosis and surgery planning. In: Proc. of the IGRT Vienna (2008)
16. Zwettler, G., Backfrieder, W., Swoboda, R., Pfeifer, F.: Fast fully-automated model-driven liver segmentation utilizing slicewise applied levelsets on large CT data. In: Proc. of the 21st European Modeling and Simulation Symposium, EMSS 2009, pp. 161–166 (2009)

A Subpixel Edge Detector Applied to Aortic Dissection Detection

A. Trujillo-Pino[1], K. Krissian[1], D. Santana-Cedrés[1], J. Esclarín-Monreal[1], and J.M. Carreira-Villamor[2]

[1] Centro de Tecnologías de la Imagen (CTIM)
Universidad de Las Palmas de Gran Canaria (ULPGC)*
[2] Universidad de Santiago de Compostela (USC)
{agustin,krissian,jesclarin}@dis.ulpgc.es, dsantana@ctim.es,
josemartin.carreira@usc.es

Abstract. The aortic dissection is a disease that can cause a deadly situation, even with a correct treatment. It consists in a rupture of a layer of the aortic artery wall, causing a blood flow inside this rupture, called dissection. The aim of this paper is to contribute to its diagnosis, detecting the dissection edges inside the aorta. A subpixel accuracy edge detector based on the hypothesis of partial volume effect is used, where the intensity of an edge pixel is the sum of the contribution of each color weighted by its relative area inside the pixel. The method uses a floating window centred on the edge pixel and computes the edge features. The accuracy of our method is evaluated on synthetic images of different thickness and noise levels, obtaining an edge detection with a maximal mean error lower than 16 percent of a pixel.

Keywords: Aortic Dissection, Subpixel Edge Detection, Anisotropic Diffusion.

1 Introduction

1.1 The Aortic Dissection

To understand the aortic dissection, we need to know the artery structure. The wall of an artery is formed by three layers, from inside to outside: the tunica intima, the tunica media and the tunica adventitia (fig. 1, left).

Under normal conditions, the blood flows inside the vessel lumen (fig. 1, center). But, in the case of an aortic dissection, the normal blood flow changes. The tunica intima breaks and the blood gets into the tunica media (fig. 1, right). Therefore, we have two flows: the normal flow inside the vessel lumen, and the flow inside the tunica media, called false vessel lumen.

At the beginning of the generation process of an aortic dissection, we have a normal flow. When the dissection occurs, in most cases, there are one or two

---

* This work has been supported by the project SIMVA, TIN2009-10770 from the Spanish Ministry of Science and Innovation.

R. Moreno-Díaz et al. (Eds.): EUROCAST 2011, Part II, LNCS 6928, pp. 217–224, 2012.

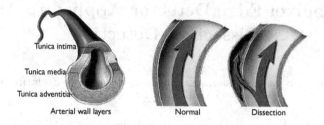

Fig. 1. Artery structure (Courtesy of A.D.A.M. Inc.) and Normal vs Dissection blood flow (Courtesy of Dr. Grasshopper)

tears (also called entry points) that connect with the vessel lumen. At this moment the false vessel lumen is created (extraluminal wall channel). A dissection may have a variable separation, length and thickness (from few millimeters to several centimeters). When there are no more entry points, we find an intramural hematoma, that can progress to a complete dissection, through a secondary rupture of the tunica media.

1.2   Aortic Dissection Classification

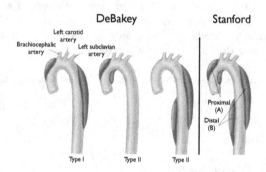

Fig. 2. DeBakey and Stanford aortic dissection classification (Courtesy of Richard J. Shemin, MD; Praveen Menon,MD; Ara Ketchedjian, MD Medscape Education (Medscape Cardiology))

There are several types of classification, based on the starting point, the type and length of the injury and the symptoms duration. Initially, the DeBakey classification was used. It was defined by Dr. Michael Ellis DeBakey, a world-renowned cardiovascular surgeon and scientist [2]. It divides the dissection in three types (fig. 2, left): Type I, type II and type III (IIIA or IIIB depending on the dissection end location).

But now, the Stanford classification, based on the prognosis differences and the therapeutic treatment, is the standard one. It divides the dissection in two types (fig. 2, right): Type A (starts at ascending aorta and can be extended to aortic arch and descending thoracic aorta) and type B (everyone else).

Based on the Stanford classification, we have the following statistics: from 58 to 72 percent of the dissections are of type A, and from 28 to 42 percent are of type B. Moreover, 70 percent of the dissections end with a rupture of the artery wall, with a bled on adjacent structures, such as pericardial bled (more frequent on type A) [1].

1.3   Diagnostic Images

Angiography has been replaced now by other imaging techniques, such as computed tomography (CT) or magnetic resonance (MRI). In the fig. 3 we can see the axial, coronal and sagittal plane of a CT; with a zoom on the dissection region. The arrow indicates the location of the aortic dissection.

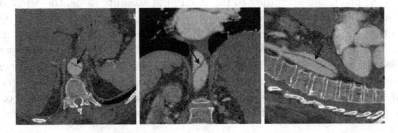

Fig. 3. Axial, coronal and sagittal plane of an aortic dissection. The black arrow indicates the location of the dissection inside the aorta.

To contribute to the diagnosis of the medical problem, the dissection must be located. The correct estimation of edge features is an important step to extract higher-level information. The subpixel edge detector proposed by Agustín Trujillo Pino[7], uses a floating window to calculate the edge features with high accuracy.

We propose to use this subpixel edge detector for locating the aortic dissection edges, because it has a thin planar structure, that divides the interior of the aorta in two or more parts. For the experiments, we use a synthetic model of the structure, and apply the method to different configurations of thickness and noise.

2   Method

2.1   The Subpixel Method

An edge is a virtual line between two regions with different intensity levels. Normally, the standard methods only indicate the edge pixels. They usually use numerical information of the pixels of a particular neighborhood to decide if it is an edge pixel or not. However, when accuracy is important, for example when measuring the dissection thickness; a pixel level detection isn't appropriate. A subpixel edge detection must be used.

The subpixel edge detection method proposed by Trujillo [7], is based on the partial volume effect inside the edge pixels. Most methods assume that an image is a continuous and differentiable function. The subpixel edge detection method assumes that an edge is a discontinuity in the intensity values of the function, delimiting the border between two objects. The intensity of an edge pixel is the sum of the contribution of each value, weighted by its relative area inside the pixel. Other methods apply any of the following techniques: moment [3], least squared [4] or interpolation [6]. The main advantage of this subpixel method is that all the edge features (sub-pixel position, orientation, curvature and change in intensity at both sides) are computed with total accuracy in ideal images.

At the beginning, the subpixel algorithm smooths the input image using a 3×3 mask obtaining the image G. Afterwards x and y derivatives are calculated at the (i, j) pixel, and according to the maximum absolute value, the orientation (vertical or horizontal) of the window centered in this pixel is decided. Once known that the partial value is greater than the threshold, the method computes the limits of the floating window (fig. 4). In the vertical case, the window width is constant, three pixels, and the maximum height is nine pixels. The height limits of the window are set to be the pixels of minimal derivative values on each side of the center pixel within each column or row of nine pixels. The use of the floating limits allows to detect close-by edges (separated by four pixels or more).

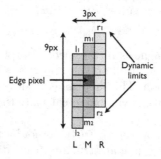

Fig. 4. Floating window of the subpixel edge detector

In the next step, the method computes the intensity values at both sides of the edge (eq. 1 and 2). This calculation is done considering the sign of the product between x and y derivatives. In all cases, the pixels used to compute the intensity are indicated by the floating limits computed before $(l_1, l_2, m_1, m_2, r_1, r_2)$.

$$B = \begin{cases} \frac{G_{i-1,j+l_1}+G_{i,j+m_1}}{2} & \text{if } G_x(i,j)G_y(i,j) > 0 \\ \frac{G_{i,j+m_1}+G_{i+1,j+r_1}}{2} & \text{if } G_x(i,j)G_y(i,j) < 0 \end{cases} \tag{1}$$

$$A = \begin{cases} \frac{G_{i,j+m_2}+G_{i+1,j+r_2}}{2} & \text{if } G_x(i,j)G_y(i,j) > 0 \\ \frac{G_{i-1,j+l_2}+G_{i,j+m_2}}{2} & \text{if } G_x(i,j)G_y(i,j) < 0 \end{cases} \tag{2}$$

There are cases where the edges are very close. For example, the dissection region could have a thickness of two or three pixels. The subpixel method can detect this type of edges from the derivative values after the limits. If these values are very high, we will be in this case, and the value of the intensity will be computed using the original image.

The last step is computing the sum of every column. This is possible using the floating limits computed in previous steps (eq. 3). With the values of the intensity at both sides of the edge pixel and the sums of the columns, we can compute the parameters of the edge. The method finds the coefficients of the parabola ($y = a + bx + cx^2$) which best fits the edge (eq. 4). Applying these steps to every edge pixel, the edges of the image are obtained with subpixel accuracy. The values of a, b and c are obtained from as follows:

$$S_L = \sum_{k=l_1}^{l_2} G_{i-1,j+k} \quad S_M = \sum_{k=m_1}^{m_2} G_{i,j+k} \quad S_R = \sum_{k=r_1}^{r_2} G_{i+1,j+k} \tag{3}$$

$$c = \frac{S_L + S_R - 2S_M}{2(A-B)} + \frac{A(2m_2 - l_2 - r_2) - B(2m_1 - l_1 - r_1)}{2(A-B)}$$

$$b = \frac{S_R - S_L}{2(A-B)} + \frac{A(l_2 - r_2) - B(l_1 - r_1)}{2(A-B)}$$

$$a = \frac{2S_M - (1+2m_2)A - (1-2m_1)B}{2(A-B)} - \frac{1 + 24a_{01} + 48a_{11}}{12}c \tag{4}$$

2.2   Noise Reduction

When the input image is noisy, it must be filtered previously to better detect the edges. For this purpose, the Noise Reducing Anisotropic Diffusion filter (NRAD) [5] is used. The NRAD method filters the noise preserving the edges, like Perona and Malik method:

$$\begin{cases} u(0) = u_0 \\ \frac{\partial u}{\partial t} = div(c\nabla u) \end{cases} \tag{5}$$

This equation (5) uses a diffusion coefficient, that is a decreasing function of the gradient norm. This diffusion function depends on a parameter related to the image gradient that must be set by the user. However, the NRAD filter (eq. 6), uses a diffusion function $1 - k$, that depends on the local statistics of the image and on the noise model.

$$\begin{cases} u(0) = u_0 \\ \frac{\partial u}{\partial t} = div((1-k)\nabla u) = div\left(\frac{\sigma_n^2}{v_g}\nabla u\right) \end{cases} \tag{6}$$

An additive noise model is used in the experiments, $g = f + n$, where the observed image, g, is equal to the sum of the ideal image, f, plus a Gaussian additive noise, n.

Equation 7 shows that the corrected image $\widehat{f}$ is calculated using an estimator, and it is the sum of the local mean $\overline{g}$ and the product between the coefficient k and the difference between the image g and its local mean $\overline{g}$.

The coefficient k (eq. 8) is the result of the division between the local variance of f, v_f, and the local variance of g, v_g. The parameter σ_n^2 is the global noise variance, computed at every iteration using a region of interest. The partial differential equation (6) is based on this estimator.

$$\widehat{f} = \overline{g} + k(g - \overline{g}) \tag{7}$$

$$k = \frac{v_f}{v_g} = \frac{v_g - \sigma_n^2}{v_g} \tag{8}$$

For this application the scalar version of this filter is used, but a matrix extension is also proposed in the original paper [5]. In the figure 5, we can see the difference of applying the edge detector without and with the NRAD filter.

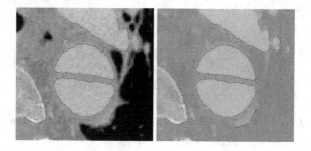

Fig. 5. Subpixel result vs Subpixel+NRAD result

3   Results

In order to run the experiments the opensource software AMILab (http://amilab.sourceforge.net) has been used. AMILab is a visualization and processing image software, but is also a complete crossplatform system that includes its own scripting language and a lot of algorithms, from simple operations like resizing an image, to segmentation algorithms.

If we look at an axial cut of a CTA of an aortic dissection, the aorta contains a thin black line. This line is the dissection wall. To measure the accuracy of the experiments, a set of synthetic images is used. These images are the combination of a circle and a ring, similar to an axial cut of an aortic dissection. As the features of the synthetic images (the radius of the circle and the internal and external radii of the ring) are known, the accuracy of the subpixel detector could be measured. The experiments made were:

- The first type tests the method with different values of the thickness of the center region, our synthetic dissection.
- In the second type, we select a thickness with a low error level and add noise to the image, from 0 to 20 (standard deviation).
- Finally, we combine all the thicknesses with all the noise levels.

Figure 6 a), represents the subpixel position error when varying the thickness of the ring inside the synthetic image. We can see a mean error lower than 0.2 and a standard deviation lower than 0.32 pixels. There is a big difference between a thickness of one and two pixels, because with one pixel one of the intensities near the edge is missed, and the initial hypothesis does not hold. However, the mean error remains lower than 0.2 pixels.

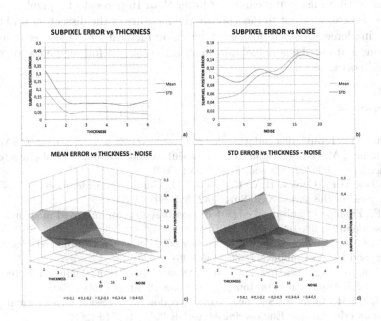

Fig. 6. Subpixel position error: a) with different thicknesses, b) with different noise levels, c) mean and d) std combining thicknesses and noise levels

Figure 6 b) represents the subpixel position error when varying the noise level on a synthetic image with a thickness of 4. In this set of tests, the NRAD method is first applied to reduce the noise, and the subpixel method is applied to detect the edges. With the highest noise value, the mean error and standard deviation obtained are lower than 0.16.

Finally, fig. 6 c) and d) represent the mean and the standard deviation when combining different thicknesses and noise levels. In both graphics, the error is still lower than 0.32 in the worst case (high level noise with a thickness of one).

4 Conclusions and Future Lines

Throughout this paper, we have described the medical problem: its definition, classification and the images used for diagnostic. Then, the need of a subpixel level edge detector has been motivated. After describing our subpixel method, we have also added to the process the NRAD method, to reduce the noise as a preprocessing step. Then, different experiments have been designed with different dissection sizes and noise levels, showing the robustness and accuracy of our method.

From this analysis, we can conclude that the combination of the subpixel detector and the NRAD method is a very accurate process for aortic dissection detection. For example, in a pixel that meets the partial volume effect with two intensities on both sides of the edge, in the worst case, an edge detection is obtained with a maximal mean error lower than 16 percent of a pixel.

In the future, we want to incorporate the measure of the dissection wall thickness, to implement the subpixel edge detection method for 3D images (subvoxel detection) and use the subpixel information to obtain a full segmentation of the dissected aorta.

References

1. Capasso, P.: Terapéutica endovascular en la aorta torácica. In: Villamor, C., Martín, J., Moliner, M. (eds.) Diagnóstico y terapéutica endoluminal. Radiología intervencionista, pp. 303–322. Masson, Barcelona (2002)
2. DeBakey, M.E., Cooley, D.A., Creech Jr., O.: Surgical considerations of dissecting aneurysms of the aorta. Ann. Surg. 142, 586–592 (1955)
3. Da, F., Zhang, H.: Sub-pixel edge detection based on an improved moment. Image Vision Comput. 28, 1645–1658 (2010)
4. Ye, J., Fu, G., Poudel, U.P.: High-accuracy edge detection with blurred edge model. Image and Vision Computing 23(5), 453–467 (2005)
5. Krissian, K., Aja-Fernández, S.: Noise-Driven Anisotropic Diffusion Filtering of MRI. IEEE Transactions on Image Processing 18(10) (October 2009)
6. Xie, Q.L.S.H., Quin, S.: Sub-pixel edge detection for precision measurement based on canny criteria. Key Engineering Materials 295, 711–716 (2005)
7. Trujillo-Pino, A.: Localización de contornos con precisión sub-pixel en imágenes bidimensionales y tridimensionales Director: Álvarez León, L. Co-directors: Esclarín Monreal, J., Alemán Flores, M., Doctoral Thesis. Universidad de las Palmas de Gran Canaria, Computer and Systems Department (2004)

Multi-dimensional Representations of Laparoscopic Simulations for SANETs

Christopher Chiu and Zenon Chaczko

Faculty of Engineering & IT, University of Technology, Sydney, Australia
{christopher.chiu,zenon.chaczko}@uts.edu.au

Abstract. This paper describes the development of a Sensor-Actuator Network (SANET) middleware environment to model laparoscopic procedures in a simulated environment. This case study examines the use of software agents to represent the organic subject (where the surgical procedure is performed) and the surgical tool/effector being manipulated by the end user (the surgeon performing the operation). Developed using the Belief-Desire-Intention (BDI) agent-based software reasoning approach by Rao and Georgeff (1995), the interaction of the agent elements in the simulation, coupled with the feedback mechanisms as the operator interacts with the simulated tissue, will aid in the simulation of laparoscopic procedures for medical training.

Keywords: Biomimetic Engineering, Medical Simulation, Multi-dimensional Modelling, Software Agents, Sensor Actuator Networks (SANET).

1 Introduction

Embedded in-situ sensors in medical instrumentation is a complimentary technology that provide real-time feedback to health professionals in the examination and diagnosis of patients. Coupled with the miniaturization and inexpensive nature of modern wireless sensors, they will become pervasive in medical apparatus. The emerging technological development for implementing wireless sensor networks in medical equipment provide the following development enhancements [1, 11]:

- **Physical Portability:** With wires and cables eliminated from the sensory device and the data collection interface, it allows for flexible usage parameters from a design and development point of view. Coupled with a rechargeable base-station and powered by lithium-ion polymer batteries, this will allow the end user of the device to operate it in a seamless manner;
- **Communication-Medium Enabler without Physical Bounds:** Wireless radio-frequency communication is unconstrained by physical wiring as well as line of sight constraints (i.e. Infrared or optic communication), so medical diagnoses can conveniently be achieved in a remote fashion;
- **Device Interactivity and Interconnectivity:** Devices sharing a common protocol standard for low-power RF communication (i.e. Bluetooth IEEE 802.15.1, ZigBee IEEE 802.15.4) [2, 7] can inter-communicate with one another, allowing for the aggregation and analysis of medical readings amongst different analytical devices for predictive end-user forecasts; and

R. Moreno-Díaz et al. (Eds.): EUROCAST 2011, Part II, LNCS 6928, pp. 225–232, 2012.
© Springer-Verlag Berlin Heidelberg 2012

- **Smart Heuristics Monitoring and Integration:** Health data that is aggregated and collated from different sources can be integrated together using data-fusion heuristics [6, 7], thus allowing professionals to be presented with a medical diagnosis containing the complete picture of health for a patient.

The main aspect to be investigated is the use of an agent-based software framework to utilize the data captured from a wireless laparoscopic probe. This data can represent different forms and means, and be presented to the end user in such a way to provide feedback of an laparoscopic trainee's performance. The main sources of feedback that can be provided to the end user's somatosensory system are as follows [3]:

- **Haptic:** The operation of the probe will be integrated with force-feedback controllers, where tension or potential detection of strain or stress will result in discrete vibrations or physical resistance against a particular direction;
- **Aural:** Aural cues to signify that a hazardous zone breach could occur, as the probe could potentially contact with a sensitive area of the body such as vital organs. These cues can vary in tone, frequency of the cue, and the volume to alert the severity of the current situation to the surgeon;
- **Visual:** Modern probes contain an optic-fiber illuminated CMOS video camera integrated at the probes receptacle, so a first-person view of the surgical procedure takes place [2]. It is critical that visual feedback is maintained in a hard real-time manner to ensure all information is presented to the end-user in an instantaneously.

The purpose of this paper is the case study into a visualization mechanism that presents the various data sources as a multi-dimensional construct to the laparoscopic surgeon in training [2, 12]. As the trainee performs a pre-defined procedure, real-time visualization indicators are presented to the user to provide guidance to their current actions and possible rectifications to prevent harm to the patient. The analytical data generated from the training session can be is replayed to the trainee and trainer, so a thorough feedback of the training session is evaluated on merit indicators of precision and expertise.

2   Visualization as an Agent-Based Process

Utilizing the Belief-Desire-Intention (BDI) software agent paradigm by Rao and Blackwell [8], a simulation model has been developed for a sensor network-enabled visualization component to model laparoscopic surgical training [3]. The agent-based architecture of the sensor-network middleware model interfaces the physical training hardware (including sensors and actuators) and associates a unique software agent for each apparatus. Each agent will be identified with unique traits, or rules, that govern the normal usage parameters and mode of operation within tolerable limits (as specified by manufacturer data sheets and physical characteristics and properties for each device).

Visualization is the agent process that will be the main focus of the case study. As the operator performs the pre-defined procedure, event-tracking heuristic selection takes place via self-organizing maps (neural networks) [5, 6], such that in multi-dimensional space the visualization of the heuristic service in execution can show the SANET network in operation in terms of allometry, ontology and hierarchy [9]. The visualization system utilizes OpenGL Hardware-accelerated graphics libraries, to reduce the processing load from the main processor and ensure overall responsiveness of the middleware environment.

In addition to the standard 3D representation of the SANET environment, surface relief maps extend the visualization in a multi-dimensional perspective, with the X and Y coordinates relative to the nth dimension. This augments the reality of the 3D space, while enabling the end-user to view the variable dimension being analyzed in the relief map (i.e. energy surface maps, sensory readings or actuator stress points). In summary, the environmental parameters driving the visualization software component combine both viewpoints to incorporate both Euclidean metrics and non-Euclidean space:

- **Agent Representations**
  Graphically rendered constructs correlate to each software agent in 3D space. By system default, this is defined as the physical position of the agent in Euclidean space; although this can be represented in non-euclidean space as a user specified instruction. The predefined settings for agent representation include 3D Euclidean space, energy plot representations of the mobile actuators and wireless sensors, and the bidirectional signal strength of the wireless sensor communicating to the actuators about the environmental space.
- **Surface/Relief Maps**
  Surface maps chart a specific attribute to each agent according to an X-Y plane; while the Z plane corresponds to the attribute value. Surface maps incorporate standardized Voronoi tessellation techniques to render the surface map overlays within each agent representation. Surface maps aid in visually identifying regions of interest where risks are likely to occur - including severity of energy depletion and wireless signal 'black spots' - such that preemptive action by a surgical student or intervention by the instructor can be achieved at the earliest opportunity.

3 Software Agent Suitability to Laparoscopic Surgical Training

Software applications designed for systemic agent approaches need to factor the following concerns: Feasibility of applying a toolkit in a given domain, such as utilizing a compliant BDI agent system versus hybrid-based models; and consideration of open-source versus closed-source frameworks. For this case study, compatibility with open source platforms was essential to ensure a standardized experimental base, hence the use of Java Standard Edition for the software implementation. The suitability of adapting software agent infrastructures involves framing the domain space within the BDI agent model, and encapsulating the available service agencies in which additional components can be developed:

- **Contextual Definition**
  As shown by the BDI agency conceptual diagram on the following page (Left), the *Plan Library* and *Belief Set* consists of rules in which the bounded

rational software agent must comply with the physical constraints of the environment space and effector specifications (such as the laws of physics); the *Desires* define the safety rules are adhered while ensuring a particular target is reached while avoiding obstacles and potential risks; the *Intentions* are the actualization of the training procedures taking place, inclusive of the haptic human user interface between the system infrastructure and end user.

- **Heuristic Integration/Augmentation**
  Depicted in the SANET network environment within a Laparoscopic surgical domain on the current page (Right), a software agent environment requires open Application Programming Interface (API) facilities to allow for heuristic integration with hardware devices. A laparoscopic effector can incorporate a variety of pressure and imaging sensors to enable real-time feedback of the operation, from the perspective of the effector itself. Hence, the services incorporated in the current version of the SANET agent infrastructure environment include data persistence services to enable data logging, multimedia records and historical data analysis for post-user feedback, while heuristic service agencies integrate Genetic Algorithm (GA) and Neural Network analytical libraries for image recognition analysis and trajectory tracking problems respectively.

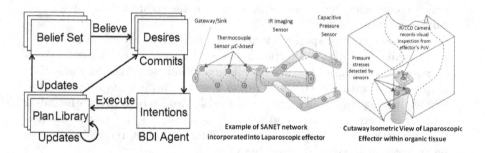

Fig. 1. *(Left)* Belief-Desire-Intention Agent; *(Right)* A Laparoscopic SANET-Effector

3.1   Agent Framework Evaluation

The software agent systems evaluated for this case study include the XJ AnyLogic Simulation Framework and the Jadex BDI Agent System. Both Java-based frameworks provide the basic libraries and software interfaces to enable development of behavioral subroutines for the laparoscopic surgical domain:

- **AnyLogic Simulation Framework by XJ Technologies**
  AnyLogic is a closed-source multi-agent paradigm system with neural network development libraries to build agent-based models for scientific and engineering concerns. The system is built with the Eclipse IDE framework for GUI design and ruleset creation, and performs automated code generation for post-project configuration and data analysis. AnyLogic is designed for multi-threading and has fixed 3D models for graphical representation.

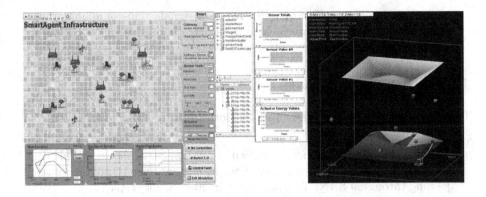

Fig. 2. *(Left)* AnyLogic Framework; *(Right)* Jadex Agency with 3D Graphics Services

The screen capture on this page (Left) shows the AnyLogic simulation from a 2D perspective.

- **Jadex BDI Agent System by Universität Hamburg**
  Jadex is an open-source Belief-Desire-Intention-compliant reasoning engine based on Jade by Telecom Italia. The underlying framework consists of four components: Jadex Agents as a software framework, Jadex Processes to execute workflow plans, Jadex Rules to define the rule engine and its execution activity, with Jadex XML for data binding and representation. The screen capture on the current page (Right) is the Jadex execution process with a middleware interface for 3D modelling of the SANET environment.

3.2   Extended Kohonen Map Heuristics Augmentation

The following algorithmic processes are considered for obstacle detection in a SANET environment for laparoscopic surgical training in the following problem statement tasks [4, 6]:

- **Feature Mapping**
  Process: For initial state described by input vector $u(0)$ in input space U
  By using a Extended Kohonen Map (EKM) [5, 10], the map self-organizes to partition continuous sensory space into discrete regions. The feature map generalization capability arises from its self-organization during training [5], when the SANET actuator is trained to map a localized sensor region. This approach increases the sensory representation's resolution in the frequently encountered stimuli regions [10].
- **Multivariate Regression**
  Process: Adapt sequence of control vectors $c(t), t = 0, \ldots, T - 1$ in sensory control space C with resultant goal state elaborated by $u(T) \in U$
  In addition, as a non-linear multi-variate regression problem uninterrupted mapping from U to C is done by training a multilayer perceptron (MLP), which offers possible generalization capability [6, 10]. The main disadvantage prior to training the network is that training samples must be collected for

each time step 't' to define quantitative error signals. This sampling process is reduced by using reinforcement learning for qualitative success or failure feedback at the end of the control sequence.

4   Experimental Results

The experimental procedure executed for both software agent platforms are as elaborated below:

1. The determination of a successful pseudo-random curve shown on this page (A) and generalized trajectory curve on the current page (B) of an actuator passing through a SANET environment in 20cm x 20cm space.
2. The maximum processor load was calculated using VisualVM Profiler Agent, which calculates processor load of the program, with 30 experimental repetitions for each node density to determine average processor loads.
3. The software platform is a Windows 7 Enterprise operating system, running Java Standard Edition 1.6 (r25); the hardware specifications is a Pentium Dual-core Processor (2.1Ghz) with 4GB of memory.
4. The number of total agents consist of the sensor network population in the SANET environment, with density and spread determined in a pseudo-random fashion via the Mersenne-twister method.

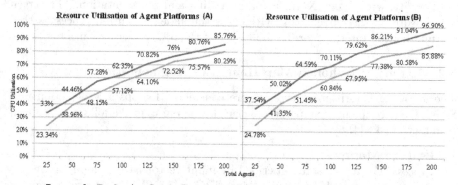

Legend: *Red* - AnyLogic Framework; *Green* - Jadex BDI Framework

Fig. 3. *(a)* Resource Utilization for Pseudo-random Trajectories; *(b)* Resource Utilization for Linear Trajectories

As evident from the results, processor load increases as sensor node densities increase, because the number of obstacles reduces the opportunity for a direct actuator trajectory. In addition, linear trajectories will require less calculation processing than pseudo-random trajectories due to simpler path calculation processes. It is noted that linear trajectory results are included as a control sample for comparative study, but in reality such actuator navigation paths is unrealistic for actual training scenarios. The interesting result is that for pseudo-random trajectories, AnyLogic requires on average 30% processing cycles than Jadex for pseudo-random paths, and 25% more processing for linear paths. As summarized on this page, the justification for these results is due to the flexibility afforded in the design of the two agent-based frameworks: while AnyLogic encapsulates code generation within its codified framework, provisioning Jadex for additional service activation is simplified due to its open-porting facilities, thus enabling distributed load handling within the Jadex engine. Thus, the BDI architecture of Jadex allows for direct relational mapping with the SANET environment, making system design flexible for service extensions in future.

Table 1. Evaluation Summary of Agent-based Framework for SANETs

	AnyLogic Framework	Jadex BDI Framework
Software Evaluation	– Closed Source Java-based Framework needs BDI compliant integration design – Eclipse user interface with encapsulated code-generation – No native support for general purpose computing on GPU's (OpenCL, CUDA)	– Open Source Java-based Framework is BDI compliant based on Jade Engine – Open-port libraries enable customization and adaption to heuristic tracking functions – Potential for supporting general purpose computing for GPU's
Technology Assessment	– Closed framework and limited customization for parallel tasks makes heuristic integration difficult for post-processing	– Flexible framework allows for customization of distributed processing tasks for a specific domain and environment space

4.1 Future Work

Future experimental work to consider in the software agent test-bed include:

- Utilizing OpenCL and CUDA processing libraries to improve parallel processing performance of tasks and heuristics;
- Improving experimental models by developing realistic a 3D mesh model to visualize real-life organic concerns to augment experimental environment;
- Optimization approach tailored for a particular service, in terms of suitability for a particular domain context (i.e. random, ad-hoc environments); and
- Development of agent-based middleware in constrained platforms, such as embedded Java frameworks (Java ME) to assess performance characteristics in ARM RISC-based hardware architectures.

5 Conclusion

The suitability of an agent-based framework should allow for distributed processing tasks from a multi-processor perspective, not just in terms of multi-threaded capability. Embedded hardware capability is becoming multi-processor intensive, and software agent-based architectures need to cater for this development shift. The main benefit of software agents utilizing multi-processor architectures is to enhance real-time performance while reducing processing load per processor, thus reducing overall power consumption. Furthermore, an agent-based framework should have open application interfaces for augmenting middleware-class services, as emerging software technologies can be integrated in a seamless and coordinated manner. The quality attributes that drive efficient software agent architectures will ultimately impact on the system environment such that within the near future, laparoscopic surgical training systems will have scope to embed software agents within the physical domain.

References

[1] Feng, C., Rozenblit, J.W., Hamilton, A.J.: A computerized assessment to compare the impact of standard. stereoscopic and high definition laparoscopic monitor displays on surgical technique, Surgical Endoscopy 24(11), 2743–2748 (2010), doi:10.1007/s00464-010-1038-6

[2] Feng, C., Rozenblit, J.W., Hamilton, A.J.: A Hybrid View in a Laparoscopic Surgery Train- ing System. In: Proc. of the 14th IEEE Intl. Conference and Workshops on the Engineering of Computer Based Systems (ECBS 2007), Tucson, Arizona, pp. 339–348 (2007)

[3] Feng, C., Rozenblit, J.W., Hamilton, A.J., Wytyczak-Partyka, A.: De_ning Spatial Regions in Computer-assisted Laparoscopic Surgical Training. In: Proc. of the 16th IEEE Intl. Conf. on Engineering of Computer Based Systems (ECBS 2009), San Francisco, USA, pp. 176–183 (2009)

[4] Halkidi, M., Batistakis, Y., Vazirgiannis, M.: Clustering Validation Techniques. Intelligent Information Systems Journal 17(2-3), 107–145 (2001)

[5] Kohonen, T.: Self-Organizing Maps, 3rd edn. Springer, New York (2000)

[6] Low, K.H., et al.: An Ensemble of Cooperative Extended Kohonen Maps for Complex Robot Motion Tasks. Neural Computation 17(6), 1411–1445 (2005)

[7] Low, K.H., et al.: Task Allocation via Self-organizing Swarm Coalitions in Distributed Sensor Networks. In: 19th Artificial Intelligence Conference, pp. 28–33 (2004)

[8] Rao, M., Georgeff, P.: BDI-agents: From Theory to Practice. In: Proceedings of the 1st International Conference on Multiagent Systems (ICMAS 1995), San Francisco, USA (1995)

[9] Ritter, H., Schulten, K., Denker, J.S.: Topology Conserving Mappings for Learning Mo- tor Tasks: Neural Networks for Computing. In: Proceedings of 151st Conference, pp. 376–380. American Institute of Physics, Snowbird (1986)

[10] Sharkey, A., et al.: Combining Diverse Neural Nets. Knowledge Eng. Rev., 231–247 (1997)

[11] Wytyczak-Partyka, A., Nikodem, J., Klempous, R., Rozenblit, J., Klempous, R., Rudas, I.: Safety Oriented Laparoscopic Surgery Training System. In: Moreno-Díaz, R., Pichler, F., Quesada-Arencibia, A. (eds.) EUROCAST 2009. LNCS, vol. 5717, pp. 889–896. Springer, Heidelberg (2009)

[12] Yang, L., Feng, C., Peng, J., Rozenblit, J.W.: A Multi-modality Framework for Energy Efficient Tracking in Large Scale Wireless Sensor Networks. In: Proc. of the 2nd IEEE Intl. Conference on Networking, Sensing and Control, Ft. Lauderdale, FL, USA, pp. 916–921 (2006)

Models and Techniques for Computer Aided Surgical Training

Jerzy W. Rozenblit

Dept. of Electrical and Computer Engineering
Dept. of Surgery
The University of Arizona,Tucson, Arizona 85721, USA
jr@ece.arizona.edu

Keywords: minimally invasive surgery, computer-guided surgery, virtually assisted training.

1 Introduction

Laparoscopic surgery, when performed by a well-trained surgeon, is a remarkably effective procedure that minimizes complications associated with large incisions, operative blood loss and post-operative pain. It also reduces the recovery time. However, the procedure is more challenging than a conventional surgery due to the restricted vision, hand-eye coordination problems, limited working space, and lack of tactile sensation. These issues make the laparoscopic surgery a more difficult technique for medical students and residents to master.

An effective training environment must provide high fidelity and repeatable exercises that are well structured to meet specific learning objectives. Analogies to the aviation world are often used as a strong motivating factor. Just as no pilot can be certified to fly a particular aircraft unless he or she has completed simulated cockpit training, no surgeon should attempt laparoscopic procedures on a patient without extensive virtual training.

Gallagher [11] posits that the goal of any surgical training program is to help surgeons automate their basic psychomotor skills before they operate on a patient (,,*the more innate visuospatial, perceptual, and psychomotor ability the surgeon has, the faster he or she will automate the surgical skills*").

One class of simulation-based training tools is called the virtual reality simulators (VRS) [4],[13],[16],[22],[23],[25],[26]. VRS systems use a computer to simulate the entire training procedure. Trainees interact with the simulator through a specially designed interface. VRS simulations often provide inadequate perception of reality and inaccurate haptic feedback. Those limitations make the performance of a VRS as a training tool questionable [24],[26].

A number of physicians prefer to use another type of a tool called the pelvic trainer. A pelvic trainer is just a box with apertures that simulates the abdomen. Trainees use real instruments to practice basic skills and observe the operating scene through a video display. The trainer provides a degree of realism and some haptic feedback. It is orders of magnitude less expensive that the VRS systems. The main limitation of this approach is the absence of an

R. Moreno-Díaz et al. (Eds.): EUROCAST 2011, Part II, LNCS 6928, pp. 233–241, 2012.

objective performance assessment. The only quantitative measurement device used frequently in the educational and clinical research is the stopwatch [12]. In the recent decade, a great number of surgical skills training tools have become commercially available that fall into the two above specified classes. We refer the reader to [4],[5],[6],[7],[8],[9],[14],[10],[18],[25] for a review of some of the existing systems.

In our work, we focus on „computer-assisted surgical training" (CAST). Our design principles and their subsequent implementation address some of the limitations of the existing systems and advance the state of the art in surgical education, assessment, and guidance in laparoscopic surgery [4],[6],[7],[8],[9],[21],[27], [28]. Our overarching vision is to develop a fully integrated training system that will serve as a „cognitive amplifier" for a practicing surgeon. Such a system will enhance training and provide assistance in real-time during an operation. Our goal is to help improve surgical outcomes and patients safety.

In this chapter, a high-level overview of our activities is given with appropriate references to various stages of CAST development. We begin with the overall design concept and its elements.

2   Design Concept and Implementation

Our CAST design concept was driven by the need to simulate surgical procedures in stages, represent anatomical variations and anomalies, permit random introduction of unforeseen crises, and to provide haptic feedback. The system should have methods and tools that track and assess trainees performance.

In [5],[6],[7],[8], we defined three fundamental design layers for CAST. Layer 1, called the *Perception Layer* embodies physical sensing devices, tracking (motion, touch accuracy, etc.) and detection algorithms. The key driving need here was to design and implement the ability to precisely track the position of surgical instruments during a training session. This allows us and the trainees to review their performance with respect to a set of metrics such as the *economy of movement, time, accuracy, direction profile, etc.* [6],[21]. This led directly to the second design layer, namely the *Comprehension Layer*, which provides a suite of metrics and algorithms for objective performance assessment.

We had commenced the initial (CAST I) system design and development by equipping surgical instruments with magnetic sensors Micro Bird [2] for precise tracking and data collection. The position data obtained from the Micro Bird sensors is used to calculate key instrument motion metrics such as total path length, average speed, instantaneous speed, average radius of motion and number of times „safety zones" were breached. Using this concept, we conducted a study [5], comparing the efficacy of a standard surgical monitor, a high definition (HD), display, and stereoscopic (3 dimensional 3D) display system.

The results of the study indicated that while the higher resolution provided by HD displays was widely favored by surgeons, it did not yield significant improvements on parameters such as the speed and movement economy. HD displays may, in fact, have detrimental effects on such parameters when compared to standard lower resolution laparoscopic or stereoscopic display systems. The 3D system was generally favored by inexperienced trainees but presented ergonomic issues [5].

Furthermore, we have refined the CAST I system to allow the trainees to work with two instruments and random "targets" for tasks such as grasping. A study was conducted to address hand-dominance in two-instrument exercises. In this study, participants were asked to grasp targets correctly using minimally-invasive surgical equipment (Karl Storz®).

There were a total of nine targets and one start point constructed out of LEGO®"bricks" for easy reconfiguration (see Figure 1). All targets had an embedded in them a metal hook surrounded by three LEDs (green, red, and yellow). The computer randomly selected a target to light up one of its LEDs. Participants were required to use the correct instrument (right instrument for the green light, left one for the red light, and both instruments for the yellow LED) to grasp the targets metal hook within ten seconds. Electromagnetic sensors (MicroBird) were used to track the instruments movements in the 3D space at 60 Hz.

We evaluated participants performance metrics based on three variables: *movement economy, time taken for completion and accuracy.*

Fig. 1. Set up for hand-dominance study

Thirty subjects participated in our study. We conducted data analysis for three group variables: dominant hand vs. non-dominant hand performance, gender effect, and previous laparoscopic training experience effect. Our initial results were in favor of the non-dominant hand, and participants who had previous laparoscopic training experience.

Our initial hypothesis was that the dominant hand performed better than the non-dominant one. However, our study disapproved the initial hypothesis as illustrated in Table 1.

Table 1. Hand dominance results

	Dominant	Non dominant
ME $\bar{x}$ ($\pm$S.E)	0.5453 ($\pm$0.0096)	0.5688 ($\pm$0.0096)
P value	p<0.0001	p<0.0001
TTC $\bar{x}$ ($\pm$S.E)	0.6797 ($\pm$0.010)	0.6753 ($\pm$0.010)
P value	p<0.4591	p<0.4591
PRO $\bar{x}$ ($\pm$S.E)	0. 3743 ($\pm$0.0099)	0.3867 ($\pm$0.0099)
P value	p<0.0464	p<0.0464

In the table above, ME stands for normalized movement economy expressed at the ratio of *actual path/ideal path*, TTC is a completion coefficient (fast movements have a higher coefficient), PRO is the aggregate measure of proficiency expressed as the product of *ME x TCC x Accuracy* (either 1, or 0 if the target was not grasped within 10 seconds).

We believe that the relationship between hand dominance and laparoscopic performance seems to be task related. Additional research using more complex surgical tasks is needed for clarification.

In the *Comprehension Layer*, we also developed the ability to assess trainees performance not only quantitatively but also qualitatively. In [18], we presented the knowledge elicitation process to model the performance metrics and the rules involved in the assessment of minimally invasive surgical skills. Our assessment model is based on fuzzy logic, so that it is easier to mimic the judgment that is already performed by experienced surgeons in qualitative terms. An empirical study to validate our approach is described in [18].

The highest, most complex element of our system, is the *Projection Layer*. Here, we work on implementing knowledge-based reasoning as well as real-time instrument guidance. We explain this concept in the following section.

2.1   Collision Free Guidance

We had further enhanced the surgical trainer with real-time guidance and navigation capabilities. This version, called CAST II, employs sensing and configuration space methods [1],[3],[17] to assist in training with a special focus on proper execution of movements and avoidance of critical zones in the operating space. An inference module is employed to determine if a particular action is potentially harmful and the reasons why the action could be harmful. Then, guidance and feedback to prevent potentially injurious actions and to reinforce correct techniques are given to the trainee. Proper guidance includes displaying the estimated optimal path and performance instructions on the screen to help the trainees know what to do, and what not to do. This concept is demonstrated in Figure 2 which depicts one of the views available in the system showing instrument tracks, and the ,,no-fly zone" (a spatial region that must not be entered by an instrument) breaches. Intrusion into ,,no-fly zones" would trigger an alert.

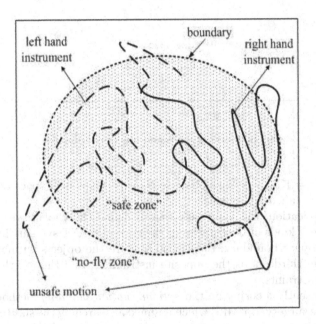

Fig. 2. "No-fly zone" diagram

In our initial study[7], [27], we used the configuration space (*C-space*) techniques to generate the estimated optimal path of the instruments [1],[17]. The first step was to model the instruments in their configuration space. As published in detail in [7], we considered the problem of a rigid instrument A moving in a Euclidean space $W = R^3$, equipped with a fixed Cartesian coordinate system, denoted by F_W . We also represented a moving coordinate system F attached to A so that each point in the instrument has consistent coordinates in F (Figure 3).

The origin of F_W is O_W, and the origin of F_A is O_A. O_A is the reference point of A.

The configuration space of A is the space C of all the possible positions of A , subject to external constraints. Now, suppose W contains a series of physical

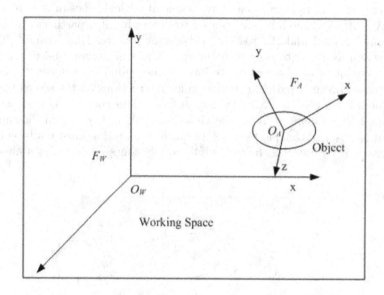

Fig. 3. Working space and object coordinates

obstacles $B_i, i = 1, 2, ..., q$. Each obstacle B_i in W maps in C space to the region CB_i , which is called a C-obstacle.

In our application, the main task was to define the C-obstacles. There are several different kinds of C-obstacles in the current CAST system. The first one is the safety space boundary; the second one are the objects within the safety boundary; the third one is the opposite instrument; and the fourth one is the additional constraints.

We are presently focusing on the *optimal motion planning* method for minimally invasive surgery (optMIS) which is aimed at searching the shortest collision-free paths for laparoscopic instruments in 3D space with multiple ,,no-fly zones''. The proposed method divides the problem into path searching and path following sub-problems. The path searching stage is used to generate the shortest path for each of the instruments to avoid breaching ,,no-fly zones''. In order to avoid collisions between the instruments, the velocity vectors are assigned to optimal paths at the path following stage. The optMIS method combines the advantages of computational geometry-based techniques, Dijkstras algorithm and evolutionary computation [19],[20].

3   Next Generation Trainer

The most likely source for a quantum leap in surgical technique is robotics. While technical and cost limitations constrain our ability to realistically perform surgery in this manner (i.e., robotically) now, the future may be markedly different. Currently, some haptic feedback devices have been introduced in virtual reality laparoscopic trainer systems. The basic idea of these devices is connecting a small robotic manipulator to surgical instruments. Therefore, force and torque can be exerted on the devices through a manipulator. The ability to link haptic devices with CAST could assist in the development of so-called "smart" instruments. "Smart" instruments are much cheaper and simpler than surgical robots.

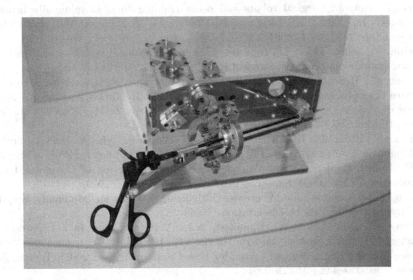

Fig. 4. CAST III device

We are developing the 3rd generation CAST system which will realize this concept (it is shown in Figure 4). It is in principle a mechatronic device that employs real surgical instruments, encoders for precise position sensing, servomotors and attendant software for motion control. We are currently completing the development of the CAST III prototype. CAST III will have embedded in it collision free and optMIS navigation.

4   Summary

In developing CAST, we take a dual position on the ultimate utility of our concept and its implementation. The foundational work focuses on providing training and assessment capabilities in a manner that is affordable, realistic, and objective. The ultimate vision behind our efforts is to transfer the technology or parts thereof to the operating room to provide computer-guided assistance in real-time.

References

1. Alterovitz, R., Goldberg, K.: Motion Planning in Medicine: Optimization and Simulation Algorithms for Image-Guided Procedures. Springer, Heidelberg (2008)
2. Ascension Technology Co., microBIRD Technical Reference Guide (2005), http://www.ascension-tech.com/
3. Cohen, J., Lin, M.C., Manocha, D., Ponamgi, M.: I-Collide: An interactive and exact collision detection system for large-scale environments. In: 1995 Proceedings of ACM I3D, pp. 189–196 (1995)
4. Dankelman, J.: Surgical robots and other training tools in minimally invasive surgery. In: 2004 IEEE International Conference on Systems, Man and Cybernetics, pp. 2459–2464 (2004)
5. Falk, V., Mintz, D., et al.: Influence of three-dimensional vision on surgical telemanipulator performance. Surgical Endoscopy 15, 1282–1288 (2001)
6. Feng, C., Rozenblit, J.W., Hamilton, A.J.: A computerized assessment to compare the impact of standard, stereoscopic and high definition laparoscopic monitor displays on surgical technique. Surgical Endoscopy 24(11), 2743–2748 (2010), doi:10.1007/s00464- 010-1038-6
7. Feng, C., Rozenblit, J.W., Hamilton, A.J., Wytyczak-Partyka, A.: Defining Spatial Regions in Computer-assisted Laparoscopic Surgical Training. In: Proc. of the 16th IEEE Intl. Conference and Workshops on the Engineering of Computer Based Systems (ECBS 2009), San Francisco, pp. 176–183 (April 2009)
8. Feng, C.: A Situational Awareness Enhancing System for Minimally Invasive Surgery Training, Ph.D. Dissertation (2007)
9. Feng, C., Rozenblit, J.W., Hamilton, A.J.: A Hybrid View in a Laparoscopic Surgery Training System. In: Proc. of the 14th IEEE Intl. Conference and Workshops on the Engineering of Computer Based Systems (ECBS 2007), Tucson, Arizona, pp. 339–348 (March 2007)
10. Feng, C., Haniffa, H., et al.: Surgical training and performance assessment using a motion tracking system. In: Proc. of the 2nd European Modeling and Simulation Symposium, EMSS 2006, October 4-6, pp. 647–652. Piera, LogiSim (2006)
11. Gallagher, A.G., McClure, N., et al.: Virtual reality training in laparoscopic surgery: a preliminary assessment of minimally invasive surgical trainer virtual reality (MIST VR). Endoscopy 31(4), 310–313 (1999)
12. Hagiike, M., Phillips, E.H., Berci, G.: Performance differences in laparoscopic surgical skills between true high-definition and three-chip CCD video system. Surgical Endoscopy 21, 1849–1854 (2007)
13. Hamilton, E.C., Scott, D.J., et al.: Comparison of video trainer and virtual reality training systems on acquisition of laparoscopic skills Journal Surgical Endoscopy. Surgical Endoscopy Journal 16, 406–411 (2002)
14. Haniffa, H., Rozenblit, J.W., Peng, J., Hamilton, A.J., Salkini, M.: Motion Planning System for Minimally Invasive Surgery. In: Proc. of the 14th IEEE Intl. Conference and Workshops on the Engineering of Computer Based Systems (ECBS 2007), Tucson, Arizona, pp. 609–610 (March 2007)
15. Hasson, H.M., Kumari, N.V., Eekhout, J.: Training simulator for developing laparoscopic skills. Journal of the Society of Laparoendoscopic Surgeons 5(3), 255–265 (2001)
16. Korndorffer Jr, J.R., Dunne, J.B., Sierra, R., et al.: Simulator training for laparoscopic suturing using performance goals translates to the operating room. J. Am. Coll. Surg. 201, 23–29 (2005)

17. Latombe, J.: Robot Motion Planning. Kluwer Academic Publishers, Norwell (1991)
18. Leonard, J.: Sensor Fusion for Surgical Applications. In: The 15th AESS/IEEE Dayton Section Symposium, pp. 37–44 (1998)
19. Napalkova, L.: Development and Application of Multi-Objective Simulation-Based Optimisation Methods. PhD Dissertation. Riga Technical University (2010)
20. Noto, M., Sato, H.: A Method for the Shortest Path Search by Extended Dijkstra Algorithm. In: IEEE International Conference on Systems, Man and Cybernetics, pp. 2316–2320 (2000)
21. Riojas, M., Feng, C., Hamilton, A.J., Rozenblit, J.W.: Knowledge Elicitation for Performance Assessment in a Computerized Surgical Training System. Applied Soft Computing 11(4), 3697–3708
22. Shrivastava, S., Sudarshan, R., et al.: Surgical Training and Performance Evaluation using Virtual Reality based Simulator. In: Virtual Concept 2003, France (2003)
23. Simbionix Co. (2007), http://www.simbionix.com
24. Spillane, L.L., Spencer, M., Maddow, C.: Simulation a Valuable Teaching Tool or a Waste of Time (Abstract). Academic Emergency Medicine 11(5), 561 (2004)
25. Stylopoulos, N., Cotin, S., et al.: Computer-enhanced laparoscopic training system (CELTS). Surgical Endoscopy 18, 782–789 (2004)
26. Waxberg, S.L., Goodell, K.H., et al.: Evaluation of Physical Versus Virtual Surgical Training Simulators. In: Human Factors and Ergonomics Society Annual Meeting Proceedings, Medical Systems and Rehabilitation, pp. 1675–1679(5) (2004)
27. Wytyczak-Partyka, A., Nikodem, J., Klempous, R., Rozenblit, J.: A novel interaction method for laparoscopic surgery training. In: Proceedings of the 8th Annual IEEE International Conference and Workshops on Human Systems Interactions, pp. 858–861 (2008)
28. Wytyczak-Partyka, A., Nikodem, J., Klempous, R., Rozenblit, J., Feng, C.: Computer-guided laparoscopic training with application of a fuzzy expert system. In: Gelbukh, A., Morales, E.F. (eds.) MICAI 2008. LNCS (LNAI), vol. 5317, pp. 965–972. Springer, Heidelberg (2008)

Application of Simulation Techniques in a Virtual Laparoscopic Laboratory

Ryszard Klempous, Jan Nikodem, and Andrzej Wytyczak-Partyka

Wroclaw University of Technology,Institute of Computer Engineering, Control and Robotics, 27 Wybrzeze Wyspianskiego St., 50-370 Wroclaw, Poland
{andrzej.wytyczak-partyka,ryszard.klempous,jan.nikodem}@pwr.wroc.pl

Abstract. This paper shows several concepts, widely known in simulation environments, applied in surgical education, with emphasis on computer graphics and image processing applications. The benefits of a training programme based on objective, simulated exercises are discussed as well as the flaws of such computer-assisted education systems. Examples of commercially available training systems are given and compared with solutions developed in research institutes.

Keywords: simulation, laparoscopic surgery, training, image processing, expert system, virtual reality.

1 Background and Motivation

In the last years patient safety has been a growing concern in health care in the developed countries. Applying simulation in surgical training has proved to improve surgical performance and thus lower the number of adverse medical events (AME) [5]. Applying several concepts from fields where simulation has been successful for years, i.e. avation, has led to development of new surgical education strategies. The model that has been in use so far, master-apprentice is gradually replaced by supervised training in simulated environments.

The medical society, since the introduction of laparoscopic surgery some 20 years ago, has developed a strong need for structured, objectively evaluated training programs. Several kinds of training curriculums have been developed and are currently in operation - some use real-life tools and objects some are completely virtual-reality based. The main benefit of employing a computer system in the training process is the objectiveness of evaluation performed by the machine and, however the pure virtual systems lack reality in perceiving the visuals and haptics, it seems especially valuable to apply them early in the training - when the basic skills are developed.

2 Simulation Concepts

The strategy of education in a simulated environment is based on several concepts:

R. Moreno-Díaz et al. (Eds.): EUROCAST 2011, Part II, LNCS 6928, pp. 242–247, 2012.

- simulated high-fidelity environment
- objective performance evaluation (time, movement error and economy)
- training scenarios
- no-fly zones.

A computer-assisted training system that implements these concepts can fulfil the demands for a skill-based, objectively evaluated education program. Several discussions of such systems were presented in [7,9,10,11]. Recent technological progress and availability of computing power provide means for creating high-fidelity simulated environments that reflect not only the 3D relations of inner anatomy, but also organ displacements due to i.e. respiratory motion.

2.1   High-Fidelity Environment

The simulated environment is usually based on textured 3D models of organs obtained from CT scans. There are commercial systems available, i.e. [1,2], that provide training scenarios with high level of detail, Fig. 1(b) 1(a), as well as simple exercises that focus on mastering the basic set of skills required to safely perform laparoscopic surgery, Fig. 1(d),1(c). Further work has to be done to provide more realistic haptic feedback and synchronization of respiratory motion. The 3D models can be also used in an augmented-reality application in conjunction with standard video imaging from a laparoscopic camera.

On the other hand there are systems like the one used at the University of Arizona [8], which use a real-life model and a computer system to calculate the performance metrics and provide an augmented reality layer, Fig. 2.

The motion of organs can be recorded using today's medical imaging techniques, such as ultrasound or CT. Moreover, motion recorded using one of these modalities can be mapped onto images recorded using a different modality, as described in [12], where we demonstrated that ultrasound images of a beating heart can be mapped onto precomputed 3D models in real time. Respiratory motion can be included in a similar manner. Another approach has been proposed in [13], where 3D models were built online, using a structure-from-motion algorithm to recover 3D coordinates from realtime images from a standard laparoscopic camera.

2.2   Augmented Reality and Guidance

Applying augmented reality and guidance in a system can be based i.e. on sound cues such as in [8], where the system provides audio tips like 'lower', 'forward', 'left', etc. to the trainee, who's trying to complete an exercise where the goal is to touch randomly selected points on a model.

By combining several data sources we are able to produces hybrid views and merge the qualities of ultrasound and CT imaging as well as high resolution positioning of the instruments inside the operating field. Positioning methods include magnetic position sensors, as well as angle sensors embedded in the trocars through which the instruments are inserted. Combining the information

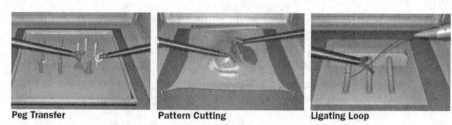

(a) Basic exercises in the Surgical Science simulator [2]

(b) Similar tasks in the Simbionix LapMentor simulator [1]

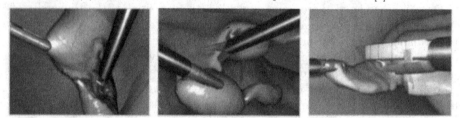

(c) High-fidelity training scenarios in the Surgical Science simulator [2]

(d) Similar tasks in the Simbionix LapMentor simulator [1]

Fig. 1. Demonstration of commercial training simulators

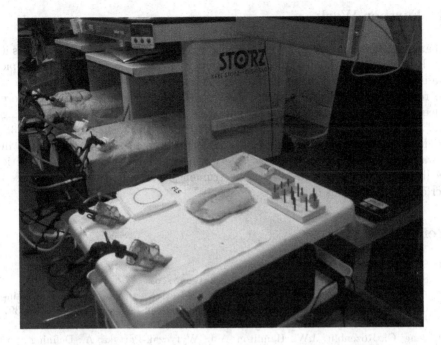

Fig. 2. Real training objects in the ASTEC simulation center

about the instrument location with predefined no-fly zones creates new opportunities for enhancing patient safety during real-life procedures [4].

An interesting application for the OR might be combining the description of no-fly zones in the operating field with a servo-mechanism embedded in the trocars, that would provide haptic feedback to the surgeon who is approaching a vital structure, outside of the scope of the planned procedure.

3   Benefits and Flaws

Training in simulated environments is a safe way to practice the skills necessary to begin participating in real procedures. Employing computer-controlled patient simulators in anaesthesiology training effected in a two-fold advantage in the skill of endotracheal intubation [3]. Equivalent studies in the field of laparoscopic surgery show similar results and therefore validate the application of Virtual Reality and simulated training in surgical education. According to the trial conducted in [6] surgeons who have received Virtual Reality training performed better in terms of procedure time, movement error and economy.

The simulated training is not designed to fully replace the part of surgical training where a real patient is involved, just to minimise the risk attached to that part. Current flaws, as reported by participants, are - not high enough fidelity, unrealistic haptic feedback.

4   Further Work

Thanks to availability of high performance graphic cards in computer systems it has been possible to create high-fidelity simulated environments for laparoscopic training. The textured 3D models already appear very life-like and leave almost no room for improvement. More emphasis should be put into providing more adequate haptic feedback as well as simulating the motion of inner organs during real procedures. Recent work on information fusion between precomputed 3D models and real-time ultrasound data [12] is a step in that direction and in a way creates possibilites for new safety-enhancing devices, such as a haptic feedback device embedded into the instrument, that would alert the surgeon performing dangerous movements.

References

1. Simbionix, http://www.simbionix.com
2. Surgical Science, http://www.surgical-science.com
3. Abrahamson, S., Denson, J.S., Wolf, R.M.: Effectiveness of a simulator in training anesthesiology residents. 1969. Quality & safety in health care 13(5), 395–397 (2004), http://qshc.bmj.com/cgi/content/abstract/13/5/395
4. Feng, C., Rozenblit, J.W., Hamilton, A.J., Wytyczak-Partyka, A.: Defining Spatial Regions in Computer-Assisted Laparoscopic Surgical Training. In: 2009 16th Annual IEEE International Conference and Workshop on the Engineering of Computer Based Systems, pp. 176–183 (April 2009), http://ieeexplore.ieee.org/lpdocs/epic03/wrapper.htmarnumber=4839244
5. Gorman, P.J., Meier, A.H., Krummel, T.M.: Computer-Assisted Training and Learning in Surgery. Computer Aided Surgery 5, 120–130 (2000)
6. Grantcharov, T.P., Kristiansen, V.B., Bendix, J., Bardram, L., Rosenberg, J., Funch-Jensen, P.: Randomized clinical trial of virtual reality simulation for laparoscopic skills training. British Journal of Surgery 91(2), 146–150 (2004)
7. Riojas, M., Feng, C., Hamilton, A., Rozenblit, J.: Knowledge elicitation for performance assessment in a computerized surgical training system. Applied Soft Computing (2011)
8. Rozenblit, J.W.: Models and techniques for computer aided surgical training. In: Proceedings of the 13th International Conference on Computer Aided Systems Theory, The Universidad de Las Palmas de Gran Canaria, pp. 370–373 (2011)
9. Wytyczak-Partyka, A., Nikodem, J., Klempous, R., Rozenblit, J., Feng, C.: Computer-guided laparoscopic training with application of a fuzzy expert system. In: Gelbukh, A., Morales, E.F. (eds.) MICAI 2008. LNCS (LNAI), vol. 5317, pp. 965–972. Springer, Heidelberg (2008)
10. Wytyczak-Partyka, A., Nikodem, J., Klempous, R., Rozenblit, J., Klempous, R., Rudas, I.: Safety Oriented Laparoscopic Surgery Training System. In: Moreno-Díaz, R., Pichler, F., Quesada-Arencibia, A. (eds.) EUROCAST 2009. LNCS, vol. 5717, pp. 889–896. Springer, Heidelberg (2009), http://www.springerlink.com/index/N115714652121637.pdf

11. Wytyczak-Partyka, A., Nikodem, J., Klempous, R., Rozenblit, J.: Surgical Training System with a Novel Approach to Human-Computer Interaction. In: Hippe, Z.S., Kulikowski, J.L. (eds.) Human-Computer Systems Interaction. AISC, vol. 60, pp. 383–393. Springer, Heidelberg (2009),
http://www.springerlink.com/index/48181687R6J86751.pdf

12. Wytyczak-Partyka, A.: Computed-tomography or Magnetic Resonance based 3D model synchronization with real-time ultrasound data. In: 2010 Fifth International Conference on Broadband and Biomedical Communications, dec 2010, pp. 1–4. IEEE, Los Alamitos (2010),
http://ieeexplore.ieee.org/lpdocs/epic03/wrapper.htmarnumber=5723616

13. Wytyczak-Partyka, A., Nikodem, J., Klempous, R.: Application of Structure-from-Motion 3D Reconstruction in Computer-Guided Surgical Training. In: 2009 16th Annual IEEE International Conference and Workshop on the Engineering of Computer Based Systems, pp. 287–290 (April 2009),
http://ieeexplore.ieee.org/lpdocs/epic03/wrapper.htmarnumber=4839255

Development of an Accurate Method for Motion Analyses of the Heart Wall Based on Medical Imagery

Bernhard Quatember[1], Martin Mayr[2], Wolfgang Recheis[1], Stefanos Demertzis[3], Giampietro Allasia[4], Alessandra De Rossi[4], Roberto Cavoretto[4], and Ezio Venturino[4]

[1] Innsbruck Medical University (Radiology), Anichstr. 35, 6020 Innsbruck, Austria
Bernhard.Quatember@uibk.ac.at, Wolfgang.Recheis@i-med.ac.at
[2] University of Applied Sciences, J. Gutenberg-Str. 3, 2700 Wiener Neustadt, Austria
Martin.Mayr@fhwn.ac.at
[3] Cardiocentro Ticino, Via Tesserete 48, 6900 Lugano, Switzerland
Stefanos.Demertzis@cardiocentro.org
[4] Universita degli Studi di Torino, Via Carlo Alberto 10, 10123 Torino, Italy
{Giampietro.Allasia,Alessandra.DeRossi,Roberto.Cavoretto,
Ezio.Venturino}@unito.it

Abstract. In the field of diagnosis and therapy of coronary artery disease, it is highly important to acquire a fair knowledge of the heart wall motion and its regional variations. Unfortunately, the accuracy of all currently applied methods for the acquisition and analysis of the regional heart wall motion is rather limited. We developed a sufficiently accurate technique for tracking and analysing the regional motion of the epicardium throughout the cardiac cycle which is based on cardiac CT and biplane angiography. In the end-diastolic position, the epicardial surface in the 3D CT data is segmented and registered to the skeleton representation of the coronary artery tree obtained from the end-diastolic frame of a biplane cineangiogram. In doing so, a landmark-based approach based on TPS transformations has been chosen. The motion tracking is accomplished by carrying out further landmark-based TPS transformations of the surface to the successive frames of the cineangiogram.

Keywords: Medical Imaging, Registration, Radial Basis Functions, Heart Motion, Cardiology.

1 Introduction

At present, cardiologists focus mainly on the patency of the coronary (epicardial) arteries. In particular, they assess the severities of the stenoses in the coronary arteries and the resulting hypoperfusion of the affected territories within the myocardium. Myocardial hypoperfusion may induce pathological processes, such as hibernation or infarction. These processes manifest themselves in abnormal (regional) motions of the heart. Motion analyses will thus enable cardiologists

R. Moreno-Díaz et al. (Eds.): EUROCAST 2011, Part II, LNCS 6928, pp. 248–255, 2012.
© Springer-Verlag Berlin Heidelberg 2012

to delve into greater detail in their diagnoses, especially in the area of coronary artery disease.

During the past decades, much effort has been devoted to capturing specific data from medical images which can be used to describe the motion of the heart and to develop clinically applicable methods which would meet the diagnostic requirements. However, the accuracy of these methods is somewhat restricted. At an early stage of heart motion analyses, biplane cineangiograms were used [1,2], but they only allow cardiologists to track the motion of the coronary arteries. Although the coronary arteries are situated at the outer surface of the myocardium, they do not allow the acquisition of the motion of the entire surface of the myocardium, since they only sparsely cover the myocardial surface. Thereafter, methods for motion tracking of the heart (more specifically, of the left ventricle) with MRI tagging imaging [3,4] and real-time motion tracking using 3D ultrasound [5,6] became the focus of interest. However, the spatial resolution of these imaging modalities is not sufficiently high. With the advent of EBCT scanners and in particular of multislice CT systems [7,8,9,3], motion analyses involving these imaging modalities have become feasible. However, the limited spatial resolution of EBCT and the insufficient temporal resolution of ECG-gated multislice CT do not yet allow cardiologists in clinical settings to carry out reliable studies of the motion of the heart.

Since, as adumbrated above, the accuracy of the known approaches to analyse the heart wall motion is somewhat restricted, we aimed at the development of an improved method of motion tracking offering a high accuracy. The pivotal point of our development efforts is the full exploitation of the synergy of two imaging modalities, viz. cardiac CT and biplane cineangiography. In the following, we will describe the conceptual basics of this method and point out its serviceability for an accurate quantitative assessment of the regional variations of ventricular motility.

2 Conceptual Basics

As already mentioned earlier, we apply a multimodal imaging approach to track and analyse the regional motion of the outer surface of the myocardium. In doing so, we fully take advantage of

- the capacity of cardiac CT (multislice CT) to retrospectively reconstruct a highly accurate 3D image of the epicardial surface at the end of the diastole where the myocardium is moving only marginally and
- the excellent motion tracking capability of biplane cineangiography which is not significantly impaired by any motion blur.

By carrying out an image registration and further transformations which we will describe in detail later, we are able to avoid the limitations of both of the employed imaging modalities, that is the insufficient temporal resolution provided by cardiac CT [8] and the imperfections caused by the sparse covering of the epicardial surface by the coronary (epicardial) arteries in biplane cineangiography [1].

It is important to note that our approach is based on medical imagery which is usually readily available in clinical settings, since it is current clinical practice to take from a patient at first a cardiac CT and, only if needed, afterwards a biplane cineangiogram, since biplane angiography is an invasive and thus a somewhat dangerous procedure; however, it is indispensable in all clinical cases relevant to our specific problem area of severe coronary artery disease [7]. The pivotal points of our approach are:

- The segmentation of the epicardial surface in the three-dimensional end-diastolic CT data set and the definition of anatomical points (selected bifurcation points of the epicardial arteries) as anatomical landmarks;
- The skeletonisation and three-dimensional reconstruction of the epicardial artery tree from all frames of the biplane cineangiogram; for the skeleton representation of the coronary artery tree we will use the abbreviation SEAT;
- The landmark-based elastic TPS (thin plate spline) registration of the segmented epicardial surface to the SEAT belonging to the end-diastolic position (landmarks are the aforementioned selected bifurcation points of the epicardial artery tree);
- The more accurate representation of the epicardial surface which has been obtained by the aforementioned registration of the segmented surface in the CT data set to the end-diastolic SEAT is subjected to repeatedly applied landmark-based TPS transformations from one SEAT to the succeeding one. As (corresponding) landmarks all bifurcation points of the individual SEATs have been chosen. The time series of these transformations ranges from the end of the diastole throughout the entire cardiac cycle.

We will here confine ourselves to the outer surface of the left ventricle, since most of the pathological changes of the myocardium, such as those caused by the aforementioned hypoperfusion (myocardial ischemia), manifest themselves primarily in a deterioration of the contractility of the left ventricle and, as a consequence, in specific regional alterations of the motility of the left ventricle.

For a reliable diagnoses and especially for an assessment of the success of therapy, cardiologists would need highly accurate data. Unfortunately, contemporary motion analysis methods cannot meet their demanding requirements. We thus aimed at an alleviation of these limitations. By processing the above-quoted multimodal imagery in the way as outlined above, the limitations of both of the employed imaging modalities, that is the insufficient temporal resolution provided by cardiac CT and the low density of the epicardial arteries on the surface of the left ventricle become irrelevant. In the next section we will describe the details of our approach.

3   Image Processing and Motion Analysis Techniques

Our research activities comprise the elaboration of image processing methods for segmentation and registration, the development of techniques for an appropriate representation of the epicardial surface, and the creation of a new approach to tracking and analysing the motion of the heart. In this section, we will deal with the most important details of our development work.

3.1 Segmentation of the Epicardial Surface in the 3D CT Image Data Set

Our segmentation method for the epicardial surface of the left ventricle is based on an ECG-gated 3D CT data set which has been retrospectively reconstructed for the end of the diastole. Such data sets usually comprise a relatively large number (k) of cross-sectional 2D images - so-called transaxial slices. As justified earlier, all our investigations are confined to the epicardial surface of the left ventricle. At this stage of development, the segmentation is carried out manually, slice by slice, by placing a sufficiently large number of points along each of the contours.

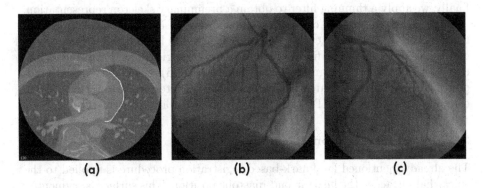

(a)   **(b)**   **(c)**

Fig. 1. Medical imagery relating to end-diastolic phase: (a)transaxial slice of CT with manually segmented ventricular wall; (b)+(c)biplane angiograms relating to end-diastolic frame of cineangiography

Figure 1(a) shows a transaxial slice of the end-diastolic CT data set. For each slice, an approximating NURBS curve is constructed which fits the placed contour points. We then use the least square fitting technique to construct an approximating NURBS curve. We thus obtain for the k slices a family of k NURBS curves. Each NURBS curve is converted into its arc-length parameterised form and equally subdivided into n equal arc-length subsegments (n is equal for all slices S_j $j = 1, 2, ..., k$). Thus, $n - 1$ subdivision points are ascribed to each slice S_j. Let $Q_j = \{q_{ij}|i \in I\}$ $I = \{0, 1, ..., n\}$ be the set of the points defined in Slice j, which comprises the two end points of the contour $q_{0j} = a_j$, $q_{nj} = b_j$, and the $n - 1$ subdivision points q_{ij} $i = 1, 2, ..., n - 1$. The points belonging to the entire surface can be represented by the set

$$Q := \{Q_j|j \in J\} J = \{1, 2, ..., k\} \tag{1}$$

As will be explained later, the k sets Q_j, together with the chosen landmarks, constitute the domain of landmark-based TPS (thin plate spline) registration.

TPS transformations are not only instrumental for the accomplishment of our image registration but also for our motion tracking task (cf. Subsection 3.4).

3.2   Computation of Skeleton Representations of the Coronary Artery Tree from Biplane Cineangiograms

For each frame of the cineangiogram, both projections of the contrast-medium-filled coronary arteries are required. In the Figures 1(b) and 1(c), both projections belonging to the frame for the end-diastolic position are depicted. We have developed a method to achieve a largely automatic segmentation of the epicardial arteries in these images.

In the first stage of our approach, we use a multi-scale Hessian filter to separate the tubular structures of the arteries from the other structures in the image. Then we carry out a conversion of these tubular structures into a binary mask, and finally, we apply a thinning filter to obtain a preliminary skeleton representation.

The second stage of the computations comprises a scan-line-based border detection procedure for an accurate determination of the boundaries of the arteries and the calculation of the final centre lines in the angiograms. From these final centre lines in both angiograms (projections A and B), space curves are three-dimensionaly reconstructed which form the 3D skeleton representations of the coronary artery tree (SEATs). For further details, please refer to [10].

3.3   Image Registration Techniques

The already mentioned landmark-based registration procedure is applied to the epicardial surface of the heart in end-diastolic position. This surface is segmented in the end-diastolic 3D CT data set as described above and then registered to the SEAT which has been computed from the end-diastolic frame in the cineangiogram.

The cineangiographic imagery comprises s frames forming the set $F^{CIN} = \{f_\sigma^{CIN} | \sigma \in S\}$ $S = \{0, 1, ..., s-1\}$, whereby Frame f_0^{CIN} which is needed in the registration procedure refers to the end of the diastole.

Localisation and Definition of 3D Anatomical Point Landmarks. We select a sufficiently large number of corresponding bifurcation points as anatomical point landmarks. This selection is first done with the cardiac CT representation. In the CT image for the end of the diastole, we thus define a set with a sufficiently large number of e point landmarks $L^{CT} = \{l_m^{CT} | m \in M\}$ $M = \{1, 2, ..., e\}$. We then select the set of corresponding landmarks $L^{SEAT} \{l_m^{SEAT} | m \in M\}$ $M = \{1, 2, ..., e\}$ in the SEAT reconstructed from both projections (angiograms) of the end-diastolic frame f_0^{CIN}.

Landmark-Based Thin Plate Spline (TPS) Transformation. Landmark-based TPS image registration is one of the most commonly used methods for non-rigid medical image registration and is well suited to our application area.

The TPS transformation yields minimal bending energy properties measured over the whole image. This properties are therefore advantageous for yielding an overall smooth deformation. We restrict the domain of our TPS transformation to the landmarks and the set Q of points of the epicardial surface as defined in Equation 1.

Given the sets of point landmarks L^{CT} and L^{SEAT} as defined above, a TPS transformation $h^{TPS(CT)}$ (vector-valued function) which maps the elements (points) of each individual set Q_j (cf. Equation 1) to points at new locations $p_{ij}^{f_0^{CIN}}$ as follows

$$p_{ij}^{f_0^{CIN}} = h^{TPS(CT)}(q_{ij}) = A^{CT} q_{ij} + B^{CT} + \sum_{m=1}^{e} w_m^{CT} \Phi\left(\left\| q_{ij} - l_m^{CT} \right\|\right) \quad (2)$$

$$\forall\, q_{ij} \in Q_j \quad j = 1, 2, ..., k$$

Thereby $\|\bullet\|$ denotes the Euclidean norm. The 3x3 matrix A^{CT} and the vector B^{CT} define an affine transformation, whereas w_m^{CT} are weighting vectors; the radial basis function $\Phi(r) = r$ (three-dimensional case) has been chosen as the kernel function Φ. The TPS transformation for each set Q_j is computed separately. For each slice S_j we thus obtain

$$P_j^{f_0^{CIN}} = \left\{ p_{ij}^{f_0^{CIN}} \,|\, i \in I \right\} \quad I = \{0, 1, ...n\} \quad (3)$$

as the set of transformed (registered) contour points. As the result of these transformations, we obtain a collection of k sets of points $P_j^{f_0^{CIN}}$ which can be represented by the set $P^{f_0^{CIN}} := \left\{ P_j^{f_0^{CIN}} \,|\, j \in J \right\}$.

For the sets of points $P_j^{f_0^{CIN}}$, we compute an interpolating NURBS curve which passes exactly through these points. We thus obtain an array of k NURBS curves as transversal contour curves of the registered epicardial surface. We also compute an array of n longitudinal interpolating NURBS curves, each of which passes through points of all slices having the same index value i. These two arrays of NURBS curves constitute a surface mesh as preliminary visual representation of the heart wall (left ventricle). The registration procedure is illustrated by Figure 2. Figure 2(a) shows the surface mesh which we achieve after having segmented the heart wall (epicadial surface of the left ventricle) in the 3D CT dataset. Figure 2(b) shows the SEAT for the end-diastolic position and the registered surface mesh. In the Figures 2(a) and 2(b), however, only the nodes of these surface meshes are depicted.

3.4 Motion Tracking and Analysis Techniques

Our motion tracking analyses are also based on TPS transformations. In the following, we assume that the SEATs are three-dimensionally reconstructed for all s frames f_σ^{CIN} $\sigma = 0, 1, ..., s-1$ (which are linearly ordered in time). Each of these

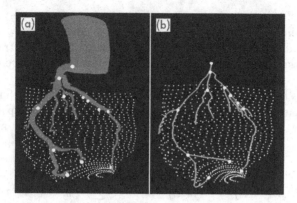

Fig. 2. Image Registration: (a)ventricular surface after segmentation in CT; (b)ventricular surface after registration to the SEAT belonging to the end-diastolic phase

transformations relate to the landmarks in two consecutive frames. The tracking procedure starts with the end-diastolic Frame f_0^{CIN} and comprises $s - 1$ individual landmark-based TPS transformations. However, the number of selected landmarks in each SEATs in this event will usually be different from that employed for the registration task described earlier. As a rule, we will include all bifurcation points which we are able to identify in the SEATs. In each frame we thus define a set of c bifurcation points (landmarks) as follows:

$$L_\sigma^{CIN} = \left\{ l_{w\sigma}^{CIN} | w \in W \right\} \tag{4}$$
$$with \ \ W = \{1, 2, ..., c\} \ \ and \ \ \sigma = 0, 1, ..., s - 1$$

Apart from this usually extended set of anatomical landmarks, the TPS transformations are carried out in full analogy with the TPS transformation used in the above-described registration procedure (cf. Subsection 3.3). We denote these TPS transformations by $h_\sigma^{TPS(CIN)}$ $\sigma = 0, 1, ..., s - 2$ and can formulate them in close conformity with Equation 2 as follows:

$$p_{ij}^{f_{\sigma+1}^{CIN}} = h_\sigma^{TPS(CIN)} \left(p_{ij}^{f_\sigma^{CIN}} \right) =$$

$$A_\sigma^{CIN} p_{ij}^{f_\sigma^{CIN}} + B_\sigma^{CIN} + \sum_{w=1}^{c} c_{w\sigma}^{CIN} \Phi \left(\left\| p_{ij}^{f_\sigma^{CIN}} - l_{w\sigma}^{CIN} \right\| \right) \tag{5}$$

$$\forall \ p_{ij}^{f_\sigma^{CIN}} \in P_j^{f_\sigma^{CIN}} \ \ \ j = 1, 2, ..., k \ \ \ \sigma = 0, 1, ..., s - 2$$

The motion tracking procedure is illustrated by Figure 3. Figure 3(a) refers to the end-diastolic position of the heart, whereas Figure 3(b) concerns the end of the systole.

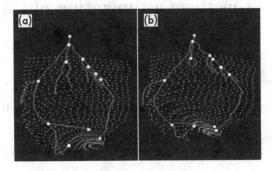

Fig. 3. Comparison between ventricular surface during end-diastolic phase and at systole: (a) end-diastolic phase; (b) end of systole

References

1. Young, A.A., Hunter, P.J., et al.: Estimation of epicardial strain using the motions of coronary bifurcations in biplane cineangiography. IEEE Transactions on Biomedical Engineering 39(5), 526–531 (1992)
2. Shechter, G., Devernay, F., et al.: Three-dimensional motion tracking of coronary arteries in biplane cineangiograms. IEEE Trans. Med. Imaging 22(4), 493–503 (2003)
3. Mahnken, A.H., Katoh, M., et al.: Acute myocardial infarction: assessment of left ventricular function with 16-detector row spiral CT versus MR imaging–study in pigs. Radiology 236(1), 112–117 (2005)
4. Caudron, J.r. m., Fares, J., et al.: Evaluation of Left Ventricular Diastolic Function with Cardiac MR Imaging. Radiographics 31(1), 239–259 (2011)
5. Herz, S.L., Ingrassia, C.M., et al.: Parameterization of Left Ventricular Wall Motion for Detection of Regional Ischemia. Annals of Biomedical Engineering 33(7), 912–919 (2005)
6. Herz, S., Hasegawa, T., et al.: Quantitative Three-Dimensional Wall Motion Analysis Predicts Ischemic Region Size and Location. Annals of Biomedical Engineering 38(4), 1367–1376 (2010)
7. Haberl, R., Tittus, J., et al.: Multislice spiral computed tomographic angiography of coronary arteries in patients with suspected coronary artery disease: An effective filter before catheter angiography? American Heart Journal 149(6), 1112–1119 (2005)
8. Brodoefel, H., Reimann, A., et al.: Sixty-four-slice CT in the assessment of global and regional left ventricular function: Comparison with MRI in a porcine model of acute and subacute myocardial infarction. European Radiology 17(11), 2948–2956 (2007)
9. Tsai, I.C., Huang, J.-L., et al.: Global and regional wall motion abnormalities of pacing-induced heart failure assessed by multi-detector row CT: a patient and canine model study. The International Journal of Cardiovascular Imaging (formerly Cardiac Imaging) 26(suppl.2), 223–235 (2010)
10. Quatember, B., Mayr, M.: Mathematical Modelling and Simulation of Coronary Blood Flow. In: Hosking, R.J., Venturino, E. (eds.) Aspects of Mathematical Modelling: Applications in Science, Medicine, Economics and Management, pp. 161–193. Birkhäuser, Basel (2008)

Multi-objective Optimization of Cancer Chemotherapy Treatment

Ewa Szlachcic, Pawel Porombka, and Jerzy Kotowski

Institute of Computer Engineering, Control and Robotics
Wrocław University of Technology
11/17 Janiszewskiego St., 50-372 Wrocław, Poland
pporombka@gmail.com, {ewa.szlachcic,jerzy.kotowski}@pwr.wroc.pl

Abstract. In cancer chemotherapy a tumor development is delivered by toxic drugs and the influence of drugs' on human body is also checked. The minimization of the tumor burden at a fixed period of time and the minimization of the toxicity of drug regimes will be sought corresponding to the mathematical Goempertz growth model. The effective treatment schedules are search with the help of Modified Differential Evolution Multi-Objective Algorithm. The numerical tests of proposed algoritm show the outcomes for each drug regimes. The tumor is eradicated through the treatment period and the toxic effects are small enough according to the strong set of constraints. The simulation of human body answering for different treatment scenarios can help to an oncologist, which can explore treatment schedules before deciding upon admissible doses regimes for suitable clinical treatment.

1 Introduction

A chemotherapy is a treatment of cancer using set of toxic drugs. They kill cancer cells but also damage patient healthy cells. A dose of drugs is given to a patient than after the period of time for the body to recover the next dose is prepared. Tumor development is delivered by toxic drugs and the influence of drugs on human body is also checked subject to a number of conflicting constraints. The introduction of toxic drugs to the human body gives the damage of different vital organs and drugs doses have to be limited according to the clinical trials and the experience of oncologists [3,5,8].

In a cancer chemotherapy optimization problem given schedules of drugs doses that can minimize the tumor size calculating toxic effects on human body as a set of constraints [1,2,7,10]. A schedule of medical treatment can be calculated based on a mathematical growth model described by a set of differential equations, when used in conjunction with an evolutionary approach [1,10,9]. In a curative cancer chemotherapy treatment the aim is to eradicate a tumor. The drug regimes tend to minimize a tumor size but the anticancer drugs are highly toxic. They have also a very negative influence on a patient quality of life and for the length of life. Moreover it can be shown that a severe drug regime fails to cure and can result in a shorter patient life [3,8].

R. Moreno-Díaz et al. (Eds.): EUROCAST 2011, Part II, LNCS 6928, pp. 256–263, 2012.

In the paper we propose to focus on a bi-criterial optimization problem of a chemotherapy dose schedules in a cancer medical treatment. Differential Evolution approach for multi-objective problem is used to calculate the set of non-dominated solutions [4].

2 Mathematical Model of a Tumor Behaviour

In curative treatment we are going to eradicate a tumor burden and to include highly toxic drug regimes. In a chemotherapy treatment the application of very toxic drugs reduces a tumor meanwhile leading to damage to the immune system and giving unacceptable effects to the patient. The schedule of multi-drugs and drug doses in time intervals to be given determines a balance between killing cancer cells and limiting the damage for human body. The toxic drugs have great influnce on a patient survival time and it is very important to define very precisely the admissible set of contraints. Several general models of growth can be applied for tumor chemotherapy modelling: exponential, von Bartalanffy, Verhulst and Gompertz models [7,9,14].

In the paper the Gompertz growth model with different constraints taking under consideration the highly toxic effects is complying based on [7,10]. Mathematical model of tumor behaviour allows to formulate an objective function calculating the behaviour of a cancer tumor corresponding to the drugs schedules in a specified period of time. The most popular model simulating the response of a tumor burden to a chemotherapy treatment is the Gompertz growth model with a linear cell-loss effect:

$$\frac{dn(x,t)}{dt} = \lambda n(x,t) ln(\frac{\theta}{n(x,t)}) - n_c(x,t), \tag{1}$$

where $n(x,t)$ represents the number of tumor cells in time t for a variables vector x. The variable x_{ij} determines a template of drug j at time interval t_i. λ and $\theta-$ are tumor parameters. $n_c(x,t)$ describes a "cell kill" term of cancer cells added to model the effect of the cytotoxic drugs on the tumor. n(0) defines the initial size of the tumor at the beginning of medical treatment and $n(0) = n_0$. The kill term for multiple drugs is shown below:

$$n_c(x,t) = n(x,t) \sum k_j(c_{2,j}(x,t) - c_{min,j}) H(c_{2,j}(x,t) - c_{min,j}) \tag{2}$$

where: $n_c(x,t)$- a cell-loss term on effective j drug concentration $(c_{2,j}(x,t) - c_{min,j})$, k_j - a parameter, expressing the constant-cell-kill hiphothesis, $c_{min,j}$ - a threshold for drug j below which no tumor cells are killed and $H(.)$ - is the Heaviside step function. The parameter k_j expects to be effective when a tumor is sensitive for anticancer toxic drug. This parameter can be calibrated according to the iterative procedure.

The multi-drug chemotherapy treatment is proposed as a discrete dosage schedules for D drugs at treatment intervals $t_1, t_2, ..., t_N$. One treatment interval is t_i for $i = 1, 2, ..., N$ and the total treatment interval is t_N. Each dose consists of D drugs characterised by the concentration level in each time period. The variable x_{ij} determines a template of drug j at time interval t_i. The x_{ij} denotes the amount of drug j infused between the start -and the end-of infusion times t_{i-1} and t_i respectively. The input function named administration protocol $u(x,t)$ characterizes a template of drug doses:

$$x = [x_{11}, x_{12}, ..., x_{ij}, ..., x_{ND}] \tag{3}$$

for D drugs in each time interval $t = [t_1, t_2, ..., t_N]$, shown below:

$$u(x,t) = \begin{cases} x_{ij}/t_i & for\ 0 < t \le t_1 \\ x_{ij}/(t_i - t_{i-1}) & for\ t_{i-1} \le t \le t_i \end{cases} \tag{4}$$

where i - index of drug dose interval for $i = [1, 2, ..., N]$ and j - index of anticancer drug for $j = [1, 2, ..., D]$. We propose the schedule of drug administration for D drugs at N switching times t_i and then compute the optimal templates x^*. A dose schedule for j drug for whole time period treatment takes the following form:

$$u_j(x,t) = \sum_{i=1}^{N} \frac{x_{ij}}{t_i - t_{i-1}} [H(t - t_i) - H(t - t_{i-1})] \tag{5}$$

and the initial value of $u_j(x,t)$ for $t = 0$ is equal $u_j(x,0) = 0$. The cancer chemotherapy treatment influnces at a tumor site but also for the normal organs. Our aim is to ensure that the human body tolerates anticancer drugs toxic side effects. The drug dose schedule will be analysed with the concentration of drug j in plasma $c_{1j}(x,t)$, defined as following:

$$\frac{dc_{1j}(x,t)}{dt} = -(k_{1j} + k_{12j})\, c_{1j}(x,t) + \frac{u_j(x,t)}{V_1} \tag{6}$$

where k_{1j} and k_{12j} define rate constraints and V_1 - parameter of drug concentration. The active concentration $c_{2j}(x,t)$ of the drug j, eliminated from the human body becomes:

$$\frac{dc_{2j}(x,t)}{dt} = k_{12j} \frac{V_1}{V_2}\, c_{1j}(x,t) - k_{2j}\, c_{2j}(x,t). \tag{7}$$

Because of the onset of toxic side effects of anticancer drugs many human body parameters falls to low level and must be taken to maintain the status of the patient [7]. Especially the White Blood Cell (WBC) count $w(x,t)$ must remain under strict control than a fixed down level. This constraint ensures necessary protection from leukopenia. The WBC count differential equation becomes:

$$\frac{dw(x,t)}{dt} = r_c - v\, w(x,t) - w(x,t) \sum_{j=1}^{D} c_{1j}(x,t)\, \mu_j \tag{8}$$

where $w(x,t)$ counts the number of WBC per unit of volume for r_c, v, μ_j as parameters of the process and $w(x,0) = w_0$. Toxicity $a_j(x,t)$ of drug j for T_{max} must not exceed limit value A_{maxj}:

$$\frac{da_j(x,t)}{dt} = c_{1j}(x,t) \tag{9}$$

and

$$a_j(x,T_{max}) \leqq A_{maxj}. \tag{10}$$

This model is formulated and tested against data from experimental and clinical tumors [5,14,10].

3 Multi-objective Optimization Problem for a Cancer Chemotherapy Treatment

In the paper we propose to focus on a bi-criterial optimization problem of a chemotherapy dose schedule in a cancer medical treatment. We used a mathematical growth model based on a set of four differential equations, which described an influence of drugs doses for the eradication of tumor burden [7]. The first optimization objective is dedicated to a curative treatment and is to minimize the number of tumor cells at a fixed period of time:

$$\min_{x \in X} n(x,t). \tag{11}$$

The second objective function will be sought to minimize the toxicity of drug regimes. The drugs should be scheduled to ensure that the patient will tolerate its toxic side effects:

$$\min_{x \in X} \sum_{i=1}^{N} \sum_{j=1}^{D} c_{1j}(x,t_j). \tag{12}$$

These two objectives conflict with each other corresponding to the set of constraints X like:

$$X = \{x : g_j(x) \leq \overline{g_j} \ for \ j = 1, 2, ..., (2 * D + N + 1)\}. \tag{13}$$

D constraints take a form of (10). Maximum j drug concentration C_{maxj} can not be exceeded for each drug, so:

$$c_{1j}(x,t) \leq C_{maxj} \ for \ j = 1, 2, ..., D. \tag{14}$$

This relation determines renal toxicity, which defines the rate of drug accumulation in urine. This toxicity is directly proportional to $c_1(x,t)$. The WBC count must be greather then a fixed down level W_D :

$$w_i(x,t_i) \geq W_D \ for \ i = 1, 2, ..., N. \tag{15}$$

The coefficient WBC count can not stay too long below a fixed upper level W_U and it is necessary to constrain the time T_U, over which the WBC count remains below W_U to be less than T_U :

$$t(x, T_{max}) \geq T_U. \tag{16}$$

The constraint (16) defines a protection against the leukopenia. The last constraint limits tumor burden during treatment process, as :

$$n(x, t) \leq N_{max}. \tag{17}$$

Finally we try to determine the input drugs schedules that minimizes the tumor size and minimizes the toxic effects on human body subjected to the set of state differential equations, while satisfying the constraints.

4 The Modified Differential Evolution Multi-objective Algorithm

Schedules of medical treatment can be calculated based on a mathematical growth model described by a set of differential equations when used in conjunction with a differential evolution approach (DE) [4,6,12,13]. The multiple use of the mathematical model in a Differential Evolution Multi-Objective Algorithm requires to evaluate a great number of objective functions and constraints. It leads to the high calculation effort. In the paper the Modified Differential Evolution Multi-Objective (MDEMO) algorithm is proposed with modifications according to the mutation operator and to the nondominated sorting in the multi-objective schedule. The intent of the proposed modifications to Differential Evolution Multi-Objective (DEMO) algorithm is to illustrate that the efficiency of the algorithm has been improved. At each step of the optimization process in a multi-objective differential evolution approach, a set of solutions is constructed, and we try to choose nondominated points among all admissible solutions.

The Pareto optimal solutions are found using the Differential Evolution algorithm for multi-objective optimization problem with the help of modified mutation operator, differential crossover DE/rand/1/bin, standarization of constraints and constrained dominance operator used in selection process. An algorithm starts with randomly generated individuals in the search space. Differential evolution employes mutation and crossover operators to produce a donor vector in the current population. The strategies are diversified by the way how to choose three vectors from the current population. A scalar rate for differential evolution idea scales the difference of any of two of the three vectors. For each chromosome the MDEMO algorithm returns the sequence of drugs doses and then the tumur size and the concentration of D drugs in plasma at the end of each interval.

5 Numerical Results

In order to investigate the performance of MDEMO algorithm according to the multi-objective optimization problems for cancer chemotherapy treatment many tests have been made prepared for curative technique. Simulations were performed for different experimental intervals: 10, 20,25 and 30 days and different drug dose scenarios.

The MDEMO algorithm was runing with the following parameters: 150 individuals in one population for 100 generations. The DE/rand/1/bin differential crossover is used with difference rate equal to 0.5 and the best value of crossover

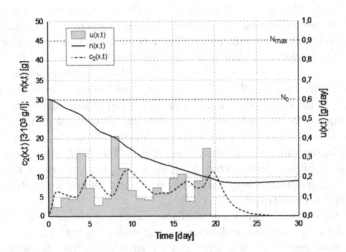

Fig. 1. Optimal dose schedules $u(x,t)$, the number of tumor cells $n(x,t)$ and toxicity effects $c_2(x,t)$ on time intervals $(0, t_1, t_2, ..., t_N)$

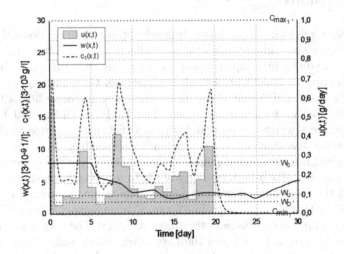

Fig. 2. Optimal dose schedules $u(x,t)$, WBC count $w(x,t)$ and the effective drug concentrations $c_1(x,t)$ in the effective compartment on time intervals $(0, t_1, t_2, ..., t_N)$

probability was fixed at 0.6, the mutation probability was equal at 0.1. In the experiments 15 independent runs were performed varying the outvalues of constraints.

The functioning of the MDEMO algorithm for cancer chemotherapy treatment is illustrated in the paper by considering the curative regime for 20 days of medical experiments. The medical parameters are taken from [5,7,10]. The Fig.1 shows the tumor response curve $n(x, t)$ against time for dose schedules described by u(x,t). Under this regime the tumor is eradicated from 30 g to 9 g through the treatment period during 20 days and the cell-loss function of $c_2(x, t)$ is also active till 23 day of treatment. After 23 day the effective concentration C_{min} is the threshold of $c_2(x, t)$, below which no tumor cells are destroyed.

The contraints are demonstrated on Fig.2 on the same time period like: optimal dose schedules $u(x, t)$, WBC count $w(x, t)$ and the effective drug concentrations $c_1(x, t)$ in the effective compartment. The optimal administration protocols are determined only by the toxicity contraints on WBC count and on C_{max}- the maximum allowed concentration for $c_1(x, t)$ levels and on C_{min} - the threshold of $c_2(x, t)$, below which no tumor cells are killed. The WBC count remains controlled at level higher than a fixed down level W_D. It is necessary to underline that the received optimal drugs doses defined by administration protocols $u(x, t)$ have to fullfill all constraints.

The simulation results are very promising according the eradication of tumor burden and to the toxicity resistance for anticancer drugs. The Pareto set of non-dominated solutions with different dose schedules gives the wide range of solutions taking under consideration by oncologists.

6   Conclusions

In the paper we determine the input drug schedules and drugs doses that minimizes the tumor size and minimizes the toxic effects on human body subjected to the set of state differential equations, while satisfying the constraints. Schedules of chemotherapy treatment are calculated based on Goempertz growth model described by a set of differential equations when used in conjuction with multi-objective differential evolution approach. The Modified Differential Evolution Multi-Objective algorithm is proposed with modifictions according to the differential mutation operator and to the nondominated sorting.

The received non-dominated points of Pareto set ensure the minimization of the tumor size and give a better quality of life to a patient with smaller toxicity of drugs at the end of the treatment period. The numerical tests for proposed MDEMO algorithm show the outcomes for each drugs regime. The algorithm will suggest an optimal chemotherapy treatment strategy. The tumor is eradicated through the treatment period and the toxic effects are small enough according to the strong set of constraints. In the moment we can simulate the answer of human body for the different treatment scenarios. The proposed algorithm gives a tool to an oncologist, which can explore a wide range of treatment schedules before deciding upon suitable doses regimes for clinical treatment.

References

1. Barbour, R., Corne, D., McCall, J.: Accelarated optimisation of chemotherapy dose schedules using fitness inheritance. In: IEEE Congress on Evolutionary Computation (2010)
2. Brownlee, A., Pelikan, M., McCall, J., Pertrovski, A.: An application of a multivariate estimation of distribution algorithm to cancer chemotherapy, Medal (2008)
3. Chingola, R., Foroni, R.I.: Estimating the growth kinetics of experimental tumors from as few as two determinations of tumor size: Implications for clinical oncology. IEEE Trans. on Biomedical Engineering 5, 808–815 (2005)
4. Das, S., Ajith, A., Amit, K.: Particle swarm optimization and differential evolution algorithms: Technical analysis, applications and hybridization perspectives. SCI, vol. 116, pp. 1–38. Springer, Heidelberg (2008)
5. Dearnaley, D., et al.: Handbook of adults cancer chemotherapy schedules. The Medicine Group (Education) Ltd., Oxfordshire (1995)
6. Gong, W., Cai, Z.: A multiobjective differential evolution algorithm for contrained optimization. In: IEEE Congress on Evolutionary Computation, pp. 181-188 (2008)
7. Iliadis, A., Barbolosi, D.: Optimizing drug regimens in cancer chemotherapy by an efficacy-toxicity mathematical model. Computers and Biomedical Research 33, 211–226 (2000)
8. Martin, R., Teo, K.: Optimal control of drug administration in cancer chemotherapy. World Scientific, Singapore (1994)
9. Petrovski, A., McCall, J.: Multi-objective Optimisation of Cancer Chemotherapy Using Evolutionary Algorithms. In: Zitzler, E., Deb, K., Thiele, L., Coello Coello, C.A., Corne, D.W. (eds.) EMO 2001. LNCS, vol. 1993, pp. 531–545. Springer, Heidelberg (2001)
10. Petrovski, A., Shakya, S., McCall, J.: Optimising cancer chemotherapy using an estimation of distribution algorithm and genetic algorithms, Medal Report No. 2008005 (January 2008)
11. Porombka, P.: A Meta-heuristic approach for the medical treatment planning, M.Sc. Thesis (unpublished), Wroclaw University of Technology, Wroclaw (2010)
12. Robič, T., Filipič, B.: DEMO: Differential evolution for multiobjective optimization. In: Coello Coello, C.A., Hernández Aguirre, A., Zitzler, E. (eds.) EMO 2005. LNCS, vol. 3410, pp. 520–533. Springer, Heidelberg (2005)
13. Santana-Quintero, L.V., Hernadez-Diaz, A.G., Molina, J., Coello Coello, C.A., Caballero, R.: DEMORS: A hybrid multi-objective optimization algorithm using differential evolution and rough set theory for constrained problems. Computers and Operations Research 37, 470–480 (2009)
14. Wheldon, T.: Mathematical models in cancer research. Adam Hilger, Bristol, Philadelphia (1988)

EDEVITALZH: Predictive, Preventive, Participatory and Personalized e-Health Platform to Assist in the Geriatrics and Neurology Clinical Scopes

Carmen Paz Suárez Araujo[1], Miguel Ángel Pérez del Pino[1], Patricio García Báez[2], and Pablo Fernández López[1]

[1] Instituto de Ciencias y Tecnologías Cibernéticas,
Universidad de Las Palmas de Gran Canaria,
35017 Las Palmas de Gran Canaria, Canary Islands, Spain
{cpsuarez,pfernandez}@dis.ulpgc.es, miguel.perez107@alu.ulpgc.es
[2] Departamento de Estadística, Investigación Operativa y Computación
Universidad de La Laguna, 38271 La Laguna, Canary Islands, Spain
pgarcia@ull.es

Abstract. This work presents an e-Health framework to aid diagnosis, prognosis and monitoring of Alzheimer's Disease and other dementias (EDEVITALZH) by interacting with Intelligent Systems for Diagnosis. Conceived as an intelligent Clinical Workstation, it provides healthcare professionals methods and tools to perform their examinations in an efficient way. Diagnosis and prognosis will be more accurate, agile and patient-dedicated, allowing time and health resources optimization. Based on Grid Computing, it can be accessed and used securely over the Internet from any healthcare center (primary or specialized care) just by using a web browser. The proposed intelligent Clinical Workstation represents a relevant contribution in Medical Informatics and Telemedicine fields.

Keywords: EDEVITALZH, e-Health, Alzheimer's Disease, Dementia, Computer-Aided Diagnosis.

1 Introduction

All the sociological studies indicate that the European population meets a remarkable aging process, due to an extraordinary increment of people's life expectancy, to a decrease of the birth rate and of child mortality [2]. The sociological importance of the elderly has grown significantly in the recent years [9,6]. This progressive inversion of the population pyramid means, to any country that suffers it, severe socio-sanitary consequences. This situation derives from the prevalence increase of neurodegenerative diseases and their secondary functional disorders. Among aging-associated diseases, there must be highlighted Dementias, especially Alzheimer's disease (AD). These pathologies and those ones related are the most interesting group, not only because they are estimated

R. Moreno-Díaz et al. (Eds.): EUROCAST 2011, Part II, LNCS 6928, pp. 264–271, 2012.
© Springer-Verlag Berlin Heidelberg 2012

to affect 5%-10% of people aging more than 65, reaching 25-30% if Mild Cognitive Impairment (MCI) is considered, but also because of the damages they cause to the patient's family, and to his/her caregiver. Detecting these disorders at an early stage will improve the patients' quality of life and provide benefits to the patients' social environment as well as to the healthcare system, assuring a better utilization of resources.

There are several open issues in the scope of Dementias and AD, among which the need of neuropathological confirmation is highlighted. Using diagnostic criteria up to date, the *ante-mortem* diagnosis of *probable AD* is currently confirmed *post-mortem* in 80-90% of cases only in specialized centers, as well as the high underdiagnosis level [7], which can reach, in certain conditions, a 95% of the cases. A new terminology has arisen out of the International Working Group for New Research Criteria for the Diagnosis of Alzheimer's Disease (IWGNRCDAD), which takes into account symptomatology and the behavioral-cognitive evolution, as well as the possibility of complementing diagnosis by employing protein biomarkers [3]; being able to arise several diagnostic cathegories, even years before the disease has started to manifest symptomatically. Other issues are the spread spectrum of ussual diagnostic criteria (CAMDEX, DSM-IV, CIE-10), the very limited coincidence between them, not higher than 5%, if taken as a set (not yet having specific clinical valid criteria for each dementia), and the clinical-pathological duality.

On the other hand, it has been estimated that the management of clinical records consumes around 25% of the healthcare system resources and time [10]. These handicaps has taken the scientific community to think of developing a series of tools which allow diagnosing the disease at the earliest possible time, with the intention of adopting the therapeutical measures that best fit. Computational intelligence allows using all the possible criteria together to assist the diagnosis, placing special emphasis on early and differential diagnosis, and patients follow-up, allowing clinicians to focus less time on data handling tasks and to dedicate more time to patients.

This work presents an e-health framework to aid diagnosis and prognosis of MCI, AD and other dementias (EDEVITALZH). EDEVITALZH is a Personalized, Predictive, Preventive, and Participatory Healthcare Delivery System (4P-HCDS) [5,6,9] following the phylosophy of Electronic Medical Records (EMR) and Clinical Workstations (CW). EDEVITALZH has been conceived as an Intelligent CW (iCW), aiding clinicians in their tasks of diagnosis, prognosis and neuropathology monitoring as well as patients follow-up by interacting with different Intelligent Systems for Diagnosis (ISD) [4,5,8,9]. It implements the Global Clinical Protocol for Dementias (GCPD) [6,9], validated by medical experts in the fields of Geriatrics and Neurology. Moreover, it empowers collaborative work between clinicians by means of an electronic interconsultation scheme. Thanks to its architecture, Internet based, and the minimal resources required, EDEVITALZH can be accessed not only from Specialized Care (SC) centers but also from Primary Care (PC) ones. Moreover, its distributed computing structure allows to have several EDEVITALZH instances in geographically distant locations.

The proposed intelligent Clinical Workstation represents a relevant contribution in Medical Informatics and Telemedicine fields and it is an optimal solution to be integrated into any health infrastructure. Diagnosis and prognosis performed by physicians will be more accurate, agile and patient-dedicated, allowing time and health resources optimization. Furthermore, it promotes the creation of a Dementias and AD knowledge database by gathering and storing information of patients anywhere in the globe, which empowers the possibility to carry out knowledge-discovering research tasks in the fields of diagnosis and prognosis of these pathologies.

2   EDEVITALZH

2.1   Fundamentals

The Healthcare IT industry agrees to differentiate, in what relates to Electronic Medical Records, two well-separated system paradigms. On one side, Patients Management Systems (PMS), which administer personal, social and administrative data of patients. On the other side, CW, that gather the set of clinical procedures, forms, tests and other diagnostic tools that healthcare professionals will employ to evaluate their patients along their clinical episodes. Despite it provides tools to manage patients' personal information, EDEVITALZH is considered an iCW based on a three-tier layout: Presentation (User Interface, UI Extension Tools & Wizards), Data Model and Technological Architecture (Computing and Security Systems, and Policies), Fig. 1:

- It implements, based on a web application model, the Global Clinical Protocol for Dementias (GCPD), a detailed set of clinical procedures, forms, tests and diagnostic criteria, which have been validated by medical experts in the fields of Geriatrics and Neurology, reflecting in an schematic way specific data of interest focused on the diagnosis of AD, MCI and other dementias and correlating clinical and therapeutical parameters simultaneously. GCPD has been tuned to be used according to each healthcare level. This way, EDEVITALZH implements two versions of GPCD, a reduced one according to PC needs and the extended one for SC, meaning this that every physician, no matter which healthcare level is at, will be able to take approach of the available resources to perform an adequate diagnosis. Regarding its electronic implementation, GCPD is represented by 2 out of 3 tiers of EDEVITALZH Logic Model Fig. 1: First tier, the Data Model (GCPD-DM); second tier, the User Interface (GCPD-UI).

- It interacts with several Intelligent Systems for Diagnosis (ISD) and other Intelligent Clinical Wizards (ICWZ), helping clinicians in decision-making tasks, reducing diagnosis time and improving the accuracy in early and differential diagnosis.

Furthermore, EDEVITALZH implements the Electronic Interconsultation, which provides clinicians the possibility to perform collaborative work between

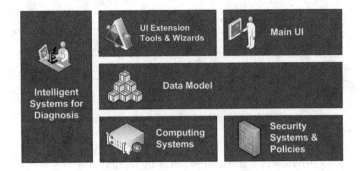

Fig. 1. EDEVITALZH Logic Model

physicians and other clinicians. Moreover, it is a powerful and valuable tool for professionals at PC and other welfare centers where there are no specialist physicians, giving them the possibility to assist patients who suffer these neurotpathologies.

EDEVITALZH web application has been developed using a Model-View-Controller (MVC) software design pattern Fig. 2, where GCPD-DM represents the Model and GCPD-UI represents the View. The Controller, *'DBengine'*, has been implemented using PHP language and AJAX. *DBengine* defines HTTP-Request parameters to handle user data requests and translate them into SQL queries. Several application interface libraries have been developed to provide the needed functionality to handle operations between the database and the user interface. Data sent between the database and the user interface follows JSON format.

This implementation scheme makes it possible to add extension tools and wizards to EDEVITALZH, improving its capabilities. Abstraction of the mechanisms to access the databases, retrieve the desired data and easily display them on the screen using YUI components, provides a powerful framework to implement as many tools as clinicians request, increasing EDEVITALZH data intelligence features and furthermore, improving user experience.

2.2 Data Model (GCPD-DM)

EDEVITALZH Data Model (GCPD-DM) was designed using the Entity-Relationship Model. GCPD-DM is based on 2 principal entities, formally named *Axis Entities*: the *'Patient'* entity and the *'Episode'* entity. Around them, another set of 9 entities coexist (listed alphabetically): *'Caregiver'*, *'Complementary Test'*, *'Diagnosis'*, *'Exploration'*, *'Interconsultation'*, *'Physician'*, *'Scale'* and *'Symptom'*. Thus, GCPD-DM consists of 11 entities, corresponding to 31 master-data and 16 activity-data SQL tables, respectively.

The developed model simplifies the way clinical data is related, encouraging information relationships to be afterwards analyzed by data exploitation. GCPD-DM empowers standarization in workflow, so does in data harvesting, according

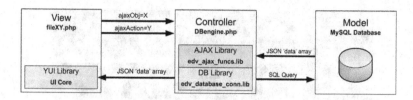

Fig. 2. EDEVITALZH Model-View-Controller Design

to specifications provided by medical experts by formalizing the way the patient is evaluated and which data must be gathered since he/she arrives to the physician's consultation for the first time. Its implementation has been performed in a powerful open-source database, MySQL Database, under Linux 2.6 operating system, because of its high performance, high reliability and high scalability. All operations regarding data rely on *DBEngine*.

2.3   User Interface (GCPD-UI)

EDEVITALZH User Interface (GCPD-UI) shapes the logical structure of the GCPD into a screen interface which users can interact with. Based on a web application model, GCPD-IU has been developed using components provided by Yahoo! User Interface Library (YUI), which provides utilities and controls written with JavaScript and Cascading Style Sheets (CSS) for building richly interactive web applications using DOM scripting, DHTML and AJAX.

Structurally speaking, GCPD is divided into the following subsections which group related parameters according to evaluation procedures, methods and techniques: *Personal Data, Social Data, Family Precedents, Habits, Episodes and Related Data, Cognitive Symptomatology, Not-Cognitive Symptomatology, Functional Symptomatology, Other Symptomatologies, Physical Explorations, Complementary Tests, Drugs Prescription, Intercurrent Diseases, Diagnosis, Disease Evolution.* According to each healthcare level, PC or SC, GCPD-UI will adapt itself, showing the specific criteria of interest for professionals so that workflow is guided to take approach of the healthcare level available resources to perform an adequate diagnosis or prognosis of the assisted patients.

GCPD subsections are visually represented as tabulators. Inside each tabulator, related parameters are shown together, displayed using datagrids. For data gathering, HTML forms according to the GCPD-DM features were implemented.

2.4   Technological Architecture

EDEVITALZH is featured as an iCW thanks to ISD which aid clinicians in their decision-making tasks. Requests to Aid Diagnosis (RAD) must be considered as execution processes (jobs) in such a way upon an user request, a new process must be executed to obtain certain results. These concepts need of a robust, scalable and fault-tolerant technological architecture which allows multiple user

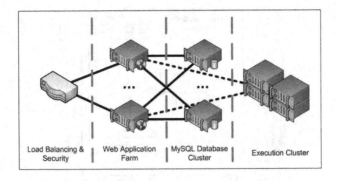

Fig. 3. EDEVITALZH Technological Architecture

connecting from anywhere and requesting aid for diagnosis, so that computing resources are managed and assigned in an accurate and efficient way to return the users' awaited results.

EDEVITALZH has been built based on the Grid Computing paradigm (GC), which makes it possible to use, in a coordinated way, all kind of computing resources (hardware and software) without being subject to any centralized control. In this sense, GC can be considered as a new type of distributed computing, where resources can be heterogeneous and are connected by wide area networks such as the Internet, empowering Cloud Computing. EDEVITALZH platform is made up of a connections load balancer, a farm of web application servers (running Apache HTTP Server), a database cluster (running MySQL Database instances) and an execution cluster, Fig. 3.

EDEVITALZH Execution Cluster has been developed using Oracle Grid Engine (OGE) because of its jobs and queues management features. These features help managing RAD jobs in a scheme of several queues according to attributes such as priority. Architecturally speaking, EDEVITALZH Execution Cluster consists of Computing Cells (C-Cell). Every C-Cell is made up of a farm of servers running Linux 2.6 operating system and connected by a high-speed communication network, linked to the Internet. The minimum EDEVITALZH C-Cell configuration according to OGE architecture considers 1 Master Node to handle job processing requests, 1 Shadow Master Node for SN fault-tolerance and n Execution Nodes to process jobs.

C-Cell hosts share a Network File System (NFS) and have been configured to improve I/O throughput according to the performed operation: NFS is only used to read and write definitive data while I/O tasks during job processing are performed locally on each execution host to reduce I/O bottlenecks. In an administration level, users, groups and operating system privileges are handled by NIS+. The whole C-Cell is monitored using SNMP protocol, checking CPU, Memory, Disk and Network Utilization every minute.

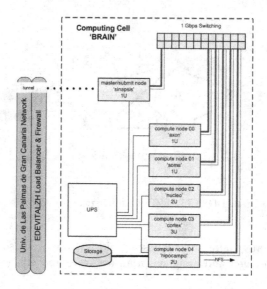

Fig. 4. 'BRAIN' Production Computing Cell at COMCIENCIA Lab, ULPGC

3 Conclusions

The e-Health plataform proposed in this paper represents an important advance in the area of Medical Informatics and Telemedicine. Thanks to its technical specifications, any healthcare center, despite its location or resources, will be able to use it; just a terminal connected to the Internet and a web browser are needed.

Healthcare system resources are managed in a more accurate and efficient way. Global Clinical Protocol for Dementias guides physicians' clinical workflow, leading the several medical examinations and helping clinicians' time to be more patient dedicated. Thanks to its Intellient Clinical Workstation features, it allows consulting and collaborative work between professional colleagues, despite their location or resources (just a terminal connected to the Internet and a web browser are needed), being of special interest the one that can be established between PC and SC clinicians. This improves diagnosis and decreases the underdiagnosis rate. Regarding decision making, EDEVITALZH interacts with Intelligent Systems for Diagnosis and other Intelligent Clinical Wizards which aid healthcare professionals in their diagnosis, prognosis and patients follow-up tasks, resulting in a more accurate and agile decision making which, in the end, means improvements differential diagnosis. Furthermore, treatments will be able to be studied in depth and patient-customized treatment strategies will be prescripted. Last, but not least, it will allow to create a knowledge-base regarding Alzheimer's Disease and other Dementias, which will allow to perform research tasks regarding these pathologies.

After all that has been stated in this paper, we conclude the most relevant aspect of the effect of this proposal is that it will ensure that no patient with dementia or with the potential to have it, will go without the adequate medical attention, without a proper diagnosis and finally, without the appropriate treatment to alleviate their condition, due to lack of human and/or necessary clinical resources.

Acknowledgments. We would like to thank Canary Islands Government, the Ministry of Science and Innovation of the Spanish Government and EU Funds (FEDER) for their support under Research Projects SolSubC200801000347 and TIN2009-13891 respectively.

References

1. Bravo-Toledo, R., Gervás-Camacho, J., Bonís-Sanz, J.: Influencia de la Informatización de la Atención Primaria en el trabajo de los profesionales y en la salud de la población. Atención Primaria 40(supl.1), 11–62 (2008)
2. Campillo Páez, M.: Hacemos correctamente la valoración geriátrica en Atención Primaria?. Revista Centro de Salud, 157-162 (March 2001)
3. Dubois, B., Feldman, H.H., et al.: Revising the definition of Alzheimer's disease: a new lexicon. The Lancet Neurology 9(11), 1118–1127 (2010)
4. García Báez, P., Fernández Viadero, C., Pérez del Pino, M.A., Prochazka, A., Suárez Araujo, C.P.: HUMANN-based systems for differential diagnosis of dementia using neuropsychological tests. In: 14th International Conference on Intelligent Engineering Systems (INES 2010), pp. 67–72 (2010); ISBN: 978-1-4244-7650-3
5. García Báez, P., Pérez del Pino, M.A., Fernández Viadero, C., Suárez Araujo, C.P.: Artificial Intelligent Systems Based on Supervised HUMANN for Differential Diagnosis of Cognitive Impairment: Towards a 4P-HCDS. In: Cabestany, J., Sandoval, F., Prieto, A., Corchado, J.M. (eds.) IWANN 2009. LNCS, vol. 5517, pp. 981–988. Springer, Heidelberg (2009)
6. Pérez del Pino, M.A., Suárez Araujo, C.P., García Báez, P., Fernández López, P.: EDEVITALZH: an e-Health Solution for Application in the Medical Fields of Geriatrics and Neurology. In: Moreno-Díaz, R., et al. (eds.) EUROCAST 2011. LNCS, vol. 6928, pp. 263–270. Springer, Heidelberg (2011)
7. Solomon, P., Murphy, C.: Should we screen for Alzh's disease? Geriatrics 60, 26–31 (2005)
8. Súarez Araujo, C.P., García Báez, P., Fernández Viadero, C.: GaNEn: A new gating neural ensemble for automatic assessment of the Severity Level of Dementia using neuropsychological tests. In: Fifth International Conference on Broadband and Biomedical Communications (IB2Com), pp. 1–6, 15–17 (2010); ISBN: 978-1-4244-6951-2
9. Suárez Araujo, C.P., Pérez del Pino, M.A., García Báez, P., Fernández López, P.: Clinical Web Environment to Assist the Diagnosis of Alzheimers Disease and other Dementias. WSEAS Transactions on Computers 6, 2083–2088 (2004); ISSN: 1109-2750
10. Terceiro, J.B.: Sociedad Digital: Del Homo Sapiens Al Homo Digitalis. Alianza Editorial (1996)

Improvements of the Construction of Exact Minimal Covers of Boolean Functions

Bernd Steinbach[1] and Christian Posthoff[2]

[1] Freiberg University of Mining and Technology, Institute of Computer Science,
D-09596 Freiberg, Germany
[2] The University of The West Indies, St. Augustine Campus, Trinidad & Tobago

Abstract. The calculation of an exact minimal cover of a Boolean function is an NP-complete problem. In this paper we introduce the definition of this problem and its basic solution. By using a slightly modified algorithm, we get a speed-up factor of more than 10^4. The main contributions of this paper are the description of an alternative approach mentioned in [15], and a remarkable improvement of this algorithm. In both cases operations of the XBOOLE library are used. Using the newly suggested algorithm, the time required for the calculation could be reduced by a factor of more than $8 * 10^8$ in comparison with the previous algorithm.

1 Introduction

There are two basic methods to synthesize combinatorial Boolean functions, *covering methods* and *decomposition methods*. Decomposition methods are more complicated than covering methods. Basic decomposition ideas were published by Ashenhurst [1], Curtis [3], and Povarov [10]. Multilevel circuits for real practical problems can be synthesized by decomposition methods suggested recently, e.g. [6], [9], or [12]. Although decomposition methods are more powerful for the synthesis of multilevel circuits, we focus in this paper on covering methods because minimal disjunctive forms (DFs) [13] go nicely with regular structures (which helps to avoid deep submicron problems).

Covering methods have been studied over a very long period of time. The well-known Quine-McCluskey method was suggested by Quine [11] and improved by Mc Cluskey [5]. Two subtasks must be solved in order to find a minimal DF for a given Boolean function. First, all prime conjunctions must be found, and second, a minimal subset of prime conjunctions must be selected to cover the given function.

The first subtask is solved by the Quine-McCluskey method such that a simpler conjunction is created from two conjunctions having a Hamming distance of 1. This method requires to start with all minterms, restricts the necessary comparisons, and guarantees that all prime conjunctions will be found.

For the second subtask Quine and McCluskey suggested to use a prime conjunction chart which allows to find a simple set of prime conjunctions (which is not for sure exactly minimal). All irredundant minimal disjunctive forms of

R. Moreno-Díaz et al. (Eds.): EUROCAST 2011, Part II, LNCS 6928, pp. 272–279, 2012.
© Springer-Verlag Berlin Heidelberg 2012

a Boolean functions can be found using the *Petrick* function [7], [8]. Among all irredundant disjunctive forms exact minimal forms can be detected by counting the number of prime conjunctions which each form uses to cover the given Boolean function.

There are drawbacks for both subtasks. The table method of Quine-McCluskey allows to find all prime conjunctions but requires to start with all minterms, the number of which grows exponentially with the number of variables. In order to find an exact minimal solution, the Petrick function must be evaluated as second subtask. The complexity of this problem for a Boolean function of n variables is $O(np^{nc})$, where $0 \leq np < 3^n$ is the number of prime conjunctions, and $0 \leq nc \leq 2^n$ is the number of values 1 for the given function. Both np and nc are typically much larger than n, therefore the problem has an exponential complexity.

There are many approaches to solve the minimization problem for large "real-world" functions. Well known is the *Espresso* program that utilizes several heuristics [2]. Other new approaches use genetic algorithms [14] or try to utilize special mathematical properties [4].

We concentrate in this paper on the second subtask, the selection of all minimal sets of prime conjunctions. We assume that all prime conjunctions are given. In order to be sure that all minimal disjunctive forms will be found, we utilize the Petrick function. We are aiming at a considerable reduction of the runtime of solution algorithms for this covering problem.

First we introduce the *unate covering problem*. Secondly we describe the classical approach for its solution in order to compare it with the new approach. As the main contribution of this paper we prove the alternative approach mentioned in [15], suggest a remarkable improvement of this algorithm, and present the experimental results.

2   Unate Covering - The Problem

Each prime conjunction covers certain function values 1 of the given Boolean function. It is evident that a disjunction of all prime conjunctions covers the given Boolean function completely. Furthermore, for each input pattern $\mathbf{x} = \mathbf{c}_0$ with $f(\mathbf{x} = \mathbf{c}_0) = 1$ exists at least one prime conjunction pc_i such that $[pc_i \wedge f(\mathbf{x})]_{\mathbf{x}=\mathbf{c}_0} = 1$. In most cases this condition will be satisfied by several prime conjunctions. Otherwise, the single prime conjunction that satisfies the condition is *essential* and must be used in each cover.

In order to solve the covering problem, we introduce Boolean *model variables* p_i. Each model variable p_i is associated with the prime conjunction pc_i. A new Boolean function $P(\mathbf{p})$ can be created as follows:

1. Generally, each $\mathbf{x} = \mathbf{c}_0$ with $f(\mathbf{x} = \mathbf{c}_0) = 1$ can be covered by several prime conjunctions. Hence, we create a disjunction of the associated model variables p_i.
2. All function values $f(\mathbf{x} = \mathbf{c}_0) = 1$ must be covered. Hence, we connect all such disjunctions by conjunctions and get the Boolean function $P(\mathbf{p})$.

The created function $P(\mathbf{p})$ is called *Petrick function*. Such a function has a conjunctive form (CF) [13].

Example 1. A simple Petrick function $P(\mathbf{p})$ of 8 variables and 8 disjunctions is shown in (1).

$$
\begin{aligned}
P(\mathbf{p}) = {}& (p_4 \vee p_6 \vee p_7) \wedge (p_4 \vee p_5 \vee p_6 \vee p_8) \wedge \\
& (p_1 \vee p_3 \vee p_4 \vee p_7 \vee p_8) \wedge (p_1 \vee p_4 \vee p_5 \vee p_7 \vee p_8) \wedge \\
& (p_1 \vee p_2 \vee p_5 \vee p_6) \wedge (p_4 \vee p_5 \vee p_6 \vee p_7 \vee p_8) \wedge \\
& (p_1 \vee p_4 \vee p_5 \vee p_6 \vee p_7 \vee p_8) \wedge (p_2 \vee p_3 \vee p_4 \vee p_7 \vee p_8)
\end{aligned} \tag{1}
$$

A complete cover is defined by equation (2). Due to the CF on the left-hand side of (2) this equation specifies a satisfiability problem (SAT). The solution of a SAT-problem are such values of the variables p_i that equation (2) is satisfied. For the wanted covers the assignments describe which prime conjunctions must be used to cover the basic function $f(\mathbf{x})$.

$$
P(\mathbf{p}) = 1 \tag{2}
$$

It is a special feature that the Petrick function is *unate*. Each variable p_i appears in a CF of a unate function with a fixed polarity. For a Petrick function all variables have even positive polarity.

The positive polarity of all variables p_i has a strong influence on the solution process. The assignment $\forall i : p_i = 1$ solves the Petrick equation (2). However, this solution means that all prime conjunctions pc_i must be used to cover the function $f(\mathbf{x})$, but the aim is to find a cover using a number of prime conjunctions pc_i which is as small as possible. We are searching for solutions of (2) where the number of assignments $p_i = 1$ is minimized.

3   Unate Covering - Classical Approach

The classical approach to solve this unate covering problem applies first the *distributive law* (3) to the clauses:

$$
(a \vee b) \wedge (c \vee d) = a\,c \vee a\,d \vee b\,c \vee b\,d \ . \tag{3}
$$

Example 2. Applying the distributive law to the first two clauses of (1) results in:

$$
\begin{aligned}
(p_4 \vee p_6 \vee p_7) \wedge (p_4 \vee p_5 \vee p_6 \vee p_8) = {}& p_4\,p_4 \vee p_4\,p_5 \vee p_4\,p_6 \vee p_4\,p_8 \vee \\
& p_6\,p_4 \vee p_6\,p_5 \vee p_6\,p_6 \vee p_6\,p_8 \vee p_7\,p_4 \vee p_7\,p_5 \vee p_7\,p_6 \vee p_7\,p_8 \ .
\end{aligned} \tag{4}
$$

Each of the 12 conjunctions of (4) means that the associated prime conjunctions must be taken to cover the same two function values 1 of $f(\mathbf{x})$. Due to (3), the number of created conjunctions of variables p_i is equal to the product of the numbers of these variables in the clauses of the Petrick function. Hence, even for the small Petrick function (1) a solution set of $3 * 4 * 5 * 5 * 4 * 5 * 6 * 5 = 180,000$ conjunctions of p_i is created.

The same variable p_i can appear in a created conjunction several times. Due to the clauses of (4), the variables p_4 and p_6 appear twice in a created conjunction. Using the *idempotence law*

$$a \wedge a = a , \tag{5}$$

each solution conjunction can be simplified such that each variable p_i appears only once.

Example 3. Applying (5) to (4) results in

$$(p_4 \vee p_6 \vee p_7) \wedge (p_4 \vee p_5 \vee p_6 \vee p_8) = p_4 \vee p_4 p_5 \vee p_4 p_6 \vee p_4 p_8 \vee \atop p_6 p_4 \vee p_6 p_5 \vee p_6 \vee p_6 p_8 \vee p_7 p_4 \vee p_7 p_5 \vee p_7 p_6 \vee p_7 p_8 . \tag{6}$$

A final stronger reduction will be reached using the *absorption law*

$$a \vee a b = a . \tag{7}$$

Example 4. Applying (7) to (6) results in

$$(p_4 \vee p_6 \vee p_7) \wedge (p_4 \vee p_5 \vee p_6 \vee p_8) = p_4 \vee p_6 \vee p_7 p_5 \vee p_7 p_8 . \tag{8}$$

Here we can see a crucial problem: the application of the absorption law requires the consideration of all pairs of existing conjunctions. In detail we observed that applying (3) and (5) to (1) results in $180,000$ conjunctions calculated in a time of 8.097 seconds. The application of (7) to the disjunction of the $180,000$ conjunctions leads to 12 conjunctions only within 75.646 seconds.

It is more efficient to apply the absorption law after each application of the distributive law instead of only once for the whole set of conjunctions.

Algorithm 1. Unate Cover of $P(\mathbf{p}) = 1$

Require: *Petrick function* $P(\mathbf{p}) = d_1(\mathbf{p}) \vee \ldots \vee d_k(\mathbf{p})$
Ensure: all minimal solutions AMS of $P(\mathbf{p}) = 1$
1: $AMS \leftarrow d_1(\mathbf{p})$
2: **for all** $i \leftarrow 2$ to k **do**
3:     $AMS \leftarrow AMS \wedge d_i(\mathbf{p})$: using law (3) and law (5)
4:     apply absorption law (7) to all pairs of conjunctions in AMS
5: **end for**

Example 5. Algorithm 1 uses the better order of the rules and finds 12 solutions (9) of the covering problem (1) within 6 milliseconds instead of 83,743 milliseconds in case of a single postponed application of the absorption law.

$$p_1 p_4 \vee p_2 p_4 \vee p_4 p_5 \vee p_4 p_6 \vee p_1 p_2 p_6 \vee p_1 p_3 p_6 \vee \atop p_3 p_5 p_6 \vee p_6 p_7 \vee p_6 p_8 \vee p_1 p_7 p_8 \vee p_5 p_7 \vee p_2 p_7 p_8 = 1 \tag{9}$$

We use Algorithm 1 (showing a speedup of more than 10^4) as reference for further comparisons. Each conjunction of the p_i (such as $p_1 p_2 p_6$ etc.) describes a complete *irredundant cover*; all the prime conjunctions selected in this way are required. In that sense all these solutions are minimal.

There may be irredundant covers with different numbers of prime conjunctions. For the Petrick function (1), there are minimal covers by 2 or 3 prime conjunctions in (9). We call an irredundant cover *exact minimal cover* when it shows the smallest possible number of prime conjunctions. This can be found out by counting the variables in each conjunction.

Example 6. There are 7 exact minimal covers (10) for the Petrick function (1) consisting of 2 prime conjunctions:

$$p_1 p_4 \vee p_2 p_4 \vee p_4 p_5 \vee p_4 p_6 \vee p_6 p_7 \vee p_6 p_8 \vee p_5 p_7 = 1 \ . \tag{10}$$

The first conjunction $p_1 p_4$ of (10) means that the prime conjunctions pc_1 and pc_4 **must** be used to cover the function. The values of the missing six variables $p_2, p_3, p_5, p_6, p_7, p_8$ are not important. Setting all of them equal to 0 (not using the respective conjunctions) results in the exact minimal cover. The same considerations apply to the other pairs.

4   Proof of the CPL(NDM(P)) - Approach

Each Petrick function (see e.g. (1)) is a conjunctive form (CF). In order to find all minimal solutions, the equation CF=1 (2) with a Petrick function on the left-hand side must be solved. The solution of this equation is a set of patterns for the variables p_i. Such a pattern includes values '1' for certain variables p_i which expresses the fact that the associated prime conjunctions pc_i must be used in the minimal cover. The remaining values for p_j of such a pattern are dashes '−' which expresses the fact that the respective prime conjunctions pc_j can be used for the representation of the function, but can be omitted without any problem. There is a direct mapping between the solution patterns and the conjunctions in the equation (9) which have a disjunctive form (DF) on the lefthand side.

Due to this transformation of the given Petrick equation CF=1 (2) into an equation of the type DF=1 (9) the CPL(NDM(P))–approach was suggested in [15]. The idea of this approach is the transformation of the Petrick function from CF into DF by (11) using the XBOOLE–operations [9], [15]

- NDM(f): negation of the function f according to *de Morgan's Law*, and
- CPL(f): complement of of the function f as orthogonal expression.

$$
\begin{aligned}
\overline{\overline{P(\mathbf{p})}} &= 1 \\
\overline{P(\mathbf{p})} &= 1 \\
NDM(\overline{P(\mathbf{p})}) &= 1 \\
CPL(NDM(\overline{P(\mathbf{p})})) &= 1
\end{aligned}
\tag{11}
$$

This core idea creates all exact minimal covers, all additional irredundant minimal covers, and all possible covers that are not minimal. In contrast to the classical approach, negated variables appear in the created DF, too. The wanted exact minimal covers can be found by selecting conjunctions of the DF having a minimal number of non-negated variables p_i as described in Algorithm 2.

Algorithm 2. All Exact Minimal Covers Defined by $P(\mathbf{p}) = 1$

Require: *Petrick function* $P(\mathbf{p}) = d_1(\mathbf{p}) \vee \ldots \vee d_k(\mathbf{p})$
Ensure: all exact minimal covers $AEMC$ of $P(\mathbf{p}) = 1$
1: $AEMC \leftarrow \text{CPL(NDM}(P(\mathbf{p})))$
2: select the exact minimal solutions of $AEMC$ by counting positive literals in each conjunction and take the smallest values
3: extend all conjunctions of $AEMC$ into minterms by adding missing negative literals

---

Theorem 1. *Algorithm 2 creates all exact minimal covers $AEMC$ expressed by $DF(P(\mathbf{p}))$ of a Boolean function $f(\mathbf{x})$ which is given by a Petrick function $CF(P(\mathbf{p}))$.*

Proof. The idea will be shown by using the following example $(a \vee b \vee c)(b \vee c \vee d)$. We use the negation according to de Morgan (NDM) in the following way:

$$\overline{CF(a,b,c,d)} = \overline{(a \vee b \vee c)(b \vee c \vee d)} = \overline{(a \vee b \vee c)} \vee \overline{(b \vee c \vee d)} = \overline{a}\overline{b}\overline{c} \vee \overline{b}\overline{c}\overline{d} \ .$$

The equation $\overline{(CF(a,b,c,d)} = 1$ has the solution vectors $(abcd) = (000-)$ and $(abcd) = (-000)$. When these solutions are compared with the original expression, then each variable of the expression is set to 0. Therefore all the disjunctions and finally $(a \vee b \vee c)(b \vee c \vee d)$ are equal to 0. That means that the XBOOLE-operation NDM sets all variables of the different disjunctions to 0 and in this way results in all vectors that are **not** a solution of the problem. Consequently the complement of this set with regard to B^n is the set of all solutions. The complement is available in XBOOLE as well (as CPL). Replacing the dashes by 0 or 1 results in three vectors $(0000), (1000), (0001)$ which are **not** a solution of the equation. The other 13 possible vectors of B^4 which are elements of the complement solve the equation.

The exact minimal covers are characterized by the smallest number of positive literals p_i in a conjunction. These exact minimal covers are selected in step 2 of Algorithm 2. Missing literals p_i in $AEMC$ allow to add unnecessary prime conjunctions to a cover. Extending all conjunctions into minterms by adding missing negative literals in step 3 prohibits all unnecessary prime conjunctions of each exact minimal cover. □

5   Improved Algorithm: DIF(S_i, NDM(P))

In a last refinement of the approach we use a partition of B^n into subsets:

$$S_i = \{\mathbf{x} = (x_1, \ldots, x_n) \mid i \text{ variables have the value } 1, i = 0, \ldots, n\}$$

with

$$B^n = S_0 \cup \ldots \cup S_n \ .$$

For a final illustration of the approach we go back to equation (1) and use again all the vectors that are **not** a solution, in the same way as before. They have been found by means of $NDM(P(\mathbf{p}))$:

(---0-00-), (---000-0), (0-00--00), (0--00-00),
(00--00--), (---00000), (0--00000), (-000--00).

The complement of $NDM(P(\mathbf{p}))$ with regard to B^n can now be replaced by a sequence of complements with regard to the sets S_i. The calculation of each difference is simpler than the calculation of the whole complement. In algorithm 3 these differences are calculated beginning with $S_i(\mathbf{p}), i = 0$. If the result of the complement is empty, then there is no cover by i prime conjunctions only. The index i is incremented by 1 after each calculation of the DIF-operation. The first $AEMC$ that is not empty includes all exact minimal covers.

Algorithm 3. Exact Minimal Coverings Defined by $P(\mathbf{p}) = 1$

Require: *Petrick function* $P(\mathbf{p}) = d_1(\mathbf{p}) \vee \ldots \vee d_k(\mathbf{p})$
Ensure: all exact minimal solutions $AEMC$ of $P(\mathbf{p}) = 1$
 1: $AEMC \leftarrow \emptyset$
 2: $i = 0$
 3: **while** $AEMC = \emptyset$ **do**
 4:    generate $S_i(\mathbf{p})$
 5:    $AEMC \leftarrow \text{DIF}(S_i(\mathbf{p}), NDM(P(\mathbf{p})))$
 6:    $i \leftarrow i + 1$
 7: **end while**

The set S_0 is not important because all variables have the value 0. Then there are n vectors with one component equal to 1, the other components are equal to 0. They cannot be orthogonal to all the vectors of the NDM vectors since in each component all of them meet at least one value $-$.

We get seven vectors with two components equal to 1 such as (10010000), (01010000) etc. They represent the combinations $(p_1 = 1, p_4 = 1)$, $(p_2 = 1, p_4 = 1)$, $(p_4 = 1, p_5 = 1)$, $(p_4 = 1, p_6 = 1)$, $(p_5 = 1, p_7 = 1)$, $(p_6 = 1, p_7 = 1)$, $(p_6 = 1, p_8 = 1)$. All of them are orthogonal to all the vectors of NDM. They are also minimal because we went from S_0 to S_1 to S_2.

6   Experimental Results

The improved classical approach in Algorithm 1 solves the simple example (1) within 6 milliseconds.

Next we tried to solve larger unate covering problems using the same algorithm. Restricted by the available memory, we could solve the benchmark of

16 p-variables and 32 clauses within 299.928 seconds using algorithm 1. The same 9 solution vectors with 3 variables were found within 3 milliseconds using Algorithm 2. This is an improvement by a factor of 99,976.

In order to exclude errors in measurement of very short time intervals we selected a much larger benchmark for the final comparison. Algorithm 2 needs 734.171 seconds to solve the benchmark of 32 p-variables and 256 clauses. The new Algorithm 3 finds the same 38 solution vectors with 5 variables within 91 milliseconds. This is an improvement of a factor of 8,068. Hence, in comparison with Algorithm 1 we reduced the runtime by a factor of more than $8 * 10^8$.

References

1. Ashenhurst, R.: The Decomposition of Switching Functions. In: International Symposium on the Theory of Switching Functions, pp. 74–116 (1959)
2. Brayton, R.K., Hachtel, G.D., McMullen, C.T., Santiovanni-Vincentelli, A.L.: Logic Minimization Algorithms for VLSI Synthesis. Kluwer Academic Publishers, Higham (1984)
3. Curtis, H.: A New Approach to the Design of Switching Circuits. Van Nostrand, Princeton (1962)
4. Galinier, P., Hertz, A.: Solution Techniques for the Large Set Covering Problem. Les Cahiers du GERAD, pp. 1–19 (2003); ISSN: 0711-2440
5. McCluskey Jr., E.J.: Minimization of Boolean Functions. Bell System Technical Journal 35(6), 1417–1444 (1956)
6. Mishchenko, A., Steinbach, B., Perkowski, M.: An Algorithm for Bi-Decomposition of Logic Functions. In: 38th Design Automation Conference 2001, Las Vegas, USA, pp. 18–22 (2001)
7. Petrick, S.K.: On the Minimization of Boolean Functions. In: Proceedings of the International Conference Information Processing, Paris, pp. 422–423 (1959)
8. Petrick, S.R.: A Direct Determination of the Irredundant Forms of a Boolean Function from the Set of Prime Implicants. Technical Report AFCRC-TR-56-110, Air Force Cambridge Research Center, Cambridge, Mass (April 1956)
9. Posthoff, C., Steinbach, B.: Logic Functions and Equations - Binary Models for Computer Science. Springer, Dordrecht (2004)
10. Povarov, G. N.: O Funkcional'noj Razdelimosti Bulevych Funkcij. DAN, tom XCIV, no 5
11. Quine, W.V.: The Problem of Simplifiying Truth Functions. The American Mathematical Monthly 59(8), 521–531 (1952)
12. Sasao, T., Matsuura, M.: A method to decompose multiple-output logic functions. In: 41st Design Automation Conference 2004, San Diego, CA, USA, pp. 428–433 (2004)
13. Steinbach, B., Posthoff, C.: An Extended Theory of Boolean Normal Forms. In: Proceedings of the 6th Annual Hawaii International Conference on Statistics, Mathematics and Related Fields, Honolulu, Hawaii, pp. 1124–1139 (2007)
14. Šeda, M.: Heuristic Set-Covering-Based Postprocessing for Improving the Quine-McCluskey Method. World Academy of Science. Engineering and Technology 29, 256–260 (2007)
15. Steinbach, B., Posthoff, C.: Logic Functions and Equations - Examples and Exercises. Springer Science + Business Media B.V. (2009)

Pattern Analysis
under Number Theoretic Transforms[*]

Claudio Moraga

European Centre for Soft Computing
33600 Mieres, Spain
Technical University of Dortmund
44221, Dortmund, Germany
mail@claudio-moraga.eu

Abstract. Number Theoretic Transforms (NTT) are integer-valued transforms that may be applied for signal processing. Particularly the Mersenne and the Fermat Transforms are interesting, since being close related to special powers of two, at the computational level, product operations needed for convolution may be efficiently reduced to shift operations. NTT exhibit, like the Fourier Transform, important properties, like the Convolution and Parseval theorems. In this paper however the focus will be on the analysis of geometric and chromatic changes on patterns using 2D-NTT.

Keywords: Number Theoretic Transforms, Pattern transformations, Pattern properties.

1 Introduction

Number Theoretic Transforms were developed in the late 60's / early 70's as an alternative to Fourier Transforms for signal processing [4], [5]. The main reason being that they operate with modular arithmetic on integers instead of complex numbers. Moreover, Fermat and Mersenne numbers –(which are most frequently used for number theoretic transforms)- are related to particular powers of two, and this may be used to reduce the complexity of computing products needed *e.g.* for convolution, to shifting operations at the bit level [1], [3], [6], [7]. It should be recalled that the IBM S/360 family of main frame computers represented the "state of the art" in those years, running from 0.034 MIPS to 0.170 MIPS with main memories in the range of 8 KB to 8 MB. It is easy to understand, that efficient bit-level arithmetic algorithms were of great importance for "computing intensive" applications, as signal processing. Even though today is easy to obtain a PC running faster than at 2 GHz with a main memory larger than 2 GB and with over 100 GB hard disk capacity, applications in the context of embedded systems have constraints in area and energy consumption. In this context, Number Theoretic Transforms may again become of interest.

---

[*] Work leading to this paper was partially supported by the Foundation for the Advance of Soft Computing, Mieres, Asturias, Spain.

R. Moreno-Díaz et al. (Eds.): EUROCAST 2011, Part II, LNCS 6928, pp. 280–287, 2012.
© Springer-Verlag Berlin Heidelberg 2012

2 Theory

Number Theoretic Transforms (NTTs) work on integer-valued discrete signals in the ring Z_M, where M is odd. This is not a severe constraint, since it is always possible to choose M to be odd and not smaller than the largest signal value. The time or space attribute of the signals is represented in the ring Z_N. M and N are related in terms of Nth primitive roots of unity modulo M.

Definition 1: α is a primitive N^{th} root of unity Modulo M, if the following conditions hold:

$$\alpha^N \equiv 1 \text{ modulo M} \tag{1}$$

$$\gcd(\alpha^k - 1, M) = 1 \quad \text{for all } k \in Z_N, \ k > 0 \tag{2}$$

E.g. if M = 5 and N = 4, then $\alpha = 2$ is a primitive 4th root of 1 modulo 5, since $2^4 \equiv 1$ mod. 5. Furthermore being 5 a prime number and being α^k-1 also a prime number for k = 1, 2 and 3, the second condition is obviously satisfied.

Definition 2: The kernel of an NTT is an N by N matrix, whose entry at the position (j,k) has the value α^{jk}, where α is a primitive N^{th} root of unity modulo M, and $j, k \in Z_N$. The notation $[\alpha^{jk}]$ will be used to denote a kernel based on α, a primitive N^{th} root of unity modulo M.

$$\left[\alpha^{jk}\right] = \begin{bmatrix} 1 & 1 & 1 & \cdots & 1 \\ 1 & \alpha & \alpha^{2\bmod N} & \cdots & \alpha^{(N-1)\bmod N} \\ 1 & \alpha^{2\bmod N} & \alpha^{4\bmod N} & \cdots & \alpha^{2(N-1)\bmod N} \\ \cdots & \cdots & \cdots & \cdots & \cdots \\ 1 & \alpha^{(N-1)\bmod N} & \alpha^{2(N-1)\bmod N} & \cdots & \alpha^{(N-1)^2\bmod N} \end{bmatrix} \tag{3}$$

Remarks

- Since α is a primitive N^{th} root of unity modulo M, all exponent calculations may be done modulo N
- It is easy to see that the kernel is symmetric: $[\alpha^{jk}] = [\alpha^{jk}]^T$
- The sub-kernel obtained by deleting the first row and the first column is also symmetric with respect of its diagonal with positive slope

Lemma 1 [8]

$$\sum_{\substack{k \in Z_N \\ j \neq 0}} \alpha^{jk} = 0 \tag{4}$$

Lemma 2

$$\left[\alpha^{jk}\right] \cdot \left[\alpha^{-jk}\right] = N \cdot \mathbf{I_N} \tag{5}$$

Proof: Let $\mathbf{I_N}$ denote the N by N identity matrix

$$[\alpha^{jk}]\cdot[\alpha^{-jk}] = [\varpi_{j,k}]$$

$$\varpi_{j,k} = \sum_{\ell\in Z_N}\alpha^{j\ell}\alpha^{-\ell k} = \sum_{\ell\in Z_N}\alpha^{(j+k)\ell \bmod N} = N \text{ if } j = -k; \text{ 0 otherwise}$$

Corollary 1.1

$$[\alpha^{jk}]^{-1} = N^{-1}[\alpha^{-jk}] \tag{6}$$

Definition 2: Let $J_K = [\varphi_{i,j}]$ be a K by K matrix such that $\varphi_{i,j} = 1$ iff $i + j = K-1$, $i, j \in Z_K$, otherwise $\varphi_{i,j} = 0$. Furthermore let $S = Diag([1], J_{N-1})$.

Notice that $J_K \cdot J_K = I_K$ and $S \cdot S = I_N$

Definition 3: Let $a = [a_{i,j}]$, $a_{i,j} \in Z_M$, $i, j \in Z_N$. Then $a^* = [a_{N-i,N-j}]$, or simply $a^* = [a_{-i,-j}]$

Lemma 2: Let $a = [a_{i,j}]$, $i, j \in Z_N$. Then $S \cdot a = [a_{N-i,\,j}]$, or simply $[a_{-i,\,j}]$

Proof: Let $S \cdot a = b = [b_{i,j}]$. From definition 2, $S = [s_{i,j}]$ where $s_{i,j} = 1$ iff $i + j \equiv 0 \bmod N$.

$$b_{i,k} = \sum_{j=0}^{N-1} s_{i,j}\cdot a_{j,k} \text{ from where } b_{i,k} = s_{i,N-i}\cdot a_{N-i,k} = a_{N-i,k}$$

Therefore $S \cdot a = S \cdot [a_{i,j}] = [a_{N-i,j}] = [a_{-i,j}]$. Similarly, $a \cdot S = [a_{i,j}]\cdot S = [a_{i,N-j}] = [a_{i,-j}]$

Corollary 2.1: $a^* = S \cdot a \cdot S$; $S \cdot [\alpha^{ij}] = [\alpha^{-ij}] = [\alpha^{ij}]\cdot S$; $[\alpha^{ij}]^* = [\alpha^{ij}]$

Definition 4 [2]: The two-sided Number Theoretic Transform of a square N by N matrix a is given by

$$T(a) = A = [\alpha^{ij}]\cdot a \cdot[\alpha^{ij}] \bmod M \tag{7}$$

Lemma 3: The inverse transform follows from Corollary 1.1 and is given by

$$T^{-1}(A) = a = N^{-2}[\alpha^{-ij}]\cdot A \cdot[\alpha^{-ij}] \bmod M \tag{8}$$

Lemma 4: Let a and b be N by N matrices with entries in Z_M. Moreover let $c \in Z_M$.

$$T(a + b \bmod M) = T(a) + T(b) \bmod M \tag{9}$$

$$T(ca) = cT(a) \bmod M \tag{10}$$

$$T(a \cdot b \bmod M) = N^{-1}T(a)\cdot S \cdot T(b) \bmod M \tag{11}$$

$$T(a^T) = (T(a))^T \,;\, T(a^*) = (T(a))^* \tag{12}$$

Proof (of (11))

$$T(a \cdot b) = [\alpha^{ij}]\cdot a \cdot b \cdot[\alpha^{ij}] = [\alpha^{ij}]\cdot a \cdot I_N \cdot b \cdot[\alpha^{ij}] = [\alpha^{ij}]\cdot a \cdot[\alpha^{ij}]\cdot N^{-1}[\alpha^{-ij}]\cdot b \cdot[\alpha^{ij}] =$$

$$= N^{-1}[\alpha^{ij}]\cdot a \cdot[\alpha^{ij}]\cdot S \cdot[\alpha^{ij}]\cdot b \cdot[\alpha^{ij}] = N^{-1}T(a)\cdot S \cdot T(b) \bmod M$$

Lemma 5: $T(S) = N \cdot I_N$; $T(J_N) = N \cdot Diag(\alpha^0, \alpha^{N-1}, \alpha^{N-2}, ..., \alpha^2, \alpha^1)$ $\tag{13}$

Proof: $T(S) = [\alpha^{ij}] \cdot S \cdot [\alpha^{ij}] = [\alpha^{ij}] \cdot [\alpha^{-ij}] = N \cdot I_N$

$$T(J_N) = [\alpha^{ij}] \cdot J_N \cdot [\alpha^{ij}] = [\alpha^{ij}] \cdot [\alpha^{(N-1-i)j}] = [\alpha^{ij}] \cdot [\alpha^{-(1+i)j}] = [\omega_{i,j}]$$

$$\omega_{k,\ell} = \sum_{u=0}^{N-1} \alpha^{ku} \cdot \alpha^{-(1+u)\ell} = \alpha^{-\ell} \sum_{u=0}^{N-1} \alpha^{(k-\ell)u} = N\alpha^{-\ell} \text{ if } k = \ell \text{ else } 0$$

$$T(J_N) = N \cdot Diag(\alpha^0, \alpha^{N-1}, \alpha^{N-2}, ..., \alpha^2, \alpha^1)$$

Note: in what follows, unless otherwise specified all operations on subindices and on superindices are done mod N and all operations on entries of matrices are done mod M.

Table 1. Basic Fermat and Mersenne NTT with $\alpha = 2$

Fermat		Mersenne	
N	M	N	M
2^{d+1} (d ≥ 1)	$F_d = 2^{2^d} + 1$	p (prime)	$\mathfrak{M}_p = 2^p - 1$
4	$F_1 = 5$	3	$\mathfrak{M}_3 = 7$
8	$F_2 = 17$	5	$\mathfrak{M}_5 = 31$
16	$F_3 = 257$	7	$\mathfrak{M}_7 = 127$

3 On Properties of Patterns and NTTs

Let patterns be square arrays of coloured pixels (or blocks of pixels). Let the cardinality of the set of colours be M, and consider a bijection between the set of colours and Z_M. Operations on patterns will be done through operations upon the corresponding numerical matrices.

Lemma 6: If a pattern is vertically symmetric then the $(N/2)^{th}$ column of its Fermat NTT is a 0-column. (Similarly a 0-row, if the pattern is horizontally symmetric.)

Proof: Let a be an N by N vertically symmetric pattern. Therefore $a = a \cdot J_N$.

$T(a \cdot J_N) = N^{-1} \cdot T(a) \cdot S \cdot T(J_N)$ (from Lemma 4)

$\qquad = N^{-1} \cdot T(a) \cdot S \cdot N \cdot Diag(\alpha^0, \alpha^{N-1}, \alpha^{N-2}, ..., \alpha^2, \alpha^1)$ (from Lemma 5)

$\qquad\qquad = T(a) \cdot S \cdot Diag(\alpha^0, \alpha^{N-1}, \alpha^{N-2}, ..., \alpha^2, \alpha^1)$ (14)

Let $T(a)_k$ denote the kth column of $T(a)$, $k \in Z_N$. Similarly for $T(a \cdot J_N)$. Then,

$T(a)\quad =\quad [T(a)_0 \quad T(a)_1 \quad ... \quad T(a)_j \quad ... \quad T(a)_{N-1}\ ]$

$T(a) \cdot S\ =\ [T(a)_0 \quad T(a)_{N-1} \quad ... \quad T(a)_{N-j} \quad ... \quad T(a)_1\ ]$

$T(a \cdot J_N) = [T(a)_0 \quad T(a)_{N-1}\alpha^{N-1} \quad ... \ T(a)_{N-j}\,\alpha^{N-j} \ ... \ T(a)_1\alpha\ ]$ (from (14))

Since $a = a \cdot J_N$, then $T(a) = T(a \cdot J_N)$. Therefore $\forall\ k \in Z_N$ holds $T(a)_k = T(a)_{N-k}\ \alpha^{N-k}$. Moreover, since in a Fermat NTT, N is even, $(N/2) \in Z_N$ and $N - (N/2) = N/2$. Hence

$$T(a)_{N/2} = T(a)_{N-(N/2)}\ \alpha^{N-(N/2)} = T(a)_{N/2}\ \alpha^{N/2} \tag{15}$$

$$0 = T(a)_{N/2}\ (\alpha^{N/2} - 1) \tag{16}$$

Since $\alpha^{N/2} \neq 1 \bmod M$, Eq. (16) can only be satisfied if $T(a)_{N/2} = [0\ 0\ \dots\ 0]^T$.

Figure 1 shows an example where M = 17, N = 8, α = 2. It is easy to see that the column with index 4 is a column of 0s. Furthermore it may be checked, that if the column with index 1 is multiplied mod 17 by α = 2, the column with index 7 is obtained. Similarly, if the column with index 2 is multiplied mod 17 by α^2 = 4, the column with index 6 is obtained. Finally, multiplying mod 17 the column with index 3 by α^3 = 8, the column with index 5 is obtained.

Should the pattern be contaminated by just one pixel of noise, the symmetry condition $a = a \cdot J_N$ will no longer hold, which is necessary for the generation of the column of 0s. (A different, but equally strong argument will be discussed after Lemma 7.)

Corollary 6.1: If a vertically symmetric pattern a is trigonometrically positive rotated by 90°, the transform of the rotated pattern equals the transposed of the transform of the original pattern.

Proof: $a = a \cdot J_N$. $Rot\ (a) = (a \cdot J_N)^T$. $T((a \cdot J_N)^T) = (T(a \cdot J_N))^T = (T(a))^T$

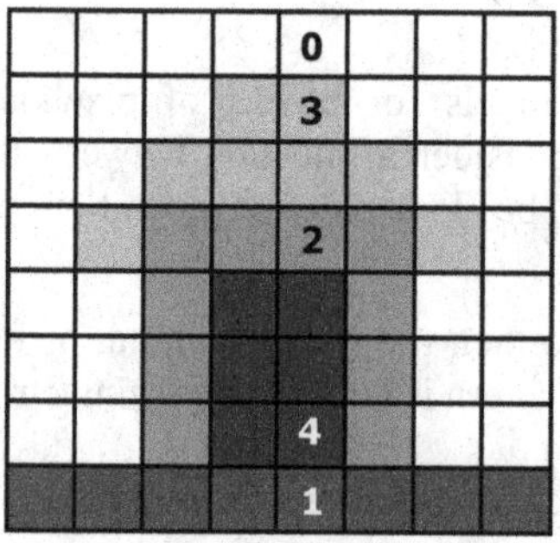

				0			
				3			
				6			
				2			
				4			
				1			

$a = a \cdot J_8$

8	3	16	9	0	4	13	6
7	5	11	7	0	5	10	10
6	1	6	11	0	3	7	2
3	9	10	12	0	11	6	1
13	9	11	15	0	1	10	1
3	10	15	14	0	10	9	3
4	13	11	4	0	15	10	9
7	1	5	13	0	2	3	2

T(a)

Fig. 1. A symmetric pattern and its transform with M = 17

Corollary 6.2 : The transform of a symmetric pattern is not affected by a rotation of 180°.

Lemma 7: Let $e_{(k,q)}$ be an N by N pattern such that the entry $e_{k,q} = 1$ and all others are 0. $T(e_{(k,q)})$ has no entry equal to 0.

Proof: i) Consider the case of $e_{(0,0)}$. $T(e_{(0,0)}) = [\alpha^{ij}] \cdot e_{(0,0)} \cdot [\alpha^{ij}] = [\omega_{i,j}]$. For all $k, q, u, v \in$ Z_N holds: $\omega_{k,q} = \sum\limits_{u=0}^{N-1}\sum\limits_{v=0}^{N-1} \alpha^{ku} e_{u,v} \alpha^{vq} = 1$, *i.e.* $T(e_{(0,0)})$ is an N by N matrix of 1s.

ii) Let a be an N by N matrix and let $P_{(k)}$ be an N by N permutation matrix such that $P_{(k)} \cdot a = [a_{(i+k),j}]$. $T(P_{(k)}) = [\alpha^{ij}] \cdot P_{(k)} \cdot [\alpha^{ij}] = [\alpha^{ij}] \cdot [\alpha^{(i+k)j}] = [\omega_{i,j}]$. For all $k, q, u, v \in Z_N$ holds:

$$\omega_{q,u} = \sum_{v=0}^{N-1} \alpha^{qv} \alpha^{(v+k)u} = \alpha^{ku} \sum_{v=0}^{N-1} \alpha^{v(q+k)} = N\alpha^{ku} \text{ if } q+k \equiv 0 \bmod N, \text{ else } 0.$$

It follows that $T(P_{(k)})$ is a generalized permutation matrix having powers of α (scaled by N) as non-zero entries.

iii) The matrix $P_{(r)} e_{(0,0)} P_{(k)}$ generates $e_{(r,k)}$, with $e_{r,k} = 1$ and all other entries equal to 0. By using twice Eq. (11), it may be obtained that $T(P_{(r)} e_{(0,0)} P_{(k)}) = N^{-2} T(P_{(r)}) \cdot S \cdot T(e_{(0,0)}) \cdot S \cdot T(P_{(k)})$. It is simple to see that $N^{-1} T(P_{(r)}) \cdot S$ is another generalized permutation matrix having powers of α as non-zero entries. Similarly for $N^{-1} S \cdot T(P_{(k)})$. Therefore since $T(e_{(0,0)}) = \mathbf{1}$, $T(e_{(r,k)}) = T(P_{(r)} e_{(0,0)} P_{(k)})$ represents a matrix all whose entries are powers of α.

Now it is possible to return to the analysis of the symmetric pattern $a = a \cdot J_8$, where $T(a)_4 = [0\ 0\ ...\ 0]^T$. Let $e_{(r,k)}$ represent one random pixel of noise. Then, from (9)

$$T(a + e_{(r,k)} \bmod M) = T(a) + T(e_{(r,k)}) \bmod M \tag{17}$$

Since all entries of $T(e_{(r,k)})$ are powers of α, the column of 0s of $T(a)$ will be completely covered by non-zero entries. Minor deviations from symmetry will immediately be detected.

Lemma 8: Let a be an N by N pattern. If all numerical values corresponding to colors are shifted by $c \bmod M$ (where $c \in Z_M$) producing the pattern a^+, then $T(a^+)$ equals $T(a)$ all over, except at the upper left corner, where it is increased by $cN^2 \bmod M$.

Proof: Let $\mathbf{1}$ denote an N by N matrix of 1s. $T(\mathbf{1}) = [\alpha^{ij}] \cdot \mathbf{1} \cdot [\alpha^{ij}] = [\omega_{i,j}]$

$$\omega_{u,v} = \sum_{q=0}^{N-1}\sum_{r=0}^{N-1} \alpha^{uq} 1_{q,r} \alpha^{rv} = \sum_{q=0}^{N-1} \alpha^{uq} \sum_{r=0}^{N-1} \alpha^{rv} = N^2 \text{ iff } u = v = 0 \tag{18}$$

$$T(a^+) = T(a + c\mathbf{1} \bmod M) = T(a) + T(c\mathbf{1}) \bmod M = T(a) + cT(\mathbf{1}) \bmod M.$$

Let $[A_{i,j}] = T(a)$ and $[A^+_{i,j}] = T(a^+)$; then $A^+_{0,0} = A_{0,0} + c \bmod M$ and for all $i, j > 0$, $A^+_{i,j} = A_{i,j}$.

Lemma 9: Let p be a 2^n by 2^n pattern and $n = q + r$. Furthermore let p consist of 2^{2r} blocks of size 2^q by 2^q. Finally assume that all blocks are identical. Then the Fermat transform $T(p)$ consists of 2^{2q} blocks of size 2^r by 2^r, where the only non-(necessarily)-zero entry of every block is the upper left one and all others are 0-entries.

Due to space limitations, the proof will be constrained to the special case $n = 2$, $q = r = 1$, and the Fermat transform with $N = 4$, $M = 5$, and $\alpha = 2$.

Proof: Let $p = [\Pi\ \Pi\ ;\ \Pi\ \Pi]$, where Π is a 2 by 2 block $[\pi_{11}\ \pi_{12}\ ;\ \pi_{21}\ \pi_{22}]$ with entries in Z_M, and let $[\alpha^{ij}]$ be partitioned into 4 square blocks $[A_1\ A_2\ ;\ A_3\ A_4]$.

$$T(p) = \begin{bmatrix} A_1 & A_2 \\ A_3 & A_4 \end{bmatrix} \cdot \begin{bmatrix} \Pi & \Pi \\ \Pi & \Pi \end{bmatrix} \cdot \begin{bmatrix} A_1 & A_2 \\ A_3 & A_4 \end{bmatrix}$$

$$= \begin{bmatrix} A_1 + A_2 & 0 \\ 0 & A_3 + A_4 \end{bmatrix} \cdot \begin{bmatrix} \Pi & \Pi \\ \Pi & \Pi \end{bmatrix} \begin{bmatrix} A_1 + A_3 & 0 \\ 0 & A_2 + A_4 \end{bmatrix}$$

$$A_1 + A_2 = \begin{bmatrix} 1 & 1 \\ 1 & 2 \end{bmatrix} + \begin{bmatrix} 1 & 1 \\ 4 & 3 \end{bmatrix} \equiv \begin{bmatrix} 2 & 2 \\ 0 & 0 \end{bmatrix} \bmod 5 \quad A_3 + A_4 = \begin{bmatrix} 1 & 4 \\ 1 & 3 \end{bmatrix} + \begin{bmatrix} 1 & 4 \\ 4 & 2 \end{bmatrix} \equiv \begin{bmatrix} 2 & -2 \\ 0 & 0 \end{bmatrix} \bmod 5$$

$$A_1 + A_3 = \begin{bmatrix} 1 & 1 \\ 1 & 2 \end{bmatrix} + \begin{bmatrix} 1 & 4 \\ 1 & 3 \end{bmatrix} \equiv \begin{bmatrix} 2 & 0 \\ 2 & 0 \end{bmatrix} \bmod 5 \quad A_2 + A_4 = \begin{bmatrix} 1 & 1 \\ 4 & 3 \end{bmatrix} + \begin{bmatrix} 1 & 4 \\ 4 & 2 \end{bmatrix} \equiv \begin{bmatrix} 2 & 0 \\ -2 & 0 \end{bmatrix} \bmod 5$$

From where $T(p) =$

$$= 4 \cdot \begin{bmatrix} 1 & 1 & 0 & 0 \\ 0 & 0 & 0 & 0 \\ 0 & 0 & 1 & -1 \\ 0 & 0 & 0 & 0 \end{bmatrix} \cdot \begin{bmatrix} \pi_{11} & \pi_{12} & \pi_{11} & \pi_{12} \\ \pi_{21} & \pi_{22} & \pi_{21} & \pi_{22} \\ \pi_{11} & \pi_{12} & \pi_{11} & \pi_{12} \\ \pi_{21} & \pi_{22} & \pi_{21} & \pi_{22} \end{bmatrix} \begin{bmatrix} 1 & 0 & 0 & 0 \\ 1 & 0 & 0 & 0 \\ 0 & 0 & 1 & 0 \\ 0 & 0 & -1 & 0 \end{bmatrix} = 4 \cdot \begin{bmatrix} \tau_{11} & 0 & \tau_{13} & 0 \\ 0 & 0 & 0 & 0 \\ \tau_{31} & 0 & \tau_{33} & 0 \\ 0 & 0 & 0 & 0 \end{bmatrix}$$

with $\quad \tau_{11} = \pi_{11} + \pi_{12} + \pi_{21} + \pi_{22} \qquad \tau_{13} = \pi_{11} - \pi_{12} + \pi_{21} - \pi_{22}$

$\qquad \tau_{31} = \pi_{11} + \pi_{12} - \pi_{21} - \pi_{22} \qquad \tau_{31} = \pi_{11} - \pi_{12} - \pi_{21} + \pi_{22}$

It is easy to see that $T(p)$ is structured in 4 blocks and only the left upper entry of each block is non-zero.

Notice that *in this case* $[\tau_{11} \ \tau_{13} \ \tau_{31} \ \tau_{33}]^T = \mathbf{W}_2 \cdot [\pi_{11} \ \pi_{12} \ \pi_{21} \ \pi_{22}]^T$ where $\mathbf{W}_2$ denotes the discrete Walsh transform [9] of dimension 2^2.

Let $e_{(r,k)}$ represent one random pixel of noise. Then, from (9)

$$T(p + e_{(r,k)} \bmod M) = T(p) + T(e_{(r,k)}) \bmod M \tag{19}$$

Since all entries of $T(e_{(r,k)})$ are powers of α, the columns and rows of 0s of $T(p)$ will be completely covered by non-zero entries. Minor deviations from modular periodicity will immediately be detected.

Figure 2 shows an example with $N = 8$, $M = 17$ and 2 by 2 blocks in the pattern:

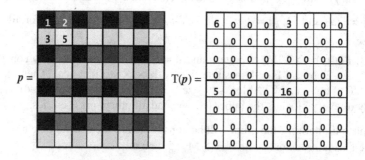

Fig. 2. Modular periodic pattern with 2 by 2 blocks

4   Conclusions

Two-sided number theoretic transforms may be applied to characterize "in the spectral domain", particular properties of patterns, like exemplarily, the symmetry or the modular regularity of a pattern. Number theoretic transforms are very sensitive to noise and may be used to detect the presence of noise pixels, for instance, in symmetric or modular regular patterns. On the other hand, this sensitivity may be used to process chromatic shifts.

References

1. Agarwal, R.C., Burrus, C.S.: Fast convolution using Fermat number transforms with applications to digital filtering. IEEE Trans. Acoust. Speech Signal Processing 22, 87–97 (1974)
2. Barthel, A.: Betrachtung von zahlentheoretischen Transformationen auf Mustern, Diplomarbeit, Fakultät Informatik, Universität Dortmund (1992)
3. Leibowitz, L.M.: Exact Fermat number transform convolution with comparison to fast Fourier transform techniques. Dissertation, The George Washington University, Dept. Computer Science (1978)
4. Nicholson, P.J.: Algebraic theory of finite Fourier Transforms. Jr. Comput. Systems Sci. 5, 524–547 (1971)
5. Pollard, J.M.: The fast Fourier Transform in a Finite Field. Math. Comput. 25, 365–374 (1971)
6. Rader, C.M.: Discrete convolutions via Mersenne transforms. IEEE Trans. Computers 21, 1269–1273 (1972)
7. Schönhage, A., Strassen, V.: Schnelle Multiplikation großer Zahlen. Computing 7, 281–292 (1971)
8. Wikipedia, http://en.wikipedia.org/wiki/Number-theoretic_transform
9. Walsh, J.L.: A closed set of orthogonal functions. Am. Jr. Math. 45, 2–5 (1923)

Remarks on Efficient Computation of the Inverse Fourier Transforms on Finite Non-Abelian Groups

Radomir S. Stanković[1], Jaakko T. Astola[2], Claudio Moraga[3],
and Stanislav Stanković[2]

[1] Dept. of Computer Science, Faculty of Electronics, Niš, Serbia
[2] Dept. of Signal Processing, Tampere University of Technology, Tampere, Finland
[3] European Center for Soft Computing, 33600 Mieres, Spain &
Technical University of Dortmund, 44221 Dortmund, Germany

Abstract. The Fourier transform is a classical method in mathematical modeling of systems. Assuming finite non-Abelian groups as the underlying mathematical structure might bring advantages in modeling certain systems often met in computer science and information technologies. Frequent computing of the inverse Fourier transform is usually required in dealing with such systems. These computations require for each function value to compute many times traces of certain matrices. These matrices are products of matrix-valued entries of unitary irreducible representations and matrix-valued Fourier coefficients. In the case of large non-Abelian groups the complexity of these computations can be a limiting factor in applications. In this paper, we present a method for speeding-up computing the traces by using decision diagrams to operate on matrix-valued group representations and related Fourier coefficients.

Keywords: Systems on groups, Fourier transform, non-Abelian groups, decision diagrams.

1 Introduction

When discussing mathematical models of systems, we do not necessarily ask for the most accurate models. Instead, we ask for a model that is most appropriate for the targeted applications. Sometimes, simpler and less accurate models serve better due to simplicity and consequently smaller computational demands, than very accurate, but complex models. Speeding up the implementation of operations involved in the model is sometimes of a crucial importance for the applicability of the model in practice.

A mathematical model is good if it captures essential features of the system and reflects its structure. In this setting, there are discrete and digital systems that are naturally modeled on finite non-Abelian groups.

An example often met in practice are various reconfigurable computing devices and related architectures. Their importance would increase in future, due to the inherent flexibility in arranging the computational process which results in

R. Moreno-Díaz et al. (Eds.): EUROCAST 2011, Part II, LNCS 6928, pp. 288–295, 2012.

computation speed-up, sometimes considerably up to an order of magnitude. See for instance a recent discussion of the subject in [3].

The input and output signals of such systems are modeled by functions f : $G \to P$, where G is a finite not necessarily Abelian group, and P is a field that can be the complex field C or a finite (Galois) field $GF(p)$ in the case of digital systems. The systems itself can be modeled by operators in function spaces $P(G)$ of such functions equipped with necessary operations.

When the Fourier analysis is used in modeling and analyzing digital systems, a frequent computation of the inverse Fourier transform for different input signals is often required. In the case of non-Abelian groups, such computation includes computing the trace of matrices, and matrices can be large, depending on the domain group selected for the system to be modeled.

In such cases, frequent computing of the inverse Fourier transform for different inputs, and in particular computing the trace of the related matrices, can be a critical factor. A considerable computation speed-up can be achieved if decision diagrams are used as the data structure to represent matrices involved and perform the required calculations.

In this paper, we propose a method to compute traces of matrices over decision diagrams, as a part of the procedure performing the inverse Fourier transforms on finite non-Abelian groups.

2   Fourier Transform on Finite Non-Abelian Groups

We assume that the group G of order $|G| = g$ is decomposable into a direct product of n constituent groups G_i of orders $|G_i| = g_i$, thus,

$$G = \times_{i=1}^{n} G_i, \quad g = \prod_{i=1}^{n} g_i, \quad g_1 \leq g_2 \leq \cdots \leq g_n.$$

The group elements $x \in G$ are expressed in terms of group elements $x_i \in G_i$ as $x = \sum_{i=1}^{n} a_i x_i, \, x \in G, \, x_i \in G_i$, and

$$a_i = \begin{cases} \prod_{j=i+1}^{n} g_j, & i = 1, \ldots, n-1 \\ 1, & i = n. \end{cases}$$

The group operation $\circ$ of G can be expressed in terms of group operations $\overset{\circ}{i}$ of the constituent groups G_i as

$$x \circ y = (x_1 \overset{\circ}{1} y_1, x_2 \overset{\circ}{2} y_2, \cdots, x_n \overset{\circ}{n} y_n), \quad x, y \in G, \quad x_i, y_i \in G_i.$$

In some applications the domain group G can be assumed as the product of constituent groups G_i where two or more of them are non-Abelian groups. In this case we speak about the generalized Fourier transforms, to keep the notation already established in the literature, see for instance [6].

The Fourier transform on finite groups is defined in terms of unitary irreducible representations as specified by the Peter-Weyl theorem [9]

Definition 1. *For a function* $f \in P(G)$, *the direct and the inverse Fourier transforms of a function* $f \in P(G)$ *are defined, respectively, by*

$$\mathbf{S}_f(w) = r_w g^{-1} \sum_{u=0}^{g-1} f(u) \mathbf{R}_w(u^{-1}), \quad f(x) = \sum_{w=0}^{K-1} Tr(\mathbf{S}_f(w) \mathbf{R}_w(x)), \quad (1)$$

where $R_w(x)$ *are group representations of* G *and* $Tr(\mathbf{A})$ *denotes the trace of the matrix* $\mathbf{A}$.

The necessity of computing the traces in the inverse Fourier transforms is obvious from (1), and the complexity of this task is illustrated by the following example.

Example 1. *Let* $S_3 = (0, (132), (123), (12), (13), (23), \circ)$ *be the symmetric group of permutations of order 3. The unitary irreducible representations of* S_3 *over the Galois field* $GF(11)$ *are shown in Table 1, where* $\mathbf{I} = \begin{bmatrix} 1 & 0 \\ 0 & 1 \end{bmatrix}$, $\mathbf{A} = \begin{bmatrix} 5 & 8 \\ 3 & 5 \end{bmatrix}$, $\mathbf{B} = \begin{bmatrix} 5 & 3 \\ 8 & 5 \end{bmatrix}$, $\mathbf{C} = \begin{bmatrix} 1 & 0 \\ 0 & 10 \end{bmatrix}$, $\mathbf{D} = \begin{bmatrix} 5 & 8 \\ 8 & 6 \end{bmatrix}$, $\mathbf{E} = \begin{bmatrix} 5 & 3 \\ 3 & 6 \end{bmatrix}$. *The Fourier transform matrix on* S_3 *is given by*

$$[\mathbf{S}_3]^{-1} = 2 \begin{bmatrix} 1 & 1 & 1 & 1 & 1 & 1 \\ 1 & 1 & 1 & 10 & 10 & 10 \\ 2\mathbf{I} & 2\mathbf{B} & 2\mathbf{A} & 2\mathbf{C} & 2\mathbf{D} & 2\mathbf{E} \end{bmatrix}.$$

Notice that $\mathbf{A} = \mathbf{B}^T$, *where* T *denotes the transposition of a matrix,* $\mathbf{C}$, $\mathbf{D}$, $\mathbf{E}$ *are symmetric matrices, and* $\mathbf{C} + \mathbf{D} + \mathbf{E} \equiv \mathbf{0} \bmod 11$.

In matrix notation, for a function $f(x)$ *defined on* S_3 *and specified by the function vector* $\mathbf{f} = [f(0), f(1), f(2), f(3), f(4), f(5)]^T$, *the Fourier spectrum is computed as*

$$[\mathbf{S}_f] = [\mathbf{S}_3]^{-1} \odot \mathbf{f}. \quad (2)$$

The inverse Fourier transform is computed as

$$\mathbf{f} = [\mathbf{S}_3] \circ [\mathbf{S}_f], \quad (3)$$

where $[\mathbf{S}_3]$ *is the* (6×3) *matrix whose columns are the group representations* $\mathbf{R}_0$, $\mathbf{R}_1$, *and* $\mathbf{R}_2$ *defined in Table 1. In (2) and (3), the symbols* $\odot$ *and* $\circ$ *denote the generalized matrix multiplications allowing to compute with vectors and matrices whose entries can be either numbers or matrices [9].*

In this example, the trace has to be computed when each function value is computed for the Fourier coefficients. In the case of the generalized Fourier transforms on finite non-Abelian groups, the unitary irreducible representations of a group G *are the Kronecker product of representations of constituent groups* G_i *and there can be many matrix-valued representations and, therefore, many matrix-valued coefficients. For each of them, the trace of the product of the value of the representation and the coefficient has to be computed for each function value.*

For example, a group $G = S_3 \times S_3$ has 9 representations. Three of them ($\mathbf{R}_2$, $\mathbf{R}_5$, $\mathbf{R}_6$, $\mathbf{R}_7$) are (2×2) matrices and $\mathbf{R}_8$ is a (4×4) matrix. Thus, for each function value, computing the trace five times is required. For larger groups that are products of some smaller non-Abelian groups, values of unary irreducible representations can be large matrices. Thus, efficient computing of traces is important for such applications.

Table 1. Unitary irreducible representations of S_3 over $GF(11)$ and computing the trace when calculating the inverse Fourier transform

x	$\mathbf{R}_0$	$\mathbf{R}_1$	$\mathbf{R}_2$
0	1	1	$\mathbf{I}$
1	1	1	$\mathbf{A}$
2	1	1	$\mathbf{B}$
3	1	10	$\mathbf{C}$
4	1	10	$\mathbf{D}$
5	1	10	$\mathbf{E}$

$$f(0) - \begin{bmatrix} 1 & 1 & \mathbf{I} \\ 1 & 1 & \mathbf{A} \\ 1 & 1 & \mathbf{B} \\ 1 & 10 & \mathbf{C} \\ 1 & 10 & \mathbf{D} \\ 1 & 10 & \mathbf{E} \end{bmatrix} \begin{bmatrix} S_f(0) \\ S_f(1) \\ S_f(2) \end{bmatrix}$$

$f(0)$ — $Tr(\mathbf{I}\, \mathbf{S}_f(2))$
$f(1)$ — $Tr(\mathbf{A}\, \mathbf{S}_f(2))$
$f(2)$ — $Tr(\mathbf{B}\, \mathbf{S}_f(2))$
$f(3)$ — $Tr(\mathbf{C}\, \mathbf{S}_f(2))$
$f(4)$ — $Tr(\mathbf{D}\, \mathbf{S}_f(2))$
$f(5)$ — $Tr(\mathbf{E}\, \mathbf{S}_f(2))$

3   Computation of Traces

For the computation of traces of a matrix that is the products of two matrices $\mathbf{A}$ and $\mathbf{C}$ over decision diagrams, we will use the equality

$$Tr(\mathbf{A} \cdot \mathbf{C}) = (vec(\mathbf{A}^T))^T (vec(\mathbf{C})), \tag{4}$$

where T denotes the transposition of a matrix, and $vec(\mathbf{X})$ is a vector obtained by concatenating the rows of $\mathbf{X}$.

In the case considered in this paper, the matrix $\mathbf{A}$ is the value of the representation $\mathbf{R}_w(x)$, $x = 0, \ldots, n$, and the matrix $\mathbf{C}$ is the value of Fourier coefficient $\mathbf{S}_f(w)$, $w = 1, \ldots, K - 1$.

In the case of large non-Abelian groups, these matrices can be large and for efficient computation with them it might be suitable to represent them by decision diagrams [7].

3.1   Representation of Matrices by Decision Diagrams

Matrices can be represented by decision diagrams such as Binary decision diagrams (BDDs) or Multi-terminal binary decision diagrams (MTBDDs), that are typically used for the representation of discrete functions, after converting matrices into vectors by concatenating either their rows or columns [7]. This way of representing matrices by decision diagrams is suitable when relationships among matrix entries result in some regularities in the produced vectors, where regularities are viewed as the appearance of identical or constant subvectors.

Quantum multiple-valued decision diagrams (QMDDs) [5], and their generalization Hybrid decision diagrams (HDDs) [4], [10], can compactly represent matrices expressing a block structure. This method of matrix representations has an advantage if a matrix consists of a large number of identical sub-matrices. We select QMDDs for applications in this paper, since QMDDs are intended to represent square matrices which is the case that we have to handle. To be represented by QMDDs, $(p^n \times p^n)$ matrices are naturally partitioned into $(p \times p)$ blocks. In a QMDD, each non-terminal node has at most p outgoing edges. For the applications considered in this paper, with each edge in a QMDT we associate the ordered pair (i_k, j_k), $i_k, j_k = 0, 1, \ldots, p - 1$, pointing to the corresponding sub-matrices at the level k.

When a group G is the direct product of smaller groups G_i, then the matrix entries of the group representations of G are the Kronecker product of the group representations of G_i, resulting in matrices which contain repeated identical blocks. In representations by QMDDs, it will be $p = r_{w_i}$, where r_{w_i} is the size of the largest unitary irreducible representations of the constituent groups G_i, $i = 1, \ldots, n$. Further, both QMDDs and HDDs are zero-suppressed type of decision diagrams [1], which makes them suitable in the application considered in this paper, due to the relatively large number of zero entries in group representations of many groups.

For more information about representation of matrices by decision diagrams, we refer to [4], [5], [10]. In this paper, the method will be illustrated by the Example 2. For clarity and generality of the presentation, this and other examples in the paper, are given on decision trees. The same, however, holds for the decision diagrams since they are derived by the reduction of the decision trees. The reduction is possible due to regularities the matrices to be represented might possess. This is certainly the case for matrices obtained as the Kronecker product of smaller matrices, which is the case considered in this paper.

In the theory of decision diagrams, the reduction rules are defined in a consistent manner, such that the entire information encoded in a decision tree is preserved in the corresponding decision diagram, and all manipulations and computations that are possible over decision trees are equally possible over the corresponding decision diagrams, see for instance [1], [2], [7].

Example 2. *Consider the representation by QMDT of a* (4×4) *matrix* $\mathbf{A}$, *and its transpose* $\mathbf{A}^T$. *The matrix* $\mathbf{A}$ *can be decomposed into* (2×2) *submatrices as:*

$$\mathbf{A} = \begin{bmatrix} a_1 & a_5 & a_9 & a_{13} \\ a_2 & a_6 & a_{10} & a_{14} \\ a_3 & a_7 & a_{11} & a_{15} \\ a_4 & a_8 & a_{12} & a_{16} \end{bmatrix} = \begin{bmatrix} \mathbf{A}_{00} & \mathbf{A}_{01} \\ \mathbf{A}_{10} & \mathbf{A}_{11} \end{bmatrix}, \tag{5}$$

where $\mathbf{A}_{00} = \begin{bmatrix} a_1 & a_5 \\ a_2 & a_6 \end{bmatrix}$, $\mathbf{A}_{01} = \begin{bmatrix} a_9 & a_{13} \\ a_{10} & a_{14} \end{bmatrix}$, $\mathbf{A}_{10} = \begin{bmatrix} a_3 & a_7 \\ a_4 & a_8 \end{bmatrix}$, *and* $\mathbf{A}_{11} = \begin{bmatrix} a_{11} & a_{15} \\ a_{12} & a_{16} \end{bmatrix}$.
This partition leads to the Quantum multiple-valued decision tree (QMDT) for $\mathbf{A}$ *as shown in Fig. 1. In the same way,*

$$\mathbf{A}^T = \begin{bmatrix} a_1 & a_2 & a_3 & a_4 \\ a_5 & a_6 & a_7 & a_8 \\ a_9 & a_{10} & a_{11} & a_{12} \\ a_{13} & a_{14} & a_{15} & a_{16} \end{bmatrix} = \begin{bmatrix} \mathbf{Q}_{00} & \mathbf{Q}_{01} \\ \mathbf{Q}_{10} & \mathbf{Q}_{11} \end{bmatrix}, \tag{6}$$

where $\mathbf{Q}_{00} = \begin{bmatrix} a_1 & a_2 \\ a_5 & a_6 \end{bmatrix}$, $\mathbf{Q}_{01} = \begin{bmatrix} a_3 & a_4 \\ a_7 & a_8 \end{bmatrix}$, $\mathbf{Q}_{10} = \begin{bmatrix} a_9 & a_{10} \\ a_{13} & a_{14} \end{bmatrix}$, *and* $\mathbf{Q}_{11} = \begin{bmatrix} a_{11} & a_{12} \\ a_{15} & a_{16} \end{bmatrix}$.

From (5) and (6) it is evident that at each level k, $\mathbf{Q}_{00}^T = \mathbf{A}_{00}$, $\mathbf{Q}_{01}^T = \mathbf{A}_{10}$, $\mathbf{Q}_{10}^T = \mathbf{A}_{01}$ and $\mathbf{Q}_{11}^T = \mathbf{A}_{11}$. This follows from the property that if $\mathbf{A} = [a_{i,j}]$, then $\mathbf{A}^T = [a_{j,i}]$. Therefore, matrices $\mathbf{A}$ and $\mathbf{A}^T$ can be represented with QMDTs identical up to the permutation of labels of edges and the same is true for the decision diagrams due to the consistency of reduction rules. Thus, Fig. 1 at the same time shows $\mathbf{A}^T$ if we refer to the labels of nodes and edges that are written in brackets. For instance, by using the pairs of labels at the edges per levels, the 0110 entry of $\mathbf{A}^T$ is a_7. It is shown in the constant nodes along the path (01)(10) in the QMDD for $\mathbf{A}$.

To perform the transposition of a matrix $\mathbf{A}$, we need to make the reordering $i_k \leftrightarrow j_k$ in edge labels at all edges at each level in the QMDD for this matrix. In a practical implementation this is equivalent to a different order of traversal of the QMDD.

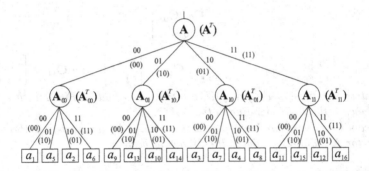

Fig. 1. Decision tree for the matrices $\mathbf{A}$ and $\mathbf{A}^T$ in Example 2.

3.2 Computation Procedure for Traces of Products of Matrices

To compute the inverse Fourier transform on finite non-Abelian groups by using the equation (4), we need a procedure for computing the trace of a matrix that is the product of two matrices $\mathbf{A}$ and $\mathbf{C}$. This procedure consists of the following steps

1. Construct the decision diagram $D_r(\mathbf{A}^T)$ for the matrix $\mathbf{A}^T$.
2. Construct the decision diagram $D_s(\mathbf{C})$ for the matrix $\mathbf{C}$.
3. Multiply $D_r(\mathbf{A}^T)$ and $D_s(\mathbf{C})$ to get the componentwise product of the corresponding pairs of values in constant nodes.
4. Determine the trace of $Tr(\mathbf{A} \cdot \mathbf{C})$ as the sum of these values.

In a practical implementation of this procedure, we construct the QMDD for $\mathbf{A}$ and then use it as the QMDD for $\mathbf{A}^T$ by the corresponding traversal procedure that it is the so-called leftmost-first traversing.

Then, we construct the QMDD for $\mathbf{C}$ and multiply these diagrams by suitably traversing each of them to get the required value for the trace $Tr(\mathbf{A} \cdot \mathbf{C})$ as in (4). The basic principle of this way of computing is illustrated by the following example.

Example 3. *Consider computing the trace of two (4×4) matrices*

$$Tr(\mathbf{A} \cdot \mathbf{C}) = Tr \left(\begin{bmatrix} a_1 & a_5 & a_9 & a_{13} \\ a_2 & a_6 & a_{10} & a_{14} \\ a_3 & a_7 & a_{11} & a_{15} \\ a_4 & a_8 & a_{12} & a_{16} \end{bmatrix} \cdot \begin{bmatrix} c_1 & c_5 & c_9 & c_{13} \\ c_2 & c_6 & c_{10} & c_{14} \\ c_3 & c_7 & c_{11} & c_{15} \\ c_4 & c_8 & c_{12} & c_{16} \end{bmatrix} \right)$$

$$= a_1c_1 + a_5c_2 + a_9c_3 + a_{13}c_4 + a_2c_5 + a_6c_6 + a_{10}c_7 + a_{14}c_8 \qquad (7)$$
$$+ a_3c_9 + a_7c_{10} + a_{11}c_{11} + a_{15}c_{12} + a_4c_{13} + a_8c_{14} + a_{12}c_{15} + a_{16}c_{16}.$$

To compute the trace with (4) over decision diagrams, we first construct the QMDTs for $\mathbf{A}^T$ and $\mathbf{C}$. The decomposition of $\mathbf{A}^T$ is given by (6) and the corresponding QMDT is shown in Fig. 1. The matrix $\mathbf{C}$ is decomposed in the same way as

$$\mathbf{C} = \begin{bmatrix} \mathbf{C}_{00} & \mathbf{C}_{01} \\ \mathbf{C}_{10} & \mathbf{C}_{11} \end{bmatrix},$$

where $\mathbf{C}_{00} = \begin{bmatrix} c_1 & c_5 \\ c_2 & c_6 \end{bmatrix}$, $\mathbf{C}_{01} = \begin{bmatrix} c_9 & c_{13} \\ c_{10} & c_{14} \end{bmatrix}$, $\mathbf{C}_{10} = \begin{bmatrix} c_3 & c_7 \\ c_4 & c_8 \end{bmatrix}$, *and* $\mathbf{C}_{11} = \begin{bmatrix} c_{11} & c_{15} \\ c_{12} & c_{16} \end{bmatrix}$.

This matrix is represented by a QMDT identical to that in Fig. 1 with constant nodes showing the corresponding entries of $\mathbf{C}$.

The componentwise product of vectors obtained by leftmost-first traversal of QMDTs for $\mathbf{A}^T$ and $\mathbf{C}$ produces the following vector:

$$S = a_1c_1 + a_2c_5 + a_5c_2 + a_6c_6 + a_3c_9 + a_4c_{13} + a_7c_{10} + a_8c_{14}$$
$$+ a_9c_3 + a_{10}c_7 + a_{13}c_4 + a_{14}c_8 + a_{11}c_{11} + a_{12}c_{15} + a_{15}c_{12} + a_{16}c_{16},$$

which is equivalent to (3) and identical to (7).

The computational complexity of this calculation is equivalent to the number of steps needed to traverse once all possible paths in QMDDs for $\mathbf{A}^T$ and $\mathbf{C}$. In more traditional computational approaches calculating $Tr(\mathbf{A} \cdot \mathbf{C})$ requires accessing once each element in matrices $\mathbf{A}$ and $\mathbf{C}$, regardless of their specific value, even zero elements have to be accessed although they do not contribute to the product. However, since QMDDs are zero-suppressed, zero valued blocks of matrices are removed during the reduction of the QMDTs. Thus, zero elements of matrices are automatically ignored during the calculation. Therefore, a significant reduction in computational time can be expected for matrices with large number of zero elements. In the worst case, for a matrix with no zero elements, the total number of paths in the full QMDT is equivalent to the number of matrix elements. Thus, the computation procedure over decision diagrams is never more complex than the computation over vectors.

4   Closing Remarks

The paper presents a method for efficient computation of traces of products of two matrices. This method is intended for speeding-up computation of the inverse Fourier transform on finite non-Abelian groups.

Further optimization will be performed by selecting decision diagrams with different number of edges per nodes, depending on the sizes of matrices to be represented [1]. For the programming implementation, we use an XML-based environment for decision diagrams [8], which makes the procedure platform independent.

References

1. Astola, J.T., Stanković, R.S.: Fundamentals of Switching Theory and Logic Design. Springer, Heidelberg (2006)
2. Berghammer, R., Leoniuk, B., Milanese, U.: Implementation of relational algebra using binary decision diagrams. In: de Swart, H. (ed.) RelMiCS 2001. LNCS, vol. 2561, pp. 241–257. Springer, Heidelberg (2002)
3. Butler, J.T.: Bent function discovery by reconfigurable computer. In: Proc. 9th Int. Workshop on Boolean Problems, Freiberg, Germany, September 16-17, pp. 1–12 (2010)
4. Miller, D.M., Stanković, R.S.: An Heterogeneous decision diagram. In: Moreno-Díaz, R., Pichler, F., Quesada-Arencibia, A. (eds.) EUROCAST 2009. LNCS, vol. 5717, pp. 540–547. Springer, Heidelberg (2009)
5. Miller, D., Thornton, M.: "QMDD: A decision diagram structure for reversible and quantum circuits. In: Proc. Int. Symp. on Multiple-Valued Logic (CD), p. 6 (2006)
6. Roziner, T.D., Karpovsky, M.G., Trachtenberg, L.A.: Fast Fourier transform over finite groups by multiprocessor systems. IEEE Trans. Acoust., Speech, Signal Processing ASSP-38(2), 226–240 (1990)
7. Sasao, T., Fujita, M. (eds.): Representations of Discrete Functions. Kluwer Academic Publishers, Dordrecht (1996)
8. Stanković, S., Astola, J.: XML Framework for various types of decision diagrams for discrete functions. IEICE - Transactions on Information and Systems E90-D(11), 1731–1740 (2007)
9. Stanković, R.S., Moraga, C., Astola, J.T.: Fourier Analysis on Finite Non-Abelian Groups with Applications in Signal Processing and System Design. Wiley/IEEE Press (2005)
10. Stanković, S., Astola, J.T., Miller, D.M., Stanković, R.S.: Heterogeneous decision diagrams for applications in Harmonic Analysis on finite non-Abelian groups. In: Proc. 40th Int. Symp. on Multiple-Valued Logic, Barcelona, Spain, May 26-18, pp. 307–312. IEEE-CS-Press, Los Alamitos (2010)

Representation of Convolution Systems on Finite Groups by Heterogeneous Decision Diagrams

Stanislav Stanković[1], Radomir S. Stanković[2],
Jaakko T. Astola[1], and Claudio Moraga[3]

[1] Dept. of Signal Processing, Tampere University of Technology, Tampere, Finland
[2] Dept. of Computer Science, Faculty of Electronics, Niš, Serbia
[3] European Centre for Soft Computing, 33600 Mieres, Spain &
Technical University of Dortmund, 44221 Dortmund, Germany

Abstract. The outputs of linear shift-invariant systems are usually defined in terms of the convolution of input signals with the impulse response functions characterizing the systems. In many areas, as for instance, electrical engineering, digital signal and image processing, statistics, physic, optics, etc., convolution systems defined on finite groups are used. Such systems can be modeled and represented by convolution matrices. The problem is that due to the complexity of systems, dealing with large matrices is required. In this paper, we discuss representation of convolution systems on finite groups by Heterogeneous decision diagrams (HDDs). Such representations permit compact representations of convolution systems, and thanks to that, efficient manipulations and computations related to investigation of features and applications of such systems.

Keywords: Convolution, Finite groups, Polynomial expressions, Spectral representations.

Signals representing information in communication and control systems demand in processing the use of strongly time-invariant systems, and shift-invariant and rotational-invariant systems in the case of speech and images, respectively. This means mathematically that the groups of real numbers R and complex numbers C are the natural domains for the definition of signals.

However, in some areas of contemporary engineering practice, as for instance, in computer engineering, consideration of systems defined on various other groups may be required [4].

Conversely, methods developed for such (generalized) systems may provide advantages in solving some particular tasks in classical system theory and applications. Due to that, generalizations of systems theory to systems described by signals on groups different from R or C are a subject of considerable research efforts in the last few decades. For instance, the dyadic systems, i.e., systems defined on dyadic groups, have been intensively studied by F. Pichler in a series of papers and by several other authors; see [3] for a bibliography up to 1989. For more recent result, we refer to [2], [12], [15].

In this paper, we consider linear convolution systems whose input and output signals are deterministic signals on finite groups. If a group G is decomposable

R. Moreno-Díaz et al. (Eds.): EUROCAST 2011, Part II, LNCS 6928, pp. 296–303, 2012.

into the direct product of some subgroups, then the input of a multi-input system S on G can be modeled by a multi-variable function $f(x_1, \ldots, x_n)$, where n is number of inputs in S. The variables x_i do not necessarily take values in the same sets. Thus, the function f can be viewed as a function defined on a decomposable group $G = \times_{i=1}^n G_i$, where $\times$ denotes the direct product and $x_i \in G_i$.

Modeling of systems in terms of the convolution product on finite groups can be performed in terms of convolution matrices. Such representations of systems usually require dealing with large matrices.

If a matrix can be partitioned in a set of matrices of different radices, it can be efficiently represented using a Heterogeneous decision diagrams (HDDs) [5], [14]. Since convolution matrices on finite decomposable groups inherently have such a property, they can be compactly represented by HDDs. This property is determined by the structure of the underlying domain group. Thanks to this observation, in this paper, we propose a method to represent convolution matrices of systems on finite groups by HDDs. For construction of HDDs we make use of the XML based framework for the representation of decision diagrams [13].

1   Convolution Systems on Finite Groups

Here we will fix the notation that will be used later in the paper. Let G be a finite, not necessarily Abelian, group of order $g = |G|$. We associate (permanently and bijectively) with each group element a non-negative integer from the set $\{0, 1, \ldots, g-1\}$, and 0 is associated with the group identity. Thus, each group element will be identified with the fixed non-negative integer associated with it and with no other element. We assume that G can be represented as a direct product of subgroups $G_1, \ldots, G_n$ of orders $g_1 = |G_1|, \ldots, g_n = |G_n|$, respectively, i.e.,

$$G = \times_{i=1}^n G_i, \quad g = \Pi_{i=1}^n g_i, \quad g_1 \leq g_2 \leq \ldots \leq g_n. \tag{1}$$

The convention adopted above for the notation of group elements applies to the subgroups G_i as well. Provided that the notational bijections of the subgroups and of G are consistently chosen, each $x \in G$ can be uniquely represented as

$$x = \sum_{i=1}^n a_i x_i, \quad x_i \in G_i, \quad x \in G, \quad a_i = \begin{cases} \Pi_{j=i+1}^n g_j, & i = 1, \ldots, n-1 \\ 1, & i = n, \end{cases} \tag{2}$$

where $g_j = |G_j|$ is the order of G_j, and $0 \leq x_i < g_i$, $i = 1, \ldots, n$.

The group operation $\circ$ of G can be expressed in terms of the group operations $\overset{\circ}{i}$ of the subgroups G_i, $i = 1, \ldots, n$ by:

$$x \circ y = (x_1 \overset{\circ}{1} y_1, \; x_2 \overset{\circ}{2} y_2, \; \ldots \; x_n \overset{\circ}{n} y_n), \quad x, y \in G, \quad x_i, y_i \in G_i. \tag{3}$$

Denote by P the complex field or a finite field and by $P(G)$ the space of functions f mapping G into P, i.e., $f : G \to P$. Due to the assumption (1) and the relation (2), each function $f \in P(G)$ can be considered as an n-variable function $f(x_1, \ldots, x_n)$, $x_i \in G_i$.

Definition 1. *A scalar linear system S over a finite not necessarily Abelian group G is defined as a quadruple $(P(G), P(G), h, *)$, where the input-output relation $*$ is the convolution product on G,*

$$y = h * f, \quad f, h, y \in P(G), \quad i.e., \quad y(\tau) = \sum_{x \in G} h(x) f(\tau \circ x^{-1}), \forall \tau \in G, \quad (4)$$

where $\circ$ is the group operation of G.

An ordered pair $(f, y) \in P(G) \times P(G)$ is exactly then an input-output pair of S if f and y fulfill equation (4). The function $h \in P(G)$ is the impulse response of S. It is easy to show that the system S is invariant against the translation of the input function. By that we mean that if y is the output to f, then $T^\tau y$ is the output to $T^\tau f$, for all $\tau \in G$, where T is the translation on G. Therefore, we denote the system S as a linear translation invariant (LTI) system.

Example 1. *Let $S_3 = (0, (132), (123), (12), (13), (23), \circ)$ be the symmetric group of permutations of order 3. According to the convention adopted in this paper, the group elements of S_3 will be denoted by 0,1,2,3,4,5, respectively. A convolution system on the group S_3 whose impulse response is $h(x)$, $x \in S_3$ is defined by the convolution matrix*

$$\mathbf{C}_{S_3} = \begin{bmatrix} h(0) & h(1) & h(2) & h(3) & h(4) & h(5) \\ h(1) & h(2) & h(0) & h(5) & h(3) & h(4) \\ h(2) & h(0) & h(1) & h(4) & h(5) & h(3) \\ h(3) & h(4) & h(5) & h(0) & h(1) & h(2) \\ h(4) & h(5) & h(3) & h(2) & h(0) & h(1) \\ h(5) & h(3) & h(4) & h(1) & h(2) & h(0) \end{bmatrix}.$$

If the input f is specified by the vector $\mathbf{F} = [f(0), f(1), f(2), f(3), f(4), f(5)]^T$, then the output of the system is the vector $\mathbf{Y} = [y(0), y(1), y(2), y(3), y(4), y(5)]^T$ defined as $\mathbf{Y} = \mathbf{C}_{S_3} \cdot \mathbf{F}$.

2   Representation of Matrices by Decision Diagrams

Quantum multiple-valued decision diagrams (QMDD) were introduced in [6] as a data structure to represent $(p^n \times p^n)$ matrices through their decomposition into p^2 submatrices of size $p^{n-1} \times p^{n-1}$, with each non-terminal vertex in a QMDD specifying a decomposition of the given matrix. The non-terminal nodes necessarily have p^2 outgoing edges. A multiplicative attribute w is assigned to each edge. In this way, an edge points to the matrix which is the submatrix rooted by the vertex it points to, multiplied by w.

If $p = 2$, i.e., when the matrix to be represented is partitioned into (2×2) submatrices, a QMDD has nodes with four outgoing edges, which reduces the dept compared with BDDs and MTBDD by a half, resulting in the corresponding speed up in matrix computations over QMDDs.

The heterogeneous decision diagrams (HDD) [5] are a generalization of QMDD derived by allowing a different number of outgoing edges for nodes at different levels in the diagram. It means that the matrix has a recursive structure consisting of submatrices of different dimensions at different levels of the decomposition of the matrix.

A level consists of nodes to which the same decision variable is assigned. In HDDs, in addition to decision variables, a radix r_i, showing the number of outgoing edges, is assigned to each non-terminal node. This is necessary in order to unambiguously specify the way a matrix is partitioned. Thus, HDDs can represent matrices that can be divided into blocks (submatrices) of different sizes. Therefore, HDDs can be used to represent convolution matrices of decomposable groups of the form (1) with subgroups of different sizes. A further generalization is proposed in [14] to represent rectangular matrices. Representation of matrices and elementary calculations, including matrix addition, multiplication Kronecker product, and Cartesian product, over HDDs and their generalizations are supported by the corresponding programming packages as reported in [5], [6], [14].

3   Representation of Convolution Matrices by HDDs

Convolution matrices on groups of the form (1) have a structure that is very suitable for representation by HDDs. This structure expresses the appearance of identical blocks. The sizes of blocks correspond to the orders of the subgroups $|G_i|$, $i = 1, \ldots, n$. Blocks are nested into each other. This corresponds to the hierarchy of levels in decision diagrams. Nodes at each level represent submatrices (blocks) in the convolution matrix. Constant nodes represent values of entries in the convolution matrix. To read a particular entry $c(j, k)$ in the convolution matrix, we follow the corresponding path from the root node to the constant node showing the value $c(j, k)$. Since the entries with the same values repeat in the convolution matrix, the number of paths to reach a constant node is equal to the number of appearances of that entry. In a decision diagram, paths consist of edges, and can be uniquely specified by ordered sets of labels at the edges a path consists of. These labels are determined as follows.

Definition 2. *If nodes at a level i represent an $(r \times r)$ submatrix consisting of $(q \times q)$ blocks, the label at the edge in the path pointing to the node $c(j, k)$ is determined as $l_i = \lfloor j/h \rfloor + q \cdot \lfloor k/h \rfloor + 1$, where $h = r/2$, and $\lfloor x \rfloor$ is the largest integer smaller than x.*

The following examples illustrate representation of convolution matrices by HDDs.

3.1   Dyadic Systems

Systems defined on dyadic groups have been introduced and greatly investigated in early seventies in the context of high interest in the discrete Walsh functions and their applications. See, for example, [2], [7], [9], [10], [11], [12].

Example 2. *For $n = 3$, the finite dyadic group of order 2^n is defined as $G = C_2^3$, where $C_2 = (\{0, 1\}, \oplus)$, and $\oplus$ denotes the addition modulo 2, (logic EXOR). A convolution system on C_2^3 is specified by the convolution matrix*

$$\mathbf{C}_{C_2^3} = \begin{bmatrix} h(0) \ h(1) & h(2) \ h(3) & h(4) \ h(5) & h(6) \ h(7) \\ h(1) \ h(0) & h(3) \ h(2) & h(5) \ h(4) & h(7) \ h(6) \\ \hline h(2) \ h(3) & h(0) \ h(1) & h(6) \ h(7) & h(4) \ h(5) \\ h(3) \ h(2) & h(1) \ h(0) & h(7) \ h(6) & h(5) \ h(4) \\ \hline h(4) \ h(5) & h(6) \ h(7) & h(0) \ h(1) & h(2) \ h(3) \\ h(5) \ h(4) & h(7) \ h(6) & h(1) \ h(0) & h(3) \ h(2) \\ \hline h(6) \ h(7) & h(4) \ h(5) & h(2) \ h(3) & h(0) \ h(1) \\ h(7) \ h(6) & h(5) \ h(4) & h(3) \ h(2) & h(1) \ h(0) \end{bmatrix}.$$

This matrix has a recursive structure that can be expressed as

$$\mathbf{C}_{C_2^3} = \begin{bmatrix} \mathbf{a} \ \mathbf{b} \\ \mathbf{b} \ \mathbf{a} \end{bmatrix}, \text{ where } \mathbf{a} = \begin{bmatrix} \mathbf{A} \ \mathbf{B} \\ \mathbf{B} \ \mathbf{A} \end{bmatrix}, \quad \mathbf{b} = \begin{bmatrix} \mathbf{C} \ \mathbf{D} \\ \mathbf{D} \ \mathbf{C} \end{bmatrix}, \text{ where }$$

$$\mathbf{A} = \begin{bmatrix} h(0) \ h(1) \\ h(1) \ h(0) \end{bmatrix}, \quad \mathbf{B} = \begin{bmatrix} h(2) \ h(3) \\ h(3) \ h(2) \end{bmatrix}, \quad \mathbf{C} = \begin{bmatrix} h(4) \ h(5) \\ h(5) \ h(4) \end{bmatrix}, \quad \mathbf{D} = \begin{bmatrix} h(6) \ h(7) \\ h(7) \ h(6) \end{bmatrix},$$

which allows to derive a compact representation for $\mathbf{C}_{C_2^3}$. Fig. 1 shows the HDD for $\mathbf{C}_{C_2^3}$. This HDD represents the matrix $\mathbf{C}_{C_2^3}$ by capturing the structure of it in the following way.

The root node has four outgoing edges labeled by 1, 2, 3, and 4. Two of them (1 and 4) point to the submatrix $\mathbf{a}$, while the other two (2 and 3) point to the submatrix $\mathbf{b}$. These submatrices are represented by subdiagrams rooted at the nodes labeled by a and b. Each of these nodes has four outgoing edges. Again pairs of them point to the same submatrices $\mathbf{A}, \mathbf{B}, \mathbf{C},$ and $\mathbf{D}$, in the left and the right subtrees, respectively. These submatrices are represented by subtrees rooted in the nodes labeled by $A, B, C,$ and D. These nodes have four outgoing edges, the pairs of which point to the same values $h(i), i = 0, 1, \ldots, 7$, that are entries of the matrix $\mathbf{C}_{C_2^3}$ and, therefore, are represented by the values assigned to constant nodes.

Consider, for example, the element $c(3, 5) \in \mathbf{C}_{C_2^3}$ to illustrate the way of reading particular entries in the convolution matrices by traversing the corresponding paths in the given HDD.

At the topmost level of the diagram in Fig. 1, the (8×8) convolution matrix is represented by a (2×2) symbolic matrix, and we obtain the appropriate edge label as $l_0 = \lfloor j/h \rfloor + q \cdot \lfloor k/h \rfloor + 1$, where $\lfloor x \rfloor$ is the largest integer smaller than x, and $q = 2$ and $h = 8/2 = 4$. For $j = 3$ and $k = 5$, we obtain $l_1 = \lfloor 3/4 \rfloor + 2 \cdot \lfloor 5/4 \rfloor = 0 + 2 + 1 = 3$.

We repeat the same process for indices j_i, k_i for each following level of HDD, where j_i is a reminder of integer division of $j_{i+1}/h_{i+1} - 1$. For the second level in this particular HDD, $j_2 = 2$, $k_2 = 0$. Since at this level, (4×4) matrix $\mathbf{a}$ is represented by a (2×2) matrix, $q_2 = 2$ and $h_2 = 4/2 = 2$. Therefore, $l_2 = \lfloor 2/2 \rfloor + 2 \cdot \lfloor 0/2 \rfloor = 1 + 0 + 1 = 2$.

Finally, in the similar manner, at the third level of the HDD we have, $j_3 = 0$, $k_3 = 0$, $q_3 = 2$, $h_3 = 1$. Thus, $l_3 = 0 + 0 + 1 = 1$.

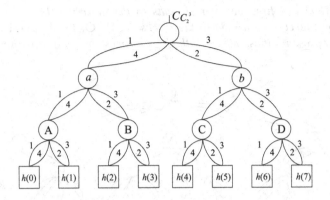

Fig. 1. HDD for the convolution matrix of dyadic systems for $n = 3$

Example 3. *Let $G_{3\times6}$ be the direct product of the group $Z_3 = (0, 1, 2, \overset{\circ}{3})$ of integers less than 3 with modulo 3 addition as the group operation, and the symmetric group of permutations of order 3, S_3 described in Example 1.*

Hence, $G_{3\times6}$ consists of pairs $(h_1, h_2) = g \in G_{3\times6}$ where $h_1 \in Z_3$ and $h_2 \in S_3$. The group operation $\circ$ of $G_{3\times6}$ is specified as follows: for $(h_1, h_2) = g \in G_{3\times6}$ and $(h'_1, h'_2) = g' \in G_{3\times6}$ we have $(h_1 \overset{\circ}{3} h'_1, h_2 \overset{\circ}{3} h'_2) = g \circ g' \in G_{3\times6}$.

For such decomposition the convolution matrix on $G_{3\times6}$ can be recursively represented as

$$\mathbf{C}_{3\times6} = \begin{bmatrix} \mathbf{a} & \mathbf{b} & \mathbf{c} \\ \mathbf{b} & \mathbf{c} & \mathbf{a} \\ \mathbf{c} & \mathbf{a} & \mathbf{b} \end{bmatrix},$$

where

$$\mathbf{a} = \begin{bmatrix} \mathbf{A} & \mathbf{B} \\ \mathbf{B} & \mathbf{A} \end{bmatrix}, \quad \mathbf{b} = \begin{bmatrix} \mathbf{C} & \mathbf{D} \\ \mathbf{D} & \mathbf{C} \end{bmatrix}, \quad \mathbf{c} = \begin{bmatrix} \mathbf{E} & \mathbf{F} \\ \mathbf{F} & \mathbf{E} \end{bmatrix},$$

and

$$\mathbf{A} = \begin{bmatrix} 0 & 1 & 2 \\ 1 & 2 & 0 \\ 2 & 0 & 1 \end{bmatrix}, \quad \mathbf{B} = \begin{bmatrix} 3 & 4 & 5 \\ 4 & 5 & 3 \\ 5 & 3 & 4 \end{bmatrix}, \quad \mathbf{C} = \begin{bmatrix} 6 & 7 & 8 \\ 7 & 8 & 6 \\ 8 & 6 & 7 \end{bmatrix},$$

$$\mathbf{D} = \begin{bmatrix} 9 & 10 & 11 \\ 10 & 11 & 9 \\ 11 & 9 & 10 \end{bmatrix}, \quad \mathbf{E} = \begin{bmatrix} 12 & 13 & 14 \\ 13 & 14 & 12 \\ 14 & 12 & 13 \end{bmatrix}, \quad \mathbf{F} = \begin{bmatrix} 15 & 16 & 17 \\ 16 & 17 & 15 \\ 17 & 15 & 16 \end{bmatrix}.$$

Fig. 2 shows the HDD for the matrix $\mathbf{C}_{3\times6}$.

*In this HDD, the first level corresponds to the matrix with entries a, b, and c. The second level corresponds to the blocks **A**, **B**, **C**, **D**, **E**, and **F**, while the third level represents these blocks with their entries shown in constant nodes.*

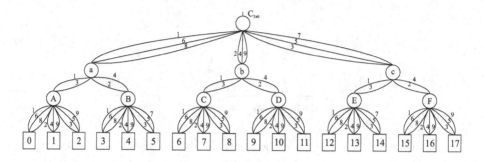

Fig. 2. HDD for the convolution matrix $\mathbf{C}_{3\times6}$

4   Experimental Results

We performed a series of experiments exploring complexity of HDDs for convolution with the specified impulse responses viewed as systems on different groups.

As system responses, we have taken integer valued switching functions from the MCNC set of benchmark functions. These functions are treated as impulse responses on groups of type C_2^n, where n is the number of input variables of the given switching function. Table 1 shows the sizes (number of nodes) of their corresponding HDDs.

Table 1. Sizes of HDDs on different groups

Function	n	Group	Number of nodes	Function	n	Group	Number of nodes
x_1	5	C_2^5	5	xor5	5	C_2^5	5
x_5	5	C_2^5	5	5xp1	7	C_2^7	127
$x_4 \oplus x_5$	5	C_2^5	5	con1	7	C_2^7	16
$x_4 \oplus \bar{x}_5$	5	C_2^5	5	rd73	7	C_2^7	26
Add2	4	C_2^4	14	rd84	8	C_2^8	34
MulL2	4	C_2^4	8	sqrt8	8	C_2^8	70
bw	5	C_2^5	25	misex1	8	C_2^8	47
maj5	5	C_2^5	5	9sym	9	C_2^9	9
rd53	5	C_2^5	13	clip	9	C_2^9	180
rd531	5	C_2^5	5	ex1010	10	C_2^{10}	561
squar53	5	C_2^5	5	sao2	10	C_2^{10}	114

As expected, linear single output switching functions such as x_1, x_5, $x_4 \oplus x_5$, $x_4 \oplus \bar{x}_5$, where $n = 5$ viewed as systems on C_2^5 exhibit a strong regularity in their corresponding convolution matrices which results in a very compact HDD representations.

References

1. Clarke, E.M., Fujita, M., Zhao, X.: Multi-terminal binary decision diagrams and hybrid decision diagrams. In: Sasao, T., Fujita, M. (eds.) Representations of Discrete Functions, pp. 93–108. Kluwer Academic Publishers, Dordrecht (1996)
2. Endow, Y.: Walsh harmonizable processes in linear system theory. Cybernetics and Systems, 489–512 (1996)
3. Gibbs, J.E., Stanković, R.S.: Why IWGD-89? a look at the bibliography of Gibbs derivatives. In: Butzer, P.L., Stanković, R.S. (eds.) Theory and Applications of Gibbs Derivatives, Belgrade, Serbia, Matematički Institut, pp. xi–xxiv (1990)
4. Karpovsky, M.G., Trachtenberg, E.A.: Some optimization problems for convolution systems over finite groups. Inf. and Control 34, 227–247 (1977)
5. Miller, D.M., Stanković, R.S.: A heterogeneous decision diagram package. In: Moreno-Díaz, R., Pichler, F., Quesada-Arencibia, A. (eds.) EUROCAST 2009. LNCS, vol. 5717, pp. 540–547. Springer, Heidelberg (2009)
6. Miller, D., Thornton, M.: QMDD: A decision diagram structure for reversible and quantum circuits. In: Proc. Int. Symp. on Multiple-Valued Logic, CD, p. 6 (2006)
7. Moraga, C.: Introduction to linear p-adic systems. In: Trappl, R. (ed.) Cybernetics and Systems Research, vol. 2. North-Holland, Amsterdam (1984)
8. Pearl, J.: Optimal dyadic models of time-invariant systems. IEEE Trans. Computers C-24 (1975)
9. Pichler, F.R.: Some aspects of a theory of correlation with respect to Walsh harmonic analysis. Univ. Maryland Tech. Res. Rept R-70-11 (1970)
10. Pichler, F.: On state space description of linear dyadic invariant systems. IEEE Trans. on Electromagnetic Compatibility EMC-13, 166 (1971)
11. Pichler, F.R.: Dyadische Faltungsoperatoren zur Beschreibung linearer Systeme. Siteber. Öst. Akad. Wiss., Math.-naturwiss. KL, Abt. II 180, Heft 1-3, 69–87 (1971)
12. Pichler, F.: Construction of dissipative dynamical system using Gibbs derivatives. In: Stanković, R.S. (ed.) Walsh and Dyadic Analysis, Elektronski fakultet, Niš, Serbia, pp. 31–36 (2008); ISBN 978-86-85195-47-1
13. Stanković, S., Astola, J.: XML Framework for various types of decision diagrams for discrete functions. IEICE - Transactions on Information and Systems E90-D(11), 1731–1740 (2007)
14. Stanković, S., Astola, J.T., Miller, D.M., Stanković, R.S.: Heterogeneous decision diagrams for applications in Harmonic Analysis on finite non-Abelian groups. In: Proc. 40th Int. Symp. on Multiple-Valued Logic, Barcelona, Spain, May 26-18, pp. 307–312. IEEE-CS-Press, Los Alamitos (2010)
15. Stanković, R.S., Stanković, M.S., Moraga, C.: Remarks on systems and differential operators on groups. Facta Universitatis (Niš), Ser. Elec. Energ. 18(3), 531–545 (2005)

Discrete Transforms Produced from Two Natural Numbers and Applications

Nikolaos Atreas[1] and Costas Karanikas[2]

[1] Aristotle University of Thessaloniki, Faculty of Engineering,
Dpt. of Mathematical, Physical and Comput. Sciences, 54124, Greece
[2] Aristotle University of Thessaloniki, Dpt. of Informatics, 54124, Greece

Abstract. Let m be a natural number and $\odot : \mathbb{R}^m \times \mathbb{R}^m \to \mathbb{R}^m$ be the usual Hadamard product operation on finite data of length m. In [1] we built a large class of $m \times m$ boolean invertible matrices (called R-matrices) determined by a pair of permutations (ρ, s) of the set $\{1, ..., m\}$. To do that we required that any pair of rows R_i, R_j, $(i, j = 1, ..., m)$ of an R-matrix satisfies either $R_i \odot R_j = R_{\max\{i,j\}}$ or $R_i \odot R_j = (0, ..., 0)$, a property mainly observed in matrices associated with multiscale linear transforms. In this paper we deal with R-transforms, i.e. linear transforms $T_R : \mathbb{C}^m \to \mathbb{C}^m$ whose corresponding matrices are R-matrices. We prove that the inverse transform T_R^{-1} has a simple representation depending only on the pair (ρ, s) identifying the matrix R. As a result we obtain a fast encoding/decoding scheme. Finally we demonstrate a method for constructing R-transforms with desired properties from a recursive equation based on dilation operators on permutations and we present applications.

1 Introduction

Let m be a natural number and A be an $m \times m$ matrix over the field $\mathbb{C}$ of complex numbers whose row vectors $A_1, ..., A_m$ satisfy

$$A_i \odot A_j = c_{ij} \, A_{g(i,j)}, \ i, j = 1, ..., m \tag{1}$$

with respect to a certain operation $g : I_m \times I_m \to I_m$ on the set $I_m = \{1, ..., m\}$ and with respect to some double-indexed sequence of scalars $\{c_{ij}\}_{i,j=1}^m$. Here and hereafter

$$A_i \odot A_j = (A_{i1}A_{j1}, ..., A_{im}A_{jm}), \ i, j = 1, ..., m$$

is the usual Hadamard product operation [8]. The notation $A = (A_1, ..., A_m)$ is used to denote an $m \times m$ matrix A with rows $A_1, ..., A_m$. We define the *support* of the i-row of an $m \times m$ matrix A by

$$supp\{A_i\} = \{k \in \{1, ..., m\} : \ A_{i,k} \neq 0\}.$$

In order to obtain efficient analysis on finite data we seek for linear transforms whose corresponding matrices have the ability to extract specific characteristics

R. Moreno-Díaz et al. (Eds.): EUROCAST 2011, Part II, LNCS 6928, pp. 304–310, 2012.
© Springer-Verlag Berlin Heidelberg 2012

from those data [2,3,4]. We mention the Fourier matrices $F_m = \{m^{-1/2}e^{2\pi ikn/m}$: $k, n = 0, ...m - 1\}$ used to extract the frequency content of a signal of length m [5], the $2^n \times 2^n$ Walsh matrices W_n ($n = 1, 2, ...$) used to measure the non-linearity of a boolean sequence of length 2^n [9] and the $2^n \times 2^n$ Haar matrices H_n providing sparse representations on finite data [6,7]. It is remarkable that these classes of matrices satisfy (1) (notice that the class of Haar matrices satisfies (1) for all $i \neq j$). In [1] we introduced and investigated a new large class of boolean matrices satisfying (1), namely the class $\mathcal{R}_m$.

Definition 1. *We say that an $m \times m$ boolean invertible matrix $R = \{R_1, ..., R_m\}$ belongs in the class $\mathcal{R}_m$ if the row vectors of R satisfy*

$$R_i \odot R_j = c_{ij} R_{\max\{i,j\}} : c_{ij} \in \{0, 1\}, i, j = 1, ..., m.$$

We study the class $\mathcal{R}_m$ because any matrix in this class contains only boolean entries and exhibits multiscale properties in the sense that if A is an $m \times m$ boolean invertible matrix and $1 \leq i < j \leq m$ then

$$A \in \mathcal{R}_m \text{ if and only if } supp\{A_j\} \subset supp\{A_i\} \text{ or } supp\{A_i\} \cap supp\{A_j\} = \oslash.$$

Therefore the class $\mathcal{R}_m$ provides natural candidates for producing multiscale transforms with desired properties. Notice that if we define by $\mathcal{A}_m$ the class of all unitriangular boolean matrices in $\mathcal{R}_m$ and by

$$\mathcal{S}_m = \{s = \{s(1), ..., s(m)\} : s(i) \in \mathbb{N}, s(i) \leq i\}$$

then in [1] we proved that the mapping $f : \mathcal{A}_m \to \mathcal{S}_m : s = f(A)$:

$$s(1) = 1, \quad s(j) = \begin{cases} k, & k = \max\{i \in \{1, ..., j-1\} : supp\{A_j\} \subset supp\{A_i\}\} \\ j, & supp\{A_i\} \cap supp\{A_j\} = \oslash \text{ for any } i = 1, ..., j-1 \end{cases} \quad (2)$$

is a bijection and provides a characterization of the class $\mathcal{R}_m$. More precisely

Theorem 1. *Every element $R \in \mathcal{R}_m$ can be uniquely written as*

$$R = A_s P_\rho : (\rho, s) \in \mathcal{P}_m \times \mathcal{S}_m,$$

where $A_s = f^{-1}(s)$ is an $m \times m$ unitriangular boolean matrix in $\mathcal{R}_m$ associated with a unique element $s \in \mathcal{S}_m$ and P_ρ is an $m \times m$ permutation matrix (permuting the columns of the identity matrix) associated with a permutation $\rho \in \mathcal{P}_m$, where $\mathcal{P}_m$ is the symmetric group of all permutations of the set $\{1, ..., m\}$.

Proof. See [1].

Remark 1. Using (2) we may easily determine the matrix A_s from s. In fact we compute the support of the columns of any element $A_s \in \mathcal{A}_m$ by

$$supp\{(A_s)_j^T\} = \{s^k(j) : 0 \leq k \leq \mu_j\}, j = 1, ..., m,$$

where $0 \leq \mu_j \leq m - 1$ is the first natural number satisfying $s^{\mu_j+1}(j) = s^{\mu_j}(j)$. Here we consider $s^0(j) = j$. Also we use the notation $s^k(j)$ $k = 2, ..., m$ to denote the composition of the sequence s with itself k times.

Remark 2. Since the sets $\mathcal{P}_m$ and $\mathcal{S}_m$ are equivalent and since the set $\mathcal{P}_m$ is enumerated, every matrix $R \in \mathcal{R}_m$ can be coded by two natural numbers between 1 and $m!$. Therefore R-matrices can be efficiently stored.

Based on the multiscale structure of R-matrices and their simple representation by two natural numbers, in section 2 we study their corresponding class of R-transforms, i.e. discrete linear invertible transforms derived from R-matrices by

$$T_R : \mathbb{C}^m \to \mathbb{C}^m : T_R(x) = x \cdot R \quad (R \in \mathcal{R}_m).$$

We prove that the inverse transform $T_R^{-1}(x) = x \cdot R^{-1}$ admits a simple representation depending only on the knowledge of the pair (ρ, s) which identifies the matrix R. As a result a fast encoding/decoding scheme is obtained.

In section 3 we exploit the results of section 2 for constructing R-transforms with desired properties on finite data of length $m = p_1 \cdots p_N$ ($p_1 \geq p_2 \ldots \geq p_N$ are prime factors of m). We do that based on an iteration process

$$\left(\rho^{(n)}, s^{(n)}\right) = \left(D_{p_n}\left(\rho^{(n-1)}\right), d_{p_n}\left(s^{(n-1)}\right)\right), \quad n = 1, ..., N,$$

where $\left(\rho^{(n)}, s^{(n)}\right) \in \mathcal{P}_{p_1 \cdots p_n} \times \mathcal{S}_{p_1 \cdots p_n}$ and $D_{p_n} : \mathcal{P}_k \to \mathcal{P}_{kp_n}$, $d_{p_n} : \mathcal{S}_k \to \mathcal{S}_{kp_n}$ are properly defined dilation operators. In each step a pair $\left(\rho^{(n)}, s^{(n)}\right)$ is generated, so a unique R-matrix matrix of order $(p_1 \cdots p_n) \times (p_1 \cdots p_n)$ is produced. Finally an $m \times m$ R-matrix is obtained and its corresponding linear transform encodes information at different scales in the following sense: any $m \times m$ R-matrix constructed via the above iteration process gives rise to a multiscale analysis $\{W_1 \subset ... \subset W_N = V_m\}$ of the space V_m of all complex valued sequences of length m. The subspaces W_i are $(p_1 \ldots p_i)$-dimensional subspaces of V_m spanned by the first $(p_1 \ldots p_i)$ row vectors of the R-matrix. Certain applications are presented to demonstrate our theory.

2   Linear Transforms Associated with R-Matrices

Let $s \in \mathcal{S}_m$ be as above. We define by T_s the set of $m \times m$ boolean matrices $T_s = \{T_s(i) : i = 1, \ldots, m\}$:

$$(T_s(i))_{k,l} = \begin{cases} \mathbf{O}, & s(i) = i \\ \begin{cases} 1, & (k,l) = (s(i), i) \\ 0 & otherwise \end{cases}, & s(i) < i \end{cases}, \quad 1 \leq k, l \leq m. \tag{3}$$

It is clear that every matrix $T_s(i)$ is either the $m \times m$ zero matrix or a boolean matrix containing one non zero element up its main diagonal.

Proposition 1. *Let $s \in \mathcal{S}_m$ and $A_s = f^{-1}(s)$ be its corresponding $m \times m$ unitriangular boolean matrix in $\mathcal{A}_m \subset \mathcal{R}_m$ as in theorem 1. Then*

$$A_s = \prod_{i=1}^m (\mathbf{I}_m + T_s(i)) \tag{4}$$

where the matrices $T_s(i)$, $i = 1,\ldots,m$ *are as in (3). Here and hereafter the symbol* $\prod$ *indicates usual matrix multiplication and* $\mathbf{I}_m$ *is the* $m \times m$ *identity matrix.*

Proof. Given an element $s \in \mathcal{S}_m$ we define a matrix $A_{s^{(j)}} = \prod_{i=1}^{m}(\mathbf{I}_m + T_{s^{(j)}}(i))$, where $s^{(j)}(i) = \begin{cases} s(i) & i \leq j \\ i & i > j \end{cases}$. Then $s^{(m)} = s$ and the following recursive equation holds for any $j = 2,\ldots,m-1$:

$$A_{s^{(j)}} = A_{s^{(j-1)}} \cdot (\mathbf{I}_m + T_s(j)),$$

where the symbol $(\cdot)$ denotes usual matrix multiplication. From (2) and (4) we deduce that the matrix $A_{s^{(j)}}$ results from the matrix $A_{s^{(j-1)}}$ by substituting only the j-column of $A_{s^{(j-1)}}$ with the sum of columns $(A_{s^{(j-1)}})_{.,j} + (A_{s^{(j-1)}})_{.,s(j)}$. Therefore if the matrix $A_{s^{(j-1)}} \in \mathcal{A}_m$ then necessarily the matrix $A_{s^{(j)}} \in \mathcal{A}_m$. Since $A_{s^{(1)}} = \mathbf{I}_m \in \mathcal{A}_m$ we are done.

Proposition 2. *Let* A_s *be as in (4). Then the* j-*column of the* $m \times m$ *inverse matrix* A_s^{-1} *is calculated by*

$$(A_s)^{-1}_{i,j} = \begin{cases} 1 & i = j \\ -1, & i = s(j) \text{ and } s(j) < j \text{ , } i = 1,...,m. \\ 0 & \text{otherwise} \end{cases} \quad (5)$$

Proof. From (2) we find that $(\mathbf{I}_m + T_s(i))^{-1} = \mathbf{I}_m - T_s(i)(1 - \delta_{i,s(i)})$, where $\delta_{i,j}$ is the Kronecker's delta. We consider $b_i = 1 - \delta_{i,s(i)}$, then we use (3) and the above equality to get

$$A_s^{-1} = \prod_{i=1}^{m}(\mathbf{I}_m - b_{m-i+1}T_s(m-i+1)) = \mathbf{I}_m - \sum_{i=1}^{m}b_i T_s(i)$$

$$+ \sum_{i=1}^{m-1}\sum_{j=i+1}^{m} b_i b_j \, T_s(j) \cdot T_s(i) + \ldots + (-1)^m b_1 ... b_m \, T_s(m) \cdots T_s(1). \quad (6)$$

Since $(T_s(j) \cdot T_s(i))_{r,v} = \delta_{r,s(j)}\delta_{j,s(i)}\delta_{i,v}$ and since by definition $s(i) \leq i$ ($i = 1,\ldots,m$) we get

$$j > i \geq s(i) \Rightarrow \delta_{j,s(i)} = 0,$$

thus all terms except for the first two terms in (6) vanish and the proof is complete.

Theorem 2. *Let* $R \in \mathcal{R}_m$. *Then the* j-*column of the inverse matrix* R^{-1} *is given by*

$$R^{-1}_{n,j} = \begin{cases} 1 & n = \rho_j \\ -1, & n = \rho_{s(j)} \text{ and } \rho_j \neq \rho_{s(j)} \text{ , } n = 1,...,m \text{ .} \\ 0 & \text{otherwise} \end{cases}$$

Proof. Combine theorem 1 and (5).

Obviously an enumerated class of simple encoding/decoding schemes naturally arises. The encoding process is defined by

$$T_R : \mathbb{C}^m \to \mathbb{C}^m : T_R(x) = x \cdot R, \ R \in \mathcal{R}_m$$

and contains only matrix multiplication involving an R-matrix. The decoding process does not involve any matrix multiplication. In fact from theorem 2 we obtain

$$T_R^{-1} : \mathbb{C}^m \to \mathbb{C}^m : \left(T_R^{-1}(x)\right)_j = x_{\rho_j} - \left(1 - \delta_{j,s(j)}\right) x_{\rho_{s(j)}}.$$

3   Multiscale Transforms on Finite Data Derived from Dilations of Permutations

In this section we demonstrate a method for constructing a variety of R-transforms on finite data from a recursion equation based on $m \times m$ R-matrices.

Let $m = p_1...p_N$ $(p_1 \geq p_2... \geq p_N)$ be the prime integer factorization of a natural number m. We present our construction in the following steps:

1st **step:** For any $\lambda = 2, 3, ...$ and for any $k \in \mathbb{N}$ we establish two dilation operators

$$D_\lambda : \mathcal{P}_k \to \mathcal{P}_{\lambda k} \text{ and } d_\lambda : \mathcal{S}_k \to \mathcal{S}_{\lambda k}.$$

2nd **step:** We select a pair $\left(\rho^{(1)}, s^{(1)}\right) \in \mathcal{P}_{p_1} \times \mathcal{S}_{p_1}$ and we define an iteration process based on the dilation operators defined in step 1:

$$\left(\rho^{(n)}, s^{(n)}\right) = \left(D_{p_n}\left(\rho^{(n-1)}\right), d_{p_n}\left(s^{(n-1)}\right)\right) \in \mathcal{P}_{p_1\cdots p_n} \times \mathcal{P}_{p_1\cdots p_n}, \ n = 2, ..., N.$$

3rd **step:** We formulate an R-matrix of order $m \times m$ corresponding to the sequence $\left(\rho^{(N)}, s^{(N)}\right)$ giving rise to a linear transform:

$$T_R : \mathbb{C}^m \to \mathbb{C}^m, \ T_R(x) = x \cdot R$$

as in section 2.

4th **step:** We define a nested sequence $\{W_1 \subset ... \subset W_N = V_m\}$ of $(p_1 \cdots p_i)$-dimensional subspaces of the space V_m of all complex valued sequences of length m such that each subspace W_i is spanned by the first $(p_1 \cdots p_i)$ row vectors of the $m \times m$ R-matrix defined in step 3. Each subspace W_i reveals information at different levels providing a multiscale analysis on data of length m.

Below we present two applications to demonstrate our theory.

Application I: *Non Orthogonal Haar-Type Multiscale Analysis*

For simplicity we present the dyadic case $m = 2^N$. Similar results can be obtained for non dyadic cases under appropriate definitions on the dilation operators. For any $k = 1, ..., N - 1$ let

$$D_2 : \mathcal{P}_k \to \mathcal{P}_{2k} : \left(D_2(\rho)\right)(n) = \begin{cases} 2\rho_n, & n = 1, ..., k \\ 2(n - k) - 1, & n = k + 1, ..., 2k \end{cases}.$$

Given the operator D_2 as above assume that $\rho^{(k)} \in \mathcal{P}_{2^k}$, $k = 1, ..., N - 1$ and define an iteration process on permutations by

$$\rho^{(k+1)} = D_2(\rho^{(k)}).$$

On the other hand if $s^{(k)} \in \mathcal{S}_{2^k}$, $k = 1, ..., N - 1$ and if $\rho^{(k)}$ are as above we define an iteration process on $\mathcal{S}_k$ by

$$s^{(k+1)} = d_{\rho^{(k)},2}(s^{(k)})$$

where

$$d_{\rho,2} : \mathcal{S}_k \to \mathcal{S}_{2k} : (d_{\rho,2}(s))(n) = \begin{cases} s(n), & n = 1, ..., k \\ \rho^{-1}(n - k), & n = k + 1, ..., 2k \end{cases}$$

and ρ^{-1} is the inverse permutation of $\rho \in \mathcal{P}_k$. If $\rho^{(1)} = \{2, 1\}$ and $s^{(1)} = \{1, 1\}$ then for any $k = 2, 3, \ldots$ we obtain

$$\left(\rho^{(2)}, s^{(2)}\right) = \{\{4, 2, 1, 3\}, \{1, 1, 2, 1\}\},$$

$$\left(\rho^{(3)}, s^{(3)}\right) = \{\{8, 4, 2, 6, 1, 3, 5, 7\}, \{1, 1, 2, 1, 3, 2, 4, 1\}\}, \ldots.$$

Since in every pair $(\rho^{(i)}, s^{(i)})$ there corresponds a unique matrix $R^{(i)}$, from theorem 1 we obtain

$$R^{(2)} = \begin{pmatrix} 1 & 1 & 1 & 1 \\ 1 & 1 & 0 & 0 \\ 1 & 0 & 0 & 0 \\ 0 & 0 & 1 & 0 \end{pmatrix}, \quad R^{(3)} = \begin{pmatrix} 1 & 1 & 1 & 1 & 1 & 1 & 1 & 1 \\ 1 & 1 & 1 & 1 & 0 & 0 & 0 & 0 \\ 1 & 1 & 0 & 0 & 0 & 0 & 0 & 0 \\ 0 & 0 & 0 & 0 & 1 & 1 & 0 & 0 \\ 1 & 0 & 0 & 0 & 0 & 0 & 0 & 0 \\ 0 & 0 & 1 & 0 & 0 & 0 & 0 & 0 \\ 0 & 0 & 0 & 0 & 1 & 0 & 0 & 0 \\ 0 & 0 & 0 & 0 & 0 & 0 & 1 & 0 \end{pmatrix}, \ldots.$$

The 2^i $(i = 1, ..., N)$ dimensional subspaces $W_i = span\left\{(R^{(i)})_k\right\}_{k=1}^{2^i}$ reveal information at different scales providing a multiscale analysis of data of length $m = 2^N$.

Application II: *Multiscale Transforms for Detecting Periodicities*

Let us define

$$D_2 : \mathcal{P}_k \to \mathcal{P}_{2k} : (D_2(\rho))(n) = \begin{cases} \rho_n + k, & n = 1, ..., k \\ n - k, & n = k + 1, ..., 2k \end{cases},$$

and keep $d_{\rho,2}$ as in application I. Then we work as in application I for $\rho^{(1)} = \{2, 1\}$ and $s^{(1)} = \{1, 1\}$ and we have

$$\left(\rho^{(2)}, s^{(2)}\right) = \{\{4, 3, 1, 2\}, \{1, 1, 2, 1\}\},$$

$$\left(\rho^{(3)}, s^{(3)}\right) = \{\{8,7,5,6,1,2,3,4\}, \{1,1,2,1,3,4,2,1\}\}, \dots$$

Therefore

$$R^{(2)} = \begin{pmatrix} 1 & 1 & 1 & 1 \\ 1 & 0 & 1 & 0 \\ 1 & 0 & 0 & 0 \\ 0 & 1 & 0 & 0 \end{pmatrix}, \quad R^{(3)} = \begin{pmatrix} 1 & 1 & 1 & 1 & 1 & 1 & 1 & 1 \\ 1 & 0 & 1 & 0 & 1 & 0 & 1 & 0 \\ 1 & 0 & 0 & 0 & 1 & 0 & 0 & 0 \\ 0 & 1 & 0 & 0 & 0 & 1 & 0 & 0 \\ 1 & 0 & 0 & 0 & 0 & 0 & 0 & 0 \\ 0 & 1 & 0 & 0 & 0 & 0 & 0 & 0 \\ 0 & 0 & 1 & 0 & 0 & 0 & 0 & 0 \\ 0 & 0 & 0 & 1 & 0 & 0 & 0 & 0 \end{pmatrix}, \dots$$

In this case the subspaces $W_i = span\left\{\left(R^{(i)}\right)_k\right\}_{k=1}^{2^i}$ contain 2^i periodic sequences. In fact W_1 is a 2-dimensional space consisting of all 2-periodic sequences. Similarly, the space W_2 is a 4-dimensional space consisting of 4-periodic sequences etc.

References

1. Atreas, N., Karanikas, C.: Boolean invertible matrices identified from two permutations and their corresponding Haar-type matrices. Linear Algebra Appl. 435(1), 95–105 (2011)
2. Atreas, N., Karanikas, C., Polychronidou, P.: A class of sparse Unimodular Matrices generating Multiresolution and Sampling analysis for data of any length. SIAM J. Matrix Anal. Appl. 30, 312–323 (2008)
3. Atreas, N., Karanikas, C.: Multiscale Haar unitary matrices with the corresponding Riesz Products and a characterization of Cantor - type languages. J. Fourier Anal. Appl. 13, 197–210 (2007)
4. Atreas, N., Polychronidou, P.: A class of sparse invertible matrices and their use for non-linear prediction of nearly periodic time series with fixed period. Numer. Funct. Anal. Optim. 29, 66–87 (2008)
5. Briggs, W.L., Van Emden, H.: An Owner's Manual for the Discrete Fourier Transform. SIAM, Philadelphia (1995)
6. Dubeau, F., Elmejdani, S., Ksantini, R.: Non-uniform Haar wavelets. Appl. Math. Comput. 159, 675–693 (2004)
7. Egiazarian, K., Astola, J.: Tree-structured Haar transforms. Non-linear image processing and pattern recognition. J. Math. Imaging Vision 16, 269–279 (2002)
8. Horn, R.A., Johnson, C.R.: Matrix Analysis. Cambridge University Press, New York (1985)
9. Rothaus, O.S.: On bent functions. Journal of Combinatorial Theory 20A, 300–305 (1976)

Reversible Synthesis in the Walsh Hadamard Domain

Milena Stanković and Suzana Stojković

Faculty of Electronic Engineering, University of Niš
A. Medvedeva 14, 18000 Niš, Serbia
{milena.stankovic,suzana.stojkovic}@elfak.ni.ac.rs

Abstract. The paper presents a method for reversible synthesis of Boolean functions based on the properties of theis Walsh-Hadamard spectra. To realize a function, each part of the reversible cascade is specified by an examination if certain appropriately defined conditions are satisfied by pairs of the Walsh-Hadamard spectral coefficients. The function to be realized is represented by a Binary Decision Diagram (BDD) and the Walsh-Hadamard spectrum is computed over this BDD. Experimental results show that the proposed method outperforms existing similar methods in terms of both the number of lines and gates.

1 Introduction

In last several years, reversible logic synthesis gained much attention primarily due to its applications in low-power computing and quantum computing. There are many synthesis approaches including these using spectral techniques. However, most of the current methods for the reversible synthesis are limited by complexity of computations and are applicable to functions of relatively small number of variables. In [1], a synthesis approach that can cope with Boolean functions of a large number of variables is proposed. The method in [1] uses BDDs to represent functions and derive reversible circuits realizing them. The basic idea is as follows: First, a BDD for the function to be synthesized is constructed. Then, each node of the BDD is substituted by a cascade of reversible gates. As a result, circuits composed of Toffoli gates are obtained within the time and memory linearly proportional to the size of the BDD.

In this paper, we propose a method for the iterative synthesis of reversible cascades by considering the properties of the function to be realized in the Walsh-Hadamard domain. BDDs are used as the data structure to represent functions and to perform all the related computations. In this sense, the proposed method can be viewed as a combination of the BDD synthesis approach proposed in [1] and [2], and the method for realization of Maitra cascades proposed in [3].

The paper is organized as follows. In the Section 2 the definition and main properties of the Walsh-Hadamard spectrum are presented. Section 3 describes the algorithm for reversible synthesis based on the Walsh-Hadamard coefficients. The algorithm in illustrated by an example in Section 4. Section 5 presents experimental results and a comparison with the results in [1].

R. Moreno-Díaz et al. (Eds.): EUROCAST 2011, Part II, LNCS 6928, pp. 311–318, 2012.
© Springer-Verlag Berlin Heidelberg 2012

2   The Walsh-Hadamard Spectrum

For a Boolean function $f(x_1, x_2, \ldots, x_n)$, the Walsh-Hadamard spectrum, represented by an integer vector $\mathbf{R}$ of length 2^n is defined as:

$$\mathbf{R}(n) = \mathbf{W}(n)\mathbf{F}(n), \quad \mathbf{W}(n) = \begin{bmatrix} 1, & 1 \\ 1 & -1 \end{bmatrix}^{\otimes n},$$

where $\otimes$ denotes the Kronecker product of matrices and $\mathbf{F}(n)$ is the truth-vector of the function $f(x_1, x_2, \ldots, x_n)$ in the $(1, -1)$ encoding.

In thus defined Walsh-Hadamard spectrum, the coefficients appear in the so-called Hadamard ordering. For $n = 3$, these coefficients are denoted as:

$$\mathbf{R}(3) = [R_0, R_3, R_2, R_{23}, R_1, R_{13}, R_{12}, R_{123}]^T.$$

In this notation, the coefficient R_0 is the zero-order coefficient. $R_1, R_2, \cdots, R_n$ are the first order coefficients, the coefficients $R_{12}, R_{13}, \cdots, R_{n,n-1}$ are the second order coefficients, while all other coefficients are the higher order coefficients. The method proposed in this paper uses the first and the second order coefficients.

It is well know that the Walsh-Hadamard coefficients are a measure of the correlation between the function and linear combinations of the input variables. For the approach proposed in this paper, the following properties of spectral coefficients are important:

1. The absolute values of spectral coefficients are limited to 2^n and the following properties are satisfied:

   - The zero-order coefficient R_0 is a measure of the correlation of f with the constants 0 and 1. Namely, for the constant function $f(x_1, x_2, \ldots, x_n) = 0$, the coefficient $R_0 = 2^n$, while for $f(x_1, x_2, \ldots, x_n) = 1$ it is $R_0 = -2^n$.
   - The first order coefficients $R_i, (i = 1, 2, \ldots, n)$ are a measure of the correlation with the variables $x_i, (i = 1, 2, \ldots, n)$. If $f(x_1, x_2, \ldots, x_n) = x_i$, then $R_i = 2^n$, and if $f(x_1, x_2, \ldots, x_n) = \bar{x}_i$, then $R_i = -2^n$.
   - The higher order coefficients $R_{ij\ldots k}$ are measures of correlations with the linear functions $(x_i \oplus x_j \cdots \oplus x_k)$. For $f(x_1, x_2, \ldots, x_n) = (x_i \oplus x_j \cdots \oplus x_k)$ it is $R_{ij\ldots k} = 2^n$, and for $f(x_1, x_2, \ldots, x_n) = (x_i \oplus x_j \cdots \oplus x_k)$, it is $R_{ij\ldots k} = -2^n$.

2. The sum of two spectral coefficients is limited to 2^n and the following properties are satisfied:

   - If $R_j + R_{ij} = 2^n$, then $f(x_i = 0) = x_j$.
   - If $R_j + R_{ij} = -2^n$, then $f(x_i = 0) = \bar{x}_j$.
   - If $R_j - R_{ij} = 2^n$, then $f(x_i = 1) = x_j$.
   - If $R_j - R_{ij} = -2^n$ then $f(x_i = 1) = \bar{x}_j$.

Table 1. Rules for reversible synthesis

	Condition	Property	Template	Residual fun.
1.	$R_0 = 2^n$	$f(x) = 0$	Template 1.	None
2.	$R_0 = -2^n$	$f(x) = 1$	Template 2.	None
3.	$R_i = 2^n$	$f(x) = x_i$	Template 3.	None
4.	$R_i = -2^n$	$f(x) = \bar{x}_i$	Template 4.	None
5.	$R_{i_1 i_2 \ldots i_k} = 2^n$	$f(x) = x_{i_1} \oplus x_{i_2} \cdots \oplus x_{i_k}$	Template 5.	None
6.	$R_{i_1 i_2 \ldots i_k} = -2^n$	$f(x) = \overline{x_{i_1} \oplus x_{i_2} \cdots \oplus x_{i_k}}$	Template 6.	None
7.	$R_0 + R_i = 2^n$	$f(x_i = 0) = 0$	Template 7.	$f(x_i = 1)$
8.	$R_0 + R_i = -2^n$	$f(x_i = 0) = 1$	Template 8.	$f(x_i = 1)$
9.	$R_0 - R_i = 2^n$	$f(x_i = 1) = 0$	Template 9.	$f(x_i = 0)$
10.	$R_0 - R_i = -2^n$	$f(x_i = 1) = 1$	Template 10	$f(x_i = 0)$
11.	$R_j + R_{ij} = 2^n$	$f(x_i = 0) = x_j$	Template 11.	$f(x_i = 1)$
12.	$R_j + R_{ij} = -2^n$	$f(x_i = 0) = \bar{x}_j$	Template 12.	$f(x_i = 1)$
13.	$R_j - R_{ij} = 2^n$	$f(x_i = 1) = x_j$	Template 13.	$f(x_i = 0)$
14.	$R_j - R_{ij} = -2^n$	$f(x_i = 1) = \bar{x}_j$	Template 14.	$f(x_i = 0)$
15.	For $R_i = R_{max}$		Template 15.	$f(x_i = 0)$ and $f(x_i = 1)$

3   Algorithm for Reversible Cascade Synthesis

Similar as for the algorithm presented in [1], if the function to be realized possesses some characteristic properties, a part of the reversible cascade is generated, and the procedure is continued by realizing the residual functions. The algorithm for the synthesis consists of the following steps:

Algorithm

1. *Input: The Walsh-Hademard spectrum* $\mathbf{R} = [R_0, R_n, R_{n-1}, \cdots R_{12 \cdots n}]^T$ *of the function* $f(x_1, x_2, \ldots, x_n)$.
2. *Output: The reversible cascade.*
3. *Step 1.* Find R_{max} - the coefficient with the maximum absolute value.
4. *Step 2.* If $|R_{max}| = 2^n$, find which of the conditions 1 to 6 in Table 1 is satisfied. Realize a part of the cascade by using the corresponding template, end go to *end*, else go to *Step 3*.
5. *Step 3.* If one of the conditions from 7 to 14 in Table 1 is satisfied, use the corresponding template to realize a part of the cascade, and go to *Step 5*, else go to *Step 4*.
6. *Step 4.* Realize a part of the cascade by using the template for the condition 15 in Table 1, and go to *Step 5*.
7. *Step 5.* Calculate spectra of the residual functions, and repeat the procedure for these spectra.
8. *end*

In this approach, the calculation of the Walsh-Hadamard spectrum is done trough the BDD for the initial function f, while the residual spectra are calculated by transforming the decision diagram representing the Walsh-Hadamard

Table 2. Templates for reversible synthesis

Rule	Template	Rule	Template	Rule	Template
1.	$0 \quad\quad f$	2.	$1 \quad\quad f$	3.	$x_i \quad\quad f$
4.	1, $x_i \oplus x_i$, f	5.	0, x_{i_1}, x_{i_2}, $\vdots$, x_{i_k} → f, x_{i_1}, x_{i_2}, x_{i_k}	6.	1, x_{i_1}, x_{i_2}, $\vdots$, x_{i_k} → f, x_{i_1}, x_{i_2}, x_{i_k}
7.	0, x_i, $f(x_i{=}1)$ → f, x_i, $f(x_i{=}1)$	8.	1, x_i, $f(x_i{=}1)$ → f, x_i, $f(x_i{=}1)$	9.	0, x_i, $f(x_i{=}0)$ → f, x_i, $f(x_i{=}0)$
10.	0, x_i, $f(x_i{=}0)$ → f, x_i, $f(x_i{=}0)$	11.	0, x_i, x_j, $f(x_i{=}1)$ → f, x_i, x_j, $f(x_i{=}1)$	12.	0, x_i, x_j, $f(x_i{=}1)$ → f, x_i, x_j, $f(x_i{=}1)$
13.	0, x_i, x_i, $f(x_i{=}0)$ → f, x_i, x_i, $f(x_i{=}0)$	14.	0, x_i, x_i, $f(x_i{=}0)$ → f, x_i, x_i, $f(x_i{=}0)$	15.	0, x_i, $f(x_i{=}0)$, $f(x_i{=}1)$ → f, x_i, $f(x_i{=}0)$, $f(x_i{=}1)$

spectrum of f. It is possible to include some optimization rules in the proposed algorithm. Some of the possible rules are shown in Table 3.

4   Illustrative Example

For an illustration of the algorithm, consider a function $f(x_1, x_2, x_3, x_4)$ defined by the truth-vector: $\mathbf{F} = [1,1,1,1,1,1,0,1,0,0,1,1,0,0,1,1]^T$. In the $(1,-1)$ coding the truth-vector of f is

$$\mathbf{F} = [-1,-1,-1,-1,-1,-1,1,-1,1,1,-1,-1,1,1,-1,-1]^T.$$

The Walsh-Hadamard spectrum of f, defined as $\mathbf{R}(4) = \mathbf{W}(4)\mathbf{F}$, is

$$\mathbf{R}(4) = [R_0, R_4, R_3, R_{34}, R_2, R_{24}, R_{23}, R_{234}, R_1, R_{14}, R_{13},$$
$$R_{134}, R_{12}, R_{124}, R_{123}, R_{1234}]^T$$
$$= [-6, 2, 6, -2, -2, -2, 2, 2, -6, 2, -10, -2, -2, -2, 2, 2]^T.$$

Since $R_3 - R_{13} = 16$ the following holds: $f(x_1 = 1) = x_3$, and it is possible to realize a part of the function f by using the template from the row 13 in Table 1, as shown in Fig 1, with the residual function $f'(x_2, x_3, x_4) = f(x_1 = 0)$.

We calculate the Walsh-Hadamard spectrum of the residual function f' from the spectrum of the function f by using the following relation:

$$\mathbf{R}' = \frac{1}{2}([\,1\ 1\,] \otimes \mathbf{I}(3))$$

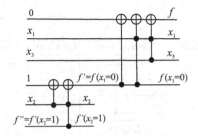

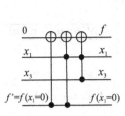

Fig. 1. The first step   **Fig. 2.** The second step

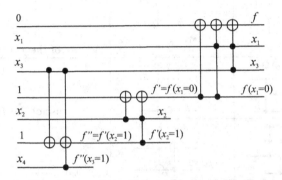

Fig. 3. The reversible cascade realizing the function f

where $\mathbf{I}(3)$ is the $(2^3 \times 2^3)$ identity matrix. The spectrum $\mathbf{R}'$ for f' is:

$$\mathbf{R}'(3) = [R'_0, R'_4, R'_3, R'_{34}, R'_2, R'_{24}, R'_{23}, R'_{234}]^T = [-6, 2, -2, -2, -2, -2, 2, 2]^T.$$

Since $R'_0 + R'_2 = -8$, the following holds: $f'(x_2 = 0) = 1$ and it is possible to use the template from the row 8 in Table 1 as shown in Fig. 2.

After this step, the residual function is $f''(x_3, x_4) = f'(x_2 = 1)$. The Walsh-Hadamard spectrum of f'', calculated from the spectrum $\mathbf{R}'$ is:

$$\mathbf{R}''(2) = [R''_0, R''_4, R''_3, R''_{34}]^T = [-2, 2, -2, -2]^T.$$

Since $R''_0 + R''_3 = -4$, the following holds: $f''(x_3 = 0) = 1$ and it is possible to use again the template from the row 8 in Table 1. After this step, the residual function is $f'''(x_4) = f''(x_3 = 1)$, and its Walsh-Hadamard spectrum is:

$$\mathbf{R}'''(2) = [R'''_0, R'''_4]^T = [0, 2]^T,$$

from where it follows $f'''(x_4) = x_4$. The final reversible cascade for the function f is shown in Fig. 3.

5   Experimental Results

Table 4 presents experimental results for a set of reversible functions from REVLib. The third and fourth column show results obtained by the algorithm

Table 3. Optimized templates

Rule	Template	Optimized template	Optimization rule
5.			Last use of the x_{i_l}
10.			Last use of the $f(x_i = 0)$
11.			Last use of the $f(x_i = 1)$ and x_j
12.			Last use of the $f(x_i = 1)$
13.			Last use of the $f(x_i = 0)$ and x_j
14.			Last use of the $f(x_i = 0)$
15.			Last use of the $f(x_i = 0)$ and $f(x_i = 1)$

proposed in [1], while the fifth and sixth column show results for the algorithm in this paper.

The proposed algorithm, can be used for reversible synthesis for realization of non-reversible functions with cascades of reversible gates. The experimental results for a set of mcnc benchmark functions are shown in Table 5.

Table 4. Experimental results for reversible functions from REVLib

Function	In/Out	Lines	Gates	Lines	Gates
3_17_6	3	10	20	5	9
4_49_7	4	18	45	19	40
4mod5_8	4/1	9	13	7	7
aj-e11_81	4	19	45	15	30
alu_9	5/1	14	29	13	22
dec24-enab_32	3/4	9	9	9	9
decod24_10	2/4	7	7	7	7
ex-1_82	3	8	13	5	6
fredkin_3	3	5	6	4	5
graycode6_11	6	16	20	6	5
ham3_28	3	10	18	7	12
ham7_29	7	36	88	26	73
hwb5_13	5	32	91	40	109
hwb6_14	6	53	167	77	239
hwb7_15	7	84	284	153	512
hwb8_64	8	129	456	240	903
miller_5	3	8	15	10	19
mini-alu_84	4/2	11	20	10	12
mod5d2_17	5	19	42	13	22
one-two-three_27	10	14	16	3	5
peres_4	3	7	9	4	5
rd32_19	3/2	8	15	5	8
rd53_68	5/3	20	49	19	40
rd73_69	7/3	38	105	45	120
rd84_70	8/4	52	140	69	192
sym6_63	6/1	17	34	19	38
sym9_71	9/1	35	79	42	102

Table 5. Experimental results for mcnc benchmark functions

function	in/out	Lines	Gates	Lines	Gates
9sym	9/1	35	79	42	102
Bw	5/28	97	286	103	258
Clip	9/5	172	597	141	436
Cordic	23/2	76	177	76	173
Ex5p	8/63	276	680	334	765
Pdc	16/40	648	2074	493	1195
Rd84	8/4	50	138	69	192
Spla	16/46	567	1422	609	1318
Sqrt8	8/4	32	84	30	65
Table3	14/14	689	2143	1340	3056
Xor5	5/1	10	19	5	4

6 Conclusion

The paper presents a method for the iterative synthesis of reversible cascade by considering properties of the function to be realized in the Walsh-Hadamard domain. The method can be viewed as an extension to reversible synthesis of the method for realization of Maitra cascades proposed in [3]. As in the case of the BDD synthesis approach proposed in [1] and [2], we use BDDs to represent the functions and its Walsh-Hadamard spectrum. Furthermore, all the computations required in the algorithm are preformed over the corresponding BDDs. Due to this, the proposed method can be used for reversible synthesis of Boolean functions of a large number of variables.

Advantages of the proposed method can be summarized as follows:

1. The optimization of the reversible network is done as a part of the synthesis algorithm.
2. The order of variables in BDDs is automatically defined by the values of the spectral coefficients.
3. The produced reversible networks can be additionally simplified by:
   (1) Deleting of unused lines. (2) Usage of shared nodes in BDDs. (3) Usage of the higher order coefficients.

Acknowledgement. This paper is realized as part of the Project No: 174026, supported by Ministry of Science, Republic of Serbia.

References

1. Wille, R., Drechsler, R.: BDD-based synthesis of reversible logic for large functions. In: Design Automation Conf. (2009)
2. Wille, R., Drechsler, R.: Effect of BDD Optimization on Synthesis of Reversible and Quantum Logic. Electronic Notes in Theoretical Computer Science (253), 57–70 (2010)
3. Stanković, M., Tišić, Ž., Nikolić, S.: Synthesis of Maitra cascades by means of spectral coefficients. In: IEEE Proceedings of Computers and Digital Techniques, vol. 130(4), pp. 101–108 (1983)

Performance Analysis of Error-Correcting Binary Decision Diagrams

Helena Astola, Stanislav Stanković, and Jaakko T. Astola

Dept. of Signal Processing, Tampere University of Technology,
FI-33101 Tampere, Finland

Abstract. Decision diagrams are an efficient way of representing switching functions and they are easily mapped to technology. A layout of a circuit is directly determined by the shape and the complexity of the decision diagram. By combining the theory of error-correcting codes with decision diagrams, it is possible to form robust circuit layouts, which can detect and correct errors. The method of constructing robust decision diagrams is analogous to the decoding process of linear codes, and is based on simple matrix and look-up operations. In this paper, the performance of robust binary decision diagrams is analyzed by determining the error probabilities for such constructions. Depending on the error-correcting properties of the code used in the construction, the error probability of a circuit can be significantly decreased by a robust decision diagram.

1 Introduction

Binary decision diagrams (BDDs) are an efficient way to represent discrete functions and they have many applications in logic design, e.g. in logic circuit minimization [2] and probabilistic analysis of digital circuits [13]. The idea of representing switching circuits using reduced BDDs was formalized by Bryant in [5], and the topic has been further explored by numerous authors. BDDs are easily mapped to technology, since the layout of a circuit is directly determined by the shape of the decision diagram and the complexity of the decision diagram determines the complexity of the final design. Decision diagrams are used for representing both binary and multiple-valued functions [4].

There are several techniques for providing tolerance against hardware component failures, the most well-known being triple modular redundancy (TMR), for which the groundwork was laid in [12]. In the TMR technique, each module of a non-redundant circuit is simply triplicated, and the output is determined by majority vote. The TMR technique has been studied and improvements have been discussed in several papers, e.g. in [1], [7]. Techniques of increasing fault-tolerance based on error-correcting codes have also been proposed in a number of papers, e.g. the (N, K) concept in [8].

In modern logic circuits, transistors are shrinking so much that even atomic-scale imperfections and variations within each transistor become a problem. This means that in addition to testing and fault detection procedures it is important to have systematic ways to increase fault tolerance already in the representations

R. Moreno-Díaz et al. (Eds.): EUROCAST 2011, Part II, LNCS 6928, pp. 319–326, 2012.

of switching functions. In [3], an approach for generating robust circuits using decision diagrams and codes was introduced. When combining decision diagrams with the theory of error-correcting codes, it is possible to form robust decision diagrams that are able to correct decision errors. The application of linear codes in decision diagrams is basically another way of representing a code, which gives robust diagrams, capable of correcting decision errors.

In Section 2 we recall the basic definitions for BDDs and error-correcting codes. In section 3 we explain the application of error-correcting codes for generating robust decision diagrams. To analyze the performance of error-correcting decision diagrams, the probabilities of incorrect outputs are computed for the examples given in Section 3 and compared with the error probabilities of traditional decision diagrams.

2   Definitions

BDDs are used to represent switching functions, i.e. functions of the form $\{0,1\}^n \rightarrow \{0,1\}$. We define BDDs using binary decision trees (BDTs), which are graphic representations of functions in the complete disjunctive normal form. For basic concepts and properties related to decision diagrams, we refer to [4], [11].

Definition 1. *A BDT is a rooted directed graph having $n+1$ levels with two different types of vertices. On levels 1 to n are the non-terminal nodes, each having two outgoing edges labeled by 0 or 1. On level $n+1$ are the terminal nodes having the label 0 or 1 and no outgoing edges.*

A BDT has a direct correspondence to the truth-table of a function. Let $f(x_1, x_2, \ldots, x_n)$ be a switching function. In the BDT of f, each node on level i corresponds to a specific variable x_i, and by following the edges the value of the function at $(x_1, x_2, \ldots, x_n)$ is found in the terminal node.

Definition 2. *A BDD is a rooted directed graph obtained from a BDT by the following reduction rules:*

1. *If two sub-graphs represent the same function, delete one, and connect the edge pointing to its root to the remaining subgraph.*
2. *If both edges of a node point to the same sub-graph, delete that node, and directly connect its edge to the sub-graph.*

The number of terminal nodes in BDDs is not limited to two nodes. Such decision diagrams are called multiterminal decision diagrams and are to represent functions with an image set having more than two elements [6]. When dealing with multi-output functions or systems of functions, we can use multiterminal decision diagrams where terminal nodes are labeled by output values.

Recall that $\mathbb{F}_2^n$ is a linear (vector) space over the field $\mathbb{F}_2$, i.e. the set $\{(x_1, x_2, \ldots, x_n) \mid x_i \in \mathbb{F}_2\}$ with vector addition and scalar multiplication satisfying the vector space axioms. In the following, for general properties of codes we refer to [9], [10].

Definition 3. *A binary code C is a subset of $\mathbb{F}_2^n$. C is called a linear code if C is a linear subspace of $\mathbb{F}_2^n$.*

The elements of C are called *codewords*. A linear code C of dimension $k \leq n$ is spanned by k linearly independent vectors of C. A matrix $\mathbf{G}$ having as rows any such k linearly independent vectors is called a *generator matrix* of the code C. If a code has length n and dimension k it is called an (n, k) code.

The code C of dimension k can equivalently be specified by listing $n - k$ linearly independent vectors of $C^\perp$, where $C^\perp$ is the subset of $\mathbb{F}_2^n$ consisting of all vectors orthogonal to C. Any matrix $\mathbf{H}$ having as rows such $n - k$ linearly independent vectors is called a *parity check matrix* of C.

The code C codes an information word $\mathbf{i} = [i_1, i_2, \dots, i_k]$ to a length n codeword $\mathbf{c} = [c_1, c_2, \dots, c_n]$ by matrix multiplication $\mathbf{c} = \mathbf{i} \cdot \mathbf{G}$. Thus, the code C can be defined as $C = \{\mathbf{iG} \mid \mathbf{i} \in \mathbb{F}_2^k\}$ and equivalently with the parity check matrix $\mathbf{H}$ as $C = \{\mathbf{c} \in \mathbb{F}_2^n \mid \mathbf{cH}^T = 0\}$.

Definition 4. *The Hamming distance $d_H(\mathbf{x}, \mathbf{y})$ of vectors $\mathbf{x}$ and $\mathbf{y}$ of length n is the number of coordinates where $\mathbf{x}$ and $\mathbf{y}$ differ, i.e. $d_H(\mathbf{x}, \mathbf{y}) = |\{i \mid x_i \neq y_i\}|$.*

Definition 5. *A code C is e-error correcting if the minimum Hamming distance between two codewords is $2e + 1$.*

3 Error-Correcting Binary Decision Diagrams

In [3], two methods of constructing robust decision diagrams were introduced. The methods are based on representing functions using error-correcting codes and constructing decision diagrams for these representations. We explain the general construction of robust BDDs and derive the construction of a robust BDD for a specific function using this general construction.

We define a robust BDD for binary functions with k variables without specifying the particular function. Consider an (n, k) error-correcting code. The idea is to map an arbitrary function $f(x_1, x_2, \dots, x_k)$ to a function $g(y_1, y_2, \dots, y_n)$ of a larger domain using error-correcting codes with parameters (n, k) and having the minimum distance $2e + 1$. This way we obtain a redundant representation for all binary functions of k variables, from which we construct a reduced BDD. This BDD will be the robust decision diagram of the k-variable binary functions.

The procedure begins by determining an (n, k)-code with minimum distance $2e + 1$ and its generator matrix $\mathbf{G}$. Then, the function $g(\mathbf{y})$ is defined as

$$g(\mathbf{y}) = \begin{cases} f(\mathbf{x}) & \text{if } d_H = (\mathbf{y}, \mathbf{xG}) \leq e \\ * & \text{otherwise.} \end{cases} \tag{1}$$

In other words, each $\mathbf{xG}$ and the vectors $\mathbf{y} \in \mathbb{F}_2^n$ within distance e from $\mathbf{xG}$ are assigned to the symbolic value $\mathbf{x}$. The vectors $\mathbf{y} \in \mathbb{F}_2^n$ at distance $> e$ from all the codewords are assigned to the label $*$. The symbol $*$ can be some arbitrary value, which can be defined in some suitable way. The function now behaves as the decoding algorithm of the code C, i.e. the vectors of $\mathbb{F}_2^n$ within distance e from a codeword $\mathbf{xG}$ are interpreted as the codeword itself when determining the function value. This is just the decoding process, where each received n-ary sequence is interpreted as the codeword within distance e from the received sequence. If the label $*$ is obtained, then more than e decision errors have been made indicating at least $e+1$ faults in the corresponding circuit.

Then the multiterminal decision tree having 2^n terminal nodes for the function g is constructed, and the obtained tree is reduced. After reducing, we have a diagram with 2^k+1 terminal nodes labeled by $f(\mathbf{x})$, $\mathbf{x} \in \mathbb{F}_2^k$ and $*$. This diagram can correct e-bit errors, since the correct function value is obtained even if a decision error occurs in $\leq e$ nodes of the diagram.

From the obtained reduced decision diagram we get a robust BDD of a specific function f by replacing the labels $f(\mathbf{x})$ by the actual values of the function f and reducing the diagram with respect to that function. This diagram will then give a robust layout for a circuit realizing the desired function of k variables.

For example, let C be a $(5,2)$-code defined by the generator matrix $\mathbf{G}$ and having the parity check matrix $\mathbf{H}$:

$$\mathbf{G} = \begin{bmatrix} 1 & 0 & 1 & 1 & 0 \\ 0 & 1 & 1 & 0 & 1 \end{bmatrix}, \ \mathbf{H} = \begin{bmatrix} 1 & 0 & 0 & 1 & 1 \\ 0 & 1 & 0 & 1 & 0 \\ 0 & 0 & 1 & 0 & 1 \end{bmatrix}.$$

Since the sum of no two columns of $\mathbf{H}$ is zero, the code has minimum distance 3 and corrects 1-bit errors. Using C, we can construct the robust decision diagram for binary 2-variable functions. Take all $\mathbf{x} \in \mathbb{F}_2^2$ and for each, compute the codeword $\mathbf{c} = \mathbf{x} \cdot \mathbf{G}$, where $\mathbf{G}$ is the generator matrix of C. To obtain g, map each of the codewords to the label $f(\mathbf{x})$. For example, $[0,1] \cdot \mathbf{G} = [0,1,1,0,1]$ is mapped to $f(0,1)$. Then, for each $\mathbf{c}$, map all the vectors $\mathbf{y} \in \mathbb{F}_2^5$ within distance 1 from $\mathbf{c} = \mathbf{xG}$ to the corresponding $f(\mathbf{x})$. The vectors $\mathbf{y} \in \mathbb{F}_2^5$ at distance > 1 from all the codewords are mapped to $*$. The MTBDD for g can be constructed and reduced to obtain the robust BDD for all 2-variable functions (Figure 1a). To get the MTBDD of a specific binary function, replace the labels $f(\mathbf{x})$ with the actual value of the function and reduce.

By using the one error correcting $(3,1)$ repetition code, we get a robust structure for a single node. This construction will have no terminal nodes labeled as $*$, since every possible sequence is always decoded to either the value 0 or 1 by majority-vote decoding, i.e., every 3-bit sequence is always at a distance ≤ 1 from the sequence 000 or 111. Using this code leads to replacing a single non-terminal node by a BDD of 4 non-terminal nodes (Figure 1b). This example is in principle similar to the TMR technique, but will produce a different circuit layout. The key difference is that once we have reduced the decision diagram, the majority vote property is already included in the structure, i.e. no voters are needed in the circuit level implementation.

The $(5,1)$ repetition code is two error correcting, and may also be used for generating a robust structure for a single node. Using a larger code increases the robustness, but consequently the complexity of the robust BDD is higher (Figure 1c).

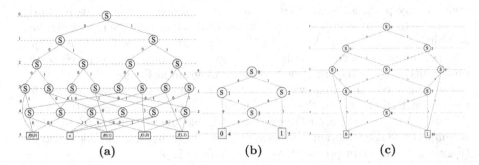

Fig. 1. A robust MTBDD for 2-variable functions (a) and robust BDDs for a single node using (3,1) and (5,1) repetition codes

4 Fault-Tolerance Analysis

In this section, the performance of robust BDDs is analyzed by determining the error probabilities for these constructions. We start by analyzing the examples given in section 3, and give an upper bound for the error probability of any robust BDD.

Denote by p the probability of an incorrect decision in a node and assume that they are independent. We call decision nodes, which make an incorrect decision, as faulty nodes. For traditional BDDs, an incorrect output is obtained whenever there is a faulty node on a path. For robust decision diagrams, there may be up to e faulty nodes on a path, and the output is still correct.

For computing the probability of a correct output, we use a brute force method to list all the combinations of nodes, for which there are up to e faulty nodes on any path. It is clear that if there are no faulty nodes in the whole diagram, we may write the output probability as

$$P\{\text{output correct for any input}\} = (1 - p)^n,$$

where n is the total number of nodes in the diagram. This gives the first term of the probability function for a correct output. Also, the following $e - 1$ terms of the function are given by the binomial expansion, i.e., $np(1-p)^{n-1}, \ldots, \binom{n}{e}p^e(1-p)^{n-e}$. The rest of the terms depend on e and the structure of the diagram. It follows, that the error probability of a robust construction is

$$P\{\text{incorrect output}\} = 1 - \left(\sum_{k=0}^{e} \binom{n}{k} p^k (1 - p)^{n-k} + \cdots \right),$$

which gives an expansion having a lowest degree term $A \cdot p^{e+1}$, where A is some constant. For a traditional diagram, since a single incorrect decision causes an incorrect output, the lowest degree term of the error probability function is always $B \cdot p$, where B is some constant.

Consider the robust BDD for a single node by the $(3, 1)$ repetition code (Figure 1b). We want to list all the possible cases for which there is at most one faulty node on any path, following that the output is always correct. This is clearly $((1-p)^4+4p(1-p)^3+p^2(1-p)^2)$, where the probability that the robust diagram is faulty is $1 - ((1-p)^4 + 4p(1-p)^3 + p^2(1-p)^2) = \tilde{p} = 5p^2 - 6p^3 + 2p^4$. The probability of a correct output $1 - \tilde{p}$ given any input is compared to the probability $1 - p$ of the single node decision diagram in Figure 2a.

By similar computations, we obtain the probability of a correct output for the robust BDD based on the $(5,1)$ repetition code, which corrects two errors (Figure 2b), and for the robust design for 2-variable functions in Figure 1a, which is compared to the traditional decision diagram for realizing 2-variable functions (Figure 2c). The error probability of a single node is p.

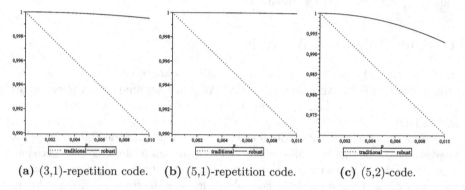

(a) $(3,1)$-repetition code.   (b) $(5,1)$-repetition code.   (c) $(5,2)$-code.

Fig. 2. Probabilities of a correct output for traditional and robust diagrams

Instead of mapping a function into a robust one by some error-correcting code, we may replace the nodes of the corresponding diagram by robust structures to obtain a robust representation for the given function. We may also replace just some of the nodes by robust structures, if it is reasonable to assume that in some parts of the circuit, errors are more likely than in others. Consider a decision diagram for some binary function f, which has k nodes in its reduced BDD. The error probability function for this diagram is $1 - (1-p)^k$. We may replace each node by the robust construction generated using the $(3,1)$-repetition code. The resulting diagram will have $4k$ nodes in total and the error probability function $1 - (1-\tilde{p})^k$. In Figure 3, the probability of a correct output of a diagram with $k = 50$ nodes is compared to the probability of a correct output of a diagram representing the same function, for which each node is replaced by the robust structure of $(3,1)$-repetition code.

Computing the exact probability of a correct output is time-consuming, but we may approximate this probability by estimating the higher order coefficients of the probability function by exploiting the structure of the general robust diagram. Since the generating matrix of a binary linear code can always be written in systematic form, the resulting robust BDD of arbitrary k-ary functions typically has a binary tree structure on levels 0 to $k+1$. To estimate the probability

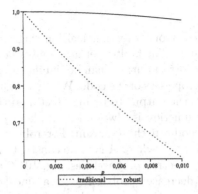

Fig. 3. The correct output probabilities of traditional BDD of $k = 50$ nodes and robust BDD with nodes replaced by the robust structures using (3,1) code

of a correct output of any robust BDD, form the first e terms using the binomial expansion and approximate the higher order coefficients by the coefficients of the probability function of the binary tree of depth $k + 1$.

Approximating only the coefficients instead of the complete terms of the polynomial of the general robust BDD ensures that the approximated coefficient will always be less or equal to the corresponding coefficient in the exact probability. Since the binary tree part of the diagram is strictly included in the whole diagram, considering faulty nodes in the binary tree part only cannot provide more allowed combinations of faulty nodes than the whole diagram.

Let n be the depth of the tree, e the number of allowed faulty nodes on a path, and r the number of faulty nodes in the whole tree. Let $S(n, e, r)$ be the number of full binary trees having r faulty nodes and up to e of them on each path. When $n = 0$, $S(n, e, r) = 1$ if $r \le e \le 1$ and 0 otherwise. When $e = 0$, $S(n, e, r) = 1$ if $r = 0$ and 0 otherwise. When $r = 0$, $S(n, e, r) = 1$. We may compute $S(n, e, r)$ for $n, e, r \ge 1$ recursively as follows:

$$S(n, e, r) = \sum_{t=0}^{r} S(n - 1, e, t)S(n - 1, e, r - t)$$

$$+ \sum_{t=0}^{r-1} S(n - 1, e - 1, t)S(n - 1, e - 1, r - 1 - t).$$

The formula is derived starting from the root of the tree, to which we add children nodes. The first convolution takes into account the parent not being faulty and the second takes into account a faulty parent node, hence we must subtract 1 from e and r. The initial values guarantee that the recursion is well-defined and stops when we reach the root node.

Now, we may approximate A of the term $Ap^r(1 - p)^{m-r}$ where m is the number of nodes in the general robust BDD by $S(n, e, r)$ of the term $S(n, e, r)p^r(1-p)^{2^n-1-r}$, where n is the depth of the binary tree and $m > 2^n - 1$.

5 Conclusions

In this paper we discussed error-correcting decision diagrams for binary logic and analyzed their performance. The fault-tolerance analysis of robust BDDs shows, that the probability of incorrect outputs can be significantly decreased depending on the error-correcting properties of the code. With traditional diagrams, a single incorrect decision causes the output to be incorrect, and the lowest degree term of the error probability function is always a multiple of p, where p is the error probability of a single node in the diagram. For robust diagrams, the lowest degree term is always $A \cdot p^{e+1}$, where A is some constant. This means, that even with moderately high gate error probabilities, e.g, 10^{-3}, a robust construction will have a significantly decreased probability for an incorrect output. However, better error-correcting properties increase the complexity of the design.

References

1. Abraham, J., Siewiorek, D.: An algorithm for the accurate reliability evaluation of triple modular redundancy networks. IEEE Transactions on Computers 23, 682–692 (1974)
2. Akers, S.B.: Binary decision diagrams. IEEE Trans. Computers C-27(6), 509–516 (1978)
3. Astola, H., Stanković, S., Astola, J.T.: Error correcting decision diagrams. In: Proceedings of The Third Workshop on Information Theoretic Methods in Science and Engineering, Tampere, Finland, August 16-18 (2010)
4. Astola, J.T., Stanković, R.S.: Fundamentals of Switching Theory and Logic Design. Springer, Heidelberg (2006)
5. Bryant, R.E.: Graph-based algorithms for Boolean functions manipulation. IEEE Trans. Computers C-35(8), 667–691 (1986)
6. Clarke, E.M., Fujita, M., Zhao, X.: Multi-terminal decision diagrams and hybrid decision diagrams. In: Sasao, T., Fujita, M. (eds.) Representation of Discrete Functions, pp. 91–108. Kluwer, Dordrecht (1997)
7. van Gils, W.: A triple modular redundancy technique providing multiple-bit error protection without using extra redundancy. IEEE Transactions on Computers 35, 623–631 (1986)
8. Krol, T.: (N, K) concept fault tolerance. IEEE Trans. Comput. 35, 339–349 (1986)
9. van Lint, J.H.: Introduction to Coding Theory. Springer, New York (1982)
10. MacWilliams, F.J., Sloane, N.J.A.: The Theory of Error-Correcting Codes. North-Holland, Amsterdam (1997)
11. Miller, D.M., Thornton, M.A.: Multiple Valued Logic: Concepts and Representations. Morgan & Claypool, San Francisco (2008)
12. von Neumann, J.: Probabilistic logics and synthesis of reliable organisms from unreliable components. In: Shannon, C., McCarthy, J. (eds.) Automata Studies, pp. 43–98. Princeton University Press, Princeton (1956)
13. Thornton, M.A., Nair, V.S.S.: Efficient calculation of spectral coefficients and their applications. IEEE Trans. Computer-Aided Design of Integrated Circuits and Systems CAD-14(11), 1328–1341 (1995)

Trading-Off Error Detection Efficiency with Implementation Cost for Sequential Circuits Implemented with FPGAs

Grzegorz Borowik and Andrzej Kraśniewski

Institute of Telecommunications,
00-665 Warsaw, Nowowiejska 15/19, Poland
{G.Borowik,andrzej}@tele.pw.edu.pl

Abstract. A number of concurrent error detection (CED) techniques have been proposed to detect transient errors in various types of circuits and systems. The CED techniques for sequential circuits (FSMs) presented in the literature are mostly aimed at implementations based on gates and flip-flops. Recently, a few techniques for circuits implemented using FPGAs have been proposed. Some of these techniques assume that an FSM is implemented using embedded memory blocks. In this paper, we present and compare a number of CED schemes for a specific design of a sequential circuit that includes the address modifier, intended for implementation in an FPGA with embedded memory blocks. The proposed set of CED schemes offers the designer an opportunity to trade-off error detection efficiency with implementation costs (circuitry overhead). In particular, some of the proposed solutions make it possible to achieve a reasonable level of error detection at the expense of less than 15% of circuitry overhead.

Keywords: dependability, concurrent error detection, transient fault, sequential circuit, FPGA, embedded memory block.

1 Introduction

Increased dependability is a highly desirable feature of today's digital circuits and systems. With technology advancements, circuits are becoming more susceptible to faults, especially transient faults [6]. The protection against such faults, in the form of concurrent error detection (CED), is becoming essential for circuits intended not only for critical, but also for less critical applications [5].

A number of CED methods have been proposed for various types of circuits and systems; these include, in particular, techniques for sequential circuits that implement finite state machines (FSMs) and sequential circuits that operate as microprogrammed control units – a short review of such techniques can be found in [4].

Most techniques for synthesis of FSMs with concurrent error detection presented in the literature are intended for circuits implemented with gates and flip-flops. Today, however, a large percentage of sequential circuits are implemented

R. Moreno-Díaz et al. (Eds.): EUROCAST 2011, Part II, LNCS 6928, pp. 327–334, 2012.

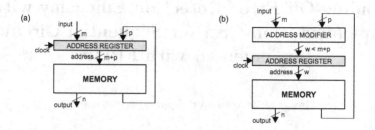

Fig. 1. Considered classes of sequential circuits: simple ROM-based implementation (a), ROM-based implementation with an address modifier (b)

using LUT-based FPGAs with embedded memory blocks (EMBs). As EMBs are more susceptible to transient faults than logic components, the development of CED schemes for sequential circuits implemented using EMBs available in FPGAs is essential.

CED schemes for sequential circuits implemented using FPGAs with embedded memory blocks were presented for a simple ROM-based implementation in which the whole combinational section of the circuit is located in the memory (Fig. 1a) [3] and for a ROM-based implementation with an address modifier (Fig. 1b) [4]. The proposed solutions were proven to guarantee on-line detection of all permanent and transient faults that affect a single input or output of any component of the circuit. Such faults are detected with a maximum latency of one clock cycle at no or negligible performance penalty and low circuitry overhead (compared to the earlier presented CED schemes for circuits implemented with gates and flip-flops).

In this paper, we show how to modify – in a variety of ways – the CED scheme for a ROM-based implementation of an FSM that includes the address modifier, so that to reduce its cost (circuitry overhead). The least expensive of the presented solutions are consistent with an idea of a "pragmatic approach" to CED, i.e. offer a reasonable error coverage at the expense of around 10% of circuitry overhead [1].

2   New CED Schemes

To define new CED schemes for a sequential circuit implemented using an FPGA with EMBs, we recall the scheme shown in Fig. 2, described in detail in [4]. In this scheme, the following error detection mechanisms are employed:

- parity checking for memory addresses – for both memory H and G; these mechanisms are denoted as CAH and CAG, respectively;
- checking of address legality – for both memory H and G; these mechanisms are denoted as CLH and CLG, respectively;
- parity checking for output; this mechanism is denoted as CY.

As an alternative to CAH and CAG, we can consider parity checking for the next state part of memory addresses only – for both memory H and G, including

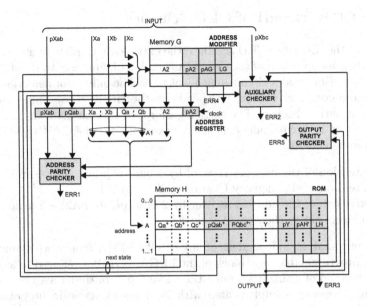

Fig. 2. CED scheme for a sequential circuit implemented using an FPGA

part A2 of memory H address (for both memories, a part of address driven by the circuit input is unprotected); these mechanisms are denoted as CAH(Q) and CAG(Q), respectively.

The various combinations of the above discussed mechanisms result in different CED schemes. The 16 CED schemes examined in this paper, denoted CED-0, ..., CED-15, are defined in Table 1. For example, CED-0 is the reference scheme shown in Fig. 2, whereas in scheme CED-8 only the parity of address for memory H is checked along with the legality of the address in memory G (there is no checking of parity of address for memory H and no checking of the output of the circuit).

Table 1. Definition of CED schemes

	CAH	CAG	CAH(Q)+CAG(Q)	CLH	CLG	CY
CED-0	+	+	-	+	+	+
CED-1	+	+	-	+	+	-
CED-2	+	+	-	-	-	+
CED-3	+	+	-	-	-	-
CED-4	+	-	-	+	+	+
CED-5	+	-	-	+	+	-
CED-6	+	-	-	-	-	+
CED-7	+	-	-	-	-	-
CED-8	+	-	-	-	+	+
CED-9	+	-	-	-	+	-
CED-10	-	-	+	+	+	+
CED-11	-	-	+	+	+	-
CED-12	-	-	+	-	-	+
CED-13	-	-	+	-	-	-
CED-14	-	-	-	+	+	+
CED-15	-	-	-	+	+	-

3 Cost (Overhead) of CED Schemes

For each of the discussed CED schemes, the extra logic consists of a part whose complexity is independent of the circuit (its number of inputs, outputs, states and FSM specification) and a circuit-dependent part. The only error detection mechanism whose complexity directly depends on the circuit to be implemented is CY (output parity checker). The extra logic for the other mechanisms in the proposed schemes is circuit-independent. For example, for the CAH(Q)+CAG(Q) mechanism it includes:

- an extension of the memory H word by 3 bits (pQab+, pQbc+, pA'),
- an extension of the memory G word by 1 bit (pA2),
- an extension of the address register by 2 bits (pQab, pA2) – 2 logic cells,
- the address parity checker – 1 logic cell.

To make our analysis independent of any specific FPGA family, we assume that the basic programmable logic block of the FPGA, hereafter referred to as a logic cell, is composed of a single 4-input LUT and a flip-flop. Under assumption that the address register is implemented with flip-flops available in programmable logic blocks, the address parity checker requires one extra logic cell. The auxiliary checker requires one extra logic cell in the case of CAG and no extra logic cells in the case of CAG(Q), and each extra bit of the address register also requires one extra logic cell.

4 Efficiency of Error Detection

We consider single-bit faults, i.e. faults that produce – in some clock cycle – an incorrect logic value at the input or output of some component of the circuit, eventually leading to an incorrect state transition. These single-bit faults may result from permanent defects or transient phenomena, such as single-event upsets (SEUs).

We define several classes of single-bit faults, affecting inputs and outputs of components comprising the functional part of the circuit of Fig. 2:

- FQa: faults associated with part Qa of the state,
- FQb: faults associated with part Qb of the state,
- FQc: faults associated with part Qc of the state,
- FXa: faults associated with part Xa of the input,
- FXb: faults associated with part Xb of the input,
- FXc: faults associated with part Xc of the input,
- FA2: faults associated with the output of the address modifier,
- FY: faults associated with the output of the circuit.

In fault class FQb (FXb respectively), the following disjoint subclasses are defined:

Table 2. Detection of various classes of faults by the proposed CED schemes

	FQa	FQb	FQc	FXa	FXb	FXc	FA2	FY
CED-0	+	+	+	+	+	+	+	+
CED-1	+	+	+	+	+	+	+	-
CED-2	+	+	+	+	+	+	+	+
CED-3	+	+	+	+	+	+	+	-
CED-4	+	+/-FQbG	+/-	+	+/-FXbG	+/-	+	+
CED-5	+	+/-FQbG	+/-	+	+/-FXbG	+/-	+	-
CED-6	+	+FQbH/-	-	+	+FXbH/-	-	+	+
CED-7	+	+FQbH/-	-	+	+FXbH/-	-	+	-
CED-8	+	+/-FQbG	+/-	+	+/-FXbG	+/-	+	+
CED-9	+	+/-FQbG	+/-	+	+/-FXbG	+/-	+	-
CED-10	+	+	+	+/-	+/-	+/-	+	+
CED-11	+	+	+	+/-	+/-	+/-	+	-
CED-12	+	+	+	-	-	-	+	+
CED-13	+	+	+	-	-	-	+	-
CED-14	+/-	+/-	+/-	+/-	+/-	+/-	+/-	+
CED-15	+/-	+/-	+/-	+/-	+/-	+/-	+/-	-

The symbols in table have the following meaning: '+' – all faults from a given class are detected, '-' – none of faults from a given class is detected, '+/-' – some of faults from a given class are detected.

The symbols in column FQb have the following meaning: '+FQbH/-' – all faults from subclass FQbH are detected and no other faults in class FQb, '+/-FQbG' – all faults from class FQb are detected, except for faults included in FQbG. The similar notation is used in column FXb.

- FQbG (FXbG): faults affecting memory G address,
- FQbH (GXbH): faults affecting memory H address,
- FQbGH (FXbGH): faults affecting both memory G and memory H address.

In Table 2 we show, for each of the proposed CED schemes, which classes of faults are detected. It is a starting point for a procedure that allows one to evaluate, for a given circuit, what fraction of faults in the assumed fault model is detected by a particular CED scheme. The most difficult part of this procedure is the calculation of the probability of producing – as a result of a fault – an illegal memory address which is then detected by checking of address legality (mechanism CLH or CLG).

Assuming that in the FSM specification, inputs are encoded, illegal addresses result, in general, from:

- illegal state codes, i.e. vectors that do not represent any element of the set of states of the FSM (with minimal-length encoding, they occur if the number of states is not equal to 2^p, where p is some natural number);
- legal state and input codes and undefined values of the next state function.

Once the FSM is implemented in the architecture of Fig. 2, the specification of both memory G and memory H is given, and for each of these two memories, one can determine the set of legal memory addresses, ADDR_LEG, and the set of illegal memory addresses, ADDR_ILL.

Let a memory address be represented in binary form as: $addr = a_{k-1} \ldots a_1 a_0$. For any address $addr \in$ ADDR_LEG and any bit position i we define $addr(i^*)$ so that $addr(i^*) = a_{k-1} \ldots a_{i+1} a_i' a_{i-1} \ldots a_0$, where a_i' is the complement of a_i and $0 \leq i \leq k-1$.

Then, the set of legal addresses with an error at position i detectable by the address legality checking mechanism is:

$$DET(i) = \{addr \in ADDR\_LEG \mid addr(i^*) \in ADDR\_ILL\}.$$

Thus, the probability of detecting an error at position i is:

$$pdet(i) = |DET(i)|/|ADDR\_LEG|. \tag{1}$$

The problem of determining the probability of detecting faults in some fault classes becomes slightly more complicated when both CLG and CLH are used.

In that case, the faults in FQc, FXc, FQbG, and FXbG which affect the output of memory G (part A2) may result in an illegal address of memory H which is detected by mechanism CLH. As the exact evaluation of the impact of a possibly incorrect value of A2 on producing an illegal address for memory H requires an examination of all possible combinations at the other subfields of the memory H address (Qa, Qb, Xa, Xb), which is quite computation-intensive, a simplified approach is taken. With this approach, the probability of detecting a single fault in FQc, FXc, FQbG, or FXbG through mechanism CLH is – for each of these faults – calculated as

$$pdet_{CLH} = |ADDR\_ILL(H)|/2^{kH}.$$

where kH is the number of address lines for memory H.

Then, the probability of detecting a fault in FQc, FXc, FQbG, or FXbG that results in an error at position i of memory G address by a "serial" combination of mechanisms CLG and CLH is

$$pdets(i) = pdet_{CLG}(i) + (1 - pdet_{CLG}(i))pdet_{CLH}. \tag{2}$$

Even more complicated is the case of faults in FQbGH and FXbGH where each fault can be detected "in parallel" by mechanism CLG or mechanism CLH. With similar simplifying assumptions as above, the probability of detecting a fault that results in an error at position i of memory G address and the corresponding position j of memory H address by a combination of mechanisms CLG and CLH is

$$pdetp(i \leftrightarrow j) = \max\{pdet_{CLG}(i) + (1 - pdet_{CLG}(i))pdet_{CLH},$$

$$pdet_{CLH}(j) + (1 - pdet_{CLH}(j))pdet_{CLG}(i)\}. \tag{3}$$

5   Experimental Results

The presented results have been obtained using a tool developed based on our proprietary system FSM*dec*, described in [2]. Using this tool, based on the analysis presented in section 4, for selected benchmark FSMs, we have calculated the fault coverage for all the considered CED schemes. The results are presented in Table 3.

Table 3. Fault coverage for CEDs for selected FSM benchmarks

	CED 0,1,2,3	CED 4	CED 5	CED 6	CED 7	CED 8	CED 9	CED 10	CED 11	CED 12	CED 13	CED 14	CED 15
cse	100	85.6	82	73.2	66.7	75.1	68.9	80.9	76.2	74.6	68.4	47.1	34.1
bbsse	100	84.2	80.4	71.8	64.9	76.5	70.8	75.7	69.7	71.8	64.9	44.1	30.4
ex1	100	92.3	88	79.2	67.6	82.9	73.4	82.9	73.4	75.5	61.8	62.2	41.1
ex4	100	92	88.9	71.2	60.4	74.2	64.6	95.3	93.5	78.8	70.8	69.9	58.6
keyb	100	87.8	87	68.1	66.2	68.1	66.2	82.9	81.8	73.9	72.3	57.6	55
mark1	100	91.5	85.9	76.5	61.2	78.1	63.8	95.2	92	87.7	79.6	71.5	52.9
sse	100	84.2	80.4	71.8	64.9	76.5	70.8	75.7	69.7	71.8	64.9	44.1	30.4

Table 4. The CED overhead for selected FSM benchmarks

	CED 0,1	CED 2,3	CED 4	CED 5	CED 6	CED 7	CED 8	CED 9	CED 10	CED 11	CED 12	CED 13	CED 14	CED 15
cse	1/2/5	1/1/5	1/1/3	1/1/3	1/1/3	0/1/3	1/1/3	0/1/3	1/1/3	1/1/3	1/1/3	1/1/3	0/1/0	0/1/0
	137.5	125	120	120	120	20	120	20	120	120	120	120	12.5	12.5
bbsse	1/3/5	1/2/5	1/2/3	1/2/3	1/2/3	0/2/3	1/2/3	0/2/3	1/2/3	1/2/3	1/2/3	1/2/3	0/1/0	0/1/0
	150	137.5	132.5	132.5	132.5	32.5	132.5	32.5	132.5	132.5	132.5	132.5	12.5	12.5
ex1	0/3/5	0/2/5	0/2/3	0/2/3	0/1/3	0/1/3	0/2/3	0/2/3	0/2/3	0/2/3	0/1/3	0/1/3	0/1/0	0/1/0
	50	37.5	32.5	32.5	20	20	32.5	32.5	32.5	32.5	20	20	12.5	12.5
ex4	1/2/5	1/2/5	1/2/3	1/2/3	1/1/3	1/1/3	1/2/3	1/2/3	1/2/3	1/2/3	1/1/3	1/1/3	1/0/0	1/0/0
	50	50	45	45	32.5	32.5	45	45	45	45	32.5	32.5	12.5	12.5
keyb	0/3/5	0/2/5	0/2/3	0/2/3	0/1/3	0/1/3	0/2/3	0/2/3	0/2/3	0/2/3	0/1/3	0/1/3	0/1/0	0/1/0
	50	37.5	32.5	32.5	20	20	32.5	32.5	32.5	32.5	20	20	12.5	12.5
mark1	1/2/5	1/1/5	1/1/3	0/1/3	0/1/3	0/1/3	0/1/3	0/1/3	1/1/3	1/1/3	1/1/3	0/1/3	0/1/0	0/1/0
	50	37.5	32.5	20	20	20	20	20	32.5	32.5	32.5	20	12.5	12.5
sse	1/2/5	1/1/5	1/1/3	1/1/3	1/1/3	0/1/3	1/1/3	0/1/3	1/1/3	1/1/3	1/1/3	1/1/3	0/1/0	0/1/0
	137.5	125	120	120	120	20	120	20	120	120	120	120	12.5	12.5
average	89.29	78.57	73.57	71.79	66.43	23.57	71.79	28.93	73.57	73.57	68.21	66.43	12.5	12.5

In Table 4 the overhead (cost) for each CED scheme is shown in terms of additional EMBs of M512 and M4K, and extra logic cells. For example, 1/2/3 in column 'CED 4' for benchmark 'bbsse' means: one extra M4K EMB, two extra M512 EMBs and 3 extra logic cells. To express the overhead with a single number, we assume that the cost of an M512 (M4K) EMB is equal to the cost of 5 logic cells (40 LCs, respectively). With this assumption, the combined overhead for scheme CED4 applied to circuit 'bbsse' is 137.5%.

In the last row of Table 4 the average combine overhead is shown. It can be seen that for the most complex scheme CED-0 scheme it is only 89.3%, and for the least complex scheme CED-15 – 12.5%.

The proposed set of CED schemes offers the designer an opportunity to trade-off on-line error detection efficiency (fault coverage) and implementation cost (circuitry overhead). This is illustrated in the Figure 3 where two sample examined benchmark circuits are shown.

As shown in Table 4 and Fig. 3, the CED implementation cost depends strongly on the selected CED scheme. This demonstrates that a set of CED schemes (and not a single scheme) is necessary if a strict limit on the cost (overhead) is imposed. Then, the designer has an opportunity to select that CED scheme that maximizes the efficiency of on-line error detection under such cost constraints.

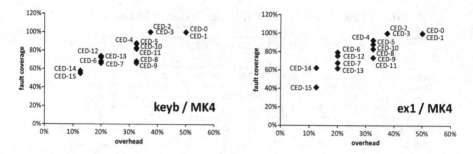

Fig. 3. Trading-off error detection efficiency and implementation cost

6   Conclusion

The presented results show that it is possible to design a low-overhead concurrent error detection scheme for a sequential circuit implemented using an FPGA with embedded memory blocks.

By means of design experiments, we show that – compared to the earlier proposed schemes for concurrent error detection in sequential circuits implemented with gates and flip-flops – the overhead for the proposed solutions intended for FPGA-based implementations can be very low.

The proposed set of CED schemes offers the designer an opportunity to trade-off error detection efficiency and implementation cost (circuitry overhead). For each scheme, both the fault coverage and circuitry overhead can be calculated based exclusively on the characteristics of the FSM and the target FPGA device. This allows the designer to select a solution that best satisfies his/her requirements and constraints, without actually designing the circuit.

References

1. Agarwal, V.: A pragmatic approach to on-line testing. In: Proc. of IEEE International On-Line Testing Symposium (keynote talk), p. 1 (2004)
2. Borowik, G.: Improved state encoding for fsm implementation in FPGA structures with embedded memory blocks. Electronics and Telecommunications Quarterly 54(1), 9–28 (2008)
3. Kraśniewski, A.: Concurrent error detection in sequential circuits implemented using FPGAs with embedded memory blocks. In: Proc. of IEEE International On-Line Testing Symposium, pp. 67–72 (2004)
4. Kraśniewski, A.: Concurrent error detection for finite state machines implemented with embedded memory blocks of SRAM-based FPGAs. Microprocessors & Microsystems 32(5-6), 303–312 (2008)
5. Mohanram, K., Sogomonyan, E.S., Gössel, M., Touba, N.A.: Synthesis of low-cost parity-based partially self-checking circuits. In: Proc. of International On-Line Test Symposium, pp. 35–40 (2003)
6. Nigh, P.: The increasing importance of on-line testing to ensure high-reliability products. In: Proc. of IEEE International Test Conference, p. 1281 (2003)

Method of Generating Irreducible Polynomials over GF(3) on the Basis of Trinomials

Grzegorz Borowik and Andrzej Paszkiewicz

Institute of Telecommunications,
00-665 Warsaw, Nowowiejska 15/19, Poland
{G.Borowik, anpa}@tele.pw.edu.pl

Abstract. The paper presents a concept design of hardware co-processor that could be used to generate irreducible primitive polynomials with coefficients over GF(3). The process of generating a primitive polynomial is done by replicating the other primitive polynomial which is fixed in the device. The implemented algorithm allows the unit to generate all possible primitive polynomials of the same degree as the stored polynomial. This approach allows us to extend the cryptographic power and capabilities of the existing cryptographic devices.

Keywords: irreducible polynomial, primitive polynomial, trinomial, linear feedback shift register, stream cipher.

1 Introduction

Primitive and irreducible polynomials over the finite fields play an important role in the coding theory [7] and cryptography [4,8]. However, in particular sparse polynomials with only a few non-zero coefficients, e.g. trinomials are most commonly used.

The designers often use a primitive polynomial as a basic unit in constructing stream ciphers for implementing linear feedback shift register (LFSR). Since linear feedback shift registers are described by coefficients of primitive polynomials, these polynomials should be treated as the key information. It would be convenient to be able to generate such information directly into the encryption device, e.g. based on the data which sites transmit to each other during the startup of a call. Such a situation is only possible when the algorithm for generating new LFSRs works efficiently.

Although general methods of generating primitive polynomials are known, they are so complex and laborious that computers have to be used when dealing with polynomials of large degrees. It is also very often not possible to store primitive polynomials in memory.

On the other hand, the popularity of irreducible polynomials over GF(2) in cryptography makes LFSRs be mostly described by sparse polynomials of the characteristic 2. Although they benefit from easy hardware implementation and bit vector representation, it is not always possible to find a primitive trinomial of a given degree.

R. Moreno-Díaz et al. (Eds.): EUROCAST 2011, Part II, LNCS 6928, pp. 335–342, 2012.

Then two solutions are possible: using other sparse polynomials, for example pentanomials, over the same field or choosing a new finite field for which irreducible trinomials exist, e.g. GF(3) instead of GF(2). In the former case it has been observed that irreducible pentanomials over GF(2) exist for all degrees between 4 and 30000 [9]. In the latter a hypothesis based on observations has been made that alongside with the increasing order of a finite field characteristic, the number of degrees for which irreducible trinomials exists increases [10].

In this paper, we focus on generating irreducible polynomials from trinomials over GF(3). The proposed method is not computationally complex and yields primitive polynomials which finally generate the feedback polynomials. Since for the ternary field $-1 = 2$, polynomials over GF(3) can be considered as binary polynomials with both positive and negative coefficients. What we need is the representative of the primitive polynomials of a certain degree to be able to generate all the other primitive polynomials of that degree. We assume that due to the need of memorizing a large number of high-degree polynomials/representatives, we are only interested to store polynomials of a small number of non-zero coefficients, i.e. trinomials.

The following aspects motivated the authors to perform the work on a cryptographic co-processor:

- the reliability of the systems designed by us is greater than the use of computing platforms based on commercial operating systems;
- stream ciphers are convenient for implementation in hardware, which explains their use in encryption/description devices;
- generating cryptographically strong primitive polynomials modulo p is not an easy task, however, replacing them in cryptographic devices frequently is preferred;
- designing stream ciphers is older and better mastered than designing block ciphers and therefore it is easier to design a strong cryptographic stream cipher than a block-cipher;
- cryptographically weak primitive polynomials, i.e. of a small number of non-zero coefficients are convenient to be implemented in software but they decrease the resistance of encryption schemes to the correlation attacks.

2   Basics

A trinomial is a polynomial consisting of three non-zero coefficient monomials of different degrees, e.g. $X^7 + 2X^2 + 1$.

A polynomial is called *irreducible* over a finite field if it cannot be factored into nontrivial polynomials over the same field. In other case polynomial is *reducible*; e.g. $X^7 + 2X^2 + 1$ is irreducible over GF(3), while $X^7 + X^2 + 1$ is reducible because $X^7 + X^2 + 1 = (X + 2)^2(X^2 + X + 2)(X^3 + X^2 + 2)$.

A *primitive polynomial* of degree n with coefficients over the field GF(p) is a polynomial such that the simplest monomial X generates all the elements of the extension field GF(p^n).

Example. Let's consider polynomial $f(X) = X^3 + 2X + 1$ over GF(3). Then $\alpha = X$ is a root of the polynomial $f(X)$. Thus, $\alpha^3 = \alpha + 2$ and similarly $\alpha^4 = \alpha^2 + 2\alpha$. All the elements of the extension field GF(3^n) generated by X are given in Table 1.

Table 1. Elements of GF(3^n) generated by X, where $f(X) = X^3 + 2X + 1$

$\alpha^3 = \alpha + 2$	$\alpha^{12} = \alpha^2 + 2$	$\alpha^{21} = \alpha^2 + 1$
$\alpha^4 = \alpha^2 + 2\alpha$	$\alpha^{13} = 2$	$\alpha^{22} = 2\alpha + 2$
$\alpha^5 = 2\alpha^2 + \alpha + 2$	$\alpha^{14} = 2\alpha$	$\alpha^{23} = 2\alpha^2 + 2\alpha$
$\alpha^6 = \alpha^2 + \alpha + 1$	$\alpha^{15} = 2\alpha^2$	$\alpha^{24} = 2\alpha^2 + 2\alpha + 1$
$\alpha^7 = \alpha^2 + 2\alpha + 2$	$\alpha^{16} = 2\alpha + 1$	$\alpha^{25} = 2\alpha^2 + 1$
$\alpha^8 = 2\alpha^2 + 2$	$\alpha^{17} = 2\alpha^2 + \alpha$	$\alpha^{26} = 1 = \alpha^0$
$\alpha^9 = \alpha + 1$	$\alpha^{18} = \alpha^2 + 2\alpha + 1$	$\alpha^1 = \alpha$
$\alpha^{10} = \alpha^2 + \alpha$	$\alpha^{19} = 2\alpha^2 + 2\alpha + 2$	$\alpha^2 = \alpha^2$
$\alpha^{11} = \alpha^2 + \alpha + 2$	$\alpha^{20} = 2\alpha^2 + \alpha + 1$	$\alpha^3 = \alpha + 2$

3   Proposed Scheme

Let $f(X)$ be a primitive polynomial of degree n over GF(p). Then $\alpha = X$ is a root of the polynomial and $\alpha^{p^1}, \alpha^{p^2}, \ldots, \alpha^{p^{n-1}}$ are the other roots of the polynomial.

Let's assume that $\beta = \alpha^k (\mathrm{mod} f(\alpha))$ and find the minimal polynomial of β a primitive element of the finite extension field GF(p^n), where k is an odd number greater than 1 and $\gcd(k, p^n - 1) = 1$. Then the minimal polynomial is a new primitive polynomial of degree n with the following roots:

$$\beta_1 = \alpha^{k \cdot p^0},$$
$$\beta_2 = \alpha^{k \cdot p^1},$$
$$\vdots$$
$$\beta_n = \alpha^{k \cdot p^{n-1}}.$$

Thus, the minimal polynomial $f_\beta(X)$ of the primitive element β is given by the following formula:

$$f_\beta(X) = (X - \beta_1)(X - \beta_2)\ldots(X - \beta_n). \tag{1}$$

Considering that for the ternary field $-1 = 2$, we have $\beta_i' = -\beta_i = 2\beta_i$, thus

$$f_\beta(X) = (X + \beta_1')(X + \beta_2')\ldots(X + \beta_n'). \tag{2}$$

Expanding the right side of the equation 2 we obtain a sum of monomials:

$$f_\beta(X) = a_n X^n + a_{n-1}X^{n-1} + \ldots + a_1 X + a_0, \quad \text{where } a_n = 1. \tag{3}$$

Coefficients $a_0, a_1, \ldots, a_{n-1}$ can be determined using the following procedure. Let $W_0(X) = 1$, $W_1(X) = X + \beta'_1$, and $W_t(X) = W_{t-1}(X)(X + \beta'_t)$, where

$$W_{t-1}(X) = b_{t-1}X^{t-1} + b_{t-2}X^{t-2} + \ldots + b_1 X + b_0,$$
$$W_t(X) = a_t X^t + a_{t-1}X^{t-1} + \ldots + a_1 X + a_0$$

and $a_t = b_{t-1} = 1$ for $t = 1, 2, \ldots, n$.

Then the polynomial $W_t(X)$ can be expressed by coefficients of the polynomial $W_{t-1}(X)$ as follows:

$$W_t(X) = (b_{t-1}X^{t-1} + b_{t-2}X^{t-2} + \ldots + b_1 X + b_0)(X + \beta'_t)$$
$$= b_{t-1}X^t + (b_{t-2} + \beta'_t b_{t-1})X^{t-1} + (b_{t-3} + \beta'_t b_{t-2})X^{t-2} +$$
$$\ldots + (b_1 + \beta'_t b_2)X^2 + (b_0 + \beta'_t b_1)X + b_0 \beta'_t.$$

Thus

$$a_0 = b_0 \beta'_t,$$
$$a_1 = b_0 + \beta'_t b_1,$$
$$\vdots$$
$$a_i = b_{i-1} + \beta'_t b_i, \quad \text{for } i = 1, 2, \ldots, t-1,$$
$$a_t = b_{t-1}$$

for $t = 1, 2, \ldots, n$.

Polynomial $W_n(X)$ obtained by applying a presented procedure is a new primitive polynomial $f_\beta(X)$ corresponding to the primitive element β.

Example. Let's consider a primitive trinomial $f(X) = X^3 + 2X + 1$ over GF(3) and parameter $k = 5$.

Then $\alpha = X$ is a root of the $f(X)$. Based on the definition of the primitive polynomial, one can easily confirm that α^5 is not a root of $f(X)$ because $5 \neq 3^n$. Let's assume $\beta_1 = \alpha^5$. Since $\gcd(5, 3^3 - 1) = 1$ the minimal polynomial of the element β is primitive.

Based on the Table 1 we have $\beta = \alpha^5 = 2\alpha^2 + \alpha + 2$. Thus, the following are the roots of a new primitive polynomial:

$$\beta_1 = 2\alpha^2 + \alpha + 2,$$
$$\beta_2 = \beta_1^3 = \alpha^{15} = 2\alpha^2,$$
$$\beta_3 = \beta_2^3 = \alpha^{45} = \alpha^{19} = 2\alpha^2 + 2\alpha + 2.$$

According to the mentioned procedure of multiplication we have:

$$W_1(X) = X - \beta_1 = X - (2\alpha^2 + \alpha + 2) = X + \alpha^2 + 2\alpha + 1,$$
$$W_2(X) = W_1(X)(X - \beta_2) = (X + \alpha^2 + 2\alpha + 1)(X - 2\alpha^2)$$
$$= (X + \alpha^2 + 2\alpha + 1)(X + \alpha^2)$$

$$= X^2 + \alpha^2 X + 2\alpha X + X + X\alpha^2 + \alpha^4 + 2\alpha^3 + \alpha^2$$
$$= X^2 + (2\alpha^2 + 2\alpha + 1)X + \alpha^2 + 2\alpha + 2\alpha + 1 + \alpha^2,$$
$$= X^2 + (2\alpha^2 + 2\alpha + 1)X + 2\alpha^2 + \alpha + 1,$$

$$
\begin{aligned}
W_3(X) &= W_2(X)(X - \beta_3) \\
&= (X^2 + (2\alpha^2 + 2\alpha + 1)X + 2\alpha^2 + \alpha + 1)(X - (2\alpha^2 + 2\alpha + 2)) \\
&= (X^2 + (2\alpha^2 + 2\alpha + 1)X + 2\alpha^2 + \alpha + 1)(X + \alpha^2 + \alpha + 1) \\
&= X^3 + (2\alpha^2 + 2\alpha + 1)X^2 + (2\alpha^2 + \alpha + 1)X \\
&\quad + X^2\alpha^2 + (2\alpha^4 + 2\alpha^3 + \alpha^2)X + 2\alpha^4 + \alpha^3 + \alpha^2 \\
&\quad + X^2\alpha + (2\alpha^3 + 2\alpha^2 + \alpha)X + 2\alpha^3 + \alpha^2 + \alpha \\
&\quad + X^2 + (2\alpha^2 + 2\alpha + 1)X + 2\alpha^2 + \alpha + 1 \\
&= X^3 + (2\alpha^2 + 2\alpha + 1)X^2 + (2\alpha^2 + \alpha + 1)X \\
&\quad + X^2\alpha^2 + (2\alpha^2 + \alpha + 2\alpha + 1 + \alpha^2)X + 2\alpha^2 + \alpha + \alpha + 2 + \alpha^2 \\
&\quad + X^2\alpha + (2\alpha + 1 + 2\alpha^2 + \alpha)X + 2\alpha + 1 + \alpha^2 + \alpha \\
&\quad + X^2 + (2\alpha^2 + 2\alpha + 1)X + 2\alpha^2 + \alpha + 1 \\
&= X^3 + (2\alpha^2 + 2\alpha + 1)X^2 + (2\alpha^2 + \alpha + 1)X \\
&\quad + X^2\alpha^2 + X + 2\alpha + 2 \\
&\quad + X^2\alpha + (2\alpha^2 + 1)X + \alpha^2 + 1 \\
&\quad + X^2 + (2\alpha^2 + 2\alpha + 1)X + 2\alpha^2 + \alpha + 1 \\
&= X^3 + 2X^2 + X + 1.
\end{aligned}
$$

Thus, a primitive polynomial corresponding to the element β is a polynomial

$$f_\beta(X) = X^3 + 2X^2 + X + 1.$$

More examples of generating primitive polynomials on the basis of trinomials are given in Table 2.

4   Practical Application

A sample application is discussed by the modification of A5/1 algorithm which is used to encrypt data in GSM systems. Until recently the strength of the algorithm has been analyzed through several studies [1,2,3,5,6] and a number of serious weaknesses in the cipher have been identified. Currently known attacks can retrieve the data sequence in real-time basing only on the ciphertext. It is therefore possible to tap GSM mobile phone conversations and decrypt them.

A5/1 is based on a combination of three linear feedback shift registers with irregular clocking. In Figure 1 the internal structure of the algorithm was shown. The three shift registers are specified by fixed primitive polynomials over GF(2), as follows:

$$R1: \ X^{19} + X^{18} + X^{17} + X^{14} + 1,$$
$$R2: \ X^{22} + X^{21} + 1,$$
$$R3: \ X^{23} + X^{22} + X^{21} + X^8 + 1.$$

Table 2. Sample primitive polynomials generated on the basis of trinomials

k	$f(X) = X^{23} + 2X^3 + 1$
5	$X^{23} + X^{19} + X^{15} + 2X^{11} + 2X^7 + 2X^3 + 1$
7	$X^{23} + X^{14} + 2X^7 + X^5 + 2X^3 + 1$
11	$X^{23} + X^{17} + 2X^{10} + 2X^5 + 2X^4 + 2X^3 + 1$
13	$X^{23} + X^{12} + X^{10} + 2X^8 + 2X^4 + 2X^3 + X^2 + 1$
17	$X^{23} + X^{11} + X^7 + X^6 + X^5 + 2X^4 + 2X^3 + 1$
19	$X^{23} + X^{15} + 2X^{10} + 2X^7 + X^6 + 2X^5 + X^4 + 2X^3 + X^2 + 1$

k	$f(X) = X^{29} + 2X^4 + 1$
5	$X^{29} + X^{24} + X^{19} + 2X^{14} + 2X^9 + 2X^4 + 1$
7	$X^{29} + X^{13} + X^{10} + X^7 + 2X^4 + 1$
11	$X^{29} + 2X^{15} + X^{12} + 2X^9 + 2X^6 + 2X^4 + 2X^3 + 1$
13	$X^{29} + X^{21} + X^7 + X^5 + 2X^4 + 1$
17	$X^{29} + 2X^{19} + X^{18} + 2X^{17} + 2X^8 + 2X^5 + 2X^4 + 1$
19	$X^{29} + X^{22} + X^{17} + 2X^{15} + X^{13} + 2X^{10} + X^8 + 2X^6 + 2X^5 + 2X^4 + X^3 + 1$

k	$f(X) = X^{31} + 2X^5 + 1$
5	$X^{31} + 2X^5 + 2X^4 + 2X^3 + X^2 + X + 1$
7	$X^{31} + X^{14} + X^{11} + X^8 + 2X^5 + 1$
11	$X^{31} + X^{23} + 2X^{14} + 2X^7 + 2X^6 + 2X^5 + 1$
13	$X^{31} + 2X^{29} + 2X^{25} + X^{23} + 2X^{13} + X^{11} + X^7 + 2X^5 + 1$
17	$X^{31} + 2X^{24} + 2X^{20} + X^{17} + X^{13} + 2X^{10} + X^9 + 2X^6 + 2X^5 + 2X^3 + 1$
19	$X^{31} + X^{28} + 2X^{25} + 2X^{22} + X^{19} + 2X^{16} + 2X^5 + X^4 + 1$

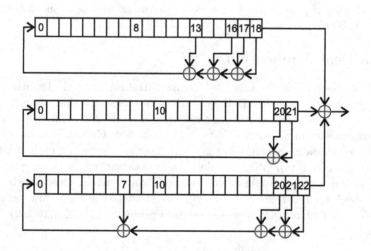

Fig. 1. Architecture of A5/1 algorithm

In [12], a modification of A5/1 algorithm has been proposed. The idea of improving the strength of the algorithm is a dynamic setting of linear feedback shift registers. This method is based on generating primitive polynomials over GF(2) and allows designers to eliminate many of the methods used to attack on the original A5/1 algorithm.

LFSRs in the structure of A5/1 are designed over binary arithmetics. However, such registers can also be considered over finite fields of a larger order, e.g. over GF(3). In this case we need two bits for each state and the addition modulo 3 feedback operation. Similarly to a binary field, some conditions of LFSR, such as period and linear complexity, depend on the feedback polynomial. In the case when the feedback polynomial is primitive, the register generates all possible states except the zero-state. It yields a period of 2^n-1 for a binary field and 3^n-1 for a ternary field. For $n = 32$, the maximal LFSR period over a binary field is 0,000231% of the maximal LSFR period over GF(3). Moreover, for the length of 32 the number of feedback polynomials which ensure the maximal register period equals 67108864 for GF(2) and for GF(3) 21158323814400, which is 0,000317% of primitive polynomials of degree 32 over a ternary field [11]. These are the arguments behind applying GF(3) instead of GF(2).

The original A5/1 algorithm controls shifting registers in a special way: the majority bit is calculated using selected bits of the registers, and subsequently the registers yielding compatible value of the selected bits to the value of the majority bit are shifted.

A new idea proposed by the authors is exchanging the majority function with the selector based on primitive polynomial over GF(3) which can be dynamically set in the device. It allows designers to extend the cryptographic power and capabilities of the old A5/1 algorithm. The new concept is presented in Figure 2.

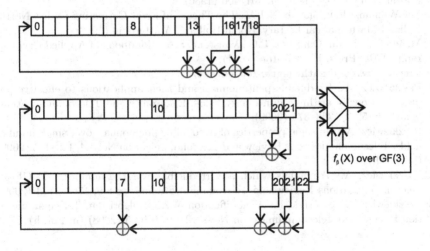

Fig. 2. Modified architecture of A5/1 algorithm

5 Conclusion

The specialized cryptographic system differs from the traditional one. It is characterized by a high security level. However, the implementation is relatively expensive and that is why one has to compromise these facts.

In this paper, we decrease the possibility of breaking into the system by limiting the knowledge of a cryptographic function. It is possible thanks to the replacement of the basic irreducible polynomial generating arithmetic of a finite field embedded in a cryptographic scheme.

Due to the fact that for a number field larger than GF(2), the probability of finding an irreducible lacunary polynomial grows, it can be assumed that fields GF(3), GF(5) and GF(7) will be applied in the near future.

References

1. Anderson, R., Roe, M.: A5 (1994), http://jya.com/crack-a5.htm
2. Babbage, S.: A space/time trade-off in exhaustive search attacks on stream ciphers. In: European Convention on Security and Detection. IEE Conference Publication 408 (May 1995)
3. Briceno, M., Goldberg, I., Wagner, D.: A pedagogical implementation of A5/1 (1999), http://cryptome.org/jya/a51-pi.htm#PI
4. von zur Gathen, J.: Irreducible trinomials over finite fields. In: Proc. of the 2001 International Symposium on Symbolic and Algebraic Computation, pp. 332–336. ACM, New York (2001)
5. Golić, J.D.: Cryptanalysis of alleged A5 stream cipher. In: Fumy, W. (ed.) EUROCRYPT 1997. LNCS, vol. 1233, pp. 239–255. Springer, Heidelberg (1997)
6. Hellman, M.E.: A cryptoanalytic time-memory trade-off. IEEE Transactions on Information Theory IT-26(4), 401–406 (1980)
7. MacWilliams, F.J., Sloane, N.J.A.: The Theory of Error-Correcting Codes. North-Holland Mathematical Library. North-Holland, Amsterdam (1988)
8. Menezes, A.J., van Oorschot, P.C., Vanstone, S.A.: Handbook of Applied Cryptography. CRC Press, Boca Raton (2001),
   http://www.cacr.math.uwaterloo.ca/hac/
9. Paszkiewicz, A.: Irreducible pentanomials and their applications to effective implementations of arithmetic in binary fields. Electronics and Telecommunications Quarterly 55(2), 363–375 (2009)
10. Paszkiewicz, A.: On some properties of irreducible polynomials over small number fields. Telecommunications Review and Telecommunication News 4, 129–135 (2009) (in Polish)
11. Paszkiewicz, A.: Trinomials which are irreducible over the number field GF(3). Telecommunications Review and Telecommunication News 8-9, 1767–1774 (2009)
12. Paszkiewicz, A., Stolarek, P.: A modification of A5/1 algorithm. Telecommunication Review and Telecommunication News 12, 1073–1075 (2008) (in Polish)

On Memory Capacity to Implement Logic Functions

Grzegorz Borowik, Tadeusz Łuba, and Paweł Tomaszewicz

Institute of Telecommunications,
00-665 Warsaw, Nowowiejska 15/19, Poland
{G.Borowik,T.Luba,P.Tomaszewicz}@tele.pw.edu.pl

Abstract. The paper presents logic synthesis method targeted at FPGA architectures with specialized embedded memory blocks (EMB). Existing tools/compilers treat ROM modules described in HDLs as indivisible entities and in consequence do not ensure effective utilization of the possibilities provided by such modules. In order to address this problem effectively we propose applying functional decomposition. The main contribution is based on the use of r-admissibility measure to guide decomposition structures for ROM-based synthesis.

Keywords: Boolean functions, technology mapping, area optimization, balanced decomposition strategy, logic synthesis, non-disjoint serial decomposition, parallel decomposition, field programmable gate arrays.

1 Introduction

In the last decade field programmable gate arrays with 4 or 5 input LUTs have been believed to be the most efficient for implementation of truth table specified designs. In current technology, FPGAs with 6 input LUTs are typical and in the future LUTs with more inputs should be available [5]. On the other hand, a common logic cell has generally one output only (some Xilinx circuits contain two-output LUTs; and some Altera's ALUTs can be configured as two-output LUTs but then the feature of implementing any given function of specified number of inputs is not available).

Alternative components to LUTs are embedded memory arrays. These arrays have been originally intended to implement storage, but recent work has shown that they can also be used to implement logic very efficiently [7]. The main feature of the memory array is that the word length can be configured by a user. Configuring the arrays as ROMs results in large multi-output lookup-tables. Thus, we can treat the memory as a logic block which can be set up with various input and output configurations. Additionally, the solution implemented in today's FPGAs is that one can configurate memory blocks that can either be combined together to make larger arrays or divided to make smaller arrays [7]. Finally, the ability to combine memory blocks with LUTs provides a user with very flexible resources from which one can create their various-sized memory arrays.

R. Moreno-Díaz et al. (Eds.): EUROCAST 2011, Part II, LNCS 6928, pp. 343–350, 2012.

In this paper we focus on a truth table implementation in embedded memory arrays and on a theory on variable partitioning of the function to be decomposed. This is possible thanks to the r-admissibility measure [1]. We study the decomposition task when the bound set and the free set of variables [6] are disjoint as well as non-disjoint sets. In the second case, the main problem of the calculation of an efficient decomposition is constructing an appropriate intersection set of the bound and the free set of variables with the minimal cardinality.

2   Functional Decomposition Using r-Admissibility Measure

Let $F(X) : B \to \{0,1\}^m$ be a multiple-output Boolean function (completely or incompletely specified), where: $B \subset \{0,1\}^n$, and values n, m denote the number of inputs and outputs respectively.

Serial functional decomposition of Boolean function relies on partitioning of input variables in such a way to obtain a two-level functional dependency $F = H(U, G(V \cup W))$ (Fig. 1).

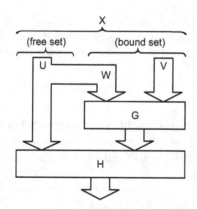

Fig. 1. Serial decomposition scheme

Partition description and partition algebra are applied to describe logic dependencies in Boolean function [2].

Theorem 1. Let P_U, P_V and P_W be partitions induced on the function F minterms by the input disjoint subsets U, V, where $X = U \cup V$, and the subset $W \subset U$; P_F be a partition induced by outputs of F. If there exists a partition P_G on the set of function F minterms such that $P_{V \cup W} \leq P_G$, and $P_U \cdot P_G \leq P_F$, then F has a serial decomposition $F = H(U, G(V \cup W))$.

Let $P_a|P_b$ denote the quotient partition and let $\varepsilon(P_a|P_b)$ be the number of elements in the largest block of $P_a|P_b$. Let $e(P_a|P_b)$ be the smallest integer equal to or larger than $\log_2(\varepsilon(P_a|P_b))$ (i.e., $e(P_a|P_b) = \lceil \log_2(\varepsilon(P_a|P_b)) \rceil$).

A *r-admissibility* of the two-block partitions' set $\{P_1, \ldots, P_k\}$ for the set $\{x_1, \ldots, x_k\}$ in relation to a partition P is defined as $r = k + e(P_1 \cdot P_2 \cdot \ldots \cdot P_k | P)$.

The r-admissibility has the following interpretation. If a set of partitions $\{P_1, \ldots, P_k\}$ calculated for selected inputs of function F is r-admissible in relation to P_F, then there might exist a serial decomposition of F in which successor function has r inputs: k primary inputs corresponding to free input variables which induce two-block partition set $\{P_1, \ldots, P_k\}$ and $r - k$ inputs which are outputs of predecessor function. Thus, to find a decomposition of F in which successor function has r inputs, we must find a set of input variables which induces an r-admissible set of input partitions.

It should be noticed that r-admissibility of a set U of k elements does not guarantee the existence of a disjoint decomposition $F = H(U, G(V))$, where the predecessor function has exactly $r - k$ outputs. It only guarantees the existence of a decomposition containing a predecessor function with arguments belonging to $V \cup W$, where $W \subseteq U$. In the best case the W set is empty, in the worst case $W = U$.

The abovementioned problems often in practice lead to the construction of a non-disjoint decomposition [4]. Then, the main problem in the construction of a non-disjoint decomposition is the computation of a W set with minimal cardinality. The selection of arguments for the W set is made based on the analysis of the P_V partition.

The main task in calculating a non-disjoint decomposition of a function F with given sets U and V, is to find a partition $P_G \geq P_{V \cup W}$, where $W \subset U$, which satisfies the conditions of Theorem 1. Roughly speaking, we construct $P_G \geq P_{V \cup W}$ by merging blocks of $P_{V \cup W}$, but in such a way that $P_U \cdot P_G \leq P_F$.

In other words, no pair of primary minterms p, q belonging to the same block of P_U and different blocks of the product $P_U \cdot P_F$ can belong to the same block of the partition P_G. Otherwise, the pair of primary minterms is a *contradictory pair*. This observation allows us to conclude that the quotient partition $P_U | P_F$ carries sufficient information about all possible contradictory pairs. With this information one can decide about the way of merging blocks of the partition P_V into blocks of the partition P_G.

The construction of the partition P_G is always possible provided that disjoint decomposition exists. If no P_G constructed satisfy $P_U \cdot P_G \leq P_F$, the disjoint decomposition does not exist. In this case some blocks of P_G contain contradictory pairs of minterms. This contradiction can be resolved by moving one of the minterms of each contradictory pair to another, specially calculated block of P_G.

Example 1. Consider function F given in Table 1, where function outputs are represented by

$$P_F = (\overline{1, 10, 17}; \overline{5, 7, 19}; \overline{6, 8, 14}; \overline{3, 12, 16}; \overline{2, 13}; \overline{4, 15}; \overline{9, 18}; \overline{11, 20}).$$

An attempt to compute a decomposition with $U = \{x_4, x_5\}$, $V = \{x_1, x_2, x_3\}$ results in

Table 1. Memory based description of Boolean function

	00	01	11	10	x_4, x_5
000	1	2	–	3	
001	4	5	6	–	
011	–	7	8	9	
010	10	–	11	12	
110	–	13	14	–	
111	15	–	–	16	
101	17	–	–	18	
100	–	19	20	–	
x_1, x_2, x_3					

$$P_U|P_F = (\overline{(1,10,17)(4,15)};\ \overline{(5,7,19)(2,13)};\ \overline{(6,8,14)(11,20)};\ \overline{(3,12,16)(9,18)},$$

$$P_V = (\overline{1,2,3};\overline{4,5,6};\overline{7,8,9};\overline{10,11,12};\overline{13,14};\overline{15,16};\overline{17,18};\overline{19,20}).$$

As the r-admissibility of the set U is $r = 3$, we should construct two-block partition $P_G \geq P_V$. Note that in this case each block B_i of $P_U|P_F$ consists of – enclosed in brackets – two sub-blocks B_i^0, B_i^1. In order to construct partition P_G at first we must merge these blocks of P_V that have a nonempty intersection with B_i^0, and similarly with B_i^1. Figure 2 shows the construction of the P_G partition.

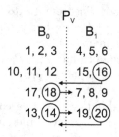

Fig. 2. Construction of the P_G partition

One can verify that the following pairs of minterms are contradictory pairs: $(6, 20)$, $(8, 20)$, $(11, 14)$, $(3, 12)$, $(12, 18)$, $(9, 16)$. We avoid this contradictions by moving the minterms 16 and 20 to the first block, and 14 and 18 to the second block (as shown in the Figure 2). This is possible if the following minterms are separated: 13 from 14, 15 from 16, 17 from 18, and 19 from 20. Table 1 shows that for each of the contradictory pairs the variable x_4 is separating their elements. In other words, the set $W = \{x_4\}$ and $F = H(x_4, x_5, G(x_1, x_2, x_3, x_4))$. In consequence

$$P_{V \cup W} = (\overline{1,2};\overline{3};\overline{4,5};\overline{6};\overline{7};\overline{8,9};\overline{10};\overline{11,12};\overline{13};\overline{14};\overline{15};\overline{16};\overline{17};\overline{18};\overline{19};\overline{20}),$$

$$P_G = (\overline{1,2,3,10,11,12,13,16,17,20};\overline{4,5,6,7,8,9,14,15,18,19}).$$

3   Parallel and Balanced Decomposition

Let's consider a multiple-output function F and assume that F has to be decomposed into two components G and H, with disjoint sets Y_G and Y_H of output variables. This problem occurs, for example, when we want to implement a large function using components with a limited number of outputs. Note that such a parallel decomposition can also alleviate the problem of an excessive number of inputs of F. This is because, for typical functions most outputs do not depend on all input variables. Therefore, the set X_G of input variables on which the outputs of Y_G depend may be smaller than X. Similarly, for the set X_H of input variables on which the outputs of Y_H depend may be smaller than X. As a result, components G and H do not only have fewer outputs, but also fewer inputs than function F. The exact formulation of the parallel decomposition problem depends on the constraints imposed by the implementation style. One possibility is to find sets Y_G and Y_H, such that, the combined cardinality of X_G and X_H is minimal. Partitioning the set of outputs into two disjoint subsets only is not an important limitation of the method, because the procedure can be applied for components G and H recursively.

In the balanced decomposition [4] the serial and parallel decompositions are intertwined in a top-down synthesis process to obtain the required circuit structure. At each step, either parallel or serial decomposition is performed, both controlled by certain input parameters. In the case of serial decomposition the parameters G_{in} and G_{out} denote the number of G inputs and outputs, respectively. In the case of parallel decomposition the parameter G_{out} represents the number of G outputs. Intertwining of serial and parallel decomposition opens up several interesting possibilities in multilevel decomposition. Experimental results show that the right balance between parallel and serial decomposition and the choice of control parameters significantly influence the area and depth of the resultant network.

Example 2. The influence of the decomposition strategy on the final result of the FPGA-based mapping process will be explained with function F representing DA logic [3] of a certain FIR filter (bla9_8) described by the following integral coefficients $[0, 10, 20, 29, 32, 29, 20, 10, 0]$.

As F is a nine-input, eight-output function, in the first step of the decomposition both the parallel and serial decomposition can be applied. Let us apply parallel decomposition at first (Fig. 3). Parallel decomposition with $G_{out} = 4$ generates two components: the first one with 7 inputs and 4 outputs, and the second with 6 inputs and 4 outputs. The first component is a subject for the two-stage serial decomposition resulting in block G with 2 inputs and 1 output – $G(2, 1)$, and block H with 6 inputs and 4 outputs – $H(6, 4)$. The second block is decomposed serially yielding $G(4, 1)$ and $H(5, 4)$. The obtained network can be built of 2 logic cells and 2 M512 ROMs. The final result of this decomposition is shown in Fig. 4.

It is worth noticing that the same function synthesized directly by commercial tool, i.e. Altera Quartus II v10.1 can be mapped onto one M4K ROM.

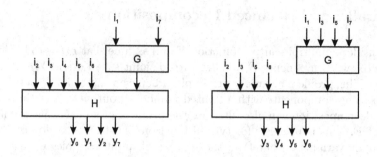

Fig. 3. Final decomposition scheme of example filter bla9_8

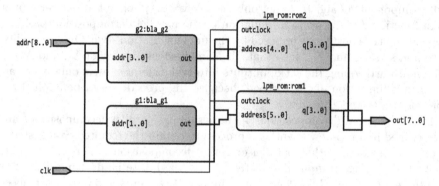

Fig. 4. Implementation of bla9_8 using Altera Quartus II supported by pre-decomposition scheme

We can estimate the result of a decomposed structure by a total *Memory Space Cost* (MSC) of all components, i.e. $\sum_i \mathrm{MSC}_i$, where MSC_i of each block with n inputs and m outputs is $m \cdot 2^n$. Then, a *Memory Space Compression Factor* (MSCF) can be viewed as the quotient of $\sum_i \mathrm{MSC}_i$ and MSC, i.e.

$$\mathrm{MSCF} = 100\% \cdot \sum_i \mathrm{MSC}_i / \mathrm{MSC},$$

where MSC is the cost of the non-decomposed function. For bla9_8 filter total MSC is the sum of the number of bits required to store components G_1, H_1, G_2, H_2, respectively, i.e.

$$\sum \mathrm{MSC}_i = 4 + 256 + 16 + 128 = 404.$$

As MSC = 4096, MSCF = 404/4096 = 9,8%.

4   Experimental Results

The decomposition method has been implemented within ROM-based Synthesis System, a modular environment integrating our own tools and providing interface to third party commercially available tools. For testing purposes we have been using a set of DA filter circuits for which their truth tables have been generated by standard DA function generator. Table 2 presents the results of decomposition applied to DA circuits of various FIR filters. Each filter is characterized by *integral filter coefficients* shown in column 2. Column 3 and 4 shows MSC of the original DA function and total MSC of the decomposed DA circuit, respectively. The last column denotes MSCF for each filter.

An interesting question is whether the decomposed structure is profitable for implementation DA circuit when using standard commercial tool, for example Altera Quartus II. The answer is yes, because commercially available tools use ROM memories in its primary fashion, i.e. no synthesis is applied for the memory content. For example: the DA circuit of bla9_8 filter can be implemented by pre-decomposition synthesis in the structure built of 2 logic cells and 2 M512 ROMs (Fig. 4). The same circuit implemented directly by Altera Quartus II v10.1 can be implemented using M4K ROM component. In other words, supporting Altera Quartus II with decomposition procedure allows users reducing 50% of memory space.

Table 2. Experimental results

Filter	Integral filter coefficients	MSC (without decomposition)	MSC (with decomposition)	MSCF [%]
bla8_8	[0,3,23,57,57,23,3,0]	2048	330	15.6
bla9_8	[0,1,14,45,64,45,14,1,0]	4096	404	9.8
bla10_8	[0,0,8,32,59,59,32,8,0,0]	8192	208	2.5
ham8_8	[1,8,32,60,60,32,8,1]	2048	276	13.4
ham9_8	[0,4,22,50,64,50,22,4,0]	4096	448	10.9
han8_8	[1,12,38,60,60,38,12,1]	2048	1156	56.4
han9_8	[0,7,27,52,64,52,27,7,0]	4096	640	15.6
rec9_8	[0,10,20,29,32,29,20,10,0]	4096	496	12.1
rec10_8	[-2,2,8,13,16,16,13,8,2,-2]	4096	2820	68.8

5   Conclusions

Taking into consideration modern FPGAs, a methodology has been proposed for flexible synthesis of designing of logic circuit onto structure composed of logic cells and EMBs. The main research concerning the use of r-admissibility to guide serial decomposition and a search scheme for finding good solutions in the large solution space has been carried out. It has been noticed that the r-admissibility value can be applied for each serial decomposition option for quick and efficient selecting of the best (or at least a good) decomposition option at each level in the search tree. So, there is no need for a full search in the solution space. Combined with parallel decomposition this allows the full range of solutions presented by the presence of configurable memory blocks to be fully explored in less time than the current methods would allow. The results show that for a set of filter benchmarks implemented using DA, the tool developed in this work outperforms the technology mapper in Altera Quartus II system.

References

1. Borowik, G., Łuba, T., Tomaszewicz, P.: A notion of r-admissibility and its application in logic synthesis. In: Proc. of the 4th IFAC Workshop on Discrete-Event System Design, DESDES 2009, Gandia Beach, Spain, pp. 207–212 (October 2009)
2. Brzozowski, J.A., Łuba, T.: Decomposition of Boolean functions specified by cubes. Journal of Multi-Valued Logic & Soft. Computing 9, 377–417 (2003)
3. Meyer-Baese, U.: Digital Signal Processing with Field Programmable Gate Arrays, Signals and Communication Technology. Springer-Verlag New York, Inc., Secaucus (2004)
4. Rawski, M., Jóźwiak, L., Nowicka, M., Łuba, T.: Non-disjoint decomposition of boolean functions and its application in fpga-oriented technology mapping. In: EUROMICRO 1997: 'New Frontiers of Information Technology', Proceedings of the 23rd EUROMICRO Conference, pp. 24–30 (September 1997)
5. Sasao, T.: On the number of LUTs to realize sparse logic functions. In: Proc. of the 18th International Workshop on Logic and Synthesis, Berkeley, CA, U.S.A., July 31-August 2, pp. 64–71 (2009)
6. Scholl, C.: Functional Decomposition With Applications to FPGA Synthesis. Kluwer Academic Publishers, Dordrecht (2001)
7. Wilton, S.: Implementing logic in fpga embedded memory arrays: architectural implications. In: Proceedings of the IEEE Custom Integrated Circuits Conference, pp. 269–272 (May 1998)

Reconstruction of Functions via Walsh-Fourier Cofficients

György Gát

College of Nyíregyháza, Inst. of Math. and Comp. Sci., Nyíregyháza,
P.O. Box 166, H–4400, Hungary
gatgy@nyf.hu

Abstract. It is of main interest in the theory and also in applications of
Fourier series that how to reconstruct a function from the partial sums
of its Walsh-Fourier series. In 1955 Fine proved the Fejér-Lebesgue theorem, that is for each integrable function we have the almost everywhere
convergence of Fejér means $\sigma_n f \to f$. It is also of prior interest that what
can be said - with respect to this reconstruction issue - if we have only
a subsequence of the partial sums. In this paper we give a brief résumé
of the recent results with respect to this issue above also regarding the
class of two-variable integrable functions.

1 Introduction

Let the numbers $n \in \mathbf{N}$ and $x \in I := [0,1)$ be expanded with respect to the
binary number system:

$$n = \sum_{k=0}^{\infty} n_k 2^k,$$

$$x = \sum_{k=0}^{\infty} x_k 2^{-k-1},$$

$(n_k, x_k \in \{0,1\})$ where if x is a dyadic rational, that is an element of the
set $\{k/2^n : k, n \in \mathbf{N}\}$, then we choose the finite expansion. Define the k -th
Rademacher function as $r_k(x) = (-1)^{x_k} (x \in I, k \in \mathbf{N})$. Let $(\omega_n, n \in \mathbf{N})$ represent the Walsh-Paley system. That is, the n-th Walsh-Paley function is

$$\omega_n(x) = \prod_{k=0}^{\infty} (-1)^{n_k x_k}.$$

Consequently, $\omega_n(x) = \prod_{k=0}^{\infty} r_k(x)$.

What is the Walsh-Paley system good for? The Walsh functions have many
possible applications. Just to mention a few:

- Data transmission [29]
- Face, fingerprint identification [14]
- Approximate solution of integral and differential equations [24].

R. Moreno-Díaz et al. (Eds.): EUROCAST 2011, Part II, LNCS 6928, pp. 351–358, 2012.
© Springer-Verlag Berlin Heidelberg 2012

A great advantage of the Walsh functions (comparing the trigonometric ones) that they can take the values +1 and −1 only. Besides, it can be determined very efficiently that which Walsh function at what point is one or minus one.

The n-th Walsh-Fourier coefficient of the integrable function $f \in L^1(I)$ is

$$\hat{f}(n) := \int_I f(x)\omega_n(x)dx.$$

The n-th partial sum of the Walsh-Fourier series of the integrable function $f \in L^1(I)$:

$$S_n f(y) := \sum_{k=0}^{n-1} \hat{f}(k)\omega_k(y).$$

It is of main interest in the theory of Fourier series that how to reconstruct the function from the partial sums of its Fourier series. It is quite well known (see e.g. [21]) that for functions belonging the Lebesgue space L^p for $1 < p < \infty$ we have the relation $S_n f \to f$ with respect to almost everywhere convergence and also with respect to the L^p-norm convergence. In the case of $p = 1$ both relation fail to hold for all integrable function. That is, it is of prior interest to discuss this case.

2   The Cesàro Means

The n-th Fejér or $(C,1)$ mean of the function f is

$$\sigma_n f := \frac{1}{n} \sum_{k=1}^{n} S_k f.$$

In 1955 Fine proved [4] for the Walsh-Paley system the well known Fejér-Lebesgue theorem. Namely, for every integrable function f we have the a.e. relation

$$\sigma_n f \to f.$$

Let have a look for the situation with the (C, α) means. What are they? Let $A_n^\alpha := \frac{(1+\alpha)...(n+\alpha)}{n!}$, where $n \in \mathbf{N}$ and $\alpha \in \mathbf{R}$ $(-\alpha \notin \mathbf{N})$. It is known, that $A_n^\alpha \sim n^\alpha$.

The n-th (C, α) mean of the function $f \in L^1(I)$:

$$\sigma_{n+1}^\alpha f := \frac{1}{A_n^\alpha} \sum_{k=0}^{n} A_{n-k}^{\alpha-1} S_k f.$$

In 1975 Schipp proved [20], that $\sigma_n^\alpha f \to f$ a.e. for each $f \in L^1(I)$ and $\alpha > 0$. In other words, the maximal convergence space of the (C, α) means is the L^1 Lebesgue space. That is, the largest possible.

The Walsh-Paley system means the set of the Walsh functions and their ordering. Another well known, widely investigated (both in theoretical and application point of view) ordering gives the so called Walsh-Kaczmarz system. This is nothing else, but a rearrangement of the Walsh-Paley system. Introduce it as follows.

If $n > 0$, then let $|n| := \max\{j \in \mathbf{N} : n_j \neq 0\}$. The n-th Walsh-Kaczmarz function is

$$\kappa_n(x) := r_{|n|}(x)(-1)^{\sum_{k=0}^{|n|-1} n_k x_{|n|-1-k}},$$

as if $n > 0$, $\kappa_0(x) := 1, x \in I$. The elements of the a Walsh-Kaczmarz system and the Walsh-Paley system is a dyadic blockwise rearrangements of each other. This means as follows:

$$\{\kappa_n : 2^k \leq n < 2^{k+1}\} = \{\omega_n : 2^k \leq n < 2^{k+1}\}.$$

We remark that the so called Hadamard matrices and transform are generated by the Walsh-Kaczmarz functions [21].

In 1998 Gát proved [6] the Fejér-Lebesgue theorem for the Walsh-Kaczmarz system. That is, $\sigma_n f \to f$ almost everywhere for each $f \in L^1(I)$. In 2004 Simon generalized [22] the result of Gát above for (C, α) summation methods.

It is also of prior interest that what can be said – with respect to this reconstruction issue – if we have only a subsequence of the partial sums. In 1936 Zalcwasser [28] asked how "rare" can be the sequence of positive integers $a(n)$ such that

$$\frac{1}{N} \sum_{n=1}^{N} S_{a(n)} f \to f. \tag{1}$$

This problem with respect to the trigonometric system was completely solved for continuous functions (uniform convergence) in [19], [27], [1], [3]. That is, if the sequence a is convex, then the condition

$$\sup_n n^{-1/2} \log a(n) < +\infty$$

is necessary and sufficient for the uniform convergence for every continuous function. For the time being, this issue with respect to the Walsh-Paley system has not been solved. Only, a sufficient condition is known, which is the same as in the trigonometric case. The paper about this is written by Glukhov [12]. See the more dimensional case also by Glukhov [13].

With respect to convergence almost everywhere, and integrable functions the situation is more complicated. Belinksky proved [2] for the trigonometric system the existence of a sequence $a(n) \sim \exp(\sqrt[3]{k})$ such that the relation (1) holds a.e. for every integrable function. In this paper Belinksky also conjectured that if the sequence a is convex, then the condition $\sup_n n^{-1/2} \log a(n) < +\infty$ is necessary and sufficient again. So, that would be the answer for the problem of Zalcwasser [28] in this point of view (trigonometric system, a.e. convergence and L^1 functions). The author of this paper proved [10] that this is not the case for the Walsh-Paley system. See below Theorem 1. On the other hand, this difference between the Walsh-Paley and the trigonometric system is not so surprising. Because of the following. Let $v(n) := \sum_{i=0}^{\infty} |n_i - n_{i+1}|, (n = \sum_{i=0}^{\infty} n_i 2^i)$ be the variation of the natural number n expanded in the number system based 2. It is a well-known result in the literature that for each sequence a tending strictly monotone increasing to plus infinity with the property $\sup_n v(a(n)) < +\infty$ we have the a.e. convergence $S_{a(n)}f \to f$ for all integrable function f. Is it also a necessary condition? This question of Balashov was answered by Konyagin [15] in the negative. He gave an example. That is, a sequence a with property $\sup_n v(a(n)) = +\infty$ and he proved that $S_{a(n)}f \to f$ a.e. for all integrable function f.

In paper [10] it is proved (see Theorem 1) that for each lacunary sequence a (that is $a(n+1)/a(n) \geq q > 1$) and each integrable function f the relation (1) holds a.e. This may also be interesting in the following point of view. If the sequence a is lacunary, then the a.e. relation $S_{a(n)}f \to f$ holds for all functions f in the Hardy space H. The trigonometric and the Walsh-Paley case can be found in [31] (trigonometric case) and [16] (Walsh-Paley case). But, the space H is a proper subspace of L^1. Therefore, it is of interest to investigate relation (1) for L^1 functions and lacunary sequence a.

In that paper - using the method of the proof of Theorem 1 one can find (Theorem 2) that for any convex sequence a (with $a(+\infty) = +\infty$ - of course) and for each integrable function the Riesz's logarithmic means of the function converges to the function almost everywhere. That is, the Riesz's logarithmic summability method can reconstruct the corresponding integrable function from any (convex) subsequence of the partial sums in the Walsh-Paley situation. For the time being there is no result known with respect to a.e. convergence of logarithmic means of subsequences of partial sums, neither in the trigonometric nor in the Walsh-Kaczmarz case.

The following a.e. convergence theorems with respect to the Fejér and logarithmic means of subsequences of the partial sums of the Walsh-Fourier series of integrable functions are proved by Gát [10].

Theorem 1. *Let* $a : \mathbf{N} \to \mathbf{N}$ *be a sequence with property* $\frac{a(n+1)}{a(n)} \geq q > 1$ $(n \in \mathbf{N})$. *Then for all integrable function* $f \in L^1(Q)$ *we have the a.e. relation*

$$\frac{1}{N} \sum_{n=1}^{N} S_{a(n)}f \to f.$$

Theorem 2. *Let* $a : \mathbf{N} \to \mathbf{N}$ *be a convex sequence with property* $a(+\infty) = +\infty$. *Then for each integrable function* f *we have the a.e. relation*

$$\frac{1}{\log N} \sum_{n=1}^{N} \frac{S_{a(n)}f}{n} \to f.$$

What can be said in the two (more) dimensional situation? This is quite a different story. Define the two-dimensional Walsh-Paley functions in the following way:

$$\omega_n(x) := \omega_{n_1}(x^1)\omega_{n_2}(x^2),$$

where $n = (n_1, n_2) \in \mathbf{N}^2$, $x = (x^1, x^2) \in I^2$. Let f be an integrable function. Its Fourier coefficients, rectangual partial sums of its Fourier series:

$$\hat{f}(n) := \int_{I^2} f(x)\omega_n(x)dx,$$

$$S_{n_1,n_2}f := \sum_{k_1=0}^{n_1-1} \sum_{k_2=0}^{n_2-1} \hat{f}(k_1, k_2)\omega_{k_1,k_2}.$$

Moreover, the two-dimensional Fejér or $(C, 1)$ means of the function $f \in L^1(I^2)$:

$$\sigma_{n_1,n_2}f := \frac{1}{n_1 n_2} \sum_{k_1=1}^{n_1} \sum_{k_2=1}^{n_2} S_{k_1,k_2}f \quad (n \in \mathbf{P}^2).$$

In 1931 Marczinkiewicz and Zygmund proved for the two-dimensional trigonometric system [17], and in 1992 Móricz, Schipp and Wade verified [18] for the two-dimensional Walsh-Paley system, that for every $f \in L\log^+ L(I^2)$ (which means $|f|\log^+|f|$ is integrable, where $\log^+ x = \max\{1, \log x\}$)

$$\sigma_{n_1,n_2}f \to f$$

a.e. as $\min\{n_1, n_2\} \to \infty$, that is, in the Pringsheim sense.

Since $L\log^+ L(I^2)$ is a proper subspace of $L^1(I^2)$, then it would be interesting to "enlarge" the convergence space, if possible. In 2000 Gát proved [7], that it is impossible. That is:

Theorem 3. *For each measurable function $\delta : [0, +\infty) \to [0, +\infty)$, $\delta(\infty) = 0$, (that is vanishing at plus infinity) there exists a*

$$f \in L\log^+ L\delta(L) \quad such \ that \quad \sigma_{n_1,n_2}f \not\to f$$

a.e. (in the Pringsheim sense).

However, what "positive" can be said for the functions in $L^1(I^2)$ as if the a.e. convergence of the two-dimensional Fejér means in the Pringsheim sense can not be said? That could be the so called restricted convergence. For the two-dimensional trigonometric system Marcinkiewicz and Zygmund proved [30] in 1939, that

$$\sigma_{n_1,n_2}f \to f$$

a.e. for every $f \in L^1(I^2)$ as if $\min\{n_1, n_2\} \to \infty$, provided that

$$2^{-\alpha} \le \frac{n_1}{n_2} \le 2^\alpha$$

for some $\alpha \ge 0$. In other words, the set of admissible indices (n_1, n_2) remains in some cone. This theorem for the two-dimensional Walsh-Paley system was verified by Móricz, Schipp and Wade [18] in 1992 in the case when n_1, n_2 both are powers of two. That is,

$$\sigma_{2^{n_1}, 2^{n_2}}f \to f$$

a.e. for every $f \in L^1(I^2)$ as if $\min\{n_1, n_2\} \to \infty$, provided that $|n_1 - n_2| \leq \alpha$ for some $\alpha \geq 0$.

The proof of the Marcinkiewicz-Zygmund theorem [30] (with respect to the Walsh-Paley system) for arbitrary set of indices remaining in some cone is due to Gát and Weisz [5], [25], separately in 1996.

It is an interesting question that it is possible to weaken somehow the "cone restriction" in a way that a.e. convergence remains for each function in L^1. Maybe for some "interim space" – if not for space L^1. The answer is negative both in the point of view of space and in the point of view of restriction. Namely, in 2001 Gát proved [8] the theorem below:

Theorem 4. *Let* $\delta : [0, +\infty) \to [0, +\infty)$ *measurable,* $\delta(+\infty) = 0$ *and let* $w : \mathbf{N} \to [1, +\infty)$ *be an arbitrary increasing function such that*

$$\sup_{x \in \mathbf{N}} w(x) = +\infty.$$

Moreover, $\vee n := \max\{n_1, n_2\}$, $\wedge n := \min\{n_1, n_2\}$. *Then, there exists a function* $f \in L \log^+ L\delta(L)$ *such that*

$$\sigma_{n_1, n_2} f \not\to f$$

a.e. as $\wedge n \to \infty$ *such that the restriction condition* $\frac{\vee n}{\wedge n} \leq w(\wedge n)$ *is also fulfilled.*

That is there is no "interim" space. Either we have space $L \log^+ L$ and "no restriction at all", or the "cone restriction" and then the maximal convergence space is L^1. As a consequence of this we have that

$$\sigma_{n_1, n_2} f \to f$$

a.e. for each $f \in L(I^2)$ as $\min\{n_1, n_2\} \to \infty$, provided that

$$\frac{\vee n}{\wedge n} \leq w(\wedge n)$$

if and only if

$$\sup w(x) < \infty.$$

Another question. What is the situation with the (C, α) summation of 2-dimensional Walsh-Fourier series? What is this?

$$\sigma^\alpha_{n_1+1, n_2+1} f = \frac{1}{A^\alpha_{n_1} A^\alpha_{n_2}} \sum_{k_1=0}^{n_1} \sum_{k_2=0}^{n_2} A^{\alpha-1}_{n_1-k_1} A^{\alpha-1}_{n_2-k_2} S_{k_1, k_2} f.$$

In 1999 Weisz proved [26], that

$$\sigma^\alpha_{n_1, n_2} f \to f$$

a.e. as $\min\{n_1, n_2\} \to \infty$ for each $f \in L \log^+ L(I^2)$ and $\alpha > 0$.

The question is that it is possible to give a "larger" convergence space for the (C, α) summability method $(\alpha > 0)$? Is there such an α? If $\alpha \leq 1$, then not. Because for the $(C, 1)$ method one can not give such a "larger" space.

Problem 1. What is the situation with the (C, α) methods, for $\alpha > 1$ in the two (more) dimensional case?

Problem 2. What is the situation with the Cesàro summation of the 2-dimensional Walsh-Kaczmarz system? There is no divergence results with respect to this system and Cesàro means.

Only we have positive results. In 2001 Simon proved [23], that $\sigma_{n_1,n_2} f \to f$ a.e. as if $\min\{n_1, n_2\} \to \infty$ (in the Pringsheim sense) for every $f \in L \log^+ L(I^2)$. He also proved the restricted "cone" convergence for functions belonging to $L^1(I^2)$.

In 2007 Gát generalized [9] the notion of cone restriction of two dimensional Fejér means used by Marcinkiewicz and Zygmund in a way that instead of straight lines he used curved lines. In this paper one can find necessary and sufficient conditions for the almost everywhere convergence of the two dimensional trigonometric Fejér means of integrable functions. Finally, I mention that the author of this paper and Nagy verified [11] the Walsh-Paley version of these results.

References

1. Belinsky, E.S.: On the summability of Fourier series with the method of lacunary arithmetic means. Anal. Math. 10, 275–282 (1984)
2. Belinsky, E.S.: Summability of Fourier series with the method of lacunary arithmetical means at the Lebesgue points. Proc. Am. Math. Soc. 125 (12), 3689–3693 (1997)
3. Carleson, L.: Appendix to the paper by J.-P. Kahane and Y. Katznelson. Series de Fourier des fonctions bornees, Studies in pure mathematics, pp. 395–413. Birkhauser, Basel-Boston (1983)
4. Fine, N.J.: Cesàro summability of Walsh-Fourier series. Proc. Nat. Acad. Sci. U.S.A. 41, 558–591 (1955)
5. Gát, G.: Pointwise convergence of the Cesàro means of double Walsh series. Ann. Univ. Sci. Budap. Rolando Eoetvoes, Sect. Comput. 16, 173–184 (1996)
6. Gát, G.: On $(C, 1)$ summability of integrable functions with respect to the Walsh-Kaczmarz system. Stud. Math. 130 (2), 135–148 (1998)
7. Gát, G.: On the divergence of the $(C, 1)$ means of double Walsh-Fourier series. Proc. Am. Math. Soc. 128 (6), 1711–1720 (2000)
8. Gát, G.: Divergence of the $(C, 1)$ means of d-dimensional Walsh-Fourier series. Anal. Math. 27 (3), 157–171 (2001)
9. Gát, G.: Pointwise convergence of cone-like restricted two-dimensional $(C, 1)$ means of trigonometric Fourier series. Journal of Approximation Theory 149 (1), 74–102 (2007)
10. Gát, G.: Almost everywhere convergence of Fejér and logarithmic means of subsequences of partial sums of the Walsh-Fourier series of integrable functions. J. Approx. Theory 162 (4), 687–708 (2010)
11. Gát, G., Nagy, K.: Pointwise convergence of cone-like restricted two-dimensional Fejér means of Walsh-Fourier series. Acta Mathematica Sinica (English series) 1, 2295–2304 (2010)
12. Glukhov, V.A.: Summation of Fourier-Walsh series. Ukr. Math. J. 38, 261–266 (1986)

13. Glukhov, V.A.: Summation of multiple Fourier series in multiplicative systems. Math. Notes 39, 364–369 (1986)

14. Jia, X., Nixon, M.S.: Analysing front view face profiles for face recognition via the Walsh transform. Pattern Recognit. Lett. 15(6), 551–558 (1994)

15. Konyagin, S.V.: The Fourier-Walsh subsequence of partial sums. Math. Notes 54(4), 1026–1030 (1993)

16. Ladhawala, N.R., Pankratz, D.C.: Almost everywhere convergence of Walsh Fourier series of H^1- functions. Stud. Math. 59, 37–92 (1976)

17. Marcinkiewicz, J.: Quelques théorèmes sur les séries orthogonales. Ann Soc. Polon. Math. 16, 85–96 (1937)

18. Móricz, F., Schipp, F., Wade, W.R.: Cesàro summability of double Walsh-Fourier series.. Trans Amer. Math. Soc. 329, 131–140 (1992)

19. Salem, R.: On strong summability of Fourier series. Am. J. Math. 77, 393–403 (1955)

20. Schipp, F.: Über gewiessen Maximaloperatoren. Annales Univ. Sci. Budapestiensis, Sectio Math. 18, 189–195 (1975)

21. Schipp, F., Wade, W.R., Simon, P.: Walsh series. An introduction to dyadic harmonic analysis. With the assistance from J. Pál (English) Bristol etc.: Adam Hilger (1990)

22. Simon, F. (C, α) summability of Walsh–Kaczmarz–Fourier series. J. Approximation Theory 127 (1), 39–60 (2000)

23. Simon, P.: Cesàro summability with respect to two-parameter Walsh systems.. Monatsh. Math. 131 (4), 321–334 (2001)

24. Sloss, B.G., Blyth, W.F.: A Walsh function method for a non-linear Volterra integral equation. J. Franklin Inst. 340(1), 25–41 (2003)

25. Weisz, F.: Cesàro summability of two-dimensional Walsh-Fourier series. Trans. Amer. Math. Soc. 348, 2169–2181 (1996)

26. Weisz, F.: Maximal estimates for the (C, α) means of d-dimensional Walsh-Fourier series. Proc. Am. Math. Soc. 128 (8), 2337–2345 (2000)

27. Zagorodnij, N.A., Trigub, R.M.: A question of Salem. Theory of functions and mappings. Collect. sci. Works, Kiev (1979)

28. Zalcwasser, Z.: Sur la sommabilité des séries de Fourier. Stud. Math. 6, 82–88 (1936)

29. Zheng, W., Su, W., Ren, F.: Theory and applications of Walsh functions. Shanghai Science-Technic Press, Shanghai (1983)

30. Zygmund, A., Marcinkiewicz, J.: On the summability of double Fourier series. Fund. Math. 32, 122–132 (1939)

31. Zygmund, A.: Trigonometric series, 2nd edn., vol. I & II. Cambridge University Press, Cambridge (1977)

Real Time Vehicle Recognition: A Novel Method for Road Detection

Adrián Peñate Sánchez[2], Alexis Quesada-Arencibia[1],
and Carlos M. Travieso González

[1] Institut de Robòtica i Informàtica Industrial, (CSIC-UPC), Barcelona, Spain
[2] Institute for Cybernetics, University of Las Palmas de Gran Canaria, Las Palmas de G.C.,
Las Palmas, España

Abstract. Knowing the location of the road in an intelligent traffic systems is one of the most used solutions to ease vehicle detection. For this purpose we propose a vehicle recognition algorithm which performs a real time automatic detection of the zones which vehicles occupy. Such algorithm is capable of functioning under extreme conditions such as low resolution, low capture angle and gray scale images.

Keywords: Automatic road detection, Intelligent transport systems, real time vehicle recognition.

1 Introduction

The purpose of this work has been the real time segmentation of vehicles in traffic environments using low resolution videos in gray scale. The method used to resolve this problem has been background subtraction with an adaptive background algorithm to learn what the background is in each moment, with this we intend to solve the problems produced by changes in the illumination.

We have developed a new method to minimize the erroneous segmentation of objects; such method consists in the determination of the probability associated with each pixel in order for it to contain a vehicle when it is segmented. These probabilities are used to relax the threshold in zones where the probability of finding a vehicle is higher. If we place the adequate global threshold we will avoid numerous false positive detections in the zones where vehicles do not transit.

The method we propose can be easily used to perform tracking by detection which has proven to be a very robust approach beacause it does not suffer from intra-frame errors due to the propagation of the error.

We are going to work with the videos used by Neeraj K. Kanhere and Stanley T. Birchfield in their paper [1], and that where kindly lent to us by them. These videos are in a 320x240 resolution with a low angle and in gray scale. We have also made use of [2] for our Matlab development.

2 Image Segmentation

We have used background subtraction for each frame of the videos. To determine the initial background we settle it as the average of the first 200 frames. From this point

R. Moreno-Díaz et al. (Eds.): EUROCAST 2011, Part II, LNCS 6928, pp. 359–364, 2012.
© Springer-Verlag Berlin Heidelberg 2012

we use the adaptive algorithm described in [3] that uses only non segmentated pixels in the background updating process.

Once extracted the background we use a similar methodology as the one described in [4], the difference consists in that we repeat the process twice, first over the segmented image in gray scale and then, after using the threshold, over the binary image that results. We also differ with [4] in that the second time we use a simple dilation and a simple erosion instead of a double closing and a double opening, and we end with a filling.

Fig. 1. Background obtained after applying the proposed techniques

Once we have obtained the blobs in the image we calculate their intrinsic parameters such its are, maximum values of x and y, the centroid and its orientation. We show over the original image a bounding box that shows the segmentation of each vehicle.

This process is thought in order to make it ready to use the temporal inference described in [4] to perform tracking and determine the grouping or splitting of blobs in critical cases such as those when partial occlusion happens between to vehicles due to perspective or shadows, or when not all blobs of the same vehicle have been grouped.

Segmentation Process

We are going to do a walk-through the whole segmentation process. In Fig. 2. we can see the original image as in one of the frames of the database of [1]. The first step would be to subtract the background as seen in Fig. 1. from the image we are going to process, the result can be seen in Fig. 3. As can be seen the result of having produced a good estimation of the background pays off at this point.

The resting part is to perform the clustering of the image in the two main steps we have mentioned earlier, once this has been done we apply the threshold to the image, we obtain the binary image, we perform the final morphological operations and we retrieve the final bloobs of the image.

Fig. 2. Original image

Fig. 3. Step 2, result of subtracting the background from the original image

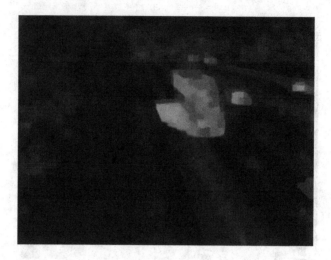

Fig. 4. Step 3, result of applying the morphological operations of filling, closing and opening

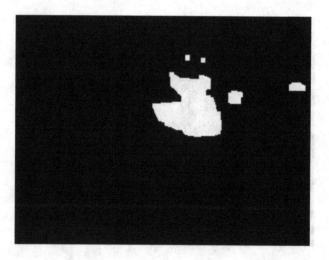

Fig. 5. Step 4, Final phase of threshold and dilation and erosion operations

Fig. 6. Final result of the segmentation and tracking by detection

3   Automatic Segmentation Zone Detection

A recurrent problem in most segmentation algorithms for traffic is appearance of noise caused by moving objects in the background, trees that are moved by the wind, pedestrians crossing a road, and so on. In contexts like this one in which objects of interest occupy a place in the frame that is completely different than the other objects that are moving, we can presuppose that it will be in this areas that we will find our objects of interest.

Fig. 7. Result of applying the probabilistic mask over the substracion of the background

To find the areas of vehicle transit, which will be the road, we suppose that they will be large areas in which the majority of the movement will be focussed. To enhance this zones we will apply a different threshold to them than to the rest of the environment.

The areas that we will enhance will be those that have a probability value higher than the mean value, and that have a big size, with this we avoid the problem derived from the movement of leaves by the wind. In order for the probability mask to be initialized properly it is necessary not to impose a very restrictive threshold to the zones that are not of interest to us.

In Fig. 7. we can observe how by applying the mask we propose the areas that contain more relevant information, pop-up from the rest hence enhancing the detection of vehicles and avoiding the detection of other moving objects such as pedestrians.

The process for the calculation of the probability mask will be to calculate and average with the previous segmented images, applying afterwards the threshold. With the binary image we will apply an erosion followed by a dilation and a filling at the end. In conclusion the novelty of our work consists in applying image processing techniques to probability distributions that enables us to detect the roads in our images in a quite consistent way.

References

1. Kanhere, N.K., Birchfield, S.T.: IEEE. Real-Time Incremental Segmentation and Tracking of Vehicles at Low Camera Angles Using Stable Features
2. Corke, P.I.: Machine Vision Toolbox, http://corkecsiro.au
3. Ha*, D.M., Lee, J.-M., Kim, Y.-D.: Neural-edge-based vehicle detection and traffic parameter extraction
4. Wei Zhang, Q.M., Wu, J., Yang, X., Fang, X.: Multilevel Framework to Detect and Handle Vehicle Occlusion

Pseudorandom Generator to Strengthen Cooperation in VANETs*

J. Molina-Gil[1], P. Caballero-Gil[1], A. Fúster-Sabater[2], and C. Caballero-Gil[1]

[1] Department of Statistics, Operations Research and Computing
University of La Laguna. 38271 La Laguna, Tenerife, Spain
{jmmolina,pcaballe,ccabgil}@ull.es
[2] Institute of Applied Physics. C.S.I.C. Serrano 144, 28006 Madrid, Spain
amparo@iec.csic.es

Abstract. A new secure communication system is here presented for spontaneous and self-managed vehicular ad-hoc networks without any infrastructure on the road or vehicles. Our proposal prevents passive behavior of users who try to take advantage of the network without co-operating in its operation. In this paper we propose the use of encrypted exchange of data as a method to strengthen cooperation in VANETs. In particular, we describe a new pseudorandom generator based on a linear feedback shift register for encrypting sent information through a stream cipher, and analyze its output statistically.

Keywords: Pseudorandom generator, VANET, Cooperation.

1 Introduction

Vehicular Ad-hoc NETworks (VANETs) are wireless networks formed between vehicles and roadside, which are used to provide drivers with information to increase safety, efficiency and comfort in road travel. VANETs do not rely on any central administration for providing communication among the so-called On Board Units (OBUs) in nearby vehicles, and between OBUs and nearby fixed infrastructure usually named Road Side Unit (RSU). In this way, VANETs combine Vehicle TO Vehicle (V2V) with Vehicle TO Infrastructure (V2I) and Infrastructure TO Vehicle (I2V) communications.

Security of communications in VANETs currently represents an important challenge to be solved because it is expected that these networks in the future will imply a major revolution for the safety and comfort of road transport. Apart from safety-related and comfort-related applications of VANETs, there are many other value-added services, like for example, the supply and demand of useful information such as alternative routes, near parking zones, gas stations, hotels, restaurants, access points to Internet, etc. In all these cases it is fundamental

---

* Research supported by the Spanish Ministry of Education and Science and the European FEDER Fund under TIN2008-02236/TSI Project and FPI scholarship BES-2009-016774, and by the Agencia Canaria de Investigación, Innovación y Sociedad de la Información under PI2007/005 Project and FPI scholarship BOC Number 60.

R. Moreno-Díaz et al. (Eds.): EUROCAST 2011, Part II, LNCS 6928, pp. 365–373, 2012.

that the information is encrypted in order to prevent access to non-authorized users who have not paid for the service. Also encryption is used in cluster-based VANETs where a secret key is shared among all members of each cluster, and used both for V2V within the cluster and for V2V between different clusters.

There are several general security requirements, such as authenticity, cooperation, scalability, privacy, anonymity, stability and low delay of communications, which must be considered in any wireless network, and which in VANETs are even more challenging than in other wireless ad-hoc networks because of their specific characteristics such as high mobility, no fixed infrastructure and frequently changing topology that range from rural roads scenarios with little traffic to cities or highways with a huge number of communications. In particular, cooperation among nodes is one of the factors to be considered for the proper performance of any VANET. Besides motivating nodes in packet retransmissions in benefit of neighboring nodes, we must ensure that only those vehicles that belong to the network and help in its operation can benefit from information relayed in it. Here the use of encrypted exchange of data is proposed as a method to strengthen cooperation and authentication in VANETs.

In order to achieve confidentiality, and also for supporting cooperation and authentication, the creation of a secure communication channel is required. Symmetric encryption is here proposed as the most efficient method to establish such a secure communication channel in a VANET because in these networks, traffic data size is generally very large. In particular, here we propose a stream cipher that uses a new pseudorandom number generator whose design is based on a nonlinear filter of a Linear Feedback Shift Register (LFSR).

A PseudoRandom Number Generator (PRNG) is an algorithm for producing a sequence of numbers that approximates the properties of random numbers. In order to be considered useful for cryptographic purposes, the resulting sequence must fulfill at least three properties: large period, pseudorandomness and high linear complexity. All these properties are here analyzed for the proposed PRNG.

This paper starts with a short revision of related work, remarking some weaknesses of existing schemes. Then Section 3 includes a detailed description of the novel pseudorandom number generator and Section 4 provides a full study about the produced sequences. The final section summarizes the conclusions.

2   Related Work

PRNGs have been traditionally used when efficient cryptographic encryption for hardware is needed in order to be used in restricted computer conditions and/or with a demand for real-time performance, like in VANETs. However, many of the pseudorandom generators that have been used or published in the past have suffered practical attacks. An example of this was the A5/1 generator used in GSM mobile phones [16]. Another example was the RC4 algorithm deployed in a multitude of applications as the standard TLS/SSL to secure communication on the Internet, in its version for Wi-Fi networks with WEP security [10]. Another widely pseudorandom generator is the E0 cipher described in the Bluetooth standard [1]. In the research field, some time ago a competition called NESSIE was launched to identify candidates for a European standard pseudorandom generator, but it had to reject all proposals [14]. More recently, another European initiative born from the ECRYPT project, called eSTREAM, identified a portfolio of new generators for stream cipher [4].

Two extremely simple PRNGs are the so-called Geffee generator [5] and the {1,2}-clocked generator [6]. Both are insecure LFSR-based PRNGs that can be cryptanalyzed through different attacks such as guess-and-determine.

In the family of LFSR-based irregularly decimated generators, we can enumerate the shrinking generator [3], the self-shrinking generator [12] and the generalized self-shrinking generator [8]. Irregularly decimated generators produce good cryptographic sequences characterized by long periods, good correlation features, excellent run distribution, balancedness, simplicity in the implementation, etc. However, also for these generators some cryptanalytic attacks have been developed [13] [17] [2]. Regarding specific encryption proposals for VANETs, almost no proposal can be found in the bibliography. [9] proposed a framework for encryption with authentication based on cellular automata.

Therefore, it can be concluded that the design of efficient and secure PRNGs continues to constitute a major challenge in cryptographic research today, and especially in VANET domain.

3 Proposal

This section describes a new PRNG proposed that can be used both for symmetric encryption through stream cipher and for challenge-response authentication based on symmetric cryptography in VANETs.

A PRNG can be seen as a deterministic function whose output is computed from the previous output. It is initialized with a randomly chosen seed. The strength of the PRNG depends on the period and the probability distribution of the output sequences. Many PRNGs are based on LFSRs because this basic generator can be applied efficiently in stream ciphers. In this paper, we define a new LFSR-based PRNG.

An LFSR is defined by a feedback function and a string of binary cells that share the same clock signal. To produce a bit, the register contents are shifted one position, extracting as output the most significant bit of the register in the previous state. The feedback function allows computing every new bit from some bits of the register, so that this new bit is the new least significant bit of the new state. The feedback function of an LFSR is basically an XOR operation on some contents of the cells of the state, given by the feedback polynomial over $GF(2)$ denoted $C(x) = 1 + c_1 x + c_2 x^2 + \cdots + c_L x^L$, whose degree L is the length of the register. The period of sequences produced with an LFSR of length L is less than or equal to $2^L - 1$, value that is reached when its feedback polynomial $C(x)$ is primitive, in which case the produced sequences have optimum statistical properties. The LFSR is commonly used as pseudorandom generator in cryptography due to the good characteristics of the produced sequences and also because its hardware implementation is efficient and its computational requirements are simple. However, LFSRs have significant drawbacks that must be solved in order to be used safely [2]. The worst problem comes from its linearity as the initial state or seed of the LFSR can be easily determined with a simple system of linear equations by using the polynomial function $C(x)$ and a $2L$-bit output keystream. Thus, in order to use an LFSR to build a PRNG, the linearity problem must be solved, what is usually performed with methods such as the so-called non-linear filtering or the non-linear combination of several LFSRs.

Our proposal is based on an LFSR mainly because it is an ideal system for both energy and computational constrained environments. The design is based on an LFSR with primitive feedback polynomial to achieve maximum period and to fulfil the pseudorandomness of the generated sequences. In particular, in the proposal the number of non zero coefficients of the LFSR feedback polynomial $C(x)$ is the smallest possible integer greater than $0.2 \cdot L$, in order to avoid correlation attacks and to ensure efficiency.

The proposed generator consists of two main building blocks: an LFSR and a filter function. The order of the nonlinear filter function has been chosen to be the greatest prime number p less than or equal to the number $L/2$, in order to ensure a large linear complexity.

The nonlinear filter function includes a linear term corresponding to the stage indicated by the function order. The number of terms in each order $i = 2, 3, ..., p$ is given by the integer part of L/i. These terms are obtained by multiplying successive disjoint stages to achieve pseudorandom and confusion.

Below we specify the concrete details of our design generally sketched in Fig. 1. The LFSR used in the exemplification of the proposed design is of length $L=16$. Its contents are denoted by $s_j, s_{j+1}, ..., s_{j+15}$. In particular, the proposed feedback polynomial $C(x)$ of the LFSR is a primitive polynomial of degree 16 defined as $C(x) = 1 + x^2 + x^7 + x^9 + x^{16}$ so that the update function is $s_{j+16} = s_{j+14} + s_{j+9} + s_{j+7} + s_j$. The contents of the 16-bit LFSR represents the state of the cipher and input of the nonlinear filter function f. In particular, from such a state, 16 variables are taken as input to the boolean function $f(x)$ of algebraic degree 7. Such a filter function has been chosen to be balanced, first-order correlation-immune, and with high nonlinearity.

The filter function is defined as

$$f(x_0, x_1, ..., x_{15}) = x_6 + \sum_{i=0}^{7} x_{2i}x_{2i+1} + \sum_{i=0}^{4} x_{3i}x_{3i+1}x_{3i+2} +$$

$$\sum_{i=0}^{3} x_{4i}x_{4i+1}x_{4i+2}x_{4i+3} + \sum_{i=0}^{2} x_{5i}x_{5i+1}x_{5i+2}x_{5i+3}x_{5i+4} +$$

$$\sum_{i=0}^{1} x_{6i}x_{6i+1}x_{6i+2}x_{6i+3}x_{6i+4}x_{6i+5} +$$

$$\sum_{i=0}^{1} x_{7i}x_{7i+1}x_{7i+2}x_{7i+3}x_{7i+4}x_{7i+5} + x_{7i+6} = x_6 +$$

$$x_0x_1 + x_2x_3 + x_4x_5 + x_6x_7 + x_8x_9 + x_{10}x_{11} + x_{12}x_{13} + x_{14}x_{15} +$$

$$x_0x_1x_2 + x_3x_4x_5 + x_6x_7x_8 + x_9x_{10}x_{11} + x_{12}x_{13}x_{14} +$$

$$x_0x_1x_2x_3 + x_4x_5x_6x_7 + x_8x_9x_{10}x_{11} + x_{12}x_{13}x_{14}x_{15} +$$

$$x_0x_1x_2x_3x_4 + x_5x_6x_7x_8x_9 + x_{10}x_{11}x_{12}x_{13}x_{14} +$$

$$x_0x_1x_2x_3x_4x_5 + x_6x_7x_8x_9x_{10}x_{11} + x_0x_1x_2x_3x_4x_5x_6 + x_7x_8x_9x_{10}x_{11}x_{12}x_{13}$$

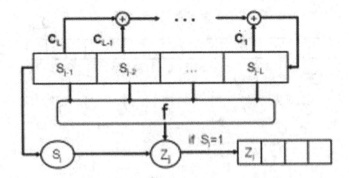

Fig. 1. General Description of the PRNG

where the variables $x_0, x_1, ..., x_{15}$ correspond to the tap positions s_j, s_{j+1}, ..., s_{j+15}, respectively. The design of the cipher, shown in Fig. 2, has been chosen to be as simple as possible for a hardware implementation. Since the LFSR in the cipher is of length 16 and its polynomial is primitive we know that the period of the LFSR keystream is $2^{16} - 1$.

In order to avoid correlation attacks, the output of the nonlinear filter is irregularly decimated so that the output of the LFSR determines whether the corresponding output of the filter function is used or discarded. Consequently, since the LFSR is regularly clocked, on average the cipher will output 0.5 bit/clock. Finally, in order to ensure a stable output, a buffer of size 4 is included.

The generator has been designed to be very small in hardware, using as few gates as possible while maintaining high security. Thus, the cipher is intended to be used in environments where gate count, power consumption and memory needs to be very small.

4   Analysis of the Generator

The most important issue of the analysis of any PRNG for stream ciphers is that any possible attacker must not be able to find any regularities in the output stream. If this were the case, a prediction attack might be launched to predict additional bits of the output stream. For this reason, it is required that the output stream is indistinguishable from a random sequence. This concept is formalized through the Golomb's randomness postulates [7], which are conditions that a sequence should fulfil in order to appear random. A binary sequence that satisfies Golomb's postulates is called a Pseudo-Noise (PN) sequence. Each postulate has an immediate translation into some test of randomness. In order to prove pseudorandomness of our generator, we have generated with it a large number of sequences and subject them to a battery of statistical tests [15]. Since most sequences pass most tests, the confidence in the pseudorandomness of the sequences is large and so is the confidence in the generator. In particular, the generator has passed the following tests: Frequency Test, Serial Test, Poker Test, Runs Test and Autocorrelation Test.

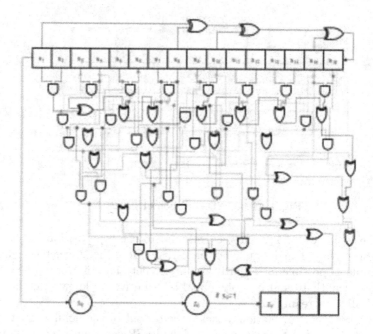

Fig. 2. Detailed Description of the PRNG

The proposed PRNG has been implemented in software to check the pseudorandomness of the output sequences. We generated 3.9 Gb of data with our PRNG in order to check its statistical properties.

Our experiments involved $2^{16} - 1$ bits produced with our generator for every possible seed of the LFSR. The results of all aforementioned statistical tests for a significance $\alpha = 0.05$, shown in Fig. 3, led to the conclusion that our proposed PRNG passes all the studied tests. In particular, the frequency test, which is based on the proportion of zeroes and ones, checks the closeness of the proportion of ones to 0.5. In this case we obtained 86,55% of positive results over all possible inputs. On the other hand, the serial test, whose focus is to determine whether the frequency of all possible 2^m m-bit overlapping patterns across the sequence is approximately the same. 100% of all possible outputs pass the serial test. For the poker test we divide the sequence into subsequences of a certain length, and then check whether these sequences appear the same number of times. It results in 80,89% of positive results with our generator over all possible inputs. The purpose of the runs test is to determine whether the number of runs of ones and zeros of various lengths is as expected for a random sequence. In particular, this test produced 97,74% of positive results for short runs, and 100% of positive results for long runs, for the sequences produced with the proposed generator over all possible inputs. Finally, in the autocorrelation test, the purpose is to check for correlations between the sequence and its shifted versions. It produces 100% positive results with the proposed generator over all possible inputs.

Test	Frequency	Serial	Poker	Short Runs	Long Runs	Autocorrelation
% of Success	86,55	100	80,89	97,74	100	100

Fig. 3. Results of Statistical Tests

Ten thousand random and different seeds have been used to initialize the PRNG and the correlation between the obtained sequences has been computed concluding that two simultaneous identical sequences do not appear.

In order to check the unpredictability property, the serial correlation test has been implemented. Such a test measures the extent to which each m-bit output depends upon the previous m-bit output. For our sequences, this value is obtained close to zero so we conclude the fulfilment of the property.

Finally, since a PRNG is a finite state machine with at most 2^L states, an output sequence must become cyclic after at most 2^L output bits. As a consequence, the more significant bits of the sequence can be modelled as a function of the less significant bits by a suitable recurrence relation. In this work we computed the period for the analyzed example and obtained always values around $2^{16} - 1$ for every possible seed.

On the other hand, the linear complexity of any sequence is the length of the smallest LFSR that generates the sequence. Thus, high linear complexity is a necessary requirement for all sequences generated by a PRNG. There exists an efficient algorithm by Berlekamp and Massey [11] that constructs the shortest linear recurrence describing the sequence. We computed the linear complexity of the produced sequences through the Berlekamp-Massey Algorithm over $2^{16} - 1$ bits of the keystream, confirming that it is always maximum and equal to half the number of analyzed bits.

We now briefly consider some general attacks on stream ciphers in order to investigate to what extent they can be applied against the proposed generator. Indeed, resistance against known cryptanalytic attacks is the most important basis for the design of a new encryption algorithm because there should be no faster successful attack than the exhaustive key search. Due to the good statistical properties of the PN-sequences produced by the basic LFSR, and because the function f is first-order correlation-immune, the correlations between the output of the generator and the bits of the LFSR are so small that they can not be exploited for correlation attacks. In addition, a filtering based on a function $f(x)$ of degree 7 is not vulnerable to algebraic attacks as the algebraic degrees of the output bits when expressed as a function of LFSR-bit are large in general, and varying in time so this defeats algebraic attacks. In addition, the cost of time/memory/data tradeoff attacks on stream ciphers is $O(2^{L/2})$, where L is the number of inner states of the stream cipher. To comply with the margins set by this attack, $L = 16$ has been chosen. The sampling resistance of $f(x)$ is reasonable because this function does not become linear in the remaining variables by fixing less than half of its 16 variables.

According to the aforementioned analysis, most sequences produced by the proposed PRNG pass most statistical analyses, have short hardware requirements and are resistant to known attacks, what confirms the validity of the proposal and the hypothesis that the proposed nonlinear filtering and decimation solve the linearity problem of LFSR-based generators.

5 Conclusions

In this work, a new PRNG whose design is based on a nonlinear filtering of a LFSR has been described. Our proposal is proposed to be used in VANETs so that it can prevent passive behavior of vehicles who try to take advantage of the network without cooperating in its operation. The new PRNG has been analyzed here and the obtained results confirm the good pseudorandomness properties of the output sequences.

References

1. Bluetooth, Specifications of the Bluetooth system, v4.0,
   http://www.bluetooth.com/
2. Caballero-Gil, P., Fúster-Sabater, A.: Improvement of the edit distance attack to clock-controlled LFSR-based stream ciphers. In: Moreno Díaz, R., Pichler, F., Quesada Arencibia, A. (eds.) EUROCAST 2005. LNCS, vol. 3643, pp. 355–364. Springer, Heidelberg (2005)
3. Coppersmith, D., Krawczyk, H., Mansour, Y.: The Shrinking Generator. In: Stinson, D.R. (ed.) CRYPTO 1993. LNCS, vol. 773, pp. 22–39. Springer, Heidelberg (1994)
4. ECRYPT Stream Cipher Project, http://www.ecrypt.eu.org/stream/index.htm
5. Geffe, P.: How to protect data with ciphers that are really hard to break. Electronics 46(1), 99–101 (1973)
6. Gollmann, D., Chambers, W.: Clock-controlled shift registers: A review. IEEE J. Selected Areas Comm. 7(4), 525–533 (1989)
7. Golomb, S.W.: Shift Register Sequences, revised edn. Aegean Park Press, Laguna Hills (1982)
8. Hu, Y., Xiao, G.: Generalized Self-Shrinking Generator. IEEE Trans. Inform. Theory 50, 714–719 (2004)
9. Jain, U.: Online Authentication with Encryption and Anonymous Authentication in Vehicular Adhoc Networks. PhD Thesis. Indian Institute of Technology (2008)
10. Mantin, I.: Analysis of the stream cipher RC4. Master's thesis. Weizmann Institute of Science, Rehovot (2001)
11. Massey, J.: Shift-register synthesis and BCH decoding. IEEE Transactions on Information Theory IT-15, 122–127 (1969)
12. Meier, W., Staffelbach, O.: The Self-shrinking Generator. In: De Santis, A. (ed.) EUROCRYPT 1994. LNCS, vol. 950, pp. 205–214. Springer, Heidelberg (1995)
13. Mihaljevic, M.J.: A Faster Cryptanalysis of the Self-Shrinking Generator. In: Pieprzyk, J.P., Seberry, J. (eds.) ACISP 1996. LNCS, vol. 1172, pp. 182–2189. Springer, Heidelberg (1996)

14. NESSIE: New european schemes for signatures, integrity, and encryption, http://www.cosic.esat.kuleuven.be/nessie/
15. NIST, Random Number Generation Technical Working Group, http://csrc.nist.gov/rng/
16. Maximov, A., Johansson, T., Babbage, S.: An improved correlation attack on A5/1. In: Handschuh, H., Hasan, M.A. (eds.) SAC 2004. LNCS, vol. 3357, pp. 1–18. Springer, Heidelberg (2004)
17. Zenner, E., Krause, M., Lucks, S.: Improved cryptanalysis of the self-shrinking generator. In: Varadharajan, V., Mu, Y. (eds.) ACISP 2001. LNCS, vol. 2119, pp. 21–35. Springer, Heidelberg (2001)

AUTOPIA Program Advances: How to Automate the Traffic?

Vicente Milanés, Enrique Onieva, Joshué Pérez, Jorge Villagrá, Jorge Godoy, Javier Alonso, Carlos González, Teresa de Pedro, and Ricardo García*

AUTOPIA program, Center for Automation and Robotics (CAR)
La Poveda-Arganda del Rey, 28500 Madrid, Spain
{vicente.milanes,enrique.onieva,joshue.perez,jorge.villagra,jorge.godoy,
javier.alonso,carlos.gonzalez,teresa.pedro,ricardo.garcia}@csic.es

Abstract. Road transport fatalities are one of the major causes of death in developed countries, so the investigation in aid systems for vehicles to reduce these figures is nowadays an open field of research. With this final goal, AUTOPIA program has been working from 1996 in the development of aid driving systems and, specifically, in autonomous systems capable of replacing the driver in some specific tasks, reducing so, the dependence on the human driver. In this paper we present some of the most relevant advances achieved using commercial vehicles. To achieve this objective, prototype vehicles have been equipped with capabilities to permit it to act over the actuators of the vehicle autonomously. Several cooperative maneuvers have been developed during last years toward a final goal: an intelligent traffic control system.

1 Introduction

The use of road networks as main transportation system causes a saturation in the vicinity of large cities. One way to try to solve this problem is based on the development of *Advanced Driver Assistance Systems* (ADAS) to relegate the drivers from some tedious driving-related tasks to make the driving easier and safer. The AUTOPIA program is focused in this line. In this connection, this paper presents the more significant advances achieved by the group in recent years toward a traffic control system on a prototype commercial car that can be easily translated to the market.

A brief summary about the main results in the ADAS field can start in the late 1950s and 1960s when speed controllers with errors up to 16 km/h were available [17]. Nowadays, *Cruise Control* (CC) systems, and its improvement to *Adaptive CC* (ACC) systems, are capable of working at speeds greater than 30 km/h either to follow a reference speed or a leading vehicle respectively. However, this systems are not available for urban traffic where the congestion is greater.

* This work was supported by the Plan Nacional, under the project Tránsito (TRA2008-06602-C03-01) and by the Comisión Interministerial de Ciencia y Tecnología under the project GUIADE (Ministerio de Fomento T9/08).

R. Moreno-Díaz et al. (Eds.): EUROCAST 2011, Part II, LNCS 6928, pp. 374–381, 2012.

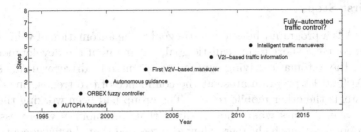

Fig. 1. AUTOPIA program advances toward a fully-automation traffic control system

Indeed, commercial systems only take into account the leading vehicle but most of traffic collisions occur at crossroads and vehicle driving in perpendicular road have to be considered.

This communication presents AUTOPIA approach to attack several of these yet unsolved topics in the automotive sector. ADAS advances, in our opinion, will cause the coexistence of vehicles that can be guided through automatic controllers and vehicles driven manually in a large-medium term. So, to validate the proposed controllers, a gas-propelled convertible Citroën C3 Pluriel has been equipped with automatic driving capabilities and another Citroën C3 is endowed with the needed equipment to be capable of sending relevant data between vehicles. The former has the throttle and brake actuators fully-automated and the latter is manually driven. Different fuzzy-logic-based controllers have been developed to deal with all these maneuvers.

2   AUTOPIA Program

Last decades have seen significant advances in the driver aid systems' field [18]. First results were obtained using on-board sensor systems – lidar, radar, ultrasounds or cameras.– to advise the driver in case of a risk situation using a human-machine interface (HMI) [1]. Next steps were focused on the development of systems capable of aiding the driver in specific driving-related tasks – cruise control (CC), lane keeping assistance (LKA) or intelligent speed assistance (ISA). Nowadays, active systems to prevent or mitigate collisions – emergency braking (EB) or collision avoidance (CA) – are being implemented in commercial vehicles. All these advances bear in mind as a long-term goal autonomous vehicles driving along the roads and, consequently, a fully-automated traffic control.

This paper presents the AUTOPIA program advances toward an automated traffic control system (see figure 1). AUTOPIA has been working in the development of intelligent transportation systems (ITS) during the last 15 years. In this time, it has designed, developed and implemented two fully-automated electric Citroën Berlingo vans [15] and a fully-automated convertible Citroën C3 Pluriel [7]. Nowadays, the automation process of a Citroën C3 and a electric minibus are in progress. These vehicles allow us to perform not only autonomous guidance but also cooperative maneuvers involving two or more than two vehicles.

2.1   First Steps

AUTOPIA is a program whose long term goal is the automation of vehicles. This is not, of course a short term realistic goal, but many of the developments necessary for the automatic driving can be implemented as driver warning systems

The AUTOPIA program arose at the confluence of two trends, one of them, fuzzy systems the other mobile robots. The group had been working these subjects for several years when they realized that automobiles where essentially mobile robots and much cheaper. They also realized that the fuzzy control techniques they had been using could perfectly be used to control the automobiles. So, the AUTOPIA program started in 1996.

The group had been working for a long time in fuzzy sets, doing projects such as the control of a special robot to tune Ultra High Frequency (UHF) amplifiers [4], a task that took a human operator about one hour and less than a minute to the robot. They also had cooperated with projects whose aim was to develop a fuzzy chip [2]. Part of these efforts consisted in the development of the ORBEX, a software system that permitted define the fuzzy control in terms of *IF ... THEN ...* sentences very similar to natural language [3].

From the very beginning the goal of the program was to perform real tests with real cars. So, the project started building a test track consisting of about 1km of roads organized to simulate three blocks of a city, the longest path being 250m long. Then the master sensor was decided it should be a real time *Kinematic-Differential Global Positioning System* (RTK-DGPS). This was not a cheap decision, but this one sensor permitted to acquire full knowledge of the position and the development of the algorithms, that would work equally well if the information was acquired by other means.

The first experiments were done on electric vans [13], but it was soon found out that there was no great difference with gasoline cars. In any case, the vehicles were equipped with WiFi and a RTK-DGPS. WiFi was used to feed the RTK corrections to the vehicles, so the GPS could achieve the centimetric precision. The equipment of the vehicle included a computer and a motor card.

2.2   Recent Years

Next step in our research was focused in the development of cooperation between two vehicles. The first implemented maneuver was and adaptive CC (ACC) [12]. To this end, the radio system was replaced by a wireless communication system that was used both to receive the differential correction and to send information between the vehicles.

Later, information coming from the infrastructure was introduced in our control system – using mainly radio frequency identification (RFID) and Zigbee technologies. This was motivated by the fact that present vehicles are not equipped with vehicle to vehicle communication ability and vehicle to infrastructure communication is needed to send information about its position, direction and intention without modifying the present vehicles. First tests with these technologies were done in 2008 [10] and 2009 [16] with encouraging results.

Fig. 2. AUTOPIA program cars. A fully-automated convertible Citroën C3 and and intelligent Citroën C3 car.

We are now working toward a new architecture [5] capable of integrating all these advances to perform an automated traffic control system. Bearing this in mind, a control station to manage a local area of traffic has been introduced and will be in charge of managing all the information coming either from the vehicles or the infrastructure with the goal of reducing the traffic accidents.

3   Vehicles

Two gas-propelled vehicles are used in the experimental phase (see Fig. 2). The former is a convertible Citroën C3 Pluriel with throttle and brake pedals modified to allow automatic driving with an on-board control unit (OCU) equipped with ORBEX. The latter – used to perform the cooperative maneuvers – is a Citroën C3 equipped with sensory information to permit exchange data about its position and speed with the autonomous car. This section describes the Pluriel's automation process and the vehicle's equipment.

3.1   Autonomous Vehicles

The Pluriel car is fully automated, i.e. the throttle and the brake are fully computer controlled [7]. As positioning sensors, the vehicle has an RTK-DGPS and an inertial measurement unit [8] connected to the OCU, capable of providing positions at a $5Hz$ rate. Data such as speed or steering wheel angle are obtained reading the vehicle's CAN bus.

The control signal of the throttle is an electric value. In the Pluriel's case, the action over the pedal is emulated using a signals computer laboratory card. The braking system was designed with the sole premise of maintaining the original car circuit operation all the time. For this reason, a selector valve was installed that allowed to merge the original braking system with the one we installed. The pressure generated is proportional to an analog signal. In case of need, the operator in the vehicle can step on the brake pedal and, should this pressure be greater than the computer generated one, the selector card would yield and the brake-by-wire would be activated [6].

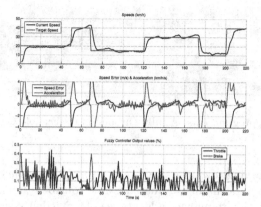

Fig. 3. Speed control experiment

3.2   Intelligent Vehicles

AUTOPIA has another type of vehicle, which can be named *intelligent* as it is carries electronic instrumentation although it is not automated. The goal of this vehicle is to cooperate with the automatic vehicle, although it is manually driven. The intelligent vehicle carries a computer, and a RTK-DGPS which is used to obtain both position and speed. This car is not modified so it can freely circulate along the roads. The communications system is identical to that of the automatic vehicle. This vehicle cooperates with the automatic one in maneuvers such as adaptive speed control or traversing crossroads.

4   Some Experimental Results

This section presents some of the achieved results during last years. Specifically, a speed control system at urban speeds, an ACC maneuver involving two vehicle and an intelligent intersection are described.

4.1   Speed Control

Figure 3 presents a trial with our convertible Citroën C3 performing a speed control experiment. The upper plot shows the current – blue line – and target – red line – speeds. The middle plot shows the values of the fuzzy input variables – Speed Error is plotted in blue line and Acceleration is plotted in red line – and, the lower plot depicts the output of the fuzzy controller, that is, the action over the throttle – blue line – and brake – red line – pedals generated by ORBEX (see [14] for more details about the controller).

One can appreciate how the fuzzy speed control is capable of following the target speed with good accuracy. Note that the obtained results are encouraging in spite of the apparently low control cycle rate – set at $5Hz$ by the on-board GPS receiver.

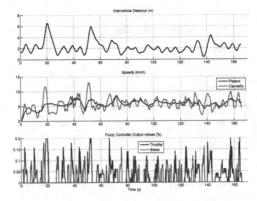

Fig. 4. Adaptive speed control experiment

4.2   Adaptive Speed Control

Figure 4 shows the behavior of the adaptive speed fuzzy controller at very low speeds. The upper plot depicts the gap between vehicles, that is, the separation distance between them. The middle plot shows the speed of both vehicles during the experiment – blue line for the leading vehicle and red line for the trailing one – and, the lower plot represents the normalized output of the ORBEX fuzzy controller over the actuators (see [9] for details).

One can appreciate how the speed of the leading vehicle is slightly higher than $5km/h$ during the experiment. Taking into account both vehicles are gas-propelled vehicles – and, consequently, the highly non-linear dynamic of this kind of vehicles at these speeds – the inter-distance is maintained during most of the time in values lower than $2m$ with maximum values of $6m$ and minimum values higher than $20cm$ to prevent a collision.

4.3   Crossroad

Figure 5 presents the behavior of the crossroad fuzzy controller for urban environments. The upper plot depicts the speed of both vehicles – blue line for the vehicle with right-of-way and red line for the vehicle without right-of-way and equipped with the fuzzy crossroad controller – in km/h. The middle plot depicts the distance of both vehicles to the cross point – red line for the vehicle without right-of-way and blue line for the vehicle with right-of-way – and, the lower plot depicts the normalized output of the ORBEX fuzzy crossroad controller over the pedals (see [11] for details). One of the vehicles is automatically driven, the other – the vehicle with the right-of-way – is manually driven.

At the beginning of the experiment both vehicles are driven at similar speeds – close to 20 km/h – and the distances to the cross point are similar. In second 10, the fuzzy crossroad controller reduced the speed of the automatic vehicle in order to permit the other vehicle to cross. About second 16, the vehicle with

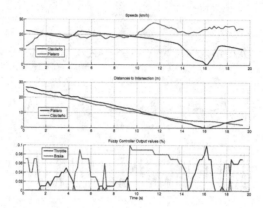

Fig. 5. Crossroad experiment

right-of-way crosses the intersection and, then the vehicle equipped with the crossroad fuzzy controller accelerates to cross safely.

5   Conclusions

This paper has presented the developments of the AUTOPIA program toward a safer road transport vehicles. In spite of the final target – a fully-automated traffic control system – can be considered a long-term goal, the presented results constitute an excellent starting point toward intelligent vehicles driving in intelligent roads.

Several controllers have been developed to face some of the most important problems in the road transportation as cruise control and adaptive cruise control at low speeds and intersection management with excellent results. These controllers have been tested using a prototype autonomous vehicle developed by the AUTOPIA program in a private driving circuit that emulates an urban traffic area. The real results obtained are promising but there is further room to improve these results searching the final goal: no accidents in roads.

References

1. Amditis, A., Pagle, K., Joshi, S., Bekiaris, E.: Driver-vehicle-environment monitoring for on-board driver support systems: Lessons learned from design and implementation. Applied Ergonomics 41(2), 225–235 (2010)
2. García, R., de Pedro, T.: Modeling a fuzzy coprocessor and its programming language. Mathware and Soft Computing 5, 167–174 (1998)
3. García, R., de Pedro, T.: First applications of the orbex coprocessor: Control of unmanned vehicles. Mathware and Soft Computing 7, 265–273 (2000)
4. Garcia, R., Fernandez, P., de Pedro, T.: Robot fingers to tune tv amplifiers using fuzzy logic. Fuzzy Sets and Systems 70, 147–153 (1995)

5. Milanés, V., Godoy, J., Pérez, J., Vinagre, B., González, C., Onieva, E., Alonso, A.: V2I-Based Architecture for Information Exchange among Vehicles. In: 7th Symposium on Intelligent Autonomous Vehicles (2010)

6. Milanés, V., González, C., Naranjo, J.E., Onieva, E., de Pedro, T.: Electro-hydraulic braking system for autonomous vehicles. International Journal of Automotive Technology 11, 1–6 (2010)

7. Milanés, V., LLorca, D., Vinagre, B., González, C., Sotelo, M.: Clavileño: Evolution of an autonomous car. In: Proc. of 13th International IEEE Conference on Intelligent Transportation Systems, pp. 1129–1134 (September 2010)

8. Milanés, V., Naranjo, J.E., Gonzánez, C., Alonso, J., de Pedro, T.: Autonomous Vehicle based in Cooperative GPS and Inertial Systems. Robotica 26, 627–633 (2008)

9. Milanés, V., Onieva, E., Pérez, J., de Pedro, T., González, C.: Control de velocidad adaptativo para entornos urbanos congestionados. Revista Iberoamericana de Automática e Informática Industrial 6(4), 66–73 (2009)

10. Milanés, V., Onieva, E., Vinagre, B., González, C., Pérez, J., Alonso, J.: Sistema de asistencia a la conducción basado en una red de comunicaciones de bajo coste. DYNA 85(3), 245–254 (2010)

11. Milanés, V., Pérez, J., Onieva, E., González, C.: Controller for urban intersections based on wireless communications and fuzzy logic. IEEE Transactions on Intelligent Transportation Systems 11(1), 243–248 (2010)

12. Naranjo, J.E., Gonzalez, C., Garcia, R., de Pedro, T.: ACC+Stop&go maneuvers with throttle and brake fuzzy control. IEEE Transactions on Intelligent Transportation Systems 7(2), 213–225 (2006)

13. Naranjo, J.E., Gonzalez, C., Garcia, R., de Pedro, T., Revuelto, J., Reviejo, J.: Fuzzy logic based lateral control for gps map tracking. In: Proc. IEEE Intelligent Vehicles Symp., pp. 397–400 (2004)

14. Onieva, E., Milanés, V., González, C., de Pedro, T., Perez, J., Alonso, J.: Throttle and brake pedals automation for populated areas. Robotica 28, 509–516 (2010)

15. Pérez, J., González, C., Milanés, V., Onieva, E., Godoy, J., de Pedro, T.: Modularity, adaptability and evolution in the autopia architecture for control of autonomous vehicles. In: Proc. IEEE International Conference on Mechatronics, ICM 2009, April 14-17, pp. 1–5 (2009)

16. Pérez, J., Seco, F., Milanés, V., Jiménez, A., Díaz, J., de Pedro, T.: An RFID-Based Intelligent Vehicle Speed Controller Using Active Traffic Signals. Sensors 10(6), 5872–5887 (2010)

17. Shaout, A., Jarrah, M.A.: Cruise control: technology review. Computers & Electrical Engineering 23(4), 259–271 (1997)

18. Zoghi, H., Hajali, M., Dirin, M., Malekan, K.: Evaluation of passive & active intelligent speed adaption system. In: Proc. 2nd Int Computer and Automation Engineering (ICCAE) Conf., vol. 4, pp. 182–186 (2010)

Study of Traffic Flow Controlled with Independent Agent-Based Traffic Signals

Enrique Onieva, Vicente Milanés, Joshué Pérez, Javier Alonso,
Teresa de Pedro, Ricardo García, Jorge Godoy, and Jorge Villagra*

AUTOPIA program, Center for Automation and Robotics (CAR)
La Poveda-Arganda del Rey, 28500 Madrid, Spain
{enrique.onieva,vicente.milanes,joshue.perez,javier.alonso,teresa.pedro,
ricardo.garcia,jorge.godoy,jorge.villagra}@csic.es

Abstract. Dealing with urban traffic is a highly complex task since it involves the coordination of many actors. Traditional approaches attempt to optimize traffic signal control for a particular vehicle density; the main disadvantage lies in the fact that traffic changes constantly. Managing traffic congestion seems to be a problem of adaptation rather than of optimization. In this work we present an agent-based traffic simulator which represents a traffic grid with two-way roads of three exclusive lanes per direction, with intersections regulated by signals. We study the repercussions on traffic flow of simple parametric behaviours when each light operates independently. A dominance analysis is applied to compare the strategies.

1 Introduction

Traffic congestion is a major recurring problem faced in many countries of the world due to the increased level of urbanization and the availability of cheaper vehicles [1].

There is no solution to the traffic congestion problem when the vehicle density saturates the streets, but there are many ways in which the vehicle flow can be constrained in order to improve traffic. Improvements aimed at reducing urban traffic congestion must focus on reducing internal bottlenecks in the network, rather than replacing the network itself. Signal (or traffic light) control is an easy way to improve traffic flow. There are basically two kinds of signal systems [2]: fixed-time and traffic-actuated. Each have their advantages and disadvantages [3]. However, their common objective is to minimize the vehicle delay and average queue length caused by intersections [4].

Since an intersection is the fundamental element of a traffic network, optimizing the performance of an isolated intersection can contribute to improving the performance of a network. Many studies in the literature have focused on

* The authors are grateful to the CYCIT (Spain) and Plan Nacional (Spain) for support from the GUIADE (P9/08) and TRANSITO (TRA2008-06602-C03-01) projects respectively, in the development of this work.

R. Moreno-Díaz et al. (Eds.): EUROCAST 2011, Part II, LNCS 6928, pp. 382–389, 2012.

isolated intersection strategies [5] [6]. Other studies, however, have been based on intersection grids [7] [8], and seem to be hopeful approaches to realistically solving the problem.

In this work we present an agent-based traffic simulator which represents a traffic grid with two-way roads of three exclusive lanes per direction and intersections regulated by signals. We study the repercussions on traffic flow of simple parametric behaviors for each light, that acts independently but respecting traffic restrictions.

Self regulated strategies [9] are implemented to model the behavior for each light. There were implemented different *selfish* strategies, where each light turns green in the moment it can; *cooperative* strategies, where lights respect other ones that need to turn green because of demand; and a classic *fixed time* strategy, where lights turn green according with a patron. Each strategy is executed under a different set of parameters and traffic grid configurations with the aim of search for the best configuration.

A dominance analysis is applied to compare strategies according with a wide set of parameters such as: number of collapsed lanes, stopped vehicles or averaged speed; with distinctions between left, straight and right lanes.

We describe first the implementation of an agent-based model (section 2), and then the design of the set of parametric strategies (section 3). In the experimental part of the work (section 4), a total of 27 strategies were tested in the simulator with different parameters values. Since it is very difficult to compare the performance of the strategies in all the measured aspects, the data were subjected to a dominance analysis (section 5). Finally, some concluding remarks and future works are presented (section 6).

2   Multiagent Model for Traffic Simulation

The simulation environment was implemented using *NetLogo* [10], a multiagent modeling environment. The developed model tries to approach a realistic traffic environment, where vehicles can turn right, left or continue straight when they reach an intersection.

The environment represents a $[n \times n]$ intersection grid controlled by light signals. Each road is divided into three exclusive lanes, one for each of the three possible manoeuvres at the next intersection: left turn, through, or right turn. Basic aspects and considerations on the agents involved are described below.

Each *vehicle* occupies the correspondent lane with the manoeuvre that intends to do. Vehicles try to go at a maximum speed but stop when a vehicle or a red/amber light is immediately in front of them. In case there is a green light in front of them, they initiates the manoeuvre.

There is a *traffic light* agent regulating each lane of each intersection. They have to satisfy the following constraints: i) amber state is maintained for a certain ammount of time (φ_{amber}). ii) traffic lights detect and count vehicles in a certain distance α in front of them, as shown in figure 1. iii) Each light has its own conflicting lights depending on the kind of manoeuvre regulated; figure 2 shows

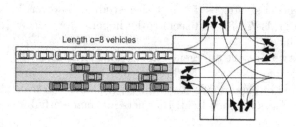

Fig. 1. Graphical representation of the *alpha* parameter which determines the detection range of the litght

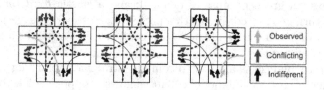

Fig. 2. Conflicting lights for a light to turn green for a left-turn (left), straight (centre), and right-turn (right) manoeuvre. A light cannot be turned green while any of its conflicting lights is green or amber.

the conflicts graphically. iv) Each light knows the state of its own conflicting lights.

Generators insert (if possible) new vehicles into the roads. The insertion is governed by three probabilities, P_r, P_s, and P_l, corresponding to the probability of creating a vehicle with a right turn, straight, or left turn intention ($P_r + P_s + P_s \leq 1$ to allow no vehicle to be created in a timestep), and γ represents the total number of vehicles to be created.

Vehicles are eliminated of the environment once they reach one road ending without intersection. Once a vehicle finalizes a manoeuvre it generates (randomly) the new desired manoeuvre to realize when reach the next intersection.

In sum, to define an environment in which to test the different strategies, the following parameters must be set: n to define the size of the world and the number of vertical and horizontal streets; φ_{amber} to define the time restriction on the amber lights; α the range of the vehicle detector in each signal; and (P_r, P_s, P_l, γ) to define the way the vehicles are generated.

3   Traffic Lights Behavior

Each traffic light agent maintains the following internal variables:

- χ represents the number of vehicles within a distance α in front of the traffic light.
- S is the current state of the light (*red, amber* or *green*).
- φ stores timesteps without the current state having changed.

- C represents the set of conflicting lights.
- NC represents the set of non-conflicting lights.
- $S_{C|NC}$ are defined as the current state of the conflicting/non-conflicting lights.

Following subsections explain in detail each one of the agent oriented light behaviors.

3.1   Fixed Time Control

This is a simple *non-adaptive* method (henceforward $Fix(\psi)$) whose main idea is to synchronize all traffic lights in time under a single pre-defined parameter ψ such that each ψ timesteps one of the four incoming roads to an intersection is assigned priority over the rest, and all traffic lights on that road change to green while the rest remain to red. Note that the traffic light on the right lane of the intersecting road to the left of the priority road can also be turned green because it generates no conflict anywhere, as can be seen in figure 3.

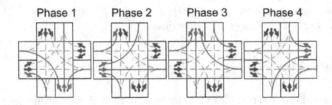

Fig. 3. Four phases used in Fixed Time Prioritization

3.2   Basic Selfish Strategy

In this strategy (henceforward $Selfish_{Basic}(\alpha, \varphi_{min})$) each traffic light turns green if there are vehicles waiting and all the conflicting lights are red; the green state is maintained while vehicles are detected within a radius α. Formally, the strategy is defined as:

- Red lights change to green if $[\chi > 0$ and $S(C) = red$ and $\varphi > \varphi_{min}]$
- Green lights change to amber if $[\chi = 0$ and $\varphi > \varphi_{min}]$
- Amber lights change to red if $[\varphi = \varphi_{amber}]$

3.3   Cooperative Selfish Strategy

This strategy (henceforward $Selfish_{Cooperative}(\alpha, \varphi_{min}, \varphi_C)$)is based on the previous one, the main idea is to maintain the same policy for switching from the red to the green state, while adding a *cooperative* situation in which green lights turn amber if any of the conflicting lights on red ($\varphi(C_{red})$) has demand during an established time φ_C. Formally, the cooperative selfish strategy is defined as:

- Red lights change to green if $[\chi > 0$ and $S(C) = red$ and $\varphi > \varphi_{min}]$
- Green lights change to amber if $[(\chi = 0$ or $\varphi(C_{red}) > \varphi_C)$ and $\varphi > \varphi_{min}]$
- Amber lights change to red if $[\varphi = \varphi_{amber}]$

4   Experimentation Setup

Each strategy is tested for in scenarios: an isolated intersection and a 4×4 intersection grid. All the cases use $\varphi_{amber} = 5$ and uniform vehicle generation probabilities ($P_r = P_s = P_l = 0.33$). Each generator inserts one vehicle/timestep into the grid until it generates $\gamma = 150$ vehicles[1]. The simulation runs until all the vehicles leave the simulation world and each run is repeated 50 times, taking averaged measures.

The following variables are used to assess the effectiveness of the considered strategy (suffices r, s, and l correspond to right-turn, straight, and left-turn lanes): (C_r, C_s, C_l) represent the average % of collapsed lanes (lanes with more than 10 vehicles stopped in front of a signal). (S_r, S_s, S_l) represent the average speed of the vehicles. (R_r, R_s, R_l) represent the average % of the time of the red state of a traffic light with demand ($\chi > 0$). A final set of variables (C, S, R) represent the respective average values independently of the lane observed.

The strategies tested are: $Fix(\psi = \{20, 50, 100\})$ for fixed time control; $Selfish_{Basic}(\alpha = \{0.5, 5, 10\}, \varphi_{min} = \{10, 20\})$ for the basic selfish strategy; and $Selfish_{Cooperative}(\alpha = \{0.5, 5, 10\}, \varphi_{min} = \{20, 50\}, \varphi_C = \{20, 50, 100\})$. That sum a total of 27 different strategies.

5   Overall Analysis

Twenty seven different strategies were tested in two different scenarios, reporting each a total of twelve variables that can be grouped in three sets (collapsed streets, vehicle speeds, and time on red with demand) of 4 elements each (the three lanes and the average).

An overall analysis to determine which strategy performs the best would involve many correlations. We therefore performed a Pareto-type [11] dominance analysis. The results are given in Table 1 grouped by four criteria: i) **Overall**: This column lists the number of strategies that dominate the given strategy in all 24 variables. ii) **Scenario**: These two columns list the number of strategies that dominate the given strategy in the 12 variables referred to the isolated intersection (D_I) and the 12 referred to the 4×4 intersection grid (D_G) separately. iii) **Aspect**: These three columns list the number of strategies that dominate the given strategy in each aspect studied. There are 8 variables for each aspect: collapsed streets (D_C), speed of the vehicles (D_S), and time on red with demand (D_T). iv) **Lane**: These three columns list the number of strategies that dominate the given strategy in the three different lanes; D_R, D_S, and D_L for right, straight, and left lanes, respectively.

The following four subsections analyze each of these criteria.

---

[1] There are 4 generators in the isolated intersection scenario (600 vehicles in total) and 16 in the intersection grid scenario (2400 vehicles in total).

Table 1. Overall Pareto analysis table

Strategy	Overall D	Scenario D_I	D_G	Aspect D_C	D_S	D_T	Lane D_R	D_S	D_L
$F(20)$	0	3	0	2	0	5	3	5	0
$F(50)$	0	0	0	1	0	3	0	1	0
$F(100)$	0	0	0	0	0	0	0	0	0
$SB(0.5, 10)$	2	5	6	19	3	5	7	2	9
$SB(5, 10)$	0	0	0	6	0	0	1	0	0
$SB(10, 10)$	0	0	0	0	0	0	0	0	0
$SB(0.5, 50)$	1	1	11	17	2	4	10	6	2
$SB(5, 50)$	0	0	7	2	1	2	3	3	0
$SB(10, 50)$	0	1	0	2	2	0	1	0	0
$SC(0.5, 10, 20)$	2	7	8	21	9	7	19	3	11
$SC(5, 10, 20)$	3	8	6	13	11	11	13	3	12
$SC(10, 10, 20)$	0	1	1	0	5	14	8	2	5
$SC(0.5, 50, 20)$	0	0	10	19	0	5	15	1	4
$SC(5, 50, 20)$	1	2	9	10	5	6	10	6	3
$SC(10, 50, 20)$	0	0	0	0	0	5	0	0	4
$SC(0.5, 10, 50)$	2	11	0	13	2	4	3	2	3
$SC(5, 10, 50)$	4	6	11	13	15	6	12	5	10
$SC(10, 10, 50)$	0	0	0	0	4	1	1	0	3
$SC(0.5, 50, 50)$	1	1	7	14	1	4	4	1	4
$SC(5, 50, 50)$	2	3	8	11	3	4	6	3	4
$SC(10, 50, 50)$	0	0	1	1	0	4	6	1	1
$SC(0.5, 10, 100)$	2	5	6	17	6	6	6	6	10
$SC(5, 10, 100)$	3	3	10	11	9	3	3	11	10
$SC(10, 10, 100)$	0	0	0	0	3	5	0	2	1
$SC(0.5, 50, 100)$	0	0	9	15	0	4	14	0	3
$SC(5, 50, 100)$	1	2	0	10	1	3	2	1	2
$SC(10, 50, 100)$	0	0	0	2	4	1	0	2	2

5.1 Overall

One observes in column D that many strategies are not dominated by any other strategy. We shall study below, however, how some of them are more suitable in a subset of these aspects. To this end, we therefore first classify as bad strategies those with a non-null D value.

Thus, the following strategies are not considered in the more detailed analyses: $Selfish_{Basic}(0.5, \{10, 50\})$, $Selfish_{Cooperative}(5, \{10, 50\}, \{20, 50, 100\})$ and $Selfish_{Cooperative}(5, 10, \{20, 50, 100\})$.

5.2 Scenario

In the scenario columns (D_I and D_G), one observes that most of the strategies with good overall suitability also present good behaviour in the isolated intersection scenario. The most important exception is $Fix(20)$ which is dominated by 3 different strategies. The other exceptions are $Selfish_{Basic}(10, 50)$ and $Selfish_{Cooperative}(10, 10, 20)$, each dominated by one other strategy.

$Selfish_{Cooperative}(10, \{10, 50\}, \{20, 50, 100\})$ show relatively good behaviour in both scenarios since they are dominated only by either 0 or 1 other strategies. The strategies $Fix(50)$, $Fix(100)$, and $Selfish_{Basic}(\{5, 10\}, 10)$ remain undominated in either scenario.

5.3   Aspect

With respect to the aspect columns (D_C, D_S, and D_T), only two strategies, $Fix(100)$ and $Selfish_{Basic}(10, 10)$, are not dominated in any aspect. None of the $Fix(\psi)$ strategies are dominated in vehicle speed.

The strategies $Selfish_{Cooperative}(0.5, 50, \{50, 100\})$ are dominated in collapsed streets by 19 and 15 strategies respectively, being hence unsuitable strategies. The same is the case with $Selfish_{Cooperative}(10, 10, 20)$ which is dominated by 14 other strategies in the time on red column. One observes that for the vehicle speeds column no strategy has such a high number of other strategies dominating it.

5.4   Lane

With respect to the lane columns (D_R, D_S, and D_L), the only strategies which are dominated by a major number of the others are $Selfish_{Cooperative}(0.5, 50, 20)$ and $Selfish_{Cooperative}(0.5, 50, 100)$, with 15 and 14 respectively in the right-turn column.

All three Fix and the four $Selfish_{Basic}(\{5, 10\}, \{10, 50\})$ strategies are undominated in the left-turn column. This is an important finding, since, as has been seen, this lane is the most conflictive, requiring most conditions to be satisfied to attain the green state.

6   Conclusions

We have here described a framework of intelligent traffic scheduling strategies using a novel agent-based simulation model to test their effectiveness. To this end, we performed experiments comparing 24 variables for each strategy, corresponding to the combinations of two scenarios, three aspects, and the three lanes and their average.

Several strategies showed good behaviour in a specific scenario, lane, or aspect. But deducing the overall effectiveness of a strategy is still an open problem in the study of systems of this kind where the number of measures of the outcome that need to be optimized conjointly can be very large. Nonetheless, the approach presented here would seem to be a good starting point for us to continue with our investigations in the field of ITS.

In future work, we shall be studying cooperative and competitive strategies for signal control in a traffic grid. It will also be interesting to study the effect of using several different strategies in the same grid, and how their distribution affects the different measures of effectiveness.

References

1. Gokulan, B.P., Srinivasan, D.: Distributed geometric fuzzy multiagent urban traffic signal control. IEEE Transactions on Intelligent Transportation Systems 11(3), 714–726 (2010)
2. Al-Khalili, A.J.: Urban traffic control- a general approach. IEEE Transactions on Systems Man and Cybernetics. 15(2), 260–271 (1985)
3. Robertson, D.I.: Traffic Models and Optimum Strategies of Control: A Review. Proceedings on Traffic Control Systems 1, 276–289 (1979)
4. Webster, F.: Traffic signal settings. In: HMSO (1958)
5. Wunderlich, R., Elhanany, I., Urbanik, T.: A stable longest queue first signal scheduling algorithm for an isolated intersection. In: IEEE International Conference on Vehicular Electronics and Safety, pp. 1–6 (2007)
6. Wunderlich, R., Liu, C., Elhanany, I., UrbanikII, T.: A novel signal-scheduling algorithm with quality-of-service provisioning for an isolated intersection. IEEE Transactions on Intelligent Transportation Systems 9(3), 536–547 (2008)
7. Sims, A., Dobinson, K.: SCAT-The Sydney Co-ordinated Adaptive Traffic System–Philosophy and Benefits. In: International Symposium on Traffic Control Systems, vol. 2 (1979)
8. Henry, J., Farges, J., Tuffal, J.: The PRODYN real time traffic algorithm. In: Proceedings of the 4th Conference on Control in Transportation Systems, vol. 2(1), p. 305 (1984)
9. Choy, M.C., Srinivasan, D., Cheu, R.: Cooperative, hybrid agent architecture for real-time traffic signal control. IEEE Transactions on Systems, Man and Cybernetics, Part A 33(5), 597–607 (2003)
10. Wilensky, U., et al.: NetLogo (1999), http://ccl.northwestern.edu/netlogo
11. Fonseca, C., Fleming, P., et al.: Genetic algorithms for multiobjective optimization: Formulation, discussion and generalization. In: Proceedings of the Fifth International Conference on Genetic Algorithms, pp. 416–423 (1993)

A Reinforcement Learning Modular Control Architecture for Fully Automated Vehicles

Jorge Villagrá, Vicente Milanés, Joshué Pérez, Jorge Godoy, Enrique Onieva,
Javier Alonso, Carlos González, Teresa de Pedro, and Ricardo Garcia*

Autopia Program, Center for Automation and Robotics, UPM-CSIC
Ctra. Campo Real km. 0.200, 28500 Arganda del Rey (Madrid), Spain
{jorge.villagra,vicente.milanes,joshue.perez,jorge.godoy,
enrique.onieva,javier.alonso,carlos.gonzalez,teresa.pedro,
ricardo.garcia}@car.upm-csic.es

Abstract. This paper proposes a modular and generic architecture to deal with
Global Chassis Control. Reinforcement learning is coupled with intelligent PID
controllers and an optimal tire effort allocation algorithm to obtain a general,
robust, adaptable, efficient and safe control architecture for any kind of automated
wheeled vehicle.

1 Introduction

In the last years a huge effort has been made both in industrial and academic environments to develop advanced driving assistance systems (ADAS). As a result of this,
several embedded control systems are already on board commercial vehicles: Adaptive Cruise Control, Lane Keeping or automatic Parking Assist systems. Most of these
systems seek to solve a specific problem by considering a particular set of car actuators -active suspensions, brakes, traction torques and steering angles of each wheel.
However, since the number of ADAS is significantly increasing, a global and modular
control architecture should be considered to rationalize and, if necessary priorize, the
use of all these actuators. Moreover, since energetic efficiency is nowadays one of the
most challenging issues for any Intelligent Transportation System (ITS), this architecture should be oriented towards an optimal use of vehicle resources.

In the past, works like [1], [4] have proposed different variants of a Global Chassis
Control (GCC). However, in all these cases the proposed architecture considered only
security functions (ESP or ABS like systems). To the best of our knowledge, the only
commercial system that introduces a general framework for an optimal use of vehicle
actuators is Toyota VDIM (Vehicle Dynamics Integrated Management, [5]), but it let
the driver to decide whether to enable or not in very specific situations. Moreover, it
does not allow the possibility to communicate with other vehicles (V2V) or with the
infrastructure (V2I). In other words, fully automated driving was not considered in none
of these cases.

---

* This work was supported by the Plan Nacional, under the project Tránsito (TRA2008-06602-
C03-01), by the Comisión Interministerial de Ciencia y Tecnología under the project GUIADE
(Ministerio de Fomento T9/08) and the Ministerio de Ciencia e Innovación under the project
CityElec (PS-370000-2009-4).

R. Moreno-Díaz et al. (Eds.): EUROCAST 2011, Part II, LNCS 6928, pp. 390–397, 2012.

This paper presents a modular control architecture for automated vehicles to fill this gap. Figure 1 schematizes an adaptation of the classical robotics paradigm perception-reasoning-action to the automatic driving context. The key issues of this contribution are located at the reasoning part, where a first work division exist at the highest level: planning and control. The planning phase will be in charge of deciding the geometrical path to track and the reference speed for each situation. To achieve such a task, all on-board sensors and V2V/V2I communication based information will be intelligently fused -perception stage- to interpret vehicle dynamics in its environment -road state, weather conditions, traffic. From these inputs, the planner will generate adequate references to the most relevant dynamic variables for vehicle handling. From this point, the

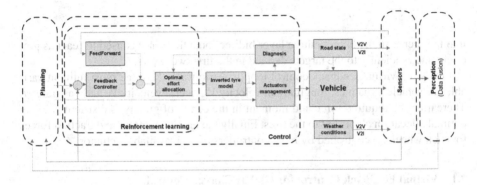

Fig. 1. Modular control architecture for automated vehicles

control layer will decide the best control action for each actuator. This modular control scheme fulfills five fundamental exigences for fully autonomous driving, that are nowadays hot topics for the ITS community and will be detailed in the following sections: efficiency, generality, adaptability, robustness and safety.

The remainder of the article is organized as follows. The basis of the allocation algorithm will be described in 2, where optimality (and therefore efficiency) issues will be discussed. Section 3 will be devoted to briefly highlight the generality of the proposed architecture. Adaptability, robustness, efficiency and safety aspects will be briefly discussed in Sections 4, 5, 6 and 7, respectively. Finally some concluding remarks will be drawn

2   A Modular Architecture: From Chassis to Tyres

The modular control architecture schematized in Fig. 1 can be reinterpreted as a sequence of tasks, as depicted in Fig. 2. Thus, from driver inputs (generally, brake, throttle and steering angle) and taking into account the perceived information from the environment (road state, weather conditions, surrounding vehicles...), a path and trajectory planner quantifies the vehicle targets, and finally the global control scheme comes

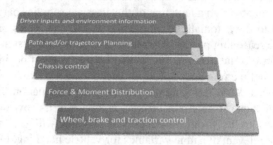

Fig. 2. Flowchart of the proposed control architecture

into the scene. In the latter, a three layer bidirectional flowchart is used to react as precisely and efficiently to the targets defined in the first two layers.

Firstly, an virtual feedback control loop is set to track the three most influent variables in vehicle dynamics: longitudinal velocity V_x, lateral velocity V_y and yaw rate $\dot{\psi}$. Thereafter, the required force and moment in the center of gravity is distributed by an optimal allocation algorithm to the tires. Finally the resulting angles and traction forces for each wheel are controlled by local controllers of each available actuator.

2.1   Virtual Feedback Control for Global Chassis Control

As previously mentioned, this first loop determines the necessary efforts (F_x and F_y) and torque (M_z) at the center of gravity to track the pre-computed V_x, V_y and $\dot{\psi}$ references. To that end, Newton's second law of motion

$$\dot{V}_{x_{ref}} = \frac{1}{M}F_x, \; \dot{V}_{y_{ref}} = \frac{1}{M}F_y, \; \dot{\psi}_{ref} = \frac{1}{I_z}M_z \qquad (1)$$

where M and I_z are the mass and the inertia moment of the vehicle. Since equation (1) is to simplistic to accurately describe vehicle's motion, three SISO robust feedback controllers (u_x, u_y, u_ψ) are added to compensate in finite time the divergences between the references and the measured values V_x, V_y and $\dot{\psi}$

$$u_x = F_x = M\dot{V}_{x_{ref}} + \text{i-PID}(e_x), e_x = V_{x_{ref}} - V_x$$

$$u_y = F_x = M\dot{V}_{y_{ref}} + \text{i-PID}(e_y), e_y = V_{y_{ref}} - V_y \qquad (2)$$

$$u_\psi = M_z = I_z\dot{\psi}_{ref} + \text{i-PID}(e_y), e_\psi = \dot{\psi}_{ref} - \dot{\psi}$$

being i-PID a robust and efficient control technique that is detailed in Section 5.

2.2   Optimal Effort Distribution

According to [3], the best solution to this problem is obtained by collectively minimizing the instantaneous friction coefficient γ_i of all wheels

$$\gamma_i = \frac{\sqrt{F_{x_i}^2 + F_{x_i}^2}}{F_{z_i}}, \ i = 1 \ldots 4$$

where F_{z_i} is the vertical load of each wheel. Therefore, the minimizing problem can be expressed by normalizing a uniform $\gamma = \gamma_{i}, 1 = \ldots 4$ with the sum of the requested moment M_0 and efforts F_0

$$\min_{q_i, \gamma} \frac{\gamma}{lF_0 + M_0}$$

where l is the wheelbase and q_i are the angles between the vertical mid-plane of each wheel and the resulting tire-road effort vector at the centre of that wheel.

Since this particular problem did not provide satisfying results for a certain number of situations where a supplementary degree of flexibility was necessary, a different optimization problem has been considered

$$\min_{q_i, \gamma_i} \frac{\sum_i (\gamma_i - \bar{\gamma})^2}{lF_0 + M_0}, \ \bar{\gamma} = \sum_i \gamma_i \tag{3}$$

A simplified SQP algorithm is applied to solve (3) in real time with the aim of finding the optimal values of γ_i and q_i at each wheel, that fulfill the following expressions

$$F_{x_i} = \gamma F_{z_i} \cos(q_i + \theta)$$
$$F_{y_i} = \gamma F_{z_i} \sin(q_i + \theta)$$

which provide the required traction efforts at each wheel F_{x_i}. Finally, the steering angles α_i are obtained via the Brush model [6]

$$\alpha = \tan^{-1} \left(\frac{\kappa_s}{\kappa_\alpha} \frac{-\kappa_i \sin(q_i + \theta)}{1 - \kappa_i \cos(q_i + \theta)} \right)$$
$$\kappa_i = \frac{3F_i}{\kappa_s} \left(1 - (1 - \gamma)^{\frac{1}{3}} \right)$$

where κ_s is the slip stiffness and κ_α the cornering stiffness Figure 3 shows two different situations in a 4 wheel driven and steering car (4WS), where the wheel on each load is different (the magenta dashed circles have the same radius). The vehicle is schematically represented in an aerial view, where the target effort torsor is represented in the gravity center by a circle arc representing M_0 and an arrow of magnitude and orientation given by F_x ana F_y. Note that while in the first case, the vehicle attains the maximum grip margin ($\gamma_i = 1, i = 1 \ldots 4$), in the second one the efforts distribution is more comfortable and only a 73% of the tire potential is used.

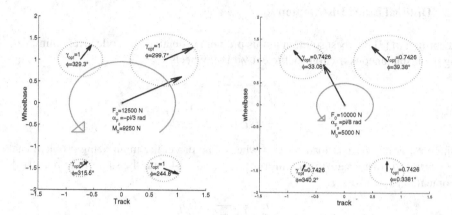

Fig. 3. Examples of efforts allocation with the same load distribution, but with different targets

3 Generality

The proposed control architecture is conceived in such a way that any control technique can be used in both the local and the high level virtual controllers. Moreover, a supplementary feedforward controller can complement the chosen feedback control law (see for instance [8]) The generality is not only related to the architecture modularity, but

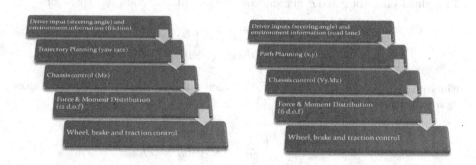

Fig. 4. Flowchart for an ESP in a 4WS vehicle (left) and a Lane Keeping in an AFS car (right)

also to the wide range of application it is useful for. In this connection, Fig. 4 shows how the generic flowchart presented in Fig. 2 may be adapted to two different ADAS with completely different actuator configurations: an ESP-like control for a 4WS vehicle and a Lane Keeping System for a Active Front Steering (AFS) vehicle.

4   Adaptability

Reinforcement Learning [10] permits to adapt on-line the controller parameters to the driver and to the vehicle. As a result, the control layer is able to adapt information provided by the driver (maximum desired velocity, acceleration, suspension behavior...) to each vehicle capabilities at any moment of its lifetime cycle. Figure 5 shows the basis of

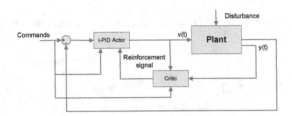

Fig. 5. Reinforcement learning scheme for Global Chassis Control

our on-line learning based control scheme. A critic learns how controller act optimally by intelligently recovering feedbacks from the environment so that desirable actions are reinforced and vice versa. To that end, 12 parameters of virtual control equations(4 control parameters for each one of the 3 degrees of freedom) are continuously tuned to adapt to pre-learnt situations. As a consequence of this, a self learning driver cognition model is transformed into an optimal control problem.

5   Robustness

Tyre and brake wear, pressure, temperature and many other factors decisively influences the dynamic behavior of a vehicle. Such effects are extremely difficult to model, and when a model is available it is not tractable for control based algorithms. Alternatively, robust model based solutions have been tested but they are not always efficient enough, because it is not easy to quantify all the unmodeled dynamics or the parametric uncertainty.

To solve this complex problem, a trajectory tracking based control, and somehow independent of the model, seems an interesting alternative to the aforementioned techniques. Therefore, intelligent PID (i-PID) controllers are used in this work because they combine the well-known PID structure with an "intelligent" term [2] that compensates the effects of nonlinear dynamics, disturbances or uncertain parameters.

As given in [2,9], a finite dimension nonlinear system can be written locally as

$$y^{(\mu)} = F + \alpha u \tag{4}$$

where $\alpha \in \mathbb{R}$ and $\mu \in \mathbb{N}$ are two constant parameters, which do not necessarily represent a physical magnitude, and whose choice is based on the following guidelines

- μ is usually 1 o 2, and it may represent the system order, but not necessarily.
- α should allow F and αu to be of the same order of magnitude.
- The term F is a sort of non-linear black box identifier [2]

If equation (4) is inverted and merged with a PID controller, the resulting i-PID control law yields (see Fig. 6 to clarify how each term is interconnected)

$$u = \frac{1}{\alpha}\left(\dot{V}_s - F\right) + K_P e + K_I \int e + K_D \frac{de}{dt}dt, e = y_r - y \qquad (5)$$

where K_P, K_I and $K_D \in \mathbb{R}^+$ are PID tuned gains and y_r is a smoothed reference.

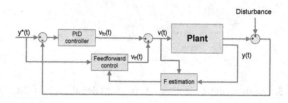

Fig. 6. i-PID control scheme

6 Efficiency

Since the optimization algorithm detailed in Section 2 takes into account the available sensors and actuators, a considerable improvement on energy consumption can be achieved. As a result, this modular architecture is specially interesting for fully actuated electric vehicles, not only in terms of energetic efficiency, but also concerning the maximum resultant forces and moments that can be handled by a vehicle. To reinforce this idea, Ono and coworkers [3] showed that with a very similar architecture the latter could be enhanced in a 18% if the vehicle was 4WS instead of a conventional one.

7 Safety

The presented control allocation scheme, based in the general architecture showed in Fig. 1 facilitates fault tolerant control [7] in case the on board diagnosis tools detects dysfunctional sensors or actuators. Figure 7 shows the basis of a fault tolerant scheme adapted to our GCC architecture, where some critic variables are on-line estimated to evaluate wether residuals are significant or not to adopt a control reconfiguration. If a failure is detected, the effort allocation stage takes into account the dysfunctional componentes to distribute the targets among the properly working actuators.

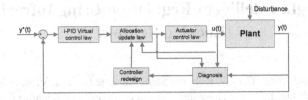

Fig. 7. Fault tolerant control for an effort allocation based control scheme

8 Concluding Remarks

A modular and generic architecture has been proposed to deal with Global Chassis Control. Different techniques are combined to provide generality, robustness, adaptability, efficiency and safety to the control architecture of any kind of wheeled vehicle. The proposed architecture is being evaluated with a realistic simulator (specially the reinforcement learning part). Moreover, the first experimental results will be soon available for very different vehicles.

References

1. Chou, H., D'Andréa-Novel, B.: Global vehicle control using differential braking torques and active suspension forces. Vehicle System Dynamics 43(4), 261–284 (2005)
2. Fliess, M., Join, C.: Intelligent PID Controllers. In: Proc. of 16th Mediterrean Conf. on Control and Automation, Ajaccio, France (2008)
3. Ono, E., Hattoria, Y., Muragishia, Y., Koibuchi, K.: Vehicle dynamics integrated control for four-wheel-distributed steering and four-wheel-distributed traction/braking systems. Vehicle System Dynamics 44(2), 139–151 (2006)
4. Poussot-Vassal, C., Sename, O., Dugard, L.: A LPV/H∞ Global Chassis Controller for handling improvements involving braking and steering systems. In: IEEE 47th Conference on Decision and Control, pp. 5366–5371 (2008)
5. Suzumura, M., Fukatani, K., Asada, H.: Current State of and Prospects for the Vehicle Dynamics Integrated Management System (VDIM). Toyota Technical Review 55(222) (2007)
6. Svendenius, J., Gäfvert, M.: A semi-empirical dynamic tire model for combined-slip forces. Vehicle System Dynamics 44(2), 189–208 (2006)
7. Tondel, P., Johansen, T.A.: Control allocation for yaw stabilization in automotive vehicles using multiparametric nonlinear programming. In: Proc. of the American Control Conference, June 8-10, pp. 453–458 (2005)
8. Villagra, J., d'Andrea-Novel, B., Mounier, H., Pengov, M.: Flatness-Based Vehicle Steering Control Strategy With SDRE Feedback Gains Tuned Via a Sensitivity Approach. IEEE Transactions on Control Systems Technology 15(3), 554–565 (2007)
9. Villagra, J., Milanes, V., Pérez, J., de Pedro, T.: Control basado en pid inteligentes: Aplicación al control de crucero de un vehículo a bajas velocidades. Revista Iberoamericana de Automática e Informática Industrial 7(4), 44–52 (2010)
10. Wang, X.S., Cheng, Y.H., Sun, W.: A Proposal of Adaptive PID Controller Based on Reinforcement Learning. Journal of China University of Mining and Technology 17(1), 40–44 (2007)

Traffic Light Intelligent Regulation Using Infrastructure Located Sensors

Javier Alonso, Jorge Godoy, Roberto Sanz, Enrique Onieva, Vicente Milanés,
Jorge Villagrá, Carlos González, Teresa de Pedro, and Ricardo García

Centro de Automática y Robótica, UPM-CSIC. Arganda del Rey,
28500 Madrid, Spain
{javier.alonso,jorge.godoy,roberto.sanz,enrique.onieva,
vicente.milanes,jorge.villagra,carlos.gonzalez,teresa.depedro,
ricardo.garcia}@car.upm-csic.es

Abstract. This paper presents a central station controlling the traffic flow of an intersection. In the proposed scenario autonomously driven and manually driven vehicles are mixed. The objective is to regulate both types of vehicles. Autonomously driven ones are controlled via wireless LAN communications; the autonomous vehicles send their positions and wait for the permission to traverse the intersection. The manually driven cars are detected in certain positions and controlled using the traffic lights. This paper presents the main idea implementation and shows the initial tests. After the discussion of the test results, some alternatives and future work lines are also exposed.

Keywords: ITS (Intelligent Transportation Systems), Safe Intersections, V2I (Vehicle to Infrastructure) and I2V Communications.

1 Introduction

The idea of using sensors to regulate the cycle time of a traffic light is starting to be used by the industry, especially in low traffic conditions. This work tries to go beyond this idea and use the perception capacity of the technology to build smart traffic lights. On our research group previous works we have achieved safe control an intersections by leaving each autonomous cars to take their own decisions [1][2]. Autonomous vehicles able to communicate each other, can share their positions, speeds, and turn intentions and use this information to determine the right of way. But with manually driven cars, and even with mixed traffic, the only way to coordinate the vehicles at an intersection is using traffic lights.

Nowadays the actual solution to control the traffic flow in an intersection is based in the cycle time of the traffic lights. This cycle times depends on a timetable. But other solutions are also available for the industry now; the cycle time of the traffic lights can be modified based on sensor inputs. The proposed idea is to use "intelligent" algorithms to directly control the traffic lights and optimize the traffic flow of the intersection.

R. Moreno-Díaz et al. (Eds.): EUROCAST 2011, Part II, LNCS 6928, pp. 398–403, 2012.
© Springer-Verlag Berlin Heidelberg 2012

2 System Deployment

The aim of the control program is to regulate the intersection where autonomous and manually driven cars are mixed. To achieve this goal a computer has been placed near the traffic light regulator and acts as central station.

The central station has access to a GPS (Global Positioning System) base station and also grants the differential correction to the autonomous vehicles involve. So, using the same Wi-Fi network used to send the differential correction to the vehicles, the central station receives the position of all the autonomous vehicles that travels near the intersection. This communications channel is also used to send the intersection traverse permission to the vehicles.

The manually driven vehicles are detected using ZigBee sensors. Other sensor has been also tested, like laser or ultrasonic sensors, and will replace the Zigbee sensors in future implementations. To send the orders to these vehicles, the central station uses the traffic lights. The permission to traverse the intersection is given by a green traffic light.

Without the use of artificial vision (we are working now in car turn lights detection), the central station can only operate in two modes. The first one, that will operate in high traffic density cases, uses the cycle times following a timetable. The second one, used in low traffic density cases, turns the traffic lights to green when a vehicle approaches and no vehicle obstructs the path.

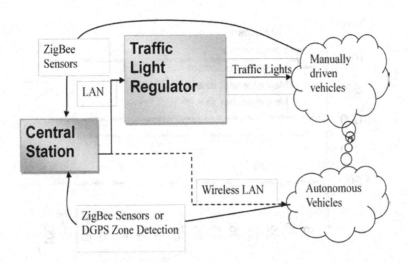

Fig. 1. System scheme: The central station get as inputs the positions of the manually and autonomously driven cars via the ZigBee sensors or the DGPS zone detections. And it sends as outputs orders directly to the vehicles via Wireless LAN or it modifies the traffic lights sending orders to the traffic light regulator via Local Area Network.

2.1 ZigBee Sensors

ZigBee is a specification for communication protocols. Its motes are used for radio-frequency (RF) applications that needs low data rate, long battery life and secure networking. These motes can use several sensors, like light, sound, temperature or magnetic sensors. In this case we have chosen to use light sensors to detect the vehicles approaching. Detection tests are shown in the next subsection.

Fig. 2. ZigBee mote

2.2 ZigBee Tests

Several tests have been made to select the best combination of the mote sensors that will permit the vehicles detection. As is shown in the figure 3, the only appreciable change, when the vehicle drive above the sensor, is shown in the light sensor. So, the mote light sensor is used to detect the presence of the vehicles.

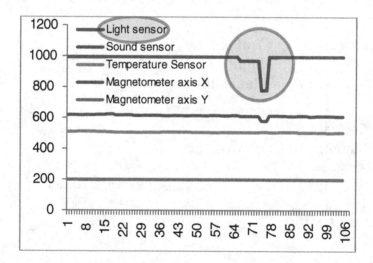

Fig. 3. Vehicle detection test: This experiment is used to choose the sensor to detect the vehicles

Once the light sensor has been selected, two ZigBee motes were deployed before each traffic light at the intersection. The setup can be seen in figure 4 left. With this setup, we started a set of experiments trying to determine at which speed the light

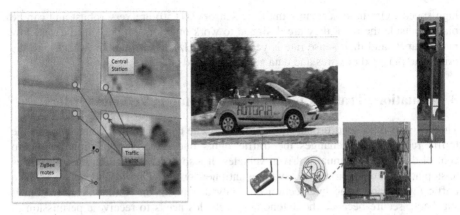

Fig. 4. Sensor test layout. This figure shows the placement of the ZigBee motes in the intersection *(left)* and the schema of the vehicle detection, and actuation over the traffic lights *(right)*.

sensors of the motes where not reliable enough. At 36 km/h, one of the two sensors was not able to detect the vehicle.

The experiments (figure 5) show a drastic reduction of the light intensity variation when the vehicle speed is 36km/h instead of 12km/h. As the vehicles that are arriving to an intersection reduce its speeds, the light intensity sensors of the ZigBee motes are good enough for this application.

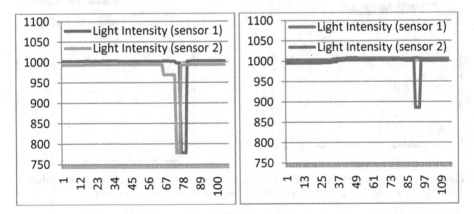

Fig. 5. The light intensity of both sensors decrease more than 200 cd when the vehicle goes above the sensor at 12km/h *(left figure)*. When de vehicle goes at a higher speed, 35 km/h, the variation of light intensity detected is only 100 cd for the second sensor, and zero for the first sensor *(right figure)*.

Some tests have been done with laser (DT50) and ultrasound sensors to replace the ZigBee motes. ZigBee motes are very cheap, there is no need of wires and work together in a mesh distribution. But they must be placed in the road, so they can be easily broken, the batteries and light sensors are needed to be replaced from time to time, and they have a very low sense rate (2Hz), so the vehicle can be undetected at high speeds. On the other hand, the laser sensors (DT50) are very robust and can be placed outside the road, they are designed to work outdoors, so they need a very low maintenance, and their sense rate is very high (50 Hz). Their main drawbacks are the price, and the need of wires and data acquisition cards.

3   Actuation: Traffic Lights and Autonomous Vehicles Orders

The last step is to send orders to the vehicles. The central station connects with the traffic regulator and changes the traffic lights under direct regulation regime to control the flow of manually driven vehicles. It also orders the autonomous vehicles to stop at a given position and stay there until new orders. This second step to achieve traffic regulation in the intersection is highly dependent on communications, but it still being secure because the autonomous vehicles needs to receive a permission to traverse the intersection.

3.1   Control Program

A control program has been made to monitorize the light intensity measurements of both motes, compared with ambient light. When a vehicle arriving to the intersection is detected, and there is no other car at the intersection (a timer is set to ensure that the previous car has had time enough to leave the intersection), the control program orders traffic lights regulator to change the lights via TCP communications.

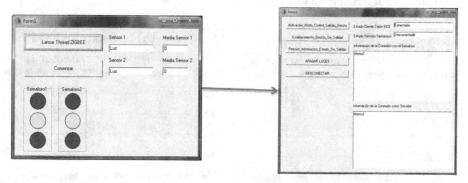

Fig. 6. The control program (*left*) set the traffic light to green or red depending on the vehicles detected. The traffic lights regulator is modified via an interface program (*right*).

The control program operates by pairs, it is the simplest way. Once a vehicle is detected in a lane, and there is no other vehicle in the right angle of that lane, the traffic lights of that lane and its opposite one are set to green, and the traffic lights of the right angle and left angle of that lane are set to red.

Autonomous vehicles are treated in the same way, if the traffic light of the lane where the vehicle is driving is set to green a message with the permission to traverse the intersection is sent to the autonomous vehicle. If the traffic light of the lane where the vehicle is driving is set to red, there is no need to send him a message denying the permission, but it still being sent for passenger's convenience.

4 Future Work

The replacement of ZigBee mote sensors with laser sensors is expected to highly improve the reliability of the detection part of the system. Initial tests made with laser sensors demonstrate high precision and reliability, even with black vehicles driving at high speeds (60 km/h).

Improvements in the actuation over the traffic light regulator are also planned. The direct traffic light modification is unsafe. Time intervals in which all traffic lights are red are needed to ensure the safety of the intersection. So, a routine to change traffic lights will be implemented.

To improve the logic of the system [3], it is planned to add cameras to the intersection. Artificial vision techniques will allow the system to know the turn intention of the vehicles and optimize middle traffic flow management. And, by adding cameras to the autonomous vehicles, the system will be able to send orders to the autonomous cars via traffic lights.

Acknowledgements. This work has been done thanks to proyects: "CITY-ELEC: Systems for Urban Enviroment Movility Electrification", Ministerio de Ciencia e Innovación, PSE-370000-2009-4; "GUIADE: Public vehicles automatic guidance system using multimodal perception to increase efficiency", Ministerio de Fomento, Ref. P9/08; and "TRÁNSITO: Local coordination between vehicles and infrastructures", CICYT, TRA 2008-06602-C03-01/AUT.

References

1. Alonso, J., Milanés, V., Onieva, E., Perez, J., García, R.: Safe Crossroads via Vehicle to Vehicle Communication. In: Moreno-Díaz, R., Pichler, F., Quesada-Arencibia, A. (eds.) EUROCAST 2009. LNCS, vol. 5717, pp. 421–428. Springer, Heidelberg (2009)
2. Alonso, J., Milanés, V., Onieva, E., Pérez, J., González, C., de Pedro, T.: Cartography For Cooperative Manoeuvres: Autopia's new Cartography System for Cooperative Manoeuvres among Autonomous Vehicles. The Journal of Navigation 64, 141–155 (2011)
3. Alonso, J.: Cooperative Driving Manouvres among Autonomous Vehicles. Phd thesis, Facultad de Informática, Universidad Politécnica de Madrid (2009)

Driving by Driverless Vehicles in Urban Environment*

Joshué Pérez, Jorge Villagrá, Enrique Onieva, Vicente Milanés,
Teresa de Pedro, and Ljubo Vlacic[1]

Robotics Department, Center for Automation and Robotics (CAR)
La Poveda-Arganda del Rey, 28500 Madrid, Spain
[1]Intelligent Control Systems Laboratory, Griffith University,
Brisbane, Australia
{joshue.perez,jorge.villagra,enrique.onieva,vicente.milanes,
teresa.pedro}@csic.es, l.vlacic@griffith.edu.au

Abstract. A number of the Intelligent Transportation System (ITS) solutions have been implemented in conventional vehicles in recent years. In the not too distant future driverless vehicles will share the roads with vehicles driven by human beings. In this paper, a novel algorithm for switching from one driving maneuver to another is proposed. The interface has been developed in C++ Visual Studio and using a 3D simulator with the data provided by a GPS and lidar sensors. Specific driving tasks such as lane following, curve driving and roundabout driving have been analyzed and tested with good simulations results obtained.

1 Introduction

Nowadays, multiple improvements in road monitoring and partial vehicle control are being deployed in conventional vehicles under the umbrella of the so called Advanced Driver Assistance systems (ADAS). Some of these solutions have been welcomed by drivers and already accepted as comfort accessories (like *Cruise Control* and *Assisted Parking* systems), while others remain important topics in the Intelligent Transportation Systems (ITS) research, such as perception systems, cooperative driving, safe and reliable driving, etc.

Most accurate vehicle control systems use global positioning (Differential GPS) data to perform the automatic control over the steering wheel [1] [2]. The need for accessing a central base station is the main weakness of GPS signal-based navigation methods. Recent research shows that this drawback could be compensated by fusing GPS with vision information, what was performed for the lane border detection task [3].

---

* This work was supported by: (i) the Plan Nacional, under the project Tránsito (TRA2008-06602-C03-01); (ii) the Comisión Interministerial de Ciencia y Tecnología under the project GUIADE (Ministerio de Fomento T9/08); (iii) the Ministerio de Ciencia e Innovación under the project CityElec (PS-370000-2009-4); and (iv) Griffith University's Intelligent Control Systems Laboratory (ICSL), Australia.

R. Moreno-Díaz et al. (Eds.): EUROCAST 2011, Part II, LNCS 6928, pp. 404–411, 2012.
© Springer-Verlag Berlin Heidelberg 2012

Lidar sensors have typically been used for the task of scanning (detection) vehicle's immediate road traffic environment, showing good results even under real-time constraints [4]. Other applications such as a car-following system to track a preceding car while maintaining a safe separation distance are also based on the lidar sensors[5].

Since DGPS and lidar sensors have both being widely accepted by the autonomous systems research community, this work is also using the lidar sensor for the purpose of detecting the presence of others vehicles and/or pedestrians while the lane following task is performed based on GPS data obtained.

The driverless vehicles-based road traffic modeling environment - ICSL Simulator - was initially developed by [6]. The simulator allows the exchange of different control strategies such as path generation methods and sensor fusion techniques based on the real data obtained from GPS and lidar sensors in real-time. An interface has been developed in C++ Visual Studio. The work presented in this paper reviews the performance of the developed modeling environment in performing both the basic driving tasks as well as high risk driving maneuvers like overtaking maneuver on two way roads.

This paper is organized as follows: section 2 explains the simulator used to test the developed driving algorithms which are described in section 3, while the obtained results are presented in section 4. Finally the conclusions are drawn in section 5.

2   ICSL Simulator

The cooperative driving paradigm has been developed for computer-assisted experimental vehicle platforms -Cybercars- [7]. Using these vehicles, the concept of decision making for driverless city vehicles has been simulated and thereafter tested on real road test tracks. These driving maneuvers have included the most basic tasks, as well as more complex ones such as: platooning, intersection crossing, emergency stopping, overtaking (but, implemented in open loop control), etc[8].

The obtained results pointed onto the possible improvements with respect to: sensor fusion, decision and control as well as driving maneuvers [6][8].

Figure 1 shows various road traffic environments and obstacles used in the simulator (from the higher left to the lower right part): roundabout, overtaking, initialization of the cybercars and path following with pedestrian detection.

The Interactive Interface

Before to start each maneuver, the following set of steps is normally required:

- To activate the simulator: different road traffic set-ups can be loaded (intersection, straight segments, urban streets, roundabouts, etc.).
- To start the program in C++: each maneuver is associated with a specific road traffic environment, and related map.

Fig. 1. 3D Simulator for Cybercars (ICSL)

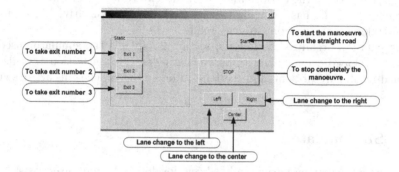

Fig. 2. Interactive interface of the roundabout maneuvers

- *To start the maneuver*: each maneuver has its own interface. For example, figure 2 shows the interface for the roundabout maneuver. All the maneuvers have a start and stop button.

3   Control Scheme

This control scheme is completely modular, so each block is added and tested. The modularity of the scheme allows the testing of different control strategies without modifying the global structure. Figure 3 shows the proposed control scheme as follow:

World Information and HMI

World information and HMI block is in charge of storing the data coming from the sensors. Moreover, previous information, such as signal position, maps or special situations, among others, are read from the initialization files. A Human-Machine Interface allows the change of preferences as well as lane reference,

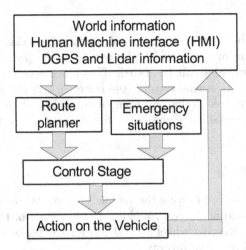

Fig. 3. Control scheme for maneuvers on urban roads

emergency stop, etc. It receives the information from the vehicle using the GPS and lidar information. The GPS gives the information a 2-dimensional Cartesian Coordinate system. The lidar information is used to stop the vehicle in a case where there is an obstacle in front of the vehicle. The driverless control is programmed to follow a route (predefined or dynamic), however, the user can change the lane, route and speed, among other parameters.

Route Planner

The Route Planner reads the information coming from the first block, and can also generate new information when or if necessary (for instance at a roundabout).The predefined points on the map come from a XML file. Each route is loaded at the beginning, though other alternative routes can be selected from other map files. For example, in the roundabout maneuver a dynamic map generator is in charge of building the roundabout points, using the parametric equations of a circle, creating the tangent line and defining the input variables for the control stage.

Emergency Situations

This block is executed in parallel with the route planner block, and it can modify the action in the actuator if an emergency situation happens. For example, when a pedestrian is crossing the street, or when another vehicle (or obstacle) is detected during a maneuver execution.

Control Stage

The Control Stage block is in charge of calculating the actions over the vehicle actuators in function of the coming information in the previous blocks. Here, different control strategies can be tested. This block receives the information according to the line reference system (the street in straight segment, and the line tangent on the curve, circles and roundabouts). For example, in case of the steering wheel, two variables have been defined: the distance to the curve and the angular error.

Action of the Vehicle

This module is in charge of moving the vehicle's actuators (steering and pedals). It receives the target from the control block. In the simulator the action interval is [-0.5 ; 0.5] for the steering wheel and [-1 ; 1] for the brake and throttle. It is totally extrapolated to a real prototype.

4   Maneuvers Simulations

Different maneuvers have been simulated, using the control scheme proposed in figure 3, as follow

Path Following

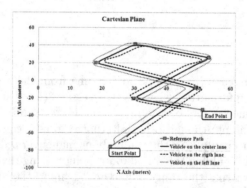

Fig. 4. Lane keeping in the central, right and left line

Figure 4 shows the path following taking into consideration three lanes: central, left and right. The reference paths are the gray lines joined to square points. The lane width is six meters, and the vehicle follows the left lane at 2.5 meters from the central lane. The square dot line shows the behavior on the left lane, the dash line shows the behavior on the right lane, and the continuous line shows the behavior on the central lane.

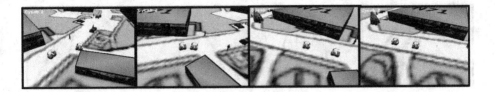

Fig. 5. Stop and go maneuver

Stop and Go, and Obstacle Detection

Figure 5 shows the sequential moments of the stop-and-go maneuvers. The first picture shows when the controlled vehicle arrives to the curve and detects another vehicle ahead of it. The next pictures show how the vehicle stops and goes when the vehicle in front restarts the driving.

Lane Change

Figure 6 shows the behavior when the reference lane is changed. The gray line is the reference line to follow, and the dashed line represents the autonomous simulated vehicle. This maneuver is the basis of overtaking.

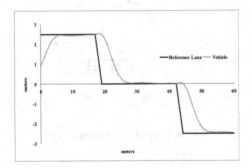

Fig. 6. Lane change in the central, right and left line

Overtaking

Figure 7 shows the sequential moments of the overtaking maneuver. When the vehicle detects a vehicle in the lane at a slower speed, it commences the overtaking maneuver. Once the faster vehicle has completed its overtaking maneuver, then the simulated cybercar returns to the start line.

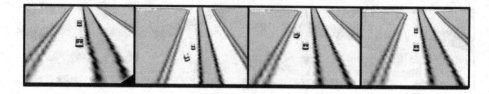

Fig. 7. Overtaking maneuver

Roundabout

Finally, figure 8 shows a simulation of the cybercar entering, driving around roundabout and exiting the roundabout. The start point determines when the cybercar enters the roundabout. Different exits can be selected (depending of the route planner), however, thanks to the interactive interface, the user can select another exit in real time. Then, a new map is generated until the vehicle leaves the roundabout.

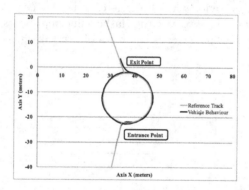

Fig. 8. Roundabout maneuver

5   Conclusion and Future Works

In this paper, different classic and new maneuvers in the ITS field have been simulated and a new control scheme for performing a variety of driving maneuvers in urban road traffic scenarios has been developed.

The control scheme is totally modular. Other control techniques, as well as map generators can be tested without great difficulties. The simulator allows the testing of these algorithms before their on-road testing is undertaken.

Future work will examine an enhanced communication among vehicles in the simulator to permit improved cooperative maneuvers (considering GPS and speed information). Furthermore, the algorithm is scheduled for on-road testing at a research facility in INRIA (France).

References

1. Xuan, Y., Coifman, B.: Lane change maneuver detection from probe vehicle dgps data, pp. 624–629 (September 2006)
2. Pérez, J., Milanés, V., Onieva, E., González, C.: Cascade architecture for lateral control in autonomous vehicle. IEEE Transactions on Intelligent Transportation Systems (6) (2010) (in Press)
3. Zhang, W., Taliwal, V.: Using lane tracker data to improve lane-level digital maps created with probe vehicle data, vol. 1, pp. 585–589 (October 2003)
4. Lindner, P., Wanielik, G.: 3d lidar processing for vehicle safety and environment recognition, pp. 66–71 (March 2009)
5. Hsu, C.W., Hsu, T.H., Chen, C.H., Kuo, Y.Y.: A path planning achievement of car following in motion control via lidar sensing, pp. 1411–1416 (June 2010)
6. Boisse, S., Benenson, L., Bouraoui, R., Parent, M., Vlacic, L.: Cybernetic transportation systems design and development: Simulation software. In: IEEE - ICRA 2007 (2007)
7. Baber, J., Kolodko, J., Noel, T., Parent, M., Vlacic, L.: Cooperative autonomous driving: intelligent vehicles sharing city roads. IEEE Robotics & Automation Magazine 12(1), 44–49 (2005)
8. Furda, A., Vlacic, L.: An object-oriented design of a world model for autonomous city vehicles. In: Proc. IEEE Intelligent Vehicles Symp (IV), pp. 1054–1059 (2010)

3D Map Building Using a 2D Laser Scanner

Á. Llamazares, E.J. Molinos, M. Ocaña,
L.M. Bergasa, N. Hernández, and F. Herranz

Department of Electronics, University of Alcalá, Madrid (Spain)
{allamazares,emolinos,mocana,bergasa,nhernandez,fherranz}@depeca.uah.es

Abstract. In this paper we present a technique to build 3D maps of
the environment using a 2D laser scanner combined with a robot's action model. This paper demonstrates that it is possible to build 3D maps
in a cheap way using an angled 2D laser. We introduce a scan matching method to minimize the odometer errors of the robotics platform
and a calibration method to improve the accuracy of the system. Some
experimental results and conclusions are presented.

1 Introduction

Laser scanners and range sensors are widely used in mobile robotics applications
such as obstacle avoidance [1], object tracking [2], map building [3], feature
extraction [4] or self-localization [5].

A 2D laser scanner provides distances and angles to the surrounding objects
by scanning the environment in a plane, usually parallel to the ground. This
technique is not enough to detect obstacles like stairs, a land irregularity or floor
level variations. These kinds of problems are overcome with the new 3D laser
scanners. With these sensors, all features are directly extracted in 3 dimensions.
In the other hand, their price is much more expensive than the first ones. Another
solution for these problems is a combination of a 2D laser and a pan-tilt unit but,
on the contrary, this system requires to spend more time to move the pan-tilt
unit [6].

There is a cheaper solution by mean of using 2D laser angled down toward
the ground, just in front of the robot, combined with the robot's action model
to extract the 3D features from movement [7]. While the sensor is scanning,
the mobile robot is moving and then the system assembles each slice into a
3D points cloud. The main problem of this cloud is that it can be affected by
the dead reckoning errors [8]. There are two kinds of errors: non-systematic and
systematic. The first ones are consequence of the slipping and skidding produced
in the turns of the robot or by the irregular ground, like cracks or bumps. The
second ones are particularly damaging because they are accumulated constantly.
The uncertainty about the laser pose in the robotics platform and the irregularity
of the robot mechanic (unequal wheel diameters, distance between contact points
of the wheels and the floor [9]) are examples of this kind of problems. Calibration
methods and scan matching techniques [10] try to solve them.

R. Moreno-Díaz et al. (Eds.): EUROCAST 2011, Part II, LNCS 6928, pp. 412–419, 2012.

In this paper we use an angled 2D laser to extract a three dimensional map of the environment and a Seekur Jr. outdoor robot platform. In addition, we propose a calibration method and a scan matching technique to improve the accuracy of the system and overcome the dead reckoning errors.

The paper is organized in the next sections: this section explains the problem and the related works, next section describes the proposed method, section 3 shows the obtained results and finally conclusions and future works are shown in section 4.

2 Description of the Proposed System

2.1 Obtaining 3D Features from a 2D Laser Sensor

When a laser sensor is placed angled towards ground, we can assume that it forms a tetrahedron like is shown in Figure 1. Figure shows an example of feature measure and the similarity of triangles to obtain the 3D pose of the measure.

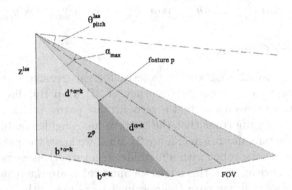

Fig. 1. Example of tetrahedron formed by laser scanner and the ground

Where z^{las} is the height of the laser, z^p is the height of the measured feature p, $d^{\alpha=k}$ is the distance from laser to ground in an angle $\alpha = k$, $d'^{\alpha=k}$ is the distance measured from laser to the feature, $b^{\alpha=k}$ and $b'^{\alpha=k}$ are the projections of the previous distances, α_{max} is the angle range of measure, θ_{pitch}^{las} is the pitch angle for the radial axis ($\alpha = 0$) and FOV is the Field of View over the ground.

If we assume that laser is in a well-known pose over the robot, the measured distance in $\alpha = 0$ shall be a constant ($d^{\alpha=0}$) and it can be obtained like (1). Using this constant, we can obtain FOV with (2). Concluding that a higher z^{las} or α_{max} and smaller θ_{pitch}^{las} can obtain a higher distance and FOV.

$$d^{\alpha=0} = \frac{z^{las}}{sin(\theta_{pitch}^{las})} \tag{1}$$

$$FOV = 2 \cdot d^{\alpha=0} \cdot tg\frac{\alpha_{max}}{2} \tag{2}$$

Using this information and the robot's action model, we can build the map assembling all the slices in a 3D points cloud. The method depends strongly on the odometry error, and then we propose a 2D scan-matching method based on [11] to correct the robot pose in the environment. This method is known like Iterative Closest Point (ICP). It is used to minimize the difference between two clouds of points. The algorithm is conceptually simple and is commonly used in real-time. It iteratively revises the transformation (translation, rotation) (3) needed to minimize the distance between the points of two raw scans.

$$
\begin{bmatrix}
cos(\theta_{yaw}^{las})cos(\theta_{pitch}^{las}) & R_{12} & R_{13} & 0 \\
-sin(\theta_{yaw}^{las}) & cos(\theta_{yaw}^{las})cos(\theta_{roll}^{las}) & cos(\theta_{yaw}^{las})sin(\theta_{roll}^{las}) & 0 \\
cos(\theta_{yaw}^{las})sin(\theta_{pitch}^{las}) & R_{32} & R_{33} & 0 \\
x^{las} & y^{las} & z^{las} & 1
\end{bmatrix}
\tag{3}
$$

$$
R_{12} = sin(\theta_{yaw}^{las})cos(\theta_{pitch}^{las})cos(\theta_{roll}^{las}) + sin(\theta_{pitch}^{las})sin(\theta_{roll}^{las})
$$
$$
R_{13} = sin(\theta_{yaw}^{las})sin(\theta_{pitch}^{las})sin(\theta_{roll}^{las}) - sin(\theta_{pitch}^{las})cos(\theta_{roll}^{las})
$$
$$
R_{32} = sin(\theta_{yaw}^{las})sin(\theta_{pitch}^{las})cos(\theta_{roll}^{las}) - cos(\theta_{pitch}^{las})sin(\theta_{roll}^{las})
$$
$$
R_{33} = sin(\theta_{yaw}^{las})sin(\theta_{pitch}^{las})sin(\theta_{roll}^{las}) + cos(\theta_{pitch}^{las})cos(\theta_{roll}^{las})
$$

2.2   Laser Pose Calibration

The laser pose is usually not known exactly, for this reason it is necessary a calibration method to improve the accuracy of 3D Map Building. To achieve this objective it is necessary to find a recognizable pattern with a single laser scan, therefore, it is important that the pattern has singular features. For this reason we use a rectangular prism (Figure 2). First we know the pattern position because it is fixed to the robot with a metallic structure, then we need to detect the 3 edges of the prism, with this edges we must calculate the measured length of each side and we will compare the obtained measures with the real length. Finally, by mean of this comparison it is possible to calculate the pitch (4) and roll (5)

$$
pitch = cos^{-1}\frac{l_3}{l_4}
\tag{4}
$$

$$
roll = cos^{-1}\frac{l_1}{l_2}
\tag{5}
$$

The three points that we have detected form a plane where the laser is placed. Then, it is possible to obtain the coordinates X and Y of the laser. Finally, we calculate the Z coordinate (height of laser) using the distance measured by the laser beam with angle $\alpha_k = 0$ (6).

$$
h = d_{\alpha=0} \cdot cos(pitch)
\tag{6}
$$

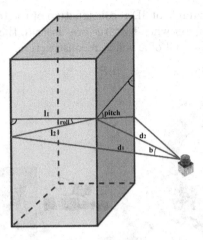

Fig. 2. Laser Calibration Pattern

3   Implementation and Results

The first Test-Bed environment was established in the surroundings of the Poly-technic School of the University of Alcal. It has a surface of 60m x 40m. The robot used in the experimentation was a Seekur Jr. by Mobilerobots, with the following configuration: MacBook Pro with Ubuntu 9.10 operating system, Player/Stage 3.0.1 control software, angled Hokuyo URG-04LX laser, bumpers and encoders in all wheels. They are shown in Figure 3.

Fig. 3. Test-bed and real prototype used in the experimentation

Figure 4 shows an example of 3D reconstruction of the test-bed with one trail of the robot. Color is clearer when features are closer to the ground. In addition, it has been extracted a detail of a bench reconstruction.

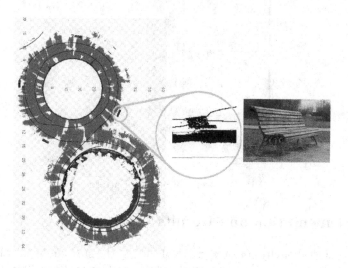

Fig. 4. 3D map building results

The second Test-Bed was the Polytechnic School entry. Figure 5, in the bottom, shows the real image of the stairs and, in the top, it shows the 3D reconstruction of the environment. In the top image, it is possible to identify the wall curvature, the back wall or the curb below the steel barrier.

Fig. 5. 3D School entry

The third Test-Bed was an indoor stairs that is shown in the bottom of the Figure 6. The top of the Figure shows a reconstruction of the stairs where it is possible to recognize the stairs in both, upper and lower angles as well as certain details of the wall.

Fig. 6. Stairs reconstruction

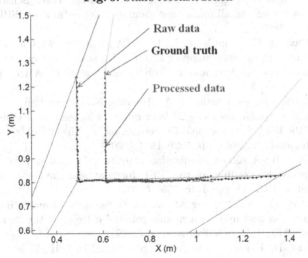

Fig. 7. Calibration results

The calibration method start with the raw data points obtained from the laser, represented in blue. Then, with the transformations mentioned before, we project the points to the floor, we call them processed data and they are represented in red. The ground truth, shown in black, is the known position of the prism. Finally, we compare the processed data and the ground truth, and obtain a mean quadratic error of 4.8 millimeters. The calibration results are shown in Figure 7.

4   Conclusions and Future Works

In this work we have presented a 3D map building using a 2D laser scanner and an action model of a real robotic platform. We have demonstrated that it is possible to build a 3D features cloud using 2D laser scanner in a real application.

In the near future, we have the intention of improving this system using a 3D scan-matching to improve the reconstruction of the 3D maps by mean of reducing the accumulative odometry error.

Acknowledgment. This work has been funded by grant S2009/DPI-1559 (Robocity2030 II Project) from the Science Department of Community of Madrid.

References

1. Chang, Y., Kuwabara, H., Yamamoto, Y.: Novel application of a laser range finder with vision system for wheeled mobile robot. In: Proc. of IEEE/ASME Int. Conf. on Advanced Intelligent Mechatronics, pp. 280–285. IEEE, Los Alamitos (2008)
2. Kogut, G., Ahuja, G., Sights, B., Pacis, E.B., Everett, H.R.: Sensor fusion for intelligent behavior on small unmanned ground vehicles. In: Proc. SPIE, Orlando, FL, vol. 6561 (2007)
3. Ueda, T., Kawata, H., Tomizawa, T., Ohya, A., Yuta, S.: Mobile sokuiki sensor system: Accurate range data mapping system with sensor motion. In: Proc. International Conference on Autonomous Robots and Agents (ICARA), pp. 309–314 (2006)
4. Nguyen, V., Gächter, S., Martinelli, A., Tomatis, N., Siegwart, R.: A comparison of line extraction algorithms using 2d laser range finder for indoor mobile robotics. In: Proc. of the IEEE International Conference on Intelligent Robots and Systems (IROS), Edmonton, Canada, pp. 1929–1934 (2005)
5. Sohn, H., Kim, B.: A robust localization algorithm for mobile robots with laser range finders. In: Proceedings of the IEEE International Conference on Robotics and Automation (ICRA), pp. 3545–3550 (2005)
6. Iocchi, L., Pellegrini, S.: Building 3d maps with semantic elements integrating 2d laser, stereo vision and imu on a mobile robot. In: Proc. of the 2nd ISPRS Int. Workshop 3D-ARCH, Zurich, Switzerland (2007)
7. Singh, S., Feng, D., Keller, P., Shaffer, G., Shi, W., Shin, D.H., West, J., Wu, B.X.: A system for fast navigation of autonomous vehicles. Technical Report CMU-RI-TR-91-20, Robotics Institute, Pittsburgh, PA (1991)

8. Zhou, Y., Chirikjian, G.S.: Probabilistic models of dead-reckoning error in non-holonomic mobile robots. In: Proc. of the IEEE International Conf. on Robotics and Automation (ICRA), Taipei, Taiwan, vol. 2, pp. 1594–1599 (2003)
9. Borenstein, J.: Internal correction of dead-reckoning errors with the smart encoder trailer. In: Proc. of the IEEE International Conference on Intelligent Robots and Systems (IROS), vol. 1, pp. 127–134. IEEE Computer Society Press, Munich (1994)
10. Thrun, S., Burgard, W., Fox, D.: A real-time algorithm for mobile robot mapping with applications to multi-robot and 3D mapping. In: Proc. of the IEEE International Conf. on Robotics and Automation (ICRA). IEEE, San Francisco (2000)
11. Censi, A., Iocchi, L., Grisetti, G.: Scan matching in the hough domain. In: Proc. of the IEEE Intern. Conference on Robotics and Automation, ICRA (2005)

Mapping Based on a Noisy Range-Only Sensor

F. Herranz, M. Ocaña, L.M. Bergasa,
N. Hernández, A. Llamazares, and C. Fernández

Department of Electronics, University of Alcalá, Madrid (Spain)
{fherranz,mocana,bergasa,nhernandez,allamazares,cfernandez}@depeca.uah.es

Abstract. Mapping techniques based on Wireless Range-Only Sensors (WROS) consist of locating the beacons using measurements of distance only. In this work we use WROS working at 2.4GHz band (same as WiFi, Wireless Fidelity), which has the disadvantage of being affected by a high noise. The goal of this paper is to study a noisy range-only sensor and its application in the development of mapping systems. A particle filter is used in order to map the environment, this technique has been applied successfully with other technologies, like Ultra-Wide Band (UWB), but we demonstrate that even using a noisier sensor this technique can be applied correctly.

1   Introduction

Vehicle navigation systems use a combination of a previous map with localization information to guide the vehicle through a mesh of connected ways. Maps are usually obtained in a semi-autonomous way process known as mapping [1]. Mapping is based on sensor observations which extract main features of the environment and allow to represent them into a topological or metric map.

Several systems for localization and mapping have been proposed and successfully deployed for indoor environments. These systems are based on: infrared sensors [2], computer vision [3], ultrasonic sensors [4], laser [5] or radio frequency (RF) [6] [7] [8] [9]. Within the last group we can find localization systems that use WiFi and UWB signal level (SL). In order to estimate the vehicle or map feature location, these systems measure the signal strength and then apply a deterministic (i.e. trilateration) or probabilistic (i.e. particle filter) algorithm to infer the estimated position. In addition, these techniques can be used in the same way in outdoor environments.

This paper addresses the problem of mapping using a noisy range-only sensor. These sensors have two important differences compared to other sensors. Firstly, using these sensors it is possible to avoid the data association problem because this kind of technology uses an unique identifier per sensor. Secondly, the measures do not provide too much information since information about the angles is not obtained. So, after measuring only one sample, the beacon could be anywhere within a ring with radius equal to the range measurement.

We have used WROS working at 2.4Ghz band, this band is affected by anything that contains water. Moreover, signal propagation is affected by reflection,

R. Moreno-Díaz et al. (Eds.): EUROCAST 2011, Part II, LNCS 6928, pp. 420–425, 2012.
© Springer-Verlag Berlin Heidelberg 2012

refraction and diffraction. This effect, known as multipath effect, turns the received SL into a complex function of the distance. In order to solve this problem, several techniques have been tested [10] [11]. In a previous work [12], authors have throughly studied the main variations that affect to this band. They identified five main variations that can appear when working with robots. Finally, they conclude that working at 2.4 GHz band the multipath effect can introduce an error of up to 10dBm to the SL measure.

In this work we employ a probabilistic technique to estimate the position of the beacons. We use a Monte Carlo algorithm like particle filter which represent multimodal distributions for position estimation [13]. Particle filters approximate distribution using a finite number of weighted samples. The estimated distribution is updated using importance sampling: new samples are drawn from the old distribution at random, propagated in accordance with robot odometry, and then weighted according to available sensor information.

The rest of the paper is organized as follows: section 2 shows the mapping process; section 3 describes the results obtained; and finally, section 4 shows some conclusions and future works.

2   Mapping with Range-Only Sensors

Mapping is the process that makes possible to estimate the position of the beacons using the distance between them and the robot. So, the knowledge of the real trajectory of the robot is one of the most important constraints of these kind of systems. Once we know the trajectory of the robot, this problem becomes similar to the localization one but with a different point of view, we suppose that the robot position is known and static at different steps, and then it seems like the beacons are moving around it.

A particle filter [14] is used to achive this aim, which is a sequential Monte Carlo algorithm, i.e., a sampling method to approximate a distribution that uses its temporal structure. A "particle representation" of distributions is used, in particular, we will be concerned with the distribution $P(X_{bt}|z_{0:t})$ where $X_{bt} = (x_{bt}, y_{bt})$ is the observed beacon state at time t, and $z_{0:t} = (r_1, r_2, ..., r_n)$ is the sequence of observations from time 0 to time t. The posterior probability, $P(X_{bt}|z_{0:t})$ is represented using a collection of N weighted samples or particles, $\{X_{bt}^{(i)}, \pi_t^{(i)}\}_{i=1}^N$ where $\pi_t^{(i)}$ is the weight of particle $X_{bt}^{(i)}$ (Equation (1)).

$$P(X_{bt}|z_{0:t}) \approx \sum_i \pi_{t-1} \delta(X_{bt} - X_{bt-1}^{(i)}) \tag{1}$$

So, the particle filter works as follows. First, the particles are uniformly distributed within a "ring" with radius equal to the first range measurement instead of covering all the space with particles, we make this "ring" wide enough in order to absorb the signal noise. Thus, taking advantage of the ring distribution it is possible to obtain better results using a small number of particles.

Second, the particles are not propagated using any motion model since the beacons are statics, instead of we apply a small random noise to the position of the particles in order to move the particles.

Finally, the particles are updated by the previous actions a_{t-1} and the actual observation z_t. This step is the main contribution of this work. Since we do not obtain information about the angle of the measurements, we build a "ring" of observations and we use this "ring" in order to weight the particles using a gaussian function. This process is described as follows:

- Measurement vectors Z are the distances between the beacons and the robot.
- The verisimilitude $P(z_t|X_{rt})$ uses a vectorial space to represent the observations. Thus, we use a circumference equation, which is written in parametric form using trigonometric function shown in equation (2). Then, 360 observations (one per angle ϕ) are generated creating a circumference with radius equal to the distance between the beacon and the robot.

$$Obs = X_{r0} + r(\cos\phi, \sin\phi) \tag{2}$$

Where X_{r0} is the robot position, r is the radius and ϕ is the angle.

Finally, it is important to highlight that this algorithm does not need to collect a high number of samples to estimate the beacon position. It is a online process and the accuracy is improving when the time is increasing.

3 Implementation and Results

We have set up a test environment outside of the Polytechnic School at the University of Alcalá (UAH), using a Seekur Jr platform (Figure 1). The robot, which is presented in Figure 1(a), has been equipped with a Waspmote device (Figure 1(a) shows a detailed view of the device) which is used as range-only sensor and a laptop using Linux Kubuntu 8.04 in order to collect the data along the paths shown in Figures 1(b), 1(c), 1(d). Thus, the environments test the algorithm in different conditions (small and big environments) and for different trajectories of the robot. The environment 1 test circular trajectories when the beacons are inside the circle. However, the environments 2 and 3 are bigger than environment 1, which theoretically has to increase the mapping error, and they place the beacons outside of the square shape. Finally, the trajectory of the robot in the environment 3 is a zig-zag pattern through the square shape.

We have performed tests varying the number of particles ranging from 100 to 1500 particles. Figure 2 shows the results of two beacons for the environment 1. Figure 2 shows the percent of error in meters less than an abscissa and the 70 and 90 percentile per experiment. Using more than 500 particles the error is less than 3 meters, moreover we have to take into account that the signal noise sometimes is more than 10 meters. Also, it is possible to notice that increasing the number of particles our solution becomes more accurate and the error decreases.

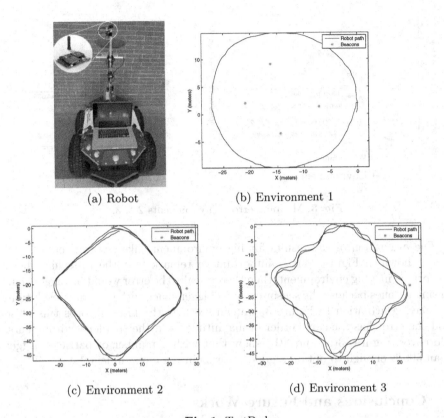

Fig. 1. TestBed

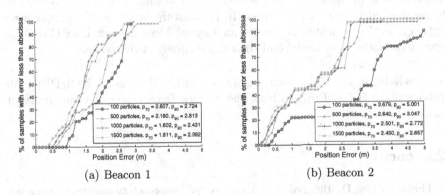

Fig. 2. Mapping error. Environment 1.

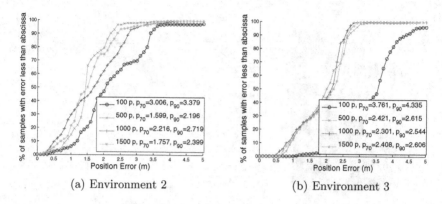

(a) Environment 2   (b) Environment 3

Fig. 3. Mapping error. Environments 2 & 3.

The evaluation of the results for big environments like environments 2 and 3 are shown in Figure 3. It is important to remark that the tests have been performed in a big environment, then theoretically the error would be bigger than in smaller ones because the sensor covers a bigger space with the same resolution. So, paying attention to Figure 3, we can see how the filter absorbs this noise and the error has the same order of magnitude as in the smaller environments. Moreover, Figures 3(a) and 3(b) show that with a number of particles bigger than 500 is enough to obtain a good error as in the environment 1.

4   Conclusions and Future Works

In this work a Wireless range-only sensor and its application to mapping system has been presented. We have proposed a solution based on a particle filter due to its ability to estimate the position of the beacons without delay and its robustness. As well, the algorithm has been tested in small and big environments obtaining good results in both cases. In near future, we have the intention to apply a SLAM algorithm and to use an Inertial Measurement Unit (IMU) to improve the movement model and then the accuracy of the system.

Acknowledgment. This work has been funded by grant S2009/DPI-1559 (Robocity2030 II-CM Project) from the Science Department of Community of Madrid.

References

1. Thrun, S., Fox, D., Burgard, W.: A probabilistic approach to concurrent mapping and localization for mobile robots. In: Machine Learning, pp. 253–271 (1998)
2. Want, R., Hopper, A., Falco, V., Gibbons, J.: The active badge location system. ACM Transactions on Information Systems 10, 91–102 (1992)

3. Krumm, J., Harris, S., Meyers, B., Brumitt, B., Hale, M., Shafer, S.: Multi-camera multi-person tracking for easy living. In: Proc. of 3rd IEEE International Workshop on Visual Surveillance, pp. 3–10 (2002)
4. Priyantha, N., Chakraborthy, A., Balakrishnan, H.: The cricket location support system. In: Proc. of the 6th ACM MobiCom, pp. 155–164 (2002)
5. Barber, R., Mata, M., Boada, M., Armingol, J., Salichs, M.: A perception system based on laser information for mobile robot topologic navigation. In: Proc. of 28th Annual Conference of the IEEE Industrial Electronics Society, pp. 2779–2784 (2002)
6. Matellán, V., Cañas, J.M., Serrano, O.: Wifi localization methods for autonomous robots. Robotica 24(4), 455–461 (2006)
7. Ocaña, M., Bergasa, L.M., Sotelo, M.Á., Flores, R., López, E., Barea, R.: Comparison of wiFi map construction methods for wiFi POMDP navigation systems. In: Moreno Díaz, R., Pichler, F., Quesada Arencibia, A. (eds.) EUROCAST 2007. LNCS, vol. 4739, pp. 1216–1222. Springer, Heidelberg (2007)
8. Jourdan, D.B., Deyst, J.J., Win, M.Z., Roy, N.: Monte carlo localization in dense multipath environments using uwb ranging. In: Proceedings of IEEE International Conference on Ultra-Wideband, pp. 314–319 (2005)
9. Blanco, J.L., Fernandez-Madrigal, J.A., Gonzalez, J.: Efficient probabilistic range-only slam. In: Proceedings of IEEE/RSJ International Conference on Intelligent Robots and Systems (IROS 2008), pp. 1017–1022 (2008)
10. Ladd, A., Bekris, K., Rudys, A., Marceu, G., Kavraki, L., Wallach, D.: Robotics-based location sensing using wireless ethernet. In: Proc. of the MOBICOM 2002 (2002)
11. Youssef, M., Agrawala, A., Shankar, A.: Wlan location determination via clustering and probability distributions. In: Proc. of the IEEE PerCom 2003 (2003)
12. Sotelo, M.A., Ocaña, M., Bergasa, L.M., Flores, R., Marrón, M., García, M.A.: Low level controller for a pomdp based on wifi observations. Robot. Auton. Syst. 55(2), 132–145 (2007)
13. Thrun, S., Fox, D., Burgard, W., Dellaert, F.: Robust monte carlo localization for mobile robots. Artificial Intelligence 128(1-2), 99–141 (2000)
14. Fox, D., Thrun, S., Dellaert, F., Burgard, W.: Particle filters for mobile robot localization. In: Doucet, A., de Freitas, N., Gordon, N. (eds.) Sequential Monte Carlo Methods in Practice. Springer, New York (2000)

U-V Disparity Analysis in Urban Environments

Basam Musleh, Arturo de la Escalera, and José María Armingol

University Carlos III of Madrid, Intelligent System Lab, Spain
{bmusleh,escalera,armingol}@ing.uc3m.es

Abstract. Traditionally obstacles detection is a great topic in computer vision applied to robotics navigation or advance driver assistance system (ADAS). Although other technologies, such as laser, obtain good results to detect obstacles in different environments, stereo vision has the advantage of providing 3D information, improving the knowledge of the environment. A study of the implementation of the u-v disparity in urban environments is presented in this paper, where several tests have been done in different situations which may be difficult to interpret by using a straightforward analysis of the u-v disparity in order to model the environment.

Keywords: Stereo vision, u-v disparity, obstacles detection.

1 Introduction

The disparity map represents the depth of every image pixel and it is possible to construct it from the images provided by the stereo rig. The depth corresponding to a pixel is proportional to the disparity between the localization of the pixel on both images, i.e the problem of obtaining the disparity map is to match each pixel of an image with the other one, called the stereo matching problem. There are a large number of methods in order to solve this problem [1], but somehow all of them are affected by occlusions, untextured areas, adverse light conditions and areas where there are repeated patterns. All these situations are common in urban environments: for example, the sky and the road are typical untextured areas, weak illumination in tunnels. On the other hand, buildings walls are a perfect example of repeating patterns.

Once the disparity map has been generated, the next step is to construct the u-v disparity [2]. The v-disparity expresses the histogram over the disparity values for every image row (v coordinate) and the u-disparity does the same but for every column (u coordinate). In short, the u-disparity is built by accumulating the pixels of each column with the same (u, d) and the v-disparity by accumulating the pixels of each row with the same (v, d). Interesting information about urban environments may be obtained from the u-v disparity. For example, in the case of the u-disparity, the perpendicular obstacles in front of the vehicle appear as horizontal lines whose pixels intensity is the height of these obstacles, whereas in the case of the v-disparity, the perpendicular obstacles appear as vertical lines whose pixels intensity is the width of the obstacles [3]. Another interesting feature is that the ground profile ahead the vehicle appears as an oblique line, this feature is very useful because the pitch of the stereo rig in relation to the ground can be measured for each frame [4].

R. Moreno-Díaz et al. (Eds.): EUROCAST 2011, Part II, LNCS 6928, pp. 426–432, 2012.
© Springer-Verlag Berlin Heidelberg 2012

A large number of different kinds of obstacles as for their size, shape, localization, colour, texture, etc. appear in urban environments and they affect to the analysis of the u-v disparity [5]. The goal of this paper is to size up what situations make difficult the interpretation of the u-v disparity and, if it is possible, how to cope with this situations. Every test has been performed by using our research platform IVVI 2.0 (Intelligent Vehicle based on Visual Information) [6] whose purpose is to test different kinds of ADAS in driving environments, such as traffic sign recognition, pedestrians and vehicles detection or a lane keeping system among others. The IVVI is a commercial vehicle (Fig. 1) which has a stereo rig and a PC in the boot of the vehicle in order to capture and process the necessary stereo images for the algorithm presented in this paper.

Fig. 1. The vehicle IVVI 2.0 (Intelligent Vehicle based on Visual Information)

Section two of this paper explains the method used to detect the obstacles and the road profile in front of the vehicle. In section three, different situations in urban environments are commented; this situations present some interesting feature that make their study interesting. The conclusions are finally commented in section four.

2 Obstacles and Road Profile Detection

As it was previously commented, the information of the environment which is possible to obtain from the disparity map and the u-v disparity are mainly the obstacles and the road profile in front of the vehicle. The method implemented in this paper in order to obtain this information will be explained in this section, where the process is divided into two steps: obstacles detection and calculation of the road profile respectively. The Fig. 2 shows different results of the algorithm applied to a urban environment.

2.1 Obstacles Detection

The method of obstacles detection is based on a preliminary detection on the u-disparity, this detection consist in thresholding the u-disparity and, in this way, every obstacle higher than a threshold measured in pixels is detected. A thresholded u-disparity is obtained thus as a result.

Fig. 2. (a) Visible left image. (b) Disparity map. (c) Obstacles map. (d) Free map. (e) v-disparity from the disparity map. (f) v-disparity from the free map.

Now, using the information from the thresholded u-disparity and the disparity map (Fig. 2(b)), it is possible to obtain the obstacles map (Fig. 2(c)), which is a dense disparity map where only the pixels of obstacles have values different from zero. In order to construct the obstacles map, it is necessary to follow this methodology: for each thresholded pixel (u, d) of the u-disparity, every pixel of the column u in the disparity map is studied. If the value of the disparity is equal to d, then the value of the disparity is conserved, but if the value of the disparity is different from d, the value is set at zero. Using the obstacles map it is possible to determine regions of interest by means of a blob analysis on the visible image and use this regions of interest in a classification task as the presented in [7].

There are other solutions to detect the obstacles in the u-v disparity [8][9], for example applying the Hough transform to detect the obstacles such as lines, the advantage of the method presented in this paper is that it is faster.

2.2 Road Profile Detection

The most straightforward way to obtain the road profile is to apply the Hough transform on the v-disparity, provided that the road profile is the most important line in the v-disparity. The problems arise when the most important line in the v-disparity is not the road profile (Fig. 2(e)), for example, when a large obstacle or several obstacles appear ahead the vehicle, situations which are extremely common in urban environments and less frequent on highways.

For this reason, our method to get the road profile uses a different v-disparity (Fig. 2(f)), which is characterized by that the obstacles have been removed from it. In order to obtain this new v-disparity, it is necessary to build the free map (Fig. 2(d)), which is the dense disparity map but all the pixels which belong to the obstacles have been deleted. In this way, the road profile becomes the most important line in the v-disparity in most of cases.

3 Different Cases Study in Urban Environments

Several common situations in urban environments are discussed in this section. These situations have a particular interest because they present some features that make difficult to analyze the information about the environment.

3.1 Large Obstacles in Front of the Vehicle

The first situation and one of the most often is when a large obstacle appears in front of the vehicle, such as another vehicle or building. Fig. 3 shows two examples of another vehicle in front. The Fig. 3(b) is a typical image of traffic jam and in the Fig. 3(a) a vehicle appears coming closer to our vehicle and a wall behind. The problem arises in principle because the line of the obstacle is the most important line in the v-disparity due to the obstacle occupies an important part of the image. Both cases the u-disparity is presented at the bottom the visible images, where it is possible to distinguish clearly the obstacles. Two different v-disparity are also shown for each case: the first one (left) is constructed by using the disparity map, and the road profile

Fig. 3. Examples of the analysis of the u-v disparity in different cases study in urban environments: (a) A vehicle and a building. (b) Traffic jam. (c) Into a tunnel. (d) Example of elevated obstacle: entrance of a tunnel.

(red line) is erroneous. However in the second one (right) the v-disparity has been constructed from the free map, where there are not any obstacles and consequently the road profile is now correct.

Another added problem is that the large obstacle in front of the vehicle has not enough texture in order to construct a good disparity map, what makes difficult to detect the obstacle and calculate the road profile because the large obstacle hides the road. This situation is common when the obstacle in front is a vehicle due to its uniform colour.

The next example is a special case of a large obstacle in front: two large walls are situated on both sides of the vehicle as the Fig. 3(c) shows. The two walls appear clearly in the u-disparity as two oblique long lines and therefore are easily detected as obstacles. The problem is that the two walls also appear in the v-disparity and the road profile obtained in the v-disparity constructed from the disparity map is erroneous. The free map and the new v-disparity are constructed to cope with this problem and then the road profile can be obtained correctly. Getting under elevated obstacles is a typical action in traffic environments, these obstacles can be traffic lights or the entrance to a tunnel (Fig. 3(d)). From the study of the u-disparity it is not possible to distinguish whether the obstacle obstructs the movement of the vehicle.

3.2 Tunnels

Several problems arise into the tunnels. The construction of the disparity map is difficult due to the weak illumination and by the fact that there are a lot of untextured areas, such as the walls, the road and the roof (Fig. 4(a)). The construction of the disparity map (Fig. 4(b)) in these conditions can be improved by increasing the size of the support region in the cost aggregation step [10]. Once the disparity map is good enough, the following problem appears on the u-v disparity because the roof of the tunnel also appears in the v-disparity (left) as an oblique long line and can be detected as if it was the road profile. When a large obstacle appears in front, it is possible to obtain correctly the road profile if the obstacle is removed from the v-disparity. It is not easy to detect the roof as an obstacle in the case of tunnels because the probability of detecting the road as an obstacle also increases, therefore one possible solution is trying to diminish its contribution as much as possible in the new v-disparity (right).

Fig. 4. (a) Analysis of the u-v disparity into a tunnel. (b) Example of the disparity map into a tunnel.

3.3 Speed Bump on the Road

As it was discussed before, once the road profile has been obtained it is possible to calculate the pitch between the stereo rig and the road. A test has been done in order to evaluate the calculation of the pitch by means of the road profile; this test consist in calculating the pitch for every frame of a sequence where a speed bump appears on the road (Fig. 5(b)). The dimensions of the speed bump are approximately 0.2 m in height and 3 m in length.

The Fig. 5(a) shows a scheme of the road and at the bottom, a graph of the pitch along the road, where the continuous line in blue represents the values of the pitch obtained by using the free map and the red dashed line the values by using the disparity map. There are not important differences between both lines except at the beginning of the speed bump, where the pitch calculated by using the disparity map (red line) is erroneous in several frames. It is important to note that the oscillations of the pitch at the beginning and at the end of the speed bump is due to the vehicle's suspension. The study about the pitch may be extended to other cases, such as a pothole on the road or sudden braking.

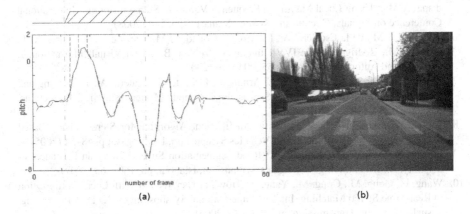

(a)   (b)

Fig. 5. (a) Scheme of the road where a speed bump appears and at the bottom, the graph of the pitch along the road. (b) One frame of the sequence where the speed bump appears.

4 Conclusions

The stereo vision in general and the u-v disparity in particular are powerful tools to obtain information of the environment, this information mainly consist in the obstacles and the road profile in front of the vehicle. However, several difficulties can appear in urban environments, difficulties that are caused in most cases by the great number and different kinds of obstacles that are in these environments.

A method to cope with these difficulties has been presented in this paper and makes possible to reduce the number of mistakes in the information acquired from the urban environments. Several cases have been presented in order to test and compare the presented method, obtaining good results. It is important to note that the system does not need any extrinsic calibration, this feature makes easy its use.

Acknowledgments. This work also was supported by Spanish Government through the CICYT projects FEDORA (Grant TRA2010-20255-C03-01) and VIDAS-DRIVER (Grant TRA2010-21371-C03-02).

References

1. Scharstein, D., Szeliski, R.: A Taxonomy and Evaluation of Dense Two-frame Stereo Correspondence Algorithms. Int. J. Comput. Vision. 47, 7–42 (2002)
2. Soquet, N., Perrollaz, R., Labayrade, R., Auber, D.: Free Space Estimation for Autonomous Navigation. In: 5th International Conference on Computer Vision System, Bielefeld, pp. 1–6 (2007)
3. Broggi, A., Caraffi, C., Fedriga, R.I., Grisleri, P.: Obstacle Detection with Stereo Vision for Off-road Vehicle Navigation. In: IEEE Conference on Computer Vision and Pattern Recognition, San Diego, pp. 65–71 (2005)
4. Labayrade, R., Aubert, D., Tarel, J.P.: Real Time Obstacles Detection in Stereovision on non Flat Road Geometry through V-disparity Representation. In: Intelligent Vehicles Symposium, Versailles, pp. 646–651 (2002)
5. Lee, C.H., Lim, Y.C., Kong, S., Lee, J.H.: Obstacle Localization with a Binarized V-disparity Map Using Local Maximum Frequency Values in Stereo vision. In: International Conference on Signals, Circuits and System, Monastir, pp. 1–4 (2008)
6. Armingol, J.M., de la Escalera, A., Hilario, C., Collado, J.M., Carrasco, J.P., Flores, M.J., Pastor, J.M., Rodriguez, F.J.: IVVI: Intelligent Vehicle Based on Visual Information. J. Robotics and Autonomous Systems 55, 904–916 (2007)
7. Musleh, B., Garcia, F., Otamendi, J., Armingol, J.M., de la Escalera, A.: Identifying and Tracking Pedestrians Based on Sensor Fusion and Motion Stability Predictions. Sensors 10, 8028–8053 (2010)
8. Hu, Z., Uchimura, K.: U_V Disparity: An Efficient Algorithm for Stereo Vision Based Scene Analysis. In: IEEE Intelligent Vehicles Symposium, Las Vegas, pp. 48–54 (2005)
9. Soquet, N., Aubert, D., Hautiere, N.: Road Segmentation Supervised by an Extended V-disparity. In: IEEE Intelligent Vehicles Symposium, Istanbul, pp. 160–165 (2007)
10. Wang, L., Gong, M., Gong, M., Yang, R.: How Far Can We Go With Local Optimization in Real-Time Stereo Matching. In: Third International Symposium on 3D Data Processing, Visualization, and Transmission, pp. 129–136 (2006)

Application of Optimization Algorithms to Trajectory Planning for Underwater Gliders

José Isern-González, Daniel Hernández-Sosa, Enrique Fernández-Perdomo,
Jorge Cabrera-Gámez, Antonio C. Domínguez-Brito, and
Víctor Prieto-Marañón

University Institute of Sistemas Inteligentes y Aplicaciones Numéricas en Ingeniería
Universidad de Las Palmas de Gran Canaria - 35017, Las Palmas, Spain
{jisern,dhernandez,efernandez,jcabrera,adominguez}@iusiani.ulpgc.es,
vprieto@ono.com

Abstract. Underwater gliders are a technology that have demonstrated
to be a valid tool for diverse applications in the oceans including validation of currents models, environmental control or security. Due to their
low speed, gliders might drift significantly from the planned trajectory
by effect of ocean currents, making path planning a crucial tool for them.
In this work, we present a novel path planning scheme for this kind of underwater agents based on optimization techniques that shows promising
results on realistic simulations, including highly time-varying ocean currents. This method models the glider as an intelligent agent that senses
the ocean currents speed and direction, and generates an path according
to the predefined objectives. The proposal reflects accurately the physical vehicle motion pattern and can be easily configured and adapted to
various optimization problems regarding underwater vehicles' missions.
This method gives a superior performance when is compared with other
approaches.

Keywords: underwater gliders, path planning.

1 Introduction

Underwater gliders constitute a technology that is being used in a wide variety
of applications in oceanography and survey (inspection) mission because they
allow to carry out long missions with low power consumption.

A glider is Autonomous Underwater Vehicle (AUV) that operates modifying
its buoyancy in a cyclic pattern. These changes produce vertical impulsion that
is transformed into horizontal speed by effect of wings and tail. The result is
a continuous climb and dive displacement (Fig. 1). These cycles are repeated
typically for 6-12 hours periods, returning then the vehicle to surface for sending
status and data communication to control room, as well as, receiving new orders,
commonly the next way-point or bearing. After 15-30 minutes in surface, the
next immersion period, also referred as stint, is started again. As gliders do not
communicate while they are submerged, the on-board navigation system simply
tries to keep the last commanded bearing during the whole stint.

R. Moreno-Díaz et al. (Eds.): EUROCAST 2011, Part II, LNCS 6928, pp. 433–440, 2012.

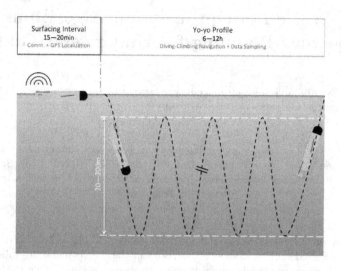

Fig. 1. Glider saw-tooth navigation pattern

Due to gliders speed is very low (aprox. 0.4 m/s), the influence of the ocean currents might force them drift significantly from their expected trajectory. This makes the paths planning a crucial tool for this type of vehicles, as it might reduce the time spent to reach a certain set of waypoints and thus the energy consumption. As a consequence, the glider autonomy gets extended. Optimal planning requires predictions maps from ocean current models as input, in order to simulate the vehicle trajectory. This numerical maps, particularly the Regional Ocean Models (ROMs), are initialized and successively corrected from teledetection data (satellite, CODAR) and in situ data (buoys, ships).

Planning for unmanned underwater vehicles has been a subject of interest for researchers since the introduction of these robotic platforms. Different approaches have been developed applying techniques that include searching algorithms based on artificial intelligence, potential field modeling, multi-objective optimization, etc. Some of the most relevant, in our opinion, are described in the following.

An influential set of planners has evolved from the A* algorithm [3] as a basis, and they operate on graphs and grids. For example, Carroll et al. [2] apply this strategy on a quad-tree search space. More recently, Garau et al. [5] propose another alternative incorporating oceanic currents on a uniform grid discretization.

The approaches based on minimization of energy functions are also worth commenting. Witt et al. [15] models time-varying obstacles using potential fields. The problem of local minima has been tackled by means of strategies based on particle swarms, simulated annealing, or genetic algorithms.

Other alternatives that also make use of continuous models are described on the works from Petres et al. [7], [8]. Later, this line has been extended to deal with the presence of strong currents [12].

Evolutionary computing has also been successfully applied to this type of problems. A significant example can be found in [1], where genetic algorithms are used for AUV trajectory planning environments characterized by time-varying currents.

The high dimensionality of the search space has led to random exploration based approaches. The rapid random trees or RRT [6] [11] are a good example of this and have been translated to the case of route planning for gliders [9].

Some authors [13] have addressed the problem using System Theory and Analytical Methods. Optimal paths are obtained solving a Boundary Value Problem (BVP). Ocean gliders can be modeled as a Dubins car, so Dubins curves are suitable in the case of steady flow, with some variants allowing for turn constraints. Zermelo's optimal navigation formula is applicable for unsteady flow, but without turn constraints. In either case, these are local planning methods that perform poorly with strong currents, so only propelled vehicles might benefit from them.

In this work, we introduce a novel path planning technique focused on underwater gliders, that bases on optimization techniques. This path planning pursues to maximize the distance traveled toward a waypoint in a fixed number of days. High frequency ROMs are used, offering hourly outputs, 1/20 deg resolution and to three days of forecast horizon. The computational cost is important because the glider is in surface a few minutes and sometimes is necessary to replan a path into this temporal window.

This paper is organized as follows: the next section the proposed method is described in detail. Section 3 presents the experiments carried out to validate our planning algorithm. Finally, section 4 contains the conclusions extracted from this work.

2   Path Planner

In this work, we introduce a new proposal based on iterative optimization to solve the path planning problem for underwater gliders. The algorithm estimates the trajectory that the vehicle will perform throughout the ocean current field obtained via ROM and generates an appropriate set of bearings to compensate for/exploit local currents to reach a given target or fulfill a certain objective.

The optimization process operates taking the commanded glider bearings of each surfacing as parameters. Additionally in this problem the number of them is known because we know the number of days of forecast. If we use stints of 8 hours with a temporal horizon of 3 days then is necessary to define 9 optimization parameters. A simple kinematic model of the glider is used in the simulator to reproduces the glider behavior in each stint combining the commanded bearing with the current model data and the nominal glider velocity. As gliders keep constant the bearing while is submersed then the temporal discretization of this method is adapted to this real behavior. As commented previously, due to their relative low speed, the resultant glider trajectory is strongly influenced by ocean currents. This effect can be observed in Fig. 2. We use the Euclidean distance to the goal of the final of the last stint as objective function. With this election, the benefit is twofold, since we avoid spatial discretization and allow for a physically realistic simulation. Both the start to goal angle or the results of a simple direct to goal strategy can be used as initial guess with good results. Classical Levenberg-Marquardt, Sequential Quadratic Programming or Quasi-Newton methods have been tested.

3   Experiments and Results

We have carried out several simulations using Matlab® to validate the proposal and test its performance. This have been done comparing the results with the ones obtained by other alternative methods:

- **Direct to goal:** This is the trivial solution to the problem. At each surfacing the next bearing is computed as the direction of the goal point.
- **Standard A*:** This method is based on the use of an uniform grid over the search space. From a given position all neighboring nodes are visited, computing a function cost for each one that integrates the measure of the time required to reach that position and an underestimation of the time required to get to the goal point. This heuristic is used to prune the non optimal trajectories from the exploring tree. Some authors [10], [14], [5] have applied this AI path planning method for gliders moving through an uniform grid of ocean currents. However, there is not trajectory integration between consecutive surfacing, this does not warrant that the glider surfaced in the corresponding node.
- **CTS-A*:** This method [4] is a variant of classic A* where the times between two consecutive surfacing are constant. It is based on the discretization of the bearings that can be commanded at each surfacing, and is suitable for both static and dynamic ocean current maps. However, as the bearings space is discretizated thus do not search in all possible routes. Additionally, if we increase the number of considered bearings, the computational cost increase exponentially.

To compare the performance of each path planning method, we have simulated 25 different missions in the Atlantic coast of the Iberian Peninsula, using ocean current maps from the ESEO-AT model. This is a ROM model that gives outputs for each hour structured in four 24h sets from now-cast to D+3 predictions. The simulations described in this paper were configured for a glider speed of 0.4 m/s and a period between surfacings of 8 hours.

Two metrics have been computed for the method comparison: path quality and computational cost. We have established as a quality measure (the lower the better), the remaining distance from the end position of planned trajectory and the target point.

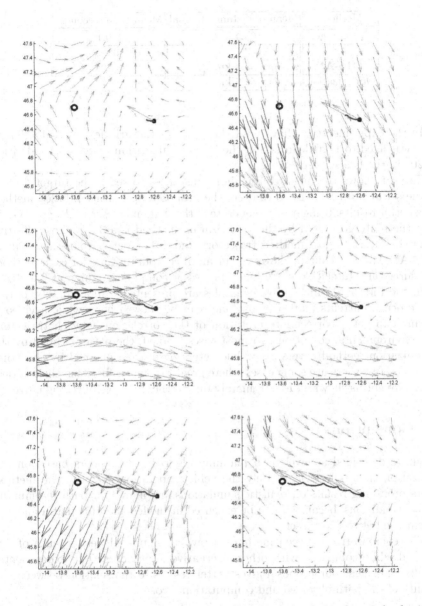

Fig. 2. Six snapshots of the optimal trajectory (blue line) simulation for a 3-day horizon with time-varying currents. Square: start point. Circle: goal point. Light blue arrows: ocean currents field. Blue arrows: ocean currents that exceed the glider speed. Orange arrows: glider bearings for each surfacing.

Table 1. Mean of remaining distance to reach the goal and computational costs

Methods	Mean of distance to goal	Mean time (seconds)
Direct to goal	65.4 km.	<0.1
A*	62.7 km.	38.4
CTS-A*	55.8 km.	342.4
Optimization	50.6 km.	8.1

In the experiments we have used the same spatial grid for A* and CTS-A* that was fixed to 1/20 degrees. For the CTS-A* algorithm we have set a division of 20° in the bearings rose.

Table 1 shows the mean of remaining distances to reach the target for the whole set of test cases. In all of them the proposed optimization-based method gets better results, being able to generate paths that end closer to the goal. Globally, the route generated by the optimization method is a 3.8 % most effective than the direct to goal method trajectory and a 3 % better than the result of CTS-A*. The last column shows the mean of computing time for each method, measured on a Intel®Core™2 Quad processor computer running at 2.5 GHz.

In the Fig. 3 two illustrative examples are presented. Unfortunately, only a static ocean currents map (the last one) can be showed here, while a video is required to get a correct interpretation of the correlation between trajectory and environmental conditions. In most cases studied, the path obtained by the optimization method covers a few kilometers more than planned by the other methods. But there are some cases where great differences between their trajectories are got as shown in Fig. 4, mainly due to the influence of strong currents.

4   Conclusions

We have described a novel path planning algorithm for gliders based on optimization that reflects accurately the vehicle operation pattern. The method offers promising results on realistic simulations and allows for path re-planning in real conditions, because it can be executed in the few minutes that a glider is on surface between transects.

The comparative between methods shows an improved performance of our method when compared with other alternative approaches. The experimental results show that our proposal gives better results in the relation between the quality of the path obtained and computational cost.

Acknowledgments. This work has been supported by the Autonomous Government of Canary Islands (Agencia Canaria de Investigación, Innovación y Sociedad de la Información) and FEDER: project ProID20100062).

The authors would like to thank Puertos del Estado for granting access to the ESEOO Regional Ocean Model.

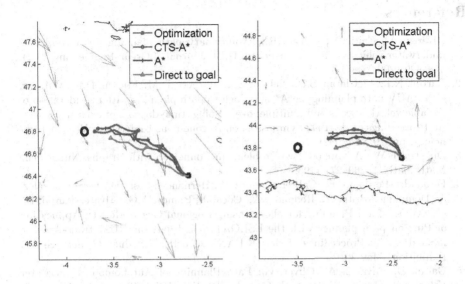

Fig. 3. Example of comparative of trajectories in two different missions of 3 days with glider speed of 0.4 m/s. Light blue arrows show the of ocean currents field. LEFT: Total distance = 95.3 km. Distance to reach the target: Optimization: 8.4 km; CTS-A*: 11.2 km; A*: 9.9 km; Direct to goal: 22.5 km. RIGHT: Total distance = 89.3 km. Optimization: 27.7 km; CTS-A*: 29.9 km; A*: 29.6 km; Direct to goal: 32.8 km.

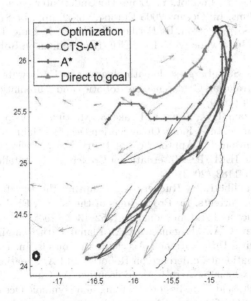

Fig. 4. Example of comparative of trajectories in a mission of 4 days. Light blue arrows show the of ocean currents field and blue arrows the ocean currents that exceed the glider speed (0.4 m/s). Total distance = 344.6 km. Distance to reach the goal point: Optimization: 68.9 km; CTS-A*: 85.1 km; A*: 169.4 km; Direct to goal: 217.6 km.

References

1. Álvarez, A., Caiti, A., Onken, R.: Evolutionary path planning for autonomous underwater vehicles in a variable ocean. IEEE Journal of Ocean Engineering 29(2), 418–429 (2004)
2. Carroll, K.P., McClaran, S.R., Nelson, E.L., Barnett, D.M., Friesen, D.K., William, G.N.: AUV path planning: an A* approach to path planning with consideration of variable vehicle speeds and multiple, overlapping, time-dependent exclusion zones. In: Proceedings of the 1992 Symposium on Autonomous Underwater Vehicle Technology, pp. 79–84 (1992)
3. Dijkstra, E.W.: A Note on Two Problems in Connexion with Graphs. Numerische Mathematik 1, 269–271 (1959)
4. Fernández-Perdomo, E., Cabrera-Gámez, J., Hernández-Sosa, D., Isern-González, J., Domínguez-Brito, A., Redondo, A., Coca, J., Ramos, A.G., Álvarez-Fanjul, E., García, M.: Path Planning for gliders using Regional Ocean Models: Application of Pinz on path planner with the ESEOAT model and the RU27 trans-Atlantic flight data. In: Proceedings of the OCEANS 2010 IEEE Sydney Conference and Exhibition (May 2010)
5. Garau, B., Álvarez, A., Oliver, G.: Path Planning of Autonomous Underwater Vehicles in Current Fields with Complex Spatial Variability: an A* Approach. In: Proc. 2005 IEEE International Conference on Robotics and Automation, pp. 194–198 (2005)
6. LaValle, S.M., Kuffner, J.J.: Randomized kinodynamic planning. In: Proceedings of the IEEE International Conference on Robotics and Automation, pp. 473–479 (1999)
7. Petres, C., Pailhas, Y., Petillot, Y., Lane, D.: Underwater path planing using fast marching algorithms. In: Oceans 2005-Europe, vol. 2, pp. 814–819 (2005)
8. Petres, C., Pailhas, Y., Patron, P., Petillot, Y., Evans, J., Lane, D.: Path Planning for Autonomous Underwater Vehicles. IEEE Transactions on Robotics 23(2), 331–341 (2007)
9. Rao, D., Williams, S.B.: Large-scale path planning for Underwater Gliders in ocean currents. In: Australasian Conference on Robotics and Automation (ACRA), Sydney, December 2-4 (2009)
10. Sathyaraj, B.M., Jain, L.C., Finn, A., Drake, S.: Multiple UAVs path planning algorithms: a comparative study. Fuzzy Optimization Decision Making 7, 257–267 (2008)
11. Simmons, R., Urmson, C.: Approaches for heuristically biasing RRT growth. In: Proceedings of the IEEE/RSJ International Conference on Intelligent Robots and Systems, pp. 1178–1183 (2003)
12. Soulignac, M., Taillibert, P., Rueher, M.: Adapting the wavefront expansion in presence of strong currents. In: Proceedings of the 2008 IEEE International Conference on Robotics and Automation, pp. 1352–1358 (2008)
13. Techy, L., Woolsey, C.A., Morgansen, K.A.: Planar Path Planning for Flight Vehicles in Wind with Turn Rate and Acceleration Bounds. In: Proceedings of the 2010 IEEE International Conference on Robotics and Automation (2010)
14. Thompson, D.R., Chien, S., Arrott, M., Balasuriya, A., Chao, Y., Li, P., Meisinger, M., Petillo, S., Schofield, O.: Mission Planning in a Dynamic Ocean Sensorweb. In: 19th International Conference on Automated Planning and Scheduling (ICAPS) - Scheduling and Planning Applications Workshop, SPARK (2009)
15. Witt, J., Dunbabin, M.: Go With the Flow: Optimal AUV Path Planning in Coastal Environments. In: Australian Conference on Robotics and Automation (2008)

Electric Scaled Vehicle as ITS Experimentation Platform

Javier J. Sanchez-Medina, Moises Diaz-Cabrera,
Manuel J. Galan-Moreno, and Enrique Rubio-Royo

Innovation Center for the Information Society (CICEI) – ULPGC, Spain
{jsanchez,erubio}@polaris.ulpgc.es, moisdc@gmail.com,
mgalan@dmat.ulpgc.es

Abstract. Intelligent Vehicle Robotics is a research area affordable only
to big size research groups, mainly because of its high costs. By the
present work we propose to develop Intelligent Vehicle Robotics research
with modest budgets using an accurately scaled platform.

We have developed a scaled intelligent vehicle model to simulate private electric vehicles. It is a low cost, flexible, expandable and open
platform that has been meant to test intelligent vehicle solutions to be,
after that tested in real scale intelligent vehicles. We have called the
model ASEIMOV, standing for Autonomous Scaled Electric Intelligent
MOnitored Vehicle.

The model consists of a scaled electric vehicle that has been equipped
with sensors, web cameras, a PC computer, batteries and ballasts to
simulate physically and through software an electric smart vehicle. A
carefully scaled vehicle means that the successful solutions tested on the
scaled platform are worthy to be tried on real scale smart vehicles in a
further step of research. Through this work we describe the ASEIMOV
model.

1 Introduction

Intelligent vehicles have being announced as the next revolution on mobility
aiming to safer and more efficient transports. There are some "intelligent" solutions already in the streets, but much more are to come. They will cover a
wide range from safety applications to unmanned navigation systems, including
collision avoidance (e.g. [11]), Lane Detection and Following (e.g. [14]), following
a leader (e.g. [10]), overtaking aid systems (e.g. [13]), etc.

To build a prototype, as a tool for testing new intelligent vehicle solutions
may be really expensive and within reach for a small list of research centers.

We have designed a new model of research platform to simulate private electric
vehicles. The aim is to have a low cost, easily implementable experimentation
device that permits researchers to test intelligent vehicle solutions.

By this work, our purpose is to present a scaled intelligent vehicle model that
could be built by a wider set of researchers to test intelligent vehicle solutions
that could be then experimented in full scale intelligent vehicles.

R. Moreno-Díaz et al. (Eds.): EUROCAST 2011, Part II, LNCS 6928, pp. 441–448, 2012.

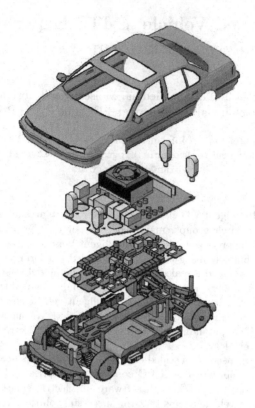

Fig. 1. ASEIMOV 3D Model

To carry out this, the proposed model needs to be as accurately scaled as possible. Its dynamic behavior – e.g. acceleration and braking curves – should be very similar to the full size intelligent vehicle where the obtained solutions, algorithms, etc., are planned to be validated.

The model consists of a scaled electric vehicle that has been equipped with sensors, web cameras, a PC computer, batteries and ballasts to simulate physically and through software an electric smart vehicle. A fine scaled vehicle makes the successful solutions tested on it good candidates to be tried on real scale smart vehicles in a further step of research.

It puts together some interesting paradigms like:

- Low Cost (but not Low Quality) Research: As a small group researching on Intelligent Transportation Systems we are aware about the importance of cheap technologies to be attainable by a bigger amount of researchers and groups from all around the world.
- Free Software: In our group we are firmly convinced about the idea of Academic Researchers should use free software for the sake of researcher independence and fair productivity feedback to global society.
- "Off-the-shelf" computer components: In the same line as above, this kind of components may be cheaper and easily obtained by researchers anywhere.

Fig. 2. First ASEIMOV Unit

Besides that, this kind of architecture has some very interesting features:

- The developed model is flexible, reusable and expandable, mainly thanks to the PC computer and PC-compatible robotic components installed.
- We used a 1/10 scale Remote Control car as a basis for the chassis – See 2.1.
- We scale a real size acceleration and braking functions (using software over the on-board PC) and its mass distribution (using ballasts)– see setion 2.6.
- We have implemented the concept of Safety Bubble using PC-compatible robotic sensors – See section 2.4.
- We have even developed a speed probe using a recycled ball mouse and the PS-2 port at the computer. With this sensor in combination with a robotic accelerometer we will face the odometry[1] of the vehicle – See 2.5.

1.1   State of the Art

There are many groups working on intelligent prototypes all around the world. Some remarkable approaches are: GRULL *Grupo de Robótica de la Universidad de La Laguna* with the project GUISTUB *Guiado de un Sistema de Transporte en una Urbanizacin Bioclimtica Cerrada*. They have designed a vehicle called Verdino [9], [6], [8].

Another remarkable research is the one from VISLAB. They are a spin-off company of the University of Parma; which is involved in basic and applied research, developing machine vision algorithms and intelligent systems for different applications, primarily for the the automotive field. They have performed several autonomous real prototypes since 1994 – e.g. [7], [5].

Other interesting research project is the so called AUTOPIA from CSIC, Madrid [12]. They have taken technology developed for mobile robots to the automotive world. They have also developed several prototypes of fuel and electric vehicles. Stanford University stands out in this area with the vehicle Stanley [1].

---

[1] Odometry: Estimation of the position and speed of a moving object.

Finally, the Japanese company ZMP.inc. [2], [3] has a very interesting scaled vehicle called Robocar Z. It is a small robotic vehicle to test autonomous navigation algorithms.

2   Model Description

In figure?? it is shown a 3D modeled ASEIMOV prototipe decomposed into its main components. In that figure can be observed from top to down, the Mini ITX computer in the top of the available space withing the vehicle. Down there there is a second platform where most of the robotic component card are placed – DC motor controller, servomotor controller, accelerometer, and sonar and infrared sensor acquisition cards. Finally, in the botton we can see all the mechanical components, the batery, webcams, and all the sensors around the custom-made supporting structure.

Every unit needs to satisfy three strong restrictions: Scarce space available, low budget and an acceptable autonomy for lab tests. Across the rest of this section we will explain the more relevant parts of the ASEIMOV model.

2.1   Chassis

In this section we will explain the main structure that supports all the elements in every ASEIMOV unit: The chassis. We need as much free volume as possible.

We realized that a good option may be to use a commercial RC vehicle as a starting point because of several reasons: RC vehicle's chassis bears a strong resemblance to a real size vehicle mechanical elements. On the other hand, this vehicle has a flat internal structure, this gives us the possibility of a free and comfortable internal space to allocate the PC and all the electronic elements needed to build an ASEIMOV unit.

For the first ASEIMOV unit we have used a Kyosho TF-5 RC electric car (1:10 scale). As can be observed in figure 1, we have designed a two shelf structure using methacrylate to hold all the electronics devices and the PC motherboard.

2.2   Locomotion

Typically, the locomotion of a vehicle requires controlling two things: traction and steering. In our model, two electric engines are used. A DC engine is used to the traction, and a servomotor is used to control the steering. Both motors are electronically controlled by the on-board computer.

To control the traction motor we have used the LV PhidgetMotorControl DC motor controller, which is connected to the on-board PC using a USB connection.

As for the steering movements we have used the servomotor included in the brand new Kyosho car that allows the right and left turn of the front wheels. That servomotor needs to be controlled by another circuit. In our case, we have used the one provided also by Phidget – PhidgetServo 1-Motor– again, connected through an USB cable to the PC motherboard.

2.3   PC Platform

A key element of the ASEIMOV model is the on-board computer. We have designed this model as a flexible research platform where different equipments can be installed depending on the specific configuration needed for every test. That is why we have included a complete PC with a Linux distribution, aiming to flexibility.

Communication. An interesting topic is the communication between our car and a remote computer. Once this communication is ensured by the constraints of speed in communication from our pc could drive the vehicle. With communication we try to touch as little as possible to ASEIMOV.

The overall control system can be administered through a Secure SHell server – OpenSSH in this case – located in the computer system of ASEIMOV.

2.4   Safety Bubble Detection

The vehicle must know what is around. Because of this, the car must be equipped in order to implement a safety bubble. This could help the implementation of intelligent algorithms ensuring a safe distance from any near obstacle or vehicle.

For the first built unit, we have installed 8 short range (10 to 80cm) IR distance sensors, a front wider range (20 to 120cm) IR distance sensor, and 7 sonars sensor (with a usable range from 0 up to 645cm) around the vehicle. All these sensors are connected to two Phidget 8/8/8 boards which are connected to the on-board PC by USB.

Fig. 3. Sensors in the Front of the Unit. From Left to Right, Top to Down, Short Range IR Sensor, Sonar Sensor, Medium Range IR and Short Range IR.

The sensors used may be easily substituted by other PC compatible ones. For instance, laser sensors may be used to get more reliable distance measures if the solution under study demands it.

2.5   Vehicle Positioning

Many vehicular robotic applications needs of tracking the vehicle position. In real scale vehicles this task use to be solved by means of GPS or similar technology.

In our case, we have included two electronic devices within the prototype we presume that could help us determining its relative position: a three axes acceleration sensor, and a home-made speed encoder.

2.6   Mass Scaling and Speed Scaling

We need our platform to be as close as possible to real size cars regarding its dynamic behavior. This is a key hypothesis of our model, since we want the successful intelligent vehicle applications developed over the ASEIMOV prototype to be then extrapolated to real size cars.

The strategy devised to get that goal is two folded:

1. First we make our prototypes to have a mass balance equivalent to the mass balance of the real size car taken as a reference.

   The dynamic response of the vehicle is directly proportional to its mass [4]. For the present work we have modeled a rough real size electric vehicle taking commercial electric vehicles currently or soon in the streets as examples – see 12. Using SolidWorks, we have calculated its center of mass. Then we calculate for that modeled real size car the mass balance between the right and the left side, and between the front and the rear of the unit. We do the same for the scaled ASEIMOV unit.

2. Second, every ASEIMOV unit needs to incorporate a closed-loop adaptive control system that adjust its longitudinal speed within a bounded range consistent with the acceleration and braking curves scaled from the real simulated car.

3   Control Application Developed

In figure 4 it is shown the control application developed for the ASEIMOV units – called JASEIMOV. This software is under GNU Public License and can be downloaded from *http://cicei.ulpgc.es/aseimov/*.

Basically, it is a user-friendly intuitive Java application using a server-client scheme where every ASEIMOV unit can be remotely controlled, and every sensor can be sampled in real time. In every ASEIMOV unit server process needs to be run and in any other PC connected to the same Wi-Fi network a JASEIMOV client can be run.

4   Conclusions and Future Research Plans

In this paper we have presented a new model of experimentation platform on intelligent vehicles, we have called ASEIMOV, standing for Autonomous Scaled Electric Intelligent MOnitored Vehicle.

The main hypothesis of the presented model is that is is possible to develop a scaled intelligent vehicle to test vehicular robotic solutions without the high costs and difficulties of real size experiments, and afterwards to extrapolate the more interesting to real size intelligent vehicles for further tests.

To achieve this goal we need the scaling process to be as accurate as possible. In the first ASEIMOV built unit we have approached that accuracy by two means: simulating the mass balance and the dynamic response of a real size vehicle, first by introducing small ballast in the platform, and second by an adaptive

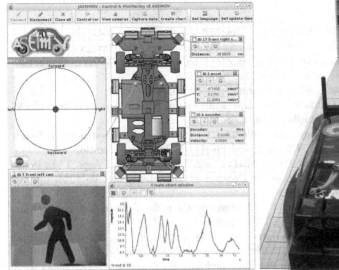

Fig. 4. Control Application   **Fig. 5.** Calibration Setup

closed-loop control software which restricts the longitudinal speed within scaled real size acceleration/braking curves.

The presented model is a low cost model that can be assumed by researching groups without huge budgets available. This would increase the number of researchers in the area, with the obvious benefits that it would bring.

Besides that, the proposed model is such a flexible one since all the components are controlled by a Linux/PC. So, it can be custom-made built for many different applications incorporating other sensors, devices, etc.

About future work plans, there is plenty of work to do now. We need to accurately define the safety bubble we can use, with the current setup of sensors. We need to fully study the vehicle positioning by the combination of the home-made speed encoder and the accelerometer, or any other technologies available. We need to test the longitudinal speed adaptive control software with real acceleration and braking curves and see how it works. We also need to improve the control application, to get more capacities from it.

After that, we will be in a position to start exploring intelligent vehicle applications. Particularly, we have keen interest in building a cluster of ASEIMOV units and developing cooperative intelligent solutions.

Acknowledgment. The authors want to thank all the people that have supported the development of the ASEIMOV project, specially all the fellows that have joined the International Advisory Board of the ASEIMOV project (http://cicei.ulpgc.es/aseimov/).

References

1. Stanford Racing Team, http://cs.stanford.edu/group/roadrunner
2. Website from ZMP.inc., http://www.zmp.co.jp/e_html/products_rc-z_en.html
3. Website about Linux, http://www.linuxfordevices.com/c/a/News/Linux-robot-car-targets-autonomous-navigation/
4. Fundamentos de mecanismos y mquinas para ingenieros (1998)
5. Automatic Vehicle Guidance: the Experience of the ARGO Autonomous Vehicle. World Scientific Co. Publisher, Singapore (1999)
6. Arnay, R., Acosta, L., Sigut, M., Toledo, J.T.: Detection of Non-structured Roads Using Visible and Infrared Images and an Ant Colony Optimization Algorithm. In: Krasnogor, N., Melián-Batista, M.B., Pérez, J.A.M., Moreno-Vega, J.M., Pelta, D.A. (eds.) NICSO 2008. Studies in Computational Intelligence, vol. 236, pp. 37–47. Springer, Heidelberg (2009)
7. Broggi, A., Bertozzi, M., Fascioli, A.: Argo and the millemiglia in automatico tour. IEEE Intelligent Systems 14(1), 55–64 (1999)
8. González, E.J., Acosta, L., Hamilton, A., Felipe, J., Sigut, M., Toledo, J., Arnay, R.: Towards a multiagent approach for the VERDINO prototype. In: Omatu, S., Rocha, M.P., Bravo, J., Fernández, F., Corchado, E., Bustillo, A., Corchado, J.M. (eds.) IWANN 2009. LNCS, vol. 5518, pp. 21–24. Springer, Heidelberg (2009)
9. Gonzlez, E., Acosta, L., Hamilton, A., Felipe, J., Sigut, M., Toledo, J., Arnay, R.: Towards a Multiagent Approach for the VERDINO Prototype. In: Distributed Computing, Artificial Intelligence, Bioinformatics, Soft Computing, and Ambient Assisted Living, June 10-12 (2009)
10. Lim, H., Kang, Y., Kim, J., Kim, C.: Formation control of leader following unmanned ground vehicles using nonlinear model predictive control. In: IEEE/ASME International Conference on Advanced Intelligent Mechatronics, AIM 2009, pp. 945–950 (July 2009)
11. Llorca, D., Sotelo, M., Parra, I., Naranjo, J., Gavilan, M., Alvarez, S.: An experimental study on pitch compensation in pedestrian-protection systems for collision avoidance and mitigation. IEEE Transactions on Intelligent Transportation Systems 10(3), 469–474 (2009)
12. Perez, J., Gonzalez, C., Milanes, V., Onieva, E., Godoy, J., de Pedro, T.: Modularity, adaptability and evolution in the autopia architecture for control of autonomous vehicles. In: IEEE International Conference on Mechatronics (2009)
13. Wang, F., Yang, M., Yang, R.: Conflict-probability-estimation-based overtaking for intelligent vehicles. IEEE Transactions on Intelligent Transportation Systems 10(2), 366–370 (2009)
14. Zhou, S., Jiang, Y., Xi, J., Gong, J., Xiong, G., Chen, H.: A novel lane detection based on geometrical model and gabor filter. In: 2010 IEEE Intelligent Vehicles Symposium (IV), pp. 59–64 (2010)

A Complete Conceptual Model for Pervasive Information Services for Public Transport

Carmelo R. García-Rodríguez, Ricardo Pérez-García, Gabino Padrón-Morales, Francisco Alayón-Hernández, and Alexis Quesada-Arencibia

University of Las Palmas de Gran Canaria, Institute of Cybernetic Science and Technology, Campus Universitario de Tafira, 35017 Las Palmas, Spain
{rgarcia,falayon,rperez,gpadron,aquesada}@dis.ulpgc.es

Abstract. The interoperability is a general requirement of the public transport information systems. This property permits them the integration with others systems that operate in different contexts. The interoperability is achieved by system components with the capacity to work autonomously in different contexts and using a common conceptual model in order to the components can collaborate together. In this work, a complete conceptual model for public information system is explained; this model permits us to develop intelligent environments where information services are provided for the actors involved in a public transport network. The main goal is provide an interoperability kernel formed by a conceptual model and system resources in order that the information systems that run in these environments have a high level of functional scalability, environmental adaptability and accessibility.

Keywords: System interoperability, ontology, public transport conceptual data models.

1 Introduction

The main goal of communication and information technologies in the public transport is the improvement of this critical service for the citizen using the information and communication technology [1]. This improvement can be expressed in terms of safety, accessibility and efficiency of the economic and environmental parameters of the transport activity [2], [3]. To achieve this main goal, the critic requirement to fulfill is the provision and management of quality data related to the different information systems of the public transport networks. For example, the management of quality data permits a more efficient use of existing transport infrastructures, enhancing efficiency and safety, as well as reducing energy consumptions and accidents. For this reason, all the transport actors (authorities, companies and citizens) are agree about the convenience of public transport networks with high level of interoperability. In this context, interoperability means the capacity to integrate the different systems implied in the transport activities (systems working in different transport areas, mode, companies and suppliers)

R. Moreno-Díaz et al. (Eds.): EUROCAST 2011, Part II, LNCS 6928, pp. 449–456, 2012.

In the context of modern systems, the interoperability is achieved providing the system components (agents) with the capacity to work autonomously in different contexts (context awareness) and using a common set of concepts (ontology) in order to the components can collaborate together. Therefore, the ontology is an important element of modern information systems for public transport. In this work a complete conceptual model for public information system is explained, this model permits us to develop intelligent environments where information services are provided for the actors involved in a public transport network, for example: guidance services for travelers, assistance systems for driving, real time systems to facilitate the technical maintenance and the operations control of the vehicles, etc. By this conceptual model, the data provided by different corporations that work in the transport network are transformed to common data entities used in the different intelligent environments. In our case, we define two environments: the onboard context and the context in transit places (stations and bus stops). The main goal is to provide a kernel of concepts about data and processes in order to achieve a high level of functional scalability, environmental adaptability and accessibility in the information systems that run in these environments. We have used the pervasive [4] and ambient intelligence [5] computing models and Transmodel [6] (European conceptual data model) Also, the mobile communication technologies and services, such as IEEE 802.11 and Bluetooth, have been considered.

2 The Problem to Solve

Several studies about data management in public information systems have concluded that many data are frequently generated by different elements (sources) and methodologies (manual measurements versus automatic processes) and these data are used by different software applications. For these reasons, the interoperability of public transport networks is an important requirement, because a lack of this property should imply, for example, a manual forms of communications between different applications and the possible incompatibility between data used by different software applications (e.g., different geographical representation of the bus stops used by the geographical information system, the passenger information system, scheduling system and the vehicle control system). Tyrinopoulos [7] studied the main problems related to the data managements in the public transport information systems dues to the lack of effective mechanisms of integration in this sector, these are: incompatibility between applications, insufficient information flow, multiple storage of common datasets, delays in information availability and high operation and maintenance costs of the applications. Therefore, the interoperability is a main requirement of the major intermodal transportation network, where different modal transport network of different cities, region and countries are integrated. But also, this is a properly characteristic of the local public transport network because achieving it the quality service to the citizen can be improved.

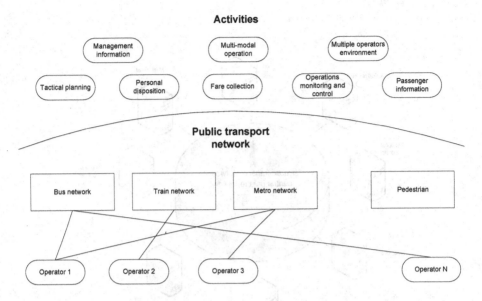

Fig. 1. Overview of a public transport network

The network integrates different transport modes (land, maritime and air) operated by several transport companies (operators). The actors of the transport network (passengers, operators and transport authorities) use the services related to the main activities of a public transport operator, for example: Tactical planning (Vehicle-Driver Scheduling and Rostering), fares, Operations monitoring and control, passenger information, etc. In this context, two classic approaches encourage the interoperability:

- Multiple interfaces between different applications. This approach has been unable to provide sufficient data sharing and communication. It is prone to errors and delays in information availability. In addition, this approach offers limited information reliability and substantially increases applications operation and maintenance costs.
- Centralized approach through data sharing and handling. The centralized approach includes unification of the technological environment of a public transport operator, integrating the various IT applications. In particular, the public transport operator stores all information in a central database, which is accessible to all related applications (see Fig. 2) The integrated computerization infrastructures based on centralized data sharing and handling are facilitated by the existence of a complete management information model. Such a model simulates the integration and data communication processes between different applications, and generates an uninterrupted and robust chain of information systems.

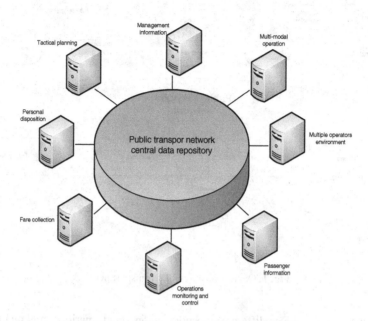

Tactical planning

Management information

Multi-modal operation

Personal disposition

Public transpor network central data repository

Multiple operators environment

Fare collection

Operations monitoring and control

Passenger information

Fig. 2. Interoperability centralized approach model

The conceptual model described in this paper is currently applied in the public transport network of Gran Canaria Island (Canary Islands). This network integrates land transport by road and in a near future train transport. Seven transport companies are the operators, six of them work in a context of urban transport and one is a metropolitan transport company. Some of these corporations are small business having a buses fleet over 15 vehicles, transporting about 100.000 passengers per year and two are medium business having a buses fleet of more than 100 vehicles, transporting more than 20.000.000 of passengers per year. This diversity is reflected also in the technological field; for example, in some of these companies the onboard ticketing activity is manually executed using as a unique payment method the cash while in others is automatically executed using different payment methods (cash, magnetic cards and contactless smart cards).

The conceptual model described in this work is a basic component of a framework where different integrated information services for the actors of the transport network can be developed. This provides the required elements (ontology, data and data schemes) to develop integrated and interoperable information services. Integrated service means a service that is accessible for the actors, for example: passengers, technical staff, in any place of the network regardless of the transport mode and company used. Interoperable service means that the service is provided regardless of the technology used. For example, nowadays three integrated services are deployed using the conceptual model proposed: a payment system based on contactless smart card, an information system for transit passengers and a web portal to provide internet information services related on public transport (fares, time tables, user opinions and complaints, etc.)

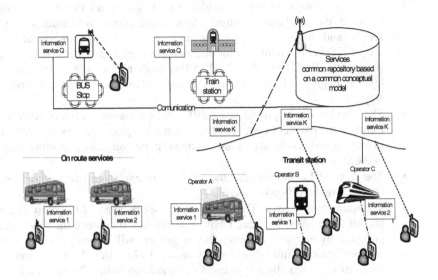

Fig. 3. System overview

3 Model Description

Our conceptual model is conceived for an information system for public transport with a high level of interoperability, that is, information services are available in every place of the public transport network (station, stops, vehicles, etc.) regardless of the technological network infrastructures (communications, hardware and software elements), user devices (cellular phone, PDA, laptop, etc.) and transport mode (bus, train, pedestrian, etc.) used. Figure 3 shows a general vision, from the infrastructure point of view, of the information system. The infrastructure technological components are deployed in the different points of the transport network permitting the access to the information services in every place and every time using different communication technologies, such as public long services, for example GPRS, or wireless local area network, for example IEEE 802.11 (Wifi), or wireless personal area network for example IEEE 802.15 (Bluetooth).

3.1 Process Conceptualization

The system has a client-server architecture. In a top-down description scheme, the model conceptualized the system architecture in two levels: the first formed by the user devices that run the client applications in order to access to the information services, this level is named user service level, and, the second, named system services level, that is formed by all the elements of the computing and communication infrastructure deployed in the transport network in order to execute the information services servers. In the next step of the top-down description the system services level is conceptualized. The elements that configure this level are structured in the following layers:

- The Infrastructure Layer provides the basic communication resources between the applications (user client applications, information services servers and infrastructure operator applications). These resources allow the use of different communication technologies, such as: GPRS, IEEE 802.11 (hereinafter WIFI) and IEEE 802.15 (hereinafter Bluetooth). Physically, this level is deployed in the transport network elements: vehicles, stations and stops.
- The Service Layer provides the different information services servers, for example the payment system or the information passenger system mentioned in section two. These agents are executed in the computer platforms installed in the vehicles.
- The Control Layer manages the whole data exchange between the agents executed in the different layers.
- Communication Layer. This layer, or transport layer, is the most complex part of the System Services Level. It is the key part since the functionality provided by any service or system in general will depend on it to a large extent. Situated just above the Control Layer, this layer is merely a specialization of a client systems communication layer. The greatest level of abstraction possible must be used here, together with the minimum amount of feedback with other parts of the system so that any change in this layer has no lateral effect on the rest of the system.
- The Information Services Provider is an application that has to make the connections between the information services servers and the client application as agile as possible. This application is executed in the transport network infrastructure both in mobile and non-mobile platforms.

The information services are provided by the different operator of the transport network. These services are accessed by user client applications running on the mobile devices, the users can be passengers, technical staff, drivers, etc. The services are available in relevant places of the transport network (vehicles, stops, station, etc.) In each of these places there is an Information Services Provider. The goal of this application is, first, to discover the available information services, and second, to facilitate the connection between service servers and user client applications.

3.2 Data Architecture

The data architecture of the model is based on three levels. The first is the Data Core Level that provides a complete data conceptual model about public transport network. A main component of this data layer is the ontology used; this ontology must be used by every transport information service. The second is the Intermediate Level that is formed by the database of each operator. The entities and relation of these database are based on the conceptual model provided by the previous level. Finally, the third is the Data Interoperability Level that is formed by components whose purpose is to reconcile the data representation of the entities, provided by the operators, required by the information service.

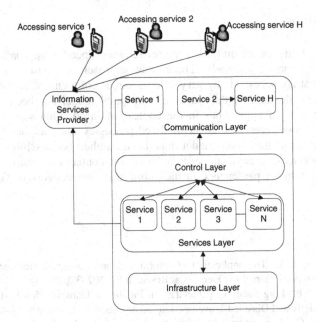

Fig. 4. Process architecture

The high level of interoperability achieved, using the components of the Data Interoperability Level, is explained bellow. In a first step, each common entity, provided by Data Core Level, is represented by two attributes that are: the entity identification and the entity description. Secondly, the data type used to represent the attributes that describe each entity is specified. This specification has three fields: the attribute identification, the name and the format. The representation of each entity is made by a set of attributes structured in two subsets: the subset of common attributes, that must be mandatory used by all the operators, and the subset of operator specific attributes that are optional in the entity representation, depending on each operator. The attributes of each entity instance are represented by the instance identification of the entity, the position in each register of representation and the value of the attribute.

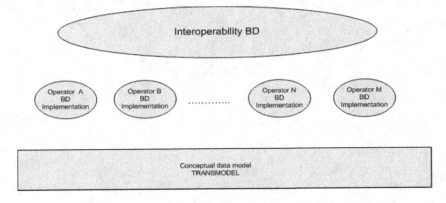

Fig. 5. Data Architecture

4 Conclusions

The interoperability in ubiquitous systems requires specific approaches that are different to the classic methods. These new approach are based on distributed components that are accessible by very heterogeneous communication infrastructures and user mobile devices. In this paper a conceptual model has been described to develop these kind of approaches in the context of information services of public transport. The model presented conceptualized processes and data, achieving a high level of interoperability. The model has been applied successfully to develop information services, a payment system based on contactless smart card and an information system for passengers, in the public transport network of Gran Canaria Island.

References

1. Giannopoulos, G.A.: The application of information and communication technologies in transport. European Journal of Operational Research 52, 302–320 (2004)
2. Mitchell, C.G.B., Ling Suen, S.: Urban Travel, Intelligent Transportation Systems, and the Safety of Elderly and Disabled Travelers. Journal of Urban Technology 5, 17–43 (1998)
3. Jakubauskas, G.: Improvement of urban transport accessibility for the passengers with reduced mobility by applying intelligent transport systems and services. In: The 8th International Conference on Reliability and Statistics in Transportation and Communication 2008, Riga, Latvia, pp. 102–108 (2008)
4. Saha, D., Ukherjee, A.: Pervasive Computing. A Paradigm for 21st Century. Computer 36(3), 25–31 (2003)
5. Emiliani, P.L., Stephanidis, C.: Universal access to ambient intelligence environments: Opportunities and challenges for people with disabilities. IBM Systems Journal 44(3), 605–619 (2005)
6. European Committee Standardization: Reference Data Model For Public Transport, Tech. Rep. CEN TC278 (2005), http://www.cenorm.be/
7. Tyrinopoulos, Y.: A Complete onceptual Model for the Integrated Management of the Transportation Work. Journal of Public Transportation 7(4), 101–121 (2004)

Constant Time Headway Control Policy in Leader Following Vehicular Platoons: 2-D Polynomial Approach

Michael Šebek and Zdeněk Hurák*

Faculty of Electrical Eng., Czech Technical University in Prague, Czech Republic
{michael.sebek,zdenek.hurak}@fel.cvut.cz
http://dce.fel.cvut.cz/

Abstract. Constant time headway policy is considered for control of vehicular platoons in future automated highway systems. 2-D polynomial approach is applied, hence dynamics is described using a fraction of two bivariate polynomials. In contrast to some previous works, the platoon here assumes a leader and an infinite number of followers. The usual bilateral z-transform used for doubly infinite vehicular strings is replaced here by a special unilateral z-transform. This naturally brings the boundary conditions into consideration through which the leader vehicle comes into the scene.

Keywords: Automated highway systems, automated guided vehicles, multidimensional systems, n-D systems, multivariable polynomials, polynomial equations, polynomial methods.

1 Introduction

In current studies automated highway systems [4], platooning is conceived as a way of expanding the envelope of capacity and safety that can be achieved by road vehicles. Vehicles organized in platoons can operate much closer together than is possible under manual driving conditions. Each highway lane can therefore carry several times as much traffic as it can today, which should make it possible to greatly reduce highway congestion. Also, at close spacing aerodynamic drag is significantly reduced, which can lead to major reductions in fuel consumption and exhaust emissions.

In the microscopic description of the highway, vehicles are individually modeled. The vehicles headway is defined as the time taken for the vehicle to traverse the intervehicle spacing ahead of it. There are various control policies for the platoon characterized by different speed-spacing relationships that the vehicle control system aims to guarantee. A popular control policy is that of constant time headway which makes the desired ranges proportional to vehicle speeds.

---

* This work has been supported by the Czech Ministry of Education within a project AMVIS ME10010.

R. Moreno-Díaz et al. (Eds.): EUROCAST 2011, Part II, LNCS 6928, pp. 457–464, 2012.

When vehicles follow each other controlled automatically in a lane, they be-
have like a coupled system of systems, the behavior of which depends on the
control actions of the individual vehicles. A phenomenon known as "slinky effect" [4] where a small tracking error or disturbance in the response of a lead
vehicle gets amplified as it propagates along the platoon or string of vehicles is
commonly observed in today's driving. The longitudinal control system of each
system has to be designed so to guarantee platoon or string stability, which in
turn implies the absence of slinky effects.

2   Leader Following Platoons

The highway lane capacity naturally increases with the length of the platoon
[4] and hence very long platoons are desirable. In literature, this demand is
approached differently: Either platoons with a finite number of cars are studied
and then the limit infinite case is taken. Or doubly infinite strings of vehicles
are considered allowing to apply bilateral transforms that neglect any boundary
conditions.

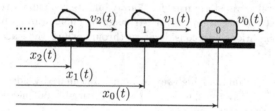

Fig. 1. Platoon of vehicles following a leader

Instead, we advocate the use of semi-infinite platoons with a leader that is
pictured in Fig. 1. Here the leading vehicle is labeled by 0 and the follow-up cars
are numbered by $1, 2, \ldots$. The leader is driven externally while the followers are
controlled by algorithms discussed in the paper.

Variables in the platoon, such as positions, inter-vehicle distances and velocities, are described by one-sided spatial sequences of time functions corresponding
to the equally indexed vehicles such as $\{f(t, k)\} = f(t, 0), f(t, 1), \ldots, t \in [0, \infty)$.

3   Temporal-Spatial Transform $\mathcal{LZ}_1$

To efficiently describe and handle the one-sided spatial sequences of time functions appearing in the platoon, we introduced an original two-dimensional transform, combining unilateral Laplace temporal transform with conveniently shifted
unilateral spatial z-transform. The new transform is denoted $\mathcal{LZ}_1$ and defined by
the following expression

$$\mathcal{LZ}_1\{f(t, k)\} = \int_{0^-}^{\infty} \left(\sum_{k=1}^{\infty} f(t, k) z^{-k} \right) e^{-st} \, dt.$$

Unlike the common unilateral z-transform definition, the discrete-space part in the $\mathcal{LZ}_1$ transform "starts" with the first follower, that is vehicle indexed by $k = 1$. This keeps the leader outside the support allowing the $\mathcal{LZ}_1$- transform to describe just the vehicles to be controlled. The leading vehicle is controlled "from outside" by another algorithm and its movement plays here the role of a boundary condition. This is revealed by the following theorem:

Theorem 1 ($\mathcal{LZ}_1$-*transform of a spatially shifted sequence*)
Given $f(t,k)$ *and its* $\mathcal{LZ}_1$-*transform* $f(s,z)$, *then*

$$\mathcal{LZ}_1\{f(t, k - 1)\} = z^{-1}f(s, z) + z^{-1}f_0(s), \tag{1}$$

where

$$f_0(s) = \int_{0^-}^{\infty} f(t, 0)e^{-st}dt \tag{2}$$

is the $\mathcal{L}$-*transform of the temporal function related to the leader.*

Other important properties to be used later are as expected:

Theorem 2 ($\mathcal{LZ}_1$-*transform of a time derivative of the sequence*)
Given $f(t,k)$ *and its* $\mathcal{LZ}_1$-*transform* $f(s,z)$, *then*

$$\mathcal{LZ}_1\left\{\frac{\partial f}{\partial t}\right\} = sf(s, z) - f_{0^-}(z), \tag{3}$$

$$\mathcal{LZ}_1\left\{\frac{\partial^2 f}{\partial t^2}\right\} = s^2 f(s, z) - sf_{0^-}(z) - \dot{f}_{0^-}(z), \tag{4}$$

assuming that the derivatives exist. Here

$$f_{0^-}(z) = \sum_{k=1}^{\infty} f(0^-, k)z^{-k}, \quad \dot{f}_{0^-}(z) = \sum_{k=1}^{\infty} \dot{f}(0^-, k)z^{-k}, \tag{5}$$

are $\mathcal{Z}_1$-*transforms of the spatial sequences of the pre-initial conditions* $f(0^-, k)$ *and* $\dot{f}(0^-, k)$, *respectively.*

Theorem 3 (*Accumulation Theorem in* $\mathcal{LZ}_1$)
$\mathcal{LZ}_1$-*transform* $g(s, z)$ *of a spatial one-sided sequence of time functions* $g(t,k)$ *is related to the* $\mathcal{LZ}_1$-*transform* $f(s, z)$ *of its accumulated sequence* $f(t, k)$ *defined by*

$$f(t, k) = \sum_{j=1}^{k} g(t, j) \tag{6}$$

by expression

$$f(s, z) = \frac{1}{1 - z^{-1}} g(s, z) \tag{7}$$

assuming that the derivatives exist.

Proofs of the $\mathcal{LZ}_1$ properties above are rather straightforward. They are provided elsewhere.

Example 1 ($\mathcal{LZ}_1$-transforms of some frequently encountered sequences)
Time-varying spatial impulse and step transform as

$$\mathcal{LZ}_1\{a(t)\delta(k)\} = a(s), \tag{8}$$

and

$$\mathcal{LZ}_1\{a(t)1(k)\} = a(s)\frac{1}{z-1} = a(s)\frac{z^{-1}}{1-z^{-1}}, \tag{9}$$

respectively, where

$$a(s) = \int_{0^-}^{\infty} a(t)e^{-st}dt \tag{10}$$

provided the integral exists.

Analogously, space-varying temporal impulse and step transform as

$$\mathcal{LZ}_1\{a(k)\delta(t)\} = a(z), \tag{11}$$

and

$$\mathcal{LZ}_1\{a(k)1(t)\} = a(z)\frac{1}{s}, \tag{12}$$

respectively, where

$$a(z) = \sum_{k=1}^{\infty} a(k)z^{-k}$$

Finally, spatial-temporal impulse and step transform as

$$\mathcal{LZ}_1\{\delta(k)\delta(t)\} = 1 \tag{13}$$

and

$$\mathcal{LZ}_1\{1(k)1(t)\} = \frac{1}{z-1}\frac{1}{s} = \frac{z^{-1}}{1-z^{-1}}\frac{1}{s}, \tag{14}$$

respectively.

The $\mathcal{LZ}_1$-transform of the sequence $\{f(t,k)\}$ expands[1] into

$$f(s,z) = \underbrace{f(s,1)}_{f_1(s)}z^{-1} + \underbrace{f(s,2)}_{f_2(s)}z^{-2} + \ldots \tag{15}$$

which is a formal power series in z^{-1} having polynomials or fractions in s as coefficients.

Application of the $\mathcal{LZ}_1$ transform opens promising door to the rich world 2-D polynomial systems theory [8], [13],[10],[11],[9],[1] etc. The 2-D polynomial approach has already been employed to solve several problems of analysis and control for platoons with leader [3,12]. In this paper, it is used with the constant time headway to derive an alternative to existing results of [4,7,6] and others.

---

[1] We are rather careless with the notation here as both the original spatiotemporal signal and its transform are labeled with the same letter, being distinguished only by their arguments (t,k) vs. (s,z) if necessary.

4 Constant Time Headway Policy

The constant time-headway policy requires not only the measurements of the inter-vehicular distances $r(t, k)$ but also the absolute velocities $\dot{x}(t, k)$ because the desired spacing is now depending on the velocity via

$$r_{\text{ref}}(t, k) = \bar{r}_0 + \bar{r}\dot{x}(t, k). \tag{16}$$

This requirement is called the constant time headway policy. Applying $\mathcal{LZ}_1$-transform, (16) turns into

$$r_{\text{ref}}(s, z) = \frac{z^{-1}}{1 - z^{-1}} \frac{\bar{r}_0}{s} + \bar{r}sx(s, z) - \bar{r}x_{0-}(z). \tag{17}$$

The platoon is then described (for $t \in [0, \infty]$, $k = 1, 2, 3, \ldots$) by

$$\ddot{x}(t, k) = \frac{1}{m}u(t, k),$$
$$\bar{y}(t, k) = x(t, k - 1) - x(t, k) - \bar{r}\dot{x}(t, k), \tag{18}$$

with the "output" $\bar{y}(t, k)$ standing for the inter-vehicular distance reduced by the velocity-dependent factor. The initial and boundary conditions are as above and the $\mathcal{LZ}_1$-transform produces

$$x(s, z) = \frac{1}{ms^2}u(s, z) + \frac{1}{s}x_{0-}(z) + \frac{1}{s^2}\dot{x}_{0-}(z),$$
$$\bar{y}(s, z) = (z^{-1} - 1 - \bar{r}s)x(s, z) + z^{-1}x_0(s) + \bar{r}x_{0-}(z),$$

and simple algebra gives rise to the single equation

$$\bar{y}(s, z) = \frac{z^{-1} - \bar{r}s - 1}{ms^2}u(s, z) \tag{19}$$
$$+ \frac{z^{-1} - 1}{s}x_{0-}(z) + \frac{z^{-1} - 1}{s^2}\dot{x}_{0-}(z) + z^{-1}x_0(s).$$

A convenient controller is here

$$p(s)u(s, z) = q(s)\left(\bar{y}_{\text{ref}}(s, z) - \bar{y}(s, z)\right), \tag{20}$$

where

$$\bar{y}_{\text{ref}}(s, z) = \frac{z^{-1}}{1 - z^{-1}} \frac{\bar{r}_0}{s}. \tag{21}$$

As no z^{-1} explicitly appears its transfer function, the controller (20) is space-invariant. In fact, it consist of identical copies of local controllers, one for each car. Every local controller operates on instant distance from the predecessor and instant velocity. It is actually driven by the regulation error as

$$e(s, z) = \bar{y}_{\text{ref}}(s, z) - \bar{y}(s, z)$$
$$= \frac{z^{-1}}{1 - z^{-1}} \frac{\bar{r}_0}{s} - \left(z^{-1} - 1 - \bar{r}s\right)x(s, z) - z^{-1}x_0(s) - \bar{r}x_{0-}(z)$$
$$= \frac{z^{-1}}{1 - z^{-1}} \frac{\bar{r}_0}{s} + \bar{r}sx(s, z) - \bar{r}x_{0-}(z) - (z^{-1} - 1)x(s, z) - z^{-1}x_0(s) \tag{22}$$
$$= r_{\text{ref}}(s, z) - r(s, z).$$

Closing the loop, the overall system equations can be derived to read

$$u(s,z) = \frac{ms^2 q(s)}{\bar{m}(s,z)} \frac{z^{-1}}{1-z^{-1}} \frac{\bar{r}_0}{s} - \frac{q(s)ms\left(z^{-1}-1\right)}{\bar{m}(s,z)} x_{0-}(z)$$

$$- \frac{q(s)m\left(z^{-1}-\bar{r}s-1\right)}{\bar{m}(s,z)} \dot{x}_{0-}(z) - \frac{q(s)ms^2 z^{-1}}{\bar{m}(s,z)} x_0(s)$$

$$e(s,z) = \frac{ms^2 p(s)}{\bar{m}(s,z)} \frac{z^{-1}}{z^{-1}-1} \frac{\bar{r}_0}{s} - \frac{p(s)ms\left(z^{-1}-1\right)}{\bar{m}(s,z)} x_{0-}(z)$$

$$- \frac{p(s)\left(z^{-1}-\bar{r}s-1\right)}{\bar{m}(s,z)} \dot{x}_{0-}(z) - \frac{p(s)ms^2 z^{-1}}{\bar{m}(s,z)} x_0(s)$$

$$r(s,z) = \frac{q(s)\left(z^{-1}-1\right)}{\bar{m}(s,z)} \frac{z^{-1}}{1-z^{-1}} \frac{\bar{r}_0}{s} + \frac{(msp(s)-\bar{r}q(s))\left(z^{-1}-1\right)}{\bar{m}(s,z)} x_{0-}(z)$$

$$+ \frac{(msp(s)-\bar{r}q(s))s}{\bar{m}(s,z)} z^{-1} x_0(s) + \frac{p(s)\left(z^{-1}-1\right)m}{\bar{m}(s,z)m} \dot{x}_{0-}(z)$$

where the common denominator is the closed-loop characteristic 2-D polynomial

$$\bar{m}(s,z) = ms^2 p(s) + \left(z^{-1}-\bar{r}s-1\right) q(s), \tag{23}$$

According to [5](Theorem 4.3, pp. 126), the overall systems is 2-D BIBO stable if

$$m(s,e^{j\omega}) \neq 0 \quad \forall s \in \mathbb{C}, \omega \in \mathbb{R} : \Re(s) \le 0, \omega \in [0,2\pi] \tag{24}$$

In other words, if it is a stable polynomial in s results from $m(s,z)$ after substituting for z any complex number from the unit circle.

In fact, this condition is not necessary and the 2-D stability can sometimes be saved by nonessential singularities of the second kind at the distinguished stability boundary (see [2]). To avoid this subtlety, all relevant coprime transfer functions are required to have a stable denominator (not vanishing on the distinguished boundary of the stability domain). Every polynomial satisfying (24) is called 2-D stable.

However, the particular 2-D polynomial (23) resulting from the constant time-headway policy happens to be 2-D unstable. Indeed, the substitution $z = 1$ converts it into 1-D unstable $\bar{m}(s,1) = s\left(msp(s) - \bar{r}q(s)\right)$. Consequently, the resulting platoon is unstable in the string sense and the unfortunate slinky effects may be expected, as shown later on.

5   Simulation Experiment

To demonstrate the constant time headway policy, a simulation experiment is conducted. At the beginning, the platoon is traveling at a constant speed $\dot{x}_{0-}$ with the vehicles evenly spaced by r_{0-}. These initial conditions are described by

$$x_{0-}(z) = -r_{0-} \frac{z^{-1}}{(1-z^{-1})^2} = -100\frac{z^{-1}}{(1-z^{-1})^2},$$

$$\dot{x}_{0-}(z) = \dot{x}_{0-} \frac{z^{-1}}{1-z^{-1}} = 30\frac{z^{-1}}{1-z^{-1}}. \tag{25}$$

With the constant time-headway policy, the desired distances between the vehicles are not prescribed from outside but result from the policy parameters $\bar{r}_0, \bar{r}$ in (16) via (17).

Besides, the vehicles should follow their leader. At the beginning, the leading vehicle is moving at the same constant speed, but then it slows down for a while and finally returns to its original velocity. This maneuver, serving as boundary condition, is described by

$$x_0\left(s\right) = \frac{30}{s^2} - \frac{10}{s^2}e^{-10s} + \frac{10}{s^2}e^{-15s}. \tag{26}$$

and visualized in Fig. 2. For constant time headway policy parameters given by

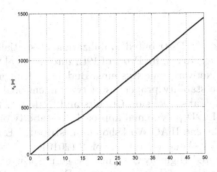

Fig. 2. Leader's maneuver $x_0(t)$ to be followed

$\bar{r}_0 = 10, \bar{r} = 3$, resulting inter-vehicular distances $r(t,k)$ and positions $x(t,k)$

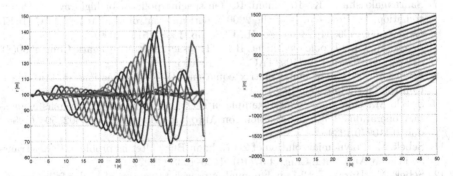

Fig. 3. Constant time-headway policy results: distances $r(t,k)$ and positions $x(t,k)$

a disturbance that evidently rises as propagating through the platoon. This actually happens for any particular local controller design. The only chance to avoid this effect to change spatial distribution of the controller.

6   Conclusions

This paper introduces a new formalism to the control of semi-infinite platoons of vehicles following their leader and it demonstrates its elegance for a classical constant time headway platooning problems

The approach is based on 2-D polynomials and their fractions resulting from a joint unilateral Laplace and z-transform – named here $\mathcal{LZ}_1$-transform. This makes it possible to model variety of platoons and controllers in a unified manner as well as to apply diverse control policies such as predecessor following, leader following, constant time-headway etc. It was pointed out that both the string instability and 2-D BIBO instability can be detected in the proposed framework investigating simple 2-D polynomials. The tools developed here are now ready to be used in the ongoing research.

References

1. Augusta, P., Hurák, Z.: Distributed stabilization of spatially invariant systems: positive polynomial approach. In: Proc. of 19th International Symposium on Mathematical Theory of Networks and Systems, Budapest, Hungary (July 2010)
2. Goodman, D.: Some stability properties of two-dimensional linear shift-invariant digital filters. IEEE Transactions on Circuits and Systems 24(4), 201–208 (1977)
3. Hurak, Z., Sebek, M.: 2D polynomial approach to stability of platoons of vehicles. In: Proceedings of the 2nd IFAC Workshop on Distributed Estimation and Control in Networked Systems, Annecy, France, vol. 2 (2010)
4. Ioannou, P.: Automated Highway Systems, 1st edn. Springer, Heidelberg (2010)
5. Kamen, E.: Stabilization of Linear Spatially-Distributed Continuous-Time and Discrete-Time systems. In: Multidimensional Systems Theory: Progress, Directions and Open Problems in Multidimensional Systems. Mathematics and Its Applications, D. Reidel Publishing Company, Boston (1985)
6. Liang, C.Y., Peng, H.: String stability analysis of adaptive cruise controlled vehicles (2000)
7. Santhanakrishnan, K., Rajamani, R.: On spacing policies for highway vehicle automation. In: Proceedings of the 2000 American Control Conference, ACC (IEEE Cat. No.00CH36334)., Chicago, IL, USA, pp. 1509–1513 (2000)
8. Sebek, M.: On 2-D pole placement. IEEE Transactions on Automatic Control 30(8), 819–822 (1985), doi:10.1109/TAC.1985.1104065
9. Sebek, M.: n-D polynomial matrix equations. IEEE Transactions on Automatic Control 33(5), 499–502 (1988)
10. Sebek, M.: One more counterexample in n-D systems-unimodular versus elementary operations. IEEE Transactions on Automatic Control 33(5), 502–503 (1988), doi:10.1109/9.1239
11. Sebek, M.: Polynomial solution of 2D Kalman-Bucy filtering problem. IEEE Transactions on Automatic Control 37(10), 1530–1533 (1992)
12. Sebek, M., Hurak, Z.: 2-D polynomial approach to control of leader following vehicular platoons. In: 18th IFAC World Congress, IFAC, Milano, Italy (submitted for publication, August 2011)
13. Šebek, M., Bisiacco, M., Fornasini, E.: Controllability and reconstructibility conditions for 2-D systems. IEEE Transactions on Automatic Control 33(5), 496–499 (1988)

User Equilibrium Study of AETROS Travel Route Optimization System

Javier J. Sanchez-Medina, Moises Diaz-Cabrera,
Manuel J. Galan-Moreno, and Enrique Rubio-Royo

Innovation Center for the Information Society (CICEI) – ULPGC, Spain
jsanchez@polaris.ulpgc.es, moisdc@gmail.com,
mgalan@dmat.ulpgc.es, erubio@polaris.ulpgc.es

Abstract. We have designed a new urban travel route optimization model in combination with a new microscopic simulation paradigm. The core of the system stands over the assumption that we can have a traffic network with an Advanced Traffic Information System (ATIS) installed that advises drivers at every intersection as to which direction to take, depending of their destination.

We have implemented a parallel Genetic Algorithm, running over a Beowulf cluster that performs a real-time optimization yielding that set of advised routes.

By these means we propose an implicitly adaptable, expandable and flexible solution for the traveler route assignment problem, in order to maximize the performance of an urban network.

Although in Dynamic Traffic Assignment (DTA) a rigorous Wardrop's User Equilibrium – [6] – cannot be fully carried out, we have developed a set of experiment aiming to see if there is a visible tendency to a User Equilibrium state for the proposed model. Results are encouraging.

1 Introduction

Traffic management is a hard task. Traffic is intrinsically unpredictable, mainly because there are human beings behind the steering wheels of the vehicles that constitute it.

Therefore, travel route planning should be faced in a dynamic way. We have developed new dynamic real-time travel route optimization model. It is based on a parallel Genetic Algorithm([2]) running over a Beowulf Cluster([5]). The evaluation performed in the Genetic Algorithm uses traffic microsimulation to predict future traffic scenarios, taking the current sensed situation as starting point.

It is a new model because it does not provide a fixed route to every entering vehicle. On the contrary, during the trip of every new vehicle, moving across the network, the optimized advised route may change as it approaches every intersection if the systems obtains a better performance solution in a changing traffic scenario.

The assignment model proposed was not meant to reach an user equilibrium (for instance Wardrop's User Equilibrium – [6]) because the optimization of

R. Moreno-Díaz et al. (Eds.): EUROCAST 2011, Part II, LNCS 6928, pp. 465–472, 2012.

paths may change so quickly, that it would not be possible to obtain enough travel time statistics to check that kind of equilibrium. It is a sacrifice made for the sake of a higher level of adaptability.

However, we have developed a set of experiment aiming to see if there is a visible tendency to a User Equilibrium state for the proposed model. Results are shared in this work.

2   Past Relevant Research

In [1] a a policy-based stochastic dynamic traffic assignment (DTA) model is proposed. Their approach is similar than ours. In both cases drivers do not have a predetermined path, but they decide at a set of intersections. The information used to make that decision is provided by the system based on the vehicles that already have driven through that link. They receive information more or less like current travel time using a path or the other.

In our case, drivers will not receive that kind of information to make their choice. They will receive the system advised option, that is obtained through a genetic algorithm global optimization, and traffic microsimulation.

In [3] it is proposed an hybrid real-time and off-line approach to the dynamic path assignment problem. The use autonomous agents and systolic parallel processing as simulation paradigms. The repertoire of predetermined paths is computed off-line using conventional optimal path-finding algorithm such as the Frank-Wolf algorithm.

This is an example of many research initiatives that implement a prefixed paths for the traffic route assignment problem. In our case, we do not have that repertoire of possible paths, but a set of possible options at the intersections of the traffic network, providing drivers through an ATIS, the optimized best option depending on their destination.

In [4] we have a beautiful work proposing an analytical solution to best path calculation in case a lane-blocking incidents happens. They presented a step-by-step methodology to cope with that situations. Moreover, they perform a set of numerical examples obtaining the best results for low-volume traffic flow conditions.

In our case, we propose a stochastic approach to cope – indirectly – with lane-blocking incidents, through a new dynamic travel route optimization model.

3   AETROS: Adaptive Evolutionary Travel Route Optimization System

Given an urban traffic network composed by lanes, intersections, access lanes through cars get into the network toward a set of destinations (outputs) the challenge consists in how can that network be managed to get the best performance from it.

We have devised an adaptive dynamic travel route model that, through an Advanced Traveler Information System (ATIS) advises drivers the best option

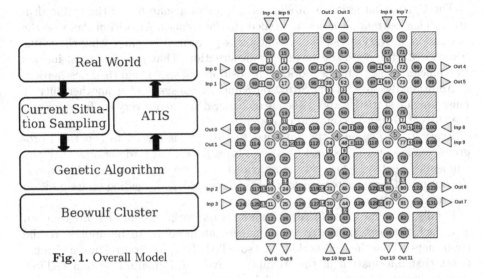

Fig. 1. Overall Model

Fig. 2. Discretized Traffic Network

at every intersection, considering their destination – previously introduced into the system. The best option – "recommended next cell" as we call it – is the result of the parallel execution of a genetic algorithm previously fed with the current traffic situation. The genetic algorithm uses a Cellular Automata based microscopic simulator within its evaluation function. All the needed software runs in a parallel program over a Beowulf Cluster.

The proposed model rests over a set of assumptions: We assume that there is an Advanced Traveler Information System (ATIS) running in the traffic network that can capture the destination of every vehicle and communicate the option they should chose at every Crossroad cell depending on the introduced destination; and we also assume that there is a sampling system based on traffic sensors that can track the position and speed of every vehicle all along its travel across the network.

Figure 1 summarizes the overall concepts of the AETROS model. First, there is a computer platform (hardware and software) module which must sample the current traffic situation in the network every T_{period} seconds.

The traffic network under study is discretized into a grid of possible vehicle positions (cells) with an approximated distance of 7 meters between each pair. This simplification is due to we use cellular automata based microscopic simulation (see 4). In figure 2 we have included the discretized network used all along through the present work.

We need the "Current Situation Sampling" module to inform about the vehicles present in the network (which cells are occupied). Furthermore, we need this module to produce an estimation of every vehicle speed and destination – output cell it is directed to.

The Current Situation Sampling module takes a snapshot of the traffic situation. That current situation is needed by the Genetic Algorithm, because the evaluation of every possible combination is performed by simulating the traffic behavior starting with the current traffic situation. That snapshot must include the vehicles in the traffic network, their position and speed, and their destination.

Additionally, the Current Situation Sampling subsystem has another duty. It must provide statistics about the current user demand at every traffic input and the current Origin-Destination probability matrix.

Every T_{period} seconds the current situation (S) is passed to a parallel program running over a Beowulf Cluster. This software has to determine the "recommended next cell" for every crossroad cell and every output. In other words, the optimized local routes are advised to every vehicle depending on its position and its destination.

Finally, once the Genetic Algorithm ends its work, the parallel program can give back the best simulated performance chromosome, to be applied to the traffic network for the next period. The so called "HW/SW control module" must inject that information in the Advance Traveler Information System (ATIS), making drivers to know the new advised next position valid just for the next T_{period} seconds.

It is important to note that there is a strong real-time restriction in this architecture. The GA must has its work finished in a less that T_{period} seconds time to be able to give the next combination on time to the control module. That is why it is so important to have a parallel and scalable architecture.

4   Microscopic Traffic Simulation Model

We have developed a new microscopic traffic model. We have no enough space for explaining it in detail, bu it is a Cellular Automata model with a set of new abstractions that we believe may yield a more flexible and accurate traffic simulation.

First we discretize a traffic network into a set of cells making a graph like the one in figure 2. As it is usually done, we sample a cell every 7 meters.

In that figure we have represented with circles the cells, or possible positions for vehicles. Not more that a vehicle per cell is permitted in the model.

Triangles mean the inputs and outputs. The inputs are places where new vehicles are created. Squares mean traffic lights.

The main feature of the proposed model is how vehicles move. We have assumed that an Advanced Traveler Information System is available at the network. Vehicles at every cell have a set of possible next cells to move, depending on its destination (output). There are two kind of cells. Plain cells, where next possible cells are the same set, no matter what is the destination of the vehicle, and Crossroad Cells (marked with hatching), where the set of possible next cells may be different depending on the destination of the vehicle.

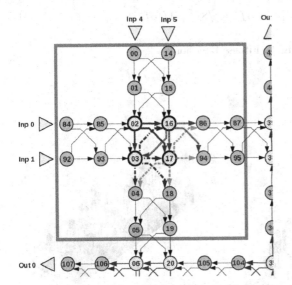

Fig. 3. Paths in our Improved Cellular Automata Model for Intersection #0

Fig. 4. Chromosome example

5   Genetic Algorithm Optimization

In figure 4 it is represented the chromosome encoding used in our model. We will explain it through an example. In figure 3 it is represented the possible next cells for the Crossroad cells 2 and 3. In our genetic algorithm, the chromosomes includes the "recommended next cell" for every Crossroad cell(CRCell) and for each output. By "recommended next cell" we mean that, when a vehicle is in a CRCell, it should chose that advised next cell, unless it is occupied.

In figure 4 it is represented that, for CRCell 2 and output 0, the advised next cell is 3. In the same row (CRCell 2), we see that for the output 1 it is also advised cell number 3. However, we see that for output 2 and 11, the advised option is cell number 16. So far, only two possible stages are considered for traffic signals: Red (0) and Green (1).

We have have chosen a Truncation and Elitism combination as selection strategy, and a standard Two Point Crossover operator. For Mutation, we have used an initial Hyper-mutation with a mutation probability that gradually decreases generation by generation aiming a $1/Population_{size}$ value at the end of the GA.

Finally, in the proposed model we use a deterministic microscopic simulator for evaluating every chromosome.

In equation 5 it is represented the fitness function used for the present work to evaluate every candidate chromosome. For N periods, the used parameter is sampled during every period. Then the resulting measurements (f_x) are combined into a polynomial function as shown in equation 5.

$$F = 1/2f_1^4 + 1/4f_2^3 + 1/8f_3^2 + 1/16f_4^1 \tag{1}$$

Fig. 5. Fitness Function

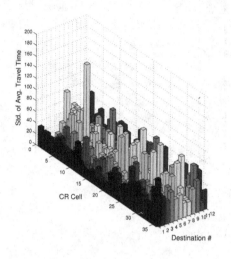

Fig. 6. STD de AVG Travel Time per CR vs Output 1000ts

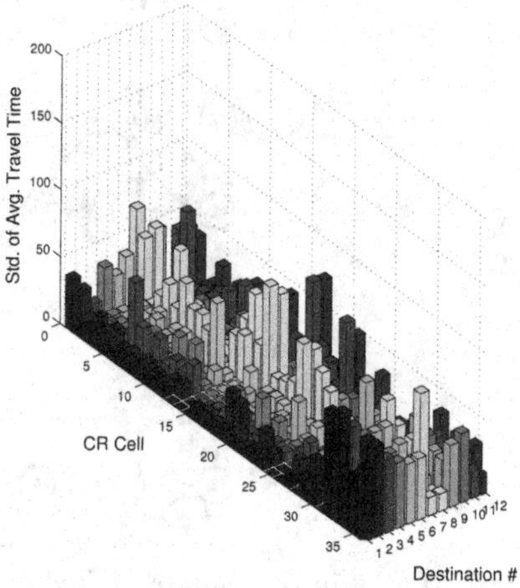

Fig. 7. STD de AVG Travel Time per CR vs Output 10000ts

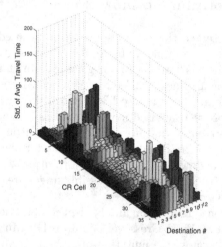

Fig. 8. STD de AVG Travel Time per CR vs Output 100000ts

6   User Equilibrium Study

The main objective of the present work is to present some results regarding a User Equilibrium study with the AETROS model.

Wardrop's User Equilibrium [6] two principles are the following: 1st – *The journey times in all routes actually used are equal and less than those which would be experienced by a single vehicle on any unused route* and 2nd – *At equilibrium the average journey time is minimum.* These can be summarized as *in equilibrium all feasible routes travel times are the same, and its value its minimum.*

In our model, since there is a set of possible options at every Crossroad Cell, we would need a very large amount of simulation time to have a significant statistical sample at every possible option. This is incompatible with our real time approach.

However, what we've done, just for this study is to run three different duration experiments and observe the standard deviation of mean travel time among every choice for every Crossroad Cell and destination pair.

For the present work we have designed a test bench using a stochastic version of the microscopic traffic simulator explained in section 4, with some key differences intending to give our Simulated Real World realism like: Random time of creation for new vehicles *arriving* the network; Random destination assignment for every new vehicle and when a driver can accelerate, a random function determines whether it will accelerate or not.

The traffic network used is the one in figure 2. It is a fictitious network with the following attributes.

- It is within a 91 m. side square.
- There are 132 cells (or possible positions for vehicles).
- It includes 18 traffic lights and 9 intersections.
- All the streets are two lane single direction streets.
- There are 12 input lanes and 12 output lanes.
- The total number of vehicles that can be in traffic light exclusive queues is 72 (54.55% of all cells).
- The Sampling Period (T_{period}) used for the tests presented is 40 time steps.

We run three different duration experiments including 1000 time steps, 10000 time steps and 100000 time steps. Then, for every (CRCell, destination) we first calculated the mean travel time (from origin to destination) for each available choice. After that, the standard deviation of those mean travel times is calculated, obtaining a value that has been represented in the bar diagrams of pictures 6, 7 and 8.

In those pictures one may observe that it seems to exist a tendency of reduction in the diversity of mean travel times, as we expand the experiment duration for the majority of CRCells and Destination pairs. This makes us confident that, at this early stage in the AETROS model development, it seems to be user equilibrium convergent.

7 Conclusion and Future Work

Through this paper we have presented some initial experimental results with the the AETROS model – Adaptive Evolutionary Travel Route Optimization System. That model has been designed to manage traffic dynamically, providing drivers destination depending optimized travel routes. To do so it uses a new microscopic simulation as evaluation function embedded into a genetic algorithm as optimization technique.

The presented experiments were focused just in User Equilibrium. We cannot run Wardrop's fully compliant exhaustive due to the dynamic nature of the AETROS model. However we have run a succession of crescent duration experiments and results seem to indicate that the new model is User Equilibrium convergent.

These modest experiments are crucial for us in the early state of development of this new model, to make us confident about its behavior, before going on with more ambitious tests.

We have some open lines and lots of work ahead. Regarding our test-bench real world simulation, we plan to implement more random variables in the stochastic simulation like hazards, vehicles passing through traffic lights with amber light on, vehicles facilitating other driver maneuvers, etc. It will mean to have a more accurate test bench in order fully study the proposed model before any real world implementation.

Regarding the validation of our model, we are contacting local government traffic departments in order to sign collaboration agreements that let us gradually implement the new technology in a real world application.

References

1. Policy-based stochastic dynamic traffic assignment models and algorithms. In: Proceedings of the IEEE 5th International Conference on Intelligent Transportation Systems, pp. 445 – 453 (2002)
2. Goldberg, D.E.: Genetic Algorithms in Search, Optimization, and Machine Learning. Addison-Wesley Professional, Reading (1989), http://www.worldcat.org/isbn/0201157675
3. Park, K., Kim, W.: A systolic parallel simulation system for dynamic traffic assignment: Spss-dta. Expert Systems with Applications 21(4), 217–227 (2001), http://www.sciencedirect.com/science/article/B6V03-447N2S6-4/2/e3a1a8f6b99706c6664c4a281aad28f4
4. Sheu, J.B.: A composite traffic flow modeling approach for incident-responsive network traffic assignment. Physica A: Statistical Mechanics and its Applications 367, 461–478 (2006), http://www.sciencedirect.com/science/article/B6TVG-4HWXJXY-1/2/2340609741f76a2b98462456703e26c1
5. Sterling, T., Becker, D.J., Savarese, D., Dorband, J.E., Ranawake, U.A., Packer, C.V.: Beowulf: A parallel workstation for scientific computation. In: Proceedings of the 24th International Conference on Parallel Processing, pp. 11–14. CRC Press, Boca Raton (1995)
6. Wardrop, J.G.: Some theoretical aspects of road traffic research. In: Proc. Inst. Civil Eng., vol. 1, pp. 325–378 (1952)

Driver Pattern Study of Las Palmas de Gran Canaria

Moises Diaz-Cabrera, Javier J. Sanchez-Medina, Idaira Perez-Armas,
Elisa Medina-Machin, Manuel J. Galan-Moreno, and Enrique Rubio-Royo

Innovation Center for the Information Society (CICEI) – ULPGC, Spain
moisdc@gmail.com, jsanchez@polaris.ulpgc.es, mgalan@dmat.ulpgc.es,
erubio@polaris.ulpgc.es

Abstract. In our group we have been dealing with traffic simulation for
a few years. We plan to develop research initiatives in order to give our
microsimulators a higher level of accuracy. We believe that it could help
to have a multimodal microsimulation, in the sense of making virtual
traffic to be composed not just by one generic vehicle type, but a set of
specific types.

Aiming to this target we have performed the research presented in
this paper. We have performed a telephone survey, and fieldwork traffic
video recordings in order to isolated some driver patterns in the traffic
of Las Palmas de Gran Canaria Canary Islands, Spain.

In this paper it is presented the methodology and the early results
of the clustering of samples into driver types, based on a small amount
of variables. They will be used later in future research to implement
multimodal traffic microsimulators. We expect that using the obtained
patterns, in the same proportions we have found them, may result in a
closer to reality microsimulation.

1 Introduction

There are lots of researchers addressing all the challenges included within traffic management. A remarkable one is traffic simulation. Traffic simulation is a
helpful ingredient, because solutions can be tested before investing in new infrastructures and avoiding the risk of a failure in real-world testings.

Hence, we need accurate simulations to produce more efficient solutions, technologies and devices. In our group we developed a Cellular Automata based microsimulator some years ago, and we used it for optimizing traffic performance
through the optimization of traffic lights programming([8] [5] [9] [10] [7]). With it
we have been able to simulate many vehicle parameters, e. g. their Green House
Emissions ([6]).

Our microsimulator is monomodal, meaning that all the virtual vehicles are of
the same type, which is defined as a general average vehicle. It seems reasonable
that if we identify driver categories and their proportion in the whole traffic,
with respect to some variables, and after that, we implement that categories in
a microsimulator, we could perform a more accurate simulation of real traffic.

R. Moreno-Díaz et al. (Eds.): EUROCAST 2011, Part II, LNCS 6928, pp. 473–480, 2012.

This is the aim of this early research: To identify possible driver patterns, their proportion, and their characteristic variable values, in order to simulate them in a multimodal microsimulation in future research.

To do so, we have captured Las Palmas de Gran Canaria – Spain – driver behavior samples. We have performed 98 telephone questionnaires, and over two hundred driver behavior samples through two different emplacement traffic recordings. So, We have performed a standard clustering process for the three cases. In this paper we present the results of that clustering.

1.1 State of the Art

In [2] driver patterns are analyzed, regarding speed and accelerations profiles. These two variables are used due to their common known relationship with emissions and fuel consumption. That study focus on finding variations between driver types (e.g. woman and men) regarding speed and mean acceleration in different scenarios: street types, peak or non-peak hour, etc.

In this work author reach the conclusion that the driver type in first place, and the street type in second place are the variables that most influence emissions and fuel consumption.

In our work we are aiming for driver patterns with a different objective. We plan to implement schematic driver patterns within a microsimulator. Therefore, the variables treated are entirely different, like the probability for a driver to accelerate when a traffic light is turning amber, or to keep the safe distance, etc.

In this ([1]) other work of Eva Ericsson it is carried out an extensive work dealing with 62 variables. After studying their possible linear dependences they become 16. The variables are related to the street type, the vehicle type and the driver type. Again, the final purpose is to discover relationships between driving patterns and emissions and fuel consumption.

In our work, so far, we are only considering the driver type influence on traffic.

In [3] it is performed an analysis of driver characteristics based on a 20 question survey fulfilled by 33 drivers. In this study they focus on driver patterns regarding driving style and skills.

The methodology of the questionnaire is similar to the one used for us, in our telephone survey.

In [4] driver patterns are defined using 60 volunteers and a sensor equipped car. The studied variables are the reaction time and the break/accelerate response to an amber traffic light.

In our work we do not use any equipped vehicle, but a telephone survey and traffic recordings. It seems logical that traffic behavior of drivers in the streets may be skewed when using an equipped car.

There is an interesting work in [12], where authors propose acquiring drivers' behavior using the steering angle when they perform a lane change as variable. Their aim is to generate a Bayesian Network model of drivers. They use a driving simulator to acquire the samples.

In that work, they do not define several driver patterns but a single model, making it as close to reality as possible.

In a microsimulation it is not easy to implement the steering angle in lane changing. Therefore, we are not interested in capturing that variable.

Finally, in [13] they try to model young driver types regarding risks assumed and response to a traffic safety campaign. They did a study including 6000 young drivers in Norway. The treated variables are related to human personality.

In our work we can not used this kind of variables, because they could not be implemented in a microsimulator.

2   Methodology

We have performed a clustering of traffic behavior samples in order to isolate some driver patterns. Both for the samples obtained from a telephone survey and fieldwork traffic recordings. In both cases, the methodology used to determine the clusters of driver types is the same, as we explain in the present subsection.

For every test case we did the following steps:

1. K-Means: In the first step we make a tentative clustering applying K-Means method, by using the *kmeans* function in Matlab. Our purpose is to make an initial estimation of the number of clusters (k) for each case. To perform this initial clustering must pass as input the number of clusters and the samples. So we tested for a range of numbers of groups. In this step no centroids[1] are provided, so the *kmeans* function will start with k randomly placed centroids.

2. Silhouette: To have an initial idea of the number of groups or clusters (k) we need to represent the Silhouette for the clusters produced by *kmeans* in the last step. The Silhouette is a representation of how well assigned is each sample to the group it has been set to belong (e.g. see 2). This representation helps us to decide k.

3. Hierarchical clustering (using the Method of SAHN[11]): After that we perform a hierarchical clustering using the *linkage* function of Matlab. In this kind of grouping every group can be included in a super-group as we increase the distance (generally euclidean distance) threshold to belong to a group. *dendrogram* function of Matlab. An example about dendrogram representation is shown in figure 2.

4. Centroids: With the help of the Dendrogram, the k value is decided. Then, the centroids of the clusters are calculated.

5. K-Means: Passing as input the calculated centroids which were calculated with hierarchical clustering, we use the K-Means method for the categorization of all the samples into the defined clusters.

3   Case Study: Results and Discussion

3.1   Telephone Questionnaire

We have applied the explained methodology a case study with data from Las Palmas de Gran Canaria, Spain. For this city we have performed a telephone

---

[1] Centroid: The center of mass of a figure, in our case, scattered samples. For instance, the centroid of a triangle is the intersection of the medians.

questionnaire. We have completed 98 successful surveys. The questions made where the following:

1. Gender
2. Age
3. Professional Driver
4. Driving License Age
5. When you encounter a traffic light in amber, Do you accelerate?
6. When there is a pedestrian waiting at an unsignalized crossing, Do you stop?
7. Do you facilitate other driver maneuvers, even when is not mandatory? (lane changes, overtaking maneuvers, etc.).
8. How often do you perform a risky overtaking?
9. Do you maintain a safe following distance?
10. Have you observed any accident provoked, at least partially, by driver reckless imprudence?

For clustering were used the variables of questions 5, 7 and 9 because it was considered variables that are easily implementable in a traffic simulation model Microscopic rate.

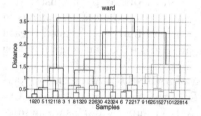

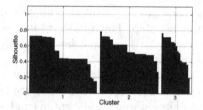

Fig. 1. Dendrogram in hierarchical clustering, *ward* algorithm (Telephone Questionnaire)

Fig. 2. Silhouette with 3 Clusters and Hierarchical Clustering Methodology *ward* (Telephone Questionnaire)

The more clear results were obtained by using the *ward* and *complete* options for *linkage*. In figure 2 it is displayed the results using *ward*.

Finally, once grouped the samples into 3 clusters, we ran again the K-means method, but using the centroids resulting from the SAHN clustering. In figure 2 it is represented the new silhouette.

In table 1 it is represented the median of any one of the variables used by the clustering. We have put the meaning of the median, instead of a numerical result. These variables will serve as category defining values of every driver patterns when we develop a multimodal version of our cellular automata microsimulator. Additionally, we have included a last column with the number of members of any cluster.

Table 1. Median Values (Meanings) for every Cluster (Telephone Questionnaire)

Question #	V5	V7	V9	# members
cluster #1	Never	Always	Always	43
cluster #2	Usually	Often	Always	37
cluster #3	Usually	Usually	Rarely	18

3.2 Traffic Video Recordings

We have performed a similar analysis using traffic recordings. The number of variables is smaller than in the case of a questionnaire. However, we do believe that recording samples are more objective.

We have captured traffic videos in two different locations in the zone so called "Siete Palmas". It is a commercial zone with an average traffic load.

First Emplacement. The variables, that were sampled, for the first emplacement are:

1. Gender
2. Professional Driver
3. Vehicle Type
4. When the driver encounters a traffic light in amber, Does He/She accelerate?
5. When the driver encounters a traffic light turning into red, Does He/She accelerate?

For this case, the variables used for the clustering where variables number 3, 4 and 5. Also for this case, the clustering results are just the same as using the 5 sampled variables.

In this case at a first glance it is difficult to determine whether to chose k=2 or k=3. However, after applying the SAHN hierarchical method, k=3 seems the best option. We have used the *single* metric for the *linkage* function. In figure 3 it is represented the dendrogram using the *single* metric. In figure 4 it is shown the silhouettes of the resulting grouping.

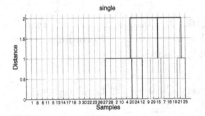

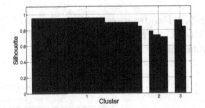

Fig. 3. Dendrogram. Method *single*. Fieldwork Traffic Recordings (1st Emplacement).

Fig. 4. 3 Clusters Silhouette (ward). Fieldwork Traffic Recordings (1st Emplacement).

Table 2. Median Values (Meanings) for every Cluster (1st Emplacement)

Question #	V3	V4	V5	# members
cluster #1	Passenger Car	True	False	30
cluster #2	Motorcycle	True	True	5
cluster #3	Taxi	True	False	3

In table 2 is represented the median (meanings) of any one of the variables used by the clustering plus the number of integrands of every category.

Second Emplacement. The following variables where sampled from the videos recorded in the second emplacement. There are a crosswalk in this emplacement.

1. Gender
2. Professional Driver
3. Vehicle Type
4. When there is a pedestrian waiting at an unsignalized crossing, Does He/She stop?

For the clustering we have chosen variables 3 and 4. Also for this test case, there is no change in the grouping using all the 4 variables captured.

In this case, the initial run of *kmeans* does not give too much light.

However, after the hierarchical clustering, it seems that k=2 may be the best option. In figure 5 it is represented the dendrogram using the *ward* metric.

Finally, in table 3 the statistics of the defining variables are shared, plus the proportion any one of the two clusters.

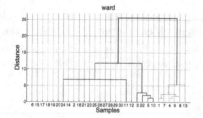

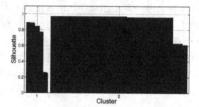

Fig. 5. Dendrogram. Method ward. Fieldwork Traffic Recordings (2nd Emplacement).

Fig. 6. 2 Clusters Silhouette (ward). Fieldwork Traffic Recordings (2nd Emplacement).

Table 3. Median Values (Meanings) for every Cluster (2nd Emplacement)

Question #	V3	V4	# members
cluster #1	Taxi	True	18
cluster #2	Passenger Car	True	112

4 Conclusions and Future Work Ideas

In our group we use traffic simulation for a number of tasks. In particular we have used a cellular automata based microsimulator embedded in the fitness function of a Genetic Algorithm to optimize traffic light programming.

We want to improve our traffic simulation including a set of different driver types in the model. We do believe that it may improve the accuracy of the model, making the simulation closer to reality.

Through this research we have developed a telephone questionnaire and two sets of fieldwork traffic recordings in order to determine possible drivers categories according to a few variables. That variables has been chosen to be easily implementable in a microsimulator.

In section 3 the representing statistics of every driver pattern are shown. A very important variable to be considered is the proportion of every pattern, since they should be simulated in the same proportions as they are present in real traffic.

The present research has been focused on the city of Las Palmas de Gran Canaria – Spain. However, the same methodology can be applied to any other city or wider area.

We plan to do a validation research: For each treated emplacement we plan to compare the simulation results from a single type of vehicle simulation (monomodal), some multimodal microsimulations and real traffic. We plan to analyze how a multimodal model may improve the accuracy of the simulation.

Also for future research we plan to study, using a wider set of samples, possible differences between driver patterns obtained from different zones or cities.

Acknowledgment. The authors would like to acknowledge the Las Palmas de Gran Canaria City Council Traffic Department for their willingness, providing us with data from "Siete Palmas" zone.

References

1. Ericsson, E.: Independent driving pattern factors and their influence on fuel-use and exhaust emission factors. Transportation Research Part D: Transport and Environment 6(5), 325–345 (2001), http://www.sciencedirect.com/science/article/B6VH8-43F8MF3-2/2/52c3be76c9fcb26eb9ad82911a2c72e9

2. Ericsson, E.: Variability in urban driving patterns. Transportation Research Part D: Transport and Environment 5(5), 337–354 (2000), http://www.sciencedirect.com/science/article/B6VH8-40CJYRS-2/2/33c71bac39659cc9b5c9dfcfbdaa0b42

3. Lei, Z., Jianqiang, W., Furui, Y., Keqiang, L.: A quantification method of driver characteristics based on driver behavior questionnaire. In: 2009 IEEE Intelligent Vehicles Symposium, pp. 616–620 (June 2009)

4. Rakha, H., El-Shawarby, I., Setti, J.: Characterizing driver behavior on signalized intersection approaches at the onset of a yellow-phase trigger. IEEE Transactions on Intelligent Transportation Systems 8(4), 630–640 (2007)

5. Medina, J.S., Moreno, M.G., Royo, E.R.: Stochastic vs deterministic traffic simulator. Comparative study for its use within a traffic light cycles optimization architecture. In: Mira, J., Álvarez, J.R. (eds.) IWINAC 2005. LNCS, vol. 3562, pp. 622–631. Springer, Heidelberg (2005)

6. Sanchez-Medina, J.J., Galan-Moreno, M.J., Rubio-Royo, E.: Study of correlation among several traffic parameters using evolutionary algorithms: Traffic flow, greenhouse emissions and network occupancy. In: Moreno Díaz, R., Pichler, F., Quesada Arencibia, A. (eds.) EUROCAST 2007. LNCS, vol. 4739, pp. 1134–1141. Springer, Heidelberg (2007)

7. Sanchez-Medina, J.J., Galan-Moreno, M.J., Rubio-Royo, E.: Traffic signal optimization in la almozara district in saragossa under congestion conditions, using genetic algorithms, traffic microsimulation, and cluster computing. IEEE Transactions on Intelligent Transportation Systems 11(1), 132–141 (2010)

8. Sanchez-Medina, J.J., Galan-Moreno, M.J., Rubio-Royo, E.: Genetic Algorithms and Cellular Automata: A New Architecture for Traffic Light Cycles Optimization. In: Proceedings of The Congress on Evolutionary Computation 2004 (CEC 2004), vol. 2, pp. 1668–1674 (2004)

9. Sanchez-Medina, J.J., Galan-Moreno, M.J., Rubio-Royo, E.: Applying a traffic lights evolutionary optimization technique to a real case: "las ramblas" area in santa cruz de tenerife. IEEE Transactions on Evolutionary Computation (2008)

10. Sanchez-Medina, J.J., Galan-Moreno, M.J., de Ugarte, N.A., Rubio-Royo, E.: Simulation times vs. network size in a genetic algorithm based urban traffic optimization architecture. In: Arabnia, H.R., Mun, Y. (eds.) Proceedings of the 2008 International Conference on Genetic and Evolutionary Methods, WORLDCOMP 2008, pp. 255–261. CSREA Press (2008)

11. Sneath, P.H.A., Sokal, R.R.: Numerical taxonomy: the principles and practice of numerical classification. Medical Research Council Microbial Systematics Unit, Univ. Leicester, England and Dept. of Ecology and Evolution, State Univ. New York, Stony Brook, NY (1973)

12. Tezuka, S., Soma, H., Tanifuji, K.: A study of driver behavior inference model at time of lane change using bayesian networks. In: IEEE International Conference on Industrial Technology, ICIT 2006, pp. 2308–2313 (2006)

13. Ulleberg, P.: Personality subtypes of young drivers. relationship to risk-taking preferences, accident involvement, and response to a traffic safety campaign. Transportation Research Part F: Traffic Psychology and Behaviour 4(4), 279–297 (2001), http://www.sciencedirect.com/science/article/B6VN8-44SK486-4/2/4dc9100dce96572fc8fd701f613b5801

Railway Field Element Simulation Tool

Miguel Villeta[1], José G. Zato Recellado[1], José E. Naranjo[1], Lourdes Cecilia[1],
Juan M. Orbegozo[2], and José A. Quintano[2]

[1] Department of Intelligent Systems, School of Computer Science,
Technical University of Madrid, Ctra. Valencia Km. 7, 28031, Madrid, Spain
mve@alumnos.upm.es, jzato@eui.upm.es, joseeugenio.naranjo@upm.es
[2] Eliop-Seinalia, C/ Sepúlveda nº 7-B. 28108 Alcobendas (Madrid)
{orbegozo,jaquintano}@eliop-seinalia.com

Abstract. This paper aims to describe the results obtained through the development of a software tool for the industrial sector. It is specifically oriented to the market focused on the railway signaling and safety. The general objective of this tool is trying to achieve an effort reduction during the testing process which is of great importance in the software development within this sector. Therefore, its specific purpose is simulating the behavior of the conventional signaling elements which rule the traffic in railways in such a way that the results obtained were as close as possible to the ideal condition. Thanks to this simulation mechanism it would be possible to reduce the number of trips to the field to do real tests. This way time and economic optimizations are achieved by the users of this tool.

Keywords: Simulation, Conventional Railway Signaling, Computer Software.

1 Introduction

The great evolution in railway signaling and safety in recent years has brought along an increase in the number of rails and a higher traffic density, thus progress in technological matters from the signaling point of view with the purpose of reducing possible traffic incoherencies which could eventually result in an accident. Concordantly every conventional signaling device which is set up on the rails, known as field elements, is subject to the commands of a mechanism called interlocking. Its main purpose is to guarantee the highest possible level of safety in the traffic it rules, avoiding incoherent maneuvers and generating dependent relationships between the movements of the mentioned devices, thanks to their cohesive behavior.

2 Description of the Problem and Proposed Technological Solution

The company Eliop-Seinalia, devoted to projects related to industrial automation and communication infrastructures management, presented a proposal for a project under the Spanish Science and Innovation Ministry Avanza 2008 Grant called "Experimental Development of Radio Blocking systems". They wanted to create a tool named

R. Moreno-Díaz et al. (Eds.): EUROCAST 2011, Part II, LNCS 6928, pp. 481–485, 2012.

"SiCam/PC" which is the acronym of "Simulador de Campo sobre PC" (PC Field Simulator) which had the objective of simulation of field elements in conventional signaling for they could be manipulated obtaining similar results to reality. The need of this tool is significant considering that the railway safety tests are fundamental when guarantying the correct running of the configuration of the interlocking installed over the rails. This fact obliged the company's engineers to travel to the test scene to set numerous anomalous situations out. This task is translated into high economic investments and time consuming activities which could be reduced by using the Si-Cam/PC.

3 Results

In this paper, the results of the work carried out with the tool SiCam/PC, obtained by the cooperation between the infrastructure R&D team of Eliop-Seinalia and the research group SIMCA (Intelligent Systems for accessible mobility and communications) from the Technical University of Madrid (UPM), are presented once the initial goals required by the project were completely achieved. The result is a tool whereby the intervention of its user with a technical knowledge on railway traffic management, allows the simulation of the typical behavior of the conventional elements that are part of the railway traffic in cooperation with a real interlocking device. This simulation system is able of supporting the laboratory tests, emulating the different behabiors of the railway field elements under a computer without necessity of on-the-field tests.

3.1 Methodology

From the tool's software development point of view, it has been important to establish structured and consistent models, as well as methodological processes which will represent good practices recollected from past experiences, with the goal of creating a sustainable and robust tool, able to respect established patterns by the CENELEC (European Committee for Electrotechnical Standardization), organization for the development of standards for applications in the railway sector [1][2].

This way, a methodology to be applied for the concept, design, development and validation of SiCam/PC was developed before the starting of the project, based in the achievement of a set of phases that include the whole lifecycle of the system. It is important to remark that this lifecycle contains a significant difference in comparison with usual software developments. This difference is related with the orientation to the industrial environment of the final system that forces to comply with severe standards in software development, in this case, the ones recommended by CENELEC. This means that the lifecycle of this simulator is different that the one of a usual software product (for example a software oriented to information systems), mainly in the product testing stage. This is important since that aim of this system is the test of railway scenarios that once tested, will be implemented in the real railway environment and, in consequence, errors in the result of this simulation can cause potentially dangerous situations in the sense of rail accidents and loss of human lives.

3.2 Architecture and Component Interaction

In figure 1 is shown the developed architecture to support the simulator of rail field elements.

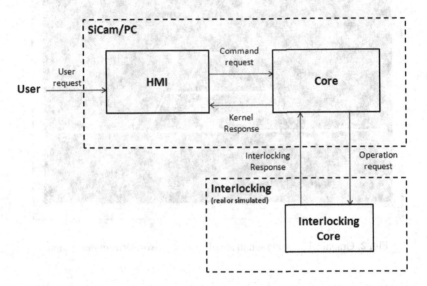

Fig. 1. SiCam/PC's software communication architecture: An overview

Considering this architecture, two fundamental subsystems, which are critical components of the main structure of the SiCam/PC, are to be enhanced: The HMI (Human-Machine Interface) and the simulation Core.

The HMI constitutes a layer which represents the interaction between the application and the user. Through this layer commands are given to the simulation Core. These commands will be interpreted by the Core and translated into a format which will be understandable for the interlocking to be sent as operations. The interlocking is an isolated system which interacts actively with the SiCam/PC indicating the operations that can be carried out and the ones which cannot. When a request is made by the user and translated into an operation form, the interlocking Core will decide if the user is making a valid request producing an answer to the subsystem of the SiCam/PC core. If the answer is positive, meaning that the user request is doable, the SiCam/PC Core will change the state charts of the elements involved and will then reply to the HMI. Finally, the HMI will modify the appropriate graphics and will show the final state to the user. It is important to mention that the appearance of the graphics of the HMI follows Spanish standards in railway information representation (figure 2) making the presented information understandable for any used trained in management of rail systems, even when this person is not an expert in computer systems.

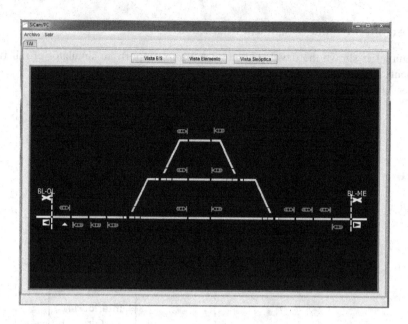

Fig. 2. Graphical presentation in simulation of a two-platform rail station

4 Conclusions and Future Works

The initially established objective of the SiCam/PC Project has been successfully achieved by the development of a software tool able of supporting simulations of rail scenarios and that allows improve the testing time – and in consequence the testing costs – in the test stage of the interlocking devices. Today, SiCam/PC is a commercial tool manufactured by Eliop-Seinalia, currently under exploitation in Spain and Egypt, with a great potential for extension to other countries.

On the one hand computing and software engineering should make their ways into the support of this kind of testing processes in which safety is a fundamental factor. On the other hand due of the need of having a unified rail traffic management system the whole European Union has to comply with the standard of the ERTMS (European Rail Traffic Management System [3]). Whereby they will achieve a strong expansion of high speed trains, using one and not many standards as it is usual nowadays. This will imply a stronger computing work which requires more attention from all the organizations belonging to this sector, therefore it is one of the fields where computing should be working from now on.

Acknowledgments. This work has been supported by the projects TRA 2009-07505, TRA 2010-15645 and TSI-020100-2009-118.

References

1. European Committee for Electrotechnical Standardization: CENELEC EN 50128, Railway Applications – Software for Railway Control and Protection Systems (1997)
2. European Committee for Electrotechnical Standardization: CENELEC EN 50129, Railway Applications – Safety-related Electronic Railway Control and Protection Systems (1999)
3. European Rail Traffic Management System: UNISIG, ERTMS Users Group: Subset026-5, System Requirements Specification SRS (2008)

Evaluation of Parameters of Functions of Cost Optimization System for Operating Systems for Carriers of Passengers by Road

Gabino Padrón-Morales, Carmelo R. García-Rodríguez,
Francisco Alayón-Hernández, and Ricardo Pérez-García

University of Las Palmas de Gran Canaria, Institute of Cybernetic Science and Technology,
Campus Universitario de Tafira, 35017 Las Palmas, Spain
{gpadron,rgarcia,falayon,rperez}@dis.ulpgc.es

Abstract. In the context of the optimization methods applicable to the carriage of passengers by road systems, this article describes a proposal to calculate and maintain automatically the parameters commonly used in the models of optimization of public transport.

Keywords: Optimization methods parameters, models, transport system.

1 Introduction

Optimization methods for operation of the processes of exploitation for the companies of carriage of passengers by road, usually use parameters that usually are not available in a clear and precise way, due to the complexity that it was supposed to have this information in the past and above all keep it updated and evaluated according to a context of changing reality. This article describes a method on the basis of the register of geographical information, obtained in successive tours made by vehicles in the fleet, allowing calculate and above all keep up to date on a statistical basis and by means of adjustment and classification set of values suited and adjusted to reality to get features of cost/benefit more faithful to the reality of those obtained with traditional.

In particular, the functions of cost optimization often move away from broken parameters that are not known with accuracy, employing statistical and heuristic criteria to model them, all of this because it does not have a faithful and peer-reviewed version of the same, we intend to introduce a system capable of providing an assessment of the parameters that in absolute terms is very approximate to the real value of the same, more approximate the greater renewed track from which the registered data are available.

2 Methods for Costs Optimization

In the context of the optimization functions based on operation parameters for the transport of passengers by road, we must cite the methods proposed by Baaj and

R. Moreno-Díaz et al. (Eds.): EUROCAST 2011, Part II, LNCS 6928, pp. 486–492, 2012.
© Springer-Verlag Berlin Heidelberg 2012

Mahmassani [1], Israeli and Assign [2], Ngamchai and Lovell [3] and Gruttner, Pinninghoff, Tudela y Díaz [4].

Baaj and Mahmassani propose a method to minimize total time of transfer of passengers and the size of the fleet required, subject to restrictions on the frequency, load factor and fleet size.

$$\min \{ C_1 \sum_{i=1}^{n} \sum_{j=1}^{n} d_{ij} t_{ij} + C_2 \sum_{k \in R} f_k t_k$$

Where $f_k \geq f_{min} \ \forall \ k \in R$ (factible frequency)

$$LF_k = \frac{(Q_k) max}{f_k CAP} \leq LF_{max} \ \forall k \in R \ (\text{load factor})$$

$$\sum_{k \in R} N_k = \sum_{k \in R} f_k t_k$$

Being the necessary data: n the number of nodes on the network, (d)ij the demand (number of trips per unit time) between nodes i and j, tij the total time of travel between i and j (in vehicle, waiting and transfer), Nk the number of buses operating on the route k, Nk = fkTk, Fk the frequency of buses operating on the route k, (f)minimum the minimum frequency of buses for entire route, tk: the total time of trip of route k, W the size of the available fleet, number of buses per hour, LFmax the load in the route k factor, (Qk) Max the maximum flow by arc en route k, CAP the capacity of passengers sitting on the bus, LFmáx the maximum permitted load factor, A the set of routes for a given solution, and C1 and C2 factors for conversion of the terms of the function target.

Israeli and Ceder propose a method to estimate the total time of transfer of passengers and the required size of the fleet, to minimize restrictions not specified with multi-objective approach.

$$\min Z_1 = a_1 \sum_{i,j \in N} PH_{ij} + a_2 \sum_{i,j \in N} WH_{ij} + a_3 \sum_{r \in R} EH_r$$

$$\min Z_2 = FS$$

Where the necessary data are: PHij is the number of passengers/hour, between nodes i and j (measured in vehicle travel time), WHij is the time-out of passengers between nodes i and j, her is the travel time vacuum, which reflects the use of buses of route r, FS the size of the fleet, A represents the set of routes for a given solution and 1,2 and3 are the weights reflecting the relative importance of the terms of the function Z1 objective.

Ngamchai and Lovell propose the following optimization function to estimate the total time of transfer of passengers and the required size of the fleet, to minimize restrictions on the factor of load with detailed approach.

$$\min\{FC + UVC + UWC\}$$

Where

$$FC = \frac{2C_v}{V}\sum_{k=1}^{R}\frac{d_k}{h_k} \qquad \text{(cost of the fleet)}$$

$$UVC = \frac{\gamma_v}{V}\sum_{i=1}^{m}\sum_{j=1}^{m}q_{ij}D_{ij} \quad \text{(cost of travel by vehicle users)}$$

$$UWC = \frac{\gamma_w}{2}\sum_{k=1}^{R}\sum_{i=1}^{m}\sum_{j=1}^{m}q_{ij}\alpha_{ij}h_k \text{(cost of waiting for users)}$$

Being the necessary data: m the amount of nodes on the network, A represents the number of routes for a given solution, (C)(V) is the cost per hour of operation of the buses, V is the speed of buses in the network, dk the length of the route k, ijq: demand between nodes i and j (number of trips per hour), (D)ij: length of the shortest route selected by passengers traveling from i to j, aIJk: is the route k using the arc (i, j), aIJk = 1, otherwise, aIJk = 0, and hk: temporal spacing of the operant service on the route (inverse of the frequency) k

$$h_k = \min\left(\sqrt{\frac{4d_k C_v}{\gamma_w V \sum_{i=1}^{m}\sum_{j=1}^{m}q_{ij}\alpha_{ijk}}}, h_k\max\right)$$

Gruttner, Pinninghoff, Tudela and Díaz propose a method to estimate the maximum benefit of operator and minimum costs of user, using restrictions on distance from origin to destination with an alternative model of allocation.

$$\max\{\alpha FO(R_i) - \beta FU(R_i)\}$$

where

$$FO = IO_L - CO_L \text{ (benefit of the operator function)}$$

$$FU = CU_L = \sum_i\sum_j\left(\delta t_{ijL}^a + t_{ijL}^v + \mu t_{ujL}^e\right) * VST * V_{ijL} \text{ (cost of the user function)}$$

In this method, the necessary data are the following: Ri is the i-th route valid set of valid paths, A and B are the coefficients for the relative importance of each goal with regard to the benefit of the FO operator function, IOL=LTLAF is the entry of the operator where AFL total influx of travel which attracts the route L, TL is the fee charged by the L line, COL= distance L KL cost operator where distance L away from the L line, KL the unit cost of operation per kilometer with respect to the cost of the FU user function, δt_{ijL}^a : access time to the line L in the arc i, j, t_{ijL}^v: tt$_{ijL}^v$ime travel in the line L from the bow i, j, μt_{ujL}^e: time of waiting in the line L from the bow i, j and VST: Subjective value of time.

In the methods proposed by these authors are among other parameters, such as: number of nodes in the network of transport, total time of the journey between two nodes, frequency of Buses on the route, minimum frequency allowed for the route, total time of route of the route, speed of Buses on the route, distance of the route, income of the route, cost of the route. When implementing any of the functions target named methods, typically, they are used as parameters estimates or approximations or values provided by the experience that sometimes are the reality with which the result proposed hardly can be considered as optimal.

Our goal is to design a system able to collect the data necessary and reliable to calculate functions optimization in a manner more faithful to reality, so that the result of applying the methods of optimization can be approached with greater certainty to the optimum. To this end, the system records the routes carried out by the vehicles according to the plan previously established for them, in addition also recorded the operations performed by the vehicle. Thus, it has a "literal" track of the position and situation in which the vehicle is at each time. For example, about the geo reference of the vehicle is registered: exact time of the registration, latitude, longitude and altitude, speed and about the operations of the vehicle for each of them is recorded: exact time of the registration, type of operation and the registered operation-specific parameters.

It is convenient to indicate that the first group of records relating to the position of the vehicles is carried out at pre-established intervals, e.g. every second, this period being a parameter setting based among other things, the ability to provide measurements of positioning device the storage capacity is available and the accuracy that you want to have on real trace of the vehicle. With respect to records that can be called operations, these occur in an asynchronous manner, i.e. is to register them at the time they occur, which can happen when a traveler cancels a title or when a driver begins or ends the route of a particular line. A main aspect of our method is to have all the operation performed by the vehicles referenced in space and time; this is achieved combining properly the geographical data and the data that represent relevant vehicles events. This functionality is achieved by the duly data registered and through the use of methods of adjustment and classification.

Moving a step forward in our goal, not only it is possible to establish a real value for a certain parameter, but that it is possible to determine a set of values, or even a function that model the behavior of the dynamic parameter according to different factors such as type of the day of the week, time zone, type of driver, vehicle type or any other factor which could be interesting. In particular, the functions of cost optimization often move away from broken parameters that are not known with accuracy, employing statistical and heuristic criteria to model them. All of this because it does not have a faithful version of the data, for this reason we introduce a system that is able to provide an assessment of the parameters that in absolute terms is very approximate to the real value of them and more approximate to the last track of the available data.

3   A Case of Use

To illustrate the method we apply it to study a specific route of the public transport network of the island of Gran Canaria. This route link town population of this island, in the outward journey the route has 30 bus stops and in the return journey it has 29 bus stop. All of these stop are properly identified in the whole of the transport network by a set of attributes, belonging of this set the precise geographic location of each bus stop. It is convenient to note that various data used are modeled according to the recommendations of the known European standard with the name of

Transmodel [5], an initiative at European level, that intend to reconcile the representation of data of transport information systems so that they can interpret and use in diverse nature systems implemented by various software developers.

The expeditions of the route are made at different times represented in the table, in the table we can see how there are three groups of scheduled time (typologies): Monday to Friday, Saturday and holidays in which Sunday is framed.

Table 1. Example of set of expeditions schedule

TYPE OF DAY	Sense	HOURS	Schedule													
			06	07	08	09	10	11	12	13	14	15	16	17	18	19
Monday to Friday	Outward		30	10	10	10	10	10	10	10	10	10	10	10	10	10
			40	40	40	40	40	40	40	40	40	40	40	40	40	40
	Return		10	10	10	10	10	10	10	10	10	10	10	10	10	10
			40	40	40	40	40	40	40	40	40	40	40	40	40	40
Saturdays	Outward				40	40	40	40	40	40	40	40	40	40	40	40
	Return			40	40	40	40	40	40	40	40	40	40	40	40	30
Bank holidays	Outward				40	40	40	40	40	40	40	40	40	40	40	40
	Return			40	40	40	40	40	40	40	40	40	40	40	40	30

Focusing on the typology of Monday to Friday, there are outward expeditions of the route in afternoon, every 60 minutes, and the frequency is variable depending on the time band of the day.

Table 3. Service sheet

FROM	TO	Itinerary	Time
14:10	14:50	Outward	00:40
14:51	15:09	Transfer and operational stop	00:18
15:10	15:50	Return	00:40
15:51	16:09	Transfer and operational stop	00:18
16:10	16:50	Outward	00:40
16:51	17:09	Transfer and operational stop	00:18
17:10	17:50	Return	00:40
17:51	18:09	Transfer and operational stop	00:18
18:10	18:50	Outward	00:40
18:51	19:09	Transfer and operational stop	00:18
19:10	19:50	Return	00:40
19:51	21:29	Transfer and operational stop	00:38
21:30	22:10	Outward	00:40
22:11	22:14	Transfer and operational stop	00:03
22:15	22:55	Return	00:40

We can see the inability to cover the scheduled planning with a single vehicle given the duration expeditions that are 40 minutes. Following a graphical representation of the duration of the expeditions is presented. It is obtained evaluating the durations of the return expeditions over a period of 3 months for the typology from Monday to Friday, for a vehicle, the times are in seconds.

Table 4. Planed and real durations of return expeditions on Monday to Friday

Hour	Planed duration	Min	Max	Average measure	Min	Sec	Deviation	Min	Sec
6:10	2400	1970	2779	2296,166667	38	16	189,536837	3	9
8:10	2400	2180	3180	2421,074074	40	21	206,029297	3	26
10:10	2400	2143	2778	2432	40	32	148,765876	2	28
12:10	2400	2166	2756	2467,724138	41	7	183,447909	3	3
14:10	2400	2002	2618	2343,04	39	3	162,55883	2	42
16:10	2400	1996	2854	2385,04	39	45	213,233729	3	33
18:10	2400	1852	2537	2251,68	37	31	154,758608	2	34
20:10	2400	1850	2674	2304,884615	38	24	215,504678	3	35

We can see how it is not possible to perform the service with a unique vehicle to affect return at the frequency required by schedule planned. These results open us a wide horizon of analysis, a common parameter is the duration of the expeditions. Table 5 presents a summary of the duration of the expeditions of the route scheduled at 16:10; the following table summarizes the data for this case.

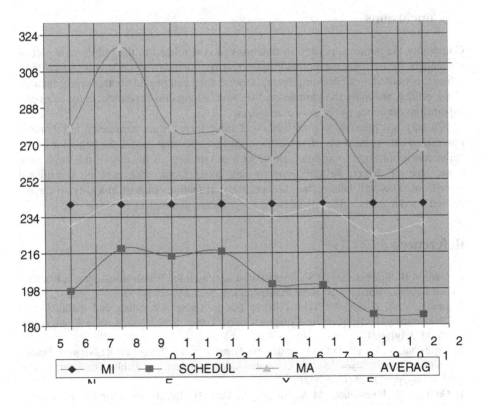

Fig. 4. Graphical representation of durations the expeditions

Table 5. Planed and real durations of return expeditions on Monday to Friday

Hour	Planned	Minimum	Maximum	Average
16:10	2400	2025	2746	2445,12
16:10	40 minutes	34 min	46 min	41 min

We appreciate as the duration of the journey the 16: 10 hours ranges between 34 minutes and 15 seconds and the 46 minutes and 16 seconds, for example, 5 minutes and 45 seconds less than planned in the case of the minimum and 6 minutes 16 seconds in the case of the maximum. This means in terms of percentage 13.62 percent lower than the planned for the minimum and 15.4 percent higher than anticipated. This means from the point of view of the company, that we are in the case of the least wasting 13.62 percent of resources every time that happens the minimum duration, while from the point of view of the user, this could mean that for any of the intermediate stops the vehicle passes ahead of schedule with the resulting inconvenience to the traveler.

4 Conclusions

Commonly the parameters used in functions of cost related to the public transport of passengers by road do not coincide with reality. For this reason seems desirable to refine the methods for obtaining them, because they can provide better representation of the reality, specially the parameters that have a temporal dependence, for example, expeditions duration, passengers demand, etc.

Not only is it possible to establish a real value for a certain parameter, but that it is possible to determine a set of values or even function, that model the behavior of the parameter according to various factors, such as typology of the day of the week time zone, type of driver, vehicle type or any other factor that may be considered significant. This will help refine the optimization features of cost in a way so far not carried out due to the difficulty of having significant parameters.

References

1. Baaj, M.H., Mahmassani, H.S.: An AI-Based Approach for Transit Route System Planning and Design. Journal of Advanced Transportation 25(2), 187–210 (1991)
2. Israeli, Y.Y., Ceder, A.: Transit Route Design Using Scheduling and multiobjective Programming Techniques. In: Computer-Aided Transit Scheduling, Lisbon Portugal, pp. 56–75 (July1993)
3. Ngamchai, S., Lovell, D.J.: Optimal Time Transfer in Bus Transit Route Network Design Using a Genetic Algorithm. In: Computer-Aided Scheduling of Public Transport, Berlin, Germany, pp. 21–23 (June 2000)
4. Gruttner, E., Pinninghoff, M.A., Tudela, A., Díaz, H.: Recorridos Optimos de Líneas de Transporte Público Usando Algoritmos Genéticos. JornadasChilenas de Computación, Copiapó, Chile (November 2002)
5. European Committee Standardization, Transmodel: Reference Data Model For Public Transport, Tech. Rep. CEN TC278 (2005), http://www.cenorm.be/

Lightweight Authentication for RFID Used in VANETs*

C. Caballero-Gil[1], P. Caballero-Gil[1], and A. Peinado-Domínguez[2],
and J. Molina-Gil[1]

[1]Department of Statistics, Operations Research and Computing.
University of La Laguna. 38271 La Laguna, Tenerife, Spain
{ccabgil,pcaballe,jmmolina}@ull.es
[2] E.T.S.I. Telecomunicación, University of Málaga, 29071 Málaga, Spain
apeinado@ic.uma.es

Abstract. This work addresses the critical problem of authentication in
RFID. It describes a new lightweight scheme for mutual authentication
between readers and tags that fulfills the EPCGen2 standard and all
practical requirements of low-cost RFID such as resource limitation of
tags and minimal interaction between tags and readers. Furthermore, the
proposal does not rely on RFID readers as they are portable, and instead
of that, it bases its security on trust in the back-end server because all
shared secrets are stored only by the tag and the back-end server, with
no possible access by the reader at any time.

1 Introduction

RFID (Radio Frequency IDentification) technology implies the use of tags and
readers for the purpose of identification through radio waves. A typical RFID
system consists of tags, readers, and a back-end server with a database containing information about the tags it manages. Tags and readers are connected
through radio communication whilst readers and the back-end server are connected through a secure channel. The standard EPC Class 1 Gen 2 (EPCGen2)
has been ratified for RFID implementations. According to it, tags are passive,
i.e. they reflect back the energy they receive from the reader, so they have their
computational capabilities very restricted. Also tag memory is limited and must
be considered unsafe and susceptible to physical attacks. In particular, according
to the EPCGen2 standard, tags only support on-chip a 16-bit Pseudo-Random
Number Generator (PRNG).

In order to illustrate the potential risks of tracking in RFID, now we describe
some examples of applications [15]. One of the main uses of RFID technology
is in products for sale, what involves several polemic issues. First, the buyer

* Research supported by the Ministerio de Ciencia e Innovación and the European
FEDER Fund under Project TIN2008-02236/TSI, and the FPI scholarship BES-
2009-016774, and by the Agencia Canaria de Investigación, Innovación y Sociedad
de la Información under PI2007/005 Project and FPI scholarship BOC Number 60.

R. Moreno-Díaz et al. (Eds.): EUROCAST 2011, Part II, LNCS 6928, pp. 493–500, 2012.
© Springer-Verlag Berlin Heidelberg 2012

of those articles does not have either to know about the presence of the tags or to be able to delete them. Also, tags might be read from a certain distance without the knowledge of the buyer, and if tagged articles are paid by credit card, it would be possible to link the unique tag IDentifications (IDs) of the articles with the identity of the buyer. Indeed, most concerns are because RFID tags in products remain functional after the products have been purchased and have carried home, and this might be used for tracking and other questionable purposes unrelated to its original inventory function. Another privacy problem comes from the possibility that a reader can list all tags that respond it without interferences among tags.

The RFID application that generates more concern is e-passport with RFID technology [18]. From 2006, U.S. requires all countries in its Visa-Waiver Program to adopt e-passports in order to increase efficiency in biometric reading machines. In particular, the corresponding standard specifies face recognition as the globally interoperable biometric for identity verification in travel documents so that all e-passports contain digitized photographic images of the faces and additionally they contain fingerprints and iris data. Protecting e-passport data against unauthorized access is a crucial part of the security of the entire system because sensitive data, such as birthdate or nationality, are carried on passports. Thus, privacy, physical safety, and psychological comfort of the users of e-passports depend on the quality of data-protection mechanisms. It is well known that RFID tags are subject to clandestine scanning. The basic guidelines of e-passports do not require authenticated or encrypted communications between passports and readers. Consequently, an unprotected e-passport chip is subject to short-range clandestine scanning with attendant leakage of sensitive personal information. The standard for e-passport stipulates the emission without authentication of a chip ID on protocol initiation. If this ID is different for every passport, it could enable tracking the movements of the passport holder by unauthorized parties. A simple solution to this problem could be the generation of a new ID after each tag reading, solution that is applied in the proposal here described. Note that although RFID technology is not the only one that allows tracking of people, what it is important is that the equipment needed to do so is not expensive and the procedure is very simple.

As RFID technology is being used increasingly, researchers are paying more attention to security and privacy problems such as the unauthorized access to tag ID information, or the existence of potential adversaries that can mislead the reader by using gathered ID information of valid tags. These problems can be solved through authentication techniques [17]. A comprehensive repository of publications on mutual authentication between tags and readers can be reached online at [2]. We can find various protocols based on different tools such as hash functions, message authentication codes, block ciphers, pseudo-random functions, etc. However, the authentication problem in EPCGen2 RFID can be considered still open because most proposals require too many resources and/or do not fulfill the standard. Here a new lightweight solution is presented for mutual authentication that fully conforms to the EPCGen2 Standard.

This paper starts with a short revision of related work, remarking some weaknesses of existing schemes. Then Sections 3 and 4 describe respectively some details of the EPCGen2 standard and characteristics of our proposal. Section 5 includes the proposed mutual authentication scheme designed to address privacy and security requirements of low-cost RFID. Conclusions close the paper.

2 Related Work

Several security schemes proposed in the literature meet the EPCGen2 standard described in the following section. In particular, some authentication proposals use pseudo-random functions [3], or PRNGs [13], but none of them are optimized for EPCGen2 compliance. The protocol proposed by Chien and Chen in [8] uses two types of keys to defend against DoS attacks that cause interruptions of synchronization between the back-end server and the tags. Furthermore, the scheme is vulnerable to information leakage and replay attacks. [7] presents a lightweight mutual authentication protocol for solving the secret disclosure problem and the replay attack in the scheme proposed in [20] by Li et al.. Nevertheless, the cloning attack problem is not yet solved for this scheme. Burmester and Munilla proposed in [4] a lightweight mutual authentication protocol compatible with session unlinkability, forward and backward secrecy. Their proposal is optimistic with constant key-lookup, and can be easily implemented on EPCGen2. Nevertheless, it is susceptible to replay and cloning attacks. Chen and Deng proposed in [6] a mutual authentication protocol that reduces the workload on the database and ensures privacy. However, they did not consider cloning attacks.

Recently many anti-counterfeiting schemes have been proposed because cloning attack issues are common in low-cost RFID tags. In [9] Choi et al. used a serial number for all tags to prevent cloning attacks. Nevertheless, the scheme does not conform exactly to EPCGen2 standard because it uses a 32-bit PRNG instead of a 16-bit PRNG. Juels proposed in [16] several simple authentication techniques for preventing skimming attacks. However, it did not consider eavesdropping and privacy invasion threats.

Mutual authentication between legitimate tags and the server has been widely studied. A comprehensive repository of published papers on the topic can be reached online at [2]. Lehtonen et al. proposed in [19] the use of synchronized secrets so that the back-end server gives through the reader to the tag a new random number every time the tag is used. This scheme seems susceptible to eavesdropping and impersonation attacks. Song and Mitchell [21] proposed a scheme based on a challenge-response approach and simple shifts and bit-wise XOR operations together with a keyed hash function. That scheme is vulnerable to tag impersonation and server impersonation attacks. In [22] Tsudik proposes an authentication protocol based on a challenge-response scheme and secret key cryptography. To protect against replay attacks, challenges are incremental sequence numbers. In this scheme a non-volatile state is required on the tag, which might be too expensive for a tag, DoS-attacks and privacy leakage are possible.

In this paper we present a new solution for mutual authentication conforming to the EPCGen2 Standard, which is completely different from all the aforementioned proposals.

3   The EPCGen2 Standard

The so-called Electronic Product Code (EPC) is fully established as standard in RFID area [11], where it has also emerged the EPCglobal Network initiative [12] to connect software and real objects. In 2004, EPCglobal ratified the standard EPC Class 1 Gen 2 (EPCGen2) for RFID implementations [1]. According to this standard, tags are passive, i.e. they reflect back the energy they receive from the reader, so they have their computational capabilities very restricted. Tags communicate with RFID readers in UHF band and its communication range can be from 2 to 10m. Furthermore, tag memory is limited and must be considered unsafe and susceptible to physical attacks.

In the EPCGen2 standard, tags only support on-chip a 16-bit Pseudo-Random Number Generator (PRNG) and a 16-bit Cyclic Redundancy Code (CRC). There is a 32-bit kill command used to disable the tag permanently, and a 32-bit access PIN to access its internal memory. Despite the large progress that the EPCGen2 standard implies in terms of communication compatibility and performance, and its significant impact for the dissemination of RFID technology, as we will see below the security level of the standard is extremely weak.

The EPCGen2 standard includes two important operations for tag management: inventory and access, and both present serious security flaws. In particular, the inventory protocol is an interactive algorithm between reader and tag with at least 4 steps that include: a Query $\in [0, 15]$, a 16-bit Random Number RN16, an ACKnowledgment ACK(RN16), and tag identifying data EPCdata. If the tag does not receive a valid ACK(RN16), it goes to its initial state and the whole process is repeated. After acknowledging a tag, a reader may choose to access it. The access command is also an interactive algorithm between reader and tag with at least 5 steps that include: ReqRN(RN16) containing the previous RN16, a new RN16 denoted Handle, ReqRN(Handle) containing the previous Handle, to which the tag responds with a new RN16'. Finally, the reader then generates a 16-bit ciphertext string with the XOR between the 16-bit word to be transmitted and this new RN16'.

In the inventory command spoofing and tracking attacks and access to private stored information are possible by simply listening to the radio channel, because the fixed EPCdata are transmitted as clear text. In the command access, security is also extremely weak because simple passive attacks can be carried out by listening in to the backward and forward channel and taking the random numbers sent by the tag in order to decrypt the ciphertext sent by the reader.

The mechanism of privacy protection in the specification implied by the kill command is perhaps too strict because in general tags should not be killed. For example in a supply chain, tags might be useful after purchase for warranty purposes. Therefore, when designing new protocols for EPCGen2 RFID, the kill command must be avoided. Moreover, the access PIN can be considered useless from security point of view since according to the standard it is XORed with a pseudorandom number sent by the tag in each session, so obtaining such a fixed PIN is easy and would endanger the entire memory of the tag.

Despite the serious security flaws of EPCGen2 standard, it can be considered a success because it has been adopted by most RFID manufacturers. In this paper, we propose a new method for authentication with privacy protection in compliance with the standard features described in EPCGen2. Our scheme does not rely on RFID readers due to their portability. Instead, our proposal bases its security on trust in the back-end server as all shared secrets (such as PIN and EPCdata) are stored only by the tag and the database in the back-end server, with no possible access by the reader at any time.

4   Basis of the Proposal

The first solutions for authentication in RFID found in the bibliography were based on unilateral authentication. However, now it is known that mutual authentication between readers and tags is necessary in such a context. Since standard cryptographic protocols such as hash functions, message authentication codes, block ciphers, etc. require too many resources to be used in low-cost RFID tags and surpass their capabilities, it is necessary to define new lightweight cryptographic protocols for the definition of mutual authentication schemes for low-cost RFID [10].

A typical mutual authentication solution based on a secret key shared between two entities consists in that each entity has to convince the other that it knows the shared secret key. Thus, to prevent tag cloning, a challenge-response scheme based on symmetric key cryptography can be used. This is the main idea behind the mutual authentication scheme here proposed.

Replay attacks represent another possible weakness of RFID technology. In order to prevent them, typical cryptographic solutions are incremental sequence numbers, clock synchronization or nonces. Passive RFID tags cannot use clocks because they do not have any power supply so clock synchronization is not feasible. On the other hand, incremental sequences are not adequate to avoid tracking. Therefore, in the scheme described in this paper we use nonces. To protect data transmitted between tag and reader against eavesdropping, the typical solution is encryption. In particular, the simplest encryption function is the XOR operation used in stream cipher. However, in that case the problem is not encryption, but key generation and management because it is necessary to produce a new encryption key for each session. This is solved with our authentication proposal. Finally, to prevent tag tracking, the update of tag ID can be used. If tag ID knowledge is only shared between the back-end server and the tag, an easy way to update it is to use the same PRNG both by the tag and by the back-end server, what implies the need for synchronization between tag and server. Such a tag ID update is used in the scheme here proposed.

5 Mutual Authentication Scheme

One of the most necessary studies in RFID is the development of strong authentication schemes for systems with resource-constrained tags. A new mechanism to provide authenticity for low-cost RFID systems fulfilling EPCGen2 is proposed below. This is a difficult task due to the relative ease with which an adversary can record or participate in a conversation between tag and reader.

The proposed method can be used by reader and tag in order to mutually authenticate each other and to establish a shared session secret key. Such a method assumes that the reader is linked through a secure communication channel to a back-end server with a database where each tag t is related to a pair given by a 16-bit secret identification number $ID_{t,i}$ and a 16-bit shared secret key $SSK_{t,i}$ for each session $i = 1, 2, \dots$. It is also assumed that both reader and tag are able to use a secure pseudorandom number generator $PRNG$, which is inmune against known attacks [14] [5].

Below the steps of the algorithm proposed for both mutual authentication and session key establishment are fully described.

Algorithm

1. The reader chooses a random $SEED1$ of length 16 to produce with the $PRNG$ a keystream sequence of length 16, and sends this $NONCE1$ to tag t.
2. Tag t sends to the reader the 16-bit output of the PRNG over its ID_t XORed with the received $NONCE1$ sequence, $PRNG(ID_{t,i}$ XOR $NONCE1) = SEED2$.
3. The reader sends $SEED2$ and $NONCE1$ to the back-end server, who compares this value with all outputs of the $PRNG$ over every $\{ID_n\}_{\forall n}$ XORed with $NONCE1$.
4. If the reader finds only one collision, then it gets the corresponding $SSK_{t,i}$, sends it to the reader, and updates in the database both values regarding tag t to $ID_{t,i+1}$ and $SSK_{t,i+1}$ by applying $PRNG$ over the previous values. Else, if the server finds more than one collision (although the probability of this case is negligible), the server informs the reader about the failure so that the process is restarted from the first step.
5. The reader sends to the tag the XOR operation between the seed originally chosen by itself and the received pairwise secret key: $SEED1$ XOR $SSK_{t,i}$.

Note that according to the above scheme we have the following properties:

– The tag obtains $SEED1$ by XORing the last received message with its $SSK_{t,i}$, and checks whether it corresponds to the initially received $NONCE1$.
– After the execution of the five steps in the above scheme, both the reader and the tag can generate the same secret session key K of length 16 through the XOR operation between the seed chosen by the reader and the seed generated by the tag, $K=SEED1$ XOR $SEED2$.
– The tag t updates its 16-bit secret identification number and its 16-bit shared secret key to $ID_{t,i+1}$ and $SSK_{t,i+1}$ respectively, by applying $PRNG$ over the previous values.

The established shared secret session key K will be then used both by the tag and by the reader to initialize the stream cipher generator PRNG in order to obtain the same key stream Z to encrypt and decrypt all messages exchanged between them during that session. K may be also used by tag and reader during that session for fast challenge-response authentication based on symmetric cryptography.

In ubiquitous environments we can assume that not many problems of connectivity exist, so for simplicity and practical security in our proposal we have assumed the existence of continuous and secure connectivity between readers and back-end server. The scheme does not provide any information useful for potential eavesdroppers of messages exchanged between tag and reader. On the other hand, without knowledge of the corresponding ID of the tag, it is very difficult to build a value that the server can recognize as valid. Therefore the proposed protocol actually provides tag authentication. Regarding tag privacy protection and tracking attack prevention, the proposed protocol protects both because the response of the tag in step 2 is random in each authentication request due to the update of its ID and the randomness of the nonce sent by the reader. Note also that the update of its secret identification number and its shared secret key involves forward security feature and resistance against replay attack. In addition, the tag never provides its ID to any reader, therefore there is no possibility that a legitimate and malicious reader can perform impersonation attacks against any tag.

Finally, Man In The Middle (MITM) attacks are impossible to cope with the proposed scheme because they require that the attacker can make independent connections with the reader and the tag in order to relay messages between them to make them believe that they are talking directly to each other when in fact the entire conversation is controlled by the attacker, and this is not possible in our proposal as either the server or the tag detect the attack due to the unknowledge of the attacker about $SEED1$. Thus, if the server detects an attack, it informs the reader that the message received in step 2 does not produce any collision by using $NONCE1$. If with a negligible probability the server finds some random collision after a MITM attack, then the tag will detect the attack when from the message received in step 5 the recovered $SEED1$ does not correspond with $NONCE1$ sent in step 1. Thus, we can conclude that the proposed mutual authentication scheme is immune to MITM attacks.

6   Conclusions

In this work, a novel lightweight mutual authentication scheme for readers and tags, which meets the EPCGen2 standard of RFID technology has been described. The proposal meets all practical requirements of low-cost RFID, and security properties such as mutual authentication and tag anonymity so that it is immune against most known attacks on authentication schemes.

References

1. Alien Technology (2004) EPCglobal Class 1 Gen 2: RFID Specification

2. Avoine, G.: (2010), http://www.avoine.net/rfid/
3. Burmester, M., Van Le, T., de Medeiros, B.: Towards provable security for ubiquitous applications. In: Batten, L.M., Safavi-Naini, R. (eds.) ACISP 2006. LNCS, vol. 4058, pp. 295–312. Springer, Heidelberg (2006)
4. Burmester, M., Munilla, J.: A Flyweight RFID Authentication Protocol. In: RFID-Sec 2009 The 5th Workshop on RFID Security. Leuven, Belgium (2009)
5. Caballero-Gil, P., Fúster-Sabater, A.: Improvement of the edit distance attack to clock-controlled LFSR-based stream ciphers. In: Moreno Díaz, R., Pichler, F., Quesada Arencibia, A. (eds.) EUROCAST 2005. LNCS, vol. 3643, pp. 355–364. Springer, Heidelberg (2005)
6. Chen, C.L., Deng, Y.Y.: Conformation of EPC Class 1 Generation 2 Standards RFID System with Mutual Authentication and Privacy Protection. Engineering Applications of Artificial Intelligence (2009)
7. Chien, H.Y., Chen, C.W.: A lightweight authentication protocol for low-cost RFID. In: Proceedings of the 2nd Workshop on RFID Security (2006)
8. Chien, H.Y., Chen, C.H.: Mutual Authentication Protocol for RFID Conforming to EPC Class 1 Generation 2 Standards. In: Computer Standards and Interfaces, vol. 29. Elsevier, Amsterdam (2007)
9. Choi, E.Y., Lee, D.H., Lim, J.I.: Anti-cloning Protocol Suitable to EPCglobal Class-1 Generation-2 RFID system. Computer Standards & Interfaces 31(6) (2009)
10. Cole, P.H., Ranasinghe, D.C.: Networked RFID System and Lightweight Cryptography. Springer, Heidelberg (2008)
11. EPCglobal. EPC radio-frequency identity protocols class-1 generation-2 UHF RFID protocol for communications at 860-960 MHz. Tech. report (2007), http://www.epcglobalinc.org/standards/
12. EPCglobal Architecture Framework EPCglobal Final Version 1.3, (1673) (2009), http://www.epcglobalinc.org
13. Eun Young Choi, D.H.L., Lim, J.I.: Anti-cloning protocol suitable to epcglobal class-1 generation-2 rfid systems. Computer Standards & Interfaces 31(6), 1124–1130 (2009)
14. Fúster-Sabater, A., Caballero-Gil, P.: Linear solutions for cryptographic nonlinear sequence generators. Physics Letters A 369(5-6), 432–437 (2007)
15. Jin, B., Zhao, X., Long, Z., Qi, F., Yu, S.: Effective and Efficient Event Dissemination for RFID Applications. The Computer Journal 52(8) (2009)
16. Juels, A.: Strengthening EPC tags against cloning. In: ACM-Workshop on Wireless Security, WiSE (2005)
17. Juels, A.: RFID security and privacy: a research survey. IEEE Journal on Selected Areas in Communications 24(2), 381–394 (2006)
18. Koscher, K., Juels, A., Kohno, T., Brajkovic, V.: EPC RFID Tags in Security Applications: Passport Cards, Enhanced Drivers Licenses, and Beyond (2008)
19. Lehtonen, M., Ostojic, D., Ilic, A., Michahelles, F.: Securing RFID systems by detecting tag cloning. In: Tokuda, H., Beigl, M., Friday, A., Brush, A.J.B., Tobe, Y. (eds.) Pervasive 2009. LNCS, vol. 5538, pp. 291–308. Springer, Heidelberg (2009)
20. Li, Y.Z., Cho, Y.B., Um, N.K., Lee, S.H.: Security and privacy on authentication protocol for low-cost RFID. In: IEEE International Conference on Computational Intelligence and Security (2006)
21. Song, B., Mitchell, C.J.: RFID Authentication Protocol for Low-cost Tags. In: WiSec 2008, Alexandria, Virginia, USA (2008)
22. Tsudik, G.: The Grid: YA-TRAP: Yet Another Trivial RFID Authentication Protocol. In: Pervasive Computing and Communications Workshops (2006)

Autonomous WLAN Sensors for Ad Hoc Indoor Localization

Heinrich Schmitzberger

Johannes Kepler University Linz, Altenbergerstr. 69, A4040 Linz, Austria
heinrich.schmitzberger@jku.at

Abstract. In mobile computing scenarios, many localization approaches have been investigated primarily on the basis of radio or sound sensor technologies. In the context of indoor localization, wireless LAN technology has proven feasible for a broad variety of localization setups with satisfactory performance and accuracy figures, not least because of its widespread availability on both infrastructure and client side. While most research concentrates on the client-based approach where the mobile device acts as sensor, this work on the contrary emphasizes infrastructure-based localization completely relying on a sensing network and shifting the computation load away from the mobile device towards a background localization infrastructure. Our main contribution is a self-contained, portable sensor network that provides indoor localization detached from stationary constraints such as an underlying backbone network or a back-end server system. We present a prototype system that realizes an ad hoc setup demanding low deployment effort and able to provide a fundament for context-aware application scenarios. We conclude this paper by highlighting the autonomy aspects of our system and discuss the issues still to solve towards an out-of-the-box localization network for indoor usage.

Keywords: Infrastructure-based indoor localization, autonomous sensor systems, ad hoc deployment, location-based services.

1 Introduction

Indoor localization has been intensively studied over the last decade. The science community has proposed solutions based on a variety of technologies (Bluetooth, WLAN, UWB, WSN, etc.). Each technology has its own characteristics and thus is suited for specific fields of application. However, indoor localization of mobile users is still considered an intricate issue with respect to real-life scenarios and has not accomplished ubiquitous availability in everyday life till today. The upcoming popularity of smart phones becoming a societal accepted companion device on the other hand claims for an applicable means to open up the indoor world for location-based services (LBS) and context-aware applications.

Concluding from the GPS story of success regarding outdoor localization, a key factor of influence is the broad availability of the respective technology in a common mobile device. In this context, WLAN technology seems to have the most promising potential as it already is present in nearly every current mobile device. In terms of

R. Moreno-Díaz et al. (Eds.): EUROCAST 2011, Part II, LNCS 6928, pp. 501–509, 2012.

indoor setups, wireless LAN offers several benefits referring to achievable accuracy, scalability, costs and deployment [10] compared to other solutions based on radio or sound sensors. Recently, commercially available WLAN localization products have been introduced [4][2] that apply client-based WLAN localization techniques to obtain the device's position indoors. Client-based localization involves a mobile device acting as a sensor and conducting location estimation by itself. In the context of real time localization, a client-based approach that continuously computes location estimates on the basis of the input from an embedded sensor noticeably stresses the limited energy resources in a twofold manner (i.e., the costly scanning effort and the increased CPU power usage for the ongoing calculations). Hence, the acceptance of such an approach declines albeit some advantages exist (e.g., privacy aspects).

In this paper, we propose a converse system where sensor hardware as well as position estimation is decoupled from the client but achieved by a WLAN sensor infrastructure, which can be categorized as infrastructure-based localization [18]. For being localized, the device produces WLAN traffic captured by networked sensors. The sensors, in turn, relay their measurements to a processor back-end that computes the emitter's estimated location. Compared to client-based localization, the main advantage is that both the signal strength sensing and the location estimation are handled by components with steady power supply. From the user's point of view, consuming LBS on top of the localization (i.e., within the browser) is the only power draining activity as it produces sufficient traffic for being localized. Moreover, the service is applicable right away without the need for additional software or specialized hardware on the client side and the WLAN interface is not blocked by scanning for AP beacons. In real life scenarios, the accuracy of infrastructural solutions [13] clearly outperforms the client-based variant, not least because a system being directly coupled to a target site is especially adapted for the respective environment (e.g., number and placement of the sensors). A major disadvantage however is the costly deployment effort needed for establishing localization infrastructure to fully cover larger target sites.

Derived from a stationary WLAN localization system we developed in the course of a campus-wide LBS project at the University of Linz [16], the sensor network described in this work realizes a self-sufficient localization infrastructure intended for ad hoc deployment, i.e., not relying on preexisting network infrastructure or back-end servers to facilitate the deployment process. In contrast to localization in wireless sensor networks (WSN) [6], our focus primarily lies on providing ubiquitous positioning for mobile users on the basis of Wi-Fi communication, which offers a bandwidth sufficient for end-user LBS applications. We contribute a system solely consisting of modified, off-the-shelf access points that act as sensor nodes and autonomously form a localization service for various mobile clients (e.g., smart phones, laptops and the alike). The extensive integration of WLAN into commercially available mobile devices allows a service architecture design that is not depending on any client prerequisites but a web browser for service consumption and the mandatory WLAN interface. Our system emphasizes autonomous operation allowing a portable solution for ad hoc indoor localization scenarios that is easy to deploy and can be adapted to arbitrary environments (e.g., conference rooms, showrooms, etc.). Thus, it is intended for spontaneously covering indoor environments with localization technology in order to quickly install a context provider for higher level applications with a primary focus on temporary installations.

The remainder of this paper is organized as follows. Section 2 discusses related work to the broad topic of indoor localization concentrating on infrastructure-based WLAN approaches. In Section 3 we describe the architecture of our system in detail and emphasize the aspects related to autonomous operation. Subsequently, Section 4 presents results from an experimental ad hoc setup at an office floor. By comparing these results to former published figures of a real-life setup at a university campus, the benefits and disadvantages of an ad hoc sensor network are illustrated. Finally, Section 5 concludes with a discussion on the issues and limits of the presented system and gives a brief outlook on future work in context of autonomous WLAN sensors.

2 Related Work

Numerous contributions have discussed the subject of indoor localization on the basis of WLAN as an indoor alternative to GPS. Most of them concentrated on signal strength localization algorithms that emphasized a client-based application. These systems broadly depend on specialized hardware in the form of tags [2][1] or native libraries supporting certain network interface card (NIC) features at client-side [17][20][21]. This paper presents a client-device independent, autonomously operating system that does not require a certain type of hardware at the user's side and consequently leverages its applicability for every setup scenario that depends on supporting various mobile platforms. To this end, the measurements used to conclude on the client's location are conducted by a WLAN sensor network consisting of modified access points that passively scan for client transmissions. This approach is often referred to as infrastructure-based localization, denoting a setup that comprises stationary sensor nodes for measuring client radio transmissions [12].

One of the first systems that falls into this category is the RADAR system presented by Bahl et. al. in [5]. The RADAR system used a setup of ordinary PCs as stationary signal strength sensors demonstrating the feasibility of WLAN technology for indoor localization. In [13], the LEASE system has been presented, an infrastructure-based framework comprising sniffers and reference-emitters. Similar to our approach, the sniffers in their setup are developed on the basis of embedded sensor platforms. An interesting aspect of LEASE with respect to our envisioned autonomous setup is the usage of the emitters as signal strength reference points to allow a dynamically rebuilding of the radio map profile necessary for location estimation. The Pinpoint system [22] is another example for using embedded devices as localization sensors. Pinpoint applies a peer-to-peer protocol to compensate clock drifts in an ad hoc network needed for mutual location estimation on the basis of a time-of-arrival technique. Opposed to Pinpoint, a more commonly applied technique for indoor WLAN localization is summarized under the term signal strength fingerprinting, i.e., matching a beforehand measured set of signal strength patterns (fingerprints) with the current sensor readings of a client in the location estimation process. The usage of modified access points as an underlying platform for signal strength fingerprinting has been discussed in [14]. Lim et. al. used a customized Kismet software on a modified access point to report signal strength measurements in the context of a calibration-free localization setup. In [7], another calibration-free fingerprinting system is proposed comprising probabilistic methods for constructing a radio profile model as a basis for position estimation. The achievement of calibration-free fingerprinting is also a premise for the fully autonomous operation in our work. However, automated radio profile generation approaches as discussed in [8] and [7] demand high computational power provoked by elaborated stochastic algorithms and are not appropriate for our setup that solely comprises embedded devices with slow CPUs. A detailed discussion on the aspects concerning autonomous operation is given in Section 3.

3 System Architecture

The system presented in this work emphasizes infrastructure-based WLAN localization - a technique that has been relegated to a niche existence [9] mainly due to cost concerns and privacy issues as of today. In terms of accuracy, applicability and maintenance efforts on the other hand, infrastructure-based localization has its advantages over client-based localization as the latter depends on signals emitted by devices that are beyond the sphere of influence of the application provider. In [16], we proposed an indoor user tracking system and discussed the advantages and the results achieved in the course of a large-scale setup covering a campus site (about 166000 aggregated square meters of floor space) by deploying 320 WLAN signal strength sensors we refer to as Sniffer Drones. Basically, a Sniffer Drone is an off-the-shelf access point (AP) comprising two separate 802.11n interfaces (2.4GHz and 5GHz). Our setups use Linksys WRT610n APs as Drones, running a Linux based Open Source firmware. To achieve real-time WLAN signal measuring we implemented sniffing software based on the received signal strength indicator (RSSI) provided by the underlying WLAN interface driver. In the campus setup, the Sniffer Drones continuously report their client measurements to a back-end server system that handles location estimation and provides an interface for LBS front-ends. In general, infrastructure-based localization systems are installed stationarily due to calibration and deployment efforts especially at large-scale sites comprising several buildings. This fact facilitates the use of a centralized backend server for costly location estimation but renders system portability hard to accomplish. In order to provide localization services in indoor environments not equipped with the required infrastructure (e.g., for pre-installation site surveys or short-run LBS setups), an ad hoc deployable system is preferable.

To this end, we adapted the architecture of the campus tracking system towards a self-organizing location providing network solely consisting of autonomously cooperating Sniffer Drones. The resulting architecture depicted in Fig. 1 sketches the three fundamental components involved in an ad hoc localization setup. The mobile client component at the upper left of Fig. 1 acts a placeholder for a variety of devices (e.g., laptops, smart phones, etc.). The minimum requirement for the client in order to participate in the envisioned ad hoc setup is a WLAN interface operating at 2.4GHz and a web browser for consuming the localization service on the one hand and implicitly producing traffic to be measured by the network composed of Sniffer Drones on the other hand. The LBS application is realized as a web service to avoid additional software installation (cf. the SIC project [16]).

The Sniffer Drone (cf. Fig. 1 lower left) architecture exploits the availability of two separate wireless LAN interfaces. The 2.4GHz interface is passively operated in the packet monitoring mode, i.e., each WLAN frame received by the driver is forwarded to a sniffing application consisting of a frame receiver, a dynamic filtering layer and the subsequent signal processor. In order to overhear all the traffic within range, the 2.4GHz interface has to stay in monitoring mode, which prevents active communication on this interface. The signal receiver is realized using the low-level packet capturing library *libpcap* [3] to obtain RSSI measurements from the interface driver. The filtering layer restrains the further processing of dispensable measurements by dynamically applying whitelist filter rules composed of the MAC addresses of actively requesting clients. The remaining measurements are collected at the signal processor that additionally averages the RSSI values using a sliding window method over the last 5 seconds and adds correct timestamp information. Finally, the measurement packet is relayed to the location estimating Master Drone utilizing the 5GHz interface as communication backbone to achieve infrastructural independence.

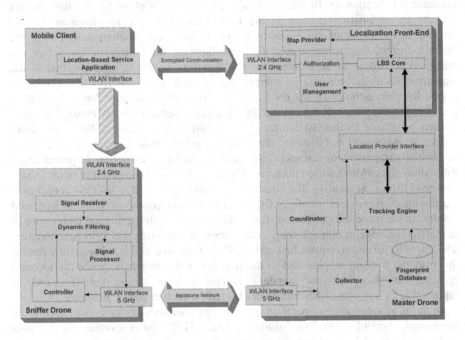

Fig. 1. Localization network architecture

For the initial organization of the autonomous sensor network a central controller process is implemented that realizes a peer-to-peer device discovery process to elect and start up a Master Drone and to initiate re-election in the case of failure. This discovery phase entails the following procedure. Every Sniffer Drone is equipped with pre-shared information on the SSID of the future backbone network and the encryption key. On startup, each Drone tries to connect to the backbone network using random timeouts between the retrying attempts. If this fails, the Drone automatically assumes its role as Master Drone, initiates the backbone network and boots the requisite services. All other Drones suddenly appearing on the network are registered at the Master. If the network collapses due to a failure at the Master Drone, the initialization process is restarted. As a further task, the controller process redirects Master Drone commands to the concerned instances (e.g., for whitelist maintenance).

The Master Drone (as depicted in Fig. 1 on the right side) is a specialization of a Sniffer Drone device augmented with features to replace a centralized back-end server as well as the needed wireless infrastructure. It provides an encrypted WLAN network on its 2.4GHz interface for client communication and LBS consumption. Furthermore, it acts as the sensor network coordinator responsible for managing the Drones operation (e.g., reacting on Drone failure, client whitelisting, etc.). At its core, the Master Drone accomplishes client position estimation in two phases. The first phase comprises a training process and an initial configuration, which defines basic site information (mainly the WGS84 coordinates of the site, a custom map and its dimensions) and splits the covered area into separate clusters. To train the system, fingerprints at selected reference points are taken all over the site and stored in a database (cf. Section 4). In the following online phase, a client localization request triggers the estimation process at the tracking engine. The measurement signals arriving at the collector are averaged for each Drone contribution representing the client's current fingerprint vector. In the following, the entries of the vector are weighted according to their intensity. The resulting vector is then matched to the fingerprint database returning an interpolation of the k nearest neighbors to produce a coarse location estimate (using the Euclidean distance as cost function and having k correlated to the Drone density at the site). If a client session already exists, this result is then compared to the last known position and time of request. Reasoning from cluster neighborhood and distance, the most probable location is returned. As a matter of limited computational resources, the tracking engine does not apply probabilistic estimation algorithms taking into account a lower accuracy compared to other related systems [13] (cf. Section 4). The consequent result is provided as WGS84 coordinates via the location provider interface. On top of this interface, the localization front-end resides. In the basic setup, the front-end is realized as a web application taking care of authorization, session management, indoor maps provisioning and LBS functionality. The client localization request first arrives at the front-end and is subsequently passed down to the tracking engine and to the network-wide whitelists. Since the location provider interface delivers standard compliant coordinates, the front-end is replaceable by any other LBS framework hosted on another device or server.

In terms of autonomous operation, several characteristics of our system need to be mentioned. According to a definition by Ibach [11], "*an autonomous distributed system consists of interacting autonomous agents which cooperatively perform a set of tasks in order to achieve a common goal. Autonomy implies independence and self government.*" This definition emphasizes the common goal of cooperating agents as a main system characteristic. With respect to our system, the global goal of each interacting Drone is to localize a mobile client. To this end, the Drones collect measurements individually and decide according to their whitelist if further processing is relevant for achieving the goal. The final location providing instance, the Master Drone, is a central element in the autonomous localization process, which rather contradicts the idea of autonomy at first. However, the election mechanism assures independence as every Drone in the network is able to fill this role. In case of a failure of the Master, the controller processes on the remaining Drones govern a coordinated take-over. The loss of one Sniffer Drone has no effect on the overall system but a decrease in localization accuracy for the respective area. Replacing the inoperative Drone with another device is just a matter of software and pre-shared configuration deployment. The only restricting aspect of a totally independent operating localization network (i.e., an out-of-the-box system) is the fact, that the system has to be trained beforehand. The infrastructural fingerprinting approach needs to assume stationary sensors and once the radio profile has been created, the setup is assumed static. Adding an additional sensor to a calibrated setup would not improve system performance unless the training process is conducted again. To solve this issue, we are currently investigating automated learning methods as described in [15].

4   Experimental Setup and Results

In order to provide the performance results of the described autonomous WLAN sensor network prototype, we compare our system with the results achieved by the stationary deployed infrastructural localization system at the campus of the University of Linz [16]. To this end, we decided for a setup on the floor of an office building that has already been measured and validated in the context of the stationary system.

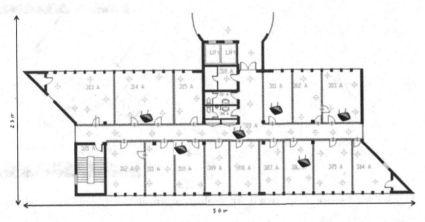

Fig. 2. Test site setup and calibration points

   The ad hoc setup uses the same spots for calibration as the stationary system does to facilitate comparison. In total, 62 calibration points were taken for covering the office site comprising an area of 50 x 23 meter. The goal was to achieve room level accuracy, i.e., the mean error distance should be in the range of 3 to 4 meter or below. For that purpose, the ad hoc setup uses 6 Drones, 5 Sniffers and one Master placed along the corridor as depicted in Fig. 2. The total calibration effort for this ad hoc setup was 30 minutes using an Android smart phone as client device emitting signals every 500 milliseconds. As the system does not require any pre-setup deployment steps besides the initial configuration and the plugging of the power supply, it is up and running in approximately 37 minutes, using 2 minutes for setting up the map and 5 minutes for device discovery including sensor boot time.

   The achieved system accuracy reveals a mean error distance of 3.24 meter, a 90% quantile of 5.93m and a standard deviation of 2.38m. The left side of Fig. 3 shows the cumulated error distance of the ad hoc setup compared to the stationary setup at the campus. The spline of the ad hoc setup has a characteristically high amount of correct location estimates up to 26% of the estimates, but displays an accuracy drift of approximately 1 meter below the stationary setup from there on. Even though the basic algorithm behind both tracking engines is similar, the stationary setup employs an additional filter mechanism on the basis of a Hidden Markov Model [19] that requires elaborated configuration (e.g., modeling the neighborhood relations among the locations). For the ad hoc system, this filter is omitted due to the design objective of a fast and simple installation. The higher rate of correct estimations of the ad hoc system is a result of the higher amount of used sensors for the covered area. The lower overall performance derives from the missing of the HMM filter, which stabilizes the location drift especially for setups with a lower sensor density. The resulting user experience is displayed in the screen dump at the right side of Fig. 3 (consumed on a tablet pc). The depicted web application hosted on the Master Drone provides a LBS environment showing the user's location through the green avatar.

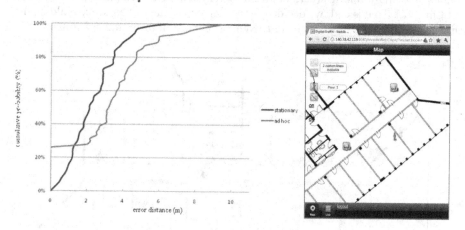

Fig. 3. Error distance comparison (left); localization providing web application (right)

5   Conclusion and Future Work

In this paper, we presented a system comprising autonomous WLAN sensors for indoor localization that allow ad hoc operation without any prerequisites at the indoor site to be covered. The presented system entails a web application front-end for location consumption and provides means to adapt to more sophisticated LBS providers. We emphasized the aspects of the system concerning autonomous operation and pointed out that the main issue to be solved for a true out-of-the-box solution relates to the generation of the radio profile that forms the basis for the signal strength fingerprint algorithm. We're currently investigating the usage of appropriate environmental signal distribution models (cf. [23]) to further improve accuracy. Even though the computational resources of the underlying hardware platform are limited, we plan on exploring probabilistic techniques to avoid the costly training phase [15] and to compensate heterogeneous client transmission characteristics by using particle filters.

References

1. Aeroscout, http://www.aeroscout.com/
2. Ekahau RTLS, http://www.ekahau.com/
3. Libpcap, http://www.tcpdump.org/
4. Skyhook wireless, http://www.skyhookwireless.com/
5. Bahl, P., Padmanabhan, V.N.: Radar: An in-building rf-based user location and tracking system. In: INFOCOM (2000)
6. Boukerche, A., Oliveira, H., Nakamura, E., Loureiro, A.: Localization systems for wireless sensor networks. IEEE Wireless Communications 14(6), 6–12 (2007)
7. De Moraes, L., Nunes, B.: Calibration-free wlan location system based on dynamic mapping of signal strength. In: MobiWac 2006: Proceedings of the 4th ACM International Workshop on Mobility Management and Wireless Access (2006)
8. El-Kafrawy, K., Youssef, M., El-Keyi, A., Naguib, A.: Propagation modeling for accurate indoor wlan rss-based localization. In: 2010 IEEE 72nd Vehicular Technology Conference Fall, VTC 2010-Fall (2010)
9. Ganu, S., Krishnakumar, A., Krishnan, P.: Infrastructure-based location estimation in wlan networks. In: Proceedings of the IEEE WCNC (2004)
10. Hazas, M., Scott, J., Krumm, J.: Location-aware computing comes of age. Computer 37(2), 95–97 (2004)
11. Ibach, P.: AUTARC, http://www2.informatik.hu-berlin.de/~ibach/autonomy.htm
12. Kjaergaard, M.: A taxonomy for radio location fingerprinting. In: Proceedings of the Third International Symposium on Location and Context Awareness (2007)
13. Krishnan, P., Krishnakumar, A., Ju, W.-H., Mallows, C., Ganu, S.: A system for lease: Location estimation assisted by stationery emitters for indoor rf wireless networks. In: Proceedings of IEEE Infocom (2004)
14. Lim, H., Kung, L., Hou, J., Luo, H.: Zero-configuration, robust indoor localization: Theory and experimentation. In: INFOCOM (2006)
15. Parodi, B., Szabo, A., Bamberger, J., Horn, J.: Indoor online learning of feature maps using spll. In: IEEE Int. Conf. on Control and Automation, ICCA 2009 (2009)
16. Schmitzberger, H., Narzt, W.: Leveraging wlan infrastructure for large-scale indoor tracking. In: Proc. of the Sixth Int. Conf. on Wireless and Mobile Communications, ICWMC 2010 (2010)
17. Sohn, T., Griswold, W., Scott, J., LaMarca, A., Chawathe, Y., Smith, I., Chen, M.: Experiences with place lab: an open source toolkit for location-aware computing. In: ICSE 2006: Proceedings of the 28th International Conference on Software Engineering (2006)
18. Varshavsky, A., Patel, S.: Ubiquitous Computing Fundamentals. In: Location in Ubiquitous Computing. ch. 7, CRC Press, Boca Raton (2010)
19. Wallbaum, M.: Indoor Geolocation Using Wireless Local Area Networks (2006)
20. Wierenga, J., Komisarczuk, P.: Simple: developing a lbs positioning solution. In MUM 2005: Proc. of the 4th Int. Conf. on Mobile and Ubiquitous Multimedia (2005)
21. Youssef, M., Agrawala, A.: The horus wlan location determination system. In: MobiSys 2005: Proceedings of the 3rd International Conference on Mobile Systems, Applications, and Services (2005)
22. Youssef, M., Youssef, A., Rieger, C., Shankar, U., Agrawala, A.: Pinpoint: An asynchronous time-based location determination system. In: MobiSys 2006: Proceedings of the 4th International Conference on Mobile Systems, Applications and Services (2006)
23. Zàruba, G., Huber, M., Kamangar, F., Chlamtac, I.: Indoor location tracking using rssi readings from a single wi-fi access point. Wirel. Netw. 13(2), 221–235 (2007)

A Compressive Sensing Scheme of Frequency Sparse Signals for Mobile and Wearable Platforms

Stephan da Costa Ribeiro, Martin Kleinsteuber,
Andreas Möller, and Matthias Kranz

Technische Universität München, Arcisstraße 21, 80333 Munich, Germany
sdcr@mytum.de, {kleinsteuber,andreas.moeller,matthias.kranz}@tum.de

Abstract. In selected scenarios, sensor data capturing with mobile devices can be separated from the data processing step. In these cases, Compressive Sensing allows a significant reduction of the average sampling rate below the Nyquist rate, if the signal has a sparse frequency representation. This can be motivated in order to increase the energy efficiency of the mobile device and extend its runtime.

Since many signals, especially in the field of motion recognition, are time-dependent, we propose a corresponding general sampling algorithm for time-dependent signals. It even allows a declining average sampling rate if the data acquisition is extended beyond a projected acquisition end.

The presented approach is testified for the purpose of motion recognition by evaluating real acceleration sensor data acquired with the proposed algorithm.

Keywords: Compressive Sensing, Motion Recognition, Data Acquisition, Signal Processing.

1 Introduction

In spite of the tremendous improvements in mobile platform technologies in recent years, the search for techniques to increase the energy efficiency of mobile devices remains an ongoing challenge. This is mainly due to the fact that a mobile device's runtime is directly dependent on a limited source of energy: the battery. For example, the runtime of smartphones has not experienced the same improvements as e.g. the device's processing power.

In many applications, especially in the context of activity recognition or skill assessment, the acquisition of sensor data can be responsible for a substantial share of the consumed energy. For the set of these applications, where it is possible to process and analyse the sensor data offline, we propose to employ the approach of Compressive Sensing[1]. If the acquired signal has a sparse frequency

---

[1] Also referred to as Compressive Sampling, see [1,2,3,4]

R. Moreno-Díaz et al. (Eds.): EUROCAST 2011, Part II, LNCS 6928, pp. 510–518, 2012.
© Springer-Verlag Berlin Heidelberg 2012

spectrum, it allows a reduction of the sensor activity and thus incites a reduction of total energy consumption on the mobile device.

Applications such as the reconstruction of activities of daily living (ADL), sports activities, or work executed to calculate calorie expenditure, reconstruct the user context, or to assess the quality of an action performed - all this can be done offline, after the actual activity has been conducted. This includes uploading the sensor data either after a certain amount of time or after the end of a sensing phase (indicated by changes in the sampled data below a certain threshold) or at the end of a day, e.g. when returning home from hiking. Many more scenarios are not demanding real-time or online data processing, and thus can benefit from the application of the theory of Compressive Sensing. Examples for the previously mentioned use cases and scenarios are following. The Sense-Cam [5] is a device hanging around the user's neck. Besides images, it records acceleration sensor data. At the end of a day, this data is downloaded and offline processed. Any subsequent recognition of activities or annotation uses the recorded sensor data. It thus would make sense, especially when the user suffers from dementia, to extend the battery life time of the mobile wearable device, and add a reconstruction step on the desktop computer prior to the activity recognition step. Another example for the offline reconstruction based on multiple, connected wearable embedded and battery powered devices is the research conducted by Laerhoven et al. [6]. They developed the Porcupine sensor platform, an ultra-low power sensing device with communication capabilities. For pure logging tasks, such as long-term activity monitoring or offline activity detection and classification [7], Compressive Sensing can be applied. We argue that, applying the theory of Compressive Sensing, the runtime of such small-scale embedded devices might significantly be increased while allowing the signal to be reconstructed nearly perfectly as we will explain later.

This paper is an extension of our previous work [8] and is structured as follows. We shortly recall the basics of CS in Sec. 2 and introduce our sampling scheme for sparse frequency signals in 3. Our method is evaluated by means of classifying three different motions which arise with the use of a rocker board and are sensed with a mobile device in Sec. 4. We conclude by discussing the strengths and limitations of the presented work in Sec. 5.

2 Compressive Sensing

The well-known Nyquist-Shannon sampling theorem states that a signal, which shall be acquired without loss of information, has to be sampled with a constant frequency that is at least twice the highest frequency present in the signal, [1]. However, an acquisition via this approach can often result in high sampling rates, since the highest frequency within the signal is often not known a priori - or it may not be opportune to exclude a high frequency from detection (e.g. for motion data originating from a specific joint of the human body). Compressive Sensing (CS) has the potential to overcome these problems if the signal that is to be acquired is sparse in the frequency domain. We shortly summarize the basic ideas of CS here in order to lay the theoretical foundation for the presented results.

The concept of CS builds on the notion that many signals of interest have a sparse representation or are compressible. For motion data, for example, the standard representation of a signal is dense. However, since human motion usually follows regular patterns, the Fourier basis typically admits a compressible representation: The important information of a sparse signal is contained in only a few dominant transform coefficients. To reconstruct the entire signal without severe loss of quality, it is sufficient to know these large coefficients together with their respective positions.

The concept of CS [4,9] offers a joint sampling and compression mechanism, which exploits a signal's sparsity to perfectly reconstruct it from a small number of acquired measurements. It allows to acquire a signal, in our example with a mobile device, only partially, and recover the complete data in its sparse representation on a stationary computer. This implies a shift of energy consumption away from the resource-constrained mobile device and onto the energy-unrestricted desktop computer.

Let $f \in \mathbb{R}^n$ be a column vector that represents a discrete n-dimensional non-sparse real-valued signal. We denote its K-sparse representation by $x^0 \in \mathbb{R}^n$, where K-sparse means that only $K < n$ entries of x^0 are nonzero. In the presented application of CS, f denotes the discretized signal in the time domain and x^0 its sparse frequency spectrum. We write the corresponding linear transformation as

$$f = \Psi x^0, \tag{1}$$

where $\Psi \in \mathbb{R}^{n \times n}$ is an orthonormal basis of $\mathbb{R}^n$, called *representation basis*. Furthermore, let $\Phi \in \mathbb{R}^{m \times n}$ be the *sampling basis* that transforms f into the vector $y \in \mathbb{R}^m$ that contains $m < n$ measurements

$$y = \Phi f = \Phi \Psi x^0. \tag{2}$$

We aim to reconstruct f by computing the approximation x^* of x^0, given only the measurements y and exploiting the fact that x^0 is sparse. Informally speaking, we are seeking the sparsest vector x that is compatible with the acquired measurements. Formally, this leads to the following minimization problem

$$\min_x \|x\|_0 \quad \text{subject to} \quad y = \Phi \Psi x, \tag{3}$$

where $\|x\|_0$ is the ℓ_0-pseudo norm of x, i.e. the number of nonzero entries.

Unfortunately, solving (3) is computationally intractable as it is a combinatorial NP-hard problem [10]. Instead, it has been shown in [3,4,11] that under some generic assumptions on the matrix $\Phi \Psi$ it is equivalent to replace the ℓ_0-pseudo norm by the ℓ_1-norm $\|x\|_1 = \sum_i |x(i)|$. Here, $x(i)$ denotes the i-th component of the vector x. This leads to the so called Basis Pursuit

$$\min_x \|x\|_1 \quad \text{subject to} \quad y = \Phi \Psi x. \tag{4}$$

This is a convex optimization problem that can be recast into a linear program, which is solved in polynomial time. The theory of CS says that if the number of measurements m is large enough compared to the sparsity factor K and the measurements are chosen *uniformly at random*, then the solution to equation (4) is exact [4]. This means that the signal is perfectly reconstructed by solving equation (1) with the computed x^*.

We now introduce an important concept, called *coherence*, that influences the amount of required samples. Suppose a signal is sampled in the basis in which it is sparse. In that case, a lot of samples are required for reconstruction, since most of the samples would be zero. Hence, it is intuitively clear that sampling and representation basis have to be *as disjoint as possible*. This is measured by the mutual coherence between Φ and Ψ

$$\mu(\Phi, \Psi) = \sqrt{n} \cdot \max_{i,j} |(\Phi\Psi)(i,j)|, \qquad (5)$$

where $X(i,j)$ denotes the (i,j)-entry of the matrix X. The coherence will take a value in $[1, \sqrt{n}]$, cf. [4], and the smaller the value $\mu(\Phi, \Psi)$ the more favorable is the pair of bases [12]. In the presented case, where the sampling and the representation bases are the standard and the Fourier basis respectively, it can be shown indeed that the two bases are maximally incoherent and hence most favorable to a low sampling rate.

The relation between the amount m of required random samples for perfect reconstruction, the coherence $\mu(\Phi, \Psi)$, the sparsity K of x^0, and the dimension n of the signal is provided by the famous formula [13]

$$m \geq C \cdot K \cdot \mu^2(\Phi, \Psi) \cdot \log n, \qquad (6)$$

where C is some positive constant. Because of this relation, Compressive Sensing describes a paradigm shift in data acquisition. According to CS, the sampling rate does not depend on the highest frequency within the signal, as stated by the Nyquist-Shannon theorem, but on the signal's sparsity.

3   Sampling a Time-Dependent Signal with Compressive Sensing

As indicated, a key concept of Compressive Sensing is that the m required samples have to be chosen from the n possible samples uniformly at random. That is, from the set $N = \{1, ..., n\}$ of possible sampling points, one of the $\binom{n}{m}$ subsets $M \subset N$, denoting the $|M| = m$ points to be sampled, is chosen randomly with equal probability.

If the samples are to be acquired from a time-dependent signal however, two inconveniences of the uniform selection model become obvious. On the one hand, the duration of the signal acquisition has to be fixed a priori. On the other hand, the random selection has to be made before the start of the signal acquisition. Since the points in time at which the signal is sampled thus have to be stored in memory, this approach can be very memory intensive for long signals. As a main result of this paper, we present a sampling algorithm which overcomes the inconveniences of the uniform probability model and is much more suited for time-dependent sampling. This algorithm is not restricted to applications in motion recognition or to data acquisitions with mobile devices, but can be generally applied in order to acquire time-dependent signals with Compressive Sensing.

In the following we introduce the Bernoulli probability model as in [3]. The set M' of points that are to be sampled is generated by first creating a sequence $I_1, I_2, ..., I_n$ of independent identically distributed random variables with $I_k \in \{0, 1\}$ and $\boldsymbol{P}(I_k = 1) = m/n$, where m and n comply with the constraints given in section 2. The set M' is then created by setting

$$M' := \{k : I_k = 1\}. \tag{7}$$

The mathematical proof that this sampling scheme also leads to a perfect signal recovery can be found in [3,4].

The Bernoulli model already inspires a very practical algorithm for sampling a signal in the time domain. Suppose a signal of a specific duration is sampled at n equidistant points in time according to the Nyquist-Shannon theorem. The Bernoulli model then suggests that the signal can be sampled at each point in time, only with a probability p satisfying the condition

$$p \geq C \cdot K \cdot \mu^2(\Phi, \Psi) \cdot \frac{\log n}{n}. \tag{8}$$

If the dominant frequencies in the signal do not change over time, we can assume an upper bound for the sparsity K which is independent of n. With the coherence $\mu^2(\Phi, \Psi) = 1$ for the bases at hand, equation (8) simplifies to

$$p \geq \text{const} \cdot \frac{\log n}{n}, \tag{9}$$

where the constant value can be estimated experimentally for specific applications. It is remarkable here, that the higher the value n, the lower we may choose the sampling probability p.

Though already providing a lower average sampling rate, this trivial randomized sampling algorithm requires that the mobile computer is reinitialized at each possible sampling point in order to calculate a pseudo-random variable. Since one can expect an even lower energy consumption if the computer is only reinitialized when a sample is actually acquired, we introduce an alternative sampling algorithm in the following. It uses only *one* pseudo-random variable to determine which of the future possible sampling points has to be sampled *next*.

Let L_k be the event that the k-th point of the future potential sampling points is the next one sampled, if randomly determined with the Bernoulli model. The probability of L_k is then given by

$$\boldsymbol{P}(L_k) = p(1 - p)^{k-1}. \tag{10}$$

A summation of these probabilities for all $k \in \mathbb{N}$ results in a geometric series which converges to $\sum_{k=1}^{\infty} p(1 - p)^{k-1} = 1$.

Since it suffices to randomly determine k, the index of the next sampling point, in accordance with the probabilities of L_k, the alternative algorithm can be stated as follows. At the beginning of the signal acquisition and after each sampled point, the mobile device creates a random variable $X \in [0, 1)$ with uniform distribution and then chooses the next sampling point following the scheme

$$k = \begin{cases} 1, & \text{if } 0 \leq X < p \\ 2, & \text{if } p \leq X < p(1-p) \\ \vdots & \\ r, & \text{if } p(1-p)^{r-2} \leq X < p(1-p)^{r-1} \\ \vdots & \end{cases} \tag{11}$$

which is also illustrated in Figure 1. Once k is determined the mobile computer

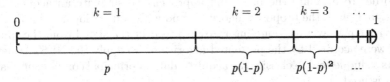

Fig. 1. Illustration of the case differentiation of the presented algorithm

may be put to sleep for the appropriate time frame. The proposed algorithm thus reduces the number of points at which the signal is sampled and at which the mobile computer is reinitialized, both by the factor of p.

The proposed sampling algorithm, together with the probability p as explained above, has two very convenient properties: Firstly, in contrast to the uniform probability model, it is possible to increase the length of the acquired signal from the value n to a higher value n' during the data acquisition procedure, which means that the end time of the acquisition process does not necessarily have to be known a priori. Secondly, we can adjust the sampling probability p over time. If the set of dominant frequencies does not vary, which is the case when human motion is considered that follows regular patterns, then by Eq. (8), p can be reduced in order $\frac{\log n}{n}$ as time goes by, without an accompanying reduction of recovery quality. This is remarkable since an acquisition of a signal over a long time period with the proposed algorithm therefore requires relatively less effort than the acquisition of a short signal.

4   Experimental Evaluation of the Proposed Approach

Two aspects need to be regarded here in order to examine the applicability of the proposed sampling scheme. On the one hand, the data recovered from a random signal acquisition has to serve its purpose in its subsequent processing steps. On the other hand, the acquisition of the partial data on the mobile device must indeed consume less energy than the conventional method, ideally proven with actual measurements. In this paper, we confine ourselves to an evaluation of the former, leaving the latter for future research. In particular, we assess how valuable recovered sensor data is for the task of motion recognition.

The dataset used for the evaluation was recorded by a smartphone which was attached to a rocker board. We recorded the orientation of the board in three different directions via acceleration sensors, as they are often a primary source for motion data on mobile devices. In this way, the orientation of the rocker board could be measured unambiguously. During the experiment, a person was standing on the board and moved the board with his/her feet, while the smartphone recorded the orientation of the board, see figure 2. This way, a total of 1540 orientation signals have been acquired with six test subjects. The participating persons always performed one of three different movements. (i) The person either moved the rocker board back and forth, (ii) left and right or (iii) the person tried to balance on the center of the board.

In order to evaluate the presented approach, we simulate an acquisition of these signals with the proposed algorithm and with conventional downsampling, both with equal average sampling rates. To recover the signal from the samples which were acquired by the presented algorithm, we apply the NESTA method [14]. As a simple tool to classify the acquired data, a principal component analysis (PCA) is used.

We use 90% of the data for training the classifier and 10% as test data. The data acquired with (a) Compressive Sensing and (b) downsampling are projected onto the first 10 principle components and the euclidean distance to the trained centers is used for classification.

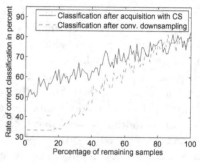

Fig. 2. The rockerboard in usage at the experiment

Fig. 3. The results of the classification for different sampling rates via Compressive Sensing and the conventional approach

Figure 3 shows the classification results of the conducted PCA. It can be seen that an acquisition of a signal with the proposed sampling algorithm leads to higher rates of correct classification, especially if the sampling rate decreases. We assume that more sophisticated classifiers amplify this promising effect.

5 Conclusion

For several mobile scenarios, sensor data capturing and data processing can be separated. For these applications, Compressive Sensing can significantly reduce the sampling rate on the mobile device. We plan, to investigate as part of our future work, to incorporate other factors influencing battery consumption, for example when and how often to communicate the acquired data for remote offline processing. Our experimental results show that a higher rate of correct classification is possible in motion recognition, if the signal is acquired with the presented approach.

We furthermore proposed a general sampling algorithm for time-dependent signals, which is not restricted to motion recognition applications. One of its interesting properties is that it even allows a reduction of the sampling rate, if the length of the data acquisition is spontaneously increased. As a downside however, the presented sampling algorithm requires the mobile device to make certain computations before each acquired sample. In the light of the promising experimental results, it therefore remains an interesting task to investigate the actual reduction in energy consumption for the presented approach.

Acknowledgments. This work has been supported in parts by the German DFG funded Cluster of Excellence "CoTeSys - Cognition for Technical Systems".

References

1. Candès, E.J., Wakin, M.B.: An introduction to compressive sampling. IEEE Signal Processing Magazine 25(2), 21–30 (2008)
2. Becker, S., Bobin, J., Candès, E.J.: Nesta: A fast and accurate first-order method for sparse recovery. SIAM J. Imaging Sciences 4(1), 1–39 (2011)
3. Candes, E.J., Romberg, J., Tao, T.: Robust uncertainty principles: exact signal reconstruction from highly incomplete frequency information. IEEE Transactions on Information Theory 52(2), 489–509 (2006)
4. Candès, E., Romberg, J.: Sparsity and incoherence in compressive sampling. Inverse Problems 23(3), 969 (2007)
5. Hodges, S., Williams, L., Berry, E., Izadi, S., Srinivasan, J., Butler, A., Smyth, G., Kapur, N., Wood, K.: SenseCam: A retrospective memory aid. In: Dourish, P., Friday, A. (eds.) UbiComp 2006. LNCS, vol. 4206, pp. 177–193. Springer, Heidelberg (2006)
6. Laerhoven, K.V., Aronsen, A.K.: Memorizing what you did last week: Towards detailed actigraphy with a wearable sensor. In: Proceedings of the 27th International Conference on Distributed Computing Systems Workshops. IEEE Computer Society, Washington, DC, USA (2007)
7. Kranz, M., Spiessl, W., Schmidt, A.: Designing ubiquitous computing systems for sports equipment. In: Proc. Fifth Annual IEEE International Conference on Pervasive Computing and Communications PerCom 2007, pp. 79–86 (2007)
8. da Costa Ribeiro, S., Kleinsteuber, M., Möller, A., Kranz, M.: Data Acquisition for Motion Recognition on Mobile Platforms via Compressive Sensing. In: Moreno-Díaz, R., et al. (eds.) EUROCAST 2011. LNCS, vol. 6928, pp. 510–517. Springer, Heidelberg (2011)

9. Donoho, D.: Compressed sensing. IEEE Transactions on Information Theory 52(4), 1289–1306 (2006)
10. Natarajan, B.K.: Sparse approximate solutions to linear systems. SIAM Journal on Computing 24(2), 227–234 (1995)
11. Donoho, D.L., Elad, M.: Optimally sparse representation in general (nonorthogonal) dictionaries via ℓ_1 minimization. Proceedings of the National Academy of Sciences of the United States of America 100(5), 2197–2202 (2003)
12. Donoho, D.L., Huo, X.: Uncertainty principles and ideal atomic decomposition. IEEE Transactions on Information Theory 47(7), 2845–2862 (2001)
13. Candès, E.J., Romberg, J.: Sparsity and incoherence in compressive sampling. Inverse Problems 23(3), 969–985 (2007)
14. Becker, S., Bobin, J., Candès, E.J.: Nesta: A fast and accurate first-order method for sparse recovery. SIAM J. Imaging Sciences 4(1), 1–39 (2011)

Evaluation of Descriptive User Interface Methodologies for Mobile Devices

Michael Tschernuth, Michael Lettner, and Rene Mayrhofer

Upper Austria University of Applied Sciences
FH OOE Forschungs & Entwicklungs GmbH, Softwarepark 11,
4232 Hagenberg, Austria
{michael.tschernuth,michael.lettner,rene.mayrhofer}@fh-hagenberg.at
http://www.fhooe.at

Abstract. The difficulty application developers in the mobile phone environment are facing is the variety of devices on the market. Since there are a few relevant global players with different operating systems and devices, it is getting more expensive to adapt applications once implemented from one hardware platform to another. To keep the costs at a minimum, a structured and reusable software architecture is crucial. Especially the maintenance of the user interface (UI) is a big challenge, thus it is beneficial to have a platform independent description of it. This paper aims at the upper layers of the software which are responsible for the user interface. A few established user interface declaration technologies and an own approach will be investigated. It is shown, that it could be beneficial when the logic—which is responsible for screen changes—is contained in the user interface description.

1 Introduction

Developers of mobile phone applications are facing the problem of implementing the same application for a variety of devices. Since there are a few relevant global players with different operating systems ([6]), more effort is needed to port applications once implemented from one platform to another. A structured and reuseable software architecture is crucial for minimizing costs for different platforms. Separating the user interface from the application logic itself can be a useful means to optimize the architecture.

A declarative approach to define the user interface independently of the application logic and following the model view controller pattern, which was introduced by Trygve Reenskaug [1], is a well established method to achieve such a separation. The implementation of the view layer is the concern of the paper. *Android OS, IPhone OS (iOS), Windows Phone 7 (WP7)* as well as the *Qt Meta-Object Language (QML)*—which is used in Qt Quick (Qt UI Creation Kit)—all provide such an architecture but the interpretation is different.

Due to a variety of screen sizes of mobile devices a UI description which is independent of the program logic, is essential if an application should be reused

R. Moreno-Díaz et al. (Eds.): EUROCAST 2011, Part II, LNCS 6928, pp. 519–526, 2012.

for different devices. Furthermore it can raise the quality of the software as layout changes do not affect the source code and the maintenance of the user interface can be done independently from the code.

The idea to separate the concerns is not a new one. Well established solutions exist in the desktop environment [7]. This research investigates declarative solutions for some of the most relevant—in terms of market share—smartphone platforms. An analysis of several mobile platform solutions and methodologies will reveal the similarities and differences regarding the user interface layer and what actually is contained in the UI description.

An own XML definition—which is used for the architecture of an embedded feature phone [5]—shows that it could be beneficial to have the information of how the screens are connected in the user interface declaration.

Which field of application our XML UI description offers is shown in Section 4, where tools—targeting the mobile software development process—of a low resource phone are presented which utilize this additional information. On of the tools is a translation tool which is used to translate the completed product into different languages. The other one shows how the description can be used to transform the UI definition to another mobile platform in a practical example. As cross-platform solutions are numerous (e.g., *RhoMobile*[1], *Titanium*[2], *WidgedPad*[3], *PhoneGap*[4], *MoSync*[5]) and already provide features for a generic user interface implementation, this should merely serve as a transformation case study and not as an actual cross-platform product.

2   Related Work

There are different approaches on how to create a user interface description. This paper describes various declarative interface description technologies with the main focus on methodologies in the mobile phone domain. In this section a short introduction into existing solutions in general is given. As additional objective it is investigated if it is possible to enhance the UI layer of the mobile phone platforms with the structural information. If that holds true, our tools presented in Section 4 can be utilized by this platform. The interface description languages based on XML are numerous [3]. However this paper investigates user interface descriptions which are used for the common available software development kits for mobile phones because it is a main objective to translate the approach proposed in Section 3 to the available platforms as a future work. Implementations which are based on modeling the user interface (e.g.,[2]) are not discussed, as there is no practical applicability in combination with our approach.

---

[1] RhoMobile: `http://rhomobile.com/`
[2] Titanium von appcelerator: `http://www.appcelerator.com/`
[3] WidgetPad:`http://widgetpad.com/`
[4] PhoneGap: `http://www.phonegap.com/`
[5] MoSync: `http://www.mosync.com/`

2.1 Android

Android uses an XML based layout file to define the user interface. The description is hierarchically organized, so every element (e.g., a Button) or *View* needs a corresponding layout type (*ViewGroup*) where it is embedded (Fig. 1). One *ViewGroup* can contain multiple *View* objects. During runtime the layout is loaded by the *Android* class that it was built for [10].

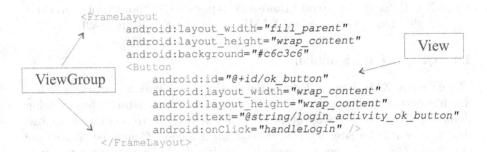

Fig. 1. XML definition of a Button (View) which is embedded in a layout (ViewGroup)

Connection of Screens. The relation between different screens cannot be derived from the XML file. It is done by starting a new Activity. During the starting process, the user interface description of the new class is loaded. The XML description of one screen is not aware of any following screens as the connections are implemented in source code (Controller). *Android* follows the MVC pattern very strictly, thus it is *not* possible to put additional information in the view layer.

2.2 IPhone

IPhone uses the *Interface Builder* for user interface creation. Outcome of this process is an XML file following the XIB syntax [11]. The description of a basic button element is depicted in Fig. 2.

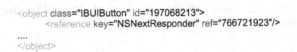

Fig. 2. Basic button definition

Connection of Screens. The architecture is similar to the *Android* concept. The user interface description has no knowledge about how the screens are connected and how the overall structure of different screens look like. Screen transitions have to be done in source code.

2.3   Windows Phone 7

The windows phone platform uses the *Extensible Application Markup Language (XAML)* as a user interface definition. The difference to the other XML descriptions is that each XAML element is a representation of a .NET object [4].

Connection of Screens. The typical way to implement screen changes is to manipulate the code-behind file from a UI element (e.g., a Button) and set the target XAML file in source code. However it is possible—although not common—to to create links between several XAML files in the XAML file itself.

2.4   *Qt Quick* for Symbian

The only not XML based UI definition in this investigation scenario is *QML*, which is part of *Qt Quick*. In *QML* it is possible to declare a user interface using *JavaScript*. Due to the usage of *JavaScript* it is possible to build more sophisticated user interfaces which already contain behavior. Compared to *Android* or *IPhone OS*, *QML* does not provide user interface elements. However, it is possible to create these elements using *JavaScript*. A set of built-in components is currently under development and will be available in future releases aka Qt Quick Components [13,14].

Connection of Screens. As *QML* can utilize *JavaScript* to introduce functionality in the user interface declaration it is possible to connect a series of screens without using the underlying platform[6]

2.5   Evaluation

The discussed platforms have been evaluated regarding their applicability for our tools presented in Section 4. Table 1 shows a comparison of the investigated declarative approaches for mobile devices. Microsoft's user interface description can be—although it is not the intended approach—adapted to work with our tools. *Android* and iOS cannot be used that easy because the controller logic has to be extracted from the source code which imposes a challenge. Qt is not XML based and therefore not applicable. The following section describes our approach where navigational context and content description are available in the XML declaration file.

3   Alternative XML description

During our project for a feature phone an XML description was developed to represent the user interface layer [5]. The previously mentioned XML descriptions are too generic to meet the requirements for the scarce resource phone. The

---

[6] Layout   Manager: `http://wiki.forum.nokia.com/index.php/Implementing_a_simple_View_Manager_with_QML`.

Table 1. Comparison of several declarative approaches for mobile devices

Platform	XML	navigational context in the view
Android	Yes	No
iOS	Yes	No
WP7	Yes	Yes
Qt	No	Yes

developed XML descriptions only contains elements of the specific system and uses an adapted MVC approach where additional information was introduced to the view layer. This section briefly describes the developed XML user interface description which contains the content of the screens as well as the information about how the screens are connected. The investigated XML descriptions from Section 2 are not—except XAML where structure information can be added to the declaration—designed to support this alteration of the MVC approach. A practical example of that idea is given in the following subsections.

3.1   Declaration of the Content

All graphical objects that appear on the screen are contained in the definition file. Elements always have to have a parent *state*, which is one single screen, where they are attached to. How the elements of the real screen are transformed into an XML description is shown in Fig. 3.

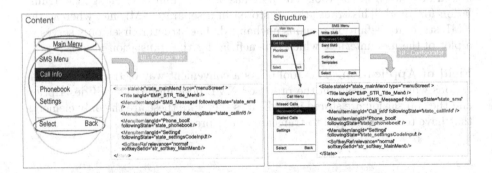

Fig. 3. Example of the content and structure definition

3.2   Declaration of the UI Structure

The connection between different *states* is achieved by adding an additional attribute to every element which is able to initiate a transition between two screens (Fig. 3).

Including the structure in the XML description offers new possibilities which resulted in a few tools which support the software engineer during the development phase. The creation of a prototype for translation purposes is one of them. The next section will present some software tools based on this XML definition.

4   Applications Based on Our XML Description

Although the description of the user interface is used as a basis for the feature phone it can be used independently of the underlying layers as well, to support the development process and to present different views of the whole system. Having navigational context available in the user interface definition resulted in a variety of tools which utilize this additional information. Within this section these tools are explained in detail.

4.1   Language Translator

For localization purposes a tool was developed to support a native speaker in translating the software into different languages. Due to the restricted screen sizes on mobile devices translations it is sometimes not sufficient to provide an as is translation. The string length has to be taken into account to match the current screen area. Under that circumstances it is beneficial that the *context* in which the current screen appears *is known*, thus the expert is able to optimize the translation for this limited space requirement.

Our developed XML description provides the navigational context, therefore it is possible to create a representation of the UI declaration for translation purposes. Fig. 4 shows how a visual representation looks like in the translation tool. Every user interface element is aware of its following screen thus it is possible to navigate along the defined structure. Ids of the translatable items for each screen are shown in the tool. The user has the possibility to change the translation for an id. This translation is stored in a separate XML file, whereas the XML structure definition remains unchanged. The structure itself only serves as a plot of the user interface which is beneficial for the translation process.

Field of Application. This tool offers a convenient way of translating applications which are based on the proposed XML description. The UI description and the translation are stored in XML files therefore these are the only elements that have to be exchanged to translate a new product.

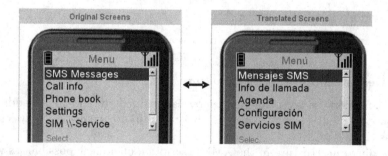

Fig. 4. Screenshot of the translation tool

4.2 Transformation to Android

As the information contained in our XML structure is a super set of the *Android* view it is possible to generate code for the *Android* platform to represent our user interface. The developed transformation tool is able to generate the XML files needed for the Android user interface on the one hand and the sourcecode for navigating between the defined screens on the other hand.

Example. Fig. 5 shows the transformation from the an XML file (*StateContent.xml*) to the Android XML description plus the source code for the navigation. The example illustrates that it is possible to transform the XML content file to Android because all the information is available in a defined format.

The other way around is more difficult as the information is not only contained in the user interface description files. The interface files lack the navigational context which has to be extracted from the sourcecode. This imposes a problem as there are numerous way to induce a screen change.

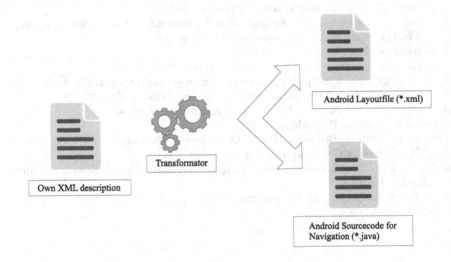

Fig. 5. Transformation overview

Field of Application. This software application serves as a case study for look and feel tests of the user interface definition on *Android*. An additional benefit this transformation tool provides is the acceleration of *Android application* development if an XML structure definition is available, because the source for the screen connections is generated automatically.

5 Future Work and Conclusion

The software tools presented in Section 4 are already used in practice and the software development is supported by their usage. To utilize those tools for the development on *Android* a structure extractor (Extracturer) is in development. With this tool it will be possible to retrieve the relevant controller parts from the source code and pack them into the view layer. An additional field of application for the user interface definition can be for documentation purposes, as the structure could be exported into a document where all the screens and their connections are printed. The transformation to other programming languages is another aspect which will be investigated in the future to benefit from the already developed toolchain.

References

1. Trygve Reenskaug. The original MVC reports (2007)
2. da Silva, A.R., Saraiva, J., Silva, R., Martins, C.: XIS UML Profile for eXtreme Modeling Interactive Systems (2007)
3. Souchon, N., Jean, V.: A review of xml-compliant user interface description languages (2003)
4. Charles, P.: Programming Windows Phone 7 (2010)
5. Lettner M., Tschernuth M.: Applied MDA for Embedded Devices: Software design and code generation for a low-cost mobile phone (2010)
6. Statistic: mobile phone market shares,
   http://www.gartner.com/it/page.jsp?id=1434613
7. Technology Report, http://xml.coverpages.org/userInterfaceXML.html
8. Developer Center - XUL, https://developer.mozilla.org/En/XUL
9. Android Developers, http://developer.android.com/guide/
10. Arno, B., Marcus, P.: Android 2 (2010)
11. Dave, M., Jeff, L.: Beginning iPhone Development: Exploring the iPhone SDK
12. QML - Reference Guide, http://doc.qt.nokia.com/
13. Fitzek, F.H.P., Mikkonen, T., Torp, T.: Qt for Symbian. Wiley & Sons Ltd, United Kingdom (2010)
14. Qt Quick, http://qt.nokia.com/qtquick/

Friends Radar: Towards a Private P2P Location Sharing Platform

Rene Mayrhofer, Clemens Holzmann, and Romana Koprivec

Upper Austrian University of Applied Sciences, Campus Hagenberg
Softwarepark 11, A-4232 Hagenberg, Austria
{rene.mayrhofer,clemens.holzmann}@fh-hagenberg.at

Abstract. In this paper, we propose a new approach to live location sharing among a group of friends that does not rely on a central server as a hub for exchanging locations messages, but is done in a peer-to-peer manner by pushing *selective location updates* via XMPP messages. That is, only those contacts specifically authorized by users will be notified of location changes via push messages, but no third-party service is involved in processing these locations. We describe an initial implementation called *Friends Radar*, and discuss the associated trade-offs between privacy and resource consumption.

1 Motivation

One of the most often asked initial question upon establishing a telephone call from or to a mobile phone is "Where are you?". As communication becomes increasingly untethered and more dynamic, the mobility aspect transforms from a hindrance to a central element. That is, location becomes the subject of communication (communication about location) to support social interactions such as micro scheduling ("I am at the main entrance, where shall we meet?") or more dynamic time frames ("I will be there in 2 minutes"). It is therefore unsurprising that – driven by broad availability of smart phones with always-on connectivity and GPS – a multitude of services for live, global location sharing have been developed in the past few years to better support or even replace textual or voice communication about location.

Google Latitude is probably the most prominent live location sharing service, but Loopt, Facebook Places, Foursquare and many others[1] work with the same principle of sending location updates to central servers and then distributing these updates to lists of contacts from there. That is, all mobile clients log in to this server, send regular updates of their own location as determined by the built-in GPS receiver, and receive push notifications or poll for the locations of other mobile devices. The server manages user accounts, lists of "friend" accounts who may query one's location, and enforces access control based on these lists. And

---

[1] A non-comprehensive list can e.g. be found at
http://bdnooz.com/lbsn-location-based-social-networking-links/.

R. Moreno-Díaz et al. (Eds.): EUROCAST 2011, Part II, LNCS 6928, pp. 527–535, 2012.

as Wagner et al. [1] have shown, people are cautious about when, with whom and at which granularity they share location information in social networks.

Although the approach protects users' location traces from other, non-"friend" users of the same system, it places implicit and irrevocable trust on the server operators and the specific server implementation. From a privacy point of view, this should be unacceptable, as it gives complete control over highly private data, namely the mobile phone users' complete location traces, to unknown operators with whom no legally binding contract will typically be created. And even if the users use pseudonyms, they may be identified just by their location traces as as has been shown recently by Krumm [2]. However, due to lack of alternatives – and, often, lack of awareness –, many users currently accept this potential intrusion into their privacy for increased convenience.

We therefore propose a platform to enable live location sharing without relying on any central servers that all users are forced to trust with their private location data. This requires a decentralized but globally scalable architecture for message transmission, management of "friends" lists on the mobile devices themselves, and peer-to-peer (P2P) location updates initiated by the respective sender. In this paper, we make the following contributions:

- We present *Friends Radar*, a live location sharing application that builds upon the globally available, distributed XMPP[2] messaging architecture, and has so far been implemented for the Google Android (see screenshot in Figure 2) and Samsung bada platforms (section 3). Friends Radar allows live location updates to be shared via extended XMPP status messages among arbitrary groups of "friends" as defined by group membership in the XMPP roster (section 3.1). The locations of friends can be visualized in different views, including an augmented reality (AR) view with friend positions overlaid on a live camera image (section 3.2).
- By exploiting the fully decentralized nature of the global XMPP infrastructure, there is no single point at which these highly sensitive messages may be logged or intercepted. The privacy of Friends Radar therefore depends on the number of servers used. If every user has their own XMPP server, perfect privacy protection (the optimum for the use case of intentionally sharing location data) is achieved (section 4.1).
- We contrast the P2P to central server approaches and present an initial, quantitative analysis of the involved overhead of the privacy-friendly XMPP approach in terms of the number and size of messages on clients and servers (section 4.2).

2   Related Work

In contrast to our recently proposed privacy-sensitive, spatial group messaging platform Air-Writing [3], the Friends Radar system does not rely on a central server infrastructure with privacy guarantees designed into the communication

---

[2] http://www.xmpp.org

protocol, but on direct peer-to-peer messaging. This is also in contrast to e.g. the mix zones model [4], which requires new and currently not widely deployed infrastructure components to mix location queries. In Friends Radar, we only build upon already existing infrastructure (namely public XMPP servers) and therefore support immediate deployment of our approach for practical use cases. The VIS system [5] also relies on existing infrastructure in the form of virtual machine hosting to improve client privacy while our approach is based only on mobile clients without additional (virtual) servers. A peer-to-peer protocol specifically designed for social networks is PeerSoN[3], which is still subject of ongoing research and not yet available for download.

The ContextContacts application[4] built on top of the ContextPhone platform [6] comes closest to our approach, but focuses on a broader sharing of contextual data without providing the ease-of-use and added features of specialized location sharing applications, and its current implementation is limited to Symbian S60 phones. Virtual Compass [7] is also highly relevant to Friends Radar, as the authors propose a method to derive in-door localization maps based on different radio links such as Bluetooth and WiFi; it is an orthogonal extension to our current use of GPS to support in-door scenarios and we plan to include this localization technique in future versions of Friends Radar.

3   The *Friends Radar* system

Friends Radar is a client application running on mobile phones with current implementations for Android and bada and an iPhone version under development. Communication between multiple clients is done via XMPP messages with an extension for transmitting structured location data. We first discuss the specific protocol and then provide a brief description of the current user interface.

3.1   Protocol

The Extensible Messaging and Presence Protocol (XMPP) is an open, extensible, real-time communication protocol that can be used to build a wide range of applications. Currently, it is mainly used for instant messaging and voice-over-IP (VoIP) connection set-up, e.g. by social networking platforms including Google Talk and Facebook, collaborative services like Google Wave, and geo-presence systems like Nokia Ovi Contacts. It evolved out of the early XML streaming technology developed by the Jabber Open Source community and is now considered the most flexible – and the only officially standardized – protocol for exchanging real-time structured data. The protocol itself is extensible and can be used to transport arbitrary XML elements for structured data.

One of the main advantages is that XMPP uses a decentralized structure with the possibility of public, private, or federated servers. Although public servers with free registration are available, every group can easily set up their own

---

[3] http://peerson.net/

[4] http://www.cs.helsinki.fi/group/context/

server and therefore remain in control of their instant messaging data. Standard client-to-server and server-to-server connection security based on TLS and X.509 certificates is already widely deployed and the default for many servers.

XMPP servers are responsible for session management, routing (forwarding) messages, and contact list storage. That is, a list of "friends" along with their categorization in groups is stored in the so-called *roster* on the server. In Friends Radar, only one group is used to hold all friends to which the user wants to send their location updates. Users can add and remove their contacts to/from the "follow" group within the friends view. Clients connect to servers using their *JabberID* (JID, e.g. username@ jabberserver.com/home), which is composed of a user name part, the domain, and an optional *resource identifier* (forming a full JID) that can be used to distinguish multiple concurrent clients using the same account (the account without the resource id is also called the bare JID). When a client sends a message to one of the contacts registered at a different domain, then the client connects to its home server, which then connects directly to the respective server responsible for the contact without intermediate hops.

All client-server communications is handled via XML streams. The basic unit of communication used in XMPP is called a *stanza* with three possible types: message, presence, and iq (Info/Query). Each kind of stanza is routed differently by servers and handled differently by clients. The <presence> stanza is used for contact on-line notification, status changes and contact exchange in the form of a specialized publish-subscribe method. Contacts may request subscription to presence and, if authorized by the account holder, will automatically receive notifications about the account status.

In Friends Radar, standard chat messages can be sent to contacts in any of the views. However, the main use case in Friends Radar is to exchange the users' geographical locations. XMPP does not implement exchanging location as a core feature, but defines an XMPP protocol extension for transmitting the current geographical or physical location of an entity [8]. This includes a <geoloc/> element that is qualified with the http://jabber.org/protocol/geoloc namespace and which supports various child elements for describing location information of the contact with different data types (altitude, building, country, floor, longitude, latitude, postal code, region, room, etc.). For the purposes of defining user location we use just 3 attributes: longitude, latitude and altitude. The proposed way to exchange location information is to use publish-subscribe (PUBSUB) or the subset specified in the Personal Eventing Protocol (PEP). Because PUBSUB and PEP are also just extensions to XMPP and not all public servers support them (for example gmail.com does not), we instead attach a location extension to standard presence stanzas for interoperability with most XMPP server implementations (Fig. 1 shows an example). In each implementation, the respective platform-specific location listener automatically distributes presence stanzas with an attached location update when the location of the user changes. Users can control the frequency of these location updates by specifying a minimal time interval between two updates.

```
<presence id="TIMW6-9" to="user@jabberservice.com">
   <geoloc xmlns="http://jabber.org/protocol/geoloc">
     <lat>48.422005</lat>
     <lon>14.084095</lon>
   </geoloc>
</presence>
```

Fig. 1. Example presence stanza with XEP-0080 user location extension as used in Friends Radar

3.2   User Interface

The user interface of Friends Radar provides multiple views to the locations of "friends". The main view is an augmented reality (AR) view with the friends' positions overlaid on a live camera image as shown in Figure 2, which provides the users with an awareness of the direction of their friends with respect to their line of sight. In addition, the positions of friends are shown in a radar view similar to that of the InfoRadar [9] system on the upper right corner of the AR view. There are two more views, namely a map which displays the positions of friends as well as a simple list, and they can all be selected via buttons on the top of the screen. A distinct feature of all three views is the appearance of a menu upon clicking on a user's portrait, which allows to establish a phone call, send a text message or an email, start a chat or view the profile details, which can also be seen in the Figure 2. Separate setting windows allow to make privacy settings (e.g. to define who can see the own position), edit the radius within which friends are shown or set the rate of position updates, among others.

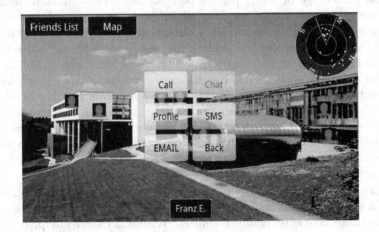

Fig. 2. Screenshot of the *Friends Radar* augmented reality view

4   Evaluation

Evaluation of Friends Radar as a system needs to cover three separate aspects: offered privacy guarantees, performance concerning network load (memory and CPU usage negligible on current smart phones), and usability. In this paper, we focus on the network aspect and therefore on privacy and performance analysis, while a future paper will more thoroughly analyze usability aspects of the different views.

4.1   Privacy

A general weakness of all friends finder type applications is that all "friends" are able to record and subsequently distribute the complete location traces they receive. An analysis of different privacy guarantees can therefore only assume other kinds of privacy threats involving third parties and explicitly exclude all contacts marked as friends by assuming them as trusted.

In all centralized approaches with caching and filtering of messages on a central server (cluster), there is an additional privacy threat that is more significant than the assumed-to-be-trusted group of friends: the server operators (which includes the administrators, company management, law enforcement, and other government bodies) have full access to *all* location traces of all users. An intentional or unintentional breach of privacy can therefore lead to large-scale profiling and detailed tracking of users, exposing their inherently private movements to unknown third parties.

Friends Radar reduces this threat significantly by eliminating this single point where all location traces are collected. The privacy guarantee offered by this decentralized approach scales directly with the number of XMPP servers (or with the percentage of direct peer-to-peer messages in contrast to using the XMPP server infrastructure, which is subject to future research). If every user runs their own XMPP server, which communicates directly and spontaneously with all other XMPP servers, we achieve the best possible privacy protection for this type of application: only the location traces of users who already marked potential attackers as a "friend" can be monitored (attackers can exploit this threat with social engineering, and this is therefore a common flaw of all social network based sharing approaches). On the other side of the spectrum, when all users connect to the same, central XMPP server (such as the services offered by Google, Facebook, or Nokia Ovi), the respective operators can again monitor and record all traces, making Friends Radar equivalent to a centralized model from a privacy point of view.

A more practical level of privacy can be achieved by running XMPP servers for coherent groups of users such as employees of a company, university students, activists in an NGO, or family members. Within a closed group, it is more likely that the server operators can be trusted not to violate user privacy. We therefore conclude that the level of privacy achieved by Friends Radar can be scaled according to user preferences by simply running private XMPP servers (which are easily set up and do not demand significant server resources).

4.2   Performance

To analyze the impact of decentralized messaging in terms of the number and size of messages in the worst-case scenario, we assume a fully-connected network of friends (i.e., each member of this group is a "friend" of all other members) of size n, in which each of the participants distributes their location with an average update frequency f (e.g. 3 updates/minute means that the current location is distributed every 20 s). We further assume the average message size to be s and be roughly constant (as it only contains the current location in terms of longitude and latitude, cf. section 3.1 for details).

   In the best-case scenario (i.e., with only few selective location updates being distributed instead of a broadcast of each location to all members of the respective group), we assume an average number m of clients that offer "interesting" location updates from the point of view of each of the local clients. Filtering interesting updates can be done manually (each user selects who they want to track) or automatically (e.g. based on a maximum destination of friends, their current activities, or common goals). Although this number can vary significantly for each of the n clients in the friends network, we define m to be the mean of all interesting (or "tracked") friends from the point of view of each client. In the worst-case scenario, $m = n$. In the best-case scenario, m does not depend on n and is assumed to be asymptotically constant. This assumption is based on the consideration that each user will typically be interested in only a limited number of friends' location updates, independently of how many friends they have in their list.

   We can now easily derive that, when using a centralized location server which handles all the location updates in terms of caching, filtering, and forwarding the update messages, each client will send $f \cdot s$ message bytes/s to the server (or, more typically, server cluster). The server will then distribute the received updates of the other group members to each client, adding an additional $(n-1) \cdot f \cdot s$ message bytes/s for each client. Therefore, each client sends or receives $n \cdot f \cdot s$ bytes/s. In a best-case analysis with centralized filtering of location updates, each client consequently sends or receives $(m+1) \cdot f \cdot s$ bytes/s, which can be a considerable improvement when compared to the worst case.

   In the Friends Radar approach, there is no centralized location server that could perform the caching and filtering of messages. For this analysis, we also assume the optimal case in terms of privacy to better highlight the penalty in terms of message overhead. That is, we assume each user to run their own XMPP server, which communicate among each other[5]. Therefore, each combination of Friends Radar client and XMPP server must generate $(n - 1) \cdot f \cdot s$ message bytes/s and send them directly to the respective recipients, causing each client to receive $(n - 1) \cdot f \cdot s$ message bytes/s in turn. Overall, each client/server combination sends or receives $2(n - 1) \cdot f \cdot s$ message bytes/s. However, our use of XMPP status messages (cf. section 3.1) allows each client to define its status message with a specific list of recipients of this status update and let the

---

[5] This assumption is unrealistic in practice, but allows us to give an upper bound on the message overhead.

Table 1. Summary of message overheads for worst-case (no filtering) and best-case (constant average number of friends each client is interested in)

	centralized location server	Friends Radar
worst-case per client	$n \cdot f \cdot s$	$2(n-1) \cdot f \cdot s$
worst-case all messages	$n^2 \cdot f \cdot s$	$n \cdot f \cdot s$ (P2P)
		$2n \cdot (n-1) \cdot f \cdot s$ (hub)
best-case per client	$(m+1) \cdot f \cdot s$	$2m \cdot f \cdot s$
best-case all messages	$n \cdot (m+1) \cdot f \cdot s$	$2n \cdot m \cdot f \cdot s$ (hub)
	$\Rightarrow O(n \cdot m)$	$\Rightarrow O(n \cdot m)$ (hub)

XMPP server generate and distribute the $n-1$ status update messages to each of the subscribers. The overhead for each client is therefore significantly smaller and is close to $f \cdot s$ message bytes/s with the overhead of attaching a recipient list of m XMPP user ids (n user ids in the worst-case scenario) to each status message. Because the decentralized model does not support centralized filtering of update messages, each client needs to decide locally to which other clients updates should be sent (assuming m for this analysis) and which updates to process (also assuming m in the best case when friend updates are co-ordinated and clients only send updates to those that will actually process them).

Considering the amount of messages in the whole network instead of a client-only point of view, the centralized case simply takes n times as many messages, resulting in a network load of $n^2 \cdot f \cdot s$ bytes/s. In the decentralized case, we need to distinguish two variations: in a fully connected peer-to-peer network (e.g. with XMPP link-local messages), we have only $n \cdot f \cdot s$ bytes/s, as each client generates one message for each update; in the XMPP infrastructure case, with XMPP servers (hubs) forwarding the messages, $2n \cdot (n-1) \cdot f \cdot s$ bytes/s are generated. For the best-case scenario, the centralized model consequently generates $n \cdot (m+1) \cdot f \cdot s$ bytes/s total messages, which is of order $O(n \cdot m)$ or $O(n)$ when m is assumed to be constant with regards to n. In the decentralized model, each client sends updates to and receives updates from all clients they are interested in, which is therefore of the same order $O(n \cdot m)$. However, taking into account the distinction between XMPP clients and XMPP servers when using status messages instead of push messages, the involved overhead can be reduced to approach the centralized case. Table 1 summarizes these analytical results.

5   Discussion and Future Outlook

In its current version, Friends Radar already supports private sharing of location among friends without relying on the trustworthiness of centralized services. It has been implemented for Android and as a prototype for Samsung bada and is currently available in a beta version from the Google Market. Next steps will include porting the Friends Radar application to other mobile platforms such as iPhone and Windows Phone 7 to make it available to a larger user base and a more systematic analysis of the different views and their advantages and disadvantages in various use cases. On the protocol side, we intend to implement the option of using XMPP link-local messages [10] based on multicast DNS and DNS-SD. In terms of localization, we will evaluate different options to make Friends Radar usable when GPS is not available or not suitable, e.g. in large in-doors environments.

Acknowledgments. The Friends Radar application code on Android and bada was developed as part of a semester project at Upper Austria University of Applied Sciences by Georg David Bauer, Matthias Braun, Daniel Fuhry, Michael Jakubec, Romana Koprivec, and Andreas Weitlaner. We are grateful to an anonymous reviewer for pointing out a flaw in our decentralized best-case performance analysis.

References

1. Wagner, D., Lopez, M., Doria, A., Pavlyshak, I., Kostakos, V., Oakley, I., Spiliotopoulos, T.: Hide and seek: location sharing practices with social media. In: Proc. MobileHCI 2010, pp. 55–58. ACM, New York (2010)
2. Krumm, J.: Inference attacks on location tracks. In: LaMarca, A., Langheinrich, M., Truong, K.N. (eds.) Pervasive 2007. LNCS, vol. 4480, pp. 127–143. Springer, Heidelberg (2007)
3. Mayrhofer, R., Sommer, A., Saral, S.: Air-Writing: A platform for scalable, privacy-preserving, spatial group messaging. In: Proc. iiWAS 2010, pp. 181–189. ACM, New York (2010)
4. Beresford, A.R., Stajano, F.: Location privacy in pervasive computing. IEEE Pervasive Computing 2(1), 46–55 (2003)
5. Cáceres, R., Shakimov, A., Cox, L., Lim, H., Varshavsky, A.: Virtual individual servers as privacy-preserving proxies for mobile devices. In: Proc. MobiHeld (2009)
6. Raento, M., Oulasvirta, A., Petit, R., Toivonen, H.: ContextPhone: A prototyping platform for context-aware mobile applications. IEEE Pervasive Computing (2005)
7. Banerjee, N., Agarwal, S., Bahl, P., Chandra, R., Wolman, A., Corner, M.: Virtual compass: Relative positioning to sense mobile social interactions. In: Floréen, P., Krüger, A., Spasojevic, M. (eds.) Pervasive Computing. LNCS, vol. 6030, pp. 1–21. Springer, Heidelberg (2010)
8. Hildebrand, J., Saint-Andre, P.: XEP-0080: User location (September 2009), http://xmpp.org/extensions/xep-0080.html; XMPP extensions standards track
9. Rantanen, M., Oulasvirta, A., Blom, J., Tiitta, S., Mäntylä, M.: Inforadar: group and public messaging in the mobile context. In: Proc. NordCHI. ACM, New York (2004)
10. Saint-Andre, P.: XEP-0174: Serverless messaging (November 2008), http://xmpp.org/extensions/xep-0174.html; XMPP extensions standards track

Hardware Sensor Aspects in Mobile Augmented Reality

Alexander Erifiu and Gerald Ostermayer

University of Applied Sciences Hagenberg
aerifiu@gmail.com,
gerald.ostermayer@fh-hagenberg.at
Softwarepark 12,
A-4232 Hagenberg, Austria

Abstract. Augmented Reality has undergone a renaissance on 3rd generation smart phones. Most of these systems heavily rely on the hardware sensory of the devices and thus are dependent on their accuracy. The paper will try to assess the quality of the sensor hardware of a 3rd generation smart phone (exemplary HTC G1/Dream) and the consequences for an Augmented Reality pedestrian navigation application (prototype). It will show that the accuracy which can be achieved by relying on sensor values is sufficient. However when testing the system prototype, it failed in certain (worst case) scenarios due to bad GPS reception or compass interference.

Keywords: Augmented reality, mobile, sensors, compass, gps, ar.

1 Introduction

With increasingly powerful hardware and the miniaturization of sensor components, Augmented Reality [3] [4] [5] has become a more and more interesting topic in mobile computing. One large field of application are pedestrian navigation applications that make heavy use of hardware sensors to render the virtual objects and paths in real-time over(laying) the camera view of the phone.

One approach to such a system was proposed by Narzt et al. [1] [2] in 2004, where nowadays smart phone hardware was still unavailable. Bringing this approach to a nowadays smart phone, the internal GPS receiver could be used to position the user, and the electronic compass and accelerometer to determine a line of vision. This means that the user is able to explore the Augmented Reality (3D–model) world by looking around freely.

If now the geographic map content is rendered into the live view of the camera the resulting question is, if the virtual objects will "match" with the ones in the real world. So to say, how accurate is an Augmented Reality navigation system that solely relies on the built in sensors of the smart phone? The paper will (exemplarily) assess the sensors from a HTC G1/Dream mobile phone to determine if the accuracy is sufficient for such an application.[1]

---

[1] These measurements were carried out as a preparation for building a Augmented Reality pedestrian navigation.

R. Moreno-Díaz et al. (Eds.): EUROCAST 2011, Part II, LNCS 6928, pp. 536–543, 2012.

2   Smartphone GPS Accuracy

To determine the GPS accuracy the deviations of latitude and longitude have to be measured. The tests took place in the open with no interfering objects and perfect reception. As reference the Garmin GPSmap 60SC was used. The Garmin device holds a differential GPS (DGPS) receiver making it highly accurate.[2]

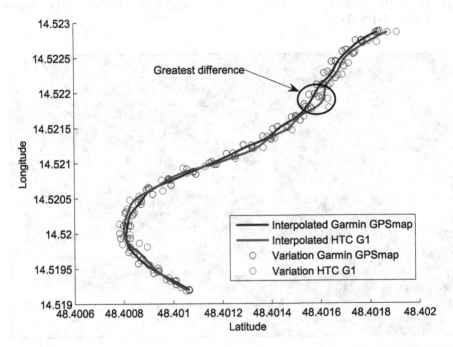

Fig. 1. Comparison of latitude / longitude between Garmin GPSmap 60SC and HTC G1. The largest difference is at 6.70 meters.

In Figure 1 the two resulting graphs from the measurements are depicted. The solid lines represent the interpolated mean values over the three measurement cycles while the circles represent the actually measured values. It can be seen that the difference between both is rather small. The greatest deviation is at 6.70 meters which already close to the defined accuracy of the Garmin device and for the usage scenario satisfactory. Moreover, the variation of the values is rather small without many discordant values. This is important because if the GPS position would be unstable so would the whole visualization, even if the user is standing still.

A scenario which also interesting when building such a system is the GPS accuracy in an urban area. To get an idea how severe the deviation compared to the ideal environment is, a second metering with the HTC G1/Dream, was

---

[2] Garmin states the values as 50% Circular Error Probable (CEP).

conducted. This time the set up was moving from and open area into an urban canyon where the GPS reception is rather weak because of shadowing and reflections. In Figure 2 the three recorded tracks (green, orange and red) can be seen, in comparison to the white line which marks the actual path. As the deviation here is rather big, a orthophoto was used to demonstrate the impact of the error. While the paths still match well in the open (upper right corner), they start to deviate once entering the urban canyon. However, on ignoring the red track, the result is acceptable although it might worsen if longer in an area with a bad GPS signal.

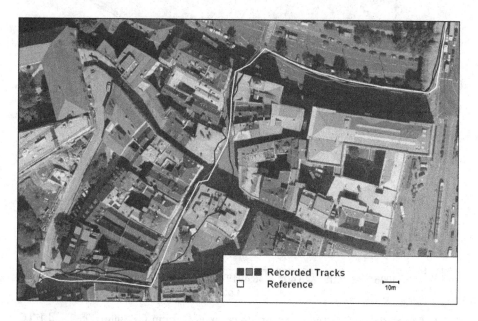

Fig. 2. Three GPS tracks recorded in central Linz (capital of Upper Austria) which show deviations on entering an urban canyon. The biggest deviation (between the red and white line) is at 20 meters. (Source: Google Earth).

Another important issue is the GPS–height, since topography is a indispensable feature in Augmented Reality. The test took place at the same location as the latitude / longitude measurements. To get a better comparison, other sources for elevation data are added. These are digital elevation models (ASTER, SRTM and GTPO30) acquired from a web service. These are not of mayor interest right now but play a significant role when creating 3D data models from 2D map systems. Analyzing the findings, it can be seen in Figure 3 that the GPS–height is quite inaccurate. Even more problematic is the very high variation of the signal, this would result in a very unstable visualization.

An alternative to bypass the erroneous GPS height would be to acquire the height from a digital elevation model via a web service. The drawback of this methods would be, that it will need more processing time than the approach

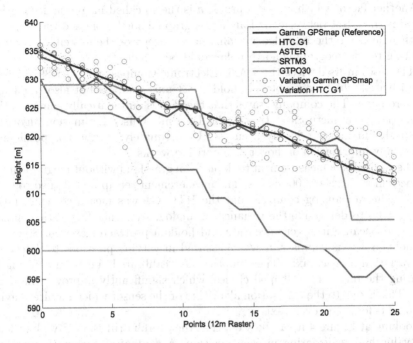

Fig. 3. Accuracy comparison of the height information between Garmin GPSmap 60SC, HTC G1 and Digital Elevation Models

based on the GPS height. Not only CPU–time, but also time to permanently request data from the web service. Moreover, the user will need a permanent data connection to acquire the height from a web service. The ideal solution would be to construct a 3D mesh representing the topography of the whole area. All the geo–objects and the user could then be placed on it.

3   Electronic Compass

Electronic compasses have been around for quite a while but are a rather new addition to smart phones. The compass holds a key role in the Augmented Reality system, for it is needed to determine in which direction the user is looking. A closer examination of the used sensor and its characteristics is therefore necessary to understand the restrictions of this technology. The electronic compass holds three magnetic sensors and three accelerometer sensors in an orthogonal configuration. As the Earth's magnetic field is a quite weak signal they are very vulnerable to distortions in this field. So the difficulty is, to measure a very weak signal while there are heavy interferences, not only from the surrounding environment but also from the phone's radio chip and other components.

Another factor which causes a problem is the so called magnetic declination, which is the offset between the Earth's geographic north pole and the magnetic north pole[3]. For the intended visualization concept of the system, a compass pointing to the geographic north pole would be beneficial.

HTC uses in its devices the 6 Axis Electronic Compass Chip AK8976A from Asahi Kasei, which does not only hold the 3–axis compass but also the 3–axis accelerometer. The company states that the chip is automatically compensating magnetic offset fluctuations trough the Dynamic Offset Estimation algorithm which should make it highly accurate. Unfortunately, it was not possible to gather any information on how this algorithm works.

The comparison measurement took place on grassland without magnetic interferences in a radius of 300 meters. The measurement set up was aligned towards north using an analog compass and the HTC G1 was measured against this fixed set up to determine the variance. A analog, liquid filled, lensatic compass was used because it is very accurate and holds a protractor as well. Since the G1 holds a 3–axis compass, it was measured in varying positions to determine the variation on each axis. The compass was "calibrated" before measuring by rotating the phone in 8–shaped circles, which significantly improves the accuracy. This is due to the calibration algorithm of the sensor which requires having reasonable forces on every axis.

Looking at Figure 4 it can be seen, that the overall drift is at 5° with at least one value highly deviating in each position. A drift of 5° means that objects in 100 meters distance are about 9 meters off their actual position while in 500 meters they are already 44 meters off.[4] This drift is not an as big problem on close distances but if trying to visualize a very distant object, for example a hiking path winding up a mountain, it can become quite an issue. If the compass error and the GPS error (which is more problematic on close distances) add up to a worst case scenario, it could result in the visualization being inaccurate on near and far. On the right side of Figure 4 it can be seen that the variance of the values is rather low. This fact could be used to further correct the values.

Further on, the compass values fluctuate at ±2° which can result in the objects slightly flickering aside. To prevent this flickering, it is obligatory for the implementation to filter the compass values. Another issue is that the compass is very sensitive to magnetic interference. Inside a car the variation shifts between 20° and 50° depending on the position in the car. Especially near (approx. 20cm) the radio, speakers, wiring loom and metal frame the deviation is very high. Large metal structures such as handrails, bridges or electricity pylons can cause heavy inaccuracies as well. Small metal objects like wrist watches can lead to the same behavior, if brought close enough (1cm) to the sensor.

Summarizing this behavior, it can be said that all (iron containing) metal structures and or magnetic fields can and do interfere with the compass, while the parameters hereby are the size of the structure and the distance to it. The characteristic of the deviation is, that at a certain distance (on the scale of the

---

[3] The distance between both north poles was 2005 approximately 800km.
[4] Calculated using the law of cosines.

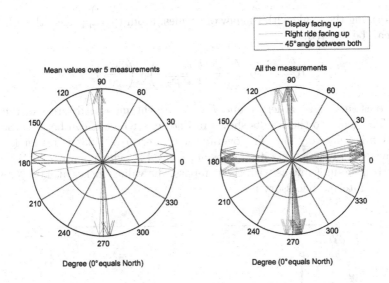

Fig. 4. Compass drift measurement on a HTC G1. As reference a analog map compass was used.

object–size) the values slightly start to drift, till they get random or the compass completely stalls.

4   Accelerometer

Acceleration sensors moved into cell phones some time ago with the Nokia 5500 released in 2006, being the first device with such a sensor. Nowadays many smart phones hold an accelerometer and many applications make use of it. In the context of the prototype the acceleration sensor is, simply put, needed to determine if the user is looking up or down – in other words the tilt of the phone. The tilt is the counter–part of the compass direction for it is used to position the objects vertically, while the compass is used for horizontal positioning. For the tilt the same restrictions apply as for the compass in terms of accuracy, only that in this situation the objects will be displayed above or under their real world position.

As described in the last Section the AK8976A chip used by HTC contains a 3–axis accelerometer. Earth's gravitational acceleration $g = 9,80665\frac{m}{s^2}$ is compared to its magnetic field rather strong and cannot be interfered with that easy. This means that the accelerometer is less vulnerable to interferences than the electronic compass. Nevertheless, it is important to determine how accurate this sensor is, as it holds a key role as well.

The measurement was set up on a carefully leveled out glass plate, where the phone was mounted with a ball bearing hinge and tilted in 10° steps between 0° and 90°. The Y–axis was hereby used to determine if the tilt was symmetric. The angle was calculated by determining the resulting force vectors and then transforming the angle with the law of cosines. From this approach the following term can be derived,

$$\alpha = \arccos\left(\frac{Fx}{\sqrt{Fx^2 + Fz^2}}\right) * \left(\frac{360}{2\pi}\right),$$

where α is the angle in degree and Fx, Fz are the measured forces of the axes in $\frac{m}{s^2}$. This leads to the results shown in Figure 5, where it can be seen that the deviation is relatively low. The overall median error of 1.38° is rather low and the deviation of the points itself does not exceed 2° which is a very satisfactory result. But again, same as with the compass, the values flicker at $\pm 0.1 \frac{m}{s^2}$, which will make filtering necessary too.

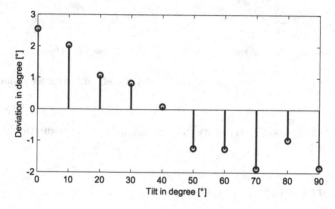

Fig. 5. Accelerometer median error measurement of the AK8976A chip. The values represent mean values over 3 measurements. The median deviation is at 1.38°.

5   Conclusion

Testing the prototype has shown that the measured accuracy of the sensors (except the GPS–height) is sufficient[5]. The GPS acquired height from the device is too inaccurate to be used, thus another source[6] for this information had to be found. Furthermore the values from the accelerometer and compass had to be filtered due to the heavy jitter and the compass heading had to be corrected to determine the geographic north pole.

The visualization itself is surprisingly accurate with proper sensor values and the mentioned corrections. Two scenarios upon use can be distinguished. The first one can be seen in Figure 6a, where the user is far away from the visualized object and the compass precision is of major concern. The second one is shown in Figure 6b where the user is standing "on the path" and the GPS position

---

[5] All the sensors might fail if strong interferences occur such as magnetic fields which affect the compass or high buildings which deflect the GPS signal.

[6] ASTER DEM data.

needs to be very accurate (±2 meters). In both scenarios the divergence in the visualization was acceptable since the virtual and "real" objects are overlapping quite well. However another issue was observed: The absolute position of the camera towards the sensor chip was off by some degrees on the tested model which created a constant offset[7] between the camera and accelerometer. This offset required a calibration and may be device dependent.

In summary it can be said that with the advancement of technology in the mobile sector the sensors might become more accurate and therefore the whole system will gain more accuracy.

(a) A distant mountain with a path (red) winding up to the top. The peak is a point of interest.

(b) A street in an urban area with a crossroad shortly ahead.

Fig. 6. Screenshots from the prototype in different situations

References

1. Narzt, W., Pomberger, G., Ferscha, A.: A New Visualization Concept for Navigation Systems, pp. 440–451. Springer, Heidelberg (2004)
2. Narzt, W., Pomberger, G., Ferscha, A.: Augmented Reality Navigation Systems, pp. 177–187. Springer, Heidelberg (2004)
3. Azuma, R.: A Survey of Augmented Reality. Teleoperators and Virtual Enviroments 6(4), 355–385 (1997)
4. Zhou, F., Duh, H.B.-L.: Trends in Augmented Reality Tracking, Interaction and Display: A Review of Ten Years of ISMAR. In: IEEE International Symposium on Mixed and Augmented Reality 2008, pp. 193–202 (2008)
5. Milgram, P., Takemura, H.: Augmented Reality: A class of displays on the Reality–Virtuality continuum. In: SPIE, vol. 2351, pp. 282–292 (1997)

---

[7] +4° vertical, +2° horizontal.

Mobile Platform Architecture Review: Android, iPhone, Qt

Michael Lettner, Michael Tschernuth, and Rene Mayrhofer

Upper Austria University of Applied Sciences, Research and Development
Softwarepark 11, 4232 Hagenberg, Austria

Abstract. The recent proliferation of mobile platforms makes it difficult for developers to find the most appropriate platform for one's needs or even target multiple ones. A review of key concepts on Android, iPhone and Qt points out important commonalities and differences that will help to better understand the respective platform characteristics. As mobility is an important aspect of such phones, the ability to access mobile-specific functionality is investigated. Implications at every concept visited will then point out things to keep in mind as a developer.

1 Motivation

The last couple of years have seen smartphone sales take off. While this hype mainly started out with the introduction of the first iPhone in 2007, more mobile platforms have been introduced since, and competition is intensifying. Due to this fragmentation, targeting an application for multiple markets, devices or operators has become increasingly difficult. As cross-platform development tools are rare yet, developers have to face a decision on which platforms their native application should be supported first, or ported to later on. Market share, ease of development, popularity, an active developer community, usability and target group are all factors for consideration when favoring one platform over the other.

Developers on the other hand would prefer to implement an application once, and deploy it for many platforms with minimal effort. To enable such a scenario, programmers must know the very differences between the platforms in question. This work will try to compare popular mobile platforms in terms of capabilities and point out the most significant differences in platform concepts (which subsequently make it difficult to enable write-once, deploy-anywhere applications). Such an analysis will help the developer to understand which parts of a system may be more suitable for reuse, and which may not—the conclusion will also try to address these questions. The work will also be beneficial for somebody trying to raise an application's abstraction level to support multiple platforms—one such project, though targeted at low-cost mobile platforms, is introduced in [5].

2 Methodology

The comparison focuses on three platforms: the underlying platform of the iPhone [2], Android [1], and Qt [3,4].

R. Moreno-Díaz et al. (Eds.): EUROCAST 2011, Part II, LNCS 6928, pp. 544–551, 2012.
© Springer-Verlag Berlin Heidelberg 2012

The first one is the one that started the recent hype, the second one is gaining more and more momentum and becoming increasingly popular, while Qt is increasingly used for Symbian development, an operating system (OS) that has been around for a much longer time, and must be taken into account not least due to its status of the system with the most widespread use. Despite the recent announcement by Nokia[1] to use Microsoft's Windows Phone OS on Nokia's devices to create a new global mobile ecosystem, Qt will still play a key role on Nokia's expected 150 million units[2] that will ship with Symbian in the years to come, and is the development environment of choice for Intel's MeeGo platform—a platform not only targeted at mobile phones or netbooks, but intended to be used in TV sets, set-top boxes or In-Vehicle Infotainment systems.

After a basic introduction to all of the beforementioned platforms, their architecture will be analyzed, and commonalities and differences in terms of platform capabilites will be pointed out.

3   Platform Introduction

Android: is an open-source software stack created for mobile phones and other devices that includes an OS, middleware and key applications [1]. It is based on Linux kernel version 2.6 to provide core system services such as security, memory management, process management, network stack, and driver model. The Dalvik virtual machine (VM)—optimized for minimal memory footprint— executes Android applications usually written in Java that were first converted into Dalvik Executable format. From a developer's perspective, it is the Android SDK that provides the tools and APIs required for developing applications.

iPhone: iOS is the mobile OS of Apple's iPhone series. It is based on the same technologies used by Mac OS X, namely the Mach kernel and BSD interfaces, thus making it a UNIX-based system [2]. Applications are primarily developed using Objective-C—a superset of ANSI C extended with syntactical and semantic features (derived from Smalltalk) to support object-oriented programming. Cocoa Touch is the application environment to build applications for iOS and consists of a suite of object-oriented libraries, a runtime, and an integrated development environment (e.g., XCode or Interface Builder). Two core frameworks are essential to application development: the Foundation and the UIKit.

Qt: Opposed to the previously discussed platforms, Qt is not limited to one specific OS. Instead, Qt is a cross-platform application and UI framework, including desktop and mobile target platforms such as Windows, Linux, Symbian or MeeGo. Qt comes with a C++ class library and integrated development tools. Bindings for a wide range of other languages exist, e.g. Java, C# or Ruby.

---

[1] http://press.nokia.com/2011/02/11/nokia-and-microsoft-announce-plans-for-a-broad-strategic-partnership-to-build-a-new-global-ecosystem/

[2] http://qt.nokia.com/products/qt-for-mobile-platforms/

4   Platform Comparison

Important concepts such as memory management, user interface realization or communication, just to name a few, are provided by all platforms in one way or the other. This section will outline these basic concepts and find differences/commonalities between the platforms in question.

4.1   OS/Platform-specific

Memory Management. Proper memory management is essential to all computer systems, but due to the memory-constrained nature of smartphones it is especially important on mobile platforms. Therefore, it is indispensable to deallocate objects that are no longer needed—which could either be taken care of by the system, or be an important necessity to be carried out by the developer.

Android: Android applications rely on automatic memory management handled by Dalvik's garbage collector (GC), which, as Google states, can sometimes cause performance issues if you are not careful with memory allocations [1]. Each process uses a separate GC instance—thus, the collectors don't interfere with instances of other applications. The type employed by Dalvik is known as tracing GC and utilizes a *mark-and-sweep* approach [6]: In a first step, the collector instance keeps mark bits to indicate that a particular object is "reachable" and therefore should not be garbage collected [7]. In a second phase all objects are collected that are marked as such. The biggest advantage of the mark-and-sweep algorithm is its ability to correctly identify and collect garbage even in the presence of reference cycles [8], whereas the major disadvantage is the fact that program execution must be halted to run the algorithm.

iPhone: Objective-C supports two concepts for memory management: automatic garbage collection and reference counting [2].

- *Garbage collection:* although introduced in Objective-C 2.0, an automatic memory management mechanism is not available on iOS (i.e., it is only supported by Mac OS X version 10.5 and higher). It would allow to pass responsibility for determining the lifetime of objects to an *automatic collector*.
- *Reference counting:* denotes a technique of memory management on iOS, where an object carries a numerical value reflecting the current claims on the object. When this value reaches zero, the object is deallocated [2]. It is the developer's responsibility to determine the lifetime of objects by balancing each call that claims object ownership (object allocation/copying, or a retain message) with a call that removes that claim (i.e., release or autorelease).

Qt: Qt follows an approach that is a certain variation of object ownership [4]: As most classes are derived from QObject, instances of all such classes are placed in a hierarchy of QObject instances. Then, when a parent object is deleted, its children are deleted, too. To mimic automatic memory management, one could allocate the parent on the stack, which would automatically destruct all dynamically allocated child objects when the parent element goes out of scope.

Implications: The platforms differ in the ways they handle memory—the biggest difference being in whether a GC is provided or not. Having one, as on Android, is not an insurance against memory leaks though[3], since references can still be held that prevent the GC from collecting certain objects. If performance is a crucial criterion in an application, the overhead of a GC might adversely affect the runtime behavior. Android's mark-and-sweep algorithm required to suspend normal program execution, disallowing any runtime predictability. Applying design principles[4] is one way to workaround performance issues. In addition, there is the possibility to develop performance-critical portions in native code. On Android, starting with Native Development Kit release r5[5], entire applications (i.e., including the whole application lifecycle) can be developed this way in C++.

When a code generator is used to generate the platform code from an abstract model (as in [5]), for languages not supporting automated garbage collection memory management design patterns [9] can be incorporated into generation rules—e.g., static or pool allocation patterns might be used internally while the implementation complexity is hidden from the programmer.

Communication between Components. This section deals with ways of communication between objects or components inside applications, from a developer's perspective. It is not meant to be understood as communication in the meaning of telecommunication and/or messaging between end users.

Android: To pass information from one screen to another, Android uses *Intents*—an asynchronous way to communicate between components (in Android terms, these are Activities, Services, Broadcast receivers and Content providers). All but the last of the beforementioned components can be activated using asynchronous messages, so-called Intents, which are objects holding the content of the message.

iPhone: On iPhone, there is not a single comparable concept of how to pass information between objects. Instead, the programmer can use the built-in capabilites of Objective C, such as Delegates, Notifications or Target/Action mechanism to pass information along screens.

Qt: Qt utilizes a concept known as *Signals and Slots* to enable communication between components—another asynchronous way of message passing between objects. Qt Widgets have either predefined signals, or can be customized with own signals. On occurrence of a specified event, a certain signal is being emitted. At the receiving end, other objects can define slots (or make use of predefined ones), which are normal C++ methods that match a signal's signature. When signals and slots are connected, code defined in slots is executed on emission of events. A strength of this scheme is that signals can be connected to multiple slots, while each slot can receive signals from multiple source objects. The execution order is not defined if multiple slots are connected to the same signal.

---

[3] http://android-developers.blogspot.com/2009/01/avoiding-memory-leaks.html

[4] http://developer.android.com/guide/practices/design/performance.html

[5] http://developer.android.com/sdk/ndk/index.html

Implications: As the mentioned communication patterns are very platform-specific, it is hard to compare them:
Commonalities:

- All three platforms have a truly asynchronous communication system in place where (multiple) events can be bound to (multiple) operations. The internal implementation is substantially different though.
- The mechanisms can be utilized to register for any notifications that report system changes to one's application (e.g., the battery level changes).
- Intents/Notifications/Signals can all be used to trigger lifecycle state changes.

Differences:

- Granularity level
  - Intents are used to pass information between Activities, Services or Broadcast receivers. They operate on a "whole screen" or service.
  - Notifications and Signals can be used to pass information between any kind of objects, be it either fine-granular to notify somebody when a single GUI element changes, or coarse-granular, e.g. on application level to react when certain system events arrive.
- Inter-process Communication (IPC)
  - Intents can be used for inter-application communication (implicit Intents, no receiving component specified, late-binding), or intra-app communication (explicit Intents, receiving component specified, early-binding).
  - Notifications are limited to intra-application communication on iOS.

Security

Android: Security mechanisms incorporated in Android span different levels [10]:

- *Operating system / VM level:* First, every application runs in its own Linux process, where each process has its own VM: Code runs isolated from all other applications' code. As each application is associated with a unique Linux user ID, permissions are set so that all application files are only visible to that user and application itself by default [1]. Together, these mechanisms create a sandbox that prevents one application from interfering with another.
- *Application level:* By explicitly declaring permissions, an application could get access to additional capabilites not provided by the basic sandbox. The user has to grant those permissions at installation time, as they have been statically declared in Android's manifest file.

iPhone: Similar to Android, iPhone applications are put in a sandbox that restricts the application to using only its own files and preferences, and limits the system resources to which the application has access. Unlike Android, there are no explicit permissions to grant on application level—all applications are equal and can use many of the provided phone capabilities (e.g., getting Internet access) without the user knowing. Due to the sandbox, they do not have direct access to the underlying communications or networking hardware though.

Qt: As Qt just comprises a cross-platform library, the security concepts inherent to the platform depend on the target OS in question. Qt itself doesn't have built-in security on a comparable level. As the focus of this review is on Qt for mobile platforms, relevant mechanisms have been discussed for Symbian [11], [12]. MeeGo will have its own security concept—still subject to definition though.

Implications

- *Open-source vs. closed-source:* Different implications of openness have been discussed. While some[6] suggest that iOS software is more secure since Android's open-source software stack can be investigated and understood by hackers, this circumstance is double-edged. It might be seen as advantage[7], since security issues can be detected and fixed faster by a bigger community. Thus, security can improve faster over time than on closed systems.
- *Approval process:* Another yet not discussed big difference on Android vs. iPhone is their strategy of application approval in their respective application stores. While Google doesn't vet applications at all, Apple is very restrictive on what is getting approved—which also adversely affects the approval time, making Android more suitable for quick prototyping, timely bugfixing or research work. Still, these measures cannot prevent somebody to publish malicious software—e.g., by activating the malicious part after a certain time period, the screening process during approval can be circumvented and tricked easily. However, what Apple could prevent is certain identity fraud—publishing an application as another author, e.g. by falsely providing the name of a big company, would most certainly be denied.
- *Sandboxing:* It should be noted that Android's and iPhone's sandbox mechanism is no means to prevent attacks, but rather a way of limiting the damage attackers could cause. Consequently, good programming practices such as carefully validating user input still apply.

4.2 Mobile-Specific

Access to Mobile-specific APIs. Functions such as telephony, texting or SIM access are at the core of each mobile phone. Their accessibility and abstraction levels are being discussed (e.g., can a call be set-up using a top-level API?).

Android: As Android was specifically designed with mobile devices in mind, the Application Framework layer in Android exports all required functionality to utilize mobile-specific services. Examples are the classes *TelephonyManager* for call- or sim-related functions (such as setting up a call, or retrieving the operator's name), the *SmsManager* (to send/receive text messages), or the *LocationManager* (e.g., to retrieve the current location).

---

[6] http://www.businessweek.com/news/2011-01-11/google-android-more-vulnerable-than-iphone-antivirus-maker-says.html

[7] http://tech.shantanugoel.com/2010/06/26/android-vs-iphone-security-models.html

iPhone: On iPhone, accessing core phone functionalities programmatically is more limited. For example, SMS can only be sent via the default SMS application, not from within an app (exception: iOS4 introduced some way of in-app form to prepopulate SMS form, but still, user must explicitly choose to send SMS). Another example is the limited access to network information—e.g., retrieving the signal strength is not officially supported (there are private frameworks that enable that—but it is not sure that Apple will approve apps that utilize such features). For access to other phone-relevant functionalities secondary frameworks exist, such as Core Location, Address Book or Map Kit.

Qt: Since Qt traditionally targets non-mobile operating systems such as Windows or Linux, too, it has not been designed specifically for mobile-specific use cases. To access specific features intrinsic to mobility, the Qt Mobility APIs have been introduced. These APIs grant access to the most commonly needed mobility features in a cross-platform fashion, i.e. without forcing the developer to implement platform-dependent native code like Symbian C++ [4].However, for not exposed functionality developers have to use platform-specific solutions. In Symbian, this could either be achieved by directly integrating Symbian C++ native code, or by using wrappers that expose those mobile extensions in a Qt-like API [4]—with the advantage of reducing native Symbian's steep learning curve.

Core Phone Functionality. The following section investigates how using certain phone functionality differs on the various platforms. A concrete example is used to illustrate this: placing a simple call from one's application.

Android: Uses Intent mechanism to notify other activities:

```
Intent i = new Intent(Intent.ACTION_CALL, Uri.parse("tel:+12345"));
i.addFlags(Intent.FLAG_ACTIVITY_NEW_TASK);
i.setClassName(mApp, PhoneApp.getCallScreenClassName());
mApp.startActivity(i);
```

Additionally, proper permissions must be granted in Manifest.xml:
```
<uses-permission id="android.permission.CALL_PHONE"/>
```

iPhone: Uses *Phone Link* concept (= URL scheme) to place a call (or SMS/email):

```
NSURL *phoneNumber = [[NSURL alloc] initWithString: @"tel:+12345"];
[[UIApplication sharedApplication] openURL: phoneNumber];
```

Qt: With the current version of Qt Mobility APIs 1.1, placing a telephone call is not yet supported (precisely speaking, the Telephony Events API from beta version has been removed/discontinued). Instead, one has to use platform-specific extensions. For Symbian, the easiest way is to utilize Qt Mobile Extensions:

```
XQTelephony *telephony = new XQTelephony(this);
telephony->call("+12345");
```

Implications: All platforms allow to incorporate basic phone functionality—although, despite Qt's claims to provide a cross-platform library, certain features could only be tapped into using platform-specific extensions. Another possible consequence was the possible exclusion from an application store if inofficial APIs were used for a certain functionality. It was pointed out that some features are not accessible on certain platforms at all—for example, an Emergency Service application on iPhone would not be able to send automated SMS notifications.

5   Conclusion

After a short introduction of the basic concepts on all three platforms key areas have been investigated in more detail. Due to certain limitations, it was pointed out that not every type of application is suited to be implemented on every platform. An unpredictable execution time resulting from Android's memory management concept suggested that the standard SDK might not be the library of choice for performance-critical applications such as games or applications with real-time constraints. Likewise, not obeying the application store rules of Apple, Google and the likes could lead to applications not being allowed or removed from the respective stores—a criterion that is better investigated thoroughly before chosing a platform. The APIs exposed to access mobile-specific functionality differ on the various platforms—it should be doublechecked whether the desired feature/information (e.g., reading phone signal strength) is accessible.

References

1. Android Developers Guide, http://developer.android.com
2. iOS Dev Center, http://developer.apple.com/devcenter/ios
3. Qt Developer Network, http://developer.qt.nokia.com/
4. Fitzek, F.H.P., Mikkonen, T., Torp, T.: Qt for Symbian. Wiley & Sons Ltd, United Kingdom (2010)
5. Lettner, M., Tschernuth, M.: Applied MDA for Embedded Devices: Software Design and Code Generation for a Low-Cost Mobile Phone. In: 34th Annual IEEE Computer Software and Applications Conference Workshops, pp. 63–68 (2010)
6. Android, D.: Source Code, http://android.git.kernel.org/?p=platform/dalvik.git;a=blob_plain;f=vm/alloc/MarkSweep.c
7. Ehringer, D.: The Dalvik Virtual Machine Architecture, Techn. report (March 2010)
8. Preiss, B.R.: Data Structures and Algorithms with Object-Oriented Design Patterns in Java. John Wiley & Sons Ltd, Chichester (1999)
9. Douglass, B.P.: Real-Time Design Patterns: Robust Scalable Architecture for Real-Time Systems. Addison-Wesley, Reading (2002)
10. IEEE Security and Privacy 8(2), 35–44 (2010)
11. Heath, C.: Symbian OS Platform Security. John Wiley & Sons, Chichester (2006)
12. Badura, T., Becher, M.: Testing the Symbian OS Platform Security Architecture. In: Advanced Information Networking and Applications, AINA 2009, pp. 838–844 (2009)

Routing with Free Geodata on Mobile Devices

Karl-Heinz Kastner[1] and Gerald Ostermayer[2]

[1] Risc Software GmbH, Softwarepark 35,
4232 Hagenberg, Austria
[2] Upper Austria University of Applied Sciences,
Mobile Computing, Softwarepark 11,
4232 Hagenberg, Austria

Abstract. Routing on mobile devices is only restrictedly realizable, because of the limited resources (memory, processor performance). On the other hand, until recently only financially strong companies were able to provide solutions for this problem because of the high costs of the geographic data involved in this task. We propose a solution consisting of a combination of hierarchical routing and shortest path bidirectional A* algorithm. When tested on the Austrian street map, our method solved routing problems about ten times faster than Dijkstra algorithm. The underlying data structure for the geo-data on the mobile device is a modified quad-tree. The basic street data has been extracted from OpenStreetMap (OSM), a project started in 2004 which provides free geographic data.

Keywords: Routing framework, Speedup technics, Mobile systems.

1 Introduction

The sale volumes of smartphones in the year 2010 increased enormously [1]. The new generation provides dual core processors, Bluetooth, GPS and operating systems like Android, IOS or w7 mobile. Their configurations satisfy all requirements for on-board or off-board routing. The advantage of on-board is the inclusion of all the maps on the mobile phone. The software causes no additional costs; off-board navigation when abroad can be very expensive because of roaming fees. The disadvantage of on-board navigation is the price of the included map data. OpenStreetMap(OSM)[1], the main provider of free geographic data, solves this problem. The project was started in the year 2004, with the aim to collect free geographical information and build up a world map. However, the raw data of OSM is not suitable for routing and too big for mobile device.

In this paper we describe our solution for routing problems on mobile devices. We combine *hierarchical routing* with *shortest path bidirectional A* algorithm*. Hierarchical routing is an approach to find the shortest path by first arranging roads in a hierarchical manner, with e.g. quadtrees as underlying data structures. Shortest path bidirectional A* algorithm searches the path by running two A*

---

[1] http://www.openstreetmap.org/

R. Moreno-Díaz et al. (Eds.): EUROCAST 2011, Part II, LNCS 6928, pp. 552–559, 2012.

in opposite directions. Applications implementing our algorithm were tested on Austrian street map data, which was extracted from OpenStreetMap. When compared to an implementation of the standard Dijkstra algorithm, our approach reached the solution about 10 times faster.

The data of OpenStreetMap requires a pre-processing step, which is explained in Section 2. It consists of generating a data structure suitable for routing, and its preparation for a mobile device – which has limited working memory [2].

In Section 3 we introduce the terms *bidirectional A* algorithm* and *hierarchical routing*. A list of relevant related works is shortly considered and the concepts are detailed, as well as the basic idea of our solution: fast bidirectional shortest path computation with a speed-up offered by hierarchical routing techniques.

Section 4, contains a detailed description of our algorithm.

In Section 5 we present the result of different applications on mobile and desktop devices. We apply our method to the computation of some long routes and record the performance.

2   Pre-processing the OSM Data

By now the data of OpenStreetMap for urban areas is quite accurate. In the rural area OSM data isn't always complete, but for the calculation of long routes this is insignificant.

The OSM data consists of *nodes, ways, relations* and *attributes*; a small example is shown in Figure 1a. This data is too rich and hardly suitable for routing. In the first step the aim of the pre-processing is the generation of a graph structure; applied to the example showed in Figure 1a, it gives the simpler structure depicted in Figure 1b.

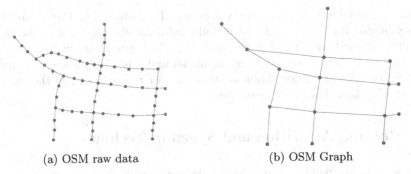

(a) OSM raw data   (b) OSM Graph

Fig. 1. Comparison of the raw data and the graph

The graph obtained after pre-processing consists of nodes and directed weighted edges. The nodes are the crossroads and endpoints and the edges are the connections between them [3] [4]. The generation comprises the following steps:

- **Extraction of streets** - The edges of the OSM data are signed with road tags.

- **Identification of crossroads** - Every node, which is used by ways two times and more is a crossroad
- **Calculation of distances between crossroads** - The distance between two crossroads is the sum of the distances between all nodes lying between them.
- **Reduction of Nodes and Edges** - A node with only two edges can be eliminated. The attributes of the edges must be combined.

This graph is suitable for routing-process but too big to handle with the memory of a smartphone. The graph must be segmented into parts. In our approach we administrate the graph in a hierarchical quad-tree shown in figure 2a.

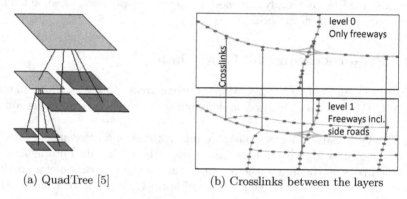

(a) QuadTree [5]   (b) Crosslinks between the layers

Fig. 2. A Quadtree with the crosslinks between the layers

In the first layer the graph only includes the motorways. The second layer is segmented into four parts and includes additionally the main roads. In the segmented third layer are all roads available. The figure 2b shows that the lower layers have additional crosslinks to the higher and every layer knows its children and its parent. This information is important for the routing and the search is not strictly bounded to one map sector.

3   Routing Algorithm and Speedup Technics

When planning holiday trips, drivers do not usually look for shortest ways; they rather prefer motorways, known roads or ways with good connectivity. The speed-up technique "hierarchical routing" incorporates these preferences and uses the following approach [6]:

- Look for the next reasonable motorway.
- Drive on motorways to a location close to the target.
- Leave the motorway and search the target starting from the motorway exit.

The technique doesn't look for shortest or fastest path; instead, it computes a good approximation. By preferring the motorways the algorithm can miss short-cuts (for example through a city); on the other hand the route avoids small city streets and makes it easier for the driver. The pre-condition of this technique is a proper development of the road network and a consistent and complete tagging of all the roads - for example main road or motorway. In the year 2002 Jagadeesh et. al.[7] developed an approach for this speed-up technique "hierarchical rout-ing". They transferred the geo-data of Singapore for the search of the shortest path in a two-layer hierarchical data structure. The second layer includes every street and the first layer only the freeways. The algorithm in a first step calcu-lates the distances to access points with Dijkstra or A*. These points have a link to nodes in the upper hierarchies. In a second step, the algorithm calculates the distances between these nodes, as elements in the first layer.

The hierarchical routing calculates paths by advancing from the start- and the end-node toward each other. In 2005 Goldberg and Harrelson[8] developed a version of the bidirectional A*, which also follows this approach. The algorithm calculates the route alternately in forward and backward search until an active node u is found from both directions. The length of current shortest path μ between the start point s and the destination point t is given with the following formula, where $g_v(u)$ is the path cost in the forward and $g_r(u)$ is the path cost in the backward search.

$$\mu = g_v(u) + g_r(u) \tag{1}$$

The computation proceeds until the following condition is fulfilled:

$$\mu \le g(u) + h(u) \tag{2}$$

Equation 2 compares the obtained shortest-path, with the sum of the path costs $g(u)$ to the current active point and the estimated costs $h(u)$ to the endpoint. The shortest path is found when the sum of these two values is equal or greater than the length of the shortest path.

4   Bidirectional Hierarchical Routing

In our work we combined the hierarchical routing from Jagadeesh et. al. and the bidirectional A* from Goldberg and Harrelson in a framework for mobile devices which optimizes the computation of long paths. Figure 3 shows this technique on a roadmap, where a search begins from the start- and the end-point marked by red dots to each other. The roads are arranged according to importance follows: side roads, main roads, highways, expressways and motorways.

In the first routing step the algorithm considers all roads in a small radius; outside this radius the algorithm does not consider the side roads. Farther away from the nodes the algorithm discards all mainroads, and then highways and so on. This procedure is ketched in Figure 3.

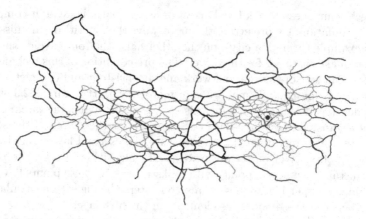

Fig. 3. Roads considered by the bidirectional hierarchical routing [9]

Algorithm 1. Hierarchical bidirectional A*-Algorithmus

1: INIT (G, Q_v, Q_r, s, t, cp)
2: **while** $Q_v \neq \emptyset \wedge Q_r \neq \emptyset$ **do**
3:     $u \leftarrow$ EXTRACT-MIN(Q_v)
4:     **for all** $v \in$ Adj(u) **do**
5:         RELAX(Q_v, u, v)
6:     **end for**
7:     $w \leftarrow$ EXTRACT-MIN(Q_r)
8:     **for all** $x \in$ Adj(w) **do**
9:         RELAX(Q_r, w, x)
10:     **end for**
11:     **if** (u visited by both searches) **then**
12:         SETCROSSPOINT$(u, w, \mu, crosspoint)$
13:     **end if**
14:     **if** ($\mu \leq g_v[u] + h_v(u) \vee \mu \leq g_r[w] + h_r(w)$) **then**
15:         **return** SHORTESTPATHCROSS$(G, crosspoint)$
16:     **end if**
17: **end while**

Our approach is presented in Algorithm 1 and is optimized for priority queues. In a first step the algorithm calls the INIT method, which initializes the forward-queue Q_v, the backward-queue Q_r, the start- and the end-point and the cross-node. Additionally the method inserts the start- and end-point into the queues. In the main step of the algorithm the search loop runs till a solution is found or one off the two queues is empty. In this loop the algorithm extracts the node u with the minimal costs, computed as the sum of the the path costs $g(u)$ and the estimated costs $h(u)$. The estimated costs are the straight line distance to the end node of the route. In the next step the Relax Method (Algorithm 2) is called. The BiStar.RELAX Method tests whether we can improve the shortest path to v found so far by going through u and if so, update the path costs g[v].

Algorithm 2. RELAX (Q, u, v)

1: **if** $(CheckNode(Q, u, v))$ **then**
2:     $BiStar.RELAX(Q, u, v)$
3: **end if**

The algorithm 2 calls before BiStar.RELAX the CheckNode Method. This function realizes the hierarchical routing. It checks one of the following verification:

Check the covered distance(DBi*) This Method checks the distance, as in the figure 3. If the path costs exceed a value, the algorithm only inserts more significant roads. $gDist(typ(u, v)) > d[u] + g(u, v)$
Check the road typ(RTBi*) The function is true, when the type of the new node is equals or higher. $typ(u) >= typ(u, v)$
Check the crosslink The search jumps in a higher layer, if a crosslink is available. $u == crosslink$

After appending new nodes into the queue, Algorithm 1 repeats the same sequence for the reverse search. In the next step the SETCROSSPOINT Method is called, if one of the active nodes is visited in both directions. The last Method SHORTESTPATHCROSS returns the shortest path, if the conditions are fulfilled.

5   Results

For testing, the routing first was developed on a desktop system. In this step of development several different algorithms and speed-up techniques were tested and analysed. Figure 4a shows the results of four different calculated routes. The chart 4b presents the calculation periods to this routes. The Algorithms are Dijkstra, A*, Bidirectional A*, Distance Bi*, Road Type Bi* and the combination of Distance and Road Typ Bi*. The diagram shows the speed-up of the hierarchical routing. The tests on the desktop device demonstrate that the speed-up techniques boosted the search to a factor of ten compared to the A* algorithm

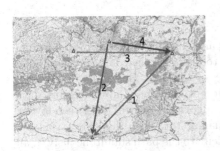

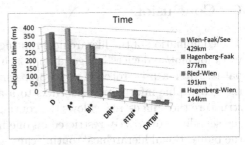

(a) Map-Overview over the routes   (b) Times of the different algorithms

Fig. 4. Test on the desktop device

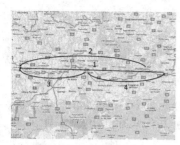
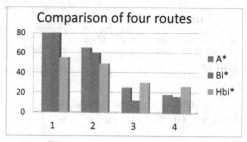
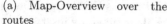

(a) Map-Overview over the   (b) Comparison of four routes
routes

Fig. 5. Test on the mobile device

and additionally the number of visited crossroads could be reduced to a factor
of twenty.

Subsequently the algorithms were ported to a Nokia C5, which is a symbian Series 60 3rd Edition smartphone. The figure 5a present the four tested
routes on the mobile device. The time and the distance of this routes are calculated with a A*, a Bidirectional A* and a Bidirectional hierarchical algorithm
and compared in the diagram 5b. The exact times are showed in the following
table 1.

Table 1. Routing on mobile devices

	start	end	path(km)	A*(ms)	Bi*(ms)	HBi*(ms)
1	St.Pölten	Ried	175	80	80	55
2	Melk	Ried	150	65	60	49
3	St.Valentin	Ried	75	25	12	30
4	St.Valentin	St.Pölten	92	18	16	26

For the tests on the mobile device, the graph only includes highways and
main roads because of the leak of working memory. The results show that the
bidirectional hierarchical algorithm is the best choice for long routes.

6   Conclusion

The combination of the hierarchical routing and the bidirectional A* in a framework for mobile devices is a good approach to optimize the computation of long
paths. After a pre-processing and preparing of the data for the mobile device,
the geographic information's shrinks to a acceptable size. The underlying data
structure the "quad-tree" allows the routing algorithm to switch between layers;
the search is not strictly restricted on one map sector. With this data structure,
the bidirectional hierarchical routing can calculate the path simultaneously in all
layers. The route can be found faster, because the algorithms only need to check
a restricted set of nodes in a map-sector and the solution is found with only one
instead of several search processes. Furthermore the structure of the algorithm

is rather simple: The framework only uses a bidirectional A*, a quad-tree and few extensions. This approach can used by existing desktop systems, as well, to speed up the search for the shortest path. The system needs only few extensions, because the desktop application works with every simple graph structures. The algorithm itself can be integrated in applications for various domains, e.g. traffic management systems and strategy games.

References

1. Canalys: Expert analysis for the high-tech industry (2010),
   http://www.canalys.com/
2. Breymann, U., Mosemann, H.: Java ME-Anwendungsentwicklung für Handys, PDA und Co, Band 2 der Reihe 2. Auflage. Carl Hanser Verlag München Wien, Google Online Books Auflage (May 2008); ISBN: 978-3-446-41376-4
3. Teschl, G., Teschl, S.: Mathematik für Informatiker - Band 1: Diskrete Mathematik und Lineare Algebra, vol. 2. Springer, Berlin (2007)
4. Dumke, R.: Algorithmen und Datenstrukturen. Otto-von-Guericke-Universität Magdeburg, Fakultät für Informatik Institut für Verteilte Systeme, AG Softwaretechnik (2001),
   http://www-ivs.cs.uni-magde-burg.de/~-dumke/-EAD/Skript41.html
5. Stout, E.Q., Stout, Q.F., De Zeeuw, D.L., Gombosi, T.I., Groth, C.P.T., Marshall, H.G., Powell, K.G.: Adaptive Blocks: A High Performance Data Structure. University of Michigan (1997)
6. Schultes, D.: Fast and exact shortest path queries using highway hierarchies. Master's thesis, Universität des Saarlandes (2005)
7. Jagadeesh, G.R., Srikanthan, T., Quek, K.H.: Heuristic techniques for accelerating hierarchical routing on road networks. IEEE Transactions on Intelligent Transportation Systems Band 3, 301–309 (2002); ISSN: 1524-9050
8. Goldberg, A.V., Harrelson, C.: Computing the Shortest Path: A* Search meets graph theory. In: Proceedings 16th Annual ACM-SIAM Symposium, pp. 156–165 (2005)
9. Schultes, D.: Route Planning in Road Networks. Doktor der Naturwissenschaften, Universität Fridericiana zu Karlsruhe (February 2008)

Usability Evaluation Framework
Automated Interface Analysis for Android Applications

Florian Lettner and Clemens Holzmann

Upper Austria University of Applied Sciences, Mobile Computing
Softwarepark 11, 4232 Hagenberg, Austria

Abstract. Usability evaluation of mobile applications can be a time-consuming task, especially due to the fact that field studies are often more suitable than laboratory evaluations. However, good user interface design can make the difference between product acceptance and rejection in the marketplace, and is therefore of high relevance for application developers. In this paper, we present an innovative approach for the automated evaluation of the usability of a mobile application, which is based on the background observation and analysis of a user's behavior when using the application under real-life conditions. We present first results of our ongoing research work on a usability evaluation framework, which should help developers to make mobile applications easier to learn, easier to use and aesthetically more pleasing, and thus lead to a higher usability and acceptance of the applications.

1 Introduction

The International Organization of Standardization defines usability as the *extent to which a product can be used by specified users to achieve specified goals with effectiveness, efficiency and satisfaction in a specified context of use.* [1]

Although this core statement about usability is both applicable to desktop as well as to mobile applications, it is more difficult for mobile applications to achieve statistically significant but also practically relevant results with conventional usability evaluation methods. According to Been-Lirn Duh [2], laboratory evaluations may reveal conceptional design flaws, but authentic data will not be provided as the application is not evaluated in real-life scenarios. He also demonstrated that some major usability issues that were not found during conventional lab tests could only be discovered in field studies, as these issues either depend on the participant's location or even on the device that has actually been used.

Based on these results, we tried to define a generic concept, which makes it possible to evaluate mobile application interfaces under real-life conditions and which also takes into account that not only users assigned to a certain user group – e.g. classified by age or previous technological knowledge – make use of certain applications. Therefore, we developed a framework that is capable of transparently monitoring a user's operational behavior by *advising* (i.e. injecting source code parts into application source code at compile time) the life cycle

R. Moreno-Díaz et al. (Eds.): EUROCAST 2011, Part II, LNCS 6928, pp. 560–567, 2012.
© Springer-Verlag Berlin Heidelberg 2012

of any Android based application to enable usability analysis under natural conditions.

The usability evaluation framework presented in this paper gives developers and designers of mobile applications the ability to enhance the quality of their software by automatically and autonomously getting feedback about design and usability issues under real-life conditions. The potential for field studies also supersedes tests under laboratory conditions, where – due to a lack of contextual information or physical limitations – simulation of real-world usage is hardly possible [3]. Instead of detecting algorithmic performance issues, this framework is able to detect design flaws based on the analysis of static metrics like the component density within a single screen on the one hand, and dynamic metrics provided by application users on the other hand, which are described in section 2.2.

The contribution of this paper is two-fold. First, it offers a general overview about the whole system including a big picture (section 2.1), followed by some definitions on usability evaluation methods (section 2.2) and concluded with an argumentation on relevant metrics for mobile applications (section 2.3). Second, the paper provides a suitable mobile framework architecture consisting of a concept that allows tracking of applications without applying changes to the host application itself (section 3.1).

2   General Approach

This chapter outlines our work and presents the big picture of the proposed usability evaluation framework. It gives a coarse overview on how the framework operates and how data is being collected and analyzed. Additionally, we present common usability evaluation methods and discuss which of them are suitable for automatic usability analysis.

2.1   Overview

During the implementation process, an Eclipse plug-in[1] is used to automatically extract so-called *activities*, which are presented as screens to the user. By taking advantage of so-called *intents*, which represent transitions between activities, the framework is capable of constructing the application's interface tree, which serves as the basis in order to present statistics and possible improvements to the designer or developer. An interface tree consists of the different activities contained in the host application, and they are connected through intents. This means that the interface tree describes the host application's user interface structure as well as possible transitions between the different activities.

Each node of the extracted tree is then augmented with static and dynamic metrics. Static metrics like the number of activities or the average number of buttons within an activity can be used to compare multiple applications with each other or to check against existing style guides. Dynamic metrics like the

---

[1] http://www.eclipse.org

observed number of clicks on a back button are then used to indicate design glitches due to bad localization or bad placement of components within a screen.

By using compile-time weaving, which is part of aspect oriented programming, aspects to record these metrics are injected into the Android application after it has been built. The injection process of source code before or after a method or event is defined as method advising. [4] So the developer's source code remains untouched and the framework acts like a remote journal. It records user interactions and transmits the logs to a server, where the data is analyzed based on predefined rule sets. The specific rule sets are based and built upon different evaluation methods and usability heuristics as described e.g. in [5], [6] and [7]. The results of this process are combined with the previously extracted interface tree to visually present design flaws and issues to the application developer or designer.

2.2   Metrics

Nielson et al. [8] identify four different groups of evaluation methods that contain rules, metrics and design principles:

– Empirically, where users are tested by e.g. performing cognitive walkthroughs during a lab-based experiment.
– Heuristically, applying predefined heuristic functions like Shneiderman's *Eight Golden Rules of Interface Design* [6].
– Formally, by checking against specific analytic functions - e.g. Fitts' Law.
– Automatically, by comparing application structures and interfaces against predefined design style guides.

According to Nielson empirical and heuristic evaluation methods are suitable to be applied at very early stages of the development process where resources are sparse, as these techniques are less time consuming compared to formal analysis methods. Additionally, Nielsen uses empirical methods to evaluate early drafts of user interfaces during the design process (e.g. paper prototypes). As a matter of fact, an implemented version of the user interface is not necessarily required for empirical or heuristic evaluation methods. As the framework we present is designed to evaluate implemented application interfaces, we aim for automatic and autonomous tests. Therefore, we need to provide formal evaluation methods and checking against existing style guides with a huge number of rules as mentioned in [9], which is not possible for manual test scenarios under laboratory conditions.

For the framework presented in this paper, we distinguish between static and dynamic metrics. Static metrics in terms of Nielson et al. are associated with automatic and formal evaluation methods. Existing style guides – for example the iOS Human Interface Guidelines [10] – can be used to test application interfaces for design consistency and structuring. Kokol [11] shows that analytic functions, like the differentiation between screens based on the relationship between data on one screen, can be measured similar to cohesion of program modules [12].

Kokol also suggests to combine this metric with the measurement of structuring, which is based on the graph theory, using his hybrid metric [13]. As for Android it is not possible to automatically extract the application tree during the development process data to evaluate static metrics like Kokol suggests can only be extracted on the device while a user is operating the application. However, as the framework consists not only of source code injected into the host application but also of an Eclipse plugin mentioned in 2.1, it is also possible to extract static metrics during the development process, which reduces the work to be done by the mobile part of the framework.

In the same terms of definition dynamic metrics are not based on the structure of an application, but on the user's behavior. Therefore, the user's navigation behavior is monitored to estimate the application's bounce rate (i.e. a user visits and immediately leaves a screen due to a navigation error), the number of screen calls per visit, the dwell time per screen and the application's conversion rate (e.g. how many visitors convert into regular users). Dynamic metrics are important to identify unused components, misleading localization and navigation glitches.

2.3 Discussion

Compared to most of the techniques Nielson [8] presents we are not limited to apply certain evaluation methods to lab-based settings only. Moreover, since the framework is able to operate completely autonomously and can perform data recording automatically and in the field, we are not restricted to a small, selected amount of users that have to match the application portfolio. Therefore, the framework provides the option for large scale field studies without even interfering with the participants or developers. At the same time, the scalability of the framework allows a generalization of usability across different user groups, which – according to Been-Lirn Duh [2] – is not applicable for mobile application evaluations under laboratory conditions. On the one hand too many users are required to cover all use cases scenarios and on the other hand experiments show that a majority of issues in mobile interfaces is only revealed under real-time conditions. Compared to other logging frameworks like e.g. Google Analytics[2] developers do not have to add function calls manually to each method and event they want to log. Moreover, the overall goal of our framework is not just to collect raw facts and figures, which have to be interpreted by the developers and application designers on their own. Instead, the framework will be able to present possible solutions on how to improve mobile applications. Moreover, existing journaling systems are mostly intended to track commercial data, latency metrics, revenue sources, application specific engangement goals, network traffic or data patterns. These data may be relevant for marketing purposes but it does not tell application designers how to improve the application visually.

However, although the framework provides possibilities to automatically perform usability tests, there are strict limitations based on the selected metrics. Sauro et al. [14] show that it is hard to relatively compare usability of different

---

[2] http://www.google.com/analytics/

features of a certain product as each metric is measured in its own scale, which makes it hard to compare correlating metrics that provide results for the same feature with each other. Therefore, Sauro et al. suggest to compare selected metrics representing effectiveness, efficiency and satisfaction of an application and then form a summated usability metric as a single percentage score metric. They measure task times, errors made during cognitive walkthroughs and record satisfaction scores using questionnaires based on the Likert scale.

Although this would be an expedient way of how to generally rate the application design, Sauro points out that it is difficult to automatically measure user satisfaction or to generalize task times, as each application differs in its purpose. For this reason single score metrics are not applicable for automatic usability evaluation methods in the way Sauro suggests it.

3   Prototype Implementation

In this section we present the architecture of our framework, how the framework is capable of automatically recording user data for usability evaluation in the next stage of development and how to monitor an arbitrary host application.

3.1   Framework Architecture and Application Tracking

In order to get access to the host application, aspect oriented programming is used. For Android AspectJ[3], which works well for Java, can be adopted and applied. An aspect is a combination of a so-called pointcut and an advice, in which the advice is the code being injected and the pointcut describes how and where the advice is added in the host application [4]. In our framework, we use aspects to inject code into the life cycle of Android applications. This is possible through the methods *OnCreate()*, *OnDestroy()*, *OnResume()* and *OnPause()*, where the pointcuts are created in order to inject advices before these methods are called (see Fig. 3.1).

The code injection works through compile time weaving, which means that a custom aspect oriented compiler is used to insert the source code at the beginning of each pointcutted method, before the actual byte code is compiled. As a result, the host application's code stays always clean, no new code is effectively added during the development process. This means that any host application running our framework can be changed and recompiled at any time without the need of changing a single line of framework code. Another benefit compared to other frameworks like *Google Analytics*[4] is that the developer does not need to call any framework functions manually, since the pointcuts are able to identify all activity classes.

These four pointcuts are the only entry points required for the framework to construct the entire application tree. Additionally, any pointcut can be added to track specific low level application events like button clicks or scroll events.

---

[3] http://www.eclipse.org/aspectj/
[4] http://www.google.com/analytics/

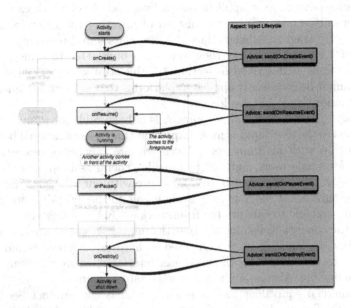

Fig. 1. Flow chart of the life cycle of an Android application, showing pointcuts and advices that are used to inject a host application's life cycle

Advices are only used to send notification events through a customized event system, which has been created according to a suitable observer pattern. A service interested in any life cycle or user event can register and listen for these events. However, for security reasons the services do neither have access to the concerned activity nor to the advice that sent the object at any time.

In order to make use of our framework, each activity has to override the previously named life cycle functions. Unfortunately, the *DalvikVM*, which is used for Android, makes use of a custom class loader and also byte code generation is different compared to the *JavaVM*. This means that load-time weaving, where code is directly injected during runtime if a certain pointcut is reached, is not possible. Therefore, the source code for pointcutted methods has to be available in the host application, otherwise the aspect oriented compiler is not able to identify pointcuts, as these methods already exist in byte code and cannot be found at compile-time. Another reason why load-time weaving is not suitable for Android is that just-in-time compiling only exists for Android since version 2.2, so the framework would only be applicable to applications running on Android Froyo or newer. [15]

4 Related Work

In 2007, Marcin Zduniak [16] presented a framework for automated GUI testing of JavaME applications. Zduniak developed a record and replay system that is able to inject source code in applications at byte code level which can be seen as a very primitive form of aspects. Instead of injecting the lifecycle directly, Zduniak directly tried to subclass JavaME core classes and to manipulate the byte code of JAR archives after they have been built. Due to some platform specific limitations as described in section 3.1, this strategy – compared to our solution – cannot be generically applied to platforms that use a class loader other than the common JavaVM class loader.

Technically speaking, Zduniak's approach is only suitable for form based applications, where the user input is more important than the operational behavior. This means that with his framework, developers are capable of reconstructing user inputs for single users, but not to provide general assumptions about an application's overall design, which we can achieve with our solution. The framework architecture is not scalable as it is close knit to the JavaME core classes, so it is hardly possible to enhance the framework easily by adding new functionality. From the concept it also follows that the main goal was to analyze mobile phone applications running on phones based on hardware keyboards and not to integrate the framework for touch based user interfaces, where the components can be more flexible. Also no metrics are taken into account.

The commercial equivalent to Zduniak's system is the product SeeTest of Experitest[5]. SeeTest is also a record and replay system but which is based on computer vision and image recognition techniques in order to extract user interface areas and to apply OCR mapping to extract strings. SeeTest has been designed for performing visual testing, functionality testing and speed performance evaluation. SeedTest provides many possibilities to evaluate graphical items but like in Zduniak's work, usability measurements and evaluation methods are not covered by the framework.

5   Conclusions and Future Work

In this paper, we presented a new way of how data for automatic usability evaluation of mobile applications can be collected automatically for a huge number of test participants. First, we presented our generic workflow and how to automatically collect mobile application data in a real-life scenario. Second, we discussed different usability evaluation techniques and identified suitable techniques that can be applied to mobile application interfaces in the next stage of development. Third, we presented our framework featuring a component based architecture to provide scalability across different usability evaluation methods using aspect oriented programming based on Android and AspectJ. Finally, we presented some related work and showed the differences to our approach.

Currently, the biggest challenge is to identify and combine different metrics in order to get significant results and to separate less useful metrics out, which was of scope for the creation of the framework. Therefore, some initial field tests for sample applications that make use of our framework are planned.

---

[5] http://www.experitest.com

References

1. Guidance on usability. International Organization for Standardization. In: Ergonomics of Human System Interaction. ISO 9241, vol. 11 (1998)
2. Duh, H.B.-L., Tan, G.C.B., Chen, V.H.-h.: Usability evaluation for mobile device: a comparison of laboratory and field tests. In: Proceedings of the 8th Conference on Human-Computer Interaction with Mobile Devices and Services, MobileHCI 2006, pp. 181–186. ACM, New York (2006)
3. Oztoprak, A., Erbug, C.: Field versus laboratory usability testing: a first comparison. Technical report, Department of Industrial Design - Middle East Technical University, Faculty of Architecture, Middle East Technical University, Faculty of Architecture Inonu Bulvari, 06531 Ankara, Turkey (2008)
4. Mens, K., Lopes, C.V., Tekinerdogan, B., Kiczales, G.: Aspect-oriented programming workshop report. In: Aksit, M., Auletta, V. (eds.) ECOOP 1997. LNCS, vol. 1241, pp. 483–496. Springer, Heidelberg (1997)
5. Nielsen, J.: Usability inspection methods. In: Conference Companion on Human Factors in Computing Systems, CHI 1994, pp. 413–414. ACM, New York (1994)
6. Shneiderman, B.: Designing the user interface: strategies for effective human-computer interaction. Addison-Wesley Longman Publishing Co., Inc., Boston (1986)
7. Tognazzini, B.: First principles of interaction design (2003)
8. Nielsen, J., Molich, R.: Heuristic evaluation of user interfaces. In: Proceedings of the SIGCHI Conference on Human Factors in Computing Systems: Empowering People, CHI 1990, pp. 249–256. ACM, New York (1990)
9. Smith, S.L., Mosier, J.N.: Guidelines for designing user interface software. The MITRE Corporation (August. 1986)
10. Apple. ios human interface guidelines (January 2011)
11. Kokol, P., Rozman, I., Venuti, V.: User interface metrics. SIGPLAN Not. 30, 36–38 (1995)
12. Conte, S.D., Dunsmore, H.E., Shen, V.Y.: Software engineering metrics and models. Benjamin-Cummings Publishing Co., Inc., Redwood City (1986)
13. Kokol, P.: Application of spreadsheet software in software engineering measurement technology. Inf. Softw. Technol. 31, 477–485 (1989)
14. Sauro, J., Kindlund, E.: A method to standardize usability metrics into a single score. In: Proceedings of the SIGCHI Conference on Human Factors in Computing Systems, CHI 2005, pp. 401–409. ACM, New York (2005)
15. Bornstein, D., Jit, D.: (May 2010),
   http://android-developers.blogspot.com/2010/05/dalvik-jit.html
16. Zduniak, M.: Automated gui testing of mobile java applications. Master's thesis, Poznan University of Technology Faculty of Computer Science and Management (2007)

Using Mobile Phone Cameras
to Interact with Ontological Data*

Pierluigi Grillo, Silvia Likavec, and Ilaria Lombardi

Università di Torino, Dipartimento di Informatica, Torino, Italy
{grillo,likavec,lombardi}@di.unito.it

Abstract. In addition to being used to access data and services on the Internet, mobile phones can also be used to retrieve information about physical objects. In this paper we present a framework and a prototype implementation of a reality browsing system that exploits mobile camera phones as access points to ontological knowledge with the corresponding physical counterparts. The use of ontologies to represent the information about the objects of the domain permits for application of reasoning and querying techniques on domain elements. Users can identify a desired product by framing its logo, obtaining further information about the object in a direct, natural and intuitive way. In addition, users can perform Web 2.0 actions on objects, contributing to the creation and development of the network of objects and users. We also provide a brief description of the implemented interface and a real world user evaluation.

1 Introduction

With the integration of cameras into mobile phones, new horizons are emerging in the world of mobile interaction. Due to the possibility of constant connection mobile phones are being more and more used to access data and services on the Internet, as well as to retrieve the information about physical objects surrounding us. On the other hand, mobile devices have limited input and output capabilities (small keyboards and screens), thus making it tedious for users to type in huge amounts of data or visualize complex information. Innovative applications and interaction techniques are needed to support usage of mobile phones as interaction devices which can be used in new contexts and environments.

Users usually access the information about objects of interest either by using an Internet search engine (e.g. Google) or by typing an exact URL into a browser. In any case, the information obtained is often overwhelming and not directly related to the object in question. We try to overcome these limitations by proposing mobile camera phones as access points to ontological knowledge. The users can identify a desired object by framing its logo with the camera phone, thus obtaining further information about the object and more interaction possibilities. In our case, not only the access to the information is faster and easier, it is also more direct, providing the users with relevant information about the

---

* This work has been supported by PIEMONTE Project - People Interaction with Enhanced Multimodal Objects for a New Territory Experience.

R. Moreno-Díaz et al. (Eds.): EUROCAST 2011, Part II, LNCS 6928, pp. 568–576, 2012.

object in question. For other approaches using camera phones to interact with physical objects and access the related information see [8,10,12,14].

We implemented *WantEat*, a prototype application [1,3] that uses the Apple iPhone integrated camera to obtain information about products in a specific domain. The work presented here is a part of PIEMONTE Project [9], in which a Social Networking Application in the domain of gastronomy is being developed, integrating the ideas of the Social Web, Semantic Web and Augmented Reality. In this way a dynamic network of people and objects of the domain emerges, where the communication is possible in both directions, thus making objects of the domain active parts of the "society". The goal of the *WantEat* application is to enable users to access information about the products they might encounter while in mobility (e.g. being at the local farmer's market or visiting the local producer of a certain product), providing them with augmented reality experience. We want to offer the users intuitive and easy access to desired information, playful and innovative at the same time. On the other hand, users should be able to tag, vote and comment the objects they interact with, contributing to the creation and enhancement of their social networks.

The main contributions of our work are:

- use of augmented reality on a mobile device for interaction with objects of interest which enables live recognition of the object in focus;
- use of Semantic Web aspects, i.e. ontologies to represent the information about the objects of the domain and their relations with other objects and users, hence having the possibility to use reasoning and querying techniques on such data;
- possibility to obtain information about the products not easily searchable with standard techniques;
- inclusion of Web 2.0 features, such as tagging, voting, and commenting on objects.

Furthermore, the prototype has been used in a real world context by a relatively large number of participants, providing realistic assessment of the approach.

The rest of the paper is organized as follows. In Section 2 we embed our work in the context of related work. Section 3 gives a brief overview of the system design, followed by the details of the recognition algorithm in Section 4. In Section 5 we present the results of the real world evaluation and we conclude in Section 6.

2   Related Work

Due to their portable nature, smartphones have always been favored candidates for ubiquitous applications. In recent years their evolution has made possible a number of advanced applications, including augmented reality (AR).

Many AR applications for mobile devices are built for commercial and social purposes. For example, the *Layar Reality Browser*[1] is a free application for

---
[1] http://www.layar.com

iPhone and Android OS smartphones that displays real time digital information on top of phone camera view. The *Layar* platform is the basis for a number of mobile location applications (such as tourist guides, live games) because the information is coded as points of interest organized in thematic layers.

Another iPhone application is proposed by the social review service *Yelp*[2]. It provides a feature called *Monocle* which uses the phone GPS and compass to display markers for restaurants, bars and other nearby businesses on top of the camera view. In a similar way, *Wikitude World Browser*[3] displays information about users' surroundings in camera view. In this case, the content comes from different sources like *Starbucks, Youtube, Qype* or *Wikipedia. Wikitude* proposes also *Wikitude Drive*, a navigation system that overlays video captured through the camera with driving instructions and other information.

The possibility to provide information about the surroundings in a natural way opens the door to discovery-based learning. The European research project *iTacitus*[4][7] studied how augmented reality can enhance user's experience in cultural heritage sites by overlaying 3D objects (like missing paintings or architecture models) or abstract context sensitive information on the real scene.

Our system does not simply provide information, it lets the user navigate the net of items (products, people, places) freely and easily, using the relations that link them. These connections are described in the domain ontology or can arise from users' actions and drive the user to serendipitous discovery and exploration of relationships among items.

Recently a number of mobile visual search applications have been developed, for example Google *Goggles*[5], *Kooaba*[6], Nokia *Point and Find*[7] and *SnapTell*[8]. In [4] the authors propose *Wikireality*, a system that, using GPS data and live camera input, recognizes a landmark and augments live video with a Wikipage icon pinned to the query object using orientation sensor data. The corresponding Wikipedia page is automatically opened in the background. The server-side image recognition has a preprocessing phase to prune the set of images used for the matching.

All these systems send a query photo to a remote server which compares it against a database. Even though various compression techniques lead to data of small dimensions, this server-centered approach suffers from network latency. On the contrary, in [13], similarly to what we propose, the recognition is performed on the mobile device. This allows the system to augment the phone camera live video with information about the objects it recognizes, in order to improve user's experience with faster live feedback.

---

[2] http://www.yelp.com
[3] http://www.wikitude.org
[4] http://www.itacitus.org/
[5] http://www.google.com/mobile/goggles/
[6] http://www.kooaba.com
[7] http://www.pointandfind.nokia.com
[8] http://www.snaptell.com

3   System Design

This section presents a short overview of the modules employed in our framework. The client-server architecture of our framework is based on the Resource Oriented Architecture approach [11] (see Figure 1). The main component of the server side is the *Service Logic Layer* which coordinates various components. The *Exposure Layer* manages the communication between the *Service Logic Layer* and the client applications from the *Application Layer*, by exposing the features of *Service Logic* and monitoring the interaction with the user. The architecture has been realized using Java Environment where the Restlet tool [6] and Apache HTTP libraries collaborate in order to answer the HTTP requests from clients.

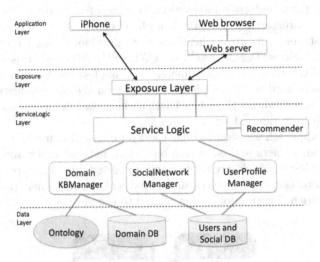

Fig. 1. System architecture

The *Data Layer* is the place where the knowledge about our system is stored. The domain ontology, represented in OWL[9], is used to model domain entities and relations among them, and is integrated with a relational MySQL database used to manage the information about the users and the social network features. The *DomainKB Manager* synthesizes a uniform representation of the two data sources in the *Data Layer* using the D2RQ tool [2] which allows to view a part of a relational database as a set of OWL individuals. Depending on the user interests, the content can be personalized employing the specialized modules *UserProfile Manager* and *Recommender*. Representing the knowledge base as ontology ensures that the domain entities are described as machine recognizable content, which facilitates querying and reasoning on them.

The domain of our application is gastronomy with many different kinds of domain items such as products (e.g. cheese or wine), actors related to products (restaurants, production companies, farms etc.), as well as recipes and geograph-

---

[9] http://www.w3.org/TR/owl2-overview/

ical data. Our domain ontology consists of one upper ontology which imports a set of light-weight ontologies, each one describing a specific part of the domain. It contains very general classes such as Salame, as well as very specific ones, such as Salame della Turgia di Bruno Tetti. Further, a set of SWRL rules is used to define associations between classes. Hence, we were able to describe the domain entities with a fine level of granularity, including the products not easily searchable with standard techniques.

4   Logo Recognition

One of the main aims of the prototype we developed is to give users tools which would help them get in touch with products and all the elements of a territory, employing natural and easy interaction. In case of a product, the main and immediately characterizing property is its label or logo.

In the last years, many applications were developed based on recognition of barcodes, such as *DataMatrix*[10] or *QRCode*[11]. Although this approach is very fast and robust, barcodes are merely meaningless black-and-white images. Moreover, users need to take a photo in order to make the application retrieve the information or redirect them to a URL, making the interaction not so natural and detached from the real world.

With our approach we want to offer users an interaction modality which uses a mobile phone camera and is, on the one hand, natural, quick and immediate and, on the other hand, closely related and immersed into the surrounding environment. Interaction takes place in augmented reality mode where real world live images are enriched with information related to the identified object (Figure 2).

Fig. 2. Logo framing

The recognition algorithm is implemented on the device using the ARToolK-itPlus library,[12] and we designed the markers, recognizable by the algorithm,

---

[10] http://www.iso.org/iso/iso_catalogue/catalogue_tc/catalogue_detail.htm?csnumber=44230
[11] http://www.qrcode.com/index-e.html
[12] http://studierstube.icg.tu-graz.ac.at/handheld_ar/artoolkitplus.php

with the logos of the products (Figure 3). With this solution users enjoy natural, immediate and simple interaction while being immersed in the real world.

The simple marker images are constrained to have a black border, needed by the algorithm to locate the marker in the scene and to primarily estimate its position with respect to the camera in order to overlay the live scene with digital information placed in the right position, in accordance with augmented reality concepts. Although complex color images affect the effectiveness of recognition, we preferred to use the logos since they enable the users to easily recognize them and get in contact with products directly. This provides the right balance between the slow full remote image recognition and a real-time experience, even though this is a limitation with respect to the number of recognizable logos, since they must be stored on the device.

Fig. 3. Logos of some products

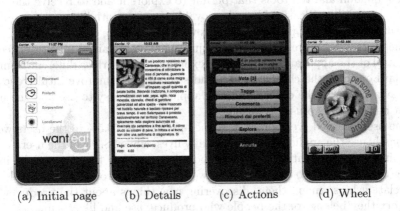

(a) Initial page   (b) Details   (c) Actions   (d) Wheel

Fig. 4. User interface

Figure 4(a) shows the application starting page where the user can select the preferred input modality to begin the exploration of the gastronomic domain. Apart from framing a product label with the phone camera, the user can start from a GPS position, a textual search or from a bookmarked or a randomly selected item. Once the object is recognized, the user can tap on the overlaid logo to show more details of the product (Figure 4(b)) or, if she isn't interested in it, she can simply frame another marker to be recognized. Further, the user can use the action sheet to perform Web 2.0 actions on the object, such as voting, tagging or commenting (Figure 4(c)). In addition, it is possible to explore the social network of the object (Figure 4(d)) with an innovative interaction model based on the metaphor of a *wheel*. This novel interface makes it possible to visualize the recognized object with some related items around it and the relationships linking them to the object in question (the description of the application interface is not the subject of this paper, for more details see [1,3]).

5   Evaluation

We evaluated our application in the real world setting, during the gastronomical fair "Salone del Gusto 2010"[13] in Torino, Italy. 684 randomly selected subjects used mobile phone cameras to obtain information about the gastronomical products at the event. Each person tried the application for 3-5 minutes and rated its four dimensions: easiness of use, comprehensibility, usefulness and pleasantness, using a 1-4 scale. The results are promising, with all average ratings over 3.

More specifically, most of the subjects (91.4%) judged the application easy to use, with the average of 3.42. In particular, regarding the interaction in augmented reality mode, 85.1% of the users found it easy and natural to use, with satisfying image recognition speed. 91% of the users found the application comprehensible, with the average of 3.46. Regarding usefulness, 78.6% of users were satisfied with the average of 3.12, This was especially due to their interest in the specific domain and the tools that permit to explore it and to receive the information in mobility. Pleasurable and enjoyable interface with innovative graphical elements had 91.8% of positive opinions with the average of 3.43.

The users, who expressed a negative judgment, complained about not feeling in control of the application, due to the experimental interface different from the standard ones for the chosen device, and suggested to improve intuitiveness of the navigation. On the other hand, the application is easy to use and the users learnt quickly how to use it efficiently.

The users showed great interest in the application: 76.5% of the users would personally use the application in their daily lives, while 88.2% of the users would recommend the application to friends and relatives. They found especially interesting the possibility to explore the network of related products and people and the relationships among them, discovering new things about the products, the territory they belong to, the people who produce, use and like them.

6   Conclusions

Mobile devices are gaining popularity due to advances in their development: bigger displays, natural interaction models through touch screens, better network capabilities, improved localization features etc. All these components and characteristics foster the implementation of new kinds of context-aware applications which can serve for information retrieval. Many of these applications allow the users to enjoy augmented reality experience through objects in the real world.

---

[13] http://www.salonedelgusto.it

Broad gastronomic domain contains many types of domain items with a great number of relations between them, not easily searchable by standard techniques. In this paper we describe a prototype mobile application for reality browsing of gastronomic products and a system architecture that supports the application. We exploit the advantages of augmented reality interaction, employing product recognition using its logo. We present a simple, innovative interaction modality to explore the network of objects and people with the support of a mobile phone. By using our prototype, users are guided in the discovery of the knowledge of a territory in a natural and serendipitous way, staying in contact with surrounding environment and interacting with it directly. In our approach, we use ontologies to represent the domain knowledge in order to enable fluid description and integration of data, as well as reasoning and querying techniques on them. The real world evaluation of our application provided a valuable feedback from users and directions for future development.

In addition, one of possible uses of logo recognition would be to insert data into a storytelling application [5]. Once the product is recognized, users can tell the system about their experience with the product, for example if they tasted or bought it. This would enable collecting structured contributions from users, which can be later aggregated into simple stories and presented to future users.

References

1. Biamino, G., Grillo, P., Lombardi, I., Marcengo, A., Rapp, A., Simeoni, R., Vernero, F.: "The Wheel": an innovative visual model for interacting with a social web of things. In: Proc. of Visual Interfaces to the Social and Semantic Web, VISSW 2011(2011)
2. Bizer, C., Seaborne, A.: D2RQ - Treating Non-RDF Databases as Virtual RDF Graphs. In: McIlraith, S.A., Plexousakis, D., van Harmelen, F. (eds.) ISWC 2004. LNCS, vol. 3298. Springer, Heidelberg (2004), http://www4.wiwiss.fu-berlin.de/bizer/d2rq/
3. Chiabrando, E., Furnari, R., Grillo, P., Likavec, S., Lombardi, I.: Dynamic interface reconfiguration based on different ontological relations. In: Smith, M.J., Salvendy, G. (eds.) HCII 2011, Part I. LNCS, vol. 6771, pp. 538–547. Springer, Heidelberg (2011)
4. Gray, D., Kozintsev, I., Wu, Y., Haussecker, H.: Wikireality: augmenting reality with community driven websites. In: Proc. of the 2009 IEEE Intl. Conf. on Multimedia and Expo., ICME 2009, pp. 1290–1293. IEEE Press, Los Alamitos (2009)
5. Likavec, S., Lombardi, I., Nantiat, A., Picardi, C., Theseider Dupré, D.: Threading facts into a collective narrative world. In: Aylett, R., Lim, M.Y., Louchart, S., Petta, P., Riedl, M. (eds.) ICIDS 2010. LNCS, vol. 6432, pp. 86–97. Springer, Heidelberg (2010)
6. Louvel, J., Boileau, T.: Restlet in Action. Manning Publications Co. (2009)
7. Megliola, M., Toffolo, S., Zoellner, M., Hodgson, B., Speller, L.: Intelligent tourism through ubiquitous services: Lessons learnt from two field studies. In: Proc. of eChallenges e-2009, IIMC (2009)
8. Pielot, M., Henze, N., Nickel, C., Menke, C., Samadi, S., Boll, S.: Evaluation of camera phone based interaction to access information related to posters. In: Proc. of Mobile Interaction with the Real World, MIRW 2008, pp. 61–72 (2008)

9. PIEMONTE Team. WantEat: interacting with social networks of intelligent things and people in the world of enogastronomy. In: Proc. of Interacting with Smart Objects Workshop 2011 (2011)
10. Rekimoto, J., Ayatsuka, Y.: Cybercode: designing augmented reality environments with visual tags. In: Proc. of DARE 2000 on Designing augmented reality environments, DARE 2000, pp. 1–10 (2000)
11. Richardson, L., Ruby, S.: RESTful web services. In: Media, O, (ed.) (2007), http://www4.wiwiss.fu-berlin.de/bizer/d2rq/
12. Rohs, M., Gfeller, B.: Using camera-equipped mobile phones for interacting with real-world objects. In: Advances in Pervasive Computing, pp. 265–271 (2004)
13. Takacs, G., Xiong, Y., Grzeszczuk, R., Chandrasekhar, V., chao Chen, W., Pulli, K., Gelfand, N., Bismpigiannis, T., Girod, B.: Outdoors augmented reality on mobile phone using loxel-based visual feature organization. In: Proc. of ACM International Conference on Multimedia Information Retrieval, pp. 427–434 (2008)
14. Toye, E., Sharp, R., Madhavapeddy, A., Scott, D., Upton, E., Blackwell, A.: Interacting with mobile services: an evaluation of camera-phones and visual tags. Personal and Ubiquitous Computing 11(2), 97–106 (2007)

The Cutting Stock Problem Recent Application in Information Technology

Jerzy Greblicki, Jerzy Kotowski, and Ewa Szlachcic

Institute of Computer Engineering, Control and Robotics,
Wrocław University of Technology,
11/17 Janiszewskiego Street, 50-372 Wrocław, Poland
{jerzy.greblicki,jerzy.kotowski,ewa.szlachcic}@pwr.wroc.pl

1 Introduction

Cloud computing is a Web-based processing, that allow to share resources, software, and information over the Internet. Cloud computing helps enterprises and other institutions like schools, universities, etc. transform business and technology. Most cloud computing infrastructures consist of services delivered through common centers and built on servers.

The two most significant components of cloud computing architecture are known as the front end and the back end. The front end is the part seen by the client, i.e. the computer user. The back end of the cloud computing architecture is the cloud itself, comprising various computers, servers and data storage devices.

Typical benefits of managing in the cloud are: reduced cost, increased storage and flexibility. Experts assume that the challenges of the cloud computing are increasing of data protection, growing data recovery and availability or the growing management capabilities. However, clouds are essentially data centers that require high energy usage to maintain operation. For a data center, the energy cost is a significant component of its operating and up-front costs.

In [4] authors show that this problem of minimizing energy consumption maps to the 2-dimensional bin-packing problem. In the modern literature papers related to this idea one may find really a lot. See [1], for example. In our paper we present the optimization problem in the cloud computing architecture that grows up at our University. Than we show it transformation to the particular cutting problem and a meta-heuristic method engaged to find an appropriate problem solution.

The paper contains two additional parts where we discuss last results found in the literature, mainly from 2011 and 2010 year. In the Section 2 we present selected papers devoted to the legal and scheduling problems that occurs in IT systems of the big size. In Section 3 we present a few papers devoted mainly to the mathematical methods useful in obtaining necessary tools to schedule/control in the cloud for example. Then we present our own algorithm for solving deployment problem in the public cloud. We used a new meta-heuristic approach, known as Improved Harmony Search Algorithm (IHSA), to obtain a numerical application. We finish with the discussion concerning our future plans.

R. Moreno-Díaz et al. (Eds.): EUROCAST 2011, Part II, LNCS 6928, pp. 577–584, 2012.

2 A Nowadays Problems in the Modern Computer Systems - A Short Survey

System virtualization provides low-cost, flexible and powerful executing environment. It plays an important role in the infrastructure of Cloud computing. In paper [8] authors propose a dynamic task scheduling scheme for virtualized data centers. Considering the availability and responsiveness performance, the general model of the task scheduling for virtual data centers is built and formulated as a two-objective optimization. A fuzzy prediction method is given to model the uncertain workload and the vague availability of virtualized server nodes. An on-line dynamic task scheduling algorithm is proposed and evaluated.

A major problem in the distributed systems is how to ensure that jobs finish their execution within the estimated completion times in the real time computing. Authors of [10] state that previously, several techniques including advance reservation, rescheduling and migration have been adopted to resolve or relieve this issue. They mention that the use of clouds may be an attractive alternative, since resources in clouds are much more reliable than those in grids. Their paper investigates the effectiveness of rescheduling using cloud resources to increase the reliability of job completion. Paper is devoted to a novel rescheduling technique, called rescheduling using clouds for reliable completion, named RC^2.

In [11] authors introduce a High Performance Computing (HPC) infrastructure architecture that provides predictable execution of scientific applications, and scales from a single resource to multiple resources. This approach allows for improving in the system different ownership, policy, and geographic locations. Authors propose their three paradigms in the evolution of HPC and high-throughput computing: owner-centric HPC (traditional), Grid computing, and Cloud computing. They analyze the synergies among HPC, Grid and Cloud computing, and finally argue for an architecture that combines the benefits of these technologies. They propose a new name for this architecture: Elastic Cluster.

Networking research funding agencies in many countries are encouraging research on revolutionary networking architectures that may or may not be bound by the restrictions of the current TCP/IP based Internet. In [13] authors present a comprehensive survey of such research projects and activities. The topics covered include various benchmarks for experimentation with the new architectures, security mechanisms, content delivery mechanisms, management and control frameworks, service architectures, as like as the routing mechanisms.

Cloud computing systems provide a new paradigm to the distributed processing of digital data. In [14] authors examine the legal aspects of digital forensic investigations of cloud computing systems. They underline that digital forensic investigations involving such systems are likely to involve more complex digital evidence acquisition and analysis. So, some public cloud computing systems may involve the storage and processing of digital data in different jurisdictions, and some organizations may choose to encrypt their data before it enters the cloud. Both of these factors in conjunction with cloud architectures may make forensic investigation of such systems more complex and time consuming.

3 Modern Methods, Algorithm and Applications in the Cutting and Packing Problems

In [2] a heuristic recursive algorithm for the two-dimensional rectangular strip packing problem is presented. It is based on a recursive structure combined with branch-and-bound techniques.

Authors of [5] formulate two-stage cutting stock problem, where the set of rectangular pieces of given dimensions are to be cut from arbitrary shaped object that may be non-convex and contain defective regions. They check the complexity of this problem and propose an optimization algorithm based on the simulation annealing technique.

In [12] authors consider two types of orthogonal, oriented, rectangular, two-dimensional packing problems. The first is the strip packing problem, for which four new and improved level-packing algorithms are presented. Two of these algorithms guarantee a packing that may be disentangled by guillotine cuts. These are combined with a two-stage heuristic designed to find a solution to the variable-sized bin packing problem, where the aim is to pack all items into bins so as to minimize the packing area.

The paper [15] deals with the general one-dimensional cutting stock problem, where optimization is not limited to a single order. Authors mention that stock cutting is treated as a permanent business process in a company in which consecutive order sets need to be fulfilled either for production needs or for its customers. They observe that exact demand for future orders is not known in advance. The unutilized and partly utilized stock lengths left after fulfilling current order sets are stored and used later. The goal is the reduction of trim loss and costs over a broader time-span. The big amount of the unutilized big elements (e.g. stock) rapidly increases the complexity of the optimization problem and finally increases calculation time.

The number of publications in the area of cutting and packing (C&P) has increased considerably over the last 25 years. The first typology of C&P problems was introduced by Dyckhoff. However, over the years also some deficiencies of this typology became evident, which created problems in dealing with recent developments and prevented it from being accepted more generally. In [16], the authors present an improved typology, which is partially based on Dyckhoff's original ideas, but introduces new categorization criteria, which define problem categories different from those of Dyckhoff. Furthermore, a new, consistent system of names is suggested for these problem categories.

In [17] authors hardly state that the task scheduling algorithm, which is an NP-completeness problem, plays a key role in modern cloud computing systems. In this paper, they propose an optimized algorithm based on genetic algorithm to schedule independent and divisible tasks adapting to different computation and memory requirements. They prompt this algorithm in heterogeneous systems, where resources are of computational and communication heterogeneity. They used genetic algorithm approach to solve obtained combinatorial optimization problem but recognize finally this approach as rather inefficient in the case where the global optimum is wanted.

4 Deployment Models

Cloud platform services computing platform and solution stack as a service, often consuming cloud infrastructure and sustaining cloud applications. It facilitates deployment of applications without the cost and complexity of buying and managing the underlying hardware and software layers.

Cloud computing is a computing model that delivers information technology (IT) as a service over the Internet. Today, cloud computing has matured to a point where it's considered a mainstream technology service. People touch the cloud every day without knowing it – by sending instant messages and sharing files easily between companies over the Internet, staying connected on projects with colleagues and other businesses through new social networking tools that take advantage of the ability to "come together in the cloud". (from CNN)

For this moment at least for deployments models of the cloud computing are available and useful. They are as follows: *a public cloud, a community cloud, a hybrid cloud* and *a private cloud. Public cloud* or external cloud describes cloud computing in the traditional mainstream sense, whereby resources are dynamically provisioned on a fine-grained, self-service basis over the Internet. *A community cloud* may be established where several organizations have similar requirements and seek to share infrastructure. The costs are spread over fewer users than a public cloud (but more than a single tenant). This option may offer a higher level of privacy, security and/or policy compliance. *Hybrid cloud* is also called hybrid delivery by the major vendors including HP, IBM, Oracle and VMware who offer technology to manage the complexity in managing the performance, security and privacy concerns that results from the mixed delivery methods of IT services. Private cloud has been described as neologism, but its concept pre-dates the term cloud by 40 years. Enterprise IT organizations use their own *private cloud*(s) for mission critical and other operational systems to protect critical infrastructures. So, *private clouds* are not an implementation of cloud computing at all, but are in fact an implementation of a technology subset: the basic concept of virtualized computing.

5 Problem Description versus Mathematical Tools

The main area of our interest is to build at the Wroclaw University of Technology the public cloud that will provide educational software to K-12 schools on the Low Silesia district. For this moment we assume that necessary back end elements of the cloud will the computers working at our University.

Existing meta-heuristic algorithms are based on ideas found in the paradigm of natural or artificial phenomena. For our purposes we reworked an optimization procedures based on the idea of Genetic Algorithm and Harmony Search Algorithm [6,7,9]. The basic concept of Genetic Algorithm is designed to simulate processes in natural system necessary for evolution. The newest method in the area of the meta-heuristic algorithms is the Harmony Search Algorithm (HSA). It was conceptualized from the musical process of searching for a perfect state of harmony, such as jazz improvisation.

5.1   Problem Description

Given:

- The number of virtual machines. Each of them is described by needed/required resources (CPU performance, memory). Required working hours are also known. It is assumed that these requirements may be different for each machine.
- There is a cloud computing system consisting of multiprocessor computers (host machines) with defined parameters.

Assumptions/restrictions:

- Each virtual machine must be deployed on a single host. It is not allow for a virtual machine to use resources from several hosts.
- The hardware resources of at least one host machines are larger than those required by the virtual machine.
- Any VM has a given priority. It is a real positive number.
- The most important parameter for the VM is its performance. The minimal feasible performance is known as like as its advisable value.
- Working hours for each VM are known.

Task:
    Deploy each virtual machine on the particular host.

5.2   Mathematical Model

To achieve an appropriate mathematical model of the problem described about first, we have to improve an appropriate notation:

n - the number of virtual machines;
m - the number of hosts;
T - time limit: $t \epsilon [0, T]$;
p_i - advisable performance of i-th VM, i=1,2,...,n;
q_i - minimal necessary performance of i-th VM, i=1,2,...,n;
c_i - the priority of i-th VM, i=1,2,...,n;
t_i - the starting time of i-th VM, i=1,2,...,n;
v_i - the ending time of i-th VM, i=1,2,...,n;
f_j - feasible performance of the j-th host, j=1,2,...,m.
    Our aim is to find the optimal value of the two sets of decision variables $x, y \epsilon R^n$, for which

$$F(x,y) = \sum_{i=1}^{n} c_i 1(x_i) \frac{y_i}{p_i} \rightarrow max \qquad (1)$$

Let $x = (x_1, x_2, ..., x_n)$ and let $y = (y_1, y_2, ..., y_n)$. For any i=1,2,...,n, x_i denotes the number of the host to which i-th virtual machine should be deployed: $x_i \epsilon \{1, 2, ..., m\}$. Similarly, for any i=1,2,...,n, y_i denotes the optimal performance of the i-th virtual machine. Of course, for each i=1,2,...,n the following local restriction: $q_i \le y_i \le p_i$ should be fulfilled. The feasible solution should also fulfill the set of m global restrictions:

$$\sum_{x_i=j} p_i \le f_j, \ j = 1, 2, ..., m \tag{2}$$

5.3 Problem Analysis

We may study two versions of the problem presented above.

- *Version I:* all parameters of the virtual machines are random numbers. Virtual machines (VM) form the stochastic process. This assumption leads to the management problem in the real time.
- *Version II:* all parameters of the virtual machines are known previously. This assumption leads to the cutting/packing problem (this paper).

One may show that this problem may be easy transformed to the Strip Packing Problem [16]. The Strip Packing Problem or Strip Cutting Problem (SCP) is formulated as follows: to pack (or cut) a set of small rectangles (pieces) into a bin (strip) of fixed width but unlimited length. The aim is to minimize the length to which the bin is filled.

Problem (1)-(2) is classified as 2/V/O/R. It was shown that SCP is NP-complete since it is a generalization of the cutting stock problem, which in turn is a generalization of the famous knapsack problem.

In classic SCP we have a single, initial strip R of fixed width W and unlimited length and a finite set S of n small rectangles (pieces) with dimensions (l_i, w_i), for i=1, . . ., n. The problem is to cut off from the strip all pieces such that: all pieces have fixed orientation, all applied cuts are of guillotine type, no overlapping between pieces and between pieces and the edges of the strip. the aim is to minimize the length to which the initial strip R is filled.

To transform problem (1)-(2) to SCP is enough to assume that we have m strips (hosts). For each strip j its width equals feasible performance of the j-th host, j=1,2,...,m and its length is related to the computing time when the host is in used. Similarly, y_i is the width of virtual machine number i=1, . . ., n.

6   The Method and the Algorithm

The problem is NP-complete. More, in practice the total number of VM goes to hundreds. Decisions variables are of integer and real type. In the problem occur many additional restrictions. We must also remember about the time consuming procedures (fitness function, decision variables coding and decoding). The final conclusion may be only one: a meta-heuristic approach should be used. Namely we decided to put into the motion the newer version of Harmony Search Algorithm (HSA) named Improved HSA (IHSA).

Classic HSA was recently developed in an analogy with music improvisation process where music players improvise the pitches of their instruments to obtain better harmony. Algorithm scheme contains the following steps:

1. Initialize the problem and algorithm parameters.
2. Initialize the harmony memory.
3. Improvise a new harmony.
4. Update the harmony memory.
5. Check the stopping criterion.

HSA uses the following parameters: HMS - The harmony memory HM size, $HMCR$ - harmony memory considering rate, PAR - pitch adjusting rate, bw - an arbitrary distance (bandwidth) and NI - the number of improvisations.

The traditional HSA algorithm uses fixed value for both PAR and bw. In the HSA method PAR and bw values were adjusted in initialization step (Step 1) and cannot be changed during new generations. The key difference between IHSA and traditional HSA method is in the way of adjusting PAR and bw. Small bw values in final generations increase the fine-tuning of solution vectors, but in early generations bw must take a bigger value to enforce the algorithm to increase the diversity of solution vectors. Large PAR values with small bw values usually cause the improvement of best solutions in final generations which algorithm converged to optimal solution vector. Usually, this parameters changes during the calculation process due to the rules presented in (3)-(4).

$$PAR(gn) = PAR_{min} + \frac{PAR_{max} - PAR_{min}}{NI} gn \tag{3}$$

$$bw(gn) = bw_{max} e^{c \cdot gn} \tag{4}$$

where c in (4) is given as:

$$c = \frac{ln\left(\frac{bw_{min}}{bw_{max}}\right)}{NI} \tag{5}$$

In (3)-(5) gn stands for the generation number.

A numerical application was written in C++, compiled and tested under Microsoft Visual Studio 2008. For the proper work an algorithm was equipped in three necessary procedures: coding and decoding procedures used after primary transformation of (3)-(4) to the permutation problem and procedure for designing the fitness value of the considered solution based on the greedy approach.

7   Conclusions

Cloud computing is a useful tool in the modern Information Technology. In this paper we consider a new model for tasks scheduling of VM deployment for business and educational purposes. We present our own algorithm for solving deployment problem in the public cloud. We mentioned that this problem is NP-hard as a specific complex mixed-integer problem with many restrictions and non-linear relations. So, meta-heuristic approach is necessary. We found Improved Harmony Search Algorithm as a very promised tool in this case.

References

1. Cagan, J., Shimada, K., Yin, S.: A survey of computational approaches to three-dimensional layout problems. Computer Aided Design 34(8), 597–611 (2002)
2. Cui, Y., Yang, Y., Cheng, X., Song, P.: A recursive branch-and-bound algorithm for the rectangular guillotine strip packing problem. Computers & Operations Research 35, 1281–1291 (2008)
3. Folino, G., Mastroianni, C.: Special section: Bio-inspired algorithms for distributed systems. Future Generation Computer Systems 26, 835–837 (2010)
4. Garg, S.K., Yeo, C.S., Anandasivam, A., Buyya, R.: Environment-conscious scheduling of HPC applications on distributed Cloud-oriented data centers. J. Parallel Distrib. Comput. (2010), doi:10.1016/j.jpdc.2010.04.004
5. Georgis, N., Petrou, M., Kittler, J.: On the generalised stock cutting problem. Machine Vision and Applications 11, 231–241 (2000)
6. Greblicki, J., Kotowski, J.: Analysis of the Properties of the Harmony Search Algorithm Carried Out on the One Dimensional Binary Knapsack Problem. In: Moreno-Díaz, R., Pichler, F., Quesada-Arencibia, A. (eds.) EUROCAST 2009. LNCS, vol. 5717, pp. 697–704. Springer, Heidelberg (2009)
7. Greblicki, J., Kotowski, J.: Automated design of totally self-checking sequential circuits. In: Moreno-Díaz, R., Pichler, F., Quesada-Arencibia, A. (eds.) EUROCAST 2009. LNCS, vol. 5717, pp. 98–105. Springer, Heidelberg (2009)
8. Kong, X., Lin, C., Jiang, Y., Yan, W., Chu, X.: Efficient dynamic task scheduling in virtualized data centers with fuzzy prediction. Journal of Network and Computer Applications (2010)
9. Kotowski, J.: The use of the method of illusion to optimizing the simple cutting stock problem. In: Proc. MMAR 2001, 7th IEEE Conference on Methods and Models in Automation and Robotics, vol. 1, pp. 149–154 (2001)
10. Lee, Y.C., Zomaya, A.Y.: Rescheduling for reliable job completion with the support of clouds. Future Generation Computer Systems 26, 1192–1199 (2010)
11. Mateescu, G., Gentzsch, W., Ribbens, C.J.: Hybrid Computing - Where HPC meets grid and Cloud Computing. In: Future Generation Computer Systems. Elsevier Ltd, Amsterdam (2010)
12. Ortmann, F.G., Ntene, N., van Vuuren, J.H.: New and improved level heuristics for the rectangular strip packing and variable-sized bin packing problems. European Journal of Operational Research 203, 306–315 (2010)
13. Paul, S., Pan, J., Jain, R.: Architectures for the future networks and the next generation Internet: A survey. Computer Communications 34, 2–42 (2011)
14. Taylor, M., Haggerty, J., Gresty, D., Hegarty, R.: Digital evidence in cloud computing systems. Computer Law & Security Review 26, 304–308 (2010)
15. Trkman, P., Gradisar, M.: One-dimensional cutting stock optimization in consecutive time periods. European Journal of Operational Research 179, 291–301 (2007)
16. Wäscher, G., Haußner, H., Schumann, H.: An improved typology of cutting and packing problems. European Journal of Operational Research 183, 1109–1130 (2007)
17. Zhao, C., Zhang, S., Liu, Q., Xie, J., Hu, J.: Independent Tasks Scheduling Based on Genetic Algorithm in Cloud Computing. In: 5th International Conference on Wireless Communications, WiCom. IEEE, Los Alamitos (2009)

Relay Identification of IPDT Plant by Analyzing Nonsymmetrical Oscillations

Mikuláš Huba[1,2] and Peter Ťapák[1]

[1] Institute of Control and Industrial Informatics
Faculty of Electrical Engineering and IT, Slovak University of Technology
Ilkovičova 3, 812 19 Bratislava, Slovakia
[2] MI/PRT, FernUniversität in Hagen, Universitätsstr. 27,
D-58084 Hagen, Germany
{peter.tapak,mikulas.huba}@stuba.sk

Abstract. The paper deals with approximation of systems with the dominant first order dynamics by the Integrator Plus Dead Time (IPDT) model based on analysis of the nonsymmetrical oscillations with possible offset arising typically under relay control. The analytical derivation is illustrated by results achieved by identification of optical plant. The results are then experimentally verified by Disturbance Observer (DOB) based controller.

Keywords: relay identification, disturbance observer, integrator plant.

1 Introduction

Relay feedback test is very popular approach used in several commercial auto-tuners. The current research in this area was closely analyzed in [10]. There are two types of relay tests, unbiased and biased. When using the unbiased test the process gain can be highly deflorated by a load disturbance. Many relay feedback methods have been proposed to reject static disturbances [1], [5], [6]. Their approaches bias the reference value of the relay on-off as much as a static disturbance (which must be known in advance), in order to achieve the same accuracy as in the case of no disturbance. None of these approaches can be applied to large static disturbance, of which the magnitude is bigger than that of the relay. By inserting a proportional integral (PI) controller behind the relay, [8] proposed an identification method for application against large static disturbance, larger than the magnitude of the relay. The drawback of the method is the necessity to tune an additional controller. Ziegler and Nichols in [9] proposed to use the sustained oscillations for process dynamics characterization giving finally PID controller tuning, whereby the process dynamics approximation was equivalent to the use of the IPDT model. It is, however, well known that the method is appropriate also for dealing with many systems with more complicated and typically static dynamics. Several papers investigate the transition point when the designer should choose to use more complex models - the First Order Plus Dead Time (FOPDT) representing the first possible extension [7], [4]. Also [2] shows

R. Moreno-Díaz et al. (Eds.): EUROCAST 2011, Part II, LNCS 6928, pp. 585–592, 2012.

that for the relatively low ratio of the dead time and the plant time constant it is enough to use the IPDT approximations also for dealing with the FOPDT processes used in this paper. However, when using the IPDT approximation for the FOPDT process, the plant feedback that is around an operating point equivalent to a load disturbance will lead to assymmetrical behavior also in the case with symmetrical relay without additional load. So, in the relay identification this oscillation asymmetry is an important issue with respect to the precision of the whole approximation. For a noncompensated disturbance the deformation of oscillations leads to increased influence of higher harmonics and to decreased precision of the identification both by using the describing functions method and the Fast Fourier Transform. The main advantage of constraining the plant approximation to the IPDT model

$$S(s) = \frac{K_s}{s} e^{-T_d s} \tag{1}$$

is that both the experiment setup and the corresponding formulas remain relatively simple and robust against measurement noise. There is no need to tune the PI controller before the identification, or to use the PI controller with an additional anti windup circuitry.

1.1   Method Derivation

Let us consider oscillations in the control loop with a relay with the output $u_r = \pm M$ and a piecewise constant input disturbance $v = const$. Then, the actual plant input will be given as a piecewise constant signal $u_A = \pm M + v$. Possible transients are shown in Fig. 2. By assuming relay switching from the

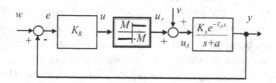

Fig. 1. Relay identification with nonsymmetrical plant input

positive relay output $u = M$ to the negative value $u = -M$ (point 1) at the time moment t_{21i-1}, due to the dead time the influence of the positive plant input $U_2 = (v + M)K_s$ will keep over interval with the length equal to the dead time value T_d. Then, after reaching output value y_{21} at the time moment τ_{21i-1} (point 2) due to the effective plant input $U_1 = (v - M)K_s$ the output starts to decrease. After the time interval t_1 it reaches the reference value w (point 3). Even though at this moment the relay switches to the positive value $u = M$ the plant output continues to fall the time T_d longer and reaches the value y_{12} (point 4). The total length of the interval with negative relay output will be denoted

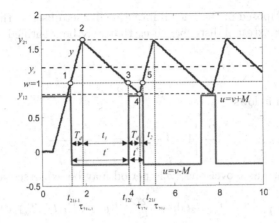

Fig. 2. Transients of basic variables of the loop in the fig 1

as t^-. Under virtue of the positive relay output the plant output starts to rise and reaches the reference value after the time t_2 (point 5). The total duration of the positive relay output may be denoted as

$$t^+ = t_2 + T_d \tag{2}$$

As a result of the time delay, the plant output turnover time instants τ_{21i} are shifted with respect to the relay reversal moments t_{21i} by T_d. Similar time shift exists among time instants τ_{12i} and t_{12i}, i.e.

$$\tau_{21i} = t_{21i} + T_d \tag{3}$$
$$\tau_{12i} = t_{12i} + T_d \tag{4}$$

For a single integrator it is possible to formulate relations

$$y_{21} - w = U_2 T_d; t_1 = (w - y_{21})/U_1$$
$$y_{12} - w = U_1 T_d; t_2 = (w - y_{12})/U_2 \tag{5}$$

Period of one cycle may be denoted as

$$P_u = t^+ + t^- = 2T_d + t_1 + t_2 = \frac{4T_d M^2}{M^2 - v^2} \tag{6}$$

For a known value of the relay amplitude M and a known ratio of the positive and negative relay output duration over one cycle

$$\epsilon = \frac{t^+}{t^-} = \frac{t_2 + T_d}{t_1 + T_d} = -\frac{v - M}{v + M} \tag{7}$$

it is possible to express the identified disturbance as

$$v = u_0 + v_n \tag{8}$$

This may be composed of the known intentionally set offset at the relay output and an unknown external disturbance v_n that may be identified as

$$v = M \frac{1 - \epsilon}{1 + \epsilon} \tag{9}$$

From (6) it then follows

$$T_d = \frac{P_u}{4} \left[1 - \left(\frac{v}{M} \right)^2 \right] = P_u \frac{\epsilon}{(1 + \epsilon)^2} \tag{10}$$

The output mean value over one cycle period may be expressed as

$$y_s = \frac{1}{P_u} \left[w + \int_0^{T_d} U_2 t \, dt + \int_{T_d}^{2T_d + t_1} (y_{21} + U_1(t - T_d)) \, dt \right]$$
$$+ \frac{1}{P_u} \left[\int_{2T_d + t_1}^{P_u} (y_{12} + U_2(t - 2T_d - t_1)) \, dt \right] \tag{11}$$

$$y_s = \frac{1}{P_u} \left[w + \int_0^{T_d} K_s(v + M)t \, dt + \int_{T_d}^{2T_d + t_1} (y_{21} + K_s(v - M)(t - T_d)) \, dt \right]$$
$$+ \frac{1}{P_u} \left[\int_{2T_d + t_1}^{P_u} (y_{12} + K_s(v + M)(t - 2T_d - t_1)) \, dt \right] \tag{12}$$

Finally, one gets formula for the plant gain

$$K_s = \frac{(1 + \epsilon)^2}{\epsilon P_u} \frac{y_s - w}{v} = \frac{(1 + \epsilon)^3}{\epsilon(1 - \epsilon) P_u} \frac{(y_s - w)}{M} \tag{13}$$

It is also possible to calculate the plant gain by using the area A limited by $y(t)$ around w over one period (6), when

$$K_s = \frac{(1 + \epsilon)^4}{\epsilon(1 + \epsilon)^2} \frac{A}{M P_u^2} \tag{14}$$

In difference to (13), this may also be used in the symmetrical case with $v = 0$ and $y_s = w$. So, to get the model parameters (1) it is enough to calculate the mean plant output value over one cycle of relay switching (12), or the equivalent area A, the period of oscillation (6) and the ratio of time slots with positive and negative relay output (7). The approximation should remain valid also in the case of constant input disturbance $v = const$. This may be considered to be composed of the intentionally introduced disturbance u_0 and of the external disturbance v_n

$$v = u_0 + v_n \tag{15}$$

In this way it is possible to introduce an additional free parameter for tuning enabling to work in any working point with arbitrarily low relay module M. After carrying out the above procedure at least for two different reference signal values w_1 and w_2 and by evaluating changes of the identified disturbance values

v_1 and v_2 in dependence on the mean output values y_{s1} and y_{s2} it is then possible to approximate the dependence

$$v = f(y_s) \tag{16}$$

If it has a negligible slope with respect to changes in y_s, the system is sufficiently well approximated by the IPDT model.

2   Real Experiment

The thermo-optical plant laboratory model (Fig.3) offers measurement of 8 process variables: controlled temperature, its filtered value, ambient temperature, controlled light intensity, its derivative and filtered value, the fan speed of rotation and current. The temperature and the light intensity control channels are interconnected by 3 manipulated voltage variables influencing the bulb (heat & light source), the light-diode (the light source) and the fan (the system cooling). Besides these, it is possible to adjust two parameters of the light intensity derivator. Within Matlab/Simulink or Scilab/Scicos schemes the plant is represented as a single block and so limiting needs on costly and complicated software packages for real time control. The (supported) external converter cards are necessary just for sampling periods below 50ms. Currently, more than 40 such plants are used in labs of several EU universities. The thermal plant consists of a halogen bulb 12V DC/20W, of a plastic pipe wall, of its internal air column containing the temperature sensor PT100, and of a fan 12V DC/0,6W (can be used for producing disturbances, but also for control). The optical channel has two outputs. The non filtered light intensity measured by a photodiode and the filtered one, where the signal is filtered by an analogue low pass filter with time constant at about 20s. The filtered optical channel was used for the experiment. We analyzed the parameters in several working points. The following tables show the average, maximal and minimal values of all parameters in all working points. The experiments ran for 30 control cycles. The sample time used for the experiments was set to 0.1 second.

3   PI$_1$ - Controller

The PI$_1$ - controller employs disturbance observer as the I-action. The controller structure consisting of P-action and DOB is presented in (Fig.4). Index "1" used in its title has to be related to one saturated pulse of the control variable that can occur in accomplishing large reference signal steps. In this way it should be distinguished from the PI$_0$ - controller reacting to a reference step by monotonic transient of the manipulated variable. To achieve fastest possible transients without overshooting the following controller tuning was used ([2]). The closed loop pole corresponding to the fastest monotonic output transients using simple P-controller

$$\alpha_e = -1/(T_d e) \tag{17}$$

Table 1. System parameters

w	M	u0	Ks	Td	v
35.000	2.500	2.500	0.602	0.538	-3.043
30.000	2.500	2.500	0.570	0.526	-2.615
20.000	2.500	2.500	0.533	0.531	-1.771
10.000	2.500	2.500	0.497	0.490	-0.913
30.000	2.000	2.000	0.590	0.456	-2.772
20.000	2.000	2.000	0.535	0.479	-1.871
10.000	2.000	2.000	0.470	0.458	-0.962
30.000	1.500	2.000	0.613	0.400	-2.886
20.000	1.500	2.000	0.586	0.408	-2.023
10.000	1.500	2.000	0.561	0.387	-1.175

Fig. 3. Thermo-optical plant

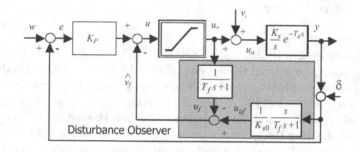

Fig. 4. PI$_1$ - controller

When using the P-controller together with the DOB based I-action, the "slower" closed loop pole should be used

$$\alpha_{eI} = \alpha_e/c = 1/(T_d ec); c = [1.3, 1.5] \tag{18}$$

The gain of P-controller corresponding to the closed loop pole (18) is then

$$K_p = -\alpha_{eI}/K_s \tag{19}$$

For the time constant of the filter used in the DOB one gets

$$T_f = -1/\alpha_{eI} \tag{20}$$

The following figure shows the real experiment results for various setpoint changes. The maximal value of process gain and the maximum value of dead time were used for the controller tuning in the first experiment. The control

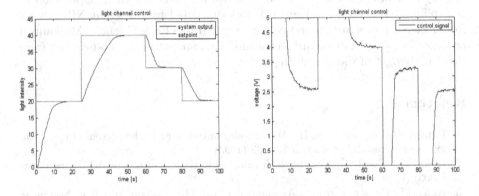

Fig. 5. Control results

gives fast transients without overshooting. The control signal consists of two control phases: one can observe an interval at the saturation followed by the control signal's monotonic transition to the new steady state value.

4   Conclusion

New relay experiment identification method has been proposed for the IPDT plant. Stable optical plant with the first order dominant dynamics was used for illustrating and verifying the method by the real experiment. The method benefits from obtaining the load disturbance value without need of tuning a PI controller firstly. Sensitivity to the measurement noise that may lead to more complicated relay output than the considered period consisting of two pulses, can be at least partially eliminated by sampled-data relay control using longer sampling periods. In applying the proposed method to controlling optical plant, the relay test yields results depending on the working point that obviously points out on nonlinear plant behaviour. In this paper, the nonlinear properties were treated by a robust controller. One of the strong advantages of the proposed method, however, is its possible extension to identifying FOPDT model, or a nonlinear model with dominant first order dynamics + dead time. Nevertheless, due to the simple analytical formulas the proposed algorithm is easy to implement online. To obtain more precise results, much faster sampling should be used. The one relay control cycle took approximately 20 samples, which does not give many combinations of t+,t-. However 0.1s sampling time is the limit for the USB soft real time control under windows operating system and as the fig. 11 and the control results show the identification precision was sufficient in this case.

Acknowledgement. This work was partially supported by the DFG Mercatorprofessur INST 219/3-1, by the project VEGA 1/0656/09 Integration and development of nonlinear and robust control methods and their application in controlling flying vehicles. The work was supported by the grant NIL-I-007-d from Iceland, Liechtenstein and Norway through the EEA Financial Mechanism and the Norwegian Financial Mechanism. This project is also co-financed from the state budget of the Slovak Republic.

References

1. Hang, C.C., Åström, K.J., Ho, W.K.: Relay auto-tuning in the present of the static load disturbance. Automatica 29, 563 (1993)
2. Huba, M.: Constrained systems design. vol.1. Basic controllers. STU Bratislava (2003) (in Slovak)
3. Huba, M.: Constrained Pole Assignment Control.In: Current Trends in Nonlinear Systems, pp. 163–183. Birkhauser, Boston (2006); ISBN10 0-8176-4383-4.-S
4. Jones, R.W., Tham, M.T.: Gain and Phase Margin Controller Tuning: FOPTD or IPDT moel-based methods. In: Annual Conference in Sapporo, August 4-6 (2004)
5. Park, J.H., Sung, S.W., Lee, I.: Improved relay auto-tuning with static load disturbance. Automatica 33, 711 (1997)
6. Shen, S., Wu, J., Yu, C.: Autotune identification under load disturbance. Industrial Engineering and Chemical Research 35, 1642 (1996)
7. Skogestad, S.: Simple Analytic Rules for Model Reduction and PID Controller tuning. Journal of process Control 13, 291–309 (2003)
8. Sung, S.W., Lee, J.: Relay feedback method under large static disturbances. Automatica 42, 353–356 (2006)
9. Ziegler, J.G., Nichols, N.B.: Optimum settings for automatic controllers. Trans. ASME 64, 759–768 (1942)
10. Liu, T., Gao, F.: A generalized relay identification method for time delay and non-minimum phase processes. Automatica 45, 1072–1079 (2009)

Modeling and Simulation of Power Yield in Thermal, Chemical and Electrochemical Systems: Fuel Cell Case

Stanislaw Sieniutycz

Faculty of Chemical Engineering, Warsaw University of Technology,
00-645 Warsaw, 1 Warynskiego Street, Poland
sieniutycz@ichip.pw.edu.pl

Abstract. This paper represents the research direction which deals with various computer aided energy converters, in particular thermal or chemical engines and fuel cells. Applying this general framework we can derive formulae for a family of converters' efficiencies and apply them to estimate irreversible power limits in practical systems. Thermal engines can be analyzed as linear units and radiation engines may be treated as Stefan-Boltzmann systems. We can also consider power limits for thermal systems as those propelled by differences of temperatures and chemical ones as those driven by differences of chemical potentials. In this paper we focus on fuel cells which are the electrochemical energy generators. We show that fuel cells satisfy the same modeling principles and apply similar computer schemes as thermal machines.

1 Introduction

In this paper power maximization approach is developed for fuel cells treated as flow engines driven by fluxes of chemical reagents . The theory combines a recent thermodynamic formalism worked out for chemical machines with the Faraday's law which determines the intensity of the electric current generation. Analyzed are performance curves of a solid oxide fuel cell (SOFC) system and the effect of typical design and operating parameters on the cell performance. Steady-state model of a high-temperature SOFC is considered, which refers to constant chemical potentials of incoming hydrogen fuel and oxidant. Lowering of the cell voltage below its reversible value is attributed to polarizations and imperfect conversions of reactions. The power formula summarizes the effect of transport laws, irreversible polarizations and efficiency of power yield. The reversible electrochemical theory is extended to the dissipative case; the efficiency decrease is linked with irreversibilities expressed in terms of polarizations (activation, concentration and ohmic). Effect of incomplete conversions is modelled assuming that substrates can be remained after the reaction and that side reactions may occur. Optimum and feasibility conditions are discussed for some input parameters such as the efficiency, power output, and electric current density of the cell.

R. Moreno-Díaz et al. (Eds.): EUROCAST 2011, Part II, LNCS 6928, pp. 593–600, 2012.

Calculations of the maximum power show that the data differ for power generated and consumed, and depend on parameters of the system, e.g., current intensity, number of mass transfer units, polarizations, electrode surface area, average chemical rate, etc.. These data provide bounds for SOFC energy generators, which are more exact and informative than reversible bounds for electrochemical transformation.

Limits for power yield are important indicators of systems' practical potential. They refer to various energy systems, in particular thermal, chemical and electrochemical engines and fuel cells. Thermal systems are easier to treat, yet, for chemical or electrochemical ones the search can involve extra, diverse aspects, such as: reaction invariants, reference components, process control, polarization data, electrochemical efficiencies, stability properties, etc.

In particular (the case of the present paper), power maximization is applied for fuel cells which are flow engines driven by fluxes of chemical reagents and electrochemical mechanism of electric current generation. The performance of a fuel cell is the effect of its design and operating parameters. In the present paper steady-state model of a SOFC is considered, which refers to constant chemical potentials of incoming hydrogen fuel and oxidant. Lowering of the cell voltage below its reversible value is attributed to polarizations and imperfect conversions of reactions.

Calculations of maximum power show that the data differ for power generated and consumed, and depend on system parameters, e.g., current intensity, number of mass transfer units, polarizations, electrode surface area, average chemical rate, etc.. These data provide bounds for SOFC energy generators, which are more exact than familiar reversible bounds for the electrochemical transformation.

2   Power Expression for Thermochemical Systems and Fuel Cells

Considerations of fuel cells leads to conclusions about a formal link between the mathematics of thermal engines and fuel cells. For simplicity we limit the related analysis below to the case of an engine propelled by a phase change or an isomerisation reaction $A_1 - A_2 = 0$ (or possibly a set of such reactions). To show a formal similarity between fuel cells and thermal machines we begin with an observation that the power producing, propelling force in an endoreversible thermal engine equals $T_{1'} - T_{2'}$, whereas the propelling force in the simplest chemical engine with the reaction $A_1 - A_2 = 0$ is $\mu_{1'} - \mu_{2'}$. The primed quantities refer to the chemically active, power producing part of the system. For the bulks of the streams or reservoirs the corresponding differences of temperature and chemical potential are respectively $T_1 - T_2$, and $\mu_1 - \mu_2$. Since the deviations of $T_{1'}$ and $\mu_{1'}$ from T_1 and μ_1 are of purely dissipative origin and the bulk differences $T_1 - T_2$, and $\mu_1 - \mu_2$ are identical with the "open circuit" (Carnot) values for the "active" differences $T_{1'} - T_{2'}$ and $\mu_{1'} - \mu_{2'}$, we may write

$$T_{1'} - T_{2'} = T_1 - T_2 - I_s(R_{1s} + R_{2s}) \tag{1}$$

$$\mu_{1'} - \mu_{2'} = \mu_1 - \mu_2 - I_n(R_{1n} + R_{2n}) \tag{2}$$

where I_s and I_n are the conserved currents of entropy and matter flowing through the energy-generating zone of the engine, and the indices 1 and 2 refer, respectively, to the resistances in the "upper" and "lower" part of the engine system. Total power production is the sum of thermal and substantial components, i.e.

$$p = p_s + p_n = (T_{1'} - T_{2'})I_s + (\mu_{1'} - \mu_{2'})I_n =$$

$$(T_1 - T_2)I_s + (\mu_1 - \mu_2)I_n - (R_{1s} + R_{2s})I_s^2 - (R_{1n} + R_{2n})I_n^2 \tag{3}$$

In terms of total resistances of the system $R_s = R_{1s} + R_{2s}$ and $R_n = R_{1n} + R_{2n}$, and after making a generalization to the case of coupled heat and mass transfer Eq. (3) reads

$$p = (T_{1'} - T_{2'})I_s + (\mu_{1'} - \mu_{2'})I_n =$$

$$(T_1 - T_2)I_s + (\mu_1 - \mu_2)I_n - R_{ss}I_s^2 - R_{sn}I_sI_n + R_{nn}I_n^2 \tag{4}$$

After introducing the enlarged flux vector $\mathbf{I} = (I_s, I_n)$, the enlarged vector of thermal potentials $\boldsymbol{\mu} = (T, \mu)$ and the resistance tensor $\mathbf{R}$, equation (4) can be written in a simple form

$$p = (\boldsymbol{\mu}_1 - \boldsymbol{\mu}_2)\mathbf{I} - \mathbf{R} : \mathbf{II} \tag{5}$$

The bulk driving forces $\boldsymbol{\mu}_1 - \boldsymbol{\mu}_2$ are given constants, whence, in linear systems with constant resistances, we are confronted with a simple maximization problem for quadratic power function p.

3   Power Limits in Energy Units and Fuel Cells

While the dimensionality of the potential vector will often be larger in real systems, the structure of Eq. (10) will be preserved whenever this equation will be considered in the vector form. Maximum power corresponds with the vanishing partial derivatives of function p. The optimal (power-maximizing) vector of currents at the maximum point of the system can be written in the form

$$I_{mp} = \frac{1}{2}\mathbf{R}^{-1}(\boldsymbol{\mu}_1 - \boldsymbol{\mu}_2) \equiv \frac{1}{2}\mathbf{I}_F \tag{6}$$

This result means that in the strictly linear systems the power-maximizing current vector is equal to one half of the purely dissipative current at the Fourier-Onsager point. The latter point refers to the system's state at which no power production occurs. Consistently, Eqs. (5) and (6) yield the following result for the maximum power

$$p_{mp} = \frac{1}{4}(\boldsymbol{\mu}_1 - \boldsymbol{\mu}_2)\mathbf{R}^{-1}(\boldsymbol{\mu}_1 - \boldsymbol{\mu}_2) \tag{7}$$

In terms of the purely dissipative flux vector at the Fourier-Onsager point, the above limit of maximum power is represented by an equation

$$p_{mp} = \frac{1}{4}\mathbf{R} : \mathbf{I}_F I_F \tag{8}$$

On the other hand, the power dissipated at the Fourier-Onsager point is

$$p_F = \mathbf{R} : \mathbf{I}_F I_F \tag{9}$$

Comparison of Eqs. (8) and (9) proves that, in linear thermo - electro - chemical systems, only at most 25% of power which is dissipated in the natural transfer process, can be transformed into the noble form of the mechanical power. This general result cannot, probably, be easily generalized to the nonlinear transfer systems where significant deviations may appear depending on the nature of diverse nonlinearities.

4   Thermodynamics of Power Yield in Fuel Cells

Fuel cells (FC) are electrochemical engines. Their role for environmental protection cannot be underestimated. Their main advantage in comparison to heat engines is that their efficiency is not a major function of device size. A fuel cell continuously transforms a part of chemical energy into electrical one by consuming fuel and oxidant. In the present paper power maximization approach is applied for the purpose of power limits in imperfect cells, where, for sufficiently large currents, power decreases with current because of prevailing effect of loss phenomena.

Temperatures T of resources were only necessary variables to describe purely thermal systems [1]. However, fuel cells are propelled by fluxes of energy and substances, so they require also chemical potentials μ_k.

Basic structure of fuel cells includes electrolyte layer in contact with a porous anode and cathode on either side. Gaseous fuels are fed continuously to the anode (negative electrode) compartment and an oxidant (i.e., oxygen from air) is fed continuously to the cathode (positive electrode) compartment. Electrochemical reactions take place at the electrodes to produce an electric current. Basic reaction is the electrochemical oxidation of fuel, usually hydrogen, and the reduction of the oxidant, usually oxygen. This principle makes a fuel cell similar to a chemical engine. In a FC process in Fig. 1 streams of fuel (H_2) and oxidant (O_2) interact; the process is propelled by diffusive and/or convective fluxes of heat and mass, transferred through the cell 'conductances' or boundary layers. The energy flux (power) is created in the cell generator which exploits the fuel stream contacting with the anode and the oxidant stream contacting with the catode. Both electrodes are separated by the electrolyte. As in thermal machines and radiation engines [2] − [7] both transfer mechanisms and properties of conducting layers influence the rate of power production.

Fuel cells performance is determined by magnitudes and directions of participating streams and by mechanism of electric current generation. Voltage lowering in a cell below its reversible value is a good measure of the cell imperfection.

The goals of the present paper include: (a) formulation of a thermo-electro-chemical model for imperfect fuel cells, especially for those with incomplete chemical conversions, (b) implementation of the model to simulate the behavior of high-T solid oxide fuel cells, (c) prediction of various losses of the voltage and their effect on the cell performance, and (d) application of fuel cell characteristics for the purpose of determining power limits.

Knowledge of operational voltage is required to define a cell efficiency as the ratio $\zeta = V/E$, where E is the reversible cell voltage or the equilibrium cell potential. For the power density in terms of ζ one has $p = iE\zeta$ or $p = \zeta p_{rev}$, which means that this efficiency is equal to the ratio of the actual power to the maximum reversible power. This definition links the fuel cell efficiency with the second law, and stresses substantial role of the operational voltage.

Assume that all incoming streams (those with "higher" Gibbs flux $G_{in} = G_{1\prime}$) represent a common phase of "substrates" (all system's components in the state before the chemical transformation, index 1′). All outgoing streams (those with "lower" Gibbs flux $G_{out} = G_{2\prime}$) represent a common phase of "products" (all system components in the state after the transformation, index 2′). The power expression follows from the entropy conservation and energy balance in the reversible part. For an isothermal reactor the power yield is

$$p = \mu_{1_1\prime} n_{1_1\prime} + \mu_{2_1\prime} n_{2_1\prime} \ldots \mu_{i_1\prime} n_{i_1\prime} \ldots + \mu_{m_1\prime} n_{m_1\prime}$$
$$-(\mu_{1_2\prime} n_{1_2\prime} + \mu_{2_2\prime} n_{2_2\prime} \ldots \mu_{i_2\prime} n_{i_2\prime} \ldots + \mu_{m_2\prime} n_{m_2\prime}) \qquad (10)$$

where the symbols n_k refer to fluxes rather than amounts of reagents. The formula shows that, in a steady and isothermal process, power yield of a chemical engine system is the difference between the input and output flux of the Gibb's function, [8] − [11].

We can transform Eq, (6) to a pronouncing form of Eq. (7) below, specific to the case of a complete conversion. In this case the components are numbered such that species 1,2 ... i are substrates and species i+1, i+2 ... m are products. Total power yield of an isothermal multi-reaction process is

$$p = \sum p_j = \sum -\{\mu_{1_1\prime} \nu_{1_j} + \mu_{2_1\prime} \nu_{2_j} \ldots + \mu_{i_1\prime} \nu_{i_j}$$
$$+\mu_{i+1_2\prime} \nu_{i+1_j} \ldots + \mu_{m-1_2\prime} \nu_{m-1_j} \ldots + \mu_{m_2\prime} \nu_{mj}\} n_j \qquad (11)$$

Quantities are molar chemical fluxes of reagents, i.e. products of the electrode surface area F and heterogeneous rates, r_j. In the case of complete conversion, power yield from the unit electrode area equals the sum of products of the affinity driving forces and the reaction rates

$$p = \sum \{A_j n_j\} = F \sum \{A_j r_j\} \qquad (12)$$

where $n_{1\prime}$ is the (positive) chemical flux defined as the product of the heterogeneous reaction rate and the electrode area. Yet, the assumption about the complete transformation of substrates into products can be relaxed. By considering the chemistry of systems with power production and transport phenomena one can quantitatively estimate effects of incomplete conversions. The related formula resembles the one which describes the effect of the internal entropy production [11]. For a single isothermal chemical reaction the corresponding power formula which subsumes the effect of incomplete conversions can be written in the form

$$p = (\Pi_{1'} - \Xi\Pi_{2'})n_{1'} = -\frac{iA}{n_eF}\Delta g^{\cdot eff}(T,p) = \Delta G^{\cdot eff} \tag{13}$$

where primed quantities refer to the inputs and outputs of the chemically active zone and $\Pi_{1'}$ is "one-way chemical affinity" attributed to reactants with known chemical potentials [8, 11]. Internal imperfection functions, Φ and Ξ, are respectively related to internal entropy production and incomplete conversion. The fraction Ξ is the reciprocity of coefficient Ψ introduced in [11]; they both characterize detrimental increase of chemical potentials of products caused by their dilution by remaining reactants.

Power formula of Eq. (9) generalizes the idealized power of an "endoreversible" system (with $\Xi = 1$) in which case difference $\Pi_{1'} - \Pi_{2'}$ is chemical affinity or $-\Delta g$. This is the chemical component of power, which describes power yield caused by chemical flux $n_{1'}$. Electrochemical power is generated with a non-ideal chemical efficiency. Effectively, in the engine mode where $\Xi < 1$, the system with internal imperfections, behalves as it would operate with a decreased affinity of an effective value $\Pi_{1'} - \Xi\Pi_{2'}$. Of course, power production is decreased by this imperfection.

5   Some Related Experiments

We have shown that a link exists between the mathematics of the thermal engines and fuel cells, and the theory of fuel cells can be unified with the theory of thermal engines. In this spirit, we present a brief analysis of some experimental data.

Voltage lowering in fuel cells below the reversible voltage is a good measure of their imperfection. Yet we need to distinguish between Nernst ideal voltage E^0 or and idle run voltage, E_0. It is the latter quantity from which all rate dependent losses of voltage should be subtracted. A number of approaches for calculating these polarization losses have been reviewed in literature by Zhao, Ou and Chen [12]. The details of calculations of the idle run voltage E_0 are discussed by Wierzbicki [13] who has implemented the Aspen Plus^{TM} software to investigate the behavior of SOFC based energy system using his own theoretical model of power yield kinetics. The model was based on equations of this paper. His calculations were compared with the experimental findings of the voltage and power in a laboratory FC system.

Sometimes, the difference between E^0 and E_0 is a current independent loss which may be described by the coefficient Ξ characterizing the detrimental increase of chemical potentials of products caused by their dilution by unreacted substrates. With the effective nonlinear resistances operating voltage can be represented as the departure from the idle run voltage E_0 (the quantity which replaces the reversible voltage E^0 in more involved situations)

$$V = E_0 - V_{int} = E_0 - V_{act} - V_{conc} - V_{ohm}$$
$$= E_0 - I(R_{act} + R_{conc} + R_{ohm}) \tag{14}$$

(Note the analogy between this equation and Eqs (1) and (2)). The losses, called polarization, include three main sources: activation polarization (V_{act}), ohmic polarization (V_{ohm}), and concentration polarization (V_{conc}). They refer to the equivalent activation resistance (R_{act}), equivalent ohmic resistance (R_{ohm}), and equivalent concentration resistance (R_{conc}). Activation and concentration polarization occur at both anode and cathode locations, while the resistive polarization represents ohmic losses throughout the fuel cell. Activation polarization V_{act} is neglected in the model of ref. [13], nonetheless the power curve is typical. As the voltage losses increase with current, the initially increasing power begins finally to decrease for sufficiently large currents, so that maxima of power are observed. The data include the losses of the idle run attributed to the flaws in electrode constructions and other imperfections which cause that the open circuit voltage is in reality lower than E^0 .

Voltage-current density and power-current density data were found for various temperatures of SOFC's. Aspen Plus^{TM} calculations testing the model versus experiments were obtained in Wierzbicki's MsD thesis [13]. They refer to experiments of Wierzbicki and Jewulski in Warsaw Institute of Energetics. In an ideal situation (no losses) the cell voltage is defined by the Nernst equation. Yet, while the first term of Eq. (14) defines the voltage without load, it nonetheless takes into account the losses of the idle run, which are the effect of flaws in electrode and other imperfections which cause that the open circuit voltage is in reality lower than the theoretical value. In the literature there are many other examples showing power maxima in fuel cells and proving the suitability of the thermodynamic theory to electrochemical systems.

The FC model describes physical and chemical performance of the irreversible fuel cells at various operating conditions. Optimum and feasibility conditions have been obtained and discussed for some input parameters such as efficiency, power output, and electric current density of the cell. Calculations of optimal power show that the data differ for power generated and consumed, and depend on parameters of the system, e.g., current intensity, number of mass transfer units, polarizations, electrode surface area, average chemical rate, etc.. They provide bounds for SOFC energy generators, which are more exact and informative than reversible bounds for electrochemical transformation.

References

[1] Sieniutycz, S.: A synthesis of thermodynamic models unifying traditional and work-driven operations with heat and mass exchange. Open Sys. & Information Dynamics 10, 31–49 (2003)

[2] Curzon, F.L., Ahlborn, B.: Efficiency of Carnot engine at maximum power output. American J. Phys. 43, 22–24 (1975)

[3] De Vos, A.: Endoreversible Thermodynamics of Solar Energy Conversion, pp. 30–41. Oxford University Press, Oxford (1994)

[4] Sieniutycz, S., Kuran, P.: Nonlinear models for mechanical energy production in imperfect generators driven by thermal or solar energy. Intern. J. Heat Mass Transfer 48, 719–730 (2005)

[5] Sieniutycz, S., Kuran, P.: Modeling thermal behavior and work flux in finite-rate systems with radiation. Intern. J. Heat and Mass Transfer 49, 3264–3283 (2006)

[6] Sieniutycz, S.: Dynamic programming and Lagrange multipliers for active relaxation of resources in non-equilibrium systems. Applied Mathematical Modeling 33, 1457–1478 (2009)

[7] Kuran, P.: Nonlinear models of production of mechanical energy in non-ideal generators driven by thermal or solar energy, PhD Thesis, Warsaw University of Technology (2006)

[8] Sieniutycz, S., Jeżowski, J.: Energy Optimization in Process Systems. Elsevier, Oxford (2009)

[9] Sieniutycz, S.: An analysis of power and entropy generation in a chemical engine. Intern. J. of Heat and Mass Transfer 51, 5859–5871 (2008)

[10] Tsirlin, A.M., Kazakov, V., Mironova, V.A., Amelkin, S.A.: Finite-time thermodynamics: conditions of minimal dissipation for thermodynamic process. Physical Review E 58, 215–223 (1998)

[11] Sieniutycz, S.: Complex chemical systems with power production driven by mass transfer Intern. J. of Heat and Mass Transfer 52, 2453–2465 (2009)

[12] Zhao, Y., Ou, C., Chen, J.: A new analytical approach to model and evaluate the performance of a class of irreversible fuel cells. International Journal of Hydrogen Energy 33, 4161–4170 (2008)

[13] Wierzbicki, M.: Optimization of SOFC based energy system using Aspen Plus^{TM}, MsD thesis, Warszawa, Supervised by S. Sieniutycz (Faculty of Chemical and Process Engineering, Warsaw University of Technology) and J. Jewulski (Laboratory of Fuel Cells, Institute of Energetics, Warsaw) (2009)

Prostheses Control with Combined Near-Infrared and Myoelectric Signals

Stefan Herrmann, Andreas Attenberger, and Klaus Buchenrieder

Universität der Bundeswehr München, Fakultät für Informatik,
Werner-Heisenberg-Weg 39, 85579 Neubiberg, Germany
{stefan.herrmann,andreas.attenberger,
klaus.buchenrieder}@unibw.de
http://www.unibw.de

Abstract. Over the last decade, technical innovations have resulted in major achievements in the field of upper limb prostheses. However, the limitation of such devices is not the electro-mechanical realization, but rather the lack of astute cutaneous control-sources. This contribution demonstrates real-time detection of muscle exertions by combining myoelectric and near-infrared signals. The presented sensor technology and classification scheme have been developed for five-finger hand prostheses but can be employed to control a variety of prosthetic devices. This control mechanism only requires a patient to individually contract extant muscles, for which a minimal-threshold myoelectric or reflected near-infrared signal can be measured on the surface of the skin. Our experimental data show that the combination of both sensor types provides better classification results and surpasses the spatial resolution of a single pickup device. Features extracted from these signals can be used as input data for our existing classifier and allow compensation of muscle fatigue effects.

Keywords: Myoelectric Signal, Near-Infrared Spectroscopy, Prosthesis Control, Sensor Fusion.

1 Introduction

A skeletal muscle consists of several muscle fibres grouped into motor units, each activated by a motor neuron. Units can be activated with a certain frequency, with which so-called action potentials propagate through the fibres [14,16]. The observed MES reflects the sum of all motor unit signals in close proximity. The amount of activated motor units and the activation frequency defines the level of muscle contraction and the resulting force [6]. Electrodes on the skin, above the muscle, can detect this difference in electric potential. In 1912 Piper started to investigate these electromyographic signals (MES) [18]. Applied research on MES processing has been pursued since the early 1960s [11,8]. An essential compendium of advances in design and technology for prostheses was compiled by Näder in 1988 [17]. Since then, technological progress in electronics, signal processing and microcontroller systems have led to numerous applications. Consummate surveys of historical developments, microprocessor control, excitation

R. Moreno-Díaz et al. (Eds.): EUROCAST 2011, Part II, LNCS 6928, pp. 601–608, 2012.

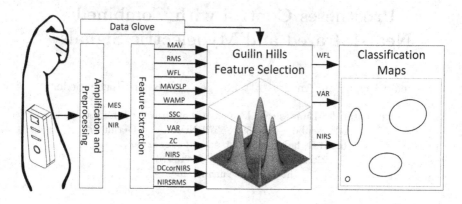

Fig. 1. Training mode of the UniBw-Hand controller

methods and state-of-the-art of upper limb prostheses are provided by Merletti, Parker, Lake, Miguelez and Muzumdar [15,13,16].

A more recent approach to measure muscle contractions is the near-infrared spectroscopy (NIRS) which offers good spatial resolution [5]. Corresponding battery-operated hardware that is safe for application can be built at low cost [1]. Biological tissue is nearly opaque to light in the visible spectrum, but it is relatively transparent for light between 700 and 900 nm [10]. Photons are only absorbed by blood chromophores, e.g., oxygenated and deoxygenated hemoglobin [1]. Contracting a muscle changes the amount of blood in the tissue and the number of backscattered photons [4].

The classification problem for prosthesis control has been structured as a multistage process by Englehart and affiliate researchers [7]. Most current control systems are based on the work of Hudgins et al. in which time-domain features and a multilayer perceptron (MLP) are used for classification [9,12]. The UniBw-Hand, developed at the Universität der Bundeswehr in Munich relies on this groundwork [2]. Our research focuses on signal acquisition, processing and classification. Our approach differs from other control methods with respect to feature processing, training methods and user comfort. As in other classification algorithms, we distinguish an operation and a training mode. During training, users exercise predefined hand and finger movements synchronously with both arms. To attain perfectly tagged classification patterns, we measure the precise, willingly synchronized gesture of the opposite, unscathed hand with a data-glove. Myoelectric and near-infrared signals (NIRS) are captured from remaining predominant muscles on the patients forearm. Since the NIRS/MES is nonlinear and stochastic, it is difficult to decide which feature subset provides best results. For this reason, we have developed the Guilin Hills selection method, which is based on a Bayesian classification scheme [2,3]. Figure 1 shows the individual steps during training mode.

Some prosthesis control mechanisms rely on Support Vector Machines (SVM), where data points are separated into two classes by hyperplanes. This approach comes with several drawbacks: (1) SVMs can only be used for two-class tasks

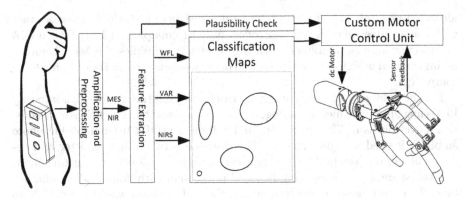

Fig. 2. Operative phase of the UniBw-hand controller

while multiclass SVMs have to be split into binary classifiers, which is computationally expensive; (2) data points are mandatorily assigned to one of the classes,
which means that outliers can easily be attributed to the wrong class; (3) it is
difficult to classify relaxed arm or hand positions as these produce only few data
points; and finally (4) data points for some movements overlap, which requires
a CPU-intensive search of kernel functions. The Guilin Hills selection method
is a much simpler statistical approach. It is based on traditional feature selection, feature projection and statistical principles. The selection process yields a
minimal subset of features necessary for a good classification. With the feature
points being normally distributed, one or more hierarchically structured classification maps can be constructed. During operation mode, as depicted in Figure
2, the NIRS/MES is measured and preprocessed exactly as in the training mode.
With the classification maps obtained during the training phase, control data
for the motor unit is generated. Via the combination of two different signals, a
plausibility check of signals can be applied, determining, for example, wether the
sensor has lost contact to the skin or surface pressure has changed. A current
sensor in the motor unit or strain gauges as integral parts of the gripper can
provide feedback and avoid grip slippage.

2 Method

During experimental trials, we found, that measuring the myoelectric signal
alone has proven insufficient for discerning individual finger movements and hand
gestures. Further experiments with MES sensors to measure the influence of
biophysical and mechanical properties, with myotonometric sensors to determine
tissue displacement due to muscle activation and with near-infrared sensors for
oximetry were investigated to provide additional data. Based on this information
and an extensive review of literature, we developed a custom miniature sensor
with a myoelectric pickup and a near- infrared sensor in a compact housing. By
adjoining two or more NIRS/MES sensors, hand and even finger motions can be

identified precisely. The myoelectric sensor consists of a single differential stage with round, silver plated, dry electrodes spaced 1 cm apart. A Burr Brown INA 121 instrumentation amplifier, with a gain of 100, amplifies the MES before it is run through a high-pass filter with a corner frequency of 15 Hz to remove DC components.

For the light source, we are using an array encapsulating twelve high intensity LEDs in a miniature metal housing, sealed with a glass top. The LEDs have emission wavelengths of 730nm, 805nm and 850nm. An OPT101 monolithic photo amplifier is used as light-detector. The distance between light emitter and detector is approximately 3,5 cm. The electronics are enclosed in a custom built, non-transparent plastic housing fastened to the skin with double sided adhesive tape. To reduce noise in the NIR signal, the pick-up area was covered with an opaque material.

Near infrared spectroscopy induces energy in the tissue and causes heat. To keep this effect to a minimum and to prevent injuries, the light source is pulsed via a trapezoidal shaped activation signal. This also allows us to estimate the amount of ambient light reaching the sensor and correct the signal. The activation frequency of the light source is 20 Hz with a duty cycle of 2.5%. Signal generation, as well as acquisition of the MES and the NIRS is achieved using Mathworks Matlab [TM](Version V.7.8) and the Data Acquisition Toolbox [TM] (Version V.2.14) using a National Instruments USB-6229 data acquisition device. For signal post-processing and generation of supply voltages for up to four combined sensors, a custom circuit was developed. Here, the MES is bandpass filtered with cutoff frequencies at 15 Hz and 512 Hz respectively, while a variable gain can be applied to adjust the signal amplitude. Digitization was carried out with a sample rate of 4096 Hz. Besides the standard time-domain features of the MES, we introduce three new features to improve the classification results.

2.1   NIRS Feature

The NIRS feature takes into account, that the light source is switched on and off periodically and eliminates ambient light from the signal. During a time window of k signal samples, the light source has to be switched at least once. $\overline{n} = \{n_1, \cdots, n_k\}$ represents the NIR signal frame and $\overline{e} = \{e_1, \cdots, e_k\}$ the enable signal for the light emitter. Therefrom follows:

$$\text{NIRS} = \text{Signal}(\overline{n}, \overline{e}) - \text{Offset}(\overline{n}, \overline{e}) \tag{1}$$

with

$$\text{Signal}(\overline{n}, \overline{e}) = \frac{\sum_{j=1}^{k} n_i \cdot \text{Ena}(e_j)}{\sum_{j=1}^{k} \text{Ena}(e_j)} \tag{2}$$

$$\text{Offset}(\overline{n}, \overline{e}) = \frac{\sum_{j=1}^{k} n_i \cdot (1 - \text{Ena}(e_j))}{\sum_{j=1}^{k} (1 - \text{Ena}(e_j))} \tag{3}$$

$\text{Ena}(e_j)$ equals 1, if the signal is greater than an upper threshold and 0, if it is below a lower threshold.

2.2 DC Corrected NIRS Feature (DCcorNIS)

Without any muscle contraction the amplitude of the NIRS feature is not equal to zero. This offset depends on the anatomy below the sensor, blood volume and blood pressure and it may change over time. It can be corrected with a recursive averaging method. In the following equation, $NIRS_i$ describes the NIRS feature in the time window i with an offset of DC_i. The parameters b_0 and a_1 must be evaluated experimentally.

$$DCcorNIRS_i = NIRS_i - DC_i \qquad (4)$$

$$DC_i = NIRS_i \cdot b_0 - DC_{i-1} \cdot a_1 \qquad (5)$$

2.3 NIRS and Myoelectric RMS Feature NIRSRMS

The NIRSRMS feature combines a weighted NIR signal with the RMS feature of the MES $\overline{m} = \{m_1, \cdots, m_k\}$:

$$NIRSRMS = RMS(\overline{m}) \cdot NIRS(\overline{n}, \overline{e}) \qquad (6)$$

3 Results

The near-infrared as well as the myoelectric signal correspond to the muscle activity. Figure 3 shows the RMS, the NIRS and the DCcorNIRS values for a muscle contraction. During this contraction, the NIRS feature shows an amplitude decay, which is caused by the blood reflux into the muscle. The amount of light, backscattered to the sensor by the non-contracted muscle, leads to a DC offset in the NIRS. This offset may vary according to arm movement or blood pressure and shows different amplitudes according to the location on the skin. With the DCcorNIRS feature, this offset can be removed successfully. Because of the recursive averaging this feature inhibits a significant decay in amplitude. A classification of finger- and hand-movements is therefore only possible for the onset of a contraction. Another possibility of dealing with the problem of amplitude decay is to alter the DCcorNIRS parameters b_0 and a_1 during a contraction.

Combining a near-infrared and an electromyographic sensor in one circuit can lead to high levels of noise in the myoelectric signal. First prototypes have shown significant artifacts when the light source of the NIR sensor is switched, due to the capacitive coupling of the digital enable signal to the skin electrodes. High currents during the phase of LED activation can cause artifacts due to reduced MES sensor supply voltage. Furthermore, noise on the ground pads can deteriorate the MES. When the combined sensor loses contact to the skin, light is reflected without penetrating the tissue and causes the measured signal to increase. This can lead to saturation of the photo amplifier and can be used as a means to avoid unwanted movements of the prostheses due to MES signal artifacts as depicted in Figure 4.

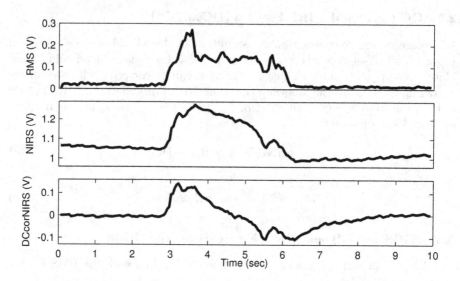

Fig. 3. RMS, NIRS and DCcorNIRS feature for a single muscle contraction

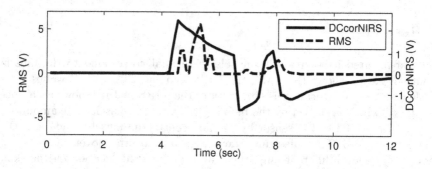

Fig. 4. Electrode Lift Artifacts can be observed in the EMG and NIR features

When the sensor shifts or moves across the skin, similar signal characteristics can be observed. Stray light reaching the sensor when the cuff is lifted can also offset the signal. Because the MES is unaffected by this kind of noise, the combination with the NIRS allows for artifact compensation. Incorporating this new, combined sensor into our existing Guilin Hills selection method is advantageous, because the new features are calculated in the same time-windows and are subjected to the feature selection. Therefore, changes in feature selection, classification map generation and operation stage are not necessary.

4 Conclusion

During our work we successfully implemented a combined NIR-MES sensor where the analog myoelectric signal is not influenced by the digital NIR measurement. Although the size of the prototype is slightly larger than standard MES-only sensors, assembly into a prosthesis is still possible. Experiments show, that the fusion of both signal types yields good results and can be incorporated into existing control schemes. Combining the digital enable signal of an LED and an analog amplifier for very weak signals in such a limited space poses various problems. To avoid and reduce artifacts, a thorough sensor layout and component placement is required. In order to acquire useful signals, the sensor must be fastened cutaneously over a muscle without applying external force and the detection area must be covered with cuff material in such a way that ambient light is reduced. The presented features can be incorporated into our classifier without any changes. Further testing with a larger number of probands is required to determine the number of times the new combined features are selected during the training phase.

In the future, we are not only planning to use this sensor for pattern recognition techniques, but also for proportional control of individual fingers. Because an active NIR Sensor allows changing the observation area, better spatial resolution compared to the MES pick-up is possible. This will make it possible to generate classification regions for finger movements which are easy to discriminate. Through a combination of a pattern recognition method at the onset of a contraction and proportional control of the selected movement with the myoelectric signal, a fine control of multi-finger devices can be achieved.

During preliminary testing, three different individual finger flections as well as hand gestures were identified using only the DCcorNIRS feature of the onset of a contraction and normal distributions as classification regions. The sensor was placed above the flexor digitorum muscle on the right forearm of a 28-year-old male volunteer. Through this one-dimensional classification map, movements could be identified correctly with a probability of 95%. Further enhancement could incorporate several optical detectors distributed across the muscle in order to acquire data from the cross section of the arm.

References

1. Bozkurt, A., Rosen, A., Rosen, H., Onaral, B.: A Portable Near Infrared Spectroscopy System for Bedside Monitoring of Newborn Brain. BioMedical Engineering onLine 4(29) (2005)
2. Buchenrieder, K.: Processing of Myoelectric Signals by Feature Selection and Dimensionality Reduction for the Control of Powered Upper-Limb Prostheses. In: Moreno Díaz, R., Pichler, F., Quesada Arencibia, A. (eds.) EUROCAST 2007. LNCS, vol. 4739, pp. 1057–1065. Springer, Heidelberg (2007)
3. Buchenrieder, K.: Dimensionality Reduction and Classification of Myoelectric Signals for the Control of Upper-Limb Prostheses. In: Proceedings of the IASTED - Human Computer Interaction 2008, pp. 113–119 (2008)

4. Bunce, S., Izzetoglu, M., Izzetoglu, K., Onaral, B., Pourrezaei, K.: Functional Near-Infrared Spectroscopy. IEEE Engineering in Medicine and Biology Magazine 25(4), 54–62 (2006)
5. Chance, B., Anday, E., Nioka, S., Zhou, S., Hong, L., Worden, K., Li, C., Murray, T., Ovetsky, Y., Pidikiti, D., Thomas, R.: A Novel Method for Fast Imaging of Brain Function, Non-Invasively, with Light. Optics Express 2, 411–423 (1998)
6. De Luca, C.: Physiology and Mathematics of Myoelectric Signals. IEEE Transactions on Biomedical Engineering BME-26(6), 313–325 (1979)
7. Englehart, K., Hudgins, B., Parker, P., Stevenson, M.: Classification of the Myoelectric Signal using Time-Frequency Based Representations. Special Issue of Medical Engineering and Physics on Intelligent Data Analysis in Electromyography and Electroneurography 21, 431–438 (1999)
8. Freedy, A., Lyman, J.: Adaptive Aiding. In: Proceedings of the 3rd International Symposium on External Control of Human Movement, pp. 155–170 (1969)
9. Hudgins, B., Parker, P., Scott, R.: A New Strategy for Multifunction Myoelectric Control. IEEE Transactions on Biomedical Engineering 40(1), 82–94 (1993)
10. Izzetoglu, M., Izzetoglu, K., Bunce, S., Ayaz, H., Devaraj, A., Onaral, B., Pourrezaei, K.: Functional Near-Infrared Neuroimaging. IEEE Transactions on Neural Systems and Rehabilitation Engineering 13(2), 153–159 (2005)
11. Kobrinski, A., Bolkovitin, S., Voskoboinikova, L.: Problems of Bioelectric Control. In: Proceedings of the 1st IFAC International Congress of Automatic and Remote Control, vol. 2 (1960)
12. Kuruganti, U., Hudgins, B., Scott, R.: Two-Channel Enhancement of a Multifunction Control System. IEEE Transactions on Biomedical Engineering 42(1), 109–111 (1995)
13. Lake, C., Miguelez, J.: Comparative Analysis of Microprocessors in Upper Limb Prosthetics. Journal of Prosthetics and Orthotics 15, 48–65 (2003)
14. Malmivuo, J., Plonsey, R.: Bioelectromagnetism, Principles and Applications of Bioelectric and Biomagnetic Fields. Oxford University Press, Oxford (2007)
15. Merletti, R., Parker, P.: Electromyography - Physiology, Engineering and Non Invasive Applications. John Wiley & Sons, Chichester (2004)
16. Muzumdar, A.: Powered Upper Limb Prostheses, Control, Implementation and Clinical Application. Springer, Heidelberg (2004)
17. Näder, M.: Prothesen-Kompendium; Prothesen der oberen Extremität. Mecke Druck und Verlag Duderstadt (1988)
18. Piper, H.: Electrophysiologie menschlicher Muskeln. Springer, Berlin (1912)

Heuristic Forecasting of Geometry Deterioration of High Speed Railway Tracks

Lisandro Quiroga and Eckehard Schnieder

Institute for Traffic Safety and Automation Engineering, TU Braunschweig
Langer Kamp 8, 38106 Braunschweig, Germany
{quiroga,schnieder}@iva.ing.tu-bs.de
http://www.iva.ing.tu-bs.de

Abstract. Travelling safely and comfortably on high speed railway lines requires excellent conditions of the whole railway infrastructure in general and of the railway track geometry in particular. In this framework, a reliable forecasting of the railway geometry ageing process is indispensable for an optimal planning and scheduling of maintenance activities. For this reason the French railway operator SNCF has been measuring periodically the geometrical characteristics of its high speed network for more than 20 years now. In this paper a hybrid system forecasting model is presented. It uses a grey-box approach: a model structure and its constraints are specified basing on previous process knowledge, then the optimal set of parameter values is searched. Since the process is non linear the parameters are searched by means of the Levenberg-Marquardt (LM) algorithm. Finally, the method is applied on real data of a French high speed TGV line and its results compared with those of benchmark approaches.

Keywords: Railway track, deterioration, forecasting, hybrid systems.

1 Introduction

Measuring and keeping railway geometry under control are fundamental tasks of the railway infrastructure maintenance process. Railway geometry is representative of the travelling comfort and the derailing risk, so if its deviation exceeds a certain limit value, the travelling speed on that sector must be reduced. Therefore, railway geometry is both a measure of travelling quality and safety. For these reasons the French railway operator SNCF has been measuring periodically the geometrical characteristics of its high speed network since its commissioning, i.e. for more than 20 years now.

The longitudinal levelling (in French *Nivellement Longitudinal*, NL) is the longitudinal mean deviation of rails respect to the ideal position, and it is considered representative of the general railway geometry deterioration [1]. By default the deterioration grade increases with time, reflecting the track geometry deterioration. Thus decrements take place only when some maintenance activity is performed. In Fig. 1 the dotted bars represent the type of maintenance that

R. Moreno-Díaz et al. (Eds.): EUROCAST 2011, Part II, LNCS 6928, pp. 609–616, 2012.

directly affect the track geometry: tamping interventions. Their heights represent the fraction of the railway sector affected by the tamping activity. Tamping yields a visually obvious effect, generating a sudden drop in NL.

Due to high logistic costs constraints, most track geometry maintenance activities need to be planned up to one year in advance. This is why a precise forecasting of the railway geometry is a key factor for effective maintenance activities planning, helping to answer the fundamental questions about when and where maintenance will be needed. In this work we present some benchmark approaches to railway track geometry degradation and restoration forecasting, and we introduce an alternative discrete-continuous (hybrid) approach. In section 3 the these models are applied on real data and the obtained results are analysed and compared.

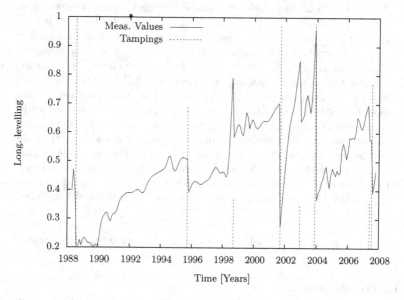

Fig. 1. Course of longitudinal levelling degradation and tamping interventions for a railroad sector

2   Applied Models

In this section the implemented grey-box models are described. We consider railway deterioration being subject to two processes: deterioration and restoration (maintenance). Different models are proposed for each of them and then put together in grey-box models.

2.1   Restoration Model

In contrast to the deterioration process, restoration process models are not numerous. In this work we consider the non linear model proposed by [9], described by (1).

$$NL_{t+1} - NL_t = \beta_0 \cdot NL_t + \beta_1 \tag{1}$$

In order to be able to apply this model on real cases, where sometimes track sectors are only partially restored (tamping is applied on only a fraction of the sector), we define u_t as in Eq. (2) as a signal with value 0 when no tamping takes place, and a value between 0 and 1 when tamping takes place in the sector, according to the fraction of the sector tamped.

$$u_t = \frac{\text{length of tamped track at time } t}{\text{total sector length}} \tag{2}$$

Then Eq. (3) is used to forecast NL after tamping.

$$NL_{t+1} = \beta_0 \cdot NL_t \cdot u_t + \beta_1 \cdot u_t + NL_t \tag{3}$$

2.2 Deterioration Models

The railway track geometry deterioration process has been deeply investigated in the last 30 years. As stated by [5], there are two main types of approaches: the engineering approach and the statistical approach.

The engineering approach aims to asses the mechanical properties of track degradation, providing a good understanding of how track responds to vehicle loading. In general, technical references agree that degradation depends on traffic intensity, travelling speed and axle load. Most of them aim to finding an equation describing deterioration rate as a function of these three variables. For an overview of the different formulas proposed see [6].

On the other hand, the statistical approach aims to analysing observations of actual geometry deviations. The latter is then considered the dependant variable and the explanatory variables can be for example accumulated axle load or simply time. The aim of this work is not to define degradation rate as a function of known variables, but to forecast degradation at l steps in time, assuming that all other variables affecting degradation remain unchanged. This is in general a valid assumption for the aimed forecasting periods, namely up to one year. Therefore, this work belongs to the statistical approach. We consider three different models: double exponential smoothing, autoregressive and hybrid. In section 5 an analysis of their performances is presented.

Exponential Smoothing. In [9] a double exponential smoothing based approach is proposed for modelling railway track geometry deterioration. Exponential smoothing is widely used for forecasting time series in the field of econometrics, and was developed by [7]. Double exponential smoothing assumes an only locally constant linear model of first order (locally constant linear trend), thus giving more weight to recent observations. At time n the parameters $\beta_{0,n}$ and $\beta_{1,n}$ are determined by minimizing expression (4).

$$\sum_{j=0}^{n-1} \omega^j [Z_{n-j} - (\beta_{0,n} - \beta_{1,n}j)]^2 \tag{4}$$

The constant ω ($\omega < 1$) is a discount factor that discounts past observations exponentially. At time n the l-step ahead forecast $\hat{Z}(n + l)$ is calculated by means of Eq. (5).

$$\hat{Z}(n + l) = \hat{\beta}_{0,n} + \hat{\beta}_{1,n} \tag{5}$$

For the model to also successfully explain the effects of degrading and restoration, it is necessary to combine the models expressed in equations 1 and 3. If the jumps caused by tamping are added to the original signal, a new signal is obtained which represents the effects of degradation only. On the other side these jumps seen as impulses make up another signal which represents the restoration process. Applying (1) on the restoration signal (here it is off course assumed that the dates of future tamping activities are known) and (3) on the degradation signal we obtain forecasts for both processes. Finally by combining again both signals, a forecast for the combined process is obtained.

Autoregressive Model. In [8] the use of ARMA (**A**uto**R**egressive **M**oving **A**verage) models for railway track geometry deterioration is proposed. To apply this model, we consider NL_t as a discrete signal sampled at regular intervals. Furthermore we define the cumulated tampint U_t as in Eq. (6).

$$U\_t = \sum_{n=0}^{t} u\_t \tag{6}$$

Then we can define the ARIMA model used in this work as Eq. (7) which is an AR model of second order plus the non-linear restoration model of (3).

$$NL\_t = \alpha\_1 NL\_t - 1 + \alpha\_2 NL\_t - 2 + \alpha\_3 U\_t - 1 + \alpha\_4 U\_t - 2 + \alpha\_5 U\_t NL\_t - 1 + \alpha\_6 \tag{7}$$

Hybrid Model. By observing track geometry degradation curves like the one of Fig. 1 and the performances of the forecasting model presented in 2.2 and 2.2, some remarks can be asserted:

- The gradient of the curve (degradation speed) between two tamping activities remains constant or at least locally constant.
- The gradient of the curve very often changes abruptly after tamping.
- The forecasting models presented so far seem to work satisfactorily for the first years, but after some tamping activities become inappropriate.

[2] argues that "*...state jumps are the basic hybrid phenomenon that cannot be represented and analysed by methods elaborated either in continuous or discrete systems theory...*". Having said this, we propose a hybrid model considering tamping activities as state jumps. For modelling the degradation process, double exponential smoothing is used. But in contrast to the model presented in 2.2, after each tamping activity the measurements before tamping are forgotten, and a new set of parameters is identified. This leads to a model adapting itself very quickly after each tamping, and very slowly between tampings.

The algorithm for obtaining the l-step forecast at time n can be described as follows:

1. **Let** $M = m_0, \ldots, m_n$ be all available measurements since the last tamping activity and $T = t_0, \ldots, t_n$ their associated times, excluding those who are too near tamping activities, i.e. excluding all measurements $m_i : \|t_i - t_{nt}\| <$ SETTLING_TIME, where m_i is a given measurement, t_i its associated time and t_{nt} is the time of the tamping activity nearest to that measurement.
2. **If** size$(M) >$ MIN_CYCLE_SIZE **then** apply double exponential smoothing with smoothing coefficient OMEGA to find the estimations $\hat{\beta}_{0,n}$ and $\hat{\beta}_{1,n}$, and go to step 5, else go to step 3.
3. **If** the current tamping cycle is not the first one **then** take the estimation of $\hat{\beta}_{1,n}$ from the tamping cycle immediately before the current one, and $\hat{\beta}_{0,n}$ such that $m_i = \hat{\beta}_{0,n} + \hat{\beta}_{1,n}t_i$ holds, where m_i is the last measured value and t_i its associated time, and go to step 6, **else** go to step 4.
4. Take $\hat{\beta}_{1,n} =$ INIT_$\beta1$ and $\hat{\beta}_{0,n}$ such that $m_i = \hat{\beta}_{0,n} + \hat{\beta}_{1,n}t_i$ holds.
5. Calculate $\hat{Z}(n + l) = \hat{\beta}_{0,n} + \hat{\beta}_{1,n}$ as the forecast at l steps.
6. **If** a tamping activity is planned within the next l steps, i.e. at step $n+k$, with $k < l$, **then** update the forecast $\hat{Z}(n + l)$ by subtracting to it the expected tamping effect given by $\Delta NL = (\hat{Z}(n + k) - $ NL_AFTER_TAMPING$)u_t$.

The algorithm uses a series of parameters, for which an explanation is next given.

- SETTLING_TIME: As can be observed in Fig. 1, in approx. the first 2 months after tamping takes place, the behaviour of the track geometry can be strongly non linear, so the measurements taking place in this lapse are discarded.
- MIN_CYCLE_SIZE: In order to perform a linear regression with a reasonable confidence, a minimal number of samples is required. In this case we take MIN_CYCLE_SIZE=5.
- OMEGA: As mentioned in section 2.2, double exponential smoothing uses a smoothing constant ω to give more weight to recent observations. [7] recommends choosing ω such that $\omega = 0.84 < \omega < 0.97$. In our work we take $\omega = 0.95$.
- INIT_$\beta0$ and INIT_$\beta1$: When there are lesser than MIN_CYCLE_SIZE sample since the last tamping available, the line gradientis taken from the last tamping cycle (we call tamping cycle the time between two consecutive tampings) and is taken such that the curve determined by and contains the last measurement. But if the current tamping cycle is the first one, the only option left is to take an arbitrary initial value . In this work we use INIT_$\beta1$=0.05, i.e. an initial degradation rate of 0.05 mm. per year.
- NL_AFTER_TAMPING: this is the typical value of NL after tamping a complete sector. In this work its value is set to 0.35.

3   Case Study

In this section we apply the models presented in section 2 to real data measured on a TGV high speed line. All forecasts are made recursively, i.e., forecasts of

NL_{t+l} are made using information in time periods $1, 2, \ldots, t$. For the forecast of NL_{t+l}, parameters are estimated using the data $NL_1, NL_2, \ldots, NL_t$. In all models, parameters are estimated by minimizing the sum of squared residuals of the l-step ahead forecast. As we use a non linear restoration model (see 2.1), for solving these minimization problems [3], an implementation of the Levenberg-Marquardt (LM) algorithm [4], is used. The LM algorithm is an iterative technique that finds a local minimum of a function that is expressed as the sum of squares of nonlinear functions.

Fig. 2 shows the achieved forecastings using the two models with best performance on the track sector of Fig. 1, namely the exponential smoothing model and the hybrid model. The hybrid model behaves better in the first year after a tamping intervention. After that, both model have similar performances.

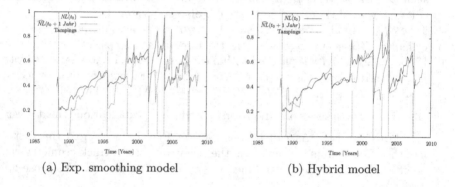

(a) Exp. smoothing model   (b) Hybrid model

Fig. 2. Forecastings of NL using the exp. smoothing (2(a)) and the hybrid (2(b)) model

Degradation and restoration of track geometry can be very different from one sector to another. Therefore, in order to asses the prediction potential and robustness of all three methods, we apply them on real data of 200 sectors of 1 km length each. We record for each model and each sector the mean absolute percentage error (MAPE) and mean square error (MSE) defined as in Eq. (8), where NL_{it} is the value measured on sector i at time t, $\widehat{NL}_{it}$ its 1-year-ahead forecast and N_i is the number of samples available for sector i.

$$MAPE_i = \frac{1}{N_i} \sum_{n=0}^{N_i-1} \left| \frac{NL_{it} - \widehat{NL}_{it}}{NL_{it}} \right| \quad \text{and} \quad MSE_i = \frac{\sum_{n=0}^{N_i-1} (NL_{it} - \widehat{NL}_{it})^2}{N_i}$$

$$(8)$$

In table 1 the estimated mean value $\hat{\mu}$ and variance $\hat{\sigma}$ for both MAPE and MSE are expressed for each of the presented methods, plus the naive forecast $\widehat{NL}_{it} = NL_{it}$. The means and variances are calculated as in Eq. (9), where X in this case are MAPE and MSE.

$$\hat{\mu}(X) = \frac{\sum_{i=1}^{200} X_i}{200} \quad \text{and} \quad \hat{\sigma}(X) = \frac{\sum_{i=1}^{200}(X_i - \bar{X})^2}{200 - 1} \tag{9}$$

The last two rows of the table shows for each model the number of sectors for which it was better than all other methods, in the sense of MAPE and MSE, respectively.

Table 1. Overview of forecasting results on 200 1-km-long track sectors with all presented process models

	Hybrid	AR	Exp. Smooth.	Naive
$\hat{\mu}$(MAPE)	16.2%	18.7%	24.7%	19.6%
$\hat{\sigma}$(MAPE)	$2.79 \cdot 10^{-3}$	$3.59 \cdot 10^{-3}$	$4.18 \cdot 10^{-3}$	$3.97 \cdot 10^{-3}$
$\hat{\mu}$(MSE)	0.0149	0.0193	0.0314	0.0225
$\hat{\sigma}$(MSE)	$3.85 \cdot 10^{-4}$	$3.44 \cdot 10^{-4}$	$3.93 \cdot 10^{-4}$	$3.36 \cdot 10^{-4}$
Sectors Best MAPE	61.5%	16.5%	10%	12%
Sectors Best MSE	66.5%	17%	8%	6.5%

The minimal mean value for both MAPE (16.2%) and MSE (0.0149) are obtained using the hybrid model. The minimal MAPE variance ($2.79 \cdot 10^{-3}$) is also achieved with the hybrid model, but in the case of MSE variance, the minimal value ($3.36 \cdot 10^{-4}$) corresponds to the naive forecasting. The hybrid model is also the most appropriate in most of the track sectors, both from the point of view of MAPE (61.5%) and MSE (66.5%). The exponential smoothing model fails to improve the overall performance of the naive model, while the hybrid model achieves a MAPE reduction of 17.3% and an MSE reduction of 33.8% respect to the naive model, and the AR model achieves a MAPE reduction of 4.59% and an MSE reduction of 14.2% respect to the naive model. The relatively low variances of MAPE and MSE achieved by the hybrid model show that the approach is robust in the sense that it can deliver satisfactory results in sectors with different degradation characteristics.

4   Conclusions

This paper presents an approach to railway track geometry forecasting modelling the degradation-restoration process as a hybrid system. The results obtained after applying this approach on the data collected in the lapse of almost 20 years on a 200 km high speed railway track are compared with the ones obtained using some benchmark approaches. This comparison shows that the hybrid model in general achieves better results than the benchmark models, due mainly to its increased adaptability after tamping activities. The approach hereby presented is intended to be used by the tamping scheduling optimization system under development at the Institute for Traffic Safety and Automation Engineering of the Technische Universität Braunschweig in cooperation with the SNCF.

References

1. Meier-Hirmer, C.: Modèles et techniques probabilistes pour loptimisation des stratégies de maintenance. Application au domaine ferroviaire. Ph.D. Thesis, Université de Marne-la-Vallée (2007)
2. Lunze, J.: What is a hybrid system? In: Engell, S., Frehse, G., Schnieder, E. (eds.) Modelling, analysis, and Design of Hybrid Systems. LNCIS, vol. 279, pp. 3–14. Springer, Heidelberg (2002)
3. Lourakis, M.I.A.: levmar: Levenberg-Marquardt nonlinear least squares algorithms in C/C++, www.ics.forth.gr/~lourakis/levmar
4. Marquardt, D.: An Algorithm for Least-Squares Estimation of Nonlinear Parameters. SIAM Journal on Applied Mathematics 11 (1963)
5. Sadeghi, J., Askarinejad, H.: Development of improved railway track degradation models. Structure and Infrastructure Engineering 6, 675–688 (2010)
6. Ubalde, L., López Pita, A., Teixeira, P., Bachiller, A., Gallego, I.: Track deterioration in high-speed railways: influence of stochastic parameters. In: Proceedins of the Railway Engineering 2005. University of Westminster, London (2005)
7. Brown, R.G.: Forecasting and Prediction of Discrete Time Series. Prentice-Hall, Englewood Cliffs (1962)
8. Hamid, A., Gross, A.: Track-quality indices and track degradation models for maintenance-of-way planning. Transportation Research Board, 2-8(802) (1981)
9. Miwa, M., Ishikawa, T., Oyama, T.: Modeling the Transition Process of Railway Track Irregularity and Its Application to the Optimal Decision-making for Multiple Tie Tamper Operations. In: 3rd International Conference Proceedings Railway Engineering 2000, London (2000)

Application of Noninteracting Control Problem to Coupled Tanks

Miroslav Halás and Vladimír Žilka

Institute of Control and Industrial Informatics
Faculty of Electrical Engineering and Information Technology
Slovak University of Technology
Ilkovičova 3, 812 19 Bratislava, Slovakia
miroslav.halas@stuba.sk

Abstract. Mathematical technicalities involved in the modern theory of nonlinear control systems often prevent a wider use of the impressive theoretical results in practice. Attempts to overlap this gap between theory and practice are usually more than welcome and form the main scope of our interest in this work. In particular, the noninteracting control problem of coupled tanks is studied. The problem is solved via regular static state feedback. It is shown that the theoretical solution to the noninteracting control problem for coupled tanks does not satisfy practical control requirements. Accordingly, the solution is modified and yields a nonlinear controller with the noninteracting control. The results are verified on the real plant.

1 Introduction

The modern theory of nonlinear systems, employing the differential geometric/algebraic methods, offers solutions to many control problems and thus form the scope of interest of many authors. To refer to a few see for instance [7,3,2] and references therein. The typical control problems are, for instance, model matching, disturbance decoupling, noninteracting control, feedback linearization, observer design and others. Many were carried not only to the case of discrete-time nonlinear systems [1,8] but also to the case of nonlinear time-delay systems [10].

However, these solutions usually involve many mathematical technicalities, mainly from abstract algebra, which prevents a wider use of the results in practice and makes the big gap between control theory and control practice even bigger. It is generally known that in practice the way of dealing with nonlinear control systems is many times based just on the linearization in a fixed operating point and then methods of linear control systems are applied. Therefore, attempts to overlap the gap are usually more than welcome, which forms the main scope of our interest in this work.

Here, the noninteracting control problem is studied which is an important and frequent control problem in practice. The laboratory model of coupled tanks, representing a demonstrative and well know system having contact points to many real control processes, is used. The theoretical solution to the noninteracting

R. Moreno-Díaz et al. (Eds.): EUROCAST 2011, Part II, LNCS 6928, pp. 617–624, 2012.

control problem as described in [2] is used to control the plant. However, it is shown that the solution, if applied directly, does not meet basic practical control requirement. Thus, additional problems, related to the difference between model and real system, constrained controller output and some others, have to be considered as well. Accordingly, the solution is modified and results in a nonlinear controller with the noninteracting control. The solution given here has contact points to that recently suggested in [12] where the similar problem, namely the disturbance decoupling, was studied.

2   Coupled Tanks

2.1   Modelling

To begin with, a mathematical model of coupled tanks has to be found. The attention is restricted to the system consisting of two tanks coupled by a valve with the flow coefficient c_{12}. In addition, each tank has a valve and a pump itself, having the flow coefficients of valves c_1 and c_2 respectively, see Fig. 1. Thus, we deal with a problem of controlling levels in each of coupled tanks by 2 independent pumps. That is, a MIMO control system with 2 inputs and 2 outputs whose state-space representation can be derived as

$$\dot{x}_1 = \frac{1}{A}u_1 - c_{12}\,\mathrm{sign}(x_1 - x_2)\sqrt{|x_1 - x_2|} - c_1\sqrt{x_1}$$
$$\dot{x}_2 = \frac{1}{A}u_2 + c_{12}\,\mathrm{sign}(x_1 - x_2)\sqrt{|x_1 - x_2|} - c_2\sqrt{x_2}$$
$$y_1 = x_1 \tag{1}$$
$$y_2 = x_2$$

where x_1 and x_2 are levels in tank 1 and tank 2 respectively and A is a tank area.

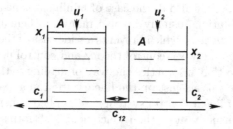

Fig. 1. Coupled tanks

2.2   Interaction in Control

The system (1) has the so-called interaction in control. That is, the different components of the output, y_1 and y_2, are not controlled separately by components of the input, u_1 and u_2. We observe that each of the inputs affects both y_1 and y_2, though it is implicit. Note that, for instance, u_1 affects x_1 which, in turn, is coupled to x_2. Therefore the interaction in control can be understood as a coupling. Either way, in such a case the direct design of a controller is not an easy task. In addition, the system (1) is, of course, nonlinear.

3   Noninteracting Control

For that reasons we proceed here with the design of noninteracting control which ensures that the output component y_i is affected only by the input component v_i for $i = 1, 2$. This could be viewed as a decoupled form. Following the lines of [2] our aim is to find, if possible, a regular static state feedback $u = \alpha(x) + \beta(x)v$ such that $dy_i^{(k)} \in \text{span}_\mathcal{K}\{dx, dv_i, \ldots, dv_i^{(k)}\}$, $k \geq 0$ and $dy_i^{(n)} \notin \text{span}_\mathcal{K}\{dx\}$ for every $i = 1, 2$. The first condition represents noninteraction constraint while the second one attains the output controllability of the closed loop [2].

The solution to the problem is given by the following necessary and sufficient condition.

The noninteracting control problem for the system (1) is solvable via regular static state feedback if and only if

$$\text{rank}_\mathcal{K} \frac{\partial(y_1^{(r_1)}, y_2^{(r_2)})}{\partial(u_1, u_2)} = 2 \tag{2}$$

where r_1 and r_2 are relative degrees of y_1 and y_2 respectively.

We observe that

$$\dot{y}_1 = \frac{1}{A}u_1 - c_{12}\,\text{sign}(x_1 - x_2)\sqrt{|x_1 - x_2|} - c_1\sqrt{x_1}$$

$$\dot{y}_2 = \frac{1}{A}u_2 + c_{12}\,\text{sign}(x_1 - x_2)\sqrt{|x_1 - x_2|} - c_2\sqrt{x_2}$$

and thus both relative degrees r_1 and r_2 equal 1. The condition (2) is clearly satisfied and the feedback that solves the noninteracting control problem can be found by solving the equations $\dot{y}_1 = v_1$, $\dot{y}_2 = v_2$ for u_1 and u_2. That is

$$u_1 = A(v_1 + c_{12}\,\text{sign}(x_1 - x_2)\sqrt{|x_1 - x_2|} + c_1\sqrt{x_1})$$

$$u_2 = A(v_2 - c_{12}\,\text{sign}(x_1 - x_2)\sqrt{|x_1 - x_2|} + c_2\sqrt{x_2}) \tag{3}$$

The closed-loop system reduces to two decoupled linear systems, both of the first order, $\dot{y}_1 = v_1$ and $\dot{y}_2 = v_2$, with the transfer functions

$$F_1(s) = \frac{Y_1(s)}{V_1(s)} = \frac{1}{s} \qquad F_2(s) = \frac{Y_2(s)}{V_2(s)} = \frac{1}{s} \tag{4}$$

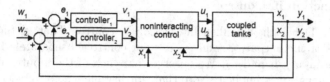

Fig. 2. Closed-loop structure with disturbance decoupling and a controller

Thus, the problem of designing a controller for the MIMO system (1) with inter-action in control is now reduced to designing controllers for two first order linear systems which is, of course, an easy task. Since we got two decoupled linear systems with the transfer functions (4) i.e. integrators, a straightforward solution is given by two P-controllers $P_1 = 1/T_1$, $P_2 = 1/T_2$ withing the standard closed-loop structure, see Fig. 2. Constants $T_1, T_2 \in R$ specify required dynamics of the closed loops $G_1(s) = \frac{P_1 F_1(s)}{1+P_1 F_1(s)} = \frac{1}{T_1 s+1}$, $G_2(s) = \frac{P_2 F_2(s)}{1+P_2 F_2(s)} = \frac{1}{T_2 s+1}$ respec-tively. However, the feedbacks (3), which achieve the noninteracting control, are not controllers actually. They only achieve the noninteracting control without any information about how successful they really are. It is thus easy to conclude that this will be sensitive not only to noise and additional disturbances, but also to the model inaccuracies. Clearly, the difference between the model (1) and the real plant causes that the compensated system does not reduce strictly to the linear systems (4) in which case the P-controllers might not be enough for controlling the systems.

4   Nonlinear Controllers with the Input Disturbance Elimination and Noninteracting Control

For this reason, the next step is to modify the both noninteracting state space feedbacks and controllers design. Since our task is to control the levels separately in each tank, it is clear that controllers should be able to control satisfactorily one-tank systems while assuming all related events just as disturbances. Then the noninteracting control can be employed as an improvement of the controller behaviour. The latter can be easily achieved by modifying the state feedbacks (3) to the form

$$u_1 = Av_1 + c_{12}A\operatorname{sign}(x_1 - x_2)\sqrt{|x_1 - x_2|}$$
$$u_2 = Av_2 - c_{12}A\operatorname{sign}(x_1 - x_2)\sqrt{|x_1 - x_2|} \tag{5}$$

Then the compensated system, i.e. the system (1) with the state feedbacks (5), reduces to two one-tank systems of the form

$$\dot{x}_1 = \tfrac{1}{A}v_1 - c_1\sqrt{x_1} \qquad \dot{x}_2 = \tfrac{1}{A}v_2 - c_2\sqrt{x_2}$$
$$y_1 = x_1 \qquad y_2 = x_2 \tag{6}$$

Note that under the state feedbacks (5) the state x_2 in the system (1) is decoupled from the first tank and in turn the state x_1 is decoupled from the second tank. The difference here is that now we do not require the compensated system takes the form of first order linear systems with the transfer functions (4) but rather take the form of standard one-tank systems (6), since for a one-tank system a plenty of controllers have been designed. This is even assumed as a trivial task and rather more complicated problems were studied for instance in [6,9,13].

Perhaps, the easiest way is to design PI-controllers based on system linearization in a fixed operating point. However, from a practical point of view this might result in a control structure having, due to the controller output constraint, wind-up effect in which case an anti-reset-wind (ARW) solution would be needed. Hence, better results can be obtained by using more sophisticated methods. Therefore, we will consider here the controller designed in [13] which adopts the control structure from [6] for linear systems and modifies to the nonlinear case, see Fig. 3. Such a structure satisfies a linearity of the closed loop, eliminates an input disturbance δ and deals with a control signal constraint. In particular, the structure has the properties of a PI-controller except that no wind-up effect might occur, in contrast to the classical PI-controller with the control signal constraint, for now there is no direct integration in the controller. For more details see [6]. Note that such a solution has been successfully employed in [12] to solve the similar problem given by the disturbance decoupling. Here, the same idea is applicable with the difference that now two decoupled one-tank systems (6) are to be controlled.

The requirement of the closed loops linearity is satisfied easily by a feedback linearization. If we want the closed loops dynamics to be determined by first order linear systems with time constants T_1 and T_2 respectively, we obtain the regular static state feedbacks

$$v_1 = \frac{w_1 A}{T_1} + A c_1 \sqrt{x_1} - \frac{x_1 A}{T_1} \qquad v_2 = \frac{w_2 A}{T_2} + A c_2 \sqrt{x_2} - \frac{x_2 A}{T_2} \qquad (7)$$

where w_1 and w_2 denote inputs to the closed loops. Under these feedbacks the input-output description of the closed loops represents linear systems with the transfer functions $G_1(s) = \frac{1}{T_1 s+1}$, $G_2(s) = \frac{1}{T_2 s+1}$. The remaining requirements are satisfied as follow. The input disturbances δ_1 and, respectively, δ_2, which represent noise, model inaccuracies and other events not having been modelled or considered, are eliminated via the feedback compensators K_{21} and K_{22}. Note that the compensators aim to reconstruct δ_1, δ_2 and subtract them from the controllers outputs. Finally, the compensators K_{11} and, respectively, K_{12} only remove the impact of K_{21} and K_{22} respectively, while controlling the systems (via the feedback linearizations (7)).

Since the models of the first and the second tank are equivalent (6) in what follows only controller for the first tank is designed in detail. That is, the compensators K_{21} and K_{22} respectively. Controller for the second tank can be derived analogically to the first one and thus will be finally only summarized.

To design the compensator K_{21} one, in linear case, simply compute the inverse transfer function which reconstructs δ_1. However, the transfer function formalism

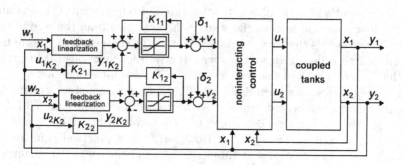

Fig. 3. Closed loop structure

is already available also for nonlinear systems [11,4]. Here, we do not enter into details, only remark that the differentials of the system variables are employed, which allows us to use linear methods, except that now the polynomial system description that relates the differentials is non-commutative. Nevertheless, such a transfer function formalism has many properties we expect, including the possibility to use the transfer function algebra when combining systems in series, parallel or feedback connection.

Following the lines of [4] the transfer function of the first system of (6) can be computed from its input-output differential equation as

$$\dot{y}_1 = \frac{1}{A}v_1 - c_1\sqrt{y_1}$$

$$d\dot{y}_1 = \frac{1}{A}dv_1 - c_1\frac{1}{2\sqrt{y_1}}dy_1$$

$$(s + \frac{c_1}{2\sqrt{y_1}})dy_1 = \frac{1}{A}dv_1$$

and the transfer function is

$$F_1(s) = \frac{1/A}{s + \frac{c_1}{2\sqrt{y_1}}} \tag{8}$$

Once the transfer function is computed we can continue with the compensator design. Of course, the ideal compensator $K_{21}(s) = \frac{1}{F_1(s)}$ is not realizable, even in linear case. Hence, we use

$$K_{21}(s) = \frac{1}{(T_{f_1}s + 1)}\frac{1}{F_1(s)} = \frac{s + \frac{c_1}{2\sqrt{y_1}}}{1/A(T_{f_1}s + 1)} \tag{9}$$

where T_{f_1} is a time constant which characterizes how fast the elimination of the disturbance δ_1 will be. The transfer function (9) corresponds to the input-output differential equation

$$T_{f_1}\dot{y}_{1K_{21}} + y_{1K_{21}} = A\dot{u}_{1K_{21}} + Ac_1\sqrt{u_{1K_{21}}} \tag{10}$$

where $u_{1K_{21}}$ and $y_{1K_{21}}$ denote input and, respectively, output to the compensator K_{21}. Note that $u_{1K_{21}} = y_1$.

The next step is to find, if possible, a state-space realization of the system (10). This is, of course, necessary when one wants to implement the compensator. To find a realization, we can follow the lines of [2] or even [5] where the nonlinear realization problem were studied directly within the transfer function formalism.

For the system (10) the following state-space realization can be found

$$\dot{x}_{1K_{21}} = -\frac{1}{T_{f_1}}x_{1K_{21}} + \frac{1}{T_{f_1}}Ac_1\sqrt{u_{1K_{21}}} + \frac{1}{T_{f_1}}Au_{1K_{21}}$$

$$y_{1K_{21}} = x_{1K_{21}} + \frac{1}{T_{f_1}}Au_{1K_{21}}$$

Finally, the compensator $K_{11}(s)$ is just a linear system with the transfer function

$$K_{11}(s) = \frac{1}{T_{f_1}s + 1}$$

As was explained, the models of the first and the second tank (6) are equivalent. So, the controller for the second tank can be derived analogically. From the input-output differential equation $\dot{y}_2 = \frac{1}{A}v_2 - c_2\sqrt{y_2}$ one can find the transfer function

$$F_2(s) = \frac{1/A}{s + \frac{c_2}{2\sqrt{y_2}}}$$

Then, the compensator K_{22} takes the form

$$K_{22}(s) = \frac{1}{(T_{f_2}s + 1)}\frac{1}{F_2(s)} = \frac{s + \frac{c_2}{2\sqrt{y_2}}}{1/A(T_{f_2}s + 1)}$$

Finally, the compensator $K_{12}(s)$ is again a linear system with the transfer function

$$K_{12}(s) = \frac{1}{T_{f_2}s + 1}$$

where T_{f_2} is a time constants which characterizes how fast the elimination of the disturbance δ_2 will be.

4.1   Experiments on the Real Plant

The compensators, together with the feedback linearizations (7) and the noninteracting control (5), can now be used to control the real plant modelled by the state-space equations (1). The whole structure was depicted in Fig. 3. The closed loop responses are shown in Fig. 4. To compare the results the experiment was repeated also without the noninteracting control (5). As can be seen, changes of the level x_1 practically do not affect the second level x_2 when the noninteracting control is employed.

Note that the same parameters were used in all experiments. The parameters A, c_1, c_{12} and c_2 were identified as $10^{-3}m^2$, 1.55×10^{-2}, 1.49×10^{-2} 1.4×10^{-2}. Time constants T_1, T_2, T_{f_1} and T_{f_2} were chosen to be $5s$, $5s$, $4s$ and $4s$ respectively.

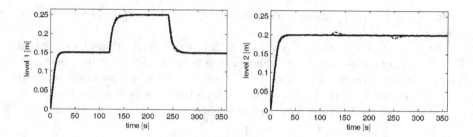

Fig. 4. The results obtained for the real plant and the nonlinear controller with (solid line) and without (dashed line) the noninteracting control

References

1. Aranda-Bricaire, E., Kotta, Ü., Moog, C.H.: Linearization of discrete-time systems. SIAM Journal of Control Optimization 34, 1999–2023 (1996)
2. Conte, G., Moog, C.H., Perdon, A.M.: Algebraic Methods for Nonlinear Control Systems. Theory and Applications (2007)
3. Fliess, M., Lévine, J., Martin, P., Rouchon, P.: Flatness and defect of non-linear systems: introductory theory and examples. Int. J. Control 61, 1327–1361 (1995)
4. Halás, M.: An algebraic framework generalizing the concept of transfer functions to nonlinear systems. Automatica 44, 1181–1190 (2008)
5. Halás, M., Kotta, Ü.: Realization problem of SISO nonlinear systems: a transfer function approac. In: 7th IEEE International Conference on Control & Automation, Christchurch, New Zealand (2009)
6. Huba, M.: Gain scheduled PI level control of a tank with variable cross section. In: 2nd IFAC Conference on Control Systems Design, Bratislava, Slovakia (2003)
7. Isidori, A.: Nonlinear systems, 2nd edn. Springer, New York (1989)
8. Kotta, Ü., Zinober, A., Liu, P.: Transfer equivalence and realization of nonlinear higher order input-output difference equations. Automatica 37, 1771–1778 (2001)
9. Pan, H., Wong, H., Kapila, V., de Queiroz, M.S.: Experimental validation of a nonlinear backstepping liquid level controller for a state coupled two tank system. Control Engineering Practice 13(1), 27–40 (2005)
10. Xia, X., Márquez-Martínez, L., Zagalak, P., Moog, C.: Analysis of nonlinear time-delay systems using modules over non-commutative rings. Automatica 38, 1549–1555 (2002)
11. Zheng, Y., Cao, L.: Transfer function description for nonlinear systems. Journal of East China Normal University (Natural Science) 2, 15–26 (1995)
12. Žilka, V., Halás, M.: Disturbance Decoupling of Coupled Tanks: From Theory to Practice. In: IFAC Symposium on System, Structure and Control, CSSS 2010, Ancona, Italy (2010) (submitted)
13. Žilka, V., Halás, M., Huba, M.: Nonlinear controllers for a fluid tank system. In: Moreno-Díaz, R., Pichler, F., Quesada-Arencibia, A. (eds.) EUROCAST 2009. LNCS, vol. 5717, pp. 618–625. Springer, Heidelberg (2009)

Description of a Low-Cost Radio-Frequency System to Detect Hydrocarbons

Francisco Cabrera[1], Víctor Araña[1], and Carlos Barrera[2]

[1] Departamento de Señales y Comunicaciones (DSC),
Instituto para el Desarrollo Tecnológico y la Innovación en las Comunicaciones (IDeTIC)
Universidad de Las Palmas de Gran Canaria (ULPGC)
Campus de Universitario de Tafira, 35017, Las Palmas de G.C., Spain
{fcabrera,varana}idetic.eu
[2] Head VIMAS (Vehicles, Instruments and Machines)
Plataforma Oceánica de Canarias (PLOCAN)
PO BOX 413, Telde, Las Palmas, Spain
carlos.barrera@plocan.eu

1 Introduction

The use of the sea is increasing in areas such as industrial, commercial transportation and sports. It is difficult to quantify the total value of the world maritime industry, and the economic relevance of a sector that affects a wide range of aspects of modern societies and their development. The need to understand the global ecosystems and environment, as well as their necessary conservation, to find the more efficient mechanisms to deal with phenomena such as climate change, ecosystem disruption, deforestation, depletion of the ozone layer or and rising sea levels have made research and study of the maritime environment a high priority issue. One of the areas of greatest current concern is the marine pollution by hydrocarbons such as control oil spills from ships. The major spills of crude oil and its products in the sea occur during their transport by oil tankers, loading and unloading operations, blowouts, etc. (Fig. 1). When introduced in the marine environment the oil goes through a variety of transformation involving physical, chemical and biological processes.

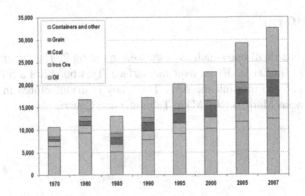

Fig. 1. Evolution of Maritime Transport billion tons between 1970-2007

R. Moreno-Díaz et al. (Eds.): EUROCAST 2011, Part II, LNCS 6928, pp. 625–632, 2012.
© Springer-Verlag Berlin Heidelberg 2012

At present, there are very few tools / methodologies for detection / measurement of hydrocarbons in general and in the seawater matrix in particular. In addition, methodologies are complex and sophisticated and expensive instruments [1,2]. The objective of this work is the development and evaluation of a hydrocarbon sensor of low cost and low power for detecting contaminants in marine and river environments. Multiple tests are conducted under different conditions and exposure times for each of the scenarios proposed marine to validate the system. This will give a true picture of the degree of implementation and maintenance costs, fundamental aspects determining the feasibility of operating the product.

2 Hydrocarbon Detection

The hydrocarbons include a wide range of products ranging from oils obtained directly from natural deposits, to the products in any mixture or degree of purity and molecular size. Together are probably the most universally substances transported, and particular way by sea [3]. As a result, the high absolute number of strokes of varying size (although a percentage is low and declining) and the characteristics of buoyancy of these substances have led them to be particularly regarding marine pollution.

Rapid and effective detection of pollutants (with special interest in mineral oil) directly under the establishment of observation and measurement systems operating. These systems provide for routine and continuous data and information in the manner and time scales required by the user of same. It also provides effective prediction of future events resulting from their discharges [4].

Technological advances in the field of monitoring environmental parameters offers a wide range of utilities, making the detection of hydrocarbons in sea water is no exception. Among the available options of systems / sensors to detect hydrocarbons in seawater that the current market offers [5], notes that most instrument systems respond to highly complex, costly operation and maintenance, which translates into high prices of acquisition and maintenance, making widespread use.

3 Buoy Platform

The buoy used is a small buoy such as is showed in the fig 2. The dimensions are: 50 cm of Diameter, 1m Large, 30 cm over the surface. This buoy has a little antenna at the top of the buoy to transmit the data. This buoy is manufactured in the Instituto Canario de Ciencias Marinas (ICCM) in Taliarte, Gran Canaria.

Fig. 2. Small Buoy

4 Radio System

The developed system for the evaluation of a simple low-cost sensor for the detection of hydrocarbons in marine and river environments is composed of two subsystems [6-7]. The first is located on the buoy "buoy subsystem" and the second is on the land "land subsystem." The first mission is to detect hydrocarbons in the marine environment, to store a certain number of samples and pass the data to another subsystem. The second subsystem complies with the functions to listen until it receives the data, process the information received and display data on screen.

4.1 Buoy Subsystem

The buoy subsystem is physically located inside a buoy and anchored at sea. It consists of three units: The Power Unit (PU), Data Acquisition Unit (DAU) and Switch Unit (SU) a. This unit is responsible for activating the acquisition unit, control and communications when hydrocarbon sensor data exceeds a threshold. The data is transmitted by a transceiver with a FSK modulation with a 64 Kbps bit rate. This data is transmitted by a acknowledgement protocol.

The buoy subsystem work in a idle mode. This mode has a low consumption in order to increase the battery life. The switch unit allows to the subsystem switch the electronic devices to transmit the data to the land subsystem. This buoy subsystem has a low consumption less 1 mA when the subsystem is in sleep mode, 20 mA when the transceiver is in rx mode and 40 mA when the subsystem is in tx mode. The life of the batteries depends on the mode of the transceiver.

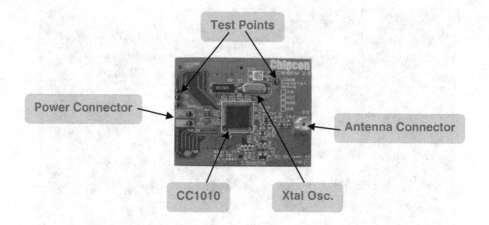

Fig. 3. CC1010 Module Board

This transceiver is the CC1010 of Texas Instruments (Formerly Chipcon). This microcontroller has a 8051 Core. It has a Flash Memory of 32 KB. Also has a SRAM of 2 KB. It has an Analogical Digital Converter of 10 bits (3 Channels), 4 Timers and 2 Serial Ports between the main characteristics. On the other hand, the transceiver is a single-conversion superheterodyne. The fig 3 shows a module board with the different parts of the buoy subsystem.

4.2 Land Subsystem

On the other hand, the land subsystem will be located anywhere within the coverage area of the buoy subsystem. This subsystem has the Power Unit (PU), Data Condition, Control and Communications (DC3U), and the Visual Display Unit (VDU). Its objective is to show the user the data that come from the RS232 serial interface or USB from the conditioning system.

The land subsystem is always in receive mode. When the data are received, these data are processed and showed in an application. Moreover, these data can be transmitted by SMS to an operator to alert the oil spill.

The power unit (PU) works with 3 V in the buoy subsystem and with 5 V in the land subsystem. The land subsystem can operate only with 2 modes (receive and transmission) because there isn't problem with the battery life. However in the buoy subsystem, we need operate with an additional mode (idle mode). This mode has a low current consumption. We switch to transmission or receive when the hydrocarbon sensor is active in order to optimize battery life.

4.3 Physical Layer

The Physical Layer consists of the basic hardware transmission technologies of the radio system. It is a fundamental layer underlying the logical data structures. The Physical Layer defines the means of transmitting raw bits rather than logical data packets over a physical link.. The bit stream may be grouped into code words or symbols and converted to a physical signal that is transmitted over a hardware transmission medium. The Physical Layer provides an electrical, mechanical, and procedural interface to the transmission medium. The shapes and properties of the electrical connectors, the frequencies to broadcast on, the modulation scheme to use are showed in the fig. 4.

Parameter	Configuration Options
Frequency	433.050 a 434.79 MHz
Modulation	FSK
Frequency Desviation	64 KHz
Bit Rate	64 Kbps
Codification	Manchester
Transmission Power	10 dBm

Fig. 4. Radiofrequency Configuration Parameters

The advantage of the asynchronous serial connection is its simplicity. We can estimate the data throughputs through the size of the data and the control data. One disadvantage is its low efficiency in carrying data. The start and end of the data are marked by the 'flag', and error detection is carried out by the frame check sequence. If the data size has a maximum sized address of 50 bits, a maximum sized control part of 16 bits and a maximum sized frame check sequence of 16 bits, the throughput of the system is 79% If the data size is increased the efficiency changes to 94%. However, it's possible that the BER is increased too. The fig 5 has a table with different data size.

Data Size (bytes)	Throughput efficiency (%)
50	79.37
100	88.50
150	92.02
204	94.01

Fig. 5. Data Size Packet

4.4 API Libraries

The CC1010IDE includes a variety of source files to ease and support the program development. Besides the standard C libraries, the source/support files are divided into 4 main groups: Hardware Definition Files (HDF), Hardware Abstraction Library (HAL), Chipcon Utility Library (CUL) and finally the application Programs as are showed in fig 6..

The Hardware Definition Files (HDF) define register addresses, interrupt vector mapping and other hardware constants. he Hardware Abstraction Library (HAL) implement a hardware abstraction interface for the user program and provides a library of macros and functions. As a result the user program can access the microcontroller peripherals, etc. Via function/macro calls, without specific knowledge about the hardware details. Besides the HAL module the CC1010IDE also provides a library of RF communication building blocks located in the Chipcon Utility Library (CUL). This library offers useful support for typical RF applications and, eventually it will provide a full RF protocol [8].

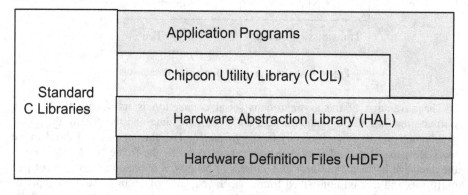

Fig. 6. Microcontroller Libraries

5   Results

The polymer sensor installed on the buoy is sensitive to very low concentrations (of the order of a few parts per billion) in times less than 35 minutes to sample the port and be able to detect from the first minute, gasoline, fuel or another type of fuel of which concentration is much higher than 15ppm as showed in fig 7.. This shows the huge advantage of this tool is available at critical points in ports or areas of special interest for their ecological value. The view of the system can be showed in fig 8.

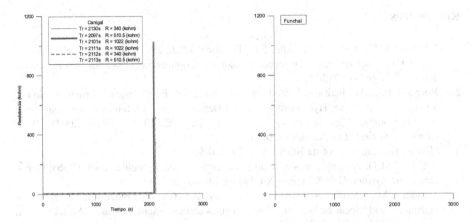

Fig. 7. Concentration of dissolved hydrocarbons. a) 2.01 ppm b) 0.11 ppm

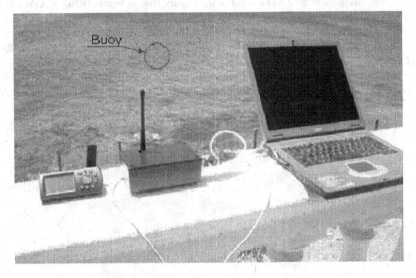

Fig. 8. View of the system in Melenara port

6 Conclusions

In this paper, we have showed a prototype of a System to detect hydrocarbons in water. This sensor will have an estimate of the type of oil found and this data is saved in the buoy subsystem. This system needn't maintenance about 1 year. It's useful in ports, around ships, beaches. It can be integrated in Sensor Network. to increase the coverage. Possibility send SMS when the sensor is activated. The coverage test was performed in Melenara with a maximum distance of 2 Km. This distance can be increased if the antenna height of the land subsystem is increased.

References

1. Ozanyan, K.B., Yeo, T.L., Hindle, F.P., Poolton, N.R.J., McCann, H., Tan, K.L.: Fiber-Based UV Laser-Diode Fluorescence Sensor for Commercial Gasolines. IEEE Sensors Journal 4(5), 681–690 (2004)
2. Rocha-Pérez, J.M., Pedraza, J., Rodríguez, F., Sandoval, F.: Electrical Characterization of a Polymeric Sensor for Hydrocarbon Spillage Detection. In: 14th International Conference on Electronics, Communications and Computers (CONIELECOMP 2004). IEEE Computer Society, Los Alamitos (2004)
3. UNCTAD, Handbook of statistics, 34, p. 536 (2009)
4. IOC-UNESCO, An implementation strategy for the coastal module of the Global Ocean Observing System. GOOS Report, No. 148, p. 141 (2005)
5. Mendoza, M., Carrillo, A., Rosas, A., Márquez, A.: New distributed optical sensor for detection and localization of liquid hydrocarbons. Sensors and Actuators, A; Physical 111(2-3), 171–182 (2004)
6. Araña, V., Cabrera, F., Déniz, A., et al.: Experimental network of marine environmental observations, surveillance and control in the Canary Islands waters (RED ACOMAR). In: 39th IEEE International Carnahan Conference on Security Technology (2005)
7. Barrera, C., Rueda, M.J., Llinás, O.: SeaMon-HC Buoy: A specific real-time lightweight moored platform for fast oil-spill detection. Ocean News and Technology 13(7), 20–22 (2007)
8. Marn, W., Rice, J., Fletcher, C., Creber, R., Babicz, R., Rogers, K.: The evolution of radio/acoustic communication gateway buoys. In: Proceedings of MTS/IEEE OCEANS (2005)

Author Index